LITERATURE FOR TODAY'S YOUNG ADULTS

Fourth Edition

Alleen Pace Nilsen
Arizona State University

Kenneth L. Donelson
Arizona State University

HarperCollinsCollegePublishers

The authors and publishers would like to thank all sources
for the use of their material. The credit lines for
copyrighted materials appearing in this work appear
in the Acknowledgments section beginning on page 597.
This section is to be considered an extension of the
copyright page.

Executive Editor: Christopher Jennison
Developmental Editor: Anita Portugal
Project Coordination and Text Adaptation: Printers Representatives, Inc.
Cover Design: Kay Petronio
Cover Illustration: Michele Barnes
Production/Manufacturing: Michael Weinstein/Linda Murray
Compositor: J. M. Post Graphics, Corp.
Printer and Binder: R. R. Donnelley & Sons Company
Cover Printer: The Lehigh Press, Inc.

Literature for Today's Young Adults, Fourth Edition
Copyright © 1993 by HarperCollins College Publishers

Library of Congress Cataloging-in-Publication Data

Nilsen, Alleen Pace.
    Literature for today's young adults / Alleen Pace Nilsen, Kenneth
  L. Donelson
      p.   cm.
    Authors' names appear in reverse order in 3rd ed.
    Includes bibliographical references and index.
    ISBN 0-673-46652-3
    I. Donelson, Kenneth L. II. Title.
Z1037.A1N55 1993
[PN1008]
016.8088'99283—dc20   92-42250
                                           CIP

93 94 95 9 8 7 6 5 4 3 2 1

Contents

PART TWO
MODERN YOUNG ADULT READING   99

FOCUS BOXES

THE PEOPLE BEHIND THE BOOKS

TABLES AND CHARTS

Preface

Revising *Literature for Today's Young Adults* is an obligation as well as an opportunity because the field of young adult books continually changes and develops. For example, since our last edition in 1988 educators and the general public have witnessed heated discussions over literature written by and about minorities and what schools promote as the literary canon. We've seen teachers adopt a whole-language approach and become adamant about using "real" literature as opposed to "dummied-down" adaptations. We've seen middle schools put a new emphasis on interdisciplinary work, thematic units, and student-centered choices.

Young adult literature has continued to gain respectability, as shown by the establishment of the Margaret A. Edwards Award sponsored by the Young Adult Library Services Association and *School Library Journal,* with the first five recipients being S. E. Hinton, Robert Cormier, Richard Peck, Lois Duncan, and M. E. Kerr. Another bit of positive evidence is crossover books—those written for teen readers, but then marketed with success to adult audiences; for example, *Ryan White: My Own Story* by AIDS victim Ryan White and Ann Marie Cunningham (Dial, 1991) and *Fallen Angels* (Scholastic, 1988), a Vietnam War story by Walter Dean Myers. His book sold 28,000 hardback copies in a standard YA format and over 200,000 in a paperback marketed to adults.

Popular culture changes include an explosive increase in the production of videotapes. People can now go to the corner rental shop and select a movie for viewing as easily as they can go to the library and select a book for reading. And with the mass marketing of paperbacks in drugstores and shopping mall bookstores, we've been pleased to see teenagers courted as serious buyers of books.

In this revision, we've tried to accommodate all of these changes and balance the need to include the latest books with the need to include the best in the field, no matter what the copyright date. For the sake of efficiency, we've put many titles and brief descriptions of recommended books, movies, and magazines in "Focus Boxes" instead of in the text. (Adults are encouraged to photocopy these focus boxes and give them to young readers.) We are constantly asked for lists of books dealing specifically with members of minority groups, so we have obliged with several such focus boxes. In trying also to provide discussions of minority issues, we happily discovered that books by and about members of minority groups are so intertwined with others that it would have been impossible—even if we thought it desirable—to treat all minority issues in a separate chapter. You'll find minority-related discussions scattered throughout nearly every chapter.

Other suggestions for revisions that we have incorporated include giving more attention to the psychology of the adolescent and to the teaching of literature in schools (see the new Chapter Eleven). To make room for the new additions, we reluctantly condensed Part Four on the history of young adult books to a single chapter. We also wish there had been room for describing classroom activities and discussion topics that have worked well with our students. We find that such activities help students share ideas and teach each other about more books than they have time to read individually. Some of these ideas are presented in an instructor's guide prepared by Elizabeth Wahlquist. It can be requested through the publisher.

We had many reasons for wanting to write this book, but chief among them was our belief that it was needed and worth doing. When in the late 1970s we surveyed teachers of YA literature in library science, English, and education departments, an overwhelming majority expressed a need for a scholarly and readable book to provide history and background for the field. One teacher wrote that her major problem "in establishing and promoting the work of the course was the sometimes skeptical view of colleagues about the worth of this literature," and added that she would welcome a book to educate professionals in related fields about the growing body of good YA books. We hope our book answers some of these needs, not just for academic classes in YA literature but also for librarians, teachers, counselors, and others working with young people between the ages of twelve and twenty.

For our purposes, we define "young adult literature" as any book freely chosen for reading by someone in this age group, which means that we do not make a distinction between books distributed by juvenile divisions and adult divisions of publishing houses. Young people read and enjoy both, and we share in the obvious goal of moving teenagers toward reading more and more adult books.

Throughout the text, we present criteria for evaluating various kinds of books, but these criteria are tentative starting places. Developing evaluation skills comes only with wide reading and practice in comparing books and matching them to particular needs. Similarly, our lists of recommended titles are only beginnings and should be supplemented by your own judgments and by current reviewing sources and annual lists of best books compiled by the Young Adult Library Services Association, *School Library Journal, Booklist,* the *ALAN Review,* the *New York Times, VOYA,* the *English Journal,* and other groups.

Although we know that paperbacks are far more widely read by young people than the original hardbound books, we show the hardback publishers (where applicable) in our book lists. We do this to give credit to the companies who found the authors and did the initial editorial and promotion work. Also, by relying on the hardback publishers, we were able to be more consistent and accurate. The paperback publishing industry is fluid, and a title may be published and then go out of print within a few months. To find paperback editions of any of the books we have listed, we recommend that readers consult the most recent issue of *Paperbound Books in Print* published annually (with periodic supplements) by R. R. Bowker Company and purchased by most libraries.

For help in preparing this fourth edition, we need to acknowledge the support of the English Department and of the central administration at Arizona State University. We thank Mary Jones and Shiela Millhollan, in particular. We also thank friends and colleagues whose ideas and words we admire and respect so much that they have probably found their way into our pages more than we realize. We are grateful to the Mesa, Arizona, Public Library and its YA librarian Diane Tucillo for serving as models of what YA services can be. We thank Nicolette Wickman for help with proofreading and indexing, and we thank Rayna Larson for help with photography. We are also grateful to critics of the third edition and to the readers of our manuscript who saved us from more errors than we might have made otherwise: Helen C. Doucet, McNeese State University; Jim Haskins, the University of Florida; Rodney D. Keller, Ricks College; Joyce C. Lackie, University of Northern Colorado; Sandra W. Lott, University of Montevallo; Muriel Radebaugh, Eastern Washington University; Robert C. Small, Radford University; and Elizabeth Wahlquist, Brigham Young University. We also thank the YA authors who contributed the "People Behind the Books" statements. Lastly, we thank HarperCollins editors Chris Jennison and Anita Portugal for supporting us on this edition and in helping us in a multitude of ways, and we thank Jeanette Ninas Johnson for bringing it all together.

Over a hundred years ago, Edward Salmon justified his work in children's literature by writing:

> It is no uncommon thing to hear children's literature condemned as wholly bad, and some people are good enough to commiserate with me on having waded through so much ephemeral matter. It may be my fault or my misfortune not to be able to see my loss. I have spent many pleasant and I may say not unprofitable hours in company with the printed thoughts of Mr. Kingston, Mr. Ballantyne, Mr. Henty, Jules Verne, Miss Alcott, Miss Mead, Miss Molesworth, Miss Doudney, Miss Younge, and a dozen others, and hope to spend as many more in the time to come as a busy life will permit.*

Today, it is heartening to consider how many talented people share Edward Salmon's feelings, and, like us, feel joy in spending their lives working in a field of literature that is always changing, exciting, and alive.

Alleen Pace Nilsen
Kenneth L. Donelson

*"Should Children Have a Special Literature?" *The Parent's Review* 1 (June 1890): 339.

UNDERSTANDING YOUNG ADULTS AND BOOKS

CHAPTER ONE

YOUNG ADULTS AND THEIR READING

"Of all passages, coming of age, or reaching adolescence, is the purest, in that it is the loneliest. In birth one is not truly conscious; in marriage one has a partner; even death is faced with a life's experience by one's side," wrote David Van Biema for a special issue of *Life* magazine devoted to *The Journey of Our Lives*.

He went on to explain that going from boy or girl to man or woman is undertaking a "huge leap on the slimmest of information." The person who fails grows older without growing wiser and faces either ostracism, insanity, or profound sorrow. Because such a debilitated or warped individual is a "drag on the community," the community bands together with the young person to see that the journey is accomplished.[1]

Initiation rites are one of the ways that communities help young people see the importance of leaving their childhood behind and taking on the mantle of adulthood. *Life* photographers traveled throughout the world to take pictures of young people undergoing such rites. Besides the expected communions, bar mitzvahs, junior proms, athletic competitions, cotillions, and graduation ceremonies, the photographers showed a virility initiation of a young boy being passed through a split sapling in an Italian forest, a boy on his first deer hunt with his father near the Pecos Bend Ranch in Texas, three Rastafarian girls partaking of "wisdom weed" (marijuana) in a Jamaican church, three Congolese Kota boys painted blue to symbolize the death of their childhoods, an Apache girl dressed in buckskin and beads and participating in a four-day celebration of her first menses, an Egyptian girl and a Turkish boy undergoing circumcisions, two Gabon girls painted white and secluded in a special hut because they had begun to menstruate, and several of Rio de Janeiro's teenage "surfers" riding the tops of speeding trains.

In affluent societies, books are one of the items that the community provides to young people in the hope of helping them succeed in their journey into adulthood. We are just as anxious as any society to help our children in this passage, but we don't have the heart—or the faith that it would work—to isolate them purposefully from us, to put them in physically dangerous situations, to confuse or disorient them, or to indoctrinate them forcefully into following in their parents' footsteps.

Undoubtedly, there are teenagers in "advanced" societies who feel isolated and in danger as well as confused and coerced. However, this isn't because their societies have planned such conditions as rites of passage; rather, it is because the societies have been unable to prevent them. Most of us feel more comfortable in offering children an intellectual approach to growing up. We want them to read about more experiences than they could have on their own. And deep in our hearts we're probably hoping that such reading will help young people mature intellectually and emotionally so that they won't feel the need to participate in the kinds of daredevil physical challenges that in 1988 cost the lives of 144 of the Rio de Janeiro train surfers. (A list of films on coming-of-age in various societies is found in Focus Box 1.1.)

The *Life* photographers did not show any teenagers reading books or any children getting their first adult library cards, a rite of passage that Robert Cormier remembers as "one of the great moments of my life, possessing my passport to a world that I still explore with wonder and delight." As a boy in the Leominster Public Library, Cormier would sneak behind the circulation desk into the adult stacks and rub his hands across the "spines of books, reading the names of the authors." Because he couldn't check the books out, he would pull them from the shelves, and sitting on the greenish, opaque glass floor with his knees jackknifed and his back against the wall, he would read. One afternoon, Miss Wheeler, the librarian, found him there and after they "talked books and authors," issued him his library card.[2]

Undoubtedly, one of the reasons the *Life* photographers didn't photograph young people reading books is that when people read, the action takes place inside their heads, which doesn't make for dramatic photos. In addition, except for textbooks, a relatively small percentage of the world's young people read books. Not all books for young people are written to help them grow into adults. Some writers simply want to share the pleasure they feel in words and story, others want to make money, and still others want to indoctrinate or educate their readers. Ever since the mid-nineteenth century, when—to the joy of the young and the anguish of the old—American publishers discovered that young people would buy dime novels by the millions, tensions have existed over which of these purposes books should serve.

The first American writers to gain national attention with books written for what today we call the "young adult audience," were Oliver Optic and Louisa May Alcott. Optic's didactic series books are almost forgotten, but Alcott's autobiographical *Little Women* is still read and loved. As famous as these two authors were in the 1860s, the terms *young adult literature, teenage books,* and

Films About That Dangerous Trip into the Rites of Passage

Desert Bloom (1986, 106 min., color: Dir: Eugene Corr; with Jon Voight and Annabeth Gish) In 1951 Las Vegas, people take the bomb as indifferently as a stepfather treats his stepdaughter.

Great Expectations (1946, 118 min., black and white; Dir: David Lean; with John Mills, Jean Simmons, and Martita Hunt) The impoverished Pip finds happiness and disillusionment in this Charles Dickens story.

High Wind in Jamaica (1965, 104 min., color; Dir: Alexander MacKendric; with Anthony Quinn) After a pirate ship captures some children, the pirate captain tries to protect their innocence, which leads to his disaster.

Intruder in the Dust (1949, 87 min., black and white; Dir: Clarence Brown; with Juano Hernandez and Claude Jarman, Jr.) Faulkner's novel about a small Southern town, racism, murder, and detection.

The Last Picture Show (1971, 118 min., black and white; Dir: Peter Bogdanovich; with Jeff Bridges, Timothy Bottoms, Ben Johnson, and Cloris Leachman) Larry McMurtry's novel about a small, dying town in west Texas with a great script and a fabulous cast. The perfect initiation novel/film.

Member of the Wedding (1952, 91 min., black and white; Dir: Fred Zimmermann; with Ethel Waters, Brandon de Wilde, and Julie Harris) The novel/play by Carson McCullers about not being wanted and growing up.

My Life as a Dog (1989, 101 min., color; Dir: Lasse Hallström) When his mother is ill, a twelve-year-old boy is shipped off to relatives. Based on the Swedish novel of the same title (recently available in this country) by Reidar Jönsson.

Pelle the Conqueror (1988, 150 min., color; Dir: Billie August; with Max von Sydow) A father can't find work in Sweden, so he and his young son come to Denmark and find farm life and work far worse than they had expected. Mostly grim, but ultimately a touching portrait of the love of father and son.

Personal Best (1982, 124 min., color; Dir: Robert Towne; with Mariel Hemingway and Patrice Donnelly) A young athlete trains for the Olympics and becomes involved in a lesbian affair.

Sons and Lovers   (1960, 103 min., black and white; Dir: Jack Cardiff; with Dean Stockwell, Trevor Howard, and Wendy Hiller) D. H. Lawrence's novel of a son trying to determine his rite of passage out of a coal-mining town.

Tex   (1982, 103 min., color; Dir: Tim Hunter; with Matt Dillon) S. E. Hinton's popular novel of two brothers finding their way in life.

Twist and Shout   (1984, 99 min., color; Dir: Billie August) Two boys mature in the early days of rock 'n roll (but you don't need to be a fan of the music to enjoy this marvelous film about love and independence).

The Yearling   (1946, 128 min., color; Dir: Clarence Brown; with Gregory Peck, Jane Wyman, and Claude Jarman, Jr.) A fine cast and a great retelling of Marjorie Kinnan Rawlings' novel about a family, a pet, and survival.

---

adolescent literature would have been strange, even meaningless, because only within the last half of the twentieth century has literature for young adults developed as a distinct unit of book publishing and promotion. Even today, an optimist might describe the field as *dynamic;* a pessimist would be more apt to say it is *unstable*.

Because of the newness of the concept and practice, there are no longstanding traditions as in children's literature, and opinions vary on whether there is even a need for a specialized approach to teenage books. The creation of such books coincided with the developing concept of adolescence as a specific and unique period of life. Puberty is a universal experience, but adolescence is not. Even today, in nontechnological societies the transition from childhood to adulthood may be quite rapid, but in the United States it begins at about age twelve or thirteen and continues through the early twenties. This stretching out of the transition between childhood and adulthood followed the Civil War. Before then, people were simply considered either children or adults. The turning point took place about age fourteen or fifteen, when children could go to work and become economic assets to the family and the community. But as the predominantly agricultural society in which children worked with their families gave way to a technological society in which people worked in factories, offices, schools, hospitals, research centers, and think-tanks, available jobs required specialized training. The more complex society became, the longer children had to go to school to prepare for their eventual adulthood. These children, waiting to be accepted as full-fledged members of society, developed their own unique society. They became *teenagers* and *young adults,* or as the psychologists prefer to call them, *adolescents*.

Any change that affects this many people in such a major way demands adjustments and a reshuffling of society's priorities and roles. Such changes do not come automatically and few believe that all the adjustments have been made.

■ *WHAT IS YOUNG ADULT LITERATURE?*

We recently heard young adults defined as "those who think they're too old to be children but who others think are too young to be adults." In this book we use the term to include students in junior high as well as those who have graduated from high school and are still finding their way into adult reading. However, we should caution that not all educators define young adults in this way. The Educational Resources Information Clearinghouse (ERIC), for example, defines young adults as those between the ages of eighteen and twenty-two, whereas the National Assessment of Educational Progress (NAEP), administered by the Educational Testing Service, refers to "young adults, ages 21 through 25."

We confess to feeling a bit pretentious when referring to a twelve- or thirteen-year-old as a young adult. However, we shy away from using the term *adolescent literature* because, as librarians have told us, "It has the ugly ring of pimples and puberty"; "It's like a conference about young adults with none present"; and "It suggests *immature*, in a derogatory sense." Still, most such college courses offered through English departments are entitled *Adolescent Literature*, and because of our English teaching backgrounds, we find ourselves using the term for variety, along with *teenage books*. However, we do not use such terms as *juvenile literature, junior novel, teen novel,* and *juvie*. These terms used to be fairly common, but today they are weighed down with negative connotations. This is unfortunate because there's often a need for communicating that a particular book is more likely to appeal to a thirteen-year-old than to a nineteen-year-old. With adults a six-year age difference may not affect choice of subject matter and intellectual and emotional response, but for teenagers even two or three years can make a tremendous difference.

By *young adult literature*, we mean anything that readers between the approximate ages of twelve and twenty choose to read (as opposed to what they may be coerced to read for class assignments). When we talk about *children's literature*, we refer to books released by the juvenile or junior division of a publisher and intended for children from prekindergarten to about sixth grade.

It wasn't until the 1920s and 1930s that most publishers divided their offerings into adult and juvenile categories. And today it is sometimes little more than chance whether an adult or juvenile editor happens to get a manuscript. Robert Cormier had never thought of himself as a writer for young people, but when his agent submitted *The Chocolate War* to Pantheon, the editor convinced Cormier that, as good as the book was, it would be simply one more in a catalog of adult books. On the other hand, if it were published for teenagers, it might sell well, and it certainly would not be one more in a long string of available adolescent novels. The editor's predictions came true, and Cormier later acknowledged that although his initial reaction to becoming a "young adult" author was one of shock followed by a month-long writer's block, he is grateful for the editorial help, which led to more attention from reviewers at the juvenile level. Although he had already published several stories and three novels, *The Chocolate War* brought him his first real financial gain. Until recently, an author who had a choice of a book coming out as either an adult or a juvenile title probably would have selected the adult division in hopes of receiving greater respect, acclaim, and financial rewards. This is less true today because of several breakthroughs. One is financial. Because we have a youth-oriented society, teenage books are popular choices for general audience movies and television specials. And as the book industry discovered that teenagers are willing to spend their own money for paperbacks in shopping mall bookstores, the financial base began to change. Developments in the 1970s already brought considerable financial success to the YA book business. Reading came into the high school curriculum as a regular class taken for at least one semester by many students. In such classes students had to read something, and in many cases this was teenage fiction. During the late 1960s, students and teachers turned away from the "classics" and the standard, required four years of English. English departments began offering electives, and courses in modern literature that included both adult and teenage fiction were popular with students. Many teachers who had previously scorned teenage books found themselves forced to take a new look and to conclude that it was better to teach adolescent literature than no literature at all.

All the interest has had a circular effect. The more important books for teenagers have become, the more respect the field has gained, and the better talent it has attracted. For example, on the basis of his Pulitzer Prize-winning play *The Effect of Gamma Rays on Man-in-the-Moon-Marigolds,* Paul Zindel was invited by Harper & Row to try teenage fiction. His first book was the well-received *The Pigman.* Both M. E. Kerr and Robert Cormier, currently two of the most respected YA authors, took positive note of this book as they pondered the effect that writing books for teenagers might have on their own careers.

A Brief Unsettled Heritage

Some writers, teachers, and other interested parties have many questions about the field of young adult literature. It is, after all, a relatively new area. An article in the *Louisville Courier-Journal* in 1951 described books written specifically for teenagers as "Flabby in content, mediocre in style, narrowly directed at the most trivial of adolescent interests." The writer went on to say, "Like a diet of cheap candies, they vitiate the appetite for sturdier food—for that bracing, ennobling and refining experience, immersion in the great stream of the English classics."[3]

Fourteen years later, J. Donald Adams, editor of the "Speaking of Books" page in *The New York Times Book Review,* pointed to adolescent literature as a symptom of what is wrong with American education and American culture:

The teen-age book, it seems to me, is a phenomenon which belongs properly only to a society of morons. I have nothing but respect for the writers of good books for children; they perform one of the most admirable functions of which a writer is capable. One proof of their value is the fact that the greatest books which children can enjoy are read with equal delight by their elders. But what person of mature years and reasonably mature understanding (for there is often a wide disparity) can read without impatience a book written for adolescents.[4]

In 1977, John Goldthwaite, writing in *Harper's,* gave as one of his nine suggestions for improving literature for young readers in particular and the world in general, the termination of teenage fiction. His reasoning was that any literate twelve-year-old could understand most science fiction and fantasy, and "As for all that novelized stuff about alienation, drugs, and pregnancy, the great bulk of it might be more enjoyable presented in comic books."[5]

Even people who are known to be committed to the concept of adolescent literature, sometimes question its authenticity. For example, in a call for papers for the April 1992 issue of the *English Journal* celebrating the fiftieth anniversary of Maureen Daly's *Seventeenth Summer* and the twenty-fifth anniversary of S. E. Hinton's *The Outsiders,* editor Ben Nelms asked, "Is the adolescent (or YA) novel simply a marketing device, or does it represent a legitimate literary genre?"[6]

Those of us who have positive attitudes about teenage books of course argue for its being a literary genre, and we think that the critics quoted earlier were not talking about the good adolescent literature published today. We can also conjecture that they were making observations based on a biased or inadequate sampling. Teenage books were never as hopelessly bad as some people claim. Criticism of any field, young adult literature or ornithology or submarine designing, begins with firsthand experience of the subject. Critics who decide to do a cursory piece on young adult literature once a year or so seldom have the reading background necessary to choose representative titles. People who generalize about an entire field of writing based on reading only five or ten books are not merely unreliable sources, but intellectual frauds. Wide knowledge surely implies a background of at least several hundred books selected from a variety of types and styles.

Although we have grounds for rejecting the kind of negative criticism quoted above, we need to be aware that it exists. Such a pessimistic view of teenage books is an unfortunate literary heritage that may well influence the attitudes of school boards, library directors, parents, teachers, and anyone else who has had no particular reason to read and examine the best of the new young adult literature. Besides, so many new books for young readers appear each year (approximately 2,000, with about one-fourth of these aimed at teenagers) that people who have already made up their minds about adolescent literature can probably find titles to support their beliefs no matter what they are. In an area as new as young adult literature, we can look at much of the disagreement and the conflicting views as inevitable. They are signs of a lively and interesting field.

CHARACTERISTICS OF THE BEST YOUNG ADULT LITERATURE

We did some research to come up with a selection of books that would be representative of what both young adults and professionals working in the field consider the best books. We should caution, however, that books are selected as "the best" on the basis of many different criteria, and one person's best will not necessarily be yours or that of the young people with whom you work. We hope that you will read many books, so that you can recommend them—not because you saw them on a list, but because you enjoyed them and believe they will appeal to a particular student.

In drawing up our list of "best books," we started with 1967, because this seemed to be a milestone year, when writers and publishers turned in new directions. We went to the Young Adult Library Services Association (formerly called the Young Adult Services Division of the American Library Association), which each January lists between thirty and eighty titles as "Best Books for Young Adults." It also produces a list of "Recommended Books for the Reluctant Young Adult Reader," published for students under the title of "Quick Picks." We also looked at the more mature titles on the list of "Notable Children's Books" distributed by the Association for Library Service to Children; at annual best book lists, such as those drawn up by *Booklist* and *School Library Journal* editors; and at such miscellaneous citings as the Newbery award, *Boston Globe–Horn Book* awards, *Horn Book* fanfare, *New York Times, Publishers Weekly,* and any lists that happen to appear such as "Best of the '80s." We've also consulted some of our colleagues, both librarians and fellow teachers of YA literature courses. Although we've used our own judgment about deleting a few of the older books, the following list includes books recommended by at least three sources. We call this our Honor Sampling. We make no claim that it includes all the good books or even the best books published each year, but we guarantee that a number of knowledgeable people were favorably impressed with each book. The value of this list is that it draws upon the judgment of a widely read group of professionals and young adults. Included in the list below are the titles and authors, hardback publishers, and where appropriate, the paperback publishers, the genre, number of pages, a notation if there has been a media production, and the ethnic group or setting if either is unusual. The books are fiction unless otherwise noted.

1992

Dear Nobody by Berlie Doherty. Orchard. Realistic, 192. pp., England.

The Harmony Arms by Ron Koertge. Little. Humorous realism, 182 pp.

The Leaving by Budge Wilson. Philomel. Short stories, 178 pp., Nova Scotia.

The Long Road to Gettysburg by Jim Murphy. Clarion. Historical nonfiction, 116 pp.

Missing May by Cynthia Rylant. Orchard. Realistic, 89 pp.

The Pigman & Me by Paul Zindel. HarperCollins. Autobiography, 160 pp.

Somewhere in the Darkness by Walter Dean Myers. Scholastic. Realistic, 224 pp., African American.

1991

Athletic Shorts: Six Short Stories by Chris Crutcher. Greenwillow. Short stories, 154 pp.

The Brave by Robert Lipsyte. HarperCollins. Realistic, 195 pp., Native American.

Black Ice by Lorene Cary. Knopf. Autobiography, 238 pp., African American.

Castle in the Air by Diana Wynne Jones. Greenwillow. Fantasy, 199 pp., Mid East.

Lyddie by Katherine Paterson. Lodestar/Dutton (Puffin pbk.). Historical, 183 pp.

Nothing But the Truth by Avi. Orchard. Realistic, 177 pp.

The Man from the Other Side by Uri Orlev. Houghton Mifflin, Historical, 186 pp., World War II Poland.

1990

Baseball in April and Other Stories by Gary Soto. Harcourt Brace Jovanovich (HBJ pbk.). Short stories, 111 pp., Hispanic.

Columbus and the World Around Him by Milton Meltzer. Franklin Watts. Nonfiction, 192 pp.

Dixie Storms by Barbara Hall. Harcourt Brace Jovanovich (Bantam pbk.). Realistic, 197 pp.

The Shining Company by Rosemary Sutcliff. Farrar, Straus, Giroux. Historical, 296 pp., seventh-century England.

The Silver Kiss by Annette Curtis Klaus. Bradbury. Occult/fantasy, 198 pp.

The True Confessions of Charlotte Doyle by Avi. Orchard (Avon pbk.). Historical, 215 pp.

White Peak Farm by Berlie Doherty. Orchard. Realistic, 86 pp., TV documentary, England.

Woodsong by Gary Paulsen. Bradbury. Personal experience, 132 pp., Alaska.

1989

And One for All by Theresa Nelson. Orchard. Realistic, 182 pp.

Blitzcat by Robert Westall. Scholastic (Scholastic pbk.). Historical/ animal, 230 pp., World War II, England.

Celine by Brock Cole. Farrar, Straus, Giroux (Farrar pbk.). Realistic, 216 pp.

Eva by Peter Dickinson. Delacorte (Dell pbk.). Science fiction, 219 pp.

Heartbeats and Other Stories by Peter D. Sieruta. HarperCollins (HarperCollins pbk.). Short stories, 216 pp.

No Kidding by Bruce Brooks. HarperCollins (HarperCollins pbk.). Dystopian future, 207 pp.

Shabanu: Daughter of the Wind by Suzanne Fisher Staples. Knopf (Knopf pbk.). Realistic, 240 pp., nomads of Cholistan Desert in Pakistan.

Stories I Ain't Told Nobody Yet by Jo Carson. Orchard (Theatre Communications pbk.). Poetry, 84 pp.

Sweetgrass by Jan Hudson. Philomel (Scholastic pbk.). Historical, 159 pp., Blackfoot Indians in 1830s.

Weetzie Bat by Francesca Lia Block. HarperCollins (HarperCollins pbk.). Realistic spoof, 88 pp.

1988

Fade by Robert Cormier. Delacorte (Dell pbk.). Fantasy/occult, 320 pp.

Fallen Angels by Walter Dean Myers. Scholastic (Scholastic pbk.). Realistic, 309 pp., mixture of ethnic groups, Vietnam War.

A Kindness by Cynthia Rylant. Orchard (Dell pbk.). Realistic, 117 pp.

Memory by Margaret Mahy. Macmillan (Dell pbk.). Realistic, 240 pp., New Zealand.

Of Such Small Differences by Joanne Greenberg. Holt. Realistic, 262 pp.

Probably Still Nick Swanson by Virginia Euwer Wolff. Macmillan (Scholastic pbk.). Realistic, 144 pp.

Say Goodnight, Gracie by Julie Reece Deaver. HarperCollins (HarperCollins pbk.), 214 pp.

Sex Education by Jenny Davis. Orchard (Dell pbk.). Realistic, 150 pp.

1987

After the Rain by Norma Fox Mazer. Morrow (Avon pbk.). Realistic, 290 pp.

The Crazy Horse Electric Game by Chris Crutcher. Greenwillow (Dell pbk.). Realistic, 224 pp., mixture of ethnic groups.

The Goats by Brock Cole. Farrar, Straus, Giroux. Realistic, 184 pp.

Permanent Connections by Sue Ellen Bridgers. HarperCollins (HarperCollins pbk.). Realistic, 164 pp.

Sons from Afar by Cynthia Voigt. Atheneum (Fawcett pbk.). Realistic, 224 pp.

The Tricksters by Margaret Mahy. Macmillan. Fantasy/occult, 266 pp., New Zealand.

1986

All God's Children Need Traveling Shoes by Maya Angelou. Random House (Random House pbk.). Autobiography, 210 pp., African American.

A Band of Angels by Julian Thompson. Scholastic (Scholastic pbk.). Realistic suspense, 294 pp., mixture of ethnic groups.

Cat Herself by Mollie Hunter. HarperCollins. Realistic, 279 pp., British nomads.

The Catalogue of the Universe by Margaret Mahy. Macmillan. Realistic, 185 pp., New Zealand.

Izzy, Willy-Nilly by Cynthia Voigt. Atheneum (Fawcett pbk.). Realistic, 288 pp.

Midnight Hour Encores by Bruce Brooks. HarperCollins (HarperCollins pbk.). Realistic, 288 pp.

1985

Betsey Brown by Ntozake Shange. St. Martin (St. Martin pbk.). Realistic, musical play, 207 pp., African American.

Beyond the Chocolate War by Robert Cormier. Knopf (Dell pbk.). Realistic, 234 pp.

Dogsong by Gary Paulsen. Bradbury (Puffin pbk.). Realistic, 177 pp., Alaska.

In Country by Bobbie Ann Mason. HarperCollins (HarperCollins pbk.). Realistic, 247 pp., movie.

The Moonlight Man by Paula Fox. Bradbury (Dell pbk.). Realistic, 192 pp., Nova Scotia.

Pocket Poems: Selected for a Journey ed. by Paul Janeczko. Bradbury. Poetry, 128 pp.

Remembering the Good Times by Richard Peck. Delacorte (Dell pbk.). Realistic, 192 pp.

1984

The Changeover: A Supernatural Romance by Margaret Mahy. Macmillan (Scholastic pbk.), Fantasy, 214 pp., New Zealand.

Cold Sassy Tree by Olive Ann Burns. Ticknor & Fields (Dell pbk.). Historical, 391 pp., TV movie, 1906 rural Georgia.

Downtown by Norma Fox Mazer. Morrow (Avon pbk.). Realistic, 216 pp.

Interstellar Pig by William Sleator. Dutton (Bantam pbk.). Science fiction, 197 pp.

A Little Love by Virginia Hamilton. Putnam. Realistic fiction, 207 pp., African American.

The Moves Make the Man by Bruce Brooks. HarperCollins (HarperCollins pbk.). Realistic fiction, 216 pp., African American and white.

One-Eyed Cat by Paula Fox. Bradbury (Dell pbk.). Realistic, 216 pp., 1934 upstate New York.

Sixteen: Short Stories by Outstanding Writers for Young Adults ed. by Donald R. Gallo. Delacorte (Dell pbk.). Short stories, 179 pp.

1983

Beyond the Divide by Kathryn Lasky. Macmillan (Dell pbk.). Historical, 254 pp., 1800s west.

The Bumblebee Flies Anyway by Robert Cormier. Pantheon (Dell pbk.). Realistic, 211 pp.

A Gathering of Old Men by Ernest J. Gaines. Knopf (Random House pbk.). Historical, 214 pp., movie, Depression South, African American.

Poetspeak: In Their Work, About Their Work ed. by Paul Janeczko, Bradbury (Macmillan pbk.). Poetry, 224 pp.

A Solitary Blue by Cynthia Voigt. Atheneum (Fawcett pbk.). Realistic, 182 pp.

1982

The Blue Sword by Robin McKinley. Greenwillow (Ace pbk.). Fantasy, 272 pp.

Class Dismissed! High School Poems by Mel Glenn. Clarion (Houghton Mifflin pbk.). Poetry, 96 pp.

The Darkangel by Meredith Ann Pierce. Atlantic. Fantasy, 223 pp.

A Formal Feeling by Zibby Oneal. Viking (Viking pbk.). Realistic, 162 pp.

Homesick: My Own Story by Jean Fritz. Putnam (Dell pbk.). Autobiographical, 163 pp., pre-war China.

A Midnight Clear by William Wharton. Knopf (Ballantine pbk.).
Realistic, 241 pp., movie, World War II.

Sweet Whispers, Brother Rush by Virginia Hamilton. Philomel (Avon
pbk.). Realistic/occult, 224 pp., African American.

1981

Let the Circle Be Unbroken by Mildred D. Taylor. Dial (Puffin pbk.).
Historical, 394 pp., Depression South, African American.

Little, Little by M. E. Kerr. HarperCollins (HarperCollins pbk.).
Humor/realistic, 183 pp.

Notes for Another Life by Sue Ellen Bridgers. Knopf (Bantam pbk.).
Realistic, 252 pp.

Rainbow Jordan by Alice Childress. Coward McCann (Avon pbk.).
Realistic, 142 pp., African American.

Stranger with My Face by Lois Duncan. Little, Brown (Dell pbk.).
Occult, 250 pp.

Tiger Eyes by Judy Blume. Bradbury (Dell pbk.). Realistic, 206 pp.,
mixed ethnic groups in New Mexico.

Westmark by Lloyd Alexander. Dutton (Dell pbk.). Historical, 184 pp.,
England.

1980

The Beginning Place by Ursula K. Le Guin. HarperCollins
(HarperCollins pbk.). Fantasy, 183 pp.

Jacob Have I Loved by Katherine Paterson. Crowell (HarperCollins
pbk.). Realistic, 216 pp., Chesapeake Bay island during World War
II.

The Quartzsite Trip by William Hogan. Atheneum. Realistic, 307 pp.

1979

After the First Death by Robert Cormier. Pantheon (Dell pbk.).
Suspense, 233 pp.

All Together Now by Sue Ellen Bridgers. Knopf (Bantam pbk.).
Realistic, 238 pp.

Birdy by William Wharton. Knopf (Avon pbk.). Realistic, 310 pp.,
movie.

The Disappearance by Rosa Guy. Delacorte (Dell pbk.). Realistic, 246
pp., African American.

The Last Mission by Harry Mazer. Delacorte (Dell pbk.). Realistic/
suspense, 182 pp., World War II.

Tex by S. E. Hinton. Delacorte (Dell pbk.). Realistic, 194 pp., movie.

Words by Heart by Ouida Sebestyen. Little, Brown (Bantam pbk.).
Historical, 162 pp., 1920s Colorado, African American.

1978

Beauty: A Retelling of the Story of Beauty and the Beast by Robin McKinley. HarperCollins. Fantasy, 247 pp.

The Book of the Dun Cow by Walter Wangerin, Jr. HarperCollins (HarperCollins pbk.). Fantasy, 255 pp.

Dreamsnake by Vonda N. McIntyre. Houghton Mifflin (Dell pbk.). Science fiction, 313 pp.

Father Figure by Richard Peck. Viking (Dell pbk.). Realistic, 192 pp., TV movie.

Gentlehands by M. E. Kerr. HarperCollins (Bantam & HarperCollins pbks.). Realistic, 183 pp.

1977

I Am the Cheese by Robert Cormier. Knopf (Dell pbk.). Realistic, 233 pp., movie.

I'll Love You When You're More Like Me by M. E. Kerr. HarperCollins (Dell & HarperCollins pbks.). Realistic, 183 pp.

Ludell & Willie by Brenda Wilkinson. HarperCollins (Bantam pbk.). Realistic, 181 pp., African American.

One Fat Summer by Robert Lipsyte. HarperCollins (HarperCollins pbk.). Realistic, 150 pp.

Winning by Robin Brancato. Knopf (Bantam pbk.). Realistic, 211 pp.

1976

Are You in the House Alone? by Richard Peck. Viking (Dell pbk.). Realistic, 156 pp., TV movie.

Dear Bill, Remember Me? by Norma Fox Mazer. Delacorte (Dell pbk.). Short stories, 195 pp.

The Distant Summer by Sarah Patterson. Simon & Schuster. Historical/romance, 153 pp., World War II.

Home Before Dark by Sue Ellen Bridgers. Knopf (Bantam pbk.). Realistic, 176 pp., migrant workers.

Never to Forget: The Jews of the Holocaust by Milton Meltzer. HarperCollins (Dell & HarperCollins pbks.). Nonfiction, 217 pp.

Ordinary People by Judith Guest. Viking. (Ballantine & Viking pbks.). Realistic, 263 pp., movie.

1975

Dragonwings by Laurence Yep. HarperCollins (HarperCollins pbk.). Historical, 248 pp., Chinese American.

Feral by Berton Roueche. HarperCollins. Horror fiction, 137 pp.

Is That You Miss Blue? by M. E. Kerr. HarperCollins (HarperCollins pbk.). Realistic, 170 pp.

The Lion's Paw by D. R. Sherman. Doubleday. Realistic, 233 pp., Africa.

Rumble Fish by S. E. Hinton. Delacorte (Dell pbk.). Realistic, 122 pp., movie.

Z for Zachariah by Robert C. O'Brien. Atheneum (Macmillan pbk.). Science fiction, 249 pp., postnuclear.

1974

The Chocolate War by Robert Cormier. Pantheon (Dell pbk.). Realistic, 253 pp., movie.

House of Stairs by William Sleator. Dutton (Puffin pbk.). Science fiction, 166 pp.

If Beale Street Could Talk by James Baldwin. Dial (Dell pbk.). Realistic, 197 pp., African American.

M. C. Higgins, the Great by Virginia Hamilton. Macmillan (Macmillan pbk.). Realistic, 278 pp., African American.

1973

A Day No Pigs Would Die by Robert Newton Peck. Knopf (Dell pbk.). Historical, 159 pp., 1920s rural Vermont.

The Friends by Rosa Guy. Holt (Bantam pbk.). Realistic, 203 pp., West Indian Black.

A Hero Ain't Nothin' But a Sandwich by Alice Childress. Coward, McCann (Avon pbk.). Realistic, 126 pp., movie, African American.

The Slave Dancer by Paula Fox. Bradbury (Dell pbk.). Historical, 176 pp., 1800s, African American and white.

Summer of My German Soldier by Bette Greene. Dial (Bantam pbk.). Historical, 199 pp., TV movie, Southern U.S./Jewish during World War II.

1972

Deathwatch by Robb White. Doubleday (Dell pbk.). Suspense, 228 pp., TV movie.

Dinky Hocker Shoots Smack! by M. E. Kerr. HarperCollins (HarperCollins pbk.). Humor/realistic, 198 pp., TV movie.

Dove by Robin L. Graham. HarperCollins (HarperCollins pbk.). Nonfiction, 198 pp., ocean voyage.

The Man Without a Face by Isabelle Holland. Lippincott (HarperCollins pbk.). Realistic, 248 pp., movie.

My Name Is Asher Lev by Chaim Potok. Knopf (Fawcett pbk.). Realistic, 369 pp., Hasidic Jewish.

Soul Catcher by Frank Herbert. Putnam (Berkley pbk.). Suspense, 250 pp., Native American.

Sticks and Stones by Lynn Hall. Follett (Dell pbk.). Realistic, 220 pp.

A Teacup Full of Roses by Sharon Bell Mathis. Viking (Puffin pbk.). 125 pp., African American.

1971

The Autobiography of Miss Jane Pittman by Ernest Gaines. Dial (Bantam pbk.). Historical, 245 pp., movie, African American.

The Bell Jar by Sylvia Plath. HarperCollins (Bantam pbk.). Realistic, 296 pp., movie.

His Own Where by June Jordan. Crowell (Dell pbk.). Realistic, 89 pp., African American.

Wild in the World by John Donovan. HarperCollins (Avon pbk.). Realistic, 94 pp., rural isolated.

1970

Bless the Beasts and Children by Glendon Swarthout. Doubleday (Simon & Schuster, pbk.). Realistic, 205 pp., movie.

I Know Why the Caged Bird Sings by Maya Angelou. Random House (Bantam pbk.). Autobiography, 281 pp., African American.

Run Softly, Go Fast by Barbara Wersba. Atheneum. Realistic, 169 pp.

1969

The Pigman by Paul Zindel. HarperCollins (Bantam). Realistic, 182 pp.

Red Sky at Morning by Richard Bradford. Lippincott (HarperCollins pbk.). Realistic, 256 pp., movie, mixed ethnic groups in New Mexico.

Soul on Ice by Eldridge Cleaver. McGraw-Hill (Dell pbk.). Autobiographical, 210 pp., African American.

1967

The Chosen by Chaim Potok. Simon & Schuster (McKay pbk.) Realistic, 284 pp., movie, Hasidic Jewish.

The Contender by Robert Lipsyte. HarperCollins (HarperCollins pbk.). Realistic, 167 pp., African American.

Mr. and Mrs. Bo Jo Jones by Ann Head. Putnam (NAL & Dutton pbks.). Realistic, 253 pp., TV movie.

The Outsiders by S. E. Hinton. Viking (Dell pbk.). Realistic, 156 pp., movie.

Reflections on a Gift of Watermelon Pickle by Stephen Dunning and others. Scott, Foresman (Scholastic pbk.). Poetry, 160 pp.

If a book is included on this honor sampling, then obviously it is outstanding in some way, but the reasons might differ considerably. One book may be here because of its originality, another for its popularity, and another for its literary

HADLEY IRWIN
on Two People Writing Under One Name

Although Hadley Irwin never had the opportunity to be a young adult—she was over the century mark when she was born—she doesn't consider herself an adult either. She knows that age isn't nearly as important as the ability to laugh, to learn, and to love.

We agree. We haven't much choice because we've been depending upon her judgment for several years. We've written problem novels (whatever they are), cross-cultural novels, historic novels, and a few books that lie buried in one of our basements. Why, we wonder, do we go on writing?

- Because life is so terribly funny. Writing is a way of saving all the ridiculous moments, ideas, quirks of thought that no one would listen to if we tried to share them in conversation. Put those bits in a story, let characters experience or see them, and maybe a reader will discover them and laugh.

- Because life is so terribly difficult. Writing is a way of mitigating pain. There are lots of bad things out there in the world, but they tend to hover over and collapse upon people called, for want of a more precise word, young adults. When awful events take place in a fictional world, maybe a reader will understand that it's possible to endure disasters of various sizes and come out alive.

- Because life is so precious. Minutes, like words, are not meant to be wasted. Neither life nor books, necessarily, have happy endings. That doesn't mean they are not worth living and reading. Neither should evoke a "So what?" at the end.

- Because life is so exciting. We want to share our delight in the differences that make the world worth exploring. In fiction, we can revel in disparities of age, sex, color, ethnicity, life style—whatever is human—and invite our readers to move out of their own lives and into someone else's.

- Because, most of all, writing allows us to live hundreds of lives, share what we know and what we guess, laugh at ourselves and the world. Sometimes we cry, too.

Hadley Irwin's books include *Moon and Me*, 1981; *Abby, My Love*, 1985; *So Long at the Fair*, 1988; and *Can't Hear You Listening*, 1990, all Macmillan.

quality. And we should warn that just because a book has not found its way to this list, it should not be dismissed as mediocre. The list covers 25 years during which there were many more outstanding books published than the 150 included here. Whenever such lists are drawn up, a degree of chance is involved.

Many of these books will be described in more detail in the following

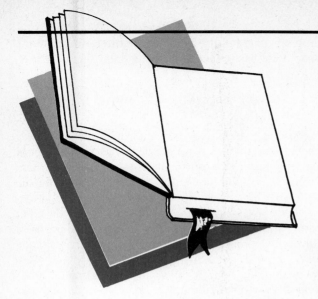

Across Generations

After the Rain by Norma Fox Mazer. Morrow, 1987. Getting to know and love a cantankerous old man just before he dies is hard, especially when he's your grandfather.

Badger on the Barge and Other Stories by Janni Howker. Greenwillow, 1985. Each of the stories in this collection explores a relationship between a teenager and an older person.

Cameo Rose by Robbie Branscum. HarperCollins, 1989. Since Grandma died, there has been no one in the Arkansas hills to teach Cam the finer points of growing into a woman. Nevertheless she's glad to work with Grandpa on the farm and even attempts to help him in his job as sheriff.

Checking on the Moon by Jenny Davis. Orchard, 1991. Cab, named after the Taxi she was born in, lived all her 13 years in Blue Cloud, Texas, but then she and her older brother are shipped off for the summer to Pittsburgh to live with her grandmother.

Gentlehands by M. E. Kerr. HarperCollins, 1978. Buddy Boyle is forced to think about more than Skye Pennington when his grandfather turns out to be guilty of crimes during World War II.

Memory by Margaret Mahy. Macmillan, 1988. Nineteen-year-old Jonny Dart and eighty-plus Sophie West, an Alzheimer's victim, both struggle with problems of time and memory.

Notes for Another Life by Sue Ellen Bridgers. Knopf, 1981. Wren and Kevin live with Bliss and Bill, a couple of really nice people who happen to be their grandparents. Their father is in a mental institution and their mother is off building a career.

The Pigman by Paul Zindel. HarperCollins, 1968. John and Lorraine are devastated at the thought that they contributed to the stress that caused their friend Mr. Pignati's heart attack.

A Summer to Die by Lois Lowry. Houghton Mifflin, 1977. Seventy-year-old Will Banks, landlord, handyman, and photographer, fills a void in Meg's life during the summer that her parents are involved in taking care of her older sister who has leukemia.

Sweet Bells Jangled Out of Tune by Robin Brancato. Knopf, 1982. Fifteen-year-old Ellen is drawn to the eccentric old bag lady that she used to know as her wealthy and elegant grandmother.

Trouble with Gramary by Betty Levin. Greenwillow, 1988. Merkka and Ben's grandmother runs a welding shop in her front yard, and Merkka is embarrassed when the townspeople complain.

chapters. Here they will simply be cited as the evidence we use to illustrate the following generalizations about the best of modern young adult literature.

Characteristic 1: YA Authors Write from the Viewpoint of Young People

A prerequisite to attracting young readers is to write through the eyes of a young person. The most consistent characteristic of the books on the Honor Sampling is the ages of the protagonists. We can count on one hand those where the protagonist is under twelve, and there are fewer than a dozen where the protagonist is over twenty.

With those over twenty, the book was most likely published for an adult audience but "found" by mature young adults because the characters are involved in the kinds of activities with which young people identify. For example, Joanne Greenberg's *Of Such Small Differences* has as its protagonist twenty-five-year-old John, who is blind and deaf. Leda, who is physically normal and a moderately successful actress and second-generation flower child, takes John as her lover. Because of the situation, the story is very different from a typical romance; nevertheless the couple is trying to solve the same problems that many young people face—living on one's own, finding someone to love, earning a living, and deciding whether money or art is the more important.

None of the fiction on the Honor Sampling focuses on characters playing the role of parents. Evidently, in the eyes of teenagers, the big dividing line—the final rite of passage—between childhood and adulthood is having children of one's own. In the personal narratives, a few of the tellers (Maya Angelou and Gary Paulsen) are parents, but the parenting role is not the part of the books with which teenagers identify.

There are adult characters who play important roles in fictional stories written for young readers, but in such situations YA authors take steps to guarantee a youthful viewpoint. For example, in *Fade,* Robert Cormier tells the life story of a man, Paul Moreaux, who inherited his family's blessing/curse of being able to make himself invisible. Cormier makes the first half of the book autobiographical, with Paul Moreaux telling about growing up in the 1930s. Then, to tell about Moreaux's adult years when he has become a successful author, Cormier switches narrators and speaks through the voice of a young female cousin who aspires to be a writer herself.

In general, authors don't have to plot so carefully if the adult characters they write about are a generation removed from teenagers (i.e., are the age of grandparents rather than parents). Perhaps because they are both on the edge of—close but not central to—the mainstream of power, young people seem able to relate more comfortably with elderly than with middle-aged adults (see Focus Box 1.2). Margaret Mahy's *Memory* lets readers get to know both nineteen-year-old Jonny Dart and eighty-plus Sophie West. In Berlie Doherty's *White Peak Farm*, the narrator of a three-generation family story set in England chooses to start the book with her grandmother's story, "Gran was a gentle soul who'd once had wild and willful ways and who had made my mother the way she is—a cut above the rest, my father says."

Other Honor Sampling books that show characters relating to elderly adults include Francesca Block's *Weetzie Bat*, Norma Fox Mazer's *After the Rain*, and Sue Ellen Bridgers *Notes for Another Life*.

Characteristic 2: "Please, Mother, I Would Rather Do It Myself!"

With formula fiction for young readers, one of the first things an author does is to figure out how to get rid of the parents so that the young person will be free to take credit for his or her own accomplishments. And although the Honor Sampling is not made up of formula fiction, there is evidence of the "Please, Mother, I would rather do it myself!" syndrome, as shown by the missing parents in Avi's *The True Confessions of Charlotte Doyle*, Francesca Block's *Weetzie Bat*, Barbara Hall's *Dixie Storms*, Brock Cole's *Celine*, Chris Crutcher's *The Crazy Horse Electric Game*, Julian Thompson's *A Band of Angels*, Norma Fox Mazer's *Downtown*, and all of S. E. Hinton's books.

A different twist to this same idea is for an author to show that the young person is smarter than the parent(s). In Cynthia Rylant's *A Kindness*, fifteen-year-old Chip Becker has been raised by his single mother, Anne. Rylant sets the stage for the story by explaining that

> Chip was brighter than his mother. His was a logical and quick mind. . . . He was a computermaestro . . . in a word, handy. He had assembled all his own Christmas toys as a child, reading lengthy directions in small print on thin paper as his mother stared helplessly at bags of colored pieces of plastic. At eleven he fixed the Hoover vacuum, and at thirteen he filled out Anne's income tax form. And for the last two years, every Sunday night he had price-compared in the Acme, making a deal with Anne that if she cooked whatever he bought, he would save her twenty dollars a week. It worked.

The conflict in the story begins on the day that Anne confides to Chip that she is pregnant and steadfastly refuses to tell him who the father is. Chip goes through some bad times feeling left out of this momentous event in their lives, but at the end of the story it's his wisdom and his speaking out that bring about a best-case ending.

Obviously, the characterization of Chip in this story is meant to appeal more to his than to his mother's generation of readers. But in keeping with the variety that exists in the Honor Sampling, many other books give more credit to parents and even call into question the idea that the teenager is always right. For example, Bruce Brooks' futuristic *No Kidding* has a protagonist, Sam, who is much like Chip in that at age eight he balanced the checkbook, at nine he bought the groceries, and at ten he conducted his own parent–teacher confer-ences. Now that he's fourteen he thinks he has the duty and the smarts to make all the decisions for his alcoholic mother and his ten-year-old brother, Ollie. Ollie has been placed with foster parents who hope to adopt him, and to the couple's amazement and sometimes irritation Sam takes it upon himself to be their supervisor. But by the end of the book he realizes that there are some things that he can't—and in fact, doesn't even want to—be in charge of.

One of the strengths of the kind of high-quality writing that appears in the Honor Sampling is that good writers will gradually lead their readers to look more realistically at themselves and at parent and child relationships. Books that feature at least one capable parent playing a strong, supportive role for a young protagonist include Berlie Doherty's *White Peak Farm*, Peter Dickinson's *Eva*, Jan Hudson's *Sweetgrass*, Virginia Euwer Wolff's *Probably Still Nick Swanson*, Bruce Brooks' *The Moves Make the Man*, Mollie Hunter's *Cat, Herself*, William Armstrong's *Sounder*, Alice Childress' *A Hero Ain't Nothin' But a Sandwich*, Kathryn Lasky's *Beyond the Divide*, and Virginia Hamilton's *M. C. Higgins, the Great*. In Robert Newton Peck's *A Day No Pigs Would Die* the boy loves his father, and in Bobbie Ann Mason's *In Country*, Bruce Brooks' *Midnight Hour Encores*, and Virginia Hamilton's *A Little Love*, the young protagonists place great importance on learning about an unknown parent.

Characteristic 3: YA Writers Avoid Speechifying

Time magazine described a 1991 off-Broadway play as "MTV drama . . . told in montage, in short riffs of scenes and crosscuts and simultaneous action instead of symphonic arcs of speechifying."[7] We're borrowing the *Time* reporter's description and applying it to YA books, because nearly all YA authors avoid "symphonic arcs of speechifying," and many of them tell their stories at the same frantic pace and with the same emphasis on powerful images as viewers have come to expect from MTV. Postindustrial countries have become hurry-up societies, and people want their stories to be presented in that same fashion.

The book from the honor listing that comes the closest to being an MTV story is Francesca Block's *Weetzie Bat*, which is eighty-eight pages long. It's a controversial book because people who read it under the expectation that it is a realistic story that will provide role models for teens come away shocked. But those who read it as an MTV story—a fairytale spoof of Hollywood and reality—come away amused with some vivid images of unforgettable teenage characters. Weetzie hangs out with homosexual Dirk, who is much admired by all the girls. However, Dirk prefers Weetzie's company not only because, "Under the pink Harlequin sunglasses, strawberry lipstick, earrings, dangling charms, and sugar-frosted eye shadow she was almost beautiful," but because she's different. On the day he meets her, she's wearing her feathered headdress and her moccasins and a pink, fringed mini-dress. "I'm into Indians," she explains. "They were here first and we treated them like shit."

We're not saying that all YA books are going to have the disjointed punch of music videos or that MTV is responsible for changing teenagers' expectations for leisure entertainment. But there's probably a circular effect in that modern mass media entertainers appeal to the same powerful emotions of adolescence— love, romance, sex, horror, and fear—as YA authors do. And as the mass media provides access to such dramatic material more quickly and more easily, writers may feel pressure to compete.

Although none of the books on the Honor Sampling are simplified for easy reading, they contain neither long, drawn-out descriptions nor pedantic or overblown language. Most YA authors try to use a natural, flowing language much like that which young adults use in their everyday conversations. The books are also limited as to number of characters and narrative events.

In 1964, when British author Leon Garfield submitted his first novel to a publishing house, it was turned down "after three or four agonizing months, when they said they couldn't quite decide whether it was adult or junior." He next submitted it to an editor who was just beginning to develop a juvenile line. Garfield said, "She suggested that, if I would be willing to cut it, then she'd publish it as a juvenile book. And of course, though I'd vowed I'd never alter a word, once the possibility of its being published became real, I cut it in about a week."[8]

Evidence from the Honor Sampling shows that long before MTV, teenagers liked their stories to be short and to the point and filled with the kinds of dramatic images that could transfer easily from words in a book to pictures in the mind or on a screen. For example, William Armstrong's 1969 *Sounder* had only 116 pages, Alice Childress' 1973 *A Hero Ain't Nothin' But a Sandwich* had 126 pages, and S. E. Hinton's 1975 *Rumble Fish* had 122 pages.

The assumption that publishers start with is that teenagers have shorter attention spans than adults and less ability to hold one strand of a plot in mind while reading about another strand. However, there's a tremendous difference in the reading abilities of young people between the ages of twelve and twenty. As students mature and become better readers, they are able to stick with longer and more complex books. Approximately a half-dozen of the Honor Sampling books have more than 300 pages. None of Robert Cormier's books is simple and straightforward. Gary Paulsen's *Dogsong* blends the past and the future with the present, whereas with Ernest Gaines' *A Gathering of Old Men*, William Wharton's *Birdy*, and Alice Childress' *A Hero Ain't Nothin' But a Sandwich*, readers must draw together and sort out alternating viewpoints and chronologies. And it is obvious from reading Ntozake Shange's *Betsey Brown*, Judith Guest's *Ordinary People*, and Chaim Potok's *My Name Is Asher Lev* that their appeal is based on something other than easy reading.

Characteristic 4: YA Literature Includes a Variety of Genres and Subjects

Because the *raison d'être* for adolescent literature is to tell a story about making the passage from childhood to adulthood, some people assume that books for

The nonfiction that appeals to enough readers to find its way to the Honor Sampling is likely to be the personal narrative, probably about events that happened during the author's youth, as in Lorene Cary's *Black Ice* (Knopf, 1991) about her attending St. Pauls prep school.

teenagers are all alike. But people who say this are revealing more about their reading patterns than about the field of adolescent literature. The Honor Sampling reveals a tremendous variety of subjects, themes, and genres. In addition, teenagers read informative nonfiction—trivia, health, history, sports, and how-to books—whose popularity is not accurately reflected because informative books are usually aimed at more specific audiences and have shorter life spans. (See Chapter 8 for a discussion.)

The kind of nonfiction that is likely to be recommended by enough people to get on the Honor Sampling is the personal narrative (e.g., Gary Paulsen's *Woodsong*, about his preparation for and participation in the Iditarod dogsled race across Alaska; Jean Fritz's *Homesick*, which tells of her childhood in China; and Maya Angelou's autobiographical *I Know Why the Caged Bird Sings* and *All God's Children Need Traveling Shoes*).

Milton Meltzer is a good enough writer of history that some of his books have been selected for several best-book lists (e.g., *Columbus and the World Around Him* and *Never to Forget: The Jews of the Holocaust*). Examples of historical fiction in the Honor Sampling include Olive Ann Burns' romantic *Cold Sassy Tree*, Kathryn Lasky's pioneer story *Beyond the Divide*, and Rosemary Sutcliff's *The Shining Company*, set in England in 600 A.D.

Short story collections include Gary Soto's *Baseball in April and Other Stories*, Peter D. Sieruta's *Heartbeats and Other Stories*, Donald R. Gallo's (ed.) *Sixteen: Short Stories by Outstanding Writers for Young Adults*, and Norma Fox Mazer's *Dear Bill, Remember Me?*

Among the poetry books are at least two that tell stories (Jo Carson's *Stories I Ain't Told Nobody Yet* and Mel Glenn's *Class Dismissed! High School Poems*), one in which poets share information about their craft (Paul Janeczko's *Poetspeak: In Their Work, About Their Work*), and one in which new standards were set (in the mid-1960s) for how to collect poems that would appeal to young readers (Stephen Dunning et al., *Reflections on a Gift of Watermelon Pickle*).

Several of the books contain elements of fantasy or science fiction that are as old as the oldest folktales (Walter Wangerin's *The Book of the Dun Cow* and Robin McKinley's *Beauty and the Beast*) and as new as nuclear war and the latest board game (Robert C. O'Briens' *Z for Zachariah* and William Sleator's *Interstellar Pig*). They are filled with romance (Annette Curtis Klause's *The Silver Kiss* and Virginia Hamilton's *Sweet Whispers, Brother Rush*) and with high-tech intrigue (Peter Dickinson's *Eva* and Robert Cormier's *The Bumblebee Flies Anyway*).

Although about half the books are contemporary realistic fiction, even these are far from identical. They range from tightly plotted suspense stories, including Julian Thompson's *A Band of Angels* and Margaret Mahy's *The Tricksters*, to serious introspections, as in Theresa Nelson's *And One for All* and Paula Fox's *One-Eyed Cat*. The theme of alienation and loneliness is seen in William Wharton's *Birdy*, John Donovan's *Wild in the World*, and Eldridge Cleaver's *Soul on Ice*. The need for a hero is seen in Robert Newton Peck's *A Day No Pigs Would Die* and Glendon Swarthout's *Bless the Beasts and Children*. Threats to the social order are explored in William Sleator's *House of Stairs* and *Interstellar Pig*. A search for values is shown in Richard Bradford's *Red Sky at Morning* and Chris Crutcher's *The Crazy Horse Electric Game*. What it means to care for others is examined in Norma Fox Mazer's *Downtown*, Virginia Hamilton's *A Little Love*, and Isabelle Holland's *The Man Without a Face*.

Characteristic 5: The Body of Work Includes Stories About Characters from Many Different Ethnic and Cultural Groups

Thirty years ago, the novels written specifically for teenagers and sold to schools and public libraries presented the same kind of middle-class, white, picket-fence neighborhoods as the one featured in the *Dick and Jane* readers from which most American children were taught to read. But the mid-1960s witnessed a striking change in attitudes. One by one, taboos on profanity, divorce, sexuality, drinking, racial unrest, abortion, pregnancy, and drugs disappeared. With this change, writers were freed to set their stories in realistic rather than romanticized neighborhoods and to explore the experiences of characters whose stories hadn't been told before.

This freedom was a primary factor in the coming of age of adolescent literature. Probably because there was such a lack of good books about

A Sampling of Books Featuring Characters Who Are African American

(Other titles are presented throughout this text.)

Annie John by Jamaica Kincaid. Farrar, Straus & Giroux, 1985. The heart of this story is Annie's seeking of independence, but she doesn't realize the pain that will come with the threat of being separated from her mother and her home on the island of Antigua.

Best Intentions: The Education and Killing of Edmund Perry by Sam Robert Anson. Random House, 1987. There's also a TV movie telling this story of a young black man who appeared to have everything going for him (he was an honors graduate from Exeter) when he was involved in an attack on a policeman in Harlem and was killed. (nonfiction)

Betsey Brown by Ntozake Shange. St. Martin's, 1985. Thirteen-year-old Betsey lives in a loving, middle-class family, but this doesn't take away all the pain when in 1959 she enters one of the first integrated schools in St. Louis.

Blue Tights by Rita Williams-Garcia. Lodestar, 1987. Fifteen-year-old Joyce Collins is an urban teenager whose physique isn't right for classical ballet. But then she finds satisfaction by joining a group of African dancers.

Bright Shadow by Joyce Carol Thomas. Avon, 1983. This love story of Abby and Carl Lee continues the Jackson family story begun in *Marked by Fire*, which won the American Book Award for its author.

Fast Talk on a Slow Track by Rita Williams-Garcia. Lodestar, 1991. Denzel Watson was class president and valedictorian when he graduated from high school. Schoolwork has always been easy for him, but when he goes to Princeton for a six-week summer program he's shocked to find that he can't just "wing it."

If Beale Street Could Talk by James Baldwin. Doubleday, 1974. In this mature story told in frank, black English, pregnant Tish loves Fonny, who has been jailed on a false charge.

Ludell by Brenda Wilkinson. HarperCollins, 1975. Ludell grows up in the South just as segregation is beginning to give way to a different social order. The sequel, *Ludell and Willie* (HarperCollins, 1977), is an exploration of first love complicated by the death of Ludell's mama, really her grandmother.

M. C. Higgins, the Great by Virginia Hamilton. Macmillan, 1974. Although M. C. doesn't leave home, he travels a road to maturity. Other excellent books by Hamilton include *A Little Love* (Philomel, 1974), and *Sweet Whispers, Brother Rush* (Philomel, 1982).

Memory of Kin: Stories About Family by Black Writers edited by Mary Helen Washington. Anchor Doubleday, 1991. This serious collection will probably be used in college literature courses, but good readers could be led to enjoy it on their own. It's an introduction to nearly twenty black authors, including several who write for young adults.

The Music of Summer by Rosa Guy. Delacorte, 1992. In this coming-of-age love story about an eighteen-year-old student at Juilliard, Guy explores diversity among African Americans, a theme she presented powerfully in her 1973 book *The Friends* (Holt).

Rainbow Jordan by Alice Childress. Putnam, 1981. In this book, as in *A Hero Ain't Nothin' But a Sandwich* (Putnam, 1973), Childress creates characters, both young and old, whom readers aren't likely to forget.

The Shimmershine Queens by Camille Yarbrough. Putnam, 1989. Angie's elderly cousin tells her about "shimmershine," her word for good feelings and pride in her African heritage. By the end of this book for younger teens, Angie begins to glow with some of her own shimmershine.

Somewhere in the Darkness by Walter Dean Myers. Scholastic, 1992. In this powerful father-and-son story, Jimmy Little meets his father for the first time and embarks on a quest to clear his father's name. Other outstanding books by Myers include *Fallen Angels* (Scholastic, 1988), *Scorpions* (HarperCollins, 1988), *The Mouse Rap* (HarperCollins, 1990), *Hoops* (Delacorte, 1981), and *The Outside Shot* (Delacorte, 1984).

---

non-middle-class protagonists and because this was where interesting things were happening, many writers during the late 1960s and the 1970s focused on minorities and on the kinds of kids that S. E. Hinton called *The Outsiders*. With the conservative swing that the country took in the 1980s, not as much attention has been paid to minority experiences; nevertheless, fourteen of the post-1980 copyrights feature minority characters. It's encouraging that they are among the most appealing of the new books, which will ensure that large numbers of teenagers of all races will read them.

Although most schools and libraries are making a concerted effort to stock and teach books reflecting minority cultures (see Focus Boxes 1.3 and 1.4, as well as Focus Boxes 2.2 and 2.3, pp. 64, 66), educators worry about marketing books directly to teenagers. They fear that publishers will not work as hard to include books about minority characters because less affluent kids, many of whom are from minorities, are not as likely to spend money on books. As publishers try to make their books more and more wish-fulfilling, they tend to return to the romanticized beautiful-people view that was characteristic of the old adolescent literature.

Another fear is that as with most television programming, everything will be watered down to suit mass tastes. But there are some crucial differences, for one person at a time reads a book, whereas television is usually viewed by a group. Even with cable television, the number of channels from which a viewer can choose is limited, but books offer a vast choice. Moreover,

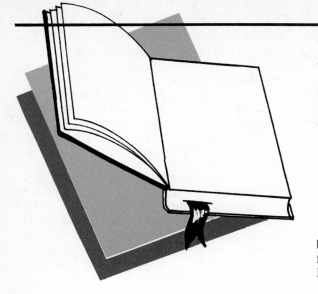

A Sampling of Books Featuring Characters Who Are Asian American

(Other titles are presented throughout this text.)

The Best Bad Thing by Yoshiko Uchida. Atheneum, 1983. For younger readers, this warm, family story tells about Rinko's growing up in the 1930s in California. Readers might enjoy comparing the fictional story to Uchida's autobiography *The Invisible Thread,* published as part of the *In My Own Words* series (Messner, 1991). Older readers will prefer her adult book, *Desert Exile: The Uprooting of a Japanese American Family* (University of Washington Press, 1982).

Children of the River by Linda Crew. Delacorte, 1989. One of the first YA novels to come to grips with the tremendous adjustments that today's refugees must make, Crew's story is about seventeen-year-old Sundara's life in Oregon after fleeing the Khmer Rouge in Cambodia.

The Floating World by Cynthia Kadohata. Viking Penguin, 1989. Olivia, who is now in her twenties, looks back on memories of her first boyfriend, Tan; her job at a chicken hatchery; and the many towns she and her family lived in because of the difficulty Japanese-Americans had finding work in the years just after World War II.

Her Own Song by Ellen Howard. Atheneum, 1988. This book for younger teens is set in Seattle in 1905, when there was widespread prejudice against the Chinese. Ten-year-old Mellie knows she's adopted, but she doesn't know that before coming to her present family she had lived with a Chinese family.

Into a Strange Land: Unaccompanied Refugee Youth in America by Brent Ashabranner and Melissa Ashabranner. Dodd, Mead, 1987. About half of the young people whose stories are told in this nonfiction book are refugees from Vietnam or Cambodia.

The Journey: Japanese Americans, Racism, and Renewal by Sheila Hamanaka. Orchard/Watts, 1990. Author/artist Hamanaka painted a mural about the experiences of Japanese Americans during World War II. The paintings and accompanying words present a dramatic yet straightforward account of a distressing chapter in American history.

The Kitchen God's Wife by Amy Tan. Putnam, 1991. A mother and her adult daughter are brought closer together as the mother shares the painful stories of her youth in China during World War II. Mature readers will also want to read Tan's earlier *The Joy Luck Club* (Putnam, 1989).

Molly by Any Other Name by Jean Davies Okomoto. Scholastic, 1990. Seventeen-year-old Molly is adopted and grows curious about her Asian heritage, which turns out to be Japanese-Canadian. When at last the court opens her records, Molly isn't so sure she wants to find the person who gave her away seventeen years ago.

The Rainbow People by Laurence Yep. HarperCollins, 1989. Yep calls these traditional stories a "peek through a keyhole into the Chinese culture." They are stories brought to the United States by Chinese immigrants. *Tongues of Jade* is a similar collection (HarperCollins, 1991).

Sea Glass by Laurence Yep. HarperCollins, 1979. Yep has said this story of a Chinese boy whose father wants him to be an athlete is his most autobiographical book. Readers might enjoy comparing it to his autobiography *The Lost Garden* (Messner, 1991). *Child of the Owl* (HarperCollins, 1977) is another modern realistic story. Yep's historical books about early Chinese immigrants include *Dragonwings* (HarperCollins, 1975), *The Serpent's Children* (HarperCollins, 1984), and *Mountain Light* (HarperCollins, 1985).

Several Kinds of Silence by Marilyn Singer. HarperCollins, 1988. Sixteen-year-old Franny Yeager's father cannot support his family in the way he would like, so he vents his frustration by blaming the Japanese. This is especially hard for Franny because she has a Japanese boyfriend.

Tales from Gold Mountain: Stories of the Chinese in the New World by Paul Yee. Macmillan, 1990. Yee's stories show how Chinese immigrants to North America mixed their folklore traditions and beliefs with their new working and living conditions.

The Woman Warrior: Memoirs of a Girlhood Among Ghosts by Maxine Hong Kingston. Knopf, 1976. Although published for adults, many older teens will relate to the author's account of growing up in California and relating to her parents and other relatives who emigrated from China. Random House has also released an audiotape of Kingston reading the book.

---

advertisers pay for most television programs, whereas readers pay the production costs of books.

Book watchers are encouraged that world events are helping teenagers to become less parochial in their reading. *Shabanu: Daughter of the Wind*, set in present-day Pakistan, was written by Suzanne Fisher Staples, a UPI news correspondent. She uses the story of a young woman's betrothal to introduce English readers to a culture very different from their own. Mollie Hunter's *Cat, Herself* is a romantic story of a Scottish gypsy; Gary Paulsen's *Dogsong* is about a young Eskimo; Margaret Mahy's books, *Memory*, *The Changeover*, and *The Tricksters* are set in New Zealand; and Berlie Doherty's *White Peak Farm* was prepared originally for a BBC documentary in Sheffield, England.

Characteristic 6: YA Books Are Basically Optimistic, with Characters Making Worthy Accomplishments

Ensuring that teenage characters are as smart as or smarter than their parents is only one of the devices that authors use to appeal to young readers. They also involve young characters in accomplishments that are challenging enough to earn the reader's respect. In the 1970s, when realism became the vogue and books were written with painful honesty about the frequently cruel world that teenagers face, some critics worried that modern young adult literature had become too pessimistic and cynical. But even in so-called downer books, authors created characters that readers could admire for the way they faced up to their challenges.

One illustration of the difference between children's and adolescent literature is a comparison between E. B. White's beloved *Charlotte's Web* and Robert Newton Peck's *A Day No Pigs Would Die*. In White's classic children's book, a beloved but useless pig wins a ribbon at the County Fair and is allowed to live a long and happy life, whereas in Peck's YA book a beloved but useless pig wins a ribbon at the County Fair but must be slaughtered anyway. Nevertheless, rather than being devastated by the death of the pig, readers identify with the boy and take pride in his ability to do what has to be done.

This kind of change and growth is the most common theme appearing in young adult literature, regardless of format. It suggests, either directly or symbolically, the gaining of maturity (i.e., the loss of innocence as part of the passage from childhood to adulthood). Such stories communicate a sense of time and change, a sense of becoming and catching glimpses of possibilities—some that are fearful and others that are awesome, odd, funny, perplexing, or wondrous.

One of the most popular ways to show change and growth is through a quest story (see Chapter 4 for discussion). Avi's *The True Confessions of Charlotte Doyle* is an almost pure example of a quest story camouflaged as a rollicking historical adventure. The intrepid narrator explains on page 1:

> . . . before I begin relating what happened, you must know something about me as I was in the year 1832—when these events transpired. At the time my name *was* Charlotte Doyle. And though I have kept the name, I am not—for reasons you will soon discover—the *same* Charlotte Doyle.

This captures the psychologically satisfying essence of quest stories, which is that over the course of the story, the protagonist will learn something and will change significantly.

Gary Paulsen introduced his autobiographical *Woodsong* with a similar promise of growth, "I understood almost nothing about the woods until it was nearly too late. And that is strange because my ignorance was based on knowledge." Other realistic quest stories include Barbara Hall's *Dixie Storms*, Teresa Nelson's *And One for All*, Cynthia Voigt's *Izzy, Willy-Nilly*, Katherine Paterson's *Lyddie*, Brock Cole's *The Goats*, Bruce Brooks' *Midnight Hour Encores*, and Bobbie Ann Mason's *In Country*. Quest stories with varying degrees of fantasy include Peter Dickinson's *Eva*, Annette Curtis Klause's *The Silver Kiss*, Mollie Hunter's *Cat, Herself*, Gary Paulsen's *Dogsong*, Lloyd Alexander's *Westmark*, and Robin McKinley's *The Blue Sword*.

Characteristic 7: YA Literature Is Influenced by Mass Marketing and Pop Culture Trends

There was a time when teachers, librarians, and book reviewers mostly controlled books for teenagers because schools and libraries had most of the money for purchasing books. But within the last decade, funding for schools and libraries has decreased and business and marketing practices have changed, so that publishers now sell directly to teenagers through shopping mall bookstores, drug and grocery stores, book clubs, and magazine and direct mail advertisements.

Of course, publishers have always been in business to make money, but two things are different today. First, publishers of books for teenagers have learned that they can make money without the help (or hindrance) of educators. Second, as big business conglomerates buy out the smaller companies, critics are concerned that educational values may take second place to concerns for profit. Major changes have occurred in both the format and the content of many of the books that are being published. Format changes include

- A higher percentage of original paperbacks
- Covers designed to inspire impulse buying
- Tie-ins with movies and television programs with covers featuring stills from the media production
- Many transitory paperbacks (i.e., ones marketed for only a few months). Those that are unsold are sent back to the distributor in the same way that magazines are returned and destroyed. The most successful of these books will be reissued in a few years with a new cover and perhaps a new title.

Another change is that books are being written, packaged, and marketed as parts of sets with easily identifiable logos which help potential readers know what to expect. In addition to predictable sets of biographies and geography books, new nonfiction sets include the beautifully prepared *Eyewitness* series from Knopf, which has been described as a museum between book covers; Lee Ames' *Draw 50* series, e.g., *Draw 50 Beasties and Yugglies and Turnover Uglies and Things That Go Bump in the Night*; Silver Burdett's *Issues for the 90s* series, e.g., *Medical Ethics* and *Managing Toxic Wastes*; and a *Make the Team* series produced by Sports Illustrated for Kids Books distributed by Little, Brown. Among the oldest and best known of the paperback sets of fiction are Bantam's *Choose Your Own Adventure, Sweet Valley High*, and *Sweet Dreams* series. Scholastic's *The Baby-Sitters Club* books by Ann Martin became so popular with junior high girls that the company is going back and printing hardbound editions for libraries. Other popular paperback series include R. L. Stine's *Fear Street* mysteries and Barbara and Scott Seigel's *The Firebrat* science fiction, both from Pocket Books/Archway. M. E. Kerr's *Fell*, followed by *Fell Back* and *Fell Down*, illustrates a new trend in which established authors plan ahead with their hardback publishers to do several books about the same main character.

Teenagers who are buying their own books will be much less likely to restrict themselves to so-called adolescent literature than will those who select books from a library where an adult has preselected "appropriate" titles. Dale Lyles, the media specialist at East Coweta High School in Sharpsburg, Georgia, sets aside $3,000 of his book budget and directs a student committee in conducting a schoolwide preference survey. Committee members check the requested titles against the library's holdings and finally make a fieldtrip to purchase the books. Lyles commented, "The titles which we end up with each year might be surprising to those who teach courses in adolescent literature. We get very few requests, almost none, for those authors usually associated with adolescent reading habits. Far more frequently students request adult trade paperbacks." Lyles is quick to explain that he allots only one-tenth of his book budget to this method of selection, probably in hopes of not having to defend the educational value of such authors as Danielle Steele, Stephen King, and V. C. Andrews.[9]

Changes in content relate to both style and subject. At an obvious level, we have seen a growing number of writers turning contemporary topics (e.g., abortion, date rape, AIDS, Alzheimer's disease, euthanasia, and homelessness) into novels. And after formula love romances became so popular in the 1970s it was hard to find a young adult novel that didn't contain at least a subplot of a love story. Now that supernatural stories are popular, we see some very good YA writers turning to this genre. For example, Annette Curtis Klause's *The Silver Kiss* is a thriller of a love story that blends a 300-year-old gothic horror story with a contemporary account of the loneliness and pain that Zoë feels as she watches her mother struggle with cancer. And when one of our classes studied Robert Cormier's *Fade*, several students made comparisons between Cormier's and Stephen King's writing.

A symbiotic relationship exists between contemporary YA books, television, and movies. In a visual medium, youthful characters are especially appealing simply because of their physical attractiveness. A second reason for the appeal of youthful characters relates as much to books as to movies. Young people's emotions are especially intense and their life-styles are undergoing the kinds of changes that form the basis for interesting plots as they make decisions, for example, about leaving home, choosing a mate, or deciding on the values they will live by for the rest of their lives.

People used to fear that if young people saw a movie based on a book they wouldn't read the book. But evidence shows that just the opposite is true. Many of the older books on the Honor Sampling have been kept alive by media-generated attention. Librarians report that interest is renewed each time a movie is re-released or shown on television for these books: *Mr. and Mrs. Bo Jo Jones, The Autobiography of Miss Jane Pittman, Red Sky at Morning, Sounder, Summer of My German Soldier, Birdy, Where the Lilies Bloom, Watership*

At last there's a real reason you shouldn't judge a book by its cover. With modern marketing techniques, the same book may have several different covers, as with Rosa Guy's *Ruby*.

Down, Dinky Hocker Shoots Smack, A Hero Ain't Nothin' But a Sandwich, The Chosen, and S. E. Hinton's *The Outsiders, Rumble Fish,* and *Tex.*

An example of the strong ties that have developed between pop culture, big business, books for teenagers, and the mass media appeared on the "People" page of *Time* magazine under the headline of "Beverly Hills Book Binge":

Lots of fab photos! Loads of sexy secrets! And many, many exclamation points! That's what you'll find in the nine new books, from five different publishers, coming out about *Beverly Hills, 90210,* the amazingly popular TV show that deals with peer pressure in a haughty high school.

Pictured with the story were the show's stars, Jason Priestley and Luke Perry, who were described as "those supercool, supersensitive pouty hunks who have teenage girls and grown-up accountants panting." Quotes included one from Elizabeth Beier of Berkley Books, which published *Luke-Mania! Jason-Fever!* "Girls want to kiss these two guys," and one from Stuart Applebaum of Bantam, "These books will not compete for the Pulitzer Prize, but I expect many young women will be doing book reports on them."[10]

IMPLICATIONS FROM ADOLESCENT PSYCHOLOGY FOR TEACHERS AND LIBRARIANS

We don't need to open a psychology book to realize that working with teenagers is a challenge, but we may feel better about our frustrations when we find that there are understandable reasons for them and that some of the best minds have offered explanations and theories. Because space in this text is too limited to include all that you need to know about adolescent psychology, we've included Focus Box 1.5, listing recommended books on adolescent psychology. Some present overviews of typical adolescence, others focus on particular problems, and still others aim at adults playing specific roles in the lives of teenagers. We recommend that, depending on the depth of your present knowledge and on the role you play in relation to young adults, you read one or more of these books.

At the least, teachers and librarians need to be aware of the emotional, intellectual, and physical changes that young adults experience, and they need to give serious thought to how they can best accommodate such changes. Growing bodies need movement and exercise but not just in ways that emphasize competition. Because they are adjusting to their new bodies and a whole host of new intellectual and emotional challenges, teenagers are especially self-conscious and need the reassurance that comes from achieving success and knowing that others admire their accomplishments. However, the typical teenage life-style is already filled with so much competition that it would be wise to plan activities where there are more winners than losers (e.g., publishing news-letters with many student-written book reviews, displaying student artwork, and sponsoring science fiction, fantasy, or other special-interest book discussion clubs). A variety of small clubs can provide multiple opportunities for leadership and for practice in successful group dynamics. Making friends is extremely important to teenagers, and many shy students need the security of some kind of organization with a supportive adult barely visible in the background.

In these activities, it is important to remember that young teens have short attention spans. A variety of activities should be organized so that participants can remain active as long as they want and then go on to something else without feeling guilty and without letting the other participants down. This does not mean that adults must accept irresponsibility. On the contrary, they can help students acquire a sense of commitment by planning for roles that are within their capabilities and their attention spans and by having clearly stated rules. Teenagers need limitations, but they also need the opportunity to help establish what these limits and expectations will be.

Adults also need to realize that the goal of most adolescents is to leave childhood behind as they move into adulthood. This has implications for whether libraries treat young adult services as a branch of the children's or the adult departments. Few teenagers want to sit on small children's chairs or to compete with nine- and ten-year-olds when they pick books off the shelves, nor are they attracted to books that use the word *children* or picture preteens on the covers.

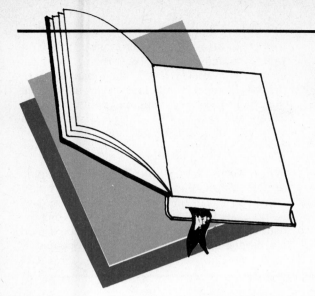

Recommended Adolescent Psychology Books*

Adolescence, 2nd edition, by L. Steinberg. New York: McGraw-Hill, 1989. This general textbook includes chapters on social and cognitive development as well as adolescents in their social contexts of school, work, family, and peer groups.

Adolescence. Adolescents, 2nd edition, by B. S. Furhmann. New York: HarperCollins, 1990. Part I treats adolescent development from historical, societal, family, peer, and school contexts; Part 2 looks at normal adolescent development; Part 3 looks at problematic responses to the pressures of adolescence.

The Adolescent: Development, Relationships, and Culture, 6th edition, by F. P. Rice. Boston: Allyn and Bacon, 1989. With a mixture of data and convincing examples, Rice draws on sociology, anthropology, education, and family studies to write about normal and atypical adolescent behavior and group life, including early marriage, nonmarital cohabitation, adolescent culture and subcultures, and participation in religion and cults.

* Thanks to Laurie Chassin, professor of psychology at Arizona State University, for help in preparing this list.

Adolescent Psychology: A Contemporary View by L. Nielson. New York: Holt, Rinehart and Winston, 1987. The readable style makes this 750-page compendium a welcome resource book. The initial overview of theories and research is especially well done.

Advances in Adolescent Development, series edited by R. Montemayor, G. R. Adams, and T. P. Gulotta. Newbury Park, CA: Sage. Volumes in this series take important topics in the area of adolescent development and present reviews of the relevant research literature.

At the Threshold: The Developing Adolescent, edited by S. S. Feldman and G. R. Elliot. Cambridge: Harvard University Press, 1990. In this comprehensive and well-received book that speaks against oversimplification, major issues are treated by the most respected writers in each area.

Being Adolescent by Mihaly Csikszentmihalyi and Reed Larson. New York: Basic Books, 1986. Based on a study of teenagers from one high school, this book identifies the patterns of adolescent life.

Consequences of Adolescent Drug Use: Impact on the Lives of Young Adults by M. D. Newcomb and P. M. Bentler. Newbury Park, CA: Sage, 1990. The results of a large-scale longitudinal study of adolescent drug use are described to show the impact of drug use on the role attainment and role functioning of young adults.

Ethnic Issues in Adolescent Mental Health, edited by A. R. Stiffman and L. E. Davis. Newbury Park, CA: Sage, 1990. Chapters on mental health issues treat antisocial behavior and substance abuse among ethnic minority adolescents.

Identity in Adolescence: Processes and Contents, edited by A. S. Waterman. San Francisco: Jossey-Bass, 1985. Waterman discusses the development of identity in relation to thinking about vocations, religion, political socialization, and choice of social roles. Especially insightful is the chapter on religious thinking and moral development.

When Teenagers Work: The Psychological and Social Costs of Adolescent Employment by E. Greenberger and L. Steinberg. New York: Basic Books, 1988. This book presents data questioning the assumption that paid work has psychological benefits for young people.

Young adults want a wide variety of informational books about aspects of their lives that are new (e.g., the physical development of their bodies, the new freedom they have to associate mainly with peers instead of family, and the added responsibilities they feel in deciding what kinds of adult roles they will fill). Cognitive or intellectual development has a tremendous influence on what young people want to read and discuss. Jean Piaget's theory that at about the age of twelve the "formal operational" stage of thinking begins to develop has important implications, because this stage of thinking gives young people the power to imagine actions and their results even though there is no way actually to try them out. Having what Boyd McCandless and Richard Coop have labeled "the powers of *if*"[11] is important not only when reading fantasy and science fiction, but when reading any literature dealing with subjects and viewpoints beyond the reader's experience. Even in realistic novels readers are asked to enter into the being and viewpoint of other characters where they must think as if they are someone else. Checking out their interpretations against those of a trusted friend or interested adult is an extension of this intellectual development. Teachers and librarians should provide ample opportunity and encouragement for this kind of discussion.

The more adults know about adolescent psychology, the better able they will be to develop relationships with students. For example, understanding the Rosenthal effect (also called mirror-imaging and self-fulfilling prophecies, in which people become what others expect) may influence what and how adults communicate with youngsters, and understanding the gender intensification hypothesis (the increasing pressures during adolescence to behave in sex-appropriate ways) may help adults deal more effectively with what looks like blatant sexism on the part of teenagers. Moreover, knowing that individuals, especially

These three young adults belong to a book reviewing group at the Mesa, Arizona, public library which for several years has produced a monthly newsletter, *Open Shelf.*

young women, may suffer from a fear of success almost as often as they suffer from a fear of failure may help adults adapt the approaches they use to involve students in activities.

How Studying Adolescent Psychology Will Make Better Readers and Evaluators of Young Adult Literature

Specialists in either adolescent literature or adolescent psychology should read widely in the other field, because although psychology provides the overall picture, honest adolescent literature provides the individual portrait. Anyone who reads widely in adolescent literature picks up information about adolescent psychology, but some concentrated study in the field will provide readers with a frame on which to hang the experiences addressed in YA books. There are good books about every conceivable problem (see Chapter 3 for a discussion), but no one can read them all. And those who will succeed in bringing young people and books together must read far more widely than just problem novels.

Often the difference in the life span between two books that are equally well written from a literary standpoint is that the ephemeral book fails to touch kids where they live, whereas the long-lasting book treats experiences that are psychologically important to young people. It's not that good authors peruse psychology books searching for case histories or symptoms of teenage problems

KATHRYN LASKY
on Profit Centers

It seems as if every time one turns around these days one hears about the fantastic boom in children's book publishing. Indeed the word *profit center* is cropping up increasingly in conjunction with the juvenile trade departments of many major publishing houses.

For so long the juvenile departments lurked in the shadowy back waters of these houses with an almost tax write-off status. So, gracious sakes and pass me my smelling salts, it does make one's head whirl to be smack dab in the middle of a profit center! Indeed, after so long as the underdog, many of us can't get used to this new lofty position.

I guess this boom has happened for all the good reasons we always knew but never dreamed other people would realize. Books don't break like plastic action figures. There are no parts to assemble, etc., etc. A lot of people credit the yuppies for bringing this about—along with their capucino machines and BMW's when they started having little yuppie babies they wanted to have well-read ones. It's kind of embarrassing to have Y.Y.'s (Yuppie Youngsters) just playing around on the floor with Teenage Ninja Mutant Turtles when there are such wonderful old tortoises like myself out there who can enrich their lives. I should be jumping for joy, right? Well, I'm not. I don't mean to look a gift horse in the mouth, but there is a dark side to this whole story. The dark side is the fact that juvenile trade publishers are starting to behave like business in the worst sense of the word. There is a crisis, and the crisis is creativity. Creativity is being threatened. I do not know how long it will take for it to move from the threatened list to the endangered list and possibly become an extinct species of sorts.

With these new profits, with all this attention focused on us, now people are hunting for formulas—what works, what does the market want? You never heard that ten years ago. You only heard of people speaking in terms of criteria of excellence—What makes a good picture book? How should illustration work with text? How does Beverly Cleary so perfectly tune into the voice of a six-year-old girl? Each book, each author was taken individually on its own. We talked way back then about books that broke out and showed courage to face real issues—*Where the Wild*

they can envision making into good stories. This would be as unlikely—and as unproductive—as it would be for a writer to study a book on literary devices and make a list: "First, I will use a metaphor, and then a bit of alliteration and some imagery, followed by personification."

The psychological aspects of well-written novels are a natural part of the story, and just as being able to recognize the way an author has brought about

Things Are or *Harriet the Spy.* We talked about authors who dared name the unnameable, reveal themselves in ways that children could not just relate to but believe in. The industry in the past has been very tolerant of risk takers. It is not so now. They have found some formulas that work—*Baby-Sitters Club* for one—that has had a huge impact on juvenile publishing along with *Sweet Valley High.*

The first victims of these new pressures are not the authors or illustrators, but the editors. They run scared. It is not simply a question of editors no longer being in the position to trust instincts; they are no longer in the position to have instincts. They have to sit on their passions, keep a tight rein on their emotional responses. There was an editor I knew who was just dying to publish my new series for middle-grade readers. She wrote me a long letter about how much she loved the characters and the story, but those settings of London in the first book and the Florida Keys for the second one were just too exotic. What I needed to do, she told me, was "to create contexts and settings more familiar to middle-grade readers, and problems that are slightly more targeted to their concerns. We need more middle America and with that I mean more shopping malls, more McDonald's. We need the children to be having real everyday problems—issues of being popular, clothes, being accepted, peer pressure—even complexion problems, after all, isn't the older set of twins on the brink of puberty?" As Dorothy Parker once said, "Constant Weader Frowed Up!"

I knew darn well that the woman who wrote me that very peculiar letter really adored those kids—the Starbuck children, all twins, and their mom and their nutty dad. But to really adore a character is getting harder and harder to defend now in an industry that deals with packagers, concept lines, and mass market series.

Today we are seeing more of something an old friend and editor of mine calls brand-name publishing—but the brand names are not necessarily Katherine Paterson or William Steig. Let's try Carly Simon, Tom Paxton, Leontyne Price, and oh dear Fergie, the duchess of York. I just can't wait for Ivana Trump to write her first children's book. I don't mean to pout about this, but it seems so unfair that somebody, for example, like Cher, might get to come into my field, but I don't get to go into hers. It's not a two-way street. I mean I know it sounds kind of silly, but then I've dreamed of my name in lights and all those neat costumes, not to mention the body. What would people do, for example, if Cher were appearing in Las Vegas, but she became ill and instead of Cher tonight it's going to be Kathryn Lasky reading excerpts to music from her most recent YA novel? I come out on stage poured into this gold lamé dress (dream on, Kathryn!) with a kind of hood ornament on my head and, talk some about children's books and then sing "I Got You, Babe." I mean people would feel ripped off, wouldn't they? Well, that's kind of the way I feel about celebrities doing children's books. Indeed, although these are boom times for the industry, I think that in a few years all of us—authors, illustrators, and more important young readers, librarians, teachers, and parents—might just begin to feel ripped off by the industry that is supposed to serve us.

Kathryn Lasky's books include *Double Trouble Squared* and *Shadows in the Water*, in the Starbuck Adventure Series, Harcourt Brace Jovanovich, 1991 and 1992; *The Bone Wars*, Morrow, 1988; *The Night Journey*, Viking, 1986; and *Pageant*, Macmillan, 1986.

a particular effect through imagery, metaphor, or allusion will bring an extra degree of pleasure and understanding, so will being able to recognize the psychological underpinnings of fictional treatments of human problems.

For example, someone familiar with gestalt psychology, with its emphasis on gaining awareness of moment-to-moment experiences and its recognition that the whole is greater than the elements that compose it will be better able to understand and appreciate Bobbie Ann Mason's *In Country*. It is the story of seventeen-year-old Sam's attempt to learn all she can about her father, who was killed in Vietnam. She reads his journal, looks at old pictures, even runs away and camps in a swamp to see if she can experience his fears and discomforts, and then in the final section of the book makes a kind of pilgrimage to the Vietnam Veterans' Memorial in Washington:

> A group of schoolkids tumble through, noisy as chickens. As they enter, one of the girls says, "Are they piled on top of each other?" They walk a few steps farther and she says, "What are all these names anyway?" Sam feels like punching the girl in the face for being so dumb. How could anybody that age not know? But she realizes that she doesn't know either. She is just beginning to understand. And she will never really know what happened to these men in the war.

Because teenagers are learning to adjust to bodies that look and feel different and because they sense different expectations from their associates, teenagers are extremely self-conscious. Many of them feel that they have an imaginary audience, that they are continually being surveyed and assessed by other people. Norma Fox Mazer shines a light on the concept of the imaginary audience in *After the Rain*, which begins as follows:

> "Look down on this scene," Rachel writes in her notebook. "Three people in a kitchen, sitting around a table. A man, a woman, and a girl." She glances up at her parents. "The three people are together but not together. The man and the woman know the girl is there, but they don't really see her. They see her, but they don't really know her."

Throughout this book, which tells the story of Rachel and her grandfather's illness and death, Rachel keeps stepping back to look at herself through the eyes of her imaginary audience. In the midst of interviewing her coach for the school newspaper, she breaks into the middle of a sentence, "My grandfather is dying," and then a few minutes later she responds to an unrelated question from her best friend with, "My grandfather is going to die":

> . . . all Rachel can think is that she's done it again. First Coach Al, now Helena. Isn't she just using Grandpa Izzy's illness to make herself important? . . . Does she plan to tell everybody? The man behind the counter when she buys a pack of gum? *My grandfather is dying.* Strangers on the street? *My grandfather is dying.* Maybe if she keeps saying it, she will feel it, she will believe it.

When reading about ego-defense mechanisms, most young readers probably do not realize that they are seeing patterns of behavior that have labels. What authors do by focusing attention on such actions is to educate their readers inductively. For example, in Richard Peck's *Remembering the Good Times*, young readers can get the point without learning the term *projection* when the narrator explains that his mother assumes that her former husband is dating because she is dating. And they don't need to know the term *repression* to understand what happened when after a classroom confrontation, a mentally disturbed student "just slid out of his desk and loped off. Everybody did. At that age, when there's something you can't explain, you walk away from it."

Whether or not young readers are looking for deeper meanings or just enjoying the surface plot of a story, they'll likely be most interested in books whose protagonists face the same kinds of challenges they are experiencing, such as the developmental tasks outlined a generation ago by Robert J. Havighurst:

1. Acquiring more mature social skills.
2. Achieving a masculine or feminine sex role.
3. Accepting the changes in one's body, using the body effectively, and accepting one's physique.
4. Achieving emotional independence from parents and other adults.
5. Preparing for sex, marriage, and parenthood.
6. Selecting and preparing for an occupation.
7. Developing a personal ideology and ethical standards.
8. Assuming membership in the larger community.[12]

Other psychologists gather all these tasks under the umbrella heading of achieving an identity, which they describe as *the* developmental task of adolescence. In the process of testing the values and ideologies of others, some young people may select a negative identity, one that is obviously undesirable in the eyes of significant others and the community as a whole. At the other extreme are those young people who adopt a foreclosed identity as a result of prematurely internalizing or adopting parents' and society's roles and values without examining them. Much of the intergenerational conflict that appears in YA books (e.g., the preceding discussion on how children are portrayed in comparison with their parents) relates to these two concepts.

In any year, dozens of young adult books touch on the problem of finding one's identity. The following quotes merely hint at the variety of ways in which the issue is approached:

> I was beginning to develop, at least physically, but nothing seemed to be the right size. Every morning I woke up, I had to check me out to see who was there. Some mornings I was a kid. Some mornings I was a maniac. Some mornings I didn't wake up at all: I just sleepwalked through the day. (From Richard Peck's *Remembering the Good Times*)

> Laura picked up her hair brush, looking into the mirror in her room. . . . She stared at herself intently. . . . Sometimes small alterations are more alarming than big ones. If Laura had been asked how she knew this reflection

ROBERT LIPSYTE
on Books for Boys

Whenever I say that boys need more good books, people roll their eyes, "C'mon, boys got it all, even now." True. But what they've got is not necessarily in all our best interests. And books can be part of the problem in a society that conditions boys to grow up to be men who beat up smaller people, including women and children, boys who become men fearful of each other, who will fight back any attempt to socialize them out of violence.

I was lucky as a kid, although I certainly didn't think so at the time. I was very fat. I might as well have been a girl. Fat boys could read; we didn't matter.

But for normal boys, not your star athletes, just your everyday boys, reading was . . . is . . . a problem. Boys typically read about sports, about specific subjects and science, but rarely about the arts or social problems. Some experts claim this comes from the difference between the sexes: Boys want to master the world; girls want to understand it.

I think that boys don't read as much as we'd like them to because (1) current books tend not to deal with the real problems and fears of boys, and (2) there is a tendency to treat boys as a group . . . which is where males are at their absolute worst . . . instead of as individuals who have to be led into reading secretly and one at a time.

Boys are afraid of being humiliated, of being hurt, of being hit by the ball, of being made to look dumb or inadequate in front of other boys and in front of girls. Most of the sports books boys are force-fed reinforce those fears with the false values of winning as the only goal, bending mindlessly to authority, preserving the status quo, often at the cost of truth. I think I was very lucky not being a sports fan as a kid and hardly reading any sports books at all.

Boys need reassurance that their fears of violence and humiliation and competition are shared fears. Books can reassure them. But to be able to read a book properly, you have to be able to sink into a scene, to absorb characters, to care, to empathize. You have to be willing to make yourself vulnerable to a book as surely as you need to make yourself vulnerable to a person. This is not easy for a male in this society to do, particularly an adolescent male who is unsure of his own identity, his sexuality, his future.

So, you say, we have to change society first, and then boys will read good books. This is true. But if we can get just a few boys to read a few good books, we will have started the change.

Cajole, coerce, do whatever needs to be done to get one book into one boy's hands, or back pocket. A book that he can make into a cave he can crawl into, roll around in, explore, for what's in there and what's in himself, find places of his own he never touched before, find out that a book is something you can do all by yourself, where no one can see you laughing or crying. It is the intellectual and emotional equivalent of safer sex.

Robert Lipyte's books include *The Brave*, HarperCollins, 1991; *The Chemo Kid*, HarperCollins, 1992; *The Contender*, HarperCollins, 1967; and *One Fat Summer*, HarperCollins, 1982.

was not hers she could not have pointed out any alien feature. The hair was hers, and the eyes were hers, hedged around with the sooty lashes of which she was particularly proud. However, for all that, the face was not her face, for it knew something that she did not. It looked back at her from some mysterious place alive with fears and pleasures she could not entirely recognize. There was no doubt about it. The future was not only warning her, but enticing her as it did so.
(From Margaret Mahy's *The Changeover: A Supernatural Romance*)

"Father, something is bothering me."
He replied around the meat. "I know. I have seen it."
"But I don't know what it is."
"I know that, too. It is part that you are fourteen and have thirteen winters and there are things that happen then which are hard to understand. But the other part that is bothering you I cannot say because I lack knowledge. You must get help from some other place. . . . I think you should go and talk to Oogruk. He is old and sometimes wise and he also tells good stories."
(From Gary Paulsen's *Dogsong*)

In life the transitions from one stage to another are likely to be continuous rather than discontinuous or abrupt, but because authors are forced by the nature of their craft to select and highlight the bits and pieces that get most quickly to the heart of a story, the transitions in books are likely to appear as specific milestones because authors must put into words what in real life may only be a vague feeling or hunch.

Chris Crutcher's *The Crazy Horse Electric Game* provides a good example of a young man finding his identity. Sixteen-year-old Willie Weaver is the pitcher—and a very good one too—for the Samson Floral team. The game that makes Willie a legend is the one that robs the Crazy Horse Electric team of its fourth straight Eastern Montana American League championship. After this game, Willie is so confident of his identity that he makes jokes with Jenny Blackburn, who on the first day back to school greets him with "Baseball hero, how you doing?" " 'Football hero,' Willie corrects her. 'New season, new image.' "

Willie's father

. . . was mythic to him; and to most other folks in Coho, Montana, too. Big Will played football for the University of Washington in the early 1960s when the Huskies beat the Michigan Wolverines 19–6 in the Rose Bowl; rushed for more than 150 yards and threw a half-back option touchdown. He was voted Most Valuable Player. . . . And when Big Will finally came back to Coho to settle and raise a family, the town was overjoyed.

Willie is on his way to adopting an identity similar to his father's, but a boating accident robs his body of its smooth and quick coordination, and Willie has to start all over to find out who he is and what he can accomplish. He leaves his small Montana town and for nearly two years struggles to find himself—with the help not of family and friends but of strangers. He succeeds, and when he returns home looking "good, much better than anyone would have expected," he is strong enough to accept weaknesses in those he loves and to go forward with his own life.

How a Well-Written Book Can Help Young Readers Mature Emotionally and Intellectually

A fairly subtle aspect of developing an identity relates to an internal versus an external locus of control. People with an external locus of control believe their lives are controlled from the outside—that is, by luck, chance, or what others do. They ask, "What will happen to me?" People with an internal locus of control believe their own actions and characteristics control their lives. They ask, "What am I going to do with my life?"

Although we all know adults who operate under an external locus of control (i.e., they blame others for whatever happens to them and take little responsibility for making their own decisions), most of us would agree that we want to help young people develop an internal locus of control (i.e., feel responsible for their own lives). But developing an internal locus of control is not something people can do simply because they are told to, nor is it something that can be learned as a skill, such as bicycle riding or swimming. Instead it is a way of looking at life, which develops slowly over many years in such infinitely small steps as three-year-olds choosing what clothes they will wear and fifteen-year-olds choosing who their friends will be. Identifying with characters in books as they develop into maturity is another of these infinitely small steps.

Certainly we aren't saying that reading books can substitute for real-life experiences, or that one or two books, no matter how well written, will be enough to change a teenager's view of life. And if authors are didactic in their messages, if they are too obvious in trying to teach a preconceived message, then readers will be turned off by what they view as preachiness. However, skilled authors are able to weave into their plots incidents about making decisions and taking responsibilities. They have several advantages over scriptwriters for television because authors can show through words what's going on in characters' minds, whereas cameras can show only what can be seen. Also, authors have more space. Most television programs that feature teens are either thirty or sixty minutes long, with time out for commercials. And most programs featuring teens are situation comedies. Sitcom writers are forced to put their primary efforts into creating humor, whereas authors have room in a book to develop both serious and humorous strands. And one of the great appeals of sitcoms is that readers know what to expect. The shows preserve the status quo, with each week's program opening with a scene of normality followed by the development and the eventual solving of a humorous problem. Although the characters attempt to solve the problem, their actions only make it worse. But finally, something or someone comes in from the outside to rescue the characters, and the show closes with a scene depicting the characters in a position similar to the one that opened the show. The identical background music and opening and closing visuals reassure viewers that they are tuning in for a repeat performance—for a variation on a story that they understand and enjoy—one that they expect to be repeated week after week.[13]

Realistic fiction for teens differs in two key ways from the preceding description of sitcoms. First, the most common genre is the coming-of-age story. In these books, young protagonists do not end up at the same place they started. They take steps toward maturity so that at the end of the book they are different in some significant way. This contrasts with series books, which are much more like sitcoms in that readers expect new incidents but with the same characters they have come to know. With coming-of-age stories, the characters change so much over the course of the story that authors will have a hard time writing a sequel and remaining true to their character. Robert Lipsyte solved the problem in writing a sequel to *The Contender* by returning twenty-five years later to write *The Brave*. Instead of having Alfred Brooks, the teenage Harlem boxer from *The Contender*, as his main character, he makes Brooks a New York City cop. His hero in the new book is Sonny Bear, a young Moscondaga Indian boxer. Brooks does for Sonny something similar to what Mr. Donatelli did for him a generation ago.

The second big difference between the TV sitcom and well-written realistic books is that in the best books the protagonists are shown solving the problem. They do not sit by waiting for something to happen. For example, near the end of Robert Cormier's *We All Fall Down*, when Jane Jerome is tied up in the "god-forsaken shed" and she realizes that Mickey Stallings, alias Mickey Looney, alias The Avenger, is really going to kill her, she thinks:

> *Give me time to say a prayer*. That was what she was about to say. One last request, beyond panic now, accepting the situation. "No," she cried out, denying her panic, her acceptance. It wasn't supposed to happen this way. *I am sixteen years old and I am not going to die this way*. This was Mickey Stallings in front of her. Not The Avenger, not some monstrous eleven-year-old. She had to make him see who he really was.

Jane's acceptance of the fact that she could and must do something is an example of the kind of taking hold of a situation that educators hope will be a model for young readers. Hundreds of books present variations on this theme of taking responsibility (i.e., developing an internal locus of control). Any author can devise plots that include such incidents, but making them believable and bringing enough life to the characters so that readers care is not easy.

In conclusion, close connections exist between adolescent literature and adolescent psychology, with psychology providing the overall picture and adolescent literature providing individual portraits. Understanding psychological concepts—something that has only been hinted at here—will help adults

- Judge the soundness of the books they read.
- Decide which ones are worthy of promotion.
- Predict which ones will last and which will be transitory.
- Make better recommendations to individuals.
- Discuss books with students from their viewpoints.
- Gain more understanding and pleasure from personal reading.

◼ NOTES

[1]David Van Biema, "The Loneliest—and Purest—Rite of Passage: Adolescence and Initiation," *The Journey of Our Lives, Life* magazine (October 1991): 31.

[2]Robert Cormier's acceptance speech for the 1991 Margaret A. Edwards Award, American Library Association Annual Conference in Atlanta, Georgia, June 30, 1991. Printed in *School Library Journal*, 37 (September 1991): 184–86.

[3]"Trash for Teen-Agers: Or Escape from Thackeray, the Brontës, and the Incomparable Jane," *Louisville Courier-Journal*, June 17, 1951. Quoted in Stephen Dunning, "Junior Book Roundup," *English Journal* 53 (December 1964): 702–703.

[4]J. Donald Adams, *Speaking of Books—and Life* (Holt, Rinehart and Winston, 1965), pp. 250–52.

[5]John Goldthwaite, "Notes on the Children's Book Trade," *Harper's* 254 (January 1977): 76, 78, 80, 84–86.

[6]Ben Nelms, "Call for Manuscripts," *English Journal* 80 (October 1991): 7.

[7]William A. Henry III, "MTV Drama: *Unidentified Human Remains and the True Nature of Love*," *Time* (September 30, 1991): 81.

[8]Justin Wintle and Emma Fisher, eds., *The Pied Pipers: Interviews with the Influential Creators of Children's Literature* (Paddington Press, 1974), p. 194.

[9]Leticia Ekhami, "Practically Speaking: Peer Review: Student Choices," *School Library Journal* 37 (September 1991): 196.

[10]Alexander Tresniowski/Reported by Wendy Cole, "People: Beverly Hills Book Binge," *Time* (October 21, 1991). 99.

[11]Boyd R. McCandless and Richard H. Coop, *Adolescents: Behavior and Development*, 2nd ed. (Holt, Rinehart and Winston, 1979), p. 160.

[12]Robert Havighurst, *Developmental Tasks and Education* (McKay, 1972).

[13]Alleen Pace Nilsen, "Why a Funny YA Novel Is Better than a TV Sitcom," *School Library Journal* 35 (March 1989): 120–123.

◼ OTHER TITLES MENTIONED IN THE TEXT OF CHAPTER ONE

(In Addition to the Honor Sampling and Focus Boxes)

Alcott, Louisa May. *Little Women: or Meg, Jo, Beth, and Amy. The Story of Their Lives. A Girl's Book.* 1868.

Ames, Lee. *Draw 50 Beasties and Yugglies and Turnover Uglies and Things That Go Bump in the Night.* Doubleday, 1988.

Cormier, Robert. *We All Fall Down.* Delacorte 1991.

Daly, Maureen. *Seventeenth Summer.* Dodd, Mead, 1942.

Jussim, Daniel. *Medical Ethics: Moral and Legal Conflicts in Health Care.* Messner, 1990.

Kerr, M. E. *Fell.* HarperCollins, 1987.

_____. *Fell Back.* HarperCollins, 1989.

_____. *Fell Down.* HarperCollins, 1991.

Kronenwetter, Michael. *Managing Toxic Wastes.* Messner, 1989.

Luke-Mania! Jason-Fever! Berkley Books, 1991.

Zindel, Paul. *The Effect of Gamma Rays on Man-in-the-Moon-Marigolds.* Dramatists, 1970.

CHAPTER TWO

LITERARY ASPECTS OF YOUNG ADULT BOOKS

In beginning the systematic study of young adult literature, we quickly discover many of the same questions and considerations we face in studying any body of literature. Writers of books for young readers work in much the same way as writers of other sorts of books. They have the same tools and largely the same intent: to evoke a response in a reader through words on a page. And young adult readers read with the same range of responses as any other group of readers.

 STAGES OF LITERARY APPRECIATION

The chart on the stages of literary appreciation (Table 2.1) outlines one view of how individuals develop reading skills and an appreciation of literature. Read the chart from the bottom up, because each level is built on the one below it. People do not go *through* these stages of development; instead they *add on* so that at each level they have all that they had before, plus a new way to gain pleasure and understanding (see also the discussion of teaching literature in Chapter Eleven).

Level 1: Understanding that there's pleasure and profit to be gained from printed words. Lucky children who have bedtime stories and make frequent visits to the library for story hour and for borrowing books, and who also have songs, nursery rhymes, and jingles woven into the fabric of everyday life are fortunate enough to develop this first stage of appreciation before they enter school. Jim Trelease, in his highly acclaimed *Read-Aloud Handbook,* explained

Table 2.1   *STAGES OF LITERARY APPRECIATION*

Read this chart from the bottom up to trace the stages of development most commonly found in the reading autobiographies of adults who love to read.

Level	Optimal Age	Stage	Sample Reading Materials	Sample Actions
7	Adulthood to death	Aesthetic appreciation	Classics Significant contemporary books	Reads constantly Dreams of writing the great American novel Enjoys literary criticism Reads fifty books a year Buys house with built-in bookshelves Rereads favorites
6	College	Reading widely	Best-sellers Acclaimed novels, poems, plays, magazines	Talks about books with friends Joins a book club Gathers a stack of books to take on vacation
5	High school	Venturing beyond self	Science fiction Social issues fiction Forbidden materials "Different" stories	Begins buying own books Gets reading suggestions from friends Reads beyond school assignments
4	Jr. high	Finding oneself in books	Realistic fiction Contemporary problem novels Wish-fulfilling stories	Hides novels inside textbooks to read during classes Stays up at night reading Uses reading as an escape from social pressures
3	Late elementary	Losing oneself in books	Series books Fantasies Animal stories Anything one can disappear into	Reads while doing chores Reads while traveling Makes friends with a librarian Checks books out regularly Gets "into" reading a particular genre or author
2	Primary grades	Learning to decode	School reading texts Easy-to-read books Signs and other real-world messages	Takes pride in reading to parents or others Enjoys reading alone Has favorite authors
1	Birth to kindergarten	Understanding of pleasure and profit from printed words	Nursery rhymes Folktales Picture books	Has favorite books for reading aloud "Reads" signs for certain restaurants and foods Memorizes favorite stories and pretends to read Enjoys listening to adults read

Fortunate children start on the long road to developing literary appreciation even before they learn to talk.

that he was not writing a book to help parents teach their children to read but to help them teach their children to *want to read*. His interest was in building a firm foundation for the development to follow.

If children are to put forth the intellectual energy required in learning to read, they need to be convinced that it is worthwhile—that pleasure awaits them— or that there are concrete benefits to be gained. In United States metropolitan areas, there's hardly a four-year-old who doesn't recognize the golden arches of a McDonald's restaurant. And toddlers too young to walk around grocery stores reach out from their seats in grocery carts to grab favorite brands of cereal. We know one child who by the time he entered first grade had taught himself to read from *TV Guide*. The format of *TV Guide* breaks almost every rule any good textbook writer would follow in designing a primer for clear and easy reading, but it had one overpowering advantage. The child could get immediate feedback. If he made a correct guess he was rewarded by getting to watch the program he wanted. If he made a mistake, he knew immediately that he had to return to the printed page to try again.

Level 2: Learning to read. Learning to decode (i.e., to turn the squiggles on a page into meaningful sounds) is the second stage of development. It gets maximum attention during the primary grades, where as much as 70 percent of the schoolday is devoted to language arts. But developing literacy is more than just decoding; it is a never-ending task for anyone who is intellectually active. Even at a mundane level, adults continue working to develop their reading skills. The owner of a new VCR trying to tape a television program, the person trying to get a new printer to "handshake" with the computer, and the person who rereads several tax guides in preparation for an audit exhibit the same symptoms of concentrated effort as do children first learning to read. They point with their fingers, move their lips, return to reread difficult parts, and in frustration slam the offending booklet to the floor. But in each case they are motivated by a vision of some benefit to be gained, and so they increase their efforts.

Those of us who learned to read with ease may lack empathy for those children who must struggle to master reading skills. In our impatience, we may forget to help them find pleasure and enjoyment. Children who learn to read easily—the girl who sits in the backseat of the car and reads all through the family vacation and the boy who reads a book while delivering the neighborhood newspapers—find their own rewards for reading. For these children, the years between seven and twelve are golden. They can read the great body of literature that the world has saved for them: *Charlotte's Web*, The Little House books, *The Borrowers, The Chronicles of Narnia, The Wizard of Oz, Where the Red Fern Grows,* and books by Beverly Cleary, Judy Blume, John Fitzgerald, and hundreds of other good writers.

At this stage children are undemanding. They are in what Margaret Early has described as a stage of unconscious enjoyment.[1] With help, they may enjoy such classics as *Alice in Wonderland, The Wind in the Willows, Treasure Island,* and *Little Women,* but by themselves they are far more likely to turn to less challenging material. Parents worry that their children are wasting time, but nearly 100 percent of our college students who say they love to read went through childhood stages of being addicted for months to one particular kind of book. Apparently, readers find comfort in knowing the characters in a book and what to expect. They develop speed and skill that stand them in good stead when they tire of a particular kind of book (they always do, sooner or later) and go on to reading some of the books parents and teachers wished they had been reading all along.

Level 3: Losing oneself in a story. Those children who read only during the time set aside in school may never get to the third stage of reading development, which is losing oneself in a book. If they do, it is likely to happen much later than in the third or fourth grades, which is typical of good readers. In this segment from *The Car Thief* by Theodore Weesner, Alex Housman, who is being kept in a detention home, is seventeen years old when he first experiences losing himself in a story (i.e., finding what we refer to as "a good read"). Someone has donated a box of books to the detention home and because there's nothing else to do

   Alex started to read a book called *Gunner Asch,* starting it mainly because he knew how to read, although he was intimidated by the mass of words. He had never read anything but the lessons in schoolbooks—assignments in history or science spaced with water colors of Washington crossing the Delaware or Thomas Edison working under candlelight. But the novel was simply written and fairly easy to understand, and he soon became interested enough in what was happening to stop reminding himself page after page that he was reading a book, to turn the pages to see what was going to happen next.

He sat on the floor reading until he grew sleepy. When his eyelids began to slide down and his head began to cloud, he lay over on his side on the floor to sleep awhile, pulling up his knees, resting his head on his arm. When he woke he got up and carried the book with him to the bathroom . . . reading the book again, he became so involved in the story that his legs fell asleep. He kept reading, intending to get up at the end of this page, then at the end of this page, if only because he would feel more comfortable with his pants up and buttoned, but he read on. He rose finally at the end of a chapter, although he read a little into the next chapter before he made himself stop. His legs were buoyant with saws and needles as he buttoned up, and he had to hold a hand against the wall not to sway from balance. Then he checked the thickness of pages he had read between his fingers, and experienced something he had never experienced before. Some of it was pride—he was reading a book—and some of it was a preciousness the book had assumed. Feeling relaxed, unthreatened, he wanted to keep the book in his hands for what it offered. He did not want to turn the pages, for then they would be gone and spent; nor did he want to do anything but turn the pages.

He stepped over legs again and sat down to read, as far from anyone as he could get, some fifteen feet, to be alone with the book. He read on. Something was happening to him, something as pleasantly strange as the feeling he had had for Irene Scheaffer. By now, if he knew a way, he would prolong the book the distance his mind could see, and he rose again, quietly, to sustain the pleasant sensation, the escape he seemed already to have made from the scarred and unlighted corridor. Within this shadowed space there were now other things—war and food and worry over cigarettes and rations, leaving and returning, dying and escaping. The corridor itself, and his own life, was less present.[2]

Level 4: Finding oneself in a story. The more experience children have with reading, the more discriminating they become. To receive pleasure they have to respect the book. In reminiscing about his childhood fondness for both *The Hardy Boys* and motorcycles, the late John Gardner remarked that his development as a literary critic took a step forward when he lost patience with the leisurely conversations that the Hardy boys were supposed to have had as they roared down country roads side by side on their motorcycles.

Good readers begin developing this critical sense in literature at about the same time they develop it in real life—at the end of childhood and the beginning of their teen years. They move away from a simple interest in what happened in a story to ask *why*. They want logical development and are no longer satisfied with stereotypes. They want characters controlled by believable human motives because now their reading has a real purpose to it. They are reading to find out about themselves, not simply to escape into someone else's experiences for a few pleasurable hours. They may read dozens of contemporary teenage novels, looking for lives as much like their own as possible. They read about real people in biographies, personal essays, and journalistic stories. They are also curious about other sides of life, and so they seek out books that present lives totally different from their own. They look for anything bizarre, unbelievable, weird, or grotesque: stories of occult happenings, trivia books, and horror stories. And of course for their leisure-time reading they may revert to level 3 of escaping into a good story. But when they are reading at the highest level of their capability, their purpose is largely one of finding themselves and their places in society.

Level 5: Venturing beyond themselves. The next stage in reading development comes when people go beyond their egocentrism and look at the larger circle of society. Senior high school English teachers have some of their best teaching experiences with books by such writers as Ernest Hemingway, John Steinbeck, Harper Lee, F. Scott Fitzgerald, Carson McCullers, William Faulkner, Arthur Miller, and Flannery O'Connor. Students respond to the way these books raise questions about conformity, social pressures, justice, and other aspects of human frailties and strengths. It is at this level that students are ready to begin looking at shades of gray rather than at black and white. Book discussions can have real meat to them because readers make different interpretations as they bring their own experiences into play against those in the books.

Obviously, getting to this level of literary appreciation is more than a matter of developing an advanced set of decoding skills. It is closely tied in with intellectual, physical, and emotional development. Teenagers face the tremendous responsibility of assessing the world around them and deciding where they will fit in. Reading at this level allows teenagers to focus on their own psychological needs in relation to society. The more directly they can do this, the more efficient they feel, which probably explains the popularity of contemporary problem novels featuring young protagonists, as in the books by Bruce Brooks, M. E. Kerr, Robert Cormier, Alice Childress, Sue Ellen Bridgers, and Richard Peck.

Although many people read fantasy and science fiction at the level of losing themselves in a good story, others may read such books as William Sleator's *House of Stairs;* Virginia Hamilton's *Sweet Whispers, Brother Rush;* and Robin McKinley's *The Blue Sword* at a higher level of reflection. They come back from spending a few hours in the imagined society with new ideas about their own society.

Levels 6 and 7: Reading widely and for aesthetic appreciation. When people have developed the skills and attitudes necessary to read at all the levels described so far, they are ready to embark on a lifetime of reading both fiction and nonfiction. They read for all the purposes described at earlier levels, but they also read for literary or aesthetic appreciation. This is the level at which authors, critics, and literary scholars concentrate their efforts. But even they don't work at this level all the time, because it is as demanding as it is rewarding. The professor who teaches Shakespeare goes home at night and loses himself in a televised rerun of "L. A. Law" or "Cheers," and the author who writes for hours in the morning might read herself to sleep that night with an Agatha Christie mystery. Reading at this highest level is an active endeavor, because the reader is doing half the work in identifying with the author and figuring out how he or she brought about a certain effect. Additional pleasure comes in knowing facts about the author's life and how the author's books have grown out of personal experiences and beliefs (see Focus Box 2.1).

In a 1983 article entitled "Finally Only the Love of the Art,"[3] poet Donald Hall wrote about his own development as a reader and writer. Except for the speed befitting his giftedness, the following excerpts show that Hall's development progressed in the same order as that described here for more typical readers.

The family lived in a variety of homes until, during Hall's early school years in the 1930s, his family assumed a mortgage on a house in Hamden that a bank had repossessed because of the Depression. Hall described it as a "bookish house" because his father read constantly and his mother recited poems to him. In the summers Hall would go to the family farm where his grandfather "said poems ('Casey at the Bat,' 'Lawyer Green,' and 'What the Deacon Said') all day long without repeating himself." His great-uncle Luther wrote verses, and so did his English-teaching Aunt Caroline, who told him "about a seafaring adventurer trapped by a cruel one-eyed giant." Hall wrote:

> ▪ . . . in Hamden from September to June I dreamed of returning to the farm. I did not enjoy the company of other children; I wanted to grow up, even to be old, like the people I loved the most. Alone after school I took pleasure in books—in the Bobbsey Twins, in the Hardy Boys, later in Roy Helton's "Jimmy Sharswood," then gradually in grown-up books. And in movies of werewolves and vampires, which when I was 12 prompted a boy next door (bless you, wherever you are) to recommend the works of Edgar Allan Poe.
>
> I swallowed Poe whole. Then I swallowed Hervey Allen's biography of Poe, "Israfel," and discovered for myself the thrilling role of *poète maudit*. . . . From 12 to 14 I wrote poems and short stories. I started novels and five-act tragedies in verse. But I had not yet committed myself wholly to writing. I entertained occasional notions of becoming an actor, or President. ("Nothing is so commonplace," Oliver Wendell Holmes said, "as to wish to be remarkable.")

When he was fourteen, Hall went to a Boy Scout meeting and happened to tell another boy that he had written a poem that day in study hall. The boy confessed that writing poems was "his profession," and he took Hall with him on poetic excursions into New Haven, where he introduced him to "Yale freshmen—18-year-olds!—who were literary geniuses."

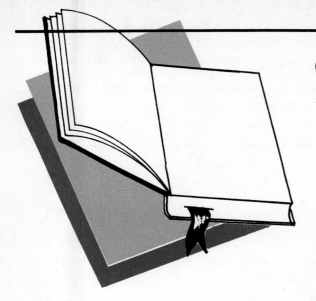

Contemporary YA Authors Tell Their Own Stories

Anonymously Yours By Richard Peck. Messner, 1991. Part of a new *In My Own Words* series, this autobiography is fairly short and easy to read.

Bill Peet, an Autobiography by Bill Peet. Houghton Mifflin, 1989. Bill Peet writes for children rather than teenagers, but many young adults have fond memories of his books and will therefore enjoy this autobiography supplemented with Peet's own cartoon-style drawings.

Boston Boy by Nat Hentoff. Knopf, 1986. Although written as an adult book, Hentoff's story of his Jewish boyhood in the anti-Semitic world of 1930s Boston will be interesting to older teens.

Chapters: My Growth as a Writer by Lois Duncan. Little, Brown, 1982. Duncan starts her story on the afternoon of her fourteenth year, when she came home from school and found that she had sold her first story to *Calling All Girls*.

A Girl from Yamhill: A Memoir by Beverly Cleary. Morrow, 1988. Cleary tells the story of her life as a child and a teenager, first on a farm and later in Portland.

Homesick: My Own Story by Jean Fritz. Putnam, 1982. Although Fritz chose to label *Homesick* "fiction," because of squeezing events from her whole childhood into a two-year story, she wrote in the foreword, "It is my story, told as truly as I can tell it."

Little by Little: A Writer's Education by Jean Little. Viking Penguin, 1988. As a child growing up in Taiwan and Canada, Jean Little was legally blind, but that didn't stop her from wanting to become a writer.

The Lost Garden by Laurence Yep. Messner, 1991. Yep's story, which is aimed at a junior high audience, will help readers empathize with a boy straddling two cultures.

Me, Me, Me, Me, Me, Not a Novel by M. E. Kerr. HarperCollins, 1983. Although this story is just as much fun to read as most of Kerr's fiction, she says that this one is a true account of the young life of Marijane Meaker, which is Kerr's real name.

The Pigman & Me by Paul Zindel. HarperCollins, 1992. Readers will both laugh and cry at this true account of a year in the teenage life of Paul Zindel.

Speaking for Ourselves: Autobiographical Sketches by Notable Authors of Books for Young Adults, edited by Donald R. Gallo. National Council of Teachers of English, 1990. Over eighty authors contributed two-page biographies to this interesting collection.

Starting from Home: A Writer's Beginnings by Milton Meltzer. Viking, 1988. Meltzer has brought different periods of history alive for thousands of young readers, and now he does the same thing for the early 1900s, as he tells about his family and his childhood.

The Times of My Life: A Memoir by Brent Ashabranner. Dutton, 1990. Ashabranner's story is interesting because of his career working in various foreign countries before he became a writer.

It was during this "heady time" that Donald Hall first began to get poems accepted by "little" magazines and eventually bigger ones. And now in his sixties, he's still aspiring for the top level of literary appreciation. He concluded his article:

> If you continue to write, you go past the place where praise, publication or admiration sustains you. The more praise the better—but it does not sustain you. You arrive at a point where only the possibilities of poetry provide food for your desires, possibilities glimpsed in great poems that you love. What began perhaps as the north wind's cooky—what continued variously as affection and self-love; what zaps crazily up and down in public recognition—finds repose only in love of art, and in the desire, if not precisely the hope, that you may make something fit to endure with the old ones.

The important points to learn from this discussion of stages of literary development are

- The ages given are the ideal; many people come to the later stages much later or not at all.
- People do not go through these stages, but instead add each one onto the foundation below. This means that those who miss a stage will be disadvantaged for all subsequent stages.
- Teachers, librarians, and parents should meet young readers where they are and help them feel comfortable at that stage before trying to move them on.
- Moving up to a new level takes not only improved reading skills, but also increased intellectual, physical, and psychological maturity.
- With an adult's help, young people can read at a higher level than they can by themselves; nevertheless, we should not push young people always to work at the highest level of their ability.
- We need to continue to provide for all the levels below the one on which we are focusing; for example, readers at any stage need to experience pleasure and profit from their reading or they may grow discouraged and join the millions of adults who have dropped off this chart and read only when they are forced to.

BECOMING A LITERARY CRITIC

As Hall indicates, the top level is not something a writer reaches effortlessly, or that once reached requires no further effort. Reaching that level as a reader means becoming a literary critic, not necessarily for other people but at least for oneself. The difference between being a critic and a reviewer is that a reviewer evaluates and makes recommendations about who would most like to read which book. Critics do more. Besides evaluating and recommending books, they give guidance. They explain. The good critic makes observations that, when shared, help others to read with understanding and insight.

Developing into the kind of reader able to derive nourishment at the highest level of literary response is a lifelong task, one that challenges all of us. The information presented in this chapter is basic to identifying with a story through the eyes of the author as well as those of the characters. We present it at the beginning of this textbook to help you

- Sharpen your insights into authors' working methods, so that you will get more out of your reading.
- Give you terminology and techniques to use in sharing your insights with young readers.
- Evaluate books and assist readers in moving up in developing their skills.
- Read reviews, articles, and critical analyses with greater understanding.

Some people speak of literature with a capital *L* to identify the kind of literature that is set apart from, or has a degree of excellence not found in, the masses of printed material that daily roll from the presses. This literature rewards study, not only because of its content, but because of its style, the techniques used, and the universality, permanence, and congeniality of the ideas expressed.

It is on the question of universality and permanence that some critics have asked whether stories written specifically for young readers can be considered Literature. Their feeling is that if a story speaks only to readers of a certain age, then it cannot really have the kind of universality required in true literature. However, every adult has lived through an adolescence and continues to experience many of the doubts, leave-takings, embarkings on new roles, and sudden flashes of joy and wonder that can be found in books with protagonists between the ages of twelve and twenty-five. Books that show the uniqueness and at the same time the universality of such experiences—*Adventures of Huckleberry Finn, The Catcher in the Rye, Little Women,* and *Lord of the Flies,* for example—are often referred to as classics. They have proven themselves with different readers across different time periods. And they are the books that readers return to for a second and third reading, each time feeling rewarded.

In contrast to literature with a capital *L,* there is formula literature and escape literature. In truth, all stories consist of variations on a limited number of plots and themes, but the difference between what is referred to simply as literature and what is referred to as formula literature is one of degree. Formula literature is almost entirely predictable. Many of the situation comedies, crime shows, and adventure shows on television are formula pieces. So are many of the books that young people—and adults—enjoy reading.

Because formula literature is highly predictable, the reader can relax and enjoy a story while expending a minimum of intellectual energy. For this reason, formula literature is often used as escape literature—something people read only for entertainment and relaxation with little or no hope of gaining insights or learning new information.

Although some significant literature will have a plot exciting enough to be read at the level of escapism and fun, the reverse isn't true. There simply isn't enough content in formula fiction to make it worthy of the kind of reading done at the upper levels. But when viewed in perspective as only part of the world's literature, there is nothing wrong with young people enjoying formula or escape literature either in books or on film.

However, it is understandable that the goal of most educators who work with young readers is to help them develop enough skill that they are not limited to this kind of reading. We want them to be able to receive pleasure from all kinds of literature, including that which offers much more than escape or amusement.

Authors of the best young adult books use the same literary techniques— though perhaps to a different degree—as the authors of the best books for adults. As will be seen in the following chapters, these literary techniques can be discussed in many different ways. Two approaches that have proven useful include classification by genre and the analysis of such essential literary elements as plot, theme, character, point of view, tone, setting, and style.

PLOT

In examining books that become popular with young adults compared to those that do not, a crucial difference often appears in the plotting. The plot of a story is the sequence of events in which the characters play out their roles in some kind of conflict. Plot is what happens.

Elements of Plot

For most young readers, there needs to be a promise within the first few pages that something exciting is going to happen, that there is going to be a believable conflict. Authors use various techniques to get this message across to their readers, or to "hook" them. S. E. Hinton did it with her first sentence in *Taming the Star Runner:* "His boot felt empty without the knife in it." Bruce Brooks did it with the first two paragraphs in *The Moves Make the Man:*

Now, Bix Rivers has disappeared, and who do you think is going to tell his story but me? Maybe his stepfather? Man, that dude does not know

Bix deep and now he never will, will he? Only thing he could say is he's probably secretly happy Bix ran away and got out of his life, but he won't tell you even that on account of he's busy getting sympathy dumped on him all over town as the poor deserted guardian.

How about Bix's momma? Can she tell you? I reckon not—she is crazy in the hospital. And you can believe, they don't let crazies have anything sharp like a pencil, else she poke out her eye or worse. So she won't be writing any stories for a long time. But me—I have plenty of pencils, number threes all sharp and dark green enamel on the outside, and I have four black and white marble composition books. Plus I can tell you some things, like Bix was thirteen last birthday (same as me), Bix was a shortstop (supreme), Bix gets red spots the size of a quarter on his cheekbones when angry and a splotch looks like a cardinal smack in the middle of his forehead when he is ashamed. I can tell a lot more, besides . . ."

Other authors use catchy titles as narrative hooks, for example, Jerry Spinelli's *There's a Girl in My Hammerlock*, Paula Fox's *The Moonlight Man*, Olive Ann Burns' *Cold Sassy Tree*, and Cynthia Voigt's *Izzy, Willy-Nilly*. Titles that are questions, such as Richard Peck's *Are You in the House Alone?* and M. E. Kerr's *If I Love You, Am I Trapped Forever?* trigger other questions in readers' minds and make them pick up the book to find the answers.

Asking questions like this works much the same as *in media res* (Latin for "in the midst of things"). It's a technique that authors use to bring the reader directly into the middle of the story. This will usually be followed by a flashback to fill in the missing details. Paul Zindel does this in *The Pigman*. Few readers put the book down after they get acquainted with two likable teenagers and then read John's statement:

Now Lorraine can blame all the other things on me, but she was the one who picked out the Pigman's phone number. If you ask me, I think he would have died anyway. Maybe we speeded things up a little, but you really can't say we murdered him.

Not murdered him.

The most exciting plots are the ones in which the action is continually rising, building suspense, and finally leading to some sort of climax. After an exciting climax, readers need to be let down gently. This brief subsiding and wrapping up of details is called the *denouement*.

In Bruce Brooks' *The Moves Make the Man*, the denouement removes any doubt as to whose story was being told. It is the narrator Jerome's as much as it is Bix's. Jerome makes the transition to his own story with, "Then it was summer and no sign of Bix and I decided to write this book. Now it is fall and you have the story." The remaining six paragraphs reassure the reader that although Bix is gone, Jerome is going to make it and without getting "all soft and mellow and full of good teary jive."

■ I got my own fakes to worry about now. I have not played ball since Bix ran away. Are my moves gone? I doubt it. But I will find out tonight. My head is healed up and the nights are getting cooler and everybody is still full of baseball and summer jive, so they won't notice old Jerome slip out in the dark with his lantern and slide across the marsh and vanish into the forest. Then it will be just Jerome and Spin Light and we will see what we can see and there will be nobody else, not for a long time.

In contrast to plots with rising action are those that are episodic. Writers of nonfiction will use many of the literary techniques discussed here so that as they describe incidents and quote dialogue, the paragraphs they write will differ little from fiction. However, rather than developing an overall plot, they are more likely to present a series of episodes. This is typical of memoirs such as James Herriot's *All Creatures Great and Small,* Maya Angelou's *I Know Why the Caged Bird Sings,* and Milton Meltzer's *The American Revolutionaries: A History in Their Own Words.*

The more unusual a plot is, the greater is the need for the author to drop hints that will prepare readers for what is ahead. This is called foreshadowing. In *Cat, Herself,* Mollie Hunter does it through fortune telling and the vision that Cat sees of herself. Robert Cormier did it in *We All Fall Down* by naming the handyman, who turns out to be a psychopath, Mickey Looney. Anyone familiar with Cormier's writing would know better than to dismiss Jane's explanation:

■ "His name is Mickey Stallings but everybody calls him Mickey Looney," she said. "Behind his back of course." Needing to explain: "Because he looks like that old movie star, Mickey Rooney. But, Looney because he is sort of odd."

Jane feels she's betrayed the neighborhood by confiding Mickey's name because the "nickname Mickey Looney was used affectionately for this gentle man who patted dogs, tousled the hair of small kids, nodded respectfully to the men and tipped his faded baseball cap to the ladies." Jane's friends say he gives them the creeps, and when Jane goes on to explain how smart he is, she is setting up an explanation that will make credible what happens 150 pages later.

In fantasy and science fiction, foreshadowing may be what identifies the genre. For example, in William Sleator's *Interstellar Pig,* the foreshadowing starts with the first sentence, "I'm telling you, there's more history to this house than any other place on Indian Neck, and that's the truth." On page 5, the landlord says about the new neighbors. "This here's the place they wanted, but they were too late. Already rented it to you folks. Man, were they ever disappointed. Never heard anybody get so upset about a summer rental."

When the neighbors arrive—two gorgeous young men and an equally gorgeous woman—they use such words as *logement, frisson,* and *beurre noir.* Barney, the teenage narrator, describes them as having a "casual, animal grace to their movements that attracted the eye simply because it was so unusual. I knew they were just three people—but somehow I felt as though I were watching three lions." There are enough such clues that by page 12, readers have figured out what Barney's parents never do figure out. The new neighbors are definitely not ordinary humans.

The effect of this foreshadowing is not to give away the ending, but to increase excitement and suspense and prepare the reader for the outcome. If authors fail to prepare readers—at least on a subconscious level—their stories may lack verisimilitude or believability. Readers want interesting and exciting plots, but they don't want to feel manipulated.

Traditionally, readers have expected to know all the answers by the end of the book, to have the plot come to a tidy close. But with some stories authors feel this is an unrealistic expectation and so they leave it up to the reader to imagine the ending. In *A Hero Ain't Nothin' But a Sandwich*, Alice Childress didn't think it fair to predict either that Benjie would become a confirmed drug addict or that he would go straight. Boys in his situation turn either way, and Childress wanted readers to think about this.

Another trend that is frustrating to some readers and critics is that as authors strive for realism, they forget about plot. Instead of writing stories, some critics say, they write case histories. Such books often have to do with a young person's struggle with drug or alcohol addiction, mental or physical illness, conflict with parents, sexual problems, or problems with the law. When an author has not planned an exciting plot, it seems that the temptation is greater to rely on unsavory details. These are the books that are often criticized for their sensationalism.

To have an interesting plot, a story must have a problem of some sort. In adult books, several problems may be treated simultaneously, but in most of the books written specifically for young adults, as well as in those that they respond to from the adult list, the focus is generally on one problem. However, authors may include a secondary or minor problem to appeal to specific readers. For example, in most of Paul Zindel's books, the primary problem is one of personal growth and development on the part of either one or two protagonists. But he tucks in an unobtrusive element of love that will bring satisfaction to romantically inclined readers without being bothersome to the rest of his audience.

Types of Plots

Basically, the problems around which plots are developed are of four types: protagonist against self, protagonist against society, protagonist against another person, and protagonist against nature.

Protagonist Against Self   A large portion of the rites-of-passage stories popular with young adults are of the protagonist-against-self type. Through the happenings in the book, the protagonist comes to some new understanding or level of maturity. For example, practically the whole story in Paula Fox's *One-Eyed Cat* takes place in the mind of eleven-year-old Ned. An uncle gives him a Daisy air rifle for his birthday, which his father puts in the attic and forbids him to use. But when Ned goes to the attic he finds "it almost at once, as though it had a voice which had called to him." He takes the gun outside and convinces himself that if he tries it just once, he will "be able to do what his father had told him to do—take his mind away from it."

Events do not turn out as Ned anticipated. It's true that after he fires the gun, he no longer has an interest in shooting, but this is because he is tortured by his memory:

> As he blinked and opened his right eye wide, he saw a dark shadow against the stones which the moon's light had turned the color of ashes. For a split second, it looked alive. Before he could think, his finger had pressed the trigger.
>
> There was a quick *whoosh,* the sound a bobwhite makes when it bursts out of underbrush, then silence. He was sure there hadn't been any loud report that would have waked anyone in the house, yet he had heard something, a kind of thin disturbance in the air. He walked over to the barn. There was no shadow now. There was nothing. He might have only dreamed that he had fired the rifle.

But within a few days when Ned is visiting the old man who lives next door, he sees a gaunt-looking cat and notices that the cat has dried blood on its face and a little hole where its left eye should be. "A thought was buzzing and circling inside his head, a thought that stung like a wasp could sting. . . . He had disobeyed his father and he had shot at something that was alive. He knew it was that cat."

The rest of the book is the story of Ned's internal anguish, his keeping the terrible secret to himself at the same time he attempts to make up for his action, and finally his coming to terms with the event and his sharing of it with his mother.

Protagonist Against Society

Protagonist-against-self stories are often, in part, protagonist-against-society stories. For example, in Sylvia Path's *The Bell Jar,* Esther Greenwood is struggling to understand herself, but the depression and the fears and doubts that she feels are brought on by her experience in New York as a college intern on a fashion magazine. Getting accepted for this position had been an important goal of hers, and she is disappointed because, when she achieves this goal, she finds that the work and the life that go with it seem frivolous and hollow.

Sue Ellen Bridgers' *Home Before Dark* is another book in which the protagonist struggles both against herself and against society. Fourteen-year-old Stella has lived most of the life she can remember in the old white station wagon that her family used for traveling from one crop to the next. When finally

Stella's father returns to the family farm that he had abandoned years before, Stella does not want to leave—ever. She refuses to leave even after her mother dies and her father remarries. And she explains:

> None of us ever owned anything until we came back to Daddy's home and Newton gave us the little house. But somehow, I felt like it had always been ours. That land out there belonged to us no matter what anyone said. Daddy was born to it, and I was born to Daddy; so the land and the house were mine. They truly belonged to me, and I belonged to them, like I had known the house and land long before and had somehow forgotten about them for a while.

Finally, Stella accepts the little house and the farm as being only one part of her life. They will always be there and she can come back to them, but she must go from them too, unless she wants to be trapped at a standstill while the rest of her family moves forward.

Books about members of minority groups (see Focus Boxes 1.3 [p. 26], 1.4 [p. 28], 2.2, and 2.3) frequently include at least some themes of protagonist against society because of the tensions that exist when members of the smaller group face choices about how much they want to try fitting into the norms of the larger group. In such books, the individuals' self-concepts as well as the problems they face are directly related to the society around them, as in Danny Santiago's *Famous All Over Town*, Joyce Carol Thomas' *Marked by Fire*, Rosa Guy's *The Friends*, and Sharon Bell Mathis' *Teacup Full of Roses*. Chaim Potok's *My Name Is Asher Lev* and *The Chosen* show boys who are trying to reach understandings of themselves, but these understandings are greatly affected by the Hasidic Jewish societies in which the boys were born and raised.

Robert Cormier's *The Chocolate War, I Am the Cheese, After the First Death,* and *Beyond the Chocolate War* all come close to being pure examples of plots in which the protagonists are in conflict with society. In *The Chocolate War* and its sequel, almost everyone in the school—faculty and students alike—goes along with the evil plans of Archie and the Vigils. The denouement of *Beyond the Chocolate War* shows that the conflict was more than a personal one between Archie and Obie. There will always be a Bunting, a Janza, and a Harley to take the place of an Archie.

In *I Am the Cheese,* Adam is left friendless and vulnerable in an institution as the result of organized crime combined with government corruption. In *After the First Death*, one young boy is betrayed by his father who is a military psychologist, while another is kept by his father in a terrible state of innocence in which he is trained as a terrorist and never allowed to experience human feelings of compassion, love, or fear. But the blame for the tragic consequences cannot be laid on the fathers' shoulders because each of them is a victim in his own way of the society to which he belongs.

A Sampling of Books Featuring Characters Who Are Hispanic

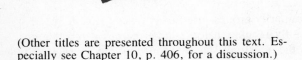

(Other titles are presented throughout this text. Especially see Chapter 10, p. 406, for a discussion.)

Across the Great River by Irene Beltran Hernandez. Arte Publico Press, 1989. Kate's father drowns as his family is led across the Rio Grande to start life in America. What Kate had envisioned as the land of opportunity becomes instead a test of endurance.

Alan and Naomi by Myron Levoy. Harper-Collins, 1977. This is as much a story of friendship as romance and includes kids from different ethnic groups trying to understand each other.

Barrio Boy by Ernesto Galarza. University of Notre Dame Press, 1977. Written in the style of a biography, this traces a boy's journey from a small village in northern Mexico to a barrio in Sacramento.

Baseball in April: And Other Stories by Gary Soto. Harcourt Brace Jovanovich, 1990. Karate lessons, Little League baseball, family problems, and relating to the opposite sex are some of the focus topics in these eleven stories about growing up in central California. Other Soto books include *A Summer Life* (Dell, 1991) and *Taking Sides* (Harcourt Brace Jovanovich, 1991).

Best Friends Tell the Best Lies by Carol Dines. Delacorte, 1989. This well-done exploration of first love, single-parent families, and social caste systems starts with fourteen-year-old Leah being upset about her mother's attraction to José.

Famous All Over Town by Danny Santiago. Simon & Schuster, 1983. In this family story set in East Los Angeles, Chato stands up against pressure not only from the neighborhood gang but also from his father.

Hunger of Memory: The Education of Richard Rodriguez an autobiography by Richard Rodriguez. David R. Godine Publisher, Inc., 1982. When Richard Rodriguez earned his Ph.D. from the University of California at Berkeley, the honor symbolized Rodriguez's assimilation into mainstream culture but alienation from his roots.

Nilda by Nicholasa Mohr. HarperCollins, 1973. The well-received *Nilda* was followed by three other books also showing what it's like to be a Puerto Rican and a New Yorker: *El Bronx Remembered* (Harper, 1975) *In Nueva York* (Dial, 1977), and *Going Home* (Dial, 1986).

Pocho by José Antonio Villarreal. Doubleday Anchor, 1989. (Originally published in 1959 by Doubleday.) Set during the Depression in California, Villarreal's story was one of the first to show the frustration and pain of trying to be part of two worlds, that of his Mexican parents and that of his new home in Sacramento.

A Shadow Like a Leopard   by Myron Levoy. HarperCollins, 1981. Fourteen-year-old Ramon is a Puerto Rican New Yorker who makes friends with an elderly painter.

Throw a Hungry Loop   by Dona Schenker. Knopf, 1990. Thirteen-year-old Texan "Tres" Bomer shares his name, but not a whole lot else, with his father and grandfather. Thanks to a heifer calf, a stubborn and unappreciated mule, and a girl named Robin, Tres's story ends on a happier note than it begins.

Protagonist Against Another   Sometimes there is a combination in which the protagonist struggles with self, and also with another person or persons. For example, in Judith Guest's *Ordinary People*, Conrad is struggling to gain his mental health after he attempts suicide, but this struggle is tied to the sibling rivalry that he felt with his older brother who was killed accidentally. And the sibling rivalry is tied to the relationship that exists between him and his parents. Because nearly everyone has experienced conflicts with family members, they can identify with the sibling rivalry in Katherine Paterson's *Jacob Have I Loved*, the tenuousness of the father/daughter relationship in Paula Fox's *The Moonlight Man*, and the family/foster child conflict in Rosa Guy's *The Disappearance*.

Adventure stories, for example, the *Rambo* movies based on David Morrell's *First Blood*, epitomize the person-against-person plot. Other examples include Julian Thompson's *A Band of Angels*, in which five young teens are unaware that they are being pursued by government agents, and Robb White's *Deathwatch*, in which the hunting guide becomes the hunting target.

Fantasy and science fiction will often have person- (or creature-) against-person plots because it is easier to personify evil when the subjects are not real people as with the aliens in William Sleator's *Interstellar Pig*, the twin in Lois Duncan's occult *Stranger with My Face*, and the evil Arawn in Lloyd Alexander's *The Black Cauldron*.

Protagonist Against Nature   Among the most exciting of the protagonist-against-nature stories are accounts of true adventures, such as Piers Paul Read's *Alive: The Story of the Andes Survivors*, Thor Heyerdahl's *The "RA" Expeditions*, and Dougal Robertson's *Survive the Savage Sea*. The stories of contemporary young adults challenging the seas include Steven Callahan's *Adrift: Seventy-Six Days Lost at Sea* and Robin Graham's *Dove*.

Within recent years, several authors have done a reverse twist on the person-against-nature plot and have made nature the protagonist and people the antagonists. This is the beginning situation in Richard Adams' *Watership Down* and throughout *The Plague Dogs*. It is also what underlies the story in John Donovan's *Family* and in Robert C. O'Brien's *Z for Zachariah*.

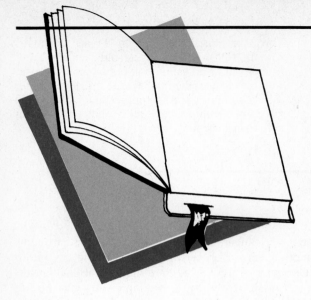

A Sampling of Books Featuring Characters Who Are Native American

(Other titles are presented throughout this text. Especially see Chapter 5 for books with mystical themes featuring American Indians.)

Bearstone by Will Hobbs. Atheneum, 1989. Cloyd, whose mother is dead and whose father is kept alive only by machines, resents being sent to spend the summer as a helper to an elderly farmer whose wife recently died.

The Brave by Robert Lipsyte. HarperCollins, 1991. Sonny Bear leaves the Moscondaga reservation and ends up in Harlem, where, fortunately, not all the people he meets are as devious as his self-appointed welcoming committee.

Ceremony by Leslie Marmon Silko. Viking/Penguin, 1977. Mature readers appreciate this story of a young Indian soldier coming home to find meaning in his life.

Dancing Teepees: Poems of American Indian Youth selected by Virginia Driving Hawk Sneve. Holiday House, 1989. The poems in this well-done collection are taken both from oral traditions and from the writings of contemporary Indian poets.

Lakota Woman by Mary Crow Dog and Richard Erdoes. Grove Weidenfeld, 1990. This mature biography tells about the author's participation in AIM, the new American Indian Movement, the stand-off at Wounded Knee, South Dakota, and her marriage to a medicine man. Written for adults, the book is harsh and graphic.

Legend Days by Jamake Highwater. HarperCollins, 1984. A young woman struggles for survival in this story which provides both historical and spiritual insights. Other historical Highwater books include *Anpao: An American Indian Odyssey* (HarperCollins, 1977) and *The Sun He Dies* (Lippincott, 1980).

Racing the Sun by Paul Pitts. Avon/Camelot, 1988. Twelve-year-old Brandon Rogers' family has adopted the culture of the white American suburbs, but then Brandon's grandfather comes to live with them and Brandon gets a chance to learn to "race the sun."

The Shadow Brothers by A. E. Cannon. Delacorte, 1990. Navajo Henry Yazzie has lived as a foster brother to Marcus Jenkins since he was seven. Now a Hopi boy comes to their high school and makes Henry take a second look at what being Indian means.

Skinwalkers by Tony Hillerman. Harper-Collins, 1987. Hillerman writes intriguing mysteries set on a Navajo reservation in Arizona. Other titles about his Navajo detectives Lieutenant Joe Leaphorn and Officer Jim Chee include *The Dance Hall of the Dead*, *The Listening Woman, People of Darkness*, *The Dark Wind*, and *The Ghostway*.

Sweetgrass by Jan Hudson. Philomel, 1989. In this historical novel, fifteen-year-old Sweetgrass lives with her tribe in western Canada. She comes of age during the terrible winter when her tribe suffers a smallpox epidemic.

The Throwing Season by Michael French. Delacorte, 1980. Henry "Indian" Chevrolet is a shot-put champion who hopes to win a college scholarship, but his plans are interrupted.

A Woman of Her Tribe by Margaret A. Robinson. Scribner's, 1990. Fifteen-year-old Annette is half-Anglo and half-Nootka Indian. She finds herself faced with demands to choose between her Indian heritage and her dreams of the future.

A Yellow Raft in Blue Water by Michael Dorris. Holt, Rinehart and Winston, 1987. Three generations of women tell their stories in this engrossing novel that centers around fifteen-year-old Rayona, who is half-Indian, half-black.

Native American authors writing for adults but whose works can be introduced to high school students include Paula Gunn Allen, Peter Blue Cloud, Michael Dorris, Anita Endrezze, Louise Erdrich, Joy Harjo, Linda Hogan, N. Scott Momaday, Simon Ortiz, Wendy Rose, Leslie Marmon Silko, Gerald Vizenor, James Welch, and Ray A. Young Bear. These authors' works were recommended by teachers Alecia Baker and Randee Browne from Boise, Idaho, at the 1991 National Council of Teachers of English annual convention.

 THEME AND MODE

Closely related to plot is theme. Theme in a book is what ties it all together and answers the questions: What does the story mean? What is it about? Theme should not be confused with a didactic moral tagged on at the end of a story, nor should it be confused with plot. Instead it is something that pervades the story and stays with the reader long after details of plot, setting, and even character have faded.

Sometimes an author will be very explicit in developing a theme, even expressing part of it in the title as with Maya Angelou's *All God's Children Need Traveling Shoes*, John Knowles' *A Separate Peace*, and S. E. Hinton's *The Outsiders*. At other times the theme is almost hidden so that young readers need help in finding it through discussion of the book with others who have read it. A book can have more than one theme, but usually the secondary themes will be less important to the story. However, because of the experiences that a reader brings to a book, it may be a secondary theme that happens to impress a particular reader. A theme must be discovered by the reader. It can't simply be told or else it is reduced to a moral.

JAY BENNETT
on The Responsibility of the Writer

This is an old, old legend and it has appeared in many diverse cultures and at different points in man's history. I'm sure it became current in violent, fragmented times when people and their leaders became confused and disoriented and didn't know where to turn. I should say, people and their leaders and their writers.

Here is one of the forms of that legend.

Long, long ago, when time was misted, there lived on a lonely, vast mountain area a prophet and his tribe. Their lives were peaceful and harmonious. They were a mild and decent people and their diet was a simple one. They grew a strain of mountain wheat that was very rare and from this wheat they made their food. But one day it was discovered that something strange had happened to the wheat. Whoever ate of the grain

immediately lost his sanity. This happened to person after person with a severe regularity.

After much thought and soul searching, the prophet decided that in order to avert total starvation, he and his people would continue to eat the strange new strain of wheat. But a carefully selected few of the tribe would still live on the limited stores of grain that had been stored in granaries. The old, pure grain.

"They will remain sane," the prophet told his tribe. "And we, looking upon them, will remember that we, too, were sane. And so, they will keep us from insane acts and so they will help us endure."

This legend came back to me with a resonance and force after I put down my newspaper the other day. I thought of the wisdom and dilemma of that old prophet, and I thought that it is up to the writer to remain sane these days.

It is up to the librarian, to the teacher to get food from the same granary the writer will be going to.

Consider the young. We all owe a grave responsibility to our young adult readers. We should be able to remind them after they've had a dose of junk television that they are sane and clear-minded and have a great stake in the world about them. The writer for the young adult readership should be a master of craft and a person of great integrity. I find that many of my colleagues are just that. I, for one, believe that the best writing these days is being done in my field. I believe that the adult readers are, in the main, being fed poisoned grain. I've picked up book after book, all highly touted and some highly praised by so-called responsible critics, and I've found that I couldn't get past the third or fourth page without seeing black spots before my eyes and feeling nausea sweep over me. That the long and ancient tradition of writing should come to this pass is tragic and shameful.

In the young adult field, I find the writers more honest, more dedicated—they're not after the main chance and the big buck—and are better masters of their craft. I say I find this today, but I'm very concerned about the future. I'm very concerned that the blight from above may hover over us like a mushroom cloud and destroy everything. The influence of bad television and bad adult books could wreak havoc with the writers and readers of our field. So I feel it's up to all of us to try to keep our grain pure.

Young adult readers should be encouraged and guided to the best of standards. If they pick up a suspense book, they should demand that it first be an entertaining one. A sight more thrilling and engrossing than most suspense television shows and feature movies. And having at one time written close to a million words for television, I can tell you that it's not a hard task for a writer who has learned his craft to beat the television boys with the product they're turning out these days.

So, the books should be entertaining in the best sense of the word. And, above all, they should have a strong and sustaining theme. I firmly believe this. Whenever I go out to meet my readers or when I read the letters they send me, I find that the themes I choose make my books extremely popular. For example, I deal with the loner in our society and show that it is impossible to survive alone. One must come to a decision, the decision to relate to the rest of humanity. Readers identify with my "loner" character and enjoy the crises of decision and at the same time find their sensibilities opened up. Readers think and feel as they enjoy, and whether or not they know it consciously, they have learned something about the world they are living in. Something that may help them develop a philosophy of decent and healthful living.

Now a word about suspense and violence.

The suspense genre, by its very nature, must deal with violence and its thread. But this does not mean that the writer should bring in violence for the sake of violence. Just to titillate, to thrill, to shock and debase the reader. This we find aplenty in movies and in quite a few television shows. When I use violence, I try to use it obliquely, rarely to state it nakedly. I always show that violence is a destroyer. Shakespeare pointed the way in *Macbeth*. Violence, he says, kills all that is human and precious in us. He takes a noble general and shows step by step how this man becomes, in Macduff's words, "A hell-hound."

All of Macbeth's humanity has completely left him. He can no longer be described in human terms.

And this brings me back to where I started. Let's keep the human terms in our young adult books. Let's keep sane. In these troubled and parlous times, let's all make sure we go to the right granary. The prophet has put upon us, teachers, librarians, and writers, all of the faith and hope of the people.

Let's not fail them.

A Word About My Craft

Some things you are born with and then develop over the years by hard work and concentration, but it was always easy and natural for me to establish mood. Mood is feeling, and I feel myself right into the thing. I get into the atmosphere so completely that a few times I have literally scared myself on hearing a sudden sound in my writing room.

My style of writing is terse, loaded with many levels. It is a style that is natural with me and took many years to develop and hone. I find it the best way to say what I have to say.

Jay Bennett's books include *The Haunted One*, 1987; *Sing Me a Death Song*, 1990; *Skinhead*, 1991; and *Coverup*, 1991, all Watts.

The kinds of themes treated in stories are closely correlated with the mode in which they are written. Mode is most commonly divided into comedy, romance, irony/satire, and tragedy. Together these make up the story of everyone's life, and in literature as in life they are interrelated, flowing one into the other. Comedy might be compared to spring, childhood, innocence, and happiness. Romance also connotes happiness and is often associated with summer, the teen years, young love, and growth. Irony and satire correlate symbolically with fall, middle age, the existence of problems, and unhappiness. Tragedy is correlated with winter, old age, suffering, and sadness.[4]

Books for children and young people have most often been written in the comic and romantic modes, because as Annie Gottlieb pointed out in "A New Cycle in 'YA' Books," "An unwritten commandment of YA fiction had always been. 'Thou shalt leave the young reader with hope.' " She credited Robert Cormier with shattering this rule in 1974, when he published *The Chocolate War,* and "The American Library Association's *Booklist* gave it a black-bordered review, suggesting an obituary for youthful optimism."[5] Throughout the 1970s the books that got the most attention from teachers, librarians, reviewers, and young readers were books in the darker modes of irony/satire and even tragedy. These included such books as the anonymous (really Beatrice Sparks')[6] *Go Ask Alice,* John Donovan's *Wild in the World,* and Jean Renvoize's *A Wild Thing.* The protagonists in these books are helpless to change the forces of the world that gather against them.

The reader of a tragedy is usually filled with pity and fear—pity for the hero and fear for oneself that the same thing might happen. The intensity of this involvement causes the reader to undergo an emotional release or catharsis that drains away subconscious fears, leaving the reader filled with pride in what the human spirit is able to undergo and still survive. Robert Cormier's books stand out as being among a very small number of YA books that come close to being tragedies. However, as shown in Chapter 3, "The New Realism," many books are written in the ironic mode.

Today it is easy to find examples of books written in the happier modes, those of comedy and romance. In these optimistic books, there are challenges to be met, but the stories have happy endings. Chapter 4, "The Old Romanticism," explores the romantic mode, which is characterized by not only happy endings but also exaggeration and wish fulfillment.

In popular culture, the term *comedy* most often refers to something funny, something that makes people laugh. But in literary criticism, *comedy* or *the comic mode* are terms that can be used as descriptors for stories that are mostly serious or even grim. What is necessary is that the events in the story move from ironic chaos to a renewal of human hope and spirit. An example is Felice Holman's *The Wild Children,* set in the postrevolutionary Russia of the 1920s. Twelve-year-old Alex comes downstairs from his attic bedroom to find that his family has been taken away. He is alone in the world, as are thousands of young Russians who make up the *bezprizorni*—the unsheltered ones. Most of the story is about Alex's terrible fear, his loneliness, and the hardships endured by these children of war. He becomes part of a gang of children who aid each other in the hard business of survival and at the end of the book escape to Finland. The closing line is a brief sentence that is almost a literal fulfillment of the definition of the comic mode, "Once again, life began." It is important to the symbolic nature of the story that it is not only Alex's life, but also the lives of the ten children who escaped with him, that can begin again. Hope for the future is made even greater by the decision of the gang's leader, fourteen-year-old Peter, to stay behind as a helper in the underground, bringing more of the orphans to freedom.

CHARACTER

The popularity of many books that do not have exciting or even interesting plots is a testament to the power of good characterization. When, through a writer's skill, readers identify closely with the protagonist, they feel as if they are living the experience. They become more interested in what is going on in the character's mind than they may be in what is happening to the character. Young adult authors who do an especially good job of developing memorable characters include Virginia Hamilton, Sue Ellen Bridgers, Katherine Paterson, Robert Cormier, Laurence Yep, and Alice Childress.

Character Development and Types

Because of the short length of most adolescent books, the author does not have space to develop fully more than a small cast of characters. There is usually a protagonist, an antagonist, and various supporting characters. The protagonist is usually the central character, the one with whom the reader identifies. Most commonly, this is a young adult, perhaps a bit older than the reader but not always. After reading a book with a fully developed protagonist, readers should know the character so well that if a situation outside of the book were described, they could predict how this character would feel and act in the new situation. They could do this because the author has developed a round character. Many sides—many different aspects—of the character have been shown. A major character can undergo changes in personality in ways a minor character cannot. Such changes are often the heart of the story, but if the character is not well developed, the changes have no meaning. Readers cannot rejoice in the arrival of a character unless they know where the character started.

A character who undergoes changes is said to be dynamic, whereas a character who stays basically the same is static. Chances are that if the focus of a story is characterization, the protagonist will be dynamic. Readers will be led to understand how and why the protagonist has changed. Background characters may change too, but in a YA book the author probably won't have the space to develop these changes, and so most background characters will remain static. And in many books where the focus is on an exciting plot or the protagonist is telling someone else's story, the main character may also be static, having much the same goals and attitudes at the end as at the beginning.

Many of the static characters found in literature are flat or stereotyped. As books (not just books for teenagers but for all ages) have gotten shorter and shorter, the literary element most affected has been characterization. For efficiency, authors have begun to rely more heavily on character types than on unique individuals.

Of course this is not entirely new. Since the beginning of literature, there have been archetypes that appear again and again. Archetypal characters include the wise and helpful older person who befriends and teaches a young protagonist, the villain or enemy, and the wicked or unsympathetic parent or stepparent. Archetypes differ from stereotypes in that they are usually main characters and they fill a symbolic as well as an active role. Stereotyped characters are in the background and little attention is given to their development. The absentminded professor, the nagging mother, and the jock are stereotypes. The hero who leaves home on a danger-fraught mission and returns as a stronger and better person is an archetype seen in stories as divergent as the biblical story of Joseph, Steven Callahan's nonfiction *Adrift: Seventy-Six Days Lost at Sea,* Robin McKinley's fantasy *The Blue Sword,* and Robert Lipsyte's realistic *The Brave.* It is because this particular archetype is a part of most readers' backgrounds that they have a good feeling at the end of Robert C. O'Brien's *Z for Zachariah.* As Ann Burden leaves the "safety" of Hidden Valley and ventures out into the radioactive world, readers feel confident that she will safely complete her quest and find other people with whom she can live and build a new society.

A reviewer is probably making a negative comment in saying that an author's characters are stereotypes, but, in reality, it is necessary that at least some characters in nearly every story be stereotyped. (The word *stereotyped* comes from the printer's world, where it used to refer to the process by which an image is created over and over again.) It would be impossible for an author to build a unique personality for every background character, and it would be too demanding for a reader to respond to a large number of fully developed characters.

The use of stock characters was always accepted as part of the act of storytelling, but in the late 1960s and 1970s, as people's social consciousness grew, so did their dislike for stereotyping. Minority groups complained that their members were stereotyped in menial roles, feminists complained that women and girls always took a back seat to men and boys, and parents complained that they were presented as unimportant or even damaging to their children's lives. Justified as these complaints were (or are), it doesn't mean that writers can get along without relying on stock characters or stereotypes. But they can feature as main characters members of those groups who have previously been ignored or relegated to stereotypes. Doing this well is always a challenge, especially when the character is someone that most young readers are not accustomed to identifying with, for example, a boy with cerebral palsy as in Jan Slepian's *The Alfred Summer,* a lesbian as in Nancy Garden's *Annie on My Mind,* and a despondent Vietnam veteran as in Bobbie Ann Mason's *In Country.*

Communicating Character

We will focus on Katherine Paterson's 1940s story set on Rass Island in the Chesapeake Bay, *Jacob Have I Loved,* to illustrate techniques authors use to help readers know and understand their characters. Characterization is crucial in this book because the problem in the story—that of sibling rivalry between the competent and practical Sara Louise and her beautiful and talented twin sister Caroline—takes place inside Sara Louise's mind. If readers don't have empathy for Sara Louise, they won't identify with her or appreciate the story.

Paterson explained in her Newbery Award acceptance speech that the conflict at the core of the book

> . . . began east of Eden, in the earliest stories of my heritage. "Cain was jealous of his brother and slew him." If, in our Freudian orientation, we speak of the basic conflict as that between parent and child, the Bible—which is the earth from which I spring—is much more concerned with the relationships among brothers and sisters. "A friend loveth at all times," says the writer of Proverbs, "but a brother is born for adversity." They never taught us the second half of that verse in Sunday School.[7]

She went on to cite the numerous fairy tales in which the youngest brother or sister must surpass the supposedly more clever elders or outwit the wicked ones, and she argued with Bruno Bettelheim's suggestion that the rivalry between brothers and sisters is actually an Oedipal conflict or is about the split self. "I do not think," she said, "we can avoid the most obvious meaning of the stories, which is that among children who grow up together in a family there run depths of feeling that will permeate their souls for both good and ill as long as they live."

Authors develop characters by telling readers what the characters do, what they say, what others say about them, what they think, and how they feel. *Jacob Have I Loved* is written in the first person, so it's easy and natural for Sara Louise to describe herself and her feelings, but notice how efficiently in this brief quote Paterson introduces Sara Louise and the secondary character McCall Purnell, and also through the dialogue presents some foreshadowing and gives readers a peek at how others relate to Sara.

> Call and I made quite a pair. At thirteen I was tall and large boned, with delusions of beauty and romance. He, at fourteen, was pudgy, bespectacled, and totally unsentimental.

"Call," I would say, watching dawn break crimson over the Chesapeake Bay, "I hope I have a sky like this the day I get married."

"Who would marry you?" Call would ask, not meanly, just facing facts.

Readers learn more about Sara Louise a few pages later when she tells Call a joke about a "p-sychiatrist," who gets into heaven because as St. Peter explains, "We got this problem. God thinks he's Franklin D. Roosevelt." Call questions Sara's use of the word "p-sychiatrist," and she explains in hindsight:

> I was an avid reader of *Time* magazine, which, besides the day-old Baltimore *Sun,* was our porthole on the world in those days, so although psychiatry was not yet a popular pastime, I was quite aware of the word, if not the fact that the p was silent.

His response to the actual joke is, "How can it be a joke? There ain't neither funny about it."

Paterson's inclusion of these two grammatical "mistakes" was an efficient way to show not only how isolated these children were but also how Call looks inward at the Island identifying with the watermen whereas Sara Louise looks outward at the world.

In the story, Call and Sara are both dynamic characters, who undergo change. Sara's sister, Caroline, is a static character, remaining much the same from beginning to end. She's almost a stereotype of the beautiful and adored child, "the kind of person other people sacrifice for as a matter of course" and the kind of person who tells other people's stories, snatching their "rights without even thinking." But Caroline sings so beautifully that on the Saturday night before Christmas, Sara Louise felt surely that she would shatter when Caroline "went up effortlessly, sweetly, and oh, so softly, to the high G, holding it just a few seconds longer than humanly possible and then returning to the last few notes and to silence."

Paterson walked a fine line in creating Caroline, who had to be irritating enough to make Sara's resentment credible, but at the same time typical enough that readers would understand the problem as representative rather than unique. One of the ways that Paterson did this was to filter everything through Sara's eyes, as on the summer day that Sara had earned extra money, and as a result her mother was making her and her father's favorite dinner. Sara was relaxed:

> [bathing her] sister and grandmother in kindly feelings that neither deserved, when Caroline said, "I haven't got anything to do but practice this summer, so I've decided to write a book about my life. Once you're known," she explained carefully as though some of us were dim-witted, "once you're famous information like that is very valuable. If I don't get it down now, I may forget."

The worst thing about this statement is that Caroline said it "in that voice of hers that made me feel slightly nauseated."

On balance, readers are also made privy to Sara's daydreams, which include catching a German spy and being honored by President Roosevelt.

There was a final touch with which I closed the award ceremony.
"Here, Mr. President," I would say, handing back the medal, "use this for our boys at the front. . . ."

She's brought back to reality when she enlists the help of Call to spy on the newcomer to Rass Island. They sneak up on his house through the marsh because "The old man would never expect people from that direction," but one of Call's shoes gets stuck in the mud so that he's left standing "on one leg like an overweight egret." He's sure that his grandmother will beat him for losing his shoe but Sara retrieves it and holds her peace about the ridiculousness of "Call's tubby little grandmother taking a switch to a large fifteen-year-old boy."

I had a greater problem than that. What would Franklin D. Roosevelt say about a spy who lost his shoe in the salt marsh and worried aloud that has grandma would beat him?

By the last quarter of the book, readers know Sara so well that they suffer along with her when the Captain, the man she thought was a spy, shares his idea of sending Caroline to music school and ironically announces that "I have Sara Louise to thank for the idea." And they react right along with Sara Louise's body when after the war Call returns home and before announcing his engagement remarks that he stopped in New York to see Caroline. "My body understood long before my mind did. First it chilled, then it began to burn, with my heart thumping overtime in alarm."

One of the advantages of books over movies and plays is that an author can more easily get inside the characters' minds and tell what they are thinking. Paterson often uses this technique, having Sara Louise carry on a continual interior monologue. In one of them she acknowledges her lack of generosity in not wanting to share Call with the Captain. "He didn't remember his own father, and if any boy needed a father, it was Call." But "Call was my only friend. If I gave him to the Captain, I'd have no one."

Authors commonly use physical attributes as a concrete substitute for less easily described abstractions. Throughout *Jacob Have I Loved*, Paterson uses descriptions of hands in this way.

Caroline would remark mildly that my fingernails were dirty. How could they be anything else but dirty? But instead of simply acknowledging the fact, I would fly into a wounded rage. . . . It wasn't my fingernails she was concerned with, that I was sure of. She was using my fingernails to indict my soul.

Midway in the book when the Captain's house is washed out to sea, Sara Louise hugs him and suddenly hears voices inside her head, one saying "Let go, stupid," while the other urges her to hold him tighter. She is terribly embarrassed and dares to look only at his hands.

> ▮   I had never noticed how long his fingers were. His nails were large, rounded at the bottom and blunt and neat at the tips. He had the cleanest fingernails of any man I'd ever seen—it was the male hand in the ad reaching to put the diamond on the Ponds-caressed female hand. Why had I never noticed before how beautiful his hands were?

In another incident, Sara Louise overreacts when Caroline borrows her hand lotion, and that fall Sara Louise studies all the hands in the classroom. "It was my current theory that hands were the most revealing part of the human body— far more significant than eyes."

Names can also be used as clues. Throughout most of the book, Sara Louise is called Wheeze because the two-year-old Caroline couldn't pronounce Sara Louise. One of the ways that Paterson shows the importance of the Captain to Sara Louise is that without appearing to give the matter much thought, he calls her by her full name: "Strange how much that meant to me."

Sara's mother and father are important background characters, but because they act much like readers expect good parents to act, Paterson does not have to devote extensive space to their development but instead relies on a few crucial details. For example, Sara's mother came to Rass Island as the schoolteacher and stayed on after falling in love with a waterman. After spending the winter on her father's boat, Sara does not want to go back to school and asks her mother to teach her at home. Her mother, who isn't good with math, says that they would have to ask the Captain to teach the math because "There is no one else with the —with the time." Sara explains that her mother "was always very careful not to seem to sneer at the rest of the islanders for their lack of education."

This brief paragraph lets readers know that Mrs. Bradshaw is not the kind of mother who would have fostered unhappiness between her daughters. She is not to blame for Sara's feelings.

The Captain and Sara's grandmother are almost archetypes. The Captain is the foolish young man who left home on a quest only to return many years later kinder and wiser than anyone dared to hope for. The grandmother is the wicked old witch, who mumbles incantations and makes wicked predictions. She's the one who, when Sara's heart is already broken because Caroline is going to be sent to the wonderful music academy in Baltimore, stands close behind her and whispers, "Romans nine thirteen, 'As it is written, Jacob have I loved, but Esau have I hated.' "

Some readers and critics have objected to these contrasting archetypes, the positive portrayal of the elderly man and the negative portrayal of the elderly woman. But the archetypes are as old as the world's literature, and at least Paterson reveals some of the reasons behind the grandmother's bad behavior.

At the very end of the book, actually in the denouement, new characters appear, including the man Sara Louise marries and the twins whose birth she attends. These characters are foils. They are there as background for the simple purpose of making Sara Louise shine. There was no need for Paterson to develop them any further than to give readers a vaguely positive feeling toward them.

This discussion has pointed out several techniques Paterson used to develop the full range of characters in *Jacob Have I Loved*. She had the narrator describe minor characters, and major characters were not only described but shown in action. Readers were allowed to listen in on their conversations and to hear what they said as well as how they said it and how others responded to them and talked about them. Readers were privy to the thoughts and daydreams of the protagonist. Other techniques Paterson used in developing her characters included Biblical allusion, foreshadowing, descriptions of physical attributes as symbols for abstract ideas, and a change in names to reflect changing attitudes. Examples of each technique have been given, but careful readers can find other equally interesting additional examples.

POINT OF VIEW

Point of view is expressed largely through the person who tells the story. A story has to be told from a consistent viewpoint. The storyteller has to decide just how far from the characters to stand, from which direction to illuminate their actions with sympathy, and when and if it is time to speak from inside one of them. The viewpoint that gives the storyteller the most freedom is the one called omniscient, or "all knowing." With this viewpoint it is as if the writer is present in all the characters, knowing what is inside their minds. This was the viewpoint that Joanne Greenberg, writing under the pseudonym Hannah Green, used when she wrote *I Never Promised You a Rose Garden*. It would hardly have been believable for the girl Deborah to tell the story, since throughout most of the book she is psychotic. Yet it is necessary that the readers be told what she is thinking since the real story takes place in her mind. Also, by using the third-person omniscient viewpoint, Green could share the thoughts of the other patients, Deborah's psychiatrist, and her parents.

Writers have much less freedom if they decide to enter into the mind and body of one of the characters and stay there, that is, to write the book in the first person. First-person narrators can describe other characters in an objective manner; that is, they can tell about whatever can be seen from the outside, but they cannot tell what is going on inside the minds of the other characters. One way to get around the limitations of a first-person book is to have the first-person chapters come alternately from different people. M. E. Kerr used this technique in *I'll Love You When You're More Like Me*, and so did Alice Childress in *A Hero Ain't Nothin' But a Sandwich*. William Wharton began *Birdy* by having Birdy's friend Al visit him in a veteran's hospital where he alternates between talking to the unresponsive Birdy and thinking his own thoughts. Birdy's thoughts—at first just fragments and pieces—are given in a slightly different style of type. By the end of the book, Birdy's thoughts have grown to whole chapters.

This technique was satisfying to readers because it put them in a better position to understand Birdy than either his friend or his psychiatrist. It also let them know things about Birdy's childhood and his family that Birdy would never have told, for example:

> Birdy's old lady'd keep any baseballs that went over the fence into their yard. Ball players didn't even try anymore. Semi-pros, everybody, gave up. Hit a homer over that fence, into Birdy's yard; good-bye, ball. Nothing to do but throw in a new one. It got to be expensive playing in that ball park if you were a long-ball-hitting right-hander.
>
> What the hell could she've done with all those baseballs? Birdy and I used to look for those baseballs everywhere around his place. Maybe she buried them, or she could've sold them; big black market source for used baseballs.

In a similar way to how William Wharton told most of Birdy's story through the eyes of his best friend, authors may use a relatively minor character to tell the story. Richard Peck has explained that he chooses to do this because the interesting stories are at the extreme ends of the normal curve. The exciting things are happening to the brilliant and successful students such as the girl that Bruce Brooks wrote about in *Midnight Hour Encores*. Or they are happening to the kids at the other end of the scale as in Fran Arrick's *Steffie Can't Come Out to Play* and S. E. Hinton's *That Was Then, This Is Now*. Peck says that these extreme characters are wonderful to write about, but they aren't the ones who will read his books. The kids at one end probably don't have the reading skill and at the other end are too busy, too involved in their own lives. Readers are most likely to come from the large group of students in between whose lives aren't full of such highs and lows.

TONE

The tone of a book is determined by the author's attitude toward subject, characters, and readers. It is difficult to pick out the exact elements that contribute to the tone of a book because many times the author is not even aware of them. If an author were speaking directly to you, tone would simply be communicated through the lilt of the voice, the lifting of an eyebrow, a twinkle in the eye, or a crease in the forehead. But when tone has to be communicated exclusively through the written word, then it is more complex.

Sometimes language reminiscent of church hymns or the Bible is used to lend weight and dignity to a book, as in the titles *All Creatures Great and*

Small by James Herriot, *Jacob Have I Loved* by Katherine Paterson, and *Manchild in the Promised Land* by Claude Brown.

The tone in these books contrasts sharply with the humorous and irreverent tone that appears in many popular new books. Americans have always been fond of exaggeration or hyperbole and its use is one way of establishing a light, humorous tone. When writers use hyperbole, readers know that what they say is not true, but they nevertheless enjoy the farfetched overstatement, as in Ellen Conford's title, *If This Is Love, I'll Take Spaghetti* and Ron Koertge's *Where the Kissing Never Stops.*

Another literary technique that authors rely on when they are establishing their desired tone is euphemistic wording. Euphemisms are words or phrases carefully chosen to avoid harsh or unpleasant concepts. In general, modern writers think it better to speak directly than to make the vague kinds of circumlocutions that used to be fashionable in writing. But some euphemisms have literary impact. For example, Margaret Craven's title *I Heard the Owl Call My Name* is more intriguing than a bald statement such as "I knew I was going to die." And Hemingway's title *For Whom the Bell Tolls* is both more euphemistic and euphonious than "the one who has died."

For certain kinds of books a reverent tone is appropriate; for example, memoirs are usually written in a loving tone, but to be successful the tone cannot be so worshipful that it becomes too sentimental. John Gunther's *Death Be Not Proud: A Memoir* telling about Gunther's teenage son's struggle against a fatal brain tumor has remained popular for four decades.

With today's emphasis on graphics and visualization, combined with improvements in the technology of reproducing paintings and photographs, publishers are producing more picture books for readers of all ages. The writers for such books face a challenge in establishing a "grown-up" tone, one that will keep such books from being classified with the more common picture books created for children. A common technique is to use photographs, rather than drawings, as in Russell Freedman's *Lincoln: A Photobiography*, Patricia Lauber's *Summer of Fire: Yellowstone*, and Philip M. Isaacson's *Round Buildings, Square Buildings, Buildings That Wiggle Like a Fish*. Picture books for older readers are also likely to have more complex subject matter, as in the Associated Press's *World War II: A 50th Anniversary* and Jan Greenberg and Sandra Jordan's *The Painter's Eye: Learning to Look at Contemporary American Art.*

Another challenge that young adult authors face is to avoid an overly didactic tone. Certainly it is the goal—conscious or unconscious—of most adults to teach worthwhile values to young people. Nevertheless, in literary criticism, calling a work "didactic" usually implies that the tone comes across as preachy. The story has been created around a message instead of having a message or a theme grow naturally out of the story. For example, Gertrude Samuels' *Run, Shelley, Run!* appears to have been written for the didactic purpose of bringing the plight of homeless girls to the public's attention, and Gloria D. Miklowitz' *Close to the Edge* is a plea for involvement and service to others as a key to good mental health.

Great literature always leaves the reader with something to think about. Lessons are taught, but they are subtle lessons, and the reader is left with the responsibility of analyzing what the writer has presented and of coming to a conclusion. *Lord of the Flies* is a book from which people learn a great deal, but is not usually considered a didactic book because the author, William Golding, does not spell out the lesson for the reader. We might contrast Golding's nondidactic tone with the didactic message that appears in an introduction written by E. M. Forster to a 1962 edition of the same book:

> It is certainly not a comforting book. But it may help a few grownups to be less complacent and more compassionate, to support Ralph, respect Piggy, control Jack, and lighten a little the darkness of man's heart. At the present moment (if I may speak personally) it is respect for Piggy that seems needed most. I do not find it in our leaders.

Forster's comments could also be described as editorializing. Notice how he asked permission to express his personal opinion. Sometimes authors will editorialize, or give their own opinions, through the voice of a character, as S. E. Hinton did in *The Outsiders* when Ponyboy explains why he wrote his story.

> I could see boys going down under street lights because they were mean and tough and hated the world, and it was too late to tell them that there was still good in it, and they wouldn't believe you if you did. It was too vast a problem to be just a personal thing. There should be some help. Someone should tell their side of the story, and maybe people would understand then and wouldn't be so quick to judge a boy by the amount of hair oil he wore.

In reality, it is probably not so much that we dislike a didactic tone as that we dislike that tone when the message is something with which we do not agree. If the message is reaffirming one of our beliefs, we identify with it and enjoy the feeling that other people are going to be convinced of the "truth."

A nostalgic tone is a potential problem in much young adult literature. Nearly all books with teenage protagonists are of potential interest to young adult readers. But one of the things that keeps some of them from reaching a large YA audience is that the authors have looked back at their own adolescence and have romanticized it. Most sixteen-year-olds interpret such a tone as condescension, which is unappealing to readers of any age.

SETTING

Setting—the context of time and place—is more important in some genres than in others. For example, it is often the setting, a time in the future or the far past or some place where people now living on this earth have never actually been, that lets readers know they are embarking on reading a fantasy. The special quality in J. R. R. Tolkien's *The Lord of the Rings* would not be possible were it not set in the mythical world of Middle Earth. Nor would many popular pieces of science fiction be possible without their outer space or futuristic settings.

Historical fiction is another genre in which the setting is important to the story. Bette Greene's *Summer of My German Soldier* could not have happened at any time other than during World War II. Without the war, there would not have been German prisoners in her hometown, nor would there have been the peculiar combination of public and private hysteria that worked on Patty Bergan's southern Christian community and her Jewish family. All of this makes it easy to think of *Summer of My German Soldier* as a historical novel. In contrast, Maureen Daly's *Seventeenth Summer* was set in approximately the same time period, but the crux of the story does not center around the war. It centers around a young girl's feelings toward the adult role that she is growing into and toward her first experience with love. Many girls who read *Seventeenth Summer* come away with the feeling that they are reading a slightly old-fashioned, but still contemporary, novel.

For our purposes, we have rather arbitrarily chosen to label any book that is set during or prior to World War II as historical fiction. Often-read books whose settings make them fall clearly into the category of historical fiction are Jack Schaefer's *Shane*, Mark Twain's *Adventures of Huckleberry Finn*, and Fred Gipson's *Old Yeller*. Of recent pieces of popular young adult fiction, good examples of how a story is controlled by its historical setting are Robert Newton Peck's *A Day No Pigs Would Die*, a 1920s family story set in a rural Vermont community of Shakers, and Jean Fritz's *Homesick: My Own Story*, the true account of Fritz's growing up in China with her American parents and their coming "home" to the United States in 1927.

Kinds of Settings

There are basically two kinds of settings in stories: one is integral and the other is backdrop. When the setting is a part of the plot, then obviously it is integral, as in the historical books and fantasies mentioned earlier. It is also integral in stories—whether fictional or true—in which the plot or problem is person against nature. In accounts of mountain climbing, survival, exploring, and other sorts of adventuring, the setting is actually the antagonist. It is interesting in and of itself, just as a character would be.

Another kind of story in which the setting is integral is the regional story. To some degree, nearly all realistic fiction is regional since the setting influences the story, but the term is usually applied to stories where the setting plays an unusually important part. For example, Hal Borland's *When the Legends Die* and Frank Herbert's *Soul Catcher* are both regional stories about young Native

GARY SOTO
on The Particulars of the World

I am new to children's writing and am only now getting to know some of the books in the field. What has struck me, now that I am reading YA novels, is that despite their other literary merits, the writing has so little that is obviously regional, obviously bent on nailing down a life that is wholly particular. Seldom are real rivers mentioned, or mountains, gangs, streets, cars; in short, the particulars of the world. Seldom do place names matter, names ringing of the familiar, such as Avocado Lake, Pinedale, Academy Cemetery,

Francher's Creek, real names that might give rise to a reader's dreaming state of mind and curiosity for a faraway place. For the most part, the novels I have been reading are homogenous and widespread in their feelings and cast of characters. They lack a sense of place. The stories could happen anywhere. And they often happen in a way that doesn't exclude anyone by race, thus, in a way, satisfying the book market, but also, in a way, dissatisfying any reader who knows what the real world is like. The characters are interchangeable, racially, that is.

I suppose because I was first trained as a poet and was told repeatedly to go to the particular—your block, your family, your friends, some dirt pile in the backyard—that I wrote about my hometown, Fresno, California. And then, more particularly, I looked to the southeast area of Fresno—the Roosevelt High area—the industrial area of south Fresno, where I grew up. My characters are Mexican-American, mostly playground kids, mostly the children of people whose parents work for Color Tile or a Safeway distribution center. I'm beginning to think that children's writing could learn to see regionality and particularity as underexplored territory. I'm beginning to think we don't have to satisfy everyone. We can remember the adult writers—Flannery O'Connor, Mark Twain, Sherwood Anderson, William Saroyan, Bernard Malamud—who had tenderness and longing toward place, even if that place scared the hell out of them when they were young.

Gary Soto's books include *Baseball in April*, Harcourt Brace Jovanovich, 1991; *A Summer Life*, Dell, 1991; *The Skirt*, Delacorte, 1992; and *The Ring*, Putnam, 1992.

American men whose searches for their own identities cannot be separated from the regions in which they grew up.

Traditionally, most regional stories have had rural settings in which the protagonists are close to nature, but as the United States has changed to an urban society and realism has become more fashionable, cities appear as important background settings, as in Nicholasa Mohr's *El Bronx Remembered* and *In Nueva York*. These are both collections of short stories that are held together by their common setting. Mohr communicates the Puerto Rican background of her stories through the touch of Spanish in the titles.

Paul Fleischman used the setting of a single room to tie together the story he wanted to tell in *The Borning Room*. It begins with a birth on January 11, 1851, and ends with a death in the same room in 1918. Although the book is specifically the life of one Ohio farm family, it is also the story of America from before the Civil War to World War I.

In contrast to stories with integral settings are those with backdrop settings. Stories of this type are set in a small town, an inner-city neighborhood, a modern suburb, or a high school. When authors establish this kind of setting, they do not want to make it so clearcut that it would be identifiable as only one place. They want to give enough details that it comes alive, but to leave it vague enough that readers can imagine the story happening, for example, in their own town or at least in one they know.

The most common backdrop setting in young adult literature is that of a high school because school is the business—the everyday life—of teenagers. The fact that there are only so many ways to describe stairways, restrooms, lockers, cafeterias, classrooms, and parking lots is one of the things that gives a sameness to books for this age group.

A refreshing change from this sameness occurs in books set outside the United States (see Focus Box 2.4). These are often among the best books published, because most of them were chosen from a much larger group as being worthy of translation and/or reprinting in American versions. Educators should encourage the reading of such books because whether the setting is integral or backdrop, readers are likely to come away feeling a little more comfortable and knowledgeable about the country where the book is set—an outcome surely to be encouraged in today's shrinking world.

How Setting Works

Sue Ellen Bridgers' *Permanent Connections* is a contemporary, realistic novel set in rural North Carolina, up along the ridges of the Appalachians. Casual readers probably take little notice of the setting, but that's because Bridgers has worked it in so skillfully that readers aren't aware of its effect. The book begins with seventeen-year-old Rob waking from a nightmare in his suburban New Jersey home. He's having a "foggy dream of being trapped somewhere, a steeply rising place tangled with rhododendron and blackberry briars." He's "disgusted with his stumbling, backsliding climb" and his mind fights to "tug him out of the nightmare, away from the rumbling sound of a storm he heard moving toward him. . . ."

When he's finally awake, he realizes that what he thought was a storm was "the grumbling thunder" of his Dad complaining about a son whose only summer job was mowing three lawns.

See Focus Box 2.4
for books set
outside the United
States. American
teenagers seem to
need extra
encouragement to
extend their reading
interests in this
direction. Gordon
Korman's *Losing
Joe's Place*
(Scholastic, 1990)
takes place in
Canada while
Beverely Naidoo's
Chain of Fire
(Lippincott, 1988)
is set in South
Africa.

Five pages after this foreshadowing, Chapter 2 begins with another description:

▪ They broke through the clouds, and there were the mountains beneath them. August green undulating, here and there open flinty shelves of yellow rock, narrow twisting ribbons of road and river splitting the valleys. Rob studied the terrain searching for landmarks, some sign that would distinguish it from other ranges in the southern Appalachians.

Rob and his father are flying to his father's childhood home because Uncle Fairlee has broken his leg and Rob's father is coming to see what needs to be done to take care of Grandpa, who is partly senile, and Aunt Coralee, who suffers from agoraphobia and has not been out of the house in the past three years.

The change in setting is crucial to the plot of *Permanent Connections* because Rob's father decides to leave him in North Carolina to help the family until Uncle Fairlee recovers, probably around Thanksgiving time. Rob resents being left "in that old falling-down excuse for a house. . . . He pushed up a window but there was no breeze. He was locked in."

His only comfort is Ellery, a neighbor girl who as a student is everything Rob isn't. What they have in common is that they both resent living in the mountains and going to the local high school. Ellery's parents have recently divorced, and her artist mother, Ginny, comes to the area and builds a house halfway up the mountain. Rob spends wakeful nights thinking about Ellery sleeping "on the edge of the mountain above him, out of reach but waiting. . . ."

All through the book, Bridgers uses descriptions of settings to reveal information about her characters. Rob's following Ellery on a long-distance run across the top of the ridge is a metaphor for the mental and emotional chase that takes up the larger part of the book but is much harder to describe. In a similar way, Aunt Coralee's struggle with agoraphobia, her fear of open space and her inability to go outside, is comparable to the emotional and mental struggles of Ginny, who whispers in the dark:

> I am afraid too. Hear me, Coralee Dickson, while you are curled like an animal in a hole away from sky and wind and sun. The demons that devour women are all the same.

When Uncle Fairlee tells Rob how Coralee's phobia developed, Bridgers' description of the setting is as important to an understanding as is Fairlee's explanation:

> "In a way it was a gradual thing," Fairlee said to Rob.
> They were on the front porch watching the creeping darkness that came from inside out—first the house and porch lost color, then the field lay in shadows and the woods blurred into solid black mounds. Now only the dense mountains themselves were separate from the pale sky, as if the dark were slowly rising out of them.

When Rob is frustrated, he runs to the barn where he leans "against the splintery wall, relishing the dark. He remembered that sudden calm in his gut when, in a game of hide and seek, he knew he'd discovered the perfect place, somewhere he couldn't be found."

His cousin's boyfriend confides to Rob that his family raises marijuana, "This land up here might not be good for much, but it's perfect for grass. On top of that, it's easier to hide than most places." Rob "cuts a deal" for two joints, smokes them after school, and then tries to drive home in the rain. He spins out on "the curve he had been warned against" and is arrested and charged with possession. On the morning he is to appear in court, "They crept through the fog, the car lights casting a narrow downward beam on the faded yellow line." But after the charge is dismissed, and Rob finds himself outside, "The sun had pierced the fog, and he blinked in the bright light," no longer feeling trapped. Uncle Fairlee is well enough now that Rob is free to decide whether to go back to Monmouth or stay in the mountains. That night he runs the ridge using the trail Ellery had made:

> Surefooted although the gravel tossed and rumbled beneath him, he started down, making his own path toward the hidden farmhouse below where his family waited with supper. His lungs and heart found that magic rhythm

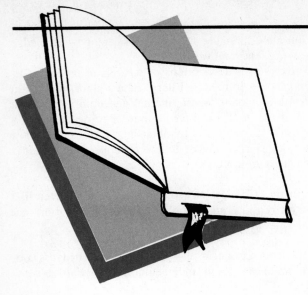

Contemporary Teens in the World Around Us

The Book of the Banshee by Anne Fine. Little, Brown, 1992. Set in Scotland, Fine's book is told through the eyes of Will Flowers, who watches his sister change from an angelic child into what he describes—through the faked persona of a war correspondent—as a screaming banshee.

Chain of Fire by Beverley Naidoo. Lipppincott, 1990. In this sequel to *Journey to Jo'Burg: A South African Story*, teenagers Naledi and Taolo help to lead a resistance movement against the forced relocation of the people in their village.

Chartbreaker by Gillian Cross. Holiday House, 1987. Finch is a singer with a rock band. Her story is told by a British author whose other well-received books include *A Map of Nowhere* and *On the Edge*.

The Forty-third War by Louise Moeri. Houghton Mifflin, 1989. Even though Uno is only twelve years old, he's forced to join a Central American army and take up soldiering.

A Hand Full of Stars by Rafik Schami, translated from Arabic by Rika Lesser. Dutton, 1990. The young narrator lives in Damascus, Syria, and aspires to be a journalist.

The Heroic Life of Al Capsella by J. Clarke. Holt, 1990. Al wants to be a normal Canadian kid, but he's hampered by a mother who writes romance novels and wears a leather jacket and a college professor father who wears the same sweater every day and seems to do nothing but drink coffee and grade papers.

In Lane Three, Alex Archer by Tessa Duder. Houghton Mifflin, 1989. Alexandra Archer is competing for the honor of representing New Zealand in the Olympics.

Losing Joe's Place by Gordon Korman. Scholastic, 1990. High school seniors Jason and his two friends get the chance to sublet his big brother's apartment in Toronto. The experience turns out to be as much challenge as fun.

Memory by Margaret Mahy. Atheneum/ Margaret K. McElderry, 1984. Mahy often includes supernatural elements in her stories, but the realistic parts of such books as *The Changeover*, *The Tricksters*, and *The Catalogue of the Universe* are set in New Zealand.

Old John by Peter Hartling. Translated from German by Elizabeth Crawford. Lothrop, Lee & Shepard, 1990 (originally published in Germany in 1981). Old John is the seventy-five-year-old grandfather of Jacob and Laura Schirmer. It's not exactly smooth sailing when Old John moves in with the family.

Rice Without Rain by Minfong Ho. Lothrop, Lee & Shepard, 1990. Seventeen-year-old Jinda falls in love with Ned, who comes from a university to help her Thai village adapt to drought and poverty.

The Secret Diary of Adrian Mole, Aged 13¾ by Sue Townsend. U.S. printing by Avon, 1984. "The biggest British sensation since the Beatles" is the way the publishers describe this popular and truly funny book, along with its sequel *The Growing Pains of Adrian Mole*.

Shabanu: Daughter of the Wind by Suzanne Fisher Staples. Knopf, 1989. The author worked for many years as a UPI news correspondent in Afghanistan, Pakistan, and India and from this experience fashioned her prize-winning story about the daughter of a nomadic family in the Cholistan desert.

Skindeep by Toeckey Jones. HarperCollins, 1986. In this South African story, upper-middle-class, white Rhonda falls in love with the pas-sionate and caring Dave, only to find out later that he is a "pass white" from a black family.

So Much to Tell You by John Marsden. Little, Brown, 1989. This winner of the Australian Book of the Year Award is the story of a fourteen-year-old girl's emotional—although not physi-cal—recovery from an attack that disfigures her face.

Two Short and One Long by Nina Ring Aamundsen. Translated from Norwegian by the author. Houghton Mifflin, 1990. Einar and Jonas are sixth-grade boys in Oslo, Norway, whose friendship is threatened when a new boy from Afghanistan comes to their school and Einar re-fuses to accept the "foreigner."

White Peak Farm by Berlie Doherty. Watts/Orchard, 1990. Jeannie tells the stories of several fiercely independent individuals who live "on a farm in the soft folding hills of Derbyshire" England, and just happen to be her family.

---

that put new spring in his legs, released his tight shoulders so his arms lifted like wings. Finally he could see the lights in brilliant, solid squares. Only he moved. There was no sound except his drumming heart and heavy breath, the dry rustle of leaf and stone beneath his feet. The world was still, waiting for him. And it seemed to him that for the first time in his life he knew where he was going.

Comparing this positive closing scene with the nightmare scene that opened the book shows how far Rob progressed during the late summer and fall. It also shows how a skilled writer uses setting to accomplish various purposes. Bridgers' descriptions make the story come alive for readers. They also serve as foreshadowing while establishing tone and mood. They allow her to be efficient in communicating the time of year, and they reveal information about the personalities of her various protagonists. The mountain setting is integral to the plot when Rob and Ellery both blame their unhappiness on being forced to move and when Rob gets the homegrown marijuana from his friend and wrecks his uncle's truck.

But probably the most important role that setting plays in *Permanent Connections* is the way it serves as a metaphor and a symbol for what is happening in people's minds. Being able to establish settings so that they accomplish multiple purposes is one of the most important skills a writer can develop. Something similar could be said for readers, who will get much more from both fiction and nonfiction if they are sensitive to the way authors incorporate setting in plot, characterization, theme, tone, and mode.

STYLE

Style is the way a story is written as contrasted to what the story is about. It is the result or effect of combining the literary aspects we have already talked about.

An Individual Matter

No two authors have exactly the same style because with writing, just as with appearance, behavior, and personal belongings, style consists of the unique blending of all the choices each individual makes. From situation to situation, these choices may differ, but they are enough alike that the styles of particular authors such as Kurt Vonnegut, Jr., Richard Brautigan, and E. L. Doctorow are recognizable from book to book. But style is also influenced by the nature of the story being told. For example, Ursula K. Le Guin used a different style when she wrote the realistic *Very Far Away from Anywhere Else* from the one she used when she wrote her fantasy *A Wizard of Earthsea*. Nevertheless, in both books she relied on the particular writing techniques that she likes and is skilled at using.

Virginia Hamilton is another author whose sense of style is evident throughout her writing, which ranges from the realistic *M. C. Higgins, the Great* to the romantic *A Little Love,* the occult *Sweet Whispers, Brother Rush,* and the science fiction Justice trilogy beginning with *Justice and Her Brothers.*

Authors' styles are influenced by such factors as their intended audience and their purpose in writing. For example, a general-information book will have a different style from that of an informative book written to persuade readers to a belief or an action. And even after an author has made the decision to write a persuasive book, the style will be affected by whether the author chooses to persuade through humor, dramatic fiction, or a logical display of evidence.

Probably the book that has had the greatest influence on the style of writing about young protagonists is J. D. Salinger's *The Catcher in the Rye.* Nearly every year, promotional materials or reviews compare five or six new young adult books to *Catcher.* Some of these comparisons are made on the basis of the subject matter, but the theme of a boy wavering between the innocence of childhood and acceptance of the adult world—imperfect as it is—is not all that unusual. It is the style of the writing that makes Salinger's book so memorable, indeed such a milestone, and has inspired other authors to imitate the colloquial speech, the candid revelations of feelings, the short snappy dialogue, the instant judgments, and the emotional extremes ranging from hostility to great tenderness.

One of the most memorable scenes in the book is the one in which the young prostitute comes to Holden's hotel room, and he is so touched by her youth and innocence that he gives up the whole idea:

> She was very nervous, for a prostitute. She really was. I think it was because she was young as hell. She was around my age. I sat down in the big chair, next to her, and offered her a cigarette. "I don't smoke," she said. She had a tiny little wheeny-whiny voice. You could hardly hear her. She never said thank you, either, when you offered her something. She just didn't know any better.
>
> "Allow me to introduce myself. My name is Jim Steele," I said.
>
> "Ya got a watch on ya?" she said. She didn't care what the hell my name was, naturally. "Hey how old are you, anyways?"
>
> "Me? Twenty-two."
>
> "Like fun you are."
>
> It was a funny thing to say. It sounded like a real kid. You'd think a prostitute and all would say, "Like hell you are" or "Cut the crap" instead of "Like fun you are."

As the girl gets ready to leave, Holden observes, "If she'd been a big old prostitute, with a lot of makeup on her face and all, she wouldn't have been half as spooky."

Teenage readers are more likely than adults to appreciate certain kinds of style. One is the hyperbole and exaggeration in Paul Zindel's books as shown through such titles as *Pardon Me, You're Stepping on My Eyeball!* and *The Amazing and Death-Defying Diary of Eugene Dingman.* Teenagers, who may have shorter attention spans than adult readers, also appreciate succinctness, as when the two protagonists in M. E. Kerr's *Night Kites* are swimming and Erick writes, "Somehow we got down to the shallow end, where we could touch, and that was what we did. We touched." Richard Peck was equally succinct in communicating the living situation of his protagonist, Buck Mendenhall, in *Remembering the Good Times.* Buck explains that what his father got out of the divorce was a "full-time trailer and a part-time kid."

Writing in dialect is an effective stylistic device to set a character apart as different from mainstream speakers, but difficulties in spelling, printing, and reading mean that most authors will use this device sparingly, and for the benefit of young readers may offer an explanation as Gary Paulsen did in *Dogsong.* The Eskimo boy, Russel, is camping in a snow-covered wilderness and he finds an ancient lamp.

Francesca Lia Block and Art Spiegelman are two authors who dared to take a chance through experimenting with literary techniques.

"See what a man has been given," he said. "By the dogs who brought me. By the night. See what a man has been given." He had dropped into the third person usage without thinking, though it was no longer used very much. He had heard the old people talk that way sometimes out of politeness.

No explanation is needed if the usage is easy to understand as in Hal Borland's *When the Legends Die,* "The Ute people have lived many generations, many grandmothers, in that land." The same can be said for most uses of black dialect, which is commonly included in the writings of June Jordan, Brenda Wilkinson, Maya Angelou, Ntozake Shange, Walter Dean Myers, and others. They use it not only for characterization but also to communicate pride in being African-Americans.

It is possible to describe the literary devices that are the basic ingredients of an author's style, but there is more to literary style than these various devices. To have a unique style, an author has to be brave enough to go beyond the tried and true. In addition, something has to click so that the devices blend together into a unified whole.

Figurative Language

Much of what determines writers' styles is how they use figurative language to set a mood, surprise the reader, create imagery, make a passage memorable, and sometimes show off their skill. Words used figuratively have different, or at least additional, meanings from those they have in standard usage. One type of figurative language—metaphors, symbols, allegories, and similes—stimulates the reader's mind to make comparisons. A second type appeals to the sense of sight or hearing. Examples include alliteration, assonance, rhyme, euphony, rhythm, and cadence. In the following sentence from Harold Brodkey's story, "Sentimental Education," both kinds of figurative language occur:

> Dimitri had a car, which Elgin borrowed—an old, weak-lunged Ford—and they could wheeze up to Marblehead and rent a dinghy and be blown around the bay, with the sunlight bright on Caroline's hair and the salt air making them hungry and the wind whipping up small whitecaps to make the day exciting.

The personification of the "weak-lunged Ford" that "wheezes" up to Marblehead helps the reader visualize the old car while the alliteration in "be blown around the bay" and "wind whipping up small whitecaps" and the rhyme in "sunlight bright" and "Caroline's hair and the salt air" affect the reader more subtly in establishing mood. The word "wheeze" is also an example of onomatopoeia, in which the sound of a word hints at its meaning.

Poetry, of course, is filled with figurative language because poets have so little space that they have to make their words do double duty. But as Maya Angelou shows in her autobiographical writing, figurative language is not limited to any one genre. She begins her *All God's Children Need Traveling Shoes* with euphonious personification:

> The breezes of the West African night were intimate and shy, licking the hair, sweeping through cotton dresses with unseemly intimacy, then disappearing into the utter blackness. Daylight was equally insistent, but much more bold and thoughtless.

And a page later:

> July and August of 1962 stretched out like fat men yawning after a sumptuous dinner. They had every right to gloat, for they had eaten me up. Gobbled me down. Consumed my spirit, not in a wild rush, but slowly, with the obscene patience of certain victors.

Metaphors are among the most common kinds of figurative language. In a metaphor, basically dissimilar things are likened to one another to give the reader a new insight. A fresh metaphor can be an effective device for making readers active instead of passive participants. Readers have to become mentally involved in order to make associations that they have not thought of before.

A metaphor can be very simple, consisting of only a word or a phrase, or it can be a series of interwoven ideas running through an entire book. In at least fourteen places in the Vietnam War story *Fallen Angels,* author Walter

Dean Myers makes comparisons to movies or television. One of the soldiers, whose uncle is a Hollywood director, keeps up a running commentary on how to make "unnatural things look *almost* natural" and on what part they should each play—whether to be Lee Marvin, one of the bad guys riding into town in a cowboy movie, the "good black guy who everybody thinks is a coward and then gets killed saving everybody else," or the "baby-faced virgin who gets killed and all you see is a pan shot of him near the end of the flick."

Seventeen-year-old Richie Perry worries about composing his letters home so that his little brother won't "think about it like you do when you go to the movies." And at night, he can't sleep because of all the short scenes that crowd into his mind:

> A few seconds of a medic putting a tag on a wounded soldier. A few seconds of a chopper taking off over the trees. A guy cradling his rifle. A body bag.

Later Richie observes that the stopping and starting of firing in a jungle battle "was as if somebody had changed channels and then switched back to the war." Ten pages later:

> The shadows moved, Peewee moved. He was getting up. I didn't want to get up. I wanted to sit there forever. Where the hell was the popcorn machine? Couldn't I just watch the rest of this f____ war? Couldn't I just be out of it for a few hours, a few minutes?

The fact that the Vietnam War was in many ways the first war fought in front of television cameras makes Myers' metaphor especially appropriate.

A technical distinction is sometimes made between metaphors and similes. Similes, like metaphors, make comparisons between basically dissimilar things, but they are literally true, whereas metaphors are only figuratively true. The creator of a simile hedges by putting in such words as *like, as, similar,* or *resembles* to indicate that a comparison is being made. In Bruce Brooks' *Midnight Hour Encores*, Sib was glad when her father told her she could choose a new name, because "I had been thrashing around inside that name like it was a wet wool coat worn inside out against my skin." A more fully developed simile appears in Zibby Oneal's *A Formal Feeling*. Sixteen-year-old Anne Cameron must let go of the dream of perfection in which she had wrapped the memories of her deceased mother. Near the end of the book, she was able at last to form the question that had bothered her since she was eight years old and her mother temporarily left the family, "If she loved me, why did she leave me?"

> That was one of the questions, but it was only one. Beneath it there was another. It had been swimming at the edges of her mind for days, darting away as a fish does, startled by a movement that comes too close. She

thought she could not avoid it any more, and so she pushed herself down one more time, like a diver. She knew the question had always been there, unspeakable, at the bottom of all she remembered and had chosen to forget. And she made herself ask: Did I ever love my mother at all?

Being able to ask this question is in effect the climax of the book, but without the interesting simile readers would have been less likely to recognize its importance. Also, since it was something that occurred in Anne's mind, the only way to make readers visualize it was through some sort of figurative language.

Allegories are extended comparisons or metaphors. They can be enjoyed on at least two levels. One is the literal or surface level on which the story is enjoyed simply for itself. On the second or deeper level, we can interpret and extend the meaning of the story, and it thereby becomes more interesting. It is in part the challenge of interpreting the allegory in William Golding's *Lord of the Flies* that makes it a good piece to read and discuss in a group.

An allegorical device that authors sometimes use is giving their characters symbolic names as Robert C. O'Brien did in *Z for Zachariah*. The title is taken from a Bible ABC book in which the first letter of the alphabet stands for Adam and the last for Zachariah. The symbolism suggests that if Adam was the first man on earth, Zachariah must be the last. The girl in the book who carries a tremendous responsibility and at the end is left with the task of rebuilding a civilization is symbolically named Ann Burden. These names may influence readers' attitudes and enhance their pleasure without their being aware of it. In a similar way, many young readers of Paula Fox's *One-Eyed Cat* probably didn't notice that when Ned confessed to shooting the cat he and his mother were sitting on the front porch of the Makepeace mansion.

Allusions work in the same way. They are an efficient way to communicate a great deal of information because one reference in a word or a phrase triggers the readers' minds to think of the whole story or idea behind the allusion. Robert Cormier's title *I Am the Cheese* is an allusion to the old nursery song and game, "The Farmer in the Dell." Besides being efficient, allusions, like metaphors, are effective in forcing readers to become actively involved in making connections. A lazy or uninterested reader might not see any allusion in Cormier's title. Someone else, especially when discovering that the family's name is Farmer, would connect the title to the nursery rhyme and perhaps think of the last line, "And the cheese stands alone!" An even more thoughtful reader might carry it back one more step and think of the next to last line, "The rat takes the cheese."

Cormier didn't leave as much for his readers to figure out in *We All Fall Down*. Fairly early in the book, he spelled out the meaning of the title when Harry Flowers explained to Buddy that the nursery rhyme "Ring Around the Rosy" referred historically to the time of the Black Plague, when people got a "rosy kind of rash and rubbed themselves with herbs and posies. Then they fell down and died." In a bit of grim foreshadowing, Buddy says to Harry, "Know what you are, Harry? . . . You're a spoiler. I always thought Ring-Around-the-Rosy was kind of a nice thing for kids to do. But now you've gone and spoiled it all."

This chapter has been little more than an introduction to—or perhaps for some of you simply a review of—the basics of literary criticism and appreciation. The concepts and the terminology will reappear throughout the rest of this textbook as well as in much of whatever else you read about books.

We placed this discussion early in the text for two reasons. First, we wanted to make it clear that authors for young adults use the same literary techniques as those used by all good writers. Second, we wanted to lay a foundation for the way you approach the reading you will do throughout this course. We want you to lose yourselves—and also find yourselves—in some very good stories. But at the same time we want to encourage you to keep a part of your mind open for looking at literature from the pleasure-giving viewpoint of the literary critic.

NOTES

[1]Margaret Early, "Stages of Growth in Literary Appreciation," *English Journal* 49 (March 1960): 163–66.

[2]First cited by G. Robert Carlsen in an article exploring stages of reading development, "Literature Is," *English Journal* 63 (February 1974): 23–27.

[3]Donald Hall, "Finally Only the Love of the Art," *New York Times Book Review*, January 16, 1983, pp. 7, 25.

[4]Glenna Davis Sloan, *The Child as Critic* (Teachers College Press, 1975).

[5]Annie Gottlieb, "A New Cycle in 'YA' Books," *New York Times Book Review*, June 17, 1984, pp. 24–25.

[6]Alleen Pace Nilsen, "The House that Alice Built: An Interview with the Author Who Brought You *Go Ask Alice*," *School Library Journal* 26 (October 1979): 109–12.

[7]Katherine Paterson, "Newbery Medal Acceptance," *Horn Book Magazine* 57 (August 1981): 385–93.

OTHER TITLES MENTIONED IN THE TEXT OF CHAPTER TWO

Adams, Richard. *The Plague Dogs*. Knopf, 1978.

———. *Watership Down*. Macmillan, 1974.

Alcott, Louisa May. *Little Women*, 1868.

Alexander, Lloyd. *The Black Cauldron*. Holt, Rinehart and Winston, 1965.

Angelou, Maya. *All God's Children Need Traveling Shoes*, Random House, 1986.

———. *I Know Why the Caged Bird Sings*. Random House, 1970.

Anonymous. *Go Ask Alice*. Prentice-Hall, 1969.

Arrick, Fran. *Steffie Can't Come Out to Play*. Bradbury, 1978.

Associated Press, foreword by Harrison Salisbury. *World War II: A 50th Anniversary*. Holt, Rinehart and Winston, 1989.

Borland, Hal. *When the Legends Die*. HarperCollins, 1963.

Bridgers, Sue Ellen. *Home Before Dark*. Knopf, 1976.

———. *Permanent Connections*. HarperCollins, 1987.

Brodkey, H. "Sentimental Education." In *First Love and Other Sorrows*. Dial Press, 1957.

Brooks, Bruce. *Midnight Hour Encores*. HarperCollins, 1986.

———. *The Moves Make the Man*. HarperCollins, 1984.

Brown, Claude. *Manchild in the Promised Land*. Macmillan, 1965.

Burns, Olive Ann. *Cold Sassy Tree*. Ticknor & Fields, 1984.

Callahan, Steven. *Adrift: Seventy-Six Days Lost at Sea*. Houghton Mifflin, 1986.

Childress, Alice. *A Hero Ain't Nothin' But a Sandwich*. Coward, McCann, 1973.

Conford, Ellen. *If This Is Love, I'll Take Spaghetti*. Four Winds, 1983.

Cormier, Robert. *After the First Death*. Pantheon, 1979.

———. *Beyond the Chocolate War*. Pantheon, 1985.

———. *The Chocolate War*. Pantheon, 1974.

———. *I Am the Cheese*. Pantheon, 1977.

———. *We All Fall Down*. Delacorte, 1991.

Craven, Margaret. *I Heard the Owl Call My Name*. Doubleday, 1973.

Daly, Maureen. *Seventeenth Summer*. Dodd, 1942.

Donovan, John. *Family*. HarperCollins, 1976.

———. *Wild in the World*. HarperCollins, 1971.

Duncan, Lois. *Stranger with My Face*. Little, Brown, 1981.

Fleischman, Paul. *The Borning Room*. HarperCollins, 1991.

Fox, Paula. *One-Eyed Cat*. Bradbury, 1985.

———. *The Moonlight Man*. Bradbury, 1985.

Freedman, Russell. *Lincoln: A Photobiography*. Clarion, 1987.

Fritz, Jean. *Homesick: My Own Story*. Putnam, 1982.

Garden, Nancy. *Annie on My Mind*. Farrar, Straus & Giroux, 1982.

Gipson, Fred. *Old Yeller*. HarperCollins, 1976.

Golding, William. *Lord of the Flies*. Coward, McCann & Geoghegan, 1955.

Graham, Robin. *Dove*. HarperCollins, 1972.

Green, Hannah. *I Never Promised You a Rose Garden*. Holt, Rinehart and Winston, 1964.

Greenberg, Jan and Sandra Jordan. *The Painter's Eye: Learning to Look at Contemporary American Art*. Delacorte, 1991.

Greene, Bette. *Summer of My German Soldier*. Dial, 1973.

Guest, Judith. *Ordinary People*. Viking, 1976.

Gunther, John. *Death Be Not Proud: A Memoir*. Modern Library, 1953.

Guy, Rosa. *The Disappearance*. Delacorte, 1979.

———. *The Friends*. Holt, Rinehart and Winston, 1973.

Hamilton, Virginia. *Justice and Her Brothers*, Greenwillow, 1978.

———. *A Little Love*. Philomel, 1984.

———. *M. C. Higgins, the Great*. Macmillan, 1974.

———. *Sweet Whispers, Brother Rush*. Philomel, 1982.

Hemingway, Ernest. *For Whom the Bell Tolls*. Scribner, 1940.

Herbert, Frank. *Soul Catcher*. Putnam, 1972.

Herriot, James. *All Creatures Great and Small*. St. Martin, 1972.

Heyerdahl, Thor. *The "RA" Expeditions*. New American Library, 1972.

Hinton, S. E. *The Outsiders*. Viking, 1967.

———. *Taming the Star Runner*, Delacorte, 1988.

———. *That Was Then, This Is Now*. Viking, 1971.

Holman, Felice. *The Wild Children*. Scribner, 1983.

Hunter, Mollie. *Cat, Herself*. HarperCollins, 1986.

Isaacson, Philip M. *Round Buildings, Square Buildings, Buildings That Wiggle Like a Fish*. Knopf, 1988.

Kerr, M. E. *If I Love You, Am I Trapped Forever?* HarperCollins, 1973.

———. *I'll Love You When You're More Like Me*. HarperCollins, 1977.

———. *Night Kites*. HarperCollins, 1986.

Knowles, John. *A Separate Peace*. Macmillan, 1960.

Koertge, Ron. *Where the Kissing Never Stops*. Little, Brown, 1987.

Le Guin, Ursula K. *Very Far Away from Anywhere Else*. Atheneum, 1976.

———. *A Wizard of Earthsea*. Parnassus, 1968.

Lipsyte, Robert. *The Brave*. HarperCollins, 1991.

Mason, Bobbie Ann. *In Country*. HarperCollins, 1985.

Mathis, Sharon Bell. *Teacup Full of Roses*. Viking, 1972.

McKinley, Robin. *The Blue Sword*. Greenwillow, 1982.

Meltzer, Milton. *The American Revolutionaries: A History in Their Own Words*. Crowell, 1987.

Miklowitz, Gloria D. *Close to the Edge*. Delacorte, 1983.

Morrell, David. *First Blood*. M. Evans, 1972.

Myers, Walter Dean. *Fallen Angels*. Scholastic, 1988.

O'Brien, Robert C. *Z for Zachariah*. Atheneum, 1975.

Oneal, Zibby. *A Formal Feeling*. Viking, 1982.

Paterson, Katherine. *Jacob Have I Loved*. HarperCollins, 1980.

Paulsen, Gary. *Dogsong*. Bradbury, 1985.

Peck, Richard. *Are You in the House Alone?* Viking, 1976.

_____. *Remembering the Good Times*. Delacorte, 1985.

Peck, Robert Newton. *A Day No Pigs Would Die*. Knopf, 1972.

Plath, Sylvia. *The Bell Jar*. HarperCollins, 1971.

Potok, Chaim. *The Chosen*. Simon & Schuster, 1967.

_____. *My Name Is Asher Lev*. Knopf, 1972.

Read, Piers Paul. *Alive: The Story of the Andes Survivors*. HarperCollins, 1974.

Renvoize, Jean. *A Wild Thing*. Little, Brown, 1971.

Robertson, Dougal. *Survive the Savage Sea*. G. K. Hall, 1974.

Salinger, J. D. *The Catcher in the Rye*. Little, Brown, 1951.

Samuels, Gertrude. *Run, Shelley, Run!* HarperCollins, 1974.

Schaefer, Jack. *Shane*. Houghton Mifflin, 1949.

Sleator, William. *House of Stairs*. Dutton, 1974.

_____. *Interstellar Pig*. Dutton, 1984.

Slepian, Jan. *The Alfred Summer*. Macmillan, 1980.

Spinelli, Jerry. *There's A Girl in My Hammerlock*. Simon and Schuster, 1991.

Thomas, Joyce Carol. *Marked by Fire*. Avon, 1982.

Thompson, Julian. *A Band of Angels*. Scholastic, 1986.

Tolkien, J. R. R. *The Lord of the Rings*. Houghton Mifflin, 1974.

Trelease, Jim. *Read-Aloud Handbook*, Penguin, 1982.

Twain, Mark. *Adventures of Huckleberry Finn*. 1884.

Voigt, Cynthia. *Izzy, Willy-Nilly*. Atheneum, 1986.

Weesner, Theodore. *The Car Thief*. Random House, 1972.

Wharton, William. *Birdy*. Knopf, 1978.

White, Rob. *Deathwatch*. Doubleday, 1972.

Zindel, Paul. *The Pigman*. HarperCollins, 1968.

_____. *Pardon Me, You're Stepping on My Eyeball!* HarperCollins, 1976.

_____. *The Amazing and Death-Defying Diary of Eugene Dingman*. HarperCollins 1987.

For information on the availability of paperback editions of these titles, please consult the most recent edition of *Paperbound Books in Print*, published annually by R. R. Bowker Company.

MODERN
YOUNG ADULT
READING

CHAPTER THREE

THE NEW REALISM
Of Life and Problems

When critic Northrop Frye used the term *realism* in his *Anatomy of Criticism,* he put it in quotation marks because when it is applied to literature the term doesn't—or shouldn't—mean the same thing that it does in other contexts. He argued that expecting literature simply to portray real life is a mistaken notion. The artist who can paint grapes so realistically that a bird will fly up and peck at the canvas is not the one most highly acclaimed. Nor would people want to listen to a symphony in which all the instruments imitated "real" sounds from nature—the cooing of doves, the rushing of a waterfall, a clap of thunder, and the wind whistling through trees.

In an interview with CNN's Larry King (November 4, 1991), Norman Mailer also commented on the concept of realism in relation to nonfiction and fiction. He claimed that as soon as a character—whether real or imagined—is written about, fiction results because the character now lives as imagined in people's minds rather than as a real person who can be talked to and touched. G. Robert Carlsen made a similar point when he said that a story exists first in the mind of its creator and then in the minds of its readers. Because it was never anything "real," it cannot be tested against an external reality, as can the plans for a building, chemical formulas, case studies, and so on.

If we evaluate literature by its realism alone, we should be forced to abandon most of the truly great literature of the world: certainly most of tragedy, much of comedy, and all of romance. We would be forced to discard the Greek plays, the great epics, Shakespeare, Molière. They succeed because they go beyond the externals of living and instead reach out and touch that imaginative life deep down inside where we live.[1]

When respected authors and critics argue against realism as a literary concept, we should explain that we are using the term in our chapter title mainly because we can't think of a better one. Besides, so many people use *realism* to describe the kinds of books being discussed in this chapter that we would be at a communication disadvantage if we tried to invent a new term.

A term that is sometimes used to describe a subset of realism is *problem novel*. We will go along with using this term for books about insurmountable problems, but again we aren't really satisfied with it because every novel includes a "problem." If it didn't, there wouldn't be a plot.

So even though we can't give a foolproof definition of the "new realism" or the "problem novel," and we're not even sure these are the best terms, that's what this chapter is about. By the end of the chapter, you should have a good idea of what such books have in common, but for now we will start by saying that realism is experientially true. It is an author's honest attempt to depict people in ordinary situations without sentimentalizing or glossing over anything. The problem novel focuses on an unfortunate event or life experience that a basically optimistic person would not foresee in his or her life, for example, experiencing an accident or grave illness, having serious troubles in one's family, being a victim of physical harm or violence, suffering from extreme forms of social pressure, or becoming addicted to drugs or alcohol.

Good YA authors treat candidly and with respect problems that belong specifically to young adults in today's world. As we pointed out in Chapter One, adolescence as a unique period of life is a fairly recent development coinciding with the growth of complex industrial societies. The problems that go along with modern adolescence did not exist in the nineteenth century, so, of course, they were not written about. At least in this one area, there is ample justification for books directed specifically to a young adult audience because there is a difference in the kinds of real-life problems that concern children, teenagers, and adults.

WHAT ARE THE PROBLEMS?

"Teens Face Whirlwind of Worries" read the headline of a newspaper story summarizing the 1991 annual convention of the American Psychological Association.[2] Conference sessions focused on the following topics:

- **Fears:** In contrast to the good old days when teenagers worried about having a boyfriend or girlfriend and getting into college, researchers at McGill University in Montreal found that the teens in their study who live in a safe, clean suburb "with parks everywhere" feared globe-threatening environmental disasters, unemployment, AIDS, World War

III, drugs, and violence. Some teenagers are so troubled by the fear of AIDS that they won't eat in restaurants.

- **Dating and Sex:** Bombarded by MTV and other sex-obsessed media almost from the cradle, some teens are dating and having sex almost as soon as their ages hit double digits. Researchers found that one-on-one dating at a tender age (fifth through eighth grades) was more likely to occur with children from broken homes and that young teens paired off with a boy- or girlfriend were not as happy as those who dated in groups.

- **Alcohol and Drugs:** The National Institute on Drug Abuse proudly touts the fact that drug use among teenagers has dropped 18 percent since the early 1980s, but these statistics are only for teenagers in school. The statistics are circular in nature, because once kids get addicted to drugs they are highly likely to drop out. Crack use among drop-outs is at epidemic proportions.

- **Money:** As the economy worsens, more kids are going to work. Two-thirds of all teens in junior and senior high have jobs. Most go to work right after school and come home too tired to read or think about homework.

- **Academics:** In this first generation growing up in a high number of single-parent families, children probably haven't had as much help with their schoolwork as children in earlier generations. One psychologist hypothesized that a contributing factor to the low number of college freshmen (only 7 percent) majoring in science and math is that young people have not been close to fathers working in such fields.

- **Independence:** Whereas rebellion and freedom were the code words of many teenagers in the 1950s and 1960s, today "there's been a revision of the model that says teenagers need to cut themselves off from their families. Now kids are saying, 'I wish there was someone I could be close to.' "

- **Mental Illness:** College counseling centers no longer treat mainly developmental issues and boyfriend/girlfriend problems. Maureen Kenny of Boston College reported that they are now dealing on a regular basis with serious mental illness and that the "kids [of divorce] suffer more than previously we had given them credit for."

Today's teenagers are not the first in history with difficult decisions to make, but certainly few of us will argue against the idea that they have a special set of problems unique to their age and to today's world. Parents, writers, and educators are eager to help young people in these decisions, and one of the ways we believe we can help is to provide books that honestly explore problems and present alternative solutions (see Focus Box 3.1). To understand the nature of the problem novel and its place in adolescent literature, it is necessary to look not only at the subject matter, but also at how the subject matter influences writing styles and how one book lays the groundwork for others. Table 3.1 lists suggestions for evaluating the problem novel.

Books That Stimulate Discussion on Decision-Making

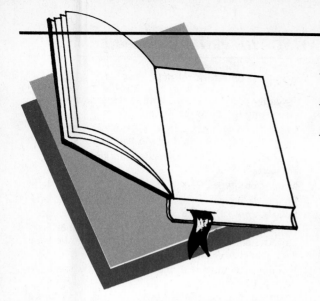

After the First Death by Robert Cormier. Pantheon, 1979. Two boys are sacrificed by their fathers, one a Middle East terrorist and one a U.S. government official.

The Bumblebee Flies Anyway by Robert Cormier. Pantheon, 1974. The grim setting of a hospital treating—or experimenting on—young adults with terminal illnesses is made more bearable by the tender love story that provides a secondary theme.

Chernowitz! by Fran Arrick. Bradbury, 1981. Emmett Sundback is a high school bully who for two years torments Bob Cherno because he's Jewish. Even when the matter comes to a head, Sundback does not change.

The Dark Behind the Curtain by Gillian Cross. Oxford, 1974. A school production of *Sweeney Todd* teaches the actors more about human frailties than about the art of acting.

I Am the Cheese by Robert Cormier. Pantheon, 1977. Seldom has there been such a powerful story of a young innocent facing incredible odds from organized crime and the U.S. Secret Service.

Incident at Loring Groves by Sonia Levitin. Dial, 1988. Based on a true story, a group of teenagers breaks into an unoccupied cottage and finds the body of a missing teenage girl. They decide to keep it a secret.

Journey of the Sparrows by Fran Leeper Buss and Daisy Cubias. Dutton/Lodestar, 1991. How to live the better life they came for and still remain invisible is the question faced by a family of illegal Hispanics trying to make it in Chicago.

Princess Ashley by Richard Peck. Delacorte, 1987. Chelsea is at first thrilled when the beautiful and rich Ashley picks her to join the "in" group; later she's devastated.

Remembering the Good Times by Richard Peck. Delacorte, 1985. Adults as well as kids suffer from social pressure. Trav's suicide reveals an ugly side of some of the adult "caregivers" connected with Trav, Kate, and Buck's junior high.

Scorpions by Walter Dean Myers. Harper-Collins, 1988. Jamal's brother is in jail and an old gang leader brings word to Jamal that he's to take over as leader of the Scorpions. He also brings Jamal a gun.

The Trial of Anna Cotman by Vivien Alcock. Delacorte, 1990. Fourteen-year-old Anna is happy to be in the secret Society of Masks, but after Yellow Lord joins, the club takes on mean and sinister tones.

Table 3.1   SUGGESTIONS FOR EVALUATING THE PROBLEM NOVEL

A good problem novel usually has:

A strong, interesting, and believable plot centering around a problem that a young person might really have.

The power to transport the reader into another person's thoughts and feelings.

Rich characterization. The characters "come alive" as believable with a balance of good and negative qualities.

A setting that enhances the story and is described so that the reader can get the intended picture.

A worthwhile theme. The reader is left with something to think about.

A smoothness of style that flows steadily and easily, carrying the reader along.

A universal appeal so that it speaks to more than a single group of readers.

A subtlety that stimulates the reader to think about the various aspects of the story.

A way of dealing with the problems so that the reader is left with insights into either society or individuals or both.

A poor problem novel may have:

A totally predictable plot with nothing new and interesting to entice the reader.

Characters who are cardboardlike exaggerations of people and are too good or too bad to be believed.

More characters than the reader can keep straight comfortably.

Many stereotypes.

Lengthy chapters or descriptive paragraphs that add bulk but not substance to the book.

A preachy message. The author spells out the attitudes and conclusions with which he or she wants each reader to leave the book.

Nothing that stays with the reader after the book has been put down.

A subject that is of interest only because it is topical or trendy.

Inconsistent points of view. The author's sympathies change with no justification.

Dialogue that sounds forced and/or inappropriate to the characters.

"Facts" that do not jibe with those of the real world.

Unlikely coincidences or changes in characters' personalities for the sake of the plot.

Exaggerations that result in sensationalism.

THE GROUND-BREAKING BOOKS

If we were to pinpoint the birth of the new realism in YA literature, the year would be 1967, which is why we chose that year as the place to begin our Honor Sampling (see p. 9). The early books on that list include S. E. Hinton's *The Outsiders,* about the Socs (the society kids) and the Greasers, and it's the Greasers' story she tells. Robert Lipsyte's *The Contender* is about a black boy hoping to use boxing as his ticket out of the slums. In Paul Zindel's *The Pigman* an alienated boy and girl make friends with a lonely old man who can't admit that his wife has died. The three of them share feelings of love and carefree playfulness, but in the end the old man dies tragically, and the boy and girl are left to ponder their role in his death and what it all means. In Richard Bradford's *Red Sky at Morning,* Southerner Josh Arnold and his mother go to a little town in New Mexico, where they are to wait out World War II. While living there, Josh gains at least a partial understanding of his Mexican-American neighbors and of himself. William Armstrong's *Sounder* is a grim historical piece about a poverty-stricken black family of tenant farmers.

These books exemplify several of the characteristics that during the 1970s came to be associated with the realistic problem novel for young adults. In addition to their candor and to the selection of subject matter, they differ from earlier books in four basic ways. The first difference lies in the choice of *characters*. These protagonists come mostly from lower-class families, which ties in with the second major difference, *setting*. Instead of living in idyllic and pleasant suburban homes, the characters in these books come from settings that are harsh, difficult places to live. To get the point across about the characters and where and how they live, authors used colloquial *language,* which is the third major difference. Authors began to write the way people really talked (e.g., in dialogue using profanity and ungrammatical constructions). That the general public allowed this change in language shows that people were drawing away from the idea that the main purpose of fictional books for young readers is to set an example of proper middle-class behavior.

The fourth difference also relates to this change in attitude, and that is the change in *mode*. As people began to think that the educational value of fiction is to provide readers with more vicarious experiences than would be either desirable or possible in real life, the mode of stories for young adults changed. It used to be that most of the books—at least most of the books approved of by parents and educators—were written in the comic and romantic modes. These were the books with upbeat, happy endings. As long as people believed that children would model their lives after what they read, then of course they wanted young people to read happy stories, because a happy life is what all of us want for our children. But the problem novel is based on a different philosophy, which is that young people will have a better chance to be happy if they have realistic expectations, if they know both the bad and the good about the society in which they live. This changed attitude opened the door to writers of irony and even tragedy for young people.

Irony differs from tragedy in that it may be less intense; similarly, instead of having heroic qualities, the protagonist is an ordinary person, much like the reader. One example used to define or illustrate irony is a "tennis serve that you can't return." You can admire its perfections, its appropriateness, and even the inevitability of the outcome, but you just can't cope with it. There's a refreshing honesty to stories that show readers they aren't the only ones who get served that kind of ball and that the human spirit, though totally devastated in this particular set, may rise again to play another match. Brock Cole's *Celine,* Cynthia Rylant's *A Kindness,* and M. E. Kerr's *Night Kites* are books of this sort.

Robert Cormier's books come closer to being tragedies. In traditional literary criticism, tragedies have three distinct elements. First, there is a noble character who, no matter what happens, maintains the qualities that the society considers praiseworthy; second, there is an inevitable force that works against the character; and third, there is a struggle and an outcome. The reader of a tragedy is usually filled with pity and fear—pity for the hero and fear for oneself that the same thing might happen. The intensity of this involvement causes the reader to undergo an emotional release as the outcome of the story unfolds. This

Through his own writing as well as what was written about him, Robert Cormier brought adolescent literature a step closer to literary respectability.

release, or catharsis, has the effect of draining away dangerous human emotions and filling the reader with a sense of exaltation or amazed pride in what the human spirit is called upon to undergo.[3]

THE CHOCOLATE WAR *AS A PROBLEM NOVEL*

Robert Cormier's *The Chocolate War* is our favorite example of a modern problem novel for young adults. It contains the kind of realism that many other books had been leading up to, and its message about conformity and human manipulation is all the more powerful because the young protagonist is so vulnerable. The religious symbolism serves as a contrasting backdrop to the terrible evil that pervades Trinity High School, where the protagonist is a freshman. The opening paragraph is the following simple line: "They murdered him." *Him* is fourteen-year-old Jerry Renault, who is being "tested" to see if he has enough guts to be on the football team.

The story begins and ends on the athletic field, where the shadows of the goalposts resemble a "network of crosses, empty crucifixes." On Jerry's third play at Trinity High he is "hit simultaneously by three of them." He blinks himself back to consciousness and jumps to his feet:

. . . intact, bobbing like one of those toy novelties dangling from car windows, but erect.

"For Christ's sake," the coach bellowed, his voice juicy with contempt. A spurt of saliva hit Jerry's cheek.

Hey coach, you spit on me, Jerry protested. Stop the spitting, coach. What he said aloud was, "I'm all right, coach," because he was a coward about stuff like that, thinking one thing and saying another, planning one thing and doing another—he had been Peter a thousand times and a thousand cocks had crowed in his lifetime.

Over the course of the book Jerry gets the courage to think and do the same thing. He refuses to sell fifty boxes of chocolate that the corrupt teacher, Brother Leon, has assigned to each student. For the first ten days of the candy campaign, he simply follows the orders of the Vigils, a gang whose members, in the words of their head man, Archie Costello, "were the school." But when the ten days are up and the Vigils order Jerry to do a reversal and participate in the selling campaign, he dares to say, "No."

At first Jerry is a hero, but because this threatens the power of the Vigils, Archie uses his full potential in people management to turn the student body against Jerry. When all the chocolates except Jerry's are sold, Archie arranges a boxing match between Jerry and a bully who is trying to work his way into the Vigils. It is supposed to be set up "with rules. Fair and square," but what Archie really masterminds is a physical and psychological battering much worse than anything Jerry underwent at football practice.

The last chapter of the book could have begun with the same line as the first chapter—"They murdered him"—except that this time it would have been less of a metaphor. Although Jerry may recover physically from a fractured jaw and internal injuries, his spirit has been murdered. In the midst of the fight:

A new sickness invaded Jerry, the sickness of knowing what he had become, another animal, another beast, another violent person in a violent world, inflicting damage, not disturbing the universe but damaging it. He had allowed Archie to do this to him.

And after the fight, when the pain—"Jesus, the pain"—brings Jerry back to consciousness, the reader sees how changed he is because of what he tries to tell his friend Goober:

They don't want you to do your thing, not unless it happens to be their thing, too. It's a laugh, Goober, a fake. Don't disturb the universe, Goober, no matter what the posters say.

In selecting *The Chocolate War* as a touchstone example, we asked ourselves several questions about the book. These same or similar questions could be asked when evaluating almost any problem novel. First, does the book make a distinctive contribution? Does it say something new or does it convey something old in a new way? And if so, is it something of value? Robert Cormier was praised by *The Kirkus Reviews* because with *The Chocolate War* he dared to "disturb the upbeat universe of juvenile books." He did not compromise by providing a falsely hopeful conclusion, nor did he sidestep the issue by leaving it open for readers to imagine their own happy ending. Until Cormier, most writers for young readers had chosen one of these two approaches. Yet Cormier was not being "difficult" just for the sake of being different. When he was questioned at a National Council of Teachers of English convention about his motives in writing such a pessimistic book for young readers, he answered that he had written three other novels and numerous short stories, all with upbeat endings, and that in *The Chocolate War* he was simply providing a balance. He then went on to say that today's young readers are a television generation. They have grown up thinking that every problem can be solved within a half-hour or an hour at the most, with time out for commercials. It's important for people to realize that all problems are not that easily solved. In real life some problems may never be solved and the solutions to others demand the utmost efforts of the most capable people in the world.

The plot of a book must be examined to see how closely it grows out of the characters' actions and attitudes. Is it an idea that could easily have been dropped into another setting or onto other characters? With Cormier's book, there wouldn't have been a story without the unique but believable personalities of both Jerry and Archie, as well as of Brother Leon. The problem was not so bizarre or unusual that it overshadowed the characters, nor were the characters so unusual that readers could not identify with them or imagine themselves having to deal with people like them. It is because the characters at first appear to be such ordinary people that readers are drawn into the story. The theme is similar to that in Golding's *Lord of the Flies,* but because Golding's book is set on a deserted island in the midst of a war it could be dismissed as unrealistic. Cormier's book has an immediacy that is hard to deny. The problem is a real one that teenagers can identify with on the first or literal level, yet it has implications far beyond one beaten-up fourteen-year-old and 20,000 boxes of leftover Mother's Day candy.

In looking at the setting, we might ask, is it just there or does it contribute something to the mood or the action or to revealing characterization? In *The Chocolate War* the story would not have been nearly so chilling without the religious setting, which provided contrast. In some ways the evil in Archie is less hideous than that in Brother Leon, the corrupt teacher who enlists Archie's help in making his unauthorized investment pay off. The Brother hides behind his clerical collar and his role of teacher and assistant headmaster, whereas Archie only identifies himself as a nonbeliever in the so-called Christian ethic. For example, when his stooge Obie asks him how he can do the things he does and still take Communion, he responds, "When you march down to the rail, you're receiving the Body, man. Me, I'm just chewing a wafer they buy by the pound in Worcester."

Another relevant question is the respect the author has for the intended audience. Cormier showed a great deal of respect for his readers: Nowhere did he write down to them. The proof of his respect is in some of the subtle symbolization that he worked into the story and the care with which he developed his style. For example, the irony of the whole situation is exemplified in the gang's name, the Vigils. He chose the name as a a shortened form of *vigilante,* an accurate description of the way the gang worked. But in response to an interview question about whether or not the name was an ironic reference to vigil lights, the candles placed devotionally before a shrine or image, he agreed that the religious connotation, the image of the boys in the gang standing like vigil lights before Archie, who basked in the glow of their admiration, "was also very much a part of my choice."[4] Another example of Cormier's subtlety is the fact that Archie's name has such meanings as "principal or chief," as in *archvillain,* and "at the extreme, that is, someone or something most fully embodying the qualities of its kind," as in *archrival.*

A question that has to be asked somewhere in the evaluation process is how many people a particular book attracts as readers. *The Chocolate War* has gone through innumerable reprintings, so it's obviously being read, although many of those who read it are doing it as a class assignment either in a college young adult literature class or in a high school English class. It's ideal for class reading and discussion because there's more in the book than any one student sees at a first reading.

HOW THE PROBLEM NOVEL HAS CHANGED

When *The Outsiders* and *The Pigman* were written, Americans had not yet sent a man to the moon, lost a war, had a president resign, been infected with AIDS, or heard of sexual harassment. It would be strange indeed for such momentous events and changes in cultural attitudes to have occurred while realistic books for young adults stayed exactly the same.

Because it was new and different and because it explored themes that intrigued and concerned both adults and young adults, publishers, authors, librarians, teachers, and critics treated the problem novel as a favored child all during the 1970s. Then in the early 1980s, changes in marketing practices and reading tastes made formula romances and other mass-produced series (horror stories, science fiction, mysteries) the favorites of young readers. That students would buy these books on their own may have delighted some publishers—or at least marketing people—but librarians and English teachers who had welcomed the YA problem novel were horrified.

They worried and wondered if serious writing for young adults was an endangered species, perhaps even close to extinction. A panel of editors touched on this at the November 1987, National Council of Teachers of English meeting in Los Angeles. HarperCollins editor Marilyn Kriney answered the question,

"Is the problem novel dead?" with another question, "What's a novel without a problem?" And she warned about the dangers of labeling books, particularly problem novels, when she said, "By pigeonholing, we're denying what makes these books great—their universality."

We agree that the YA realistic problem novel is alive and well, and for us it's still the most intriguing YA reading. We also think that some but not all of the changes that have occurred within the last twenty-five years have made for better books. One such change is that the modern problem novel is no longer so shocking to young adults. In her 1979 May Hill Arbuthnot lecture, Sheila Egoff conjectured that problem novels were popular with young readers because they featured the unknown and exotic, they flattered readers by making the audience feel grown-up, they appealed to prurient interests, and they were promoted through peer pressure: "Not to have read Judy Blume seems as socially unacceptable as not being familiar with the latest 'in' television show."[5]

Ignoring for the moment that adults choose their best-sellers for the same reasons, most of Egoff's comments seem dated. Perhaps the books have changed; society certainly has. In 1971, *Go Ask Alice* shocked many adults and some adolescents because they had no idea that "nice, middle-class, white girls did such things" (the *things* being sex and drugs). Readers were virtuously allowed, or encouraged, to relish all those gorgeous, salacious details because the author was preaching a moral message. Today's television documentaries and magazines and newspapers leave little in the "unknown and exotic" category. In the early 1990s, Marshall McLuhan's idea of the global village took on added meaning as the world watched and listened to Anita Hill charge Clarence Thomas with sexual harassment and Magic Johnson explain how he came to carry the HIV virus. The AIDS epidemic was scary enough to bring sex education out into the open, and when a demonstration was given on national television of how to put on a condom, the only loud protest came from banana growers, who objected to their merchandise being used as a model.

All of this has had a numbing effect. Almost daily we see publicly displayed bumper stickers, T-shirt messages, and tabloid headlines that a few years ago would have been considered so off-color that their messages would have been whispered among close friends. And if pornographic books and magazines, sexually explicit cable television or videos, and telephone scoop lines devoted to sexual talk are available to adults in a community, they are also available to young adults. Obviously, whether we like it or not, young people today have been exposed to information and opinions about all sorts of things, precisely the kinds of sensitive issues treated in YA problem novels. This means that today's books have to offer more than titillation, which is exactly what the best ones have always done.

Recent problem novels are also likely to contain more excitement, romance, and optimism. Being forced to compete with the unrealistic wish fulfillment of formula romances, as well as the equally unrealistic chills of occult and horror tales, has made authors less likely to write starkly grim stories. This was brought forcefully home to us when we looked for a new touchstone example of modern tragedy and then decided to keep Robert Cormier's 1974 *The Chocolate War*. We couldn't find a new book we liked that was a pure example of a tragedy. Today's authors soften their stories with motifs supporting wishful thinking. The most common is for a wonderful boy to come along and help a girl solve her problems. Another technique is to create problems that young readers can be enticed into wishing they had a chance to solve. For example, the protagonist in Sandy Asher's *Everything Is Not Enough* is so wealthy and spoiled that he has to go against his father's wishes to take a summer job as a busboy. The "problems" in Robin Brancato's *Uneasy Money* result from a high school senior winning the New Jersey lottery.

Another trend is for authors to cram more and more into each book. For example, Julian F. Thompson's 1986 *A Band of Angels* begins with an orphaned boy caught in a political situation somewhat like Cormier's 1977 *I Am the Cheese*. But in Thompson's novel, the boy and the warm and supportive friends that he picks up are largely unaware and untouched by any danger. They camp in the woods and hatch plans to have every kid sign a petition against nuclear war. Al Muller, in *The ALAN Review* (Fall 1986), criticized the fact that on the way to the happy ending, readers meet not only the main characters, but also a hippie college professor who takes advantage of teenage runaways, a jailed teenager's suicide, Vietnam veterans hiding in a wilderness, materialistic and capitalistic adults and parents, industrial-strength profanity, and historical and literary allusions to Bob Dylan, *Shane,* the Children's Crusade, Descartes, *The Sun Also Rises,* and Marlin Perkins.

Joan Kaywell criticized Isabelle Holland's *The Island* for much the same reason in the spring 1985 *ALAN Review:* "a heart attack here, a murder there," then some "drugs and an arranged marriage." Kaywell argued that the elements didn't work well together, "especially when the characters are so bland." She compared her disappointment to what she would have felt had she gone to Julia Child's house and been served "chicken cordon bleu à la TV dinner."[6]

The result of both of these trends is a blurring of the dividers between problem novels and other types of stories, such as romances, historical fiction, and adventure stories. This has forced us to make some arbitrary decisions because many of the books we discuss here could also be discussed in other sections, and vice versa.

A positive result from authors' attempts to give their readers more is less stereotyping of characters and plots, and the kinds of problems that contemporary teenagers face are being written about in a variety of settings. Readers are learning about teenagers' lives in other countries (see Focus Box 2.4, p. 86). YA authors are also concentrating more attention on characters of different ages (see "Across Generations," Focus Box 1.2, p. 19) and are developing parents who are not quite as one-sided as they used to be.

Sexual stereotyping is also less apparent in the new books. For example, in 1967, when teenager S. E. Hinton wrote the autobiographical *The Outsiders,* her publishers suggested that she go by her initials rather than by her name of Susan Elizabeth. They feared that readers wouldn't respect a "macho" story if they knew it was written by a woman, but in 1985, when Cin Forshay-Lunsford published the autobiographical *Walk Through Cold Fire,* a book with a plot and characters that several reviewers compared to *The Outsiders,* no one suggested that the author take a masculine-sounding pen name or that the main character in the book be changed from a girl to a boy.

Of course, we expect changes in books focusing on issues related to racial and ethnic differences. Among the most critically acclaimed books of the 1960s and early 1970s that young adults responded to were Eldridge Cleaver's *Soul on Ice,* William H. Armstrong's *Sounder,* Maya Angelou's *I Know Why the Caged Bird Sings,* Sharon Bell Mathis' *Teacup Full of Roses,* Alice Childress' *A Hero Ain't Nothin' But a Sandwich,* and Rosa Guy's *The Friends.* As powerful as these books were, they had a grimness and a sameness to them, and it's refreshing today to have them supplemented by books in which a variety of characters from different backgrounds face problems, sometimes separately but sometimes together (see Focus Boxes 1.3, 1.4, 2.2, and 2.3 on minority characters in YA books, pp. 26, 28, 64, and 66).

In conclusion, although there will be exceptions, realistic problem novels of today will generally have

- Less reliance for interest on shock and titillation
- More excitement, romance, and optimism
- More of a world view
- Less stereotyping of characters, plots, and settings
- A more balanced and convincing view of parents
- More sophisticated and varied approaches to problems connected with racism and ethnic identification

CATEGORIES OF CONCERN IN REALISTIC NOVELS

Our original subtitle for this chapter was "Of Life and Other Sad Songs." But now that "realistic" novels for young adults have become less pessimistic and less focused on insurmountable problems, it's no longer appropriate to imply that the message of realism for teenagers is that life is one long, sad song. As this chapter shows, there are still plenty of worthwhile problem novels, but there are also many other realistic novels treating topics and themes that we would prefer to view simply as parts of life rather than as problems. And since there are more of these then can fit comfortably in one chapter, we've scattered some of our "realistic" Focus Boxes throughout the rest of this textbook.

One of the identifying characteristics of YA literature is that the problems that authors choose to write about are those most likely to be met by contemporary teenagers. Because today's society is so different from what it was two or three generations ago, young readers aren't likely to find their kinds of problems in many of the classics. Nor are they likely to find their kinds of problems in contemporary problem novels written for adults, because these books are likely to focus on marital problems, mature sexual relationships, disappointments in careers, and adjustments to growing old. Teenagers are more interested in how they relate to their parents, siblings, and friends; in how they are going to adjust to society; and in the kinds of sexual experiences and relationships they might expect to have.

Family Relationships

A look at mythology, folklore, and classical and religious literature shows that the subject of family relationships is not what's new about the new realism. One could find virtually thousands of stories touching on the theme (see Focus Box 3.2). Inadequate or absent parents appeal to young adult readers who are desperately involved with changing from someone's child to an individual with rights.

Relative newcomers to YA books are parents who are or have been hippies. Sharon Leezer, one of our graduate students who is a teacher and librarian in Phoenix, wrote a paper asking, "Have the Flower Children Sprouted Weeds in the Garden of Motherhood?" She became interested in the ways parents were portrayed when she noticed how many older men and women came to parent/teacher conferences in her suburban, middle-class school. To her surprise, she learned that these were usually grandparents raising offspring left behind as their flower children turned into hard-core, absent hippies. She set out to find how this new reality was portrayed in contemporary fiction.

She found that a common way for authors to indicate the flower child background of parents is to have the children address them by first names: Melody, Taxi, Courtney, Saffron. These parents in turn give their children unusual names: Galadrial, Pax, Joshua Fortune, Sara Sunshine, Tie-Dye, and Esalen Starness Blue. The parents are away from home for long periods of time; they send postcards, usually with no return address; they raise false hopes by professing love and a desire to see the child; and they make their children wait for calls by public telephones. For example, in Betsy Byars' *The Two-Thousand-Pound Goldfish*, Weezie stands in the designated phone booth at the designated time for 156 weeks but receives only five calls. In Stephanie Tolan's *A Good Courage*, Tie-Dye's flower child mother takes him to yet another commune, and in Cynthia Voigt's *A Solitary Blue*, when Melody leaves her son, seven-year-old Jeff, she explains in a note that she is needed by hungry people and little hunted-down animals. Years later, when Jeff visits his mother at her grandmother's house, she exchanges his plane ticket home for a bus ticket, explaining that the extra money could be better spent on poor, starving children. Since she leaves him no money for meals, he becomes one of the starving children she professes to be so concerned about.

However, not all hippie parents are presented negatively. The plot in Thelma Hatch Wyss' *Here at the Scenic-Vu Motel* revolves around the fact that the

Parents and Kids

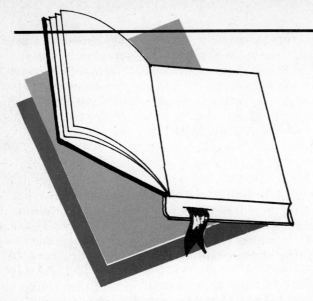

A Day No Pigs Would Die by Robert Newton Peck. Knopf, 1973. The love that the boy Robert feels for his Pa is only one of the themes in this powerful story of a Vermont farm family from the 1920s.

Dinky Hocker Shoots Smack by M. E. Kerr, HarperCollins, 1972. The first of M. E. Kerr's YA books was inspired by her watching a do-gooder mother solving everyone's problems except those of her own daughter.

Father Figure by Richard Peck. Viking, 1978. In this split family, seventeen-year-old Jim thinks of himself as a substitute father for his little brother. When circumstances change, Jim is jealous and hurt because his brother chooses the real father over him.

Good-bye and Keep Cold by Jenny Davis. Orchard, 1987. Edda's father was killed in a Kentucky strip-mining accident and Edda looks back on the aftermath and what it meant to her growing up.

The Great Gilly Hopkins by Katherine Paterson. Crowell, 1979. Gilly manipulates her caregivers until she gets the wise and wonderful Trotter as a foster mother. But when Gilly's attempt to find her flower-child mother backfires, not even Trotter can help.

Journey to an 800 Number by E. L. Konigsburg. Atheneum, 1982. When Max is sent to live with his father, who travels around the country selling rides on his camel, Max is at first humiliated at what he considers a difference in class.

Keep Laughing by Cynthia Grant. Atheneum, 1991. Fifteen-year-old Shep Young is almost swept off his feet when his famous comedian father comes roaring back into his life after a long absence.

A Kindness by Cynthia Rylant. Orchard, 1988. Fifteen-year-old Chip is accustomed to handling all the practical matters in his single-parent family and is shocked when his pregnant mother won't confide in him.

Midnight Hour Encores by Bruce Brooks. HarperCollins, 1986. In this far from typical family—a remnant of the 1960s—it's refreshing to read about a positive father/daughter relationship.

The Moonlight Man by Paula Fox. Bradbury, 1986. In a memorable summer visit, Catherine ends up playing the role of the grown-up when she discovers that her father is a "falling-down-drunk."

The Outside Child by Nina Bawden. Lothrop, Lee and Shepard, 1989. When thirteen-year-old Jane accidentally discovers that her father has a second family, she is hurt and angry.

Pillow of Clouds   by Marc Talbert. Dial, 1991. After his thirteenth birthday, Chester has to choose whether to live with his father in New Mexico or his mother in Iowa. Their differences in personalities and life-styles are as great as the physical differences between Iowa and New Mexico.

Rainbow Jordan   by Alice Childress. Putnam, 1981. Although Rainbow's mother fails in playing her role, readers still learn something about what "family" means.

Rear-View Mirror   by Paul Fleischman. HarperCollins, 1986. Olivia Tate spends the summer with a father that until now she knew "neither by sight nor by scent, but solely by report. He was like a distant land known only through traveller's tales. . . ."

Return to Bitter Creek   by Doris Buchanan Smith. Viking, 1986. In this witty and honest book, Lacey's unwed mother decides to take Lacey back to their hometown and their family.

Send No Blessings   by Phyllis R. Naylor. Macmillan, 1990. As the oldest of eight children, fifteen-year-old Beth struggles to understand why her parents keep bringing more "blessings" into their already cramped double-wide trailer.

Somewhere in the Darkness   by Walter Dean Myers. Scholastic, 1992. Jimmy arrives home from school to find a tall, thin man waiting to introduce himself as the father who's been gone so long that Jimmy has to look at a photograph to verify the truth of what the man says.

Sydney, Herself   by Colby Rodowsky. Farrar, Straus & Giroux, 1989. Readers of Sydney's self-awareness journey will get to know a likable girl and see how she and her mother come to terms with their relationship and their individual dreams.

---

teenagers' parents, mostly refugees from the 1960s, are seeking the simple life in Bear Flats, Idaho. It's not their fault that the school board decides to quit bussing the seven kids to the nearest school. The solution is for the teenage children to live Monday through Friday in a motel. In *The Great Gilly Hopkins,* Katherine Paterson portrays Courtney Rutherford Hopkins as a "flower child gone to seed," but in *Bridge to Terabithia* she portrays Leslie's parents, Bill and Judy Burke, as an intelligent, creative couple, who come in their "little Italian car . . . to reassess their value structure" by living in a rundown farmhouse with lots of books and no television set. They wear old jeans, write instead of "work," and eat clabber.

In Norma Fox Mazer's *Downtown,* Hal and Laura Connors are fugitives from the F.B.I. because they were leaders of an antiwar protest that went awry and killed two people. Their son, named Pax but now called Pete, is left with a bachelor uncle and in general has a good life—except for when he's awakened by what he calls the White Terror or when he's followed by government agents or when he can't tell his girlfriend about his family. When his mother turns herself in and sends for him to visit her in jail, he is exuberantly happy, but as he and his uncle get closer to New York he is overcome with doubts and realizes that he no longer knows where home is, "I finally understand that there is no ending for my story . . . no perfect ending . . . no little-Pax-happy-at-last ending."

In Bruce Brooks' *Midnight Hour Encores,* sixteen-year-old Sib asks her unorthodox father, Taxi, to take her to California to visit the flower child mother, who gave her away on the day she was born. To Sib's surprise, her mother is now a successful businesswoman, open and warm and at least willing to try being a mother. But in the end, Sib decides to return to Washington, D.C., with Taxi. This refreshing change from the unrealistic child-centeredness of the old problem novels is possible because Sib, along with readers, realizes that contrary to what she would like to think, she did not raise herself with only a little help from Taxi.

In Sonia Levitin's *A Season for Unicorns,* fourteen-year-old Ingrid is embittered when she learns that her father casually engages in extramarital sex. Learning something similar is even more traumatic for seventeen-year-old Alan in John Rowe Townsend's *Downstream.* Alan is in love with his twenty-three-old tutor and is devastated when he learns that she is having an affair with his father.

YA authors have not developed the mother/daughter relationship as fully as they have father/son and father/daughter relationships. However, Jamaica Kincaid's *Annie John,* set on the Caribbean Island of Antigua, is a powerful new exploration of a daughter's painful gaining of emotional independence from her mother. And books by Norma Klein, Norma Fox Mazer, and Judy Blume often feature mothers and daughters.

In Paula Fox's *A Place Apart* and in Judy Blume's *Tiger Eyes,* the fathers of the families die unexpectedly (a heart attack and a shooting, respectively) and the mothers and daughters move to new locales, almost as if they are embarking on dual quests in search of a way to put their lives back together. In neither book is it easy, as shown by the climax of *Tiger Eyes,* when Davey's mother invites her out to a special dinner.

"This is nice," I say. What I mean is that it is nice to be alone with my mother. This is the first time since we came to Los Alamos that it is just the two of us.

"Yes," Mom says. "It's very nice."

"It's been a long time."

"Yes," Mom says. "And I've wanted to explain that to you, Davey."

She is arranging and rearranging her silverware, moving the spoon into the fork's place, then the fork into the spoon's. "Up until now, I've been afraid to be alone with you."

"Afraid?"

"Yes."

"But why?"

"I was afraid you'd ask me questions and I wouldn't have any answers. I've been afraid you'd want to talk about Daddy . . . and the night he was killed . . . and the pain would be too much for me."

"I did want to talk about it," I tell her. "For a long time . . . and it hurt me that you wouldn't."

"I know," she says, reaching across the table and touching my hand. "But I had to come to terms with it myself, first. Now I think I'm ready . . . now I can talk about it with you."

"But now I don't need to," I say.

The absence of a fulfilling relationship between a parent and child sometimes opens the way for the young protagonist to establish a friendship with a surrogate parent, or more commonly a surrogate grandparent. Also, when the adults in children's lives are either absent, preoccupied, or flawed in some way, space is cleared for fully developed sibling relationships. For example, Cynthia Voigt's Newbery Award–winning *Dicey's Song* begins as follows:

> ■ AND THEY LIVED HAPPILY EVER AFTER
> Not the Tillermans, Dicey thought. That wasn't the way things went for the Tillermans, ever. She wasn't about to let that get her down. She couldn't let it get her down—that was what had happened to Momma.

Dicey's view that when parents are weak the children have to be that much stronger is a theme often illustrated through the way brothers and sisters pull together to close gaps in the family circle, as in Betsy Byars' *The Night Swimmers,* Vera and Bill Cleaver's *Where the Lilies Bloom* and *Trial Valley,* and S. E. Hinton's *Tex.* Harry Mazer's *When the Phone Rang* is a more mainstream exploration of three young people's (ages twelve, sixteen, and twenty-one) struggle to keep their family together after their parents were killed in a plane crash.

Jean Ferris' *Across the Grain* focuses on a less successful brother-sister relationship. When their mother dies, Will promises that he will watch over his older sister Paige—an awkward arrangement, since Paige is the legal guardian. Paige makes several decisions that are obviously bad for both of them, so after Will turns eighteen he leaves Paige and goes to U.C.L.A. to build his own life. Julie Reece Deaver's *First Wedding, Once Removed* is the touching story of how thirteen-year-old Pokie comes to terms with the courtship and marriage of her older brother Gib, and Barbara Hall's *Dixie Storms* is Dutch's story of her fifteenth summer, when a cousin comes to visit and upsets the balance that Dutch's atypical family had achieved.

Writers who consistently show strong family relationships include Sue Ellen Bridgers, Paula Fox, Virginia Hamilton, Katherine Paterson, Ouida Sebestyen, Mildred Taylor, and Cynthia Voigt.

Friends and Society

Peer groups become increasingly important to teenagers as they move beyond a social and emotional dependence on their parents. By becoming part of a group, clique, or gang, teenagers take a step toward emotional independence.

Even though they aren't making truly independent decisions about such social conventions as clothing, language, and entertainment, it's no longer their parents who are deciding on and enforcing their behavior. As part of a group, they try out various roles ranging from conformist to nonconformist, from follower to leader. These roles can be acted out by individuals within the group or they can be acted out by the group as a whole, as, for example, when one gang challenges another gang. Group members in such a situation are caught up in a kind of emotional commitment that they would seldom feel as individuals.

But it isn't automatic that all teenagers find groups to belong to, and even if they do, they are still curious about other groups. This is where young adult literature comes in. It extends the peer group, giving teenagers a chance to participate vicariously in many more personal relationships than are possible for most youngsters in the relatively short time that they spend in high school. By reading about other individuals trying to find places for themselves, teenagers begin answering such questions as: Who is making the "right" decisions? What values and attitudes are "best"? How will I be judged by other groups and by other individuals? What are the possible results of certain choices? And what are attractive and reasonable alternatives?

The whole area of making friends is a challenge to teenagers. When they were very young, it was a simple matter of playing with whoever happened to be nearby. Parents were responsible for locating in the "right" neighborhood near "good schools," so that children had no reason to give particular thought to differences in social and economic classes or ethnic backgrounds. But the older children get, the more they become responsible for making their own friends. Quite suddenly their environments are expanded not only through larger, more diverse schools, but also through jobs, extracurricular activities, public entertainment, shopping in malls, and church or community activities.

Throughout elementary school, young people are taught that America is a democracy and that we do not have a caste system. Any boy—and maybe today, any girl—can grow up to be president. But real-life observations don't support this, and that may be why books exploring differences in social classes are especially popular with young adults, who as they emerge from childhood begin making observations about social class structures.

One of the most perceptive and at the same time humorous explorations of the topic is E. L. Konigsburg's *Journey to an 800 Number*. When Maximillian Stubbs' divorced mother remarries and leaves for a long honeymoon, he takes his prep school jacket and fifty dollars and goes off to spend time with his father. Woody, the father, makes a living by traveling to tourist and convention centers, where he sells rides on the camel he keeps. Max is horrified at what he perceives as a difference in class between his father and himself, but in the words of one reviewer, he gradually learns "to separate the outward, lavish trappings of class from the simple meaning of the word."[7]

Naturally, school is a common topic for teenage books, since this is what young people are involved in on a daily basis. Compassionate teachers include Ann Treer in Robin Brancato's *Winning*, Nigeria Greene and Bernard Cohen in Alice Childress' *A Hero Ain't Nothin' But a Sandwich*, Miss Stevenson and Miss Widmer in Nancy Garden's *Annie on My Mind*, P. J. Cooper in William Hogan's *The Quartzsite Trip*, and the school nurse in Phyllis Reynolds Naylor's *The Keeper*, but these are the exceptions. Society forces young people to treat authority figures—teachers, librarians, ministers, housemothers, coaches, parole officers, and so on—with respect. Because young people aren't allowed to discuss differences of opinion or "quarrel" with these adults as they might with their parents, hostilities undoubtedly build up. It's therefore fairly common for authors to tap into this reservoir of resentment to bring smiles to young readers, as when in Paul Zindel's *Confessions of a Teenage Baboon*, fatherless Chris relates his conversation with a solicitous police officer:

> "What you need is the PAL or a Big Brother," he advised, squeezing my shoulder. "If you were my kid you'd be playing football." "If I were your kid I'd be playing horse," I said. "Horse?" he said, looking a little puzzled as he opened the patrol-car door. "You know," I clarified. "I'd be the front end—and you could just be yourself."

Although this kind of humor is both unfair and irritating to adults, it serves as a respite and a refreshing change of pace that is necessary to keep some problem novels from becoming too depressing.

The problem of group identification is a part of all of S. E. Hinton's books, especially *The Outsiders*, where the *greasers* (i.e., *the dirt heads*) are in conflict with the *socs* (i.e., *the society kids*). Myron Levoy's *A Shadow Like a Leopard* is a grim, but at the same time upbeat, story of fourteen-year-old Ramon Santiago, who makes friends with an old man who is a painter. Ramon is a Puerto Rican living in the slums of New York, and in one scene, when people stare at him as he walks through a hotel lobby, he feels ashamed "of his clothing, of his face, of his very bones. Ashamed to be Puerto Rican." In Glendon Swarthout's *Bless the Beasts and Children*, the outsiders are five leftover boys at a summer camp in Arizona. They are known as "the bedwetters," and end up aligning with a herd of mistreated buffaloes.

It's a mark of maturity in the field of young adult literature that no longer are just the big group distinctions being made. In *Tiger Eyes*, Judy Blume includes many subtle observations, which lead readers to see and judge inductively various status symbols in the high-tech, scientific community of Los Alamos (e.g., Bathtub Row, gunracks in pickup trucks, and tell-tale comments about Native Americans and Chicanos). In *Remembering the Good Times*, Richard Peck's narrator has fun describing the various groups in his new school:

> There were suburbanites still maintaining their position and their Izod-and-L.L. Bean image. . . . a few authentic Slos, the polyester people. . . . punk. . . . funk. . . . New Wave. . . . Spaces. . . . people at the top of the line looked a lot like the Pine Hill Slos down at the bottom who'd been having to wear this type gear all along except with different labels.

In *The Friends*, Rosa Guy does a masterful job of leading her readers to see how Phyllisia is taught that she's too good for the neighborhood. Her family has immigrated to Harlem from the West Indies, and her overly strict, restaurant-owner father constantly instills in her a feeling of superiority. He is horrified when Phyllisia brings home poor "ragamuffin" Edith, with her ragged coat, holey socks, turned-over shoes, and matted hair. In her more recent *The Music of Summer*, Guy explores relationships among African Americans with varying degrees of assimilation into white society and how this assimilation affects every other aspect of their lives.

Adolescence is commonly thought to end when a young person marries, becomes a parent, or gains financial independence, which usually means having full-time employment. The children of affluent parents can take longer to choose and prepare for their life's work, which gives them alternatives not open to the youngster who must be self-supporting at age sixteen, eighteen, or even twenty. Also, if a middle-class teenager gets into some kind of trouble, chances are that the parents will be able to cushion the blow and provide a second chance, while youngsters without an adult support system may prematurely brand themselves as losers.

A less disturbing aspect of fitting into society is that of gaining financial independence. For young people this is a two-pronged issue. First, they must get enough money to achieve the degree of independence considered appropriate in their peer groups. It may be only enough money to buy soda pop and an occasional ticket to the movies, or with other kids the goal may be to acquire enough money to pay for clothing, entertainment, and transportation, or even to take themselves away from parental control by moving out. Achieving this kind of immediate financial independence usually means having a job, which is a secondary theme in several contemporary books, e.g., Cynthia Rylant's *Soda Jerk* and Robert Lipsyte's *The Summerboy*. The development of a talent may also be a secondary theme in an accomplishment story, as for the artists in Brock Cole's *Celine* and Zibby Oneal's *In Summer Light*. Several of the books in Focus Box 10.2 on page 419 show young people growing through their development of musical talents.

The responsibilities of individuals in relation to social problems around them are explored for young readers in James Lincoln Collier's *When the Stars Begin to Fall*. When fourteen-year-old Harry tries to reveal the local carpet factory's part in polluting a river, he learns that not all adults are as honest or as committed as he expected. Dean Hughes' *Family Pose* treats the problem of homelessness through eleven-year-old Davis's attempt to live on the streets of Seattle. He sneaks into the Hotel Jefferson and falls asleep next to the warm Coke machine, where Paul, the night bellboy, finds him.

In Joan Phipson's *Hit and Run*, a sixteen-year-old Australian boy comes of age through his acceptance of social responsibility. He was driving carelessly and hit a baby carriage. He flees in panic, sure that his wealthy and unethical father will solve the problem for him. But by the end of the book, the boy is ready to begin relying on his own judgment and strength. In books set outside the United States, readers get the added bonus of learning about other cultures (see Focus Box 2.4, "Contemporary Teens in the World Around Us," on p. 86.)

Racial, Ethnic, and Class Relationships

The demographic makeup of the United States is undergoing considerable change with both long- and short-term effects. Some of those changes were outlined by George Keller, director of strategic planning for the University of Pennsylvania, in a workshop at Arizona State University (February 14, 1992). They include:

- Declining birth and death rates. If it were not for immigration, the United States would have a net loss in population growth.
- Rapidly increasing numbers of foreign-born Americans. In 1970, 4.7 percent of Americans were foreign born; in 1990, the figure was 8.6 percent and in 2040 it is predicted to be 14.2 percent.[8]
- Immigrants bringing in different family values, religion, and attitudes toward education. Over 80 percent of today's immigrants are Hispanic or Asian, as compared with the "old days," when most immigrants came from Europe.
- An older population. The United States is becoming one of the oldest populations in the world. By the year 2020, the fastest-growing segment of the population will be the really old—those over age 80.
- Single-parent families. In 1990, 24 percent of all new births occurred outside of marriage.
- Working mothers. In 1990, 66 percent of women with children under age eighteen were working outside the home.
- Higher birth rates among poor women. In 1990, 19 percent of new births were to women in the lowest income range.
- A population that is being divided into extremes. While the size of the middle class shrinks, the number of those in "permanent" poverty and in "permanent" affluence grows. This is especially true for African Americans, where there are now large numbers of well-educated professionals whose lives are in sharp contrast with large numbers of people living under conditions as painful as anything known since the days of slavery.

Although few people have these specific facts at hand, almost everyone realizes that changes are occurring, and to many people these changes are threatening, especially when coupled with bad economic conditions. One of the results has been an increase in incidents of racism on high school and college campuses. Even more frightening is the racism among disaffected young people who have dropped out from society and are expressing their rebellion through acts of aggression against minorities. These disaffected youths shave their heads, decorate their bodies with garish tattoos, and dress in white T-shirts, black work boots, and flight jackets. Their emulation of Nazi beliefs and actions led the editors of *Time* magazine to write:

> . . . more than anything else, the skinheads are a frightening, pathetic reminder that the U.S. has not solved its racial problems—and that it is time the subject once more take a prominent place on the national agenda.[9]

Faced with problems of this magnitude, it seems overly optimistic and even naive to suggest that teenage books can be a help. Even the best of teachers isn't likely to change a skinhead into a library groupie or a kid who would rather sit home and read books. But for the large majority of young readers, teenage books can be one way of focusing needed attention on the matter of racism.

In the 1960s, when civil rights activists inspired authors, publishers, librarians, teachers, and critics to look at the racial makeup of books presented to young readers, the findings were disturbing. Rather than enriching and extending young readers' views of the world and the people around them, many of the books reinforced prejudices and relied heavily on negative stereotypes. This was more apparent in juvenile than in adult books for several reasons. First, books for young people are often illustrated with either drawings or photographs, and when nearly all the people in the illustration are white, it is more difficult for nonwhite readers to identify with the characters and to imagine that the books are about them and their friends. Second, juvenile books tend to be condensed. With less space in which to develop characters, authors are forced to develop background characters as efficiently as possible. One way to be efficient is to use stereotypes that readers already recognize, for example, the stoic Indian, the happy black, the dumb blonde, the insensitive jock, and so forth, down the line through many other demeaning and offensive overgeneralizations. When positive portrayals were made of blacks, Indians, Asians, and other minority group members, the stories were most often historical or set in some faraway place. The characters were written about as "foreigners."

A third contributing factor is that much of what young people read is from the popular culture which is even less likely than school materials to have been created with care and thought given to the presentation of minority members. As Australian writer Ivan Southall said in the 1974 May Hill Arbuthnot Honor Lecture at the University of Washington:

> From our English comics we learned the fundamental truths of life: for instance, people with yellow skins were inscrutable and cunning, people with brown skins were childlike and apt to run amok, people with black skins were savages, but, if tamed, made useful carriers of heavy loads on great expeditions of discovery by Englishmen. It was in order for black people to be pictured without clothes, after all, they didn't know what clothes were and didn't count, somehow.[10]

Today there's a visible cadre of authors writing good books featuring characters from different ethnic groups, for example, Gary Soto's *A Summer Life* (Dell, 1991) about his Hispanic childhood in Los Angeles and Linda Crew's *Children of the River* (Dell, 1989) about a Cambodian refugee trying to fit into an Oregon high school.

A difference between the YA book world of today and that of the 1960s is that today there is a visible cadre of stars writing consistently fine books featuring characters from different ethnic groups. Not all the books are problem novels (thank goodness), but nearly all of them help to break down the old, negative stereotypes. Black authors of star status include Alice Childress, Rosa Guy, Virginia Hamilton, James Haskins, Walter Dean Myers, Mildred Taylor, and Brenda Wilkinson. Nicholasa Mohr and Myron Levoy write about Puerto Ricans living in the States; Danny Santiago, T. Ernesto Bethancourt, and Gary Soto write about Hispanics; Jamake Highwater writes about American Indians; and Laurence Yep describes Chinese Americans. Although their books are not directly about ethnic differences, Judy Blume's, Norma Klein's, M. E. Kerr's, and Robert Lipsyte's books often include details that increase readers' awareness of what it means to be Jewish.

In this section, we are not including descriptions of all the books that we think do a good job of exploring racial and ethnic differences. Instead such books are scattered throughout all the other chapters, but because we were so frequently asked to provide lists of books about members of minority groups, we have created Focus Boxes on American Indians (p. 66), Asian Americans (p. 28), African Americans (p. 26), and Hispanics (p. 64). These should be viewed as samplings rather than as comprehensive lists.

NICHOLASA MOHR
on The American Child

Who is the American child? The American experience is not a monolithic structure. American children, and especially those children who fill our public schools in urban America, are not typically white . . . or middle class. This was true when my first book, *Nilda,* was published as young adult literature back in 1973. There were few or no books representing an accurate and engaging account of the lives of Hispanic-American children and their families.

Sadly, the same is true in the 1990s. Not much has changed in the mainstream publishing community of Children and Young Adult literature.

Finding picture books, middle-grade, and young adult books that accurately represent our multicultural population is difficult, if not almost impossible. The few serious and very good African-American writers who continue to produce important and valuable books are not widely distributed. Asian, Native American, or Hispanic writers seem to be nonexistent in the mainstream publishing community.

In spite of this reality, I am among the few who continues to write about an American Hispanic experience that is a vital part of the variety that makes up our population. *All* our children have a right to see and read about themselves. They have a right to enjoy learning about the dynamic differences inherent in this vast nation of ours . . . to understand, respect, and enjoy the diversity of their neighbors. And those more accepted white, middle-class children should not have to grow up suspicious, fearful, and rejecting anyone different from themselves.

How can our children know who they are and seek their rightful place in society if they have no role models and remain invisible? As this generation of Hispanic children as well as other children of color grow up and become adults, their visibility, I believe . . . will be critical to the future of these United States. It is only when these youngsters finally begin to see themselves in books in the many positive ways that they and their families participate in this nation's development and growth that we can expect to see them become an integral part in the successful shaping of this country's destiny.

We have both philosophical and pedagogical reasons for not wanting to lump together all the books about minorities. Although some of them focus on interracial relationships or problems connected with being a minority, others focus on the same kinds of problems that are treated in nonminority books. In addition, there's a welcome trend for "differentness" not to be treated as just a matter of skin color. Good authors explore the issue of differentness in a variety of ways and with a variety of groups. For example, Kevin Major's *Far from Shore* is set in Newfoundland; one Canadian reviewer praised it because

His picture of life in Newfoundland is bright and sharp, not, thank God, that salty picaresque pastich we mainlanders so often get to chuckle indulgently over.[11]

Some authors prefer to focus on the similarities among all people rather than on differences between particular groups. For example, black author Lorenz Graham is quoted in Anne Commire's *Something About the Author* as saying:

My personal problem with publishers has been the difference between my image and theirs. Publishers have told me that my characters, African and Negro, are "too much like white people." And I say, "If you look closely you will see that people are people."[12]

Jamake Highwater expresses a counterbalancing view:

In the process of trying to unify the world we must be exceedingly careful not to destroy the diversity of the many cultures of man that give human life meaning, focus, and vitality. . . .

Today we are beginning to look into the ideas of groups outside the dominant culture, and we are finding different kinds of "truth" that make the world we live in far bigger than we ever dreamed it could be—for the greatest distance between people is not geographical space but culture.[13]

Something that probably wouldn't have been in a YA book twenty-five years ago is the following line from Barbara Ann Porte's *I Only Made Up the Roses:* "Like everybody else in the room of relatives, except mother and me, Perley is black. . . . " This line is indicative of one of the biggest changes that has occurred in YA books treating ethnic minorities. Most of the early books were clearly segregated. Characters came from a single race. And when authors chose to write about characters from outside their own groups, they were met with hostility. Fortunately, that kind of parochialism has disappeared and the result has been more books that include characters from different groups interacting with each other in a variety of ways.

By having characters from different groups involved in the same activities, authors can show a wide spectrum of actions and attitudes. Early in his career, Walter Dean Myers was one of the few black writers who wrote upbeat, positive stories about "good, lovable kids." His *Fast Sam, Cool Clyde, and Stuff; It Ain't All for Nothin'; The Young Landlords;* and *Motown and Didi* are among the warmest and most enjoyable of those stories about black kids living in inner cities. But just as white authors are getting braver about extending their stories to include blacks, so is Myers becoming more courageous about including whites. His *Crystal* is the story of a black model whose biggest worry is not what color she is but what kinds of pictures she should pose for. His *Fallen Angels* is about an integrated groups of soldiers in Vietnam whose biggest challenge is pulling together for their mutual survival.

In a similar way, Laurence Yep has written several realistic books about young Chinese Americans, but he also writes fantasy and suspense stories. His *Liar, Liar* is a teenage mystery featuring Marsh Weiss and Sean Pierce, two Caucasian boys. In *A White Romance*, Virginia Hamilton writes about Talley's experience when his all-black high school is integrated and he becomes friends with Didi, a white girl, who, like him, is a runner. Hamilton reverses the stereotyping, because Talley gets involved with drugs through Didi. Cynthia Voigt has taken black characters with minor roles in her books about the Till-ermans (*Homecoming, Dicey's Song,* and *Sons from Afar*) and given them major roles in *Come a Stranger* and *The Runner*.

Bruce Brooks' *The Moves Make the Man* is basically a quest story of accomplishment, and it almost doesn't matter that with the two best friends, one is black and the other is white. But when white Bix comes to dinner at black Jerome's house, big brother and future psychologist Maurice is disappointed that they are going to have a white guest because he had hoped for some "in-house observation." The rest of Jerome's family laughs at Maurice's disappointment and his pretentious pronouncement that, "Counseling across the color line is notoriously fruitless, due to preconditions of mistrust." But when Bix arrives, Jerome is surprised to see that his old friend has equally strange expectations. When he is introduced to younger brother Henri, Bix gives Henri an awkward high-five and says, "Dig it."

> Now, dig it is a very stupid thing to say when being introduced. Henri did not notice, but I did, and I thought it was queer. But when Maurice was there and I introduced him and he peered at Bix like to see if there was any chance of busting the color line with a little counseling anyway, and Bix grinned right into his stare and held out his hand and said, What be happening, Maurice my man?
>
> Maurice, who does not know jive talk from bird song, just looked confused and said Fine thank you and shook hands, but I was nearabout flipped. What be happening, Maurice my man? Where did Bix get this jive talking junk? It was ridiculous.

This light-hearted counterbalancing of stereotypes is possible because today's young readers are more sophisticated about ethnic and racial differences. A generation ago, many white, middle-class readers had been so isolated from other racial groups that learning the generalities—what some would call the stereotypes—was a kind of progress. Today most teenagers are ready to go beyond those stereotypes. For example, in Chris Crutcher's *The Crazy Horse Electric Game*, white Willie is rescued by Lacey Casteel, a black bus driver in

Oakland, California, who also happens to be a pimp. Readers, along with Willie, get to know Lacey as much more than a stereotype.

In her novels about white, middle-class kids, M. E. Kerr often includes shrewd observations about prejudice. For example, in *If I Love You, Am I Trapped Forever?* Alan's grandfather teaches him not to call anyone a Jew. Instead he is to describe people as being "of the Jewish persuasion." Once a year in Cayuta, Rabbi Goldman gives the Sunday sermon at the Second Presbyterian Church while Reverend Gosnell speaks to the Saturday congregation at Temple Emmanuel. Still Jews do not belong to the Cayuta North Country Club and "No one's exactly pushing for intermarriage. . . ."

In *Little Little,* black Calpurnia Dove and white Little Little are in the same English class, where they compete as writers. When Miss Grossman reads aloud one of Calpurnia's essays, Little Little thinks that the teacher is only being nice to Calpurnia because she's black. In her heart, Little Little recognizes the ridiculousness of her assumption and conjectures that Calpurnia probably "decides Miss Grossman is only being nice to me because I'm a dwarf." Little Little goes on to explain that most of the black teenagers in town go to Commercial High to learn business skills or trades. Of the few who do go to her high school, "one is always elected to some office, unanimously. But that high honor rarely gets one of them a seat saved at noon in the cafeteria among the whites, or even a particularly warm hello."

One of the advantages of authors including racism as a secondary, as opposed to a primary theme, is that more readers will meet the issue and be led to think about it. Both adults and young readers tend to color-code books, thinking that books about blacks or Hispanics, for example, are only for black or Hispanic readers, respectively. Walter Dean Myers has pointed out the ridiculousness of such a notion by asking why those librarians in white, middle-class neighborhoods who refuse to buy books about minority characters keep purchasing Dickens' novels even though they have no nineteenth-century English children in their schools.

Another damaging tendency is for teachers, librarians, and reviewers to present books and discuss them as if they represent *the* black point of view or *the* Asian-American point of view. Adults need to help young readers realize that people are individuals first and members of particular groups second. In John Patrick's play *The Teahouse of the August Moon* one of the lines that gets a big laugh from the white middle-class American audiences is about all Americans looking alike. The audience laughs because the tables are turned on an old joke, and a glimpse is provided of how ridiculous it is to think of any group of individuals as carbon copies of one another.

Perhaps for the sake of efficiency, history and social studies textbooks have to lump people together and talk about them according to the characteristics of the majority in the group, but good literature can counterbalance these generalizations and show individual perspectives. When students have read enough to go beyond the stereotypes of at least one group, they will be more aware that the study of people as groups needs to be filled in with individual portrayals.

Body and Self

Books that treat problems related to accepting and effectively using one's physical body are treated in several sections of this text and in Focus Boxes 3.3 and 3.4. When the physical problem is relatively minor, or is at least one that can be corrected, it might be treated as an accomplishment-romance. Also, many nonfiction books as well as sports stories focus on the physical body, and in many realistic novels physical problems serve as a concrete or visible symbol for mental growth, which is harder to show.

It is almost obligatory in realistic fiction for young protagonists to express dissatisfaction with their appearance. Part of this is because hardly anyone has a perfect body or hasn't envied others for their appearance or physical skill. A bigger part is that adolescent bodies are changing so fast that their owners have not yet had time to adjust. The reason they spend so much time looking in mirrors is to reassure themselves, "Yes, this is me!"

In 1970, Judy Blume surprised the world of juvenile fiction by writing a book that gave major attention to physical aspects of growing up. In *Are You There, God? It's Me, Margaret,* Margaret Simon worries because her breasts are small and because she's afraid she will be the last one in her crowd to begin menstruating. A later Blume book, *Then Again, Maybe I Won't,* features Tony Miglione and his newly affluent family. He too worries about his developing body. In fact, he carries a jacket even on the warmest days so that he will have something to hide behind in case he has an erection. These books are read mostly by younger adolescents. But both junior and senior high students read Blume's *Deenie.* It is about a pretty teenager whose mother wants her to be a model, but then it's discovered that she has scoliosis and must wear an unsightly back brace. A minor point that goes unnoticed by some readers (but not by censors) is Deenie's worry that her back problems might be related to the fact that she masturbates. Because Blume ties physical development in with emotional and social development, her books are more fun to read (and more controversial) than are factual books about the development of the human body.

The problem novel does not stop with treating the more or less typical problems of growing up. Authors explore the effects of parents' mental illness on their children as in A. E. Cannon's *Amazing Gracie,* Jocelyn Riley's *Crazy Quilt,* and Phyllis Naylor's *The Keeper.* They also explore mental illness in teenagers as in Hannah Green's well-known *I Never Promised You a Rose Garden* and Rebecca Stowe's 1992 *Not the End of the World.* On the first page of Stowe's extraordinary and powerful coming-of-age story, Maggie's grandmother jovially explains to her tittering bridge friends that Maggie's crazy. All the way through, readers—along with Maggie—wonder about the truth of the "joke."

Problems of addiction are looked at in Gloria D. Miklowitz's *Anything to Win* (steroids), Hadley Irwin's *Can't Hear You Listening* (drugs), Amy Ehrlichs's *The Dark Card* (gambling), Alden Carter's *Up Country* (parental alcoholism), and Robert Cormier's *We All Fall Down* (teenage alcoholism). See

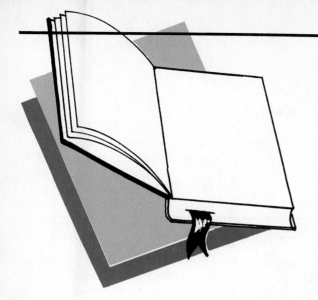

Dying Is Easy—Surviving Is Hard

A Begonia for Miss Applebaum by Paul Zindel. HarperCollins, 1989. Henry and Zelda are permanently changed when their favorite teacher develops terminal cancer.

A Blues I Can Whistle by A. E. Johnson. Four Winds, 1969. After Cody's suicide attempt fails, he tries to explain to doctors why he did it. More than twenty years old and still worth reading.

Bridge to Terabithia by Katherine Paterson. HarperCollins, 1977. Two children create a perfect world. One dies, and the other tries to live.

Close Enough to Touch by Richard Peck. Delacorte, 1981. Long after the funeral, Matt tries desperately to get over the death of his first love.

A Day No Pigs Would Die by Robert Newton Peck. Knopf, 1972. Death is always near in the Depression (children die early, his father is a hog killer, starvation happens), but Rob and his family also find joy and love together.

The Language of Goldfish by Zibby Oneal. Viking, 1980. Carrie struggles to sort out the feelings that she hid away when her mother died.

My Brother Stealing Second by Jim Naughton. HarperCollins, 1989. Billy kills himself and a couple celebrating their wedding anniversary while he's drunk and driving. His parents and brother and the daughter of the couple suffer and survive somehow.

Ordinary People by Judith Guest. Viking, 1976. The popularity of this story of Conrad Jarrett's inability to adjust to his older brother's accidental death has been helped by the fact that the 1980 movie was so well done that it won four Academy Awards.

Saint Maybe by Anne Tyler. Knopf, 1991. In Tyler's typically appealing style, she tells a powerful story of what happens to a family after a brother's suicide.

Say Goodnight, Gracie by Julie Reece Deaver. HarperCollins, 1988. When Jimmy is killed by a drunk driver, Morgan realizes how much he meant to her, then and now.

Sex Education by Jenny Davis. Orchard, 1988. Following the accidental death of her boyfriend, Livvie mostly sleeps for seven months in the University Psychiatric Institute, but she's at last ready to tell her story as part of recovering.

Sheila's Dying by Alden R. Carter. Putnam, 1987. Just as Jerry and Sheila are about to break up, Sheila learns she's dying and Jerry cannot leave her.

Tiger Eyes   by Judy Blume. Bradbury, 1981. After her father is killed in a senseless robbery, Davey and her mother and her little brother try to exist before they can learn to survive.

Tunnel Vision   by Fran Arrick. Bradbury, 1980. Anthony hangs himself and leaves a distraught family and friends trying vainly to puzzle out why a bright and popular young person would take his own life.

Wild in the World   by John Donovan. HarperCollins, 1971. Of a family of eleven brothers and sisters who die of capricious deaths, John alone survives on a lonely mountain.

You Take the High Road   by Mary K. Pershall. Dial, 1990. When Sammy (age fourteen) learns her mother is pregnant, that's tough to take, but not nearly as tough as her baby brother's sudden death.

Focus Box 3.4 for books treating disabilities and Focus Box 3.3 for books on death. The openness with which such a subject as death is discussed is shown in Gunnel Beckman's *Admission to the Feast*. In it, nineteen-year-old Annika Hallin accidentally learns from a substitute doctor that she has leukemia. She flees by herself to her family's summer cottage, where she tries to sort out her reactions:

> I don't think I understood it until last night . . . that I, Anika, . . . will just be put away, wiped out, obliterated. . . . And here on earth everything will just go on. . . . I shall never have more than this little scrap of life.

Although Katherine Paterson's *Bridge to Terabithia* is considered a children's book because it's about two fifth-graders, we know several young adults who have read it and wept, as have many adults. Jean Ferris' *Invincible Summer* is a restrained but sad love story about two teenagers with leukemia. The boy, Rick, dies, but the book ends with readers and the girl, Robin, still uncertain about her prognosis and her future. Of course, she wants to live, but she consoles herself by thinking that if the treatments are unsuccessful, as Rick's were, if it were truly going to be "lights out, the end, eternal sleep, then what was there to worry about?" On the other hand, if she were going to be someplace, then Rick would be there too.

The value of such fictional treatments as the ones cited in this section is that they involve readers in the problem from many different viewpoints, and they show relationships between physical and emotional problems. For example, one of the strong points of Robin Brancato's *Winning,* the story of a football player paralyzed in a game, is that it shows the ripple effect of Gary's accident: how it changes his friends, his parents, his girlfriend, and his teacher. In one brief moment their definition of winning is forever changed. In the new situation, surviving—just wanting to survive—means winning, and readers cheer with Gary when he makes it through the depression that causes some of his hospital mates to commit suicide.

Characters with Disabilities

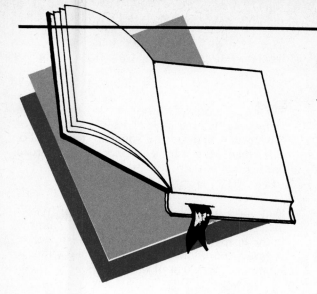

The Alfred Summer by Jan Slepian. Macmillan, 1980. Once readers get to know Alfred, they will think differently about people with cerebral palsy.

All Together Now by Sue Ellen Bridgers. Knopf, 1979. When Casey Flanagan goes to spend the summer with her grandparents, she makes friends with thirty-three-year-old Dwayne Pickens, who is retarded. Dwayne is just one of several fascinating characters in this big family story.

Commander Coatrack Returns by Joseph McNair. Houghton Mifflin, 1989. Lisa takes over the care of her baby brother, who has something a little wrong with him, and when her parents decide it's really their job, she goes on to develop another relationship with a boy at school who also has something a "little wrong."

The Crazy Horse Electric Game by Chris Crutcher. Greenwillow, 1987. Willie Weaver is on his way to becoming a star athlete when a boating accident leaves him with severe physical problems.

Deenie by Judy Blume. Bradbury, 1973. Deenie's mother wants her beautiful daughter to be a model, but then Deenie is diagnosed as having scoliosis and must wear an unsightly brace.

Halsey's Pride by Lynn Hall. Scribner's, 1990. March Halsey is thirteen and epileptic. When she moves to a new school to live with her father, she wants desperately to keep her condition secret.

Little Little by M. E. Kerr. HarperCollins, 1981. Little Little is a PF (Perfectly Formed) dwarf whose mother wants her to marry another PF, Lionel Knox. Little Little prefers Sidney Applebaum, whose back is more crooked but whose morals are more straight than those of Lionel (also known as Opportunity) Knox.

Lizard by Dennis Covington. Delacorte, 1991. Lizard is a deformed boy who escapes into a world of acting and dreams when he runs away with a man who claims to be his father.

M.E. and Morton by Sylvia Cassedy. Crowell, 1987. The lives of a lonely child and her older retarded brother are enriched by a bossy newcomer to the neighborhood.

Of Such Small Differences   by Joanne Greenberg. Holt, 1988. Twenty-five-year-old John is deaf and blind, but that doesn't stop him from loving sighted and hearing Leda, a moderately successful actress and second-generation flower child.

Probably Nick Swanson   by Virginia Euwer Wolff. Macmillan, 1988. Nick has "minimal brain damage" and at school is doomed to being in Room 19, home of the "droolers" and other misfits. Shana is on her way back to regular classes when she accepts Nick's invitation for a star-crossed date to the junior prom.

Risk n' Roses   by Jan Slepian. Philomel, 1990. Having just moved to the Bronx, Skip is anxious to join the "in" group on her street, but she sees her retarded sister as a drawback to being accepted.

Sweet Whispers, Brother Rush   by Virginia Hamilton. Philomel, 1982. An important part of this story, which contains some mysteriously occult strands, is a sister's devotion to her retarded brother.

Winning   by Robin Brancato. Knopf, 1977. When football star Gary Madden finds himself in the hospital, he relies on his English teacher to bring him information that will allow him to figure out the extent of his injuries.

Sexual Relationships

Here we will give some examples of different kinds of sexual relationships treated in problem novels, but lest we leave the impression that we look at sex only as a problem, we hasten to add that discussions of the matter also appear in Chapter Four ("The Love Romances") and in Chapter Eight ("Informational Books").

In trying to satisfy their curiosity, teenagers seek out and read the vivid descriptions of sexual activity in such books as Scott Spencer's *Endless Love* and William Hogan's *The Quartzsite Trip*, both published for adults but featuring young protagonists. Male and female readers have also been intrigued by Don Bredes' *Hard Feelings*, Terry Davis' *Vision Quest*, Jay Daly's *Walls*, and Aidan Chambers' *Breaktime*, all coming-of-age stories that focus on young men's sexual desires. Books that are intended primarily for young female audiences are more likely to focus on romantic elements of a story while only hinting at the characters' sexuality.

In our first edition of this textbook, we wrote that the three sexual issues treated in YA problem novels were rape, homosexuality, and premarital sex resulting in pregnancy. Today we need to add disease, incest, and child abuse. Among the best of several books exploring this latter theme is Hadley Irwin's *Abby, My Love*. The story is told from the viewpoint of college student Chip, who at age thirteen fell in love with Abby. She was only twelve, but in Chip's words she "sounded so much older, like she was an adult and I was the kid. She wasn't condescending or anything. She was just different." Over their high school years, they develop a close friendship, but her overprotective dentist father won't allow normal dating. Chip is frequently puzzled by Abby's behavior, and then one day she confides in him about her father's sexual abuse. Through the help of Chip's mother, steps are taken to help Abby's family face up to the problem and begin a healing process.

Reviewers used such terms as "admirable restraint and sensitivity," "tender, moving love story," "humor, wit, courage and compassion," "well drawn, plausible, and likable characters," and "a credible, optimistic resolution." The only hint of a negative comment came in a *Booklist* review, where the writer questioned Chips long-term obsession with the changeable Abby.[14] The author most likely used the wish-fulfilling romantic element to soften the awfulness of the problem.

Katherine Martin's *Night Riding* is a powerful story set in rural Tennessee during the 1950s. Prin's family struggles through a difficult summer when her mother is pregnant and her father is hospitalized with tuberculosis. But her family's troubles are small compared to those of the family next door in which the father sexually abuses the daughter.

Michael Borich's *A Different Kind of Love* is about a fourteen-year-old girl's ambivalence about her affection for the twenty-five-year-old rock star uncle who has come to live with her and her mother. Fran Arrick's *Steffie Can't Come Out to Play* is a sympathetic portrayal of a teenage prostitute, and Richard Peck's *Are You in the House Alone?* and Patricia Dizenso's *Why Me?* treat the physical, emotional, and societal aspects of rape.

One of the early criticisms of the new realism was that the whole area of sexuality was treated so negatively. For example, in 1975, when W. Keith Kraus analyzed several books about premarital pregnancy—including Ann Head's *Mr. and Mrs. Bo Jo Jones*, Zoa Sherburnes's *Too Bad About the Haines Girl*, Jean Thompson's *House of Tomorrow*, Margaret Maze Craig's *It Could Happen to Anyone*, Nora Stirling's *You Would if You Loved Me*, Jeannette Eyerly's *A Girl Like Me*, Paul Zindel's *My Darling, My Hamburger*, and John Neufield's *For All the Wrong Reasons*—he concluded that the "old double standard is reinforced by the so-called new realism." He compared the stories to the old romances in which the girl is at the beginning an outsider who is discovered by a popular athlete. As she begins to date, a whole new social world opens up to her. But the dating leads to petting, and then to sex, and finally pregnancy and unhappiness. He lamented that the "sexual act itself is never depicted as joyful, and any show of intimacy carries a warning of future danger."[15] Many of the authors whose books will be treated in the next chapter under "The Love Romance" purposely set out to counterbalance the negative images that Kraus and other critics noted.

In the problem novel, the emphasis is usually on the physical aspect of the problem, but it's really the emotional aspects that interest most readers. When Paul Zindel was speaking in Arizona in the late 1970s, he commented on the fact that next to *The Pigman*, his most popular book was *My Darling, My Hamburger*, which is about pregnancy and abortion. Soon after the book was published in 1969, a Supreme Court decision made most abortions legal, and

Zindel thought that would be the end of all sales because his book would seem terribly old-fashioned. However, it didn't turn out this way, because rather than settling the issue, the legalization of abortions increased interest in the moral and psychological aspects of the problem. Decision making was passed from the courts to every female with an unwanted pregnancy. And it isn't just the woman herself who is involved; it's the father, the grandparents, and the friends.

Even in books where the main focus is not on whether someone is going to have an abortion, it may be mentioned as a possibility. For example, in Judy Blume's *Forever*, one of Katherine's friends has an abortion. In *Love Is One of the Choices*, Norma Klein told the story of two close friends and their first sexual loves. One of them chooses to marry and become pregnant right away, but the other gets pregnant, refuses to marry, and has an abortion.

Three landmark books opened the door to the treatment of homosexuality in books for young readers. They were John Donovan's *I'll Get There. It Better Be Worth the Trip* in 1969, Isabelle Holland's *The Man Without a Face*, and Lynn Hall's *Sticks and Stones,* both in 1972. The protagonists are male and in all three books an important character dies. In none can a direct cause-and-effect relationship be charted between the death and the homosexual behavior, but possibilities for blame are there. And because the three books were all published within a relatively short period, critics were quick to object to the cumulative implications that homosexual behavior will be punished with some dreadful event. In spite of this criticism, Sandra Scoppettone's *Trying Hard to Hear You*, published in 1974, was surprisingly similar, ending in an automobile accident that killed one of the teenage male lovers.

Books featuring female homosexuals were almost a decade behind the ones about males. In 1976, Rosa Guy published *Ruby*, which was a sequel to *The Friends*. Ruby is Phyllisia's older sister, and in the book she had a lesbian relationship with a beautiful classmate. *Publishers Weekly* described the homosexuality in the book as "perhaps just a way-step toward maturity." This relaxed attitude toward female homosexuality was reflected in Deborah Hautzig's 1978 *Hey Dollface* and in Nancy Garden's 1982 *Annie on My Mind*, which was praised for its strong characterization and tender love story.

Both *Publishers Weekly* and *School Library Journal* gave the equivalent of starred reviews to A. M. Homes' 1989 *Jack*. Fifteen-year-old Jack is devastated when after his parents' divorce he learns that his father is gay. But in the course of the book, his shame and bewilderment are gradually replaced by understanding and acceptance, not only of his father but also of the fact that people's lives come with problems and that it does no good to try to hide from them.

Since it isn't the shocking topic that it used to be, sexual preference now appears in some books as a secondary rather than as a primary theme, as in Myron Levoy's *Three Friends*, when Lori's bisexuality is acknowledged, and in Hila Colman's *Happily Ever After*, when Melanie and Paul's friendship survives his confession that he is gay. M. E. Kerr's well-written *Night Kites* starts out as a romance between seventeen-year-old Erick and a Madonna look-alike. But what readers remember from the book is Erick's relationship with

FRANCESCA LIA BLOCK
on Facing the Darkness

There is so much sorrow surrounding us today, and I believe that the first step toward healing is confrontation. I hope that my work can both help readers confront pain and offer the possibility of solace through love and art.

Weetzie Bat has been considered controversial by some people, but when I wrote it, I wanted to present the most truthful expression of what I have seen, which includes bitterness and sweetness, disillusion, and magic. *Weetzie* is about creating your own family in a world of broken bonds and loss. *Witch Baby* deals with a girl who is constantly revealing and expressing everyone's sadness. It is because of this that she is eventually able to overcome her isolation and bring others together. And in *Cherokee Bat and the Goat Guys* the characters spiral toward a destructive sexual awakening until they learn to understand and honor the power of nature.

The book I am currently working on is a post-apocalyptic love story in which a boy and girl, separated by disaster, overcome amnesia and illness to be reunited. Although this may cause some controversy as well, I feel it is more positive to read about love that survives destruction than about the numbness of denial. I've written about incest and the death of loved ones, but also about angels, genies, enchanted animals, and magical cures.

Luckily, I have had the support of my parents and of my editor, Joanna Cotler at HarperCollins, who have always encouraged my work, no matter how controversial or offbeat. Charlotte Zolotow, who recently retired from HarperCollins, also made me feel free to explore issues that had real relevance for me. These open-minded attitudes have made it possible for me to grow as a writer and a person.

Although my work is often a dark journey, especially by the standards of much Young Adult fiction, I believe that it is also a primarily life-affirming one in which the spirit triumphs through the use of the imagination, self-expression, and bonding with others. We have all been exposed to hell as reality through images of war and suffering. We can't ignore these things, but we can address them and create new, more peaceful, healing worlds in our art and in our lives.

Francesca Lia Block's books include *Weetzie Bat*, 1989; *Witch Baby*, 1991; and *Cherokee Bat and the Goat Guys*, 1992, all HarperCollins.

---

his older brother, Pete, who midway through the story is diagnosed as having AIDS. The family has to absorb simultaneously the news of his impending death and the fact that for years this favored son has been hiding his gay lifestyle from them.

In actuality, the big sex-related problems—rape, abuse, disease, homosexuality, and unwanted pregnancy—are experienced by few teenagers, but nearly all young people wonder abut the moral and social implications of experimenting with sexual activity, whether or not it leads to intercourse. Todd Strasser's *A Very Touchy Subject* and Norma Fox Mazer's *Up in Seth's Room* do a good job of showing the magnitude of teenagers' concerns. As Jean Fritz said when she reviewed Mazer's book for the *New York Times Book Review:*

> The questions we follow relentlessly from beginning to end are the perennial ones of adolescence: Will she or won't she? And what's it like? . . . Everyone should be pleased with the outcome. Finn sticks to her guns, although the fact that she "doesn't" is hardly more than a technicality. There are enough explicit scenes to give young readers, who don't know, a good idea of "what it's like."[16]

Mazer said she wrote the book as an antidote to all the "realistic" books implying that having sexual relationships is the norm for high school kids. Half of the kids in high school are not sexually intimate,[17] and even the half that are have dozens of unanswered questions and worries.

To get direct answers to their questions, young readers can turn to the informational books discussed in Chapter Eight. But because the questions they are most concerned with involve moral, emotional, and psychological issues, the fuller kinds of fictional treatments described here will continue to be popular.

NOTES

[1]G. Robert Carlsen, "Bait/Rebait: Literature Isn't Supposed to Be Realistic," *English Journal* 70 (January 1981): 8–12.

[2]Bernard Bauer, *San Jose Mercury News,* reprinted in *The Arizona Republic,* August 23, 1991.

[3]Glenna Davis Sloan, *The Child as Critic* (Teachers College Press, 1975), pp. 19–21.

[4]Alleen Pace Nilsen, "The Poetry of Naming in Young Adult Books," *ALAN Review 7* (Spring 1980): 3–4, 31.

[5]Sheila Egoff, "May Hill Arbuthnot Honor Lecture: Beyond the Garden Wall," *Top of the News* 35 (Spring 1979): 257–71.

[6]Joan F. Kaywell, Review of *The Island, ALAN Review* 12 (Spring 1985): 29.

[7]Hazel Rochman, "The YA Connection: Choosing to Stay Home," *Booklist* 83 (February 1, 1987): 837.

[8]"Immigrant Impact Grows on U.S. Population," *Wall Street Journal,* March 16, 1992.

[9]"A Chilling Wave of Racism," *Time* 131 (January 25, 1988): 57.

[10]Ivan Southall, "Real Adventure Belongs to Us," *A Journey of Discovery on Writing for Children* (Macmillan, 1976), p. 69.

[11]Janet Lunn, *Books in Canada* 9 (December 1980): 21.

[12]Anne Commire, *Something about the Author,* Vol. 2 (Gale Research, 1971), pp. 122–23.

[13]Jamake Highwater, *Many Smokes, Many Moons* (Lippincott, 1978), pp. 13–14.

[14]Review of *Abby, My Love, Booklist* 81 (March 1, 1985): 944.

[15]W. Keith Kraus, "Cinderella in Trouble: Still Dreaming and Losing," *School Library Journal* 21 (January 1975): 18–22.

[16]Jean Fritz, review of *Up in Seth's Room, New York Times Book Review* (January 20, 1980), p. 30.

[17]The Federal Center for Disease Control conducted a 1990 study released January 3, 1992, and reported in various news media the following day. Findings were that 54 percent of high school students have had sexual experiences, 39 percent within the last three months. The percentage climbed from 40 percent of ninth graders to 72 percent of twelfth graders. One in twenty-five students reported having a sexually transmitted disease, and 78 percent of the students reporting intercourse said they had recently used some form of contraception.

OTHER TITLES MENTIONED IN THE TEXT OF CHAPTER THREE

Angelou, Maya. *I Know Why the Caged Bird Sings.* Random House, 1976.

Anonymous. *Go Ask Alice.* Prentice-Hall, 1971.

Armstrong, William. *Sounder.* HarperCollins, 1969.

Arrick, Fran. *Steffie Can't Come Out to Play.* Bradbury, 1978.

Asher, Sandy. *Everything Is Not Enough.* Delacorte, 1987.

Beckman, Gunnel. *Admission to the Feast.* Holt, 1972.

Blume, Judy. *Are You There God? It's Me, Margaret.* Bradbury, 1970.

———. *Deenie.* Bradbury, 1973.

———. *Forever.* Bradbury, 1975.

_____. *Then Again, Maybe I Won't.* Bradbury, 1971.

_____. *Tiger Eyes.* Bradbury, 1981.

Borich, Michael. *A Different Kind of Love.* Holt, 1985.

Bradford, Richard. *Red Sky at Morning.* Lippincott, 1968.

Brancato, Robin. *Uneasy Money.* Knopf, 1986.

_____. *Winning.* Knopf, 1977.

Bredes, Don. *Hard Feelings.* Atheneum, 1977.

Brooks, Bruce. *Midnight Hour Encores.* HarperCollins, 1987.

_____. *The Moves Make the Man.* HarperCollins, 1986.

Byars, Betsy. *The Night Swimmers.* Delacorte, 1980.

_____. *The Two-Thousand-Pound Goldfish.* HarperCollins, 1982.

Cannon, A. E. *Amazing Grace.* Delacorte, 1991.

Carter, Alden. *Up Country.* Putnam, 1989.

Chambers, Aidan. *Breaktime.* HarperCollins, 1979.

Childress, Alice. *A Hero Ain't Nothin' But a Sandwich.* Coward, McCann, 1973.

Cleaver, Eldridge. *Soul on Ice.* McGraw-Hill, 1968.

Cleaver, Vera and Bill. *Trial Valley.* Lippincott, 1977.

_____. *Where the Lilies Bloom.* HarperCollins, 1969.

Cole, Brock. *Celine.* Farrar, Straus & Giroux, 1989.

Collier, James Lincoln. *When the Stars Begin to Fall.* Delacorte, 1986.

Colman, Hila. *Happily Ever After.* Scholastic, 1984.

Cormier, Robert. *The Chocolate War.* Pantheon, 1974.

_____. *I Am the Cheese.* Pantheon, 1977.

_____. *We All Fall Down.* Delacorte, 1991.

Craig, Margaret Maze. *It Could Happen to Anyone.* Berkeley, 1970.

Crutcher, Chris. *The Crazy Horse Electric Game.* Greenwillow, 1987.

Daly, Jay. *Walls.* HarperCollins, 1980.

Davis, Terry. *Vision Quest.* Viking, 1979.

Deaver, Julie Reece. *First Wedding, Once Removed.* HarperCollins, 1988.

Dizenzo, Patricia. *Why Me? The Story of Jenny.* Avon, 1976.

Donovan, John. *I'll Get There. It Better Be Worth the Trip.* HarperCollins, 1969.

Ehrlich, Amy. *The Dark Card.* Viking, 1991.

Eyerly, Jeannette. *A Girl Like Me.* Lippincott, 1966.

Ferris, Jean. *Across the Grain.* Farrar, Straus & Giroux, 1990.

_____. *Invincible Summer.* Farrar, Straus & Giroux, 1987.

Forshay-Lunsford, Lin. *Walk Through Cold Fire.* Dell, 1986.

Fox, Paula. *A Place Apart.* Farrar, Straus & Giroux, 1982.

Frye, Northrop. *Anatomy of Criticism.* Princeton University Press, 1957.

Garden, Nancy. *Annie on My Mind.* Farrar, Straus & Giroux, 1982.

Golding William. *Lord of the Flies.* Putnam, 1955.

Green, Hannah. *I Never Promised You a Rose Garden.* Holt, 1964.

Guy, Rosa. *The Friends.* Holt, 1973.

_____. *The Music of Summer.* Delacorte, 1992.

_____. *Ruby.* Viking, 1976.

Hall, Barbara. *Dixie Storms.* Harcourt Brace Jovanovich, 1990.

Hall, Lynn. *Sticks and Stones.* Follett, 1972.

Hamilton, Virginia, *A White Romance.* Putnam, 1987.

Hautzig, Deborah. *Hey Dollface.* Morrow, 1978.

Head, Ann. *Mr. and Mrs. Bo Jo Jones.* Putnam, 1967.

Hinton, S. E. *The Outsiders.* Viking, 1967.

_____. *Tex.* Delacorte, 1979.

Hogan, William. *The Quartzsite Trip*. Atheneum, 1980.

Holland, Isabelle. *The Island*. Little, Brown, 1984.

———. *The Man Without a Face*. Lippincott, 1972.

Homes, A. M. *Jack*. Macmillan, 1989.

Hughes, Dean. *Family Pose* (published in paperback as *Family Picture*). Atheneum, 1989.

Irwin, Hadley. *Abby, My Love*. Macmillan, 1985.

———. *Can't Hear You Listening*. McElderry Books, 1990.

Kerr, M. E. *If I Love You, Am I Trapped Forever?* HarperCollins, 1973.

———. *Little Little*. HarperCollins, 1981.

———. *Night Kites*. HarperCollins, 1986.

Kincaid, Jamaica. *Annie John*. Farrar, Straus & Giroux, 1985.

Klein, Norma. *Love Is One of the Choices*. Dial, 1979.

Konigsburg, E. L. *Journey to an 800 Number*. Atheneum, 1982.

Levitin, Sonia. *A Season for Unicorns*. Atheneum, 1986.

Levoy, Myron. *A Shadow Like a Leopard*. HarperCollins, 1981.

———. *Three Friends*. HarperCollins, 1984.

Lipsyte, Robert. *The Contender*. HarperCollins, 1967.

———. *The Summer Boy*. HarperCollins, 1982.

Major, Kevin. *Far from Shore*. Delacorte, 1981.

Martin, Katherine. *Night Riding*. Knopf, 1989.

Mathis, Sharon Bell. *Teacup Full of Roses*. Viking, 1975.

Mazer, Harry. *When the Phone Rang*. Scholastic, 1985.

Mazer, Norma Fox. *Downtown*. Morrow, 1984.

———. *Up in Seth's Room*. Delacorte, 1979.

Miklowitz, Gloria D. *Anything to Win*. Delacorte, 1989.

Myers, Walter Dean. *Crystal*. Viking, 1987.

———. *Fallen Angels*. Scholastic, 1988.

———. *Fast Sam, Cool Clyde, and Stuff*. Viking, 1975.

———. *It Ain't All for Nothin'*. Viking, 1978.

———. *Motown and Didi: A Love Story*. Viking, 1984.

———. *The Young Landlords*. Viking, 1979.

Naylor, Phyllis Reynolds. *The Keeper*. Atheneum, 1986.

Neufeld, John. *For All the Wrong Reasons*. NAL Penguin, 1980.

Oneal, Zibby. *In Summer Light*. Viking, 1985.

Paterson, Katherine. *Bridge to Terabithia*. Crowell, 1977.

———. *The Great Gilly Hopkins*. Crowell, 1979.

Patrick, John. *The Teahouse of the August Moon*. Dramatists, 1953.

Peck, Richard. *Are You in the House Alone?* Viking, 1976.

———. *Remembering the Good Times*. Delacorte, 1985.

Phipson, Joan. *Hit and Run*. Macmillan, 1985.

Porte, Barbara Ann. *I Only Made Up the Roses*. Greenwillow, 1987.

Riley, Jocelyn. *Crazy Quilt*. Morrow, 1983.

Rylant, Cynthia. *A Kindness*. Orchard, 1988.

———. *The Soda Jerk*. Orchard, 1990.

Scoppettone, Sandra. *Trying Hard to Hear You*. HarperCollins, 1974.

Sherburne, Zoa. *Too Bad About the Haines Girl*. Morrow, 1967.

Spencer, Scott. *Endless Love*. Knopf, 1979.

Stirling, Nora. *You Would If You Loved Me*. Evans, 1969.

Stowe, Rebecca. *Not the End of the World*. Pantheon, 1992.

Strasser, Todd. *A Very Touchy Subject*. Delacorte, 1985.

Swarthout, Glendon. *Bless the Beasts and Children*. Doubleday, 1970.

Thompson, Jean. *House of Tomorrow*. HarperCollins, 1967.

Thompson, Julian F. *A Band of Angels.* Scholastic, 1986.

Tolan, Stephanie. *A Good Courage.* Morrow, 1988.

Townsend, John Rowe. *Downstream.* Lippincott, 1987.

Voigt, Cynthia. *Come a Stranger.* Atheneum, 1986.

————. *Dicey's Song.* Atheneum, 1982.

————. *Homecoming.* Atheneum, 1981.

————. *The Runner.* Atheneum, 1985.

————. *A Solitary Blue.* Atheneum, 1983.

————. *Sons from Afar.* Atheneum, 1981.

Wyss, Thelma Hatch. *Here at the Scenic-Vu Motel.* HarperCollins, 1988.

Yep, Laurence. *Liar, Liar.* Morrow, 1983.

Zindel, Paul. *Confessions of a Teenage Baboon.* HarperCollins, 1977.

————. *My Darling, My Hamburger.* HarperCollins, 1969.

————. *The Pigman.* HarperCollins, 1968.

For information on the availability of paperback editions of these titles, please consult the most recent edition of *Paperbound Books in Print,* published annually by R. R. Bowker Company.

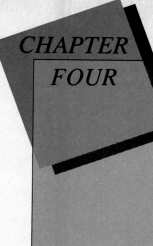

THE OLD
ROMANTICISM
Of Wishing and Winning

Romances serve as a counterbalance to the depressing realism of the problem novel. They have happy endings and their tellers can exaggerate just enough to make the stories more interesting than real life. There is usually a quest of some sort in which the protagonist experiences doubts and undergoes severe trials, but he or she is successful in the end. This success is all the more appreciated because of the difficulties the protagonist has suffered. In bad moments the extremes of suffering resemble a nightmare, but in good times the successes are like happy daydreams.

The word *romance* comes from the Latin adverb *romanice,* which means "in the Roman, [i.e., the Latin] manner." It is with this meaning that Latin, Italian, Spanish, and French are described as romance languages. The literary meaning of *romance* grew out of its use by English speakers to refer to French dialects, which were much closer to Latin than was their own Germanic language of English. Later, it was used to refer to Old French and finally to anything written in French.

Many of the French stories read by English speakers were tales about knights who set out on bold adventures, slaying dragons, rescuing princesses from ogres, and defeating the wicked enemies of a righteous king. Love was often an element in these stories, for the knight was striving to win the hand of a beloved maiden. So, today, when a literary piece is referred to as a romance, it usually contains either adventure or love, or both.

The romance is appealing to teenagers because many romantic symbols relate to youthfulness and hope, and many of the protagonists even in traditional and classic tales are in their teens. They have reached the age at which they leave home or anticipate leaving to embark on a new way of life. This is more likely to be called "moving out" than "going on a romantic quest," but the results are much the same (see Focus Box 4.1). And seeking and securing a "true love" usually—but not always—takes up a greater proportion of the time and energy of the young than of middle-aged adults. The exaggeration that is part of the romantic mode is quite honestly felt by young people. At no other stage of life do people feel their emotions quite so intensely. Robert Cormier once commented that he began writing about young protagonists when he observed that in one afternoon at the beach his own children could go through what to an adult would be a whole month of emotional experiences.

Another teenage characteristic particularly appropriate to the romantic mode is the optimism of youth. Even though many young people may not be more optimistic than their elders, they are presumed to be so. This means that a writer working with basically the same plot in a story for adults might be inclined to present the adult story in an ironic mode but the young adult story in a romantic mode. For example, three popular quest stories about young protagonists that were published as somber adult books are J. D. Salinger's *The Catcher in the Rye*, Hannah Green's *I Never Promised You a Rose Garden,* and Judith Guest's *Ordinary People*. In all three, worthy young heroes set out to find wisdom and understanding. They make physical sacrifices, including suicide attempts, and the wise and kindly psychiatrists serve as today's counterpart to the white witches, the wizards, and the helpful gods and goddesses of traditional romances. The difference is that the realistic helpers of today rely on science instead of magic. But just as in the old days, hard, painstaking work is also required. This is what Deborah Blau's psychiatrist communicates in the phrase used for the book's title, *I Never Promised You a Rose Garden*. If Green's book had been a romance, there would have been no such reminder of life's difficulties. Readers could have imagined Deborah leaving the mental institution and living "happily ever after."

THE ADVENTURE/ACCOMPLISHMENT ROMANCE

The great satisfaction of the adventure or the accomplishment romance lies in its wish fulfillment, as when David slays Goliath, when Cinderella is united with the noble prince and given the fitting role of queen, and when Dorothy and Toto find their way back to Kansas. In every culture there are legends, myths, and folk and fairy tales that follow the pattern of the adventure/accomplishment romance. In the Judeo-Christian culture, the biblical story of Joseph is a prime example. Early in life, Joseph was chosen and marked as a special person. When his brothers sold him as a slave to the Egyptian traders, he embarked on his quest for wisdom and knowledge. Just when all seemed lost, he received divine help—being blessed with the ability to interpret dreams. This got him out of prison and into the pharaoh's court. The climax of the story

Accomplishment Quests

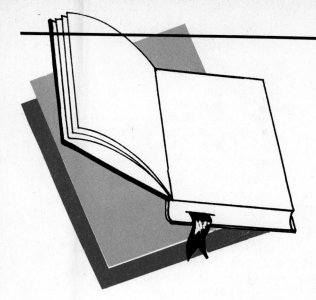

Catalogue of the Universe   by Margaret Mahy. Macmillan, 1986. Angela is disappointed when she contrives to meet her father, a man she's never seen, but her friendship with Tycho helps her move past the disappointment.

The Crazy Horse Electric Game   by Chris Crutcher. Greenwillow, 1987. All those things that aren't supposed to happen to a nice, normal family do, and the misfortunes leave Willie Weaver to work out his own healing.

Dogsong   by Gary Paulsen. Bradbury, 1985. Dreams and real life swirl together like heavy fog and steam rising from the ocean as Russel, an Eskimo boy, journeys alone on a dogsled.

The Goats   by Brock Cole. Farrar, Straus & Giroux, 1987. The other campers strip Laura and Howie of their clothes and leave them on an island, where, to their surprise, they manage to survive both physically and emotionally.

Good-bye and Keep Cool   by Jenny Davis. Orchard 1987. Bidding farewell to childhood and to the Kentucky mining town where she has lived with her mother makes for a poignant coming of age for Edda Combs.

In Country   by Bobbie Ann Mason. Harper-Collins, 1985. A teenage girl's acceptance and partial understanding of her father's death comes through a trip that she takes with her uncle and her grandmother to the Vietnam War Memorial in Washington.

Looking for Home   by Jean Ferris. Farrar, Straus & Giroux, 1989. Daphne does not dare to tell her father that she's pregnant, nor does she want to tell the boy who is the father of her child, and so she moves to the city and gets a job as a waitress, finding herself a substitute family.

One Fat Summer   by Robert Lipsyte. Harper Collins, 1977. Bobby's story shows that a heroic quest doesn't have to take a person far from home. He goes only to the other side of the island, where he works for Dr. Kahn. Sequels include *The Summer Boy* and *Summer Rules*.

Rear-View Mirror   by Paul Fleischman. HarperCollins, 1986. Seventeen-year old Olivia Tate sets out on a commemorative bike trip in remembrance of the father she learned to love only a few months before his death.

Sons from Afar   by Cynthia Voigt. Atheneum, 1987. In this continuation of the story of the Tillermans from *Homecoming* and *Dicey's Song*, brothers James and Sammy go looking for the father they never knew.

The True Confessions of Charlotte Doyle by Avi. Orchard, 1990. The difference between this and most historical sailing adventures is that the heroine is a twelve-year-old girl, who, on her journey from England to America in 1802, turns into a competent sailor and manager of human affairs.

The Voyage of the Frog by Gary Paulsen. Orchard, 1989. David inherits his beloved Uncle Owen's old sailboat named *The Frog*. He takes the boat out to fulfill his uncle's final request and ends up facing not only his grief but nine days of life-threatening troubles.

What I Did for Roman by Pam Conrad. HarperCollins, 1987. In this love and family story, sixteen-year old Darcie frees herself from the unhealthy emotional bonds that tied her to a young zookeeper.

---

came years later, during the famine that brought his brothers to Egypt and the royal palace. Without recognizing Joseph, they begged for food. His forgiveness and his generosity were final proofs of his worthiness.

A distinguishing feature of such romances is the happy ending, achieved only after the hero's worth is proven through a crisis or an ordeal. Usually as part of the ordeal the hero must make a sacrifice, be wounded, or leave some part of his or her body, even if it is only sweat or tears. The real loss is that of innocence, but it is usually symbolized by a physical loss, as in Norse mythology, when Odin gave one of his eyes to pay for knowledge, or in J. R. R. Tolkien's *The Lord of the Rings*, when Frodo, who has already suffered many wounds, found that he could not throw the ring back and so must let Gollum take his finger along with the ring. The suffering of the hero nearly always purchases some kind of wisdom, even though wisdom is not what the hero set out to find.

The adventure/accomplishment romance has elements applicable to the task of entering the adult world, which all young people anticipate. The story pattern includes the three stages of formal initiation as practiced in many cultures. First, the young and innocent person is separated both physically and spiritually from the nurturing love of friends and family. Then, during this separation, the hero, who embodies noble qualities, undergoes a test of courage and stamina that may be either mental, psychological, or physical. In the final stage, the young person is reunited with former friends and family in a new role of increased status.

Izzy, Willy-Nilly *as an Adventure/Accomplishment Romance*

Authors often dramatize mental accomplishments as physical ones because it is extremely hard to show something occurring inside someone's head. The physical challenge serves as a symbol for the mental one. The effect of this has been that adventure romances are more likely to feature males than females, because males' life-styles usually include more physically challenging activities (e.g., athletic competition, war, physical labor, and surviving on one's own). However, authors are consciously trying to write adventure/accomplishment stories about females (e.g. Jean George's *Julie of the Wolves,* Deborah Savage's *A Rumour of Otters,* and Bobbie Ann Mason's *In Country*).

Cynthia Voigt's *Izzy, Willy-Nilly* is a good illustration of how traditional archetypal initiation rites can be translated into a modern and appealing story. It begins as follows:

> "Isobel? I'm afraid we're going to have to take it off."
>
> "Take it off, take it off," I sang, like a vamp song; but I don't think I actually did, and I know my laughter stayed locked inside my head. I think my voice did too.
>
> "Isobel. Can you hear me?" I didn't know. I didn't think so. *It* was my leg. I went to sleep.

Izzy wakes up enough to tell the doctor, "My name's Izzy," and then she falls back to sleep, thinking that by correcting the name he called her, she had also corrected the "disturbing, frightening feeling that something was wrong."

Tenth-grader–cheerleader–nice-girl Izzy has been in a serious automobile accident, and before she is really conscious, her leg is being amputated. Chapter Two is a flashback to before the accident. The author uses this chapter to set the background and to show readers that Izzy Lingard is a special person worthy of the challenge she will face. Izzy is the first of her group to be asked out by a senior, and she is strong enough not to succumb to the boy's teasing her because she has to ask her parents' permission before she accepts.

Since a romance is essentially the story of one person's achievement and development, everything else is a condensation. For the sake of efficiency, the personalities of the supporting characters are shown through symbols, metaphors, and significant details, all of which highlight the qualities that are important to the story. It is not really the villain the hero must ultimately defeat, but the villain stands in the way of the true accomplishment and gives the hero an enemy upon whom to focus. Without some scary, nightmarish, and usually life-threatening incident, the happy ending could not be appreciated.

The boy who asked Izzy for a date is the villain of the story. He is a "notorious flirt," who at the party gets so drunk that although he isn't hurt when he plows his car into a tree, he does nothing to help Izzy. Then he lies to the police about Izzy doing the driving, and instead of apologizing for what happened, he manipulates Izzy's friend, hoping to influence what Izzy will tell the police.

Izzy faces the physical loss of her leg and the challenge of learning to walk with a prosthesis, but the real challenge is the emotional one of acceptance. In the daytime, at least in front of other people, Izzy is cheerful. The first day that she dares to look down at the blanket covering her "leg-and-a-half" she begins her quest for emotional peace. Heroes in traditional romances often had visions or visits from divine beings. Izzie's "vision" comes through her mental image of a tiny little Izzy doll:

■ My brain wasn't working. It was as if the little Izzy was running around and around in circles, some frantic wind-up Izzy, screeching *No, no, no.*
But it was *Yes, yes, yes.*
And I knew it.
I knew it, but I couldn't believe it.

Izzy lays her head on the formica hospital table over her bed, and although she is not asleep, she has a nightmare:

■ I felt as if a huge long slide was slipping up past me, and I was going down it. I couldn't stop myself, and I didn't even want to. . . . Something heavy and wet and cold and gray was making me go down, pushing at the back of my bent neck and at my shoulders. At the bottom, wherever that was, something heavy and wet and cold and gray waited for me. It was softer than the ground when I hit it. I went flying off the end of the slide and fell into the gray. The gray reached up around me and closed itself over me and swallowed me up.

When a nurse comes in, Izzy wishes she would leave because she is afraid she might cry, and, "We didn't cry, not the Lingards. We were brave and made jokes about things hurting. . . ." The nurse is a physical therapist who gives Izzy painful massages to toughen up her skin and muscles so she will be ready for the prosthesis. Izzy is hurt that the woman concentrates on her work and doesn't look at Izzy's face or talk with her. In her depressed mood, Izzy decides that it is because she is no longer a whole person. "I guessed if you'd finished working on the pizza dough, you wouldn't bend over and say goodbye to it. You don't talk to *things*. And that's what I was, a thing, a messed-up body."
The worst times for Izzy are at night, when she wakes up alone and can't keep her "mind from going down that slide thinking of all the things that I managed not to think about during the days." She never knew until then, never even suspected, how it felt to be depressed.

■ I'd been miserable. I'd been blue. But depressed, no, I hadn't been that. I never knew how it felt to sigh out a breath so sad you could almost see tears in it. I never knew the way tears would ooze and ooze out of your eyes. I never knew the way something could hang like a gray cloud over all of your mind and you could never get away from it, never forget it.

Help comes to Izzy, not from her old friends, who are too involved in their own lives and too uncomfortable with her misfortune to stay long, but from the strange misfit Rosamunde—"not at all like Lisa and the rest"—who arrives to decorate Izzy's hospital room and to play Yahtze and bring fruit, good conversation, homemade turnovers, and piroshki.
When Izzy is released from the hospital, she doesn't go back to her old room on the second floor. Instead she is given her parents' bedroom on the first floor,

and it's here in the middle of the nights that Izzy, isolated from her family and in a strange and lonely place, undergoes the suffering that makes her eventual victory that much sweeter. On the outside, Izzy's victory is shown through her return to school and her eventual confrontation of the boy who caused her to lose her leg. But her more important challenge is an internal one. Voigt uses a conversation between Izzy and Rosamunde to help readers understand:

> "I used to really like watching you move around, because you always seemed so comfortable in your own body, and it wasn't anything you thought about, or even noticed; it was just the way you were, that was what was so great about it."
>
> "You're talking in the past tense," I said, carefully keeping my eyes on the ribbon I was tying, thinking how much I'd changed.
>
> "No, that's not true. I mean, I *was*. I mean, it was the past tense, but you still have that way of being—comfortable to be with. Only it used to show, anybody who saw you saw it, just looking at you. Because it wasn't just being comfortable with your body that made you so nice. But I really mind that."
>
> Then I did look at her. "I mind it too," I said.

During a particularly bad time, Izzy sees the little doll in her head "standing there waving her detached leg at a crowd of people, like a safety monitor waving her stop sign." In contrast, the first day that someone at school forgets about Izzy's crutches, the little doll "gathered herself up and did an impossible back-flip, and then another and another." The book ends with Izzy seeing the little doll:

> . . . standing alone, without crutches. . . . Her arms were spread out slightly. She looked like she was about to dance, but really her arms were out for balance. . . . The little Izzy balanced there briefly and then took a hesitant step forward—ready to fall, ready not to fall.

OTHER QUEST STORIES OF ACCOMPLISHMENT

The motif of a worthy young hero embarking on a quest of wisdom appears in many more good books than those mentioned in this chapter, because it fits well in biographies, adventure stories, historical fiction, fantasy, science fiction, and problem novels. Even when the quest is not the main part of a story, motifs that fit the quest romance are incorporated. For example, in traditional romances the protagonist usually receives the vision or insight in a "high or isolated place like a mountain top, an island, or a tower."[1] In Virginia Hamilton's *M. C. Higgins, the Great*, the boy, M. C., comes to his realizations about his family and his role while he contemplates the surrounding countryside from a special

HARRY MAZER
on Surrendering Ourselves

I write novels, yet, inevitably, I find my books listed as useful for various kinds of readers. For instance, my book *The Island Keeper* was described in a single review as useful for "overweight teens, teens with parental or guardian conflicts, teens experiencing the death of a sibling, teens interested in the running away theme, and teens interested in camping or nature."

Somehow this misses by a mile what I had in mind when I wrote this book. I had in mind to write a novel that captured the reader, engaged her, involved her, moved her to tears or laughter or exaltation. Usefulness was low on the list.

I try not to write useful books. There are enough of them in the world. Textbooks, handbooks, manuals, travel guides, stories of great men— and lately great women. I have no argument with them, and they are indeed useful.

But what is the use of fiction, that peculiar long narrative story we call a novel? As a book, a novel can be used to build a wall, hold a door open, balance a rickety table, or throw in anger or defense. Dogs sometimes will accept a book as a substitute for a bone, and cats have been known to dig into a novel. Kids are notorious unless corrected for turning novels into coloring books.

To spend our time in useless pursuits makes adults uneasy. This is how you distinguish the kids from the grown-ups. Grown-ups work, raise families, have activities and hobbies, useful pursuits that justify their existence. Travel is educational, climbing rocks increases your cardiovascular capacity and white water canoeing stretches your psychic limits. But what does lying in a hammock reading a novel do for you? It's too easy, too much fun, too enjoyable. What can be the use of it? It won't put money in your pocket, it won't advance your career or make you a measurably better or healthier or handsomer person.

For what is the use of a story, but in itself? In the telling . . . and in the listening, in the reading and losing oneself in the unexpected. The novel puts us into a world we can't alter, a world more interesting, intense, and moving than the real world. A world where nothing useful is expected of us, where things happen that we need only observe, wonder at, and think about.

When we read a novel, when we surrender ourselves to the story, our guard drops, and we abandon our slit-eyed purposefulness. We don't have to pretend, we don't have to put on masks, we don't have to posture and behave usefully. We are released.

There we have it—the true use of a novel—it gives us back our purest selves.

Harry Mazer's books include *The Girl of His Dreams,* Crowell, 1987; *City Light,* Scholastic, 1988; *Someone's Mother Is Missing,* Delacorte, 1990; and with Norma Fox Mazer, *Heartbeat,* Bantam, 1989.

Accomplishment romances are among the most requested compact disks at the Mesa, Arizona, Public Library.

bicycle seat affixed to the top of a tall steel pole standing in the yard of his mountain home. The pole is unique and intriguing, and M.C. earned it as a reward from his father for swimming across the Ohio River.

Robert Lipsyte's *The Contender* opens with Mr. Donatelli, the manager of a boxing gym, listening to the confident sound of young, black Alfred Brooks climbing the steps to his gym. Mr. Donatelli says he can tell who has what it takes to be a contender (readers are to interpret this as meaning a contender in life as well as in the boxing ring) by how they climb those stairs. A generation later, in another quest story, *The Brave*, this same Alfred Brooks helps Sonny Bear, a seventeen-year-old boxer from the Moscondaga Indian reservation, change the monster he feels inside himself into the dignified Hawk spirit of his people.

A railroad lantern named Spin Light that Jerome wins with his basketball skill is an intriguing symbol in Bruce Brooks' *The Moves Make the Man*. It enables him to go to a hidden and lonely court and play basketball after dark, but by the end of the book, readers share in Jerome's optimism that Spin Light will enable him to see more than his way around the basketball court.

In Chris Crutcher's *The Crazy Horse Electric Game*, pitching star Willie Weaver is seriously injured in a water-skiing accident. He runs away when it appears that on top of losing his athletic and speaking abilities, he is also losing his girlfriend. At first, he is concerned with only surviving, but then he gets involved with other people and attends an alternative school where, with help, he recovers many of his motor skills. He returns home strong enough to cope with all the changes that have occurred.

Some critics fear that when authors use such physical changes as Willie Weaver's almost miraculous recovery as a tangible or metaphorical way to communicate emotional or mental accomplishment, young readers will interpret the physical achievement literally rather than figuratively. Teenagers are already overly concerned about their bodies and any defects that they might have. Many physical challenges, including the common motif of obesity, cannot be totally overcome, so these critics prefer stories in which the protagonist comes to terms with the problem, as does Izzy in *Izzy, Willy-Nilly* and the young Indian boy in Anne Eliot Crompton's historical *The Sorcerer*. The boy is named Lefthand because he was injured by a bear and cannot hunt. In his tribe, this is a serious problem, because hunting is what the men do. There is no miraculous cure for his disability, but he gains both his own and his tribe's respect when he develops enough skill as an artist to draw the pictures of animals needed for the tribe's hunting rituals.

The acceptance of the compromised dream is an element of the romance pattern that is particularly meaningful to young adults. Many of them are just beginning to achieve some of their lifelong goals, and they are discovering the illusory nature of the end of the rainbow, which is a symbolic way of saying such things as, "When I graduate," "When we get married," "When I'm eighteen," or "When I have my own apartment." Like the characters in the romances, they are not sorry they have ventured, for they have indeed found something worthwhile, but it is seldom the pot of gold they had imagined.

Since the pattern of the romance has been outlined so clearly by critics, and since its popularity has passed the test of time with honors, it would seem to be a very easy story to write. The plot has already been worked out. An author needs only to develop a likable protagonist, determine a quest, fill in the supporting roles with stock characters, and then supply a few interesting details. But it is far from being this simple. Sometimes, as in dance, the things that look the simplest are the hardest to execute. The plot must not be so obvious that the reader recognizes it as the same old thing. The really good author will develop a unique situation that on the surface appears to be simply a good story. Its appeal as a romantic quest should be at a deep, almost subconscious level, with readers experiencing a sense of *déjà vu*. It is as if their own life story is being told, because the romantic quest is everyone's story.

Westerns

The conquering of the American West is one of the great romantic quests of all time. As such it caught the imagination not only of America but of the entire world. Dime novelists of the 1870s and 1880s glorified the wildness and vitality of miners, cowboys, mountain men, soldiers, and outlaws. In 1902, Owen

Wister's *The Virginian: A Horseman of the Plains* established the genre of the quiet and noble hero, the schoolmarm heroine, the hero's weak friend, and villains galore. Wister set up the archetypal showdown between good guys and bad guys. Jack Shaeffer's 1949 *Shane,* helped along by the Alan Ladd movie, added to the myth of the western loner-hero. All through the first third of the twentieth century, Zane Grey published his romanticized and highly popular westerns, a tradition carried on more recently by Louis L'Amour, but with more skill and attention to historical detail.

Literally hundreds of writers have published westerns, stories set roughly between 1880 and 1895 (see Focus Box 4.2). Equally important in establishing the genre of the West have been movies and television. In 1990, Kevin Costner's *Dances with Wolves* surprised movie makers and critics when it became the most successful film of the year. Expectations were that people had seen, heard, or read so many westerns that they wouldn't come to see another one. But Costner's story had a new plot plus all the elements of the adventure/accomplishment romance, one of the oldest stories in the world. Its popularity shows that readers and viewers don't want a new story as much as they want a variation on a familiar theme.

In *Dances with Wolves,* a young soldier decides to volunteer for duty on the western frontier because he wants to see buffalos. He embarks on a more difficult task than anything he could have imagined. He arrives at the North Dakota post to find it abandoned, which results in the traditional period of isolation and contemplation necessary for the development of a hero. The fact that he works hard to salvage the abandoned post and do his duty as a completely unsupervised soldier shows viewers that he's a special person worthy of the friendships that develop, first with the wolf who plays with him and then with the Sioux Indians who are supposed to be his enemies.

By the time the other soldiers arrive and accuse the hero of treason because he has become friends with the Indians, viewers have no doubt who is the hero and who are the villains. They suffer with the hero when the villains shoot his wolf, and by the end they are clearly on his side when they see him riding off with the young woman whose life he has saved. It's appropriate that he looks different and that he's called by a new name, because the ordeal he endured transformed him from a curious young soldier into a wise and caring man.

Of course, not all westerns follow the pattern of the romantic quest as closely as does *Dances with Wolves,* but most of them have some aspects of the adventure romance (e.g., the embarking on a literal journal that carries over into an intellectual and psychological journey, the exaggerated differences between the good guys and the bad guys, the taking of risks, the existence of life-threatening dangers, and the winning of someone's love).

Most writers of westerns are aiming for a popular culture audience and therefore use a straightforward style that's easy to read. And it is endemic to the genre that the heroes are involved in the same kinds of tasks as today's young adults—they are unencumbered individuals setting forth to find

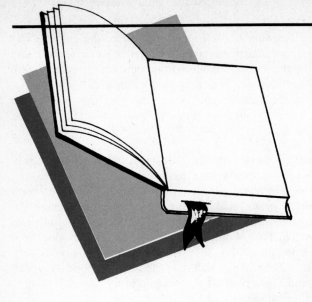

Western Novels That'll Stick to Your Ribs

Journal of the Gun Years by Richard Matheson. Evans, 1991. A young man leaves his farm life and goes west, where he becomes a gunman with a legendary reputation that he begins to believe.

The Last Picture Show by Larry McMurtry. Dial, 1966. The end of the West comes to dusty and drying-up Thalia, Texas, and the movie theater shuts down as well.

The Man Who Killed the Deer by Frank Waters. Farrar, Straus & Giroux, 1942. A young Indian is caught between two cultures.

North to Yesterday by Robert Flynn. Knopf, 1967. Some romantics take off on a cattle drive years after the cattle trails have all dried up.

Outlaw by Warren Kiefer. Donald I. Fine, 1989. Lee Garland tells his story of a man who lives by his own rules for ninety years, beginning with New Mexico in 1894, then the Spanish-American War, and beyond.

The Ox-Bow Incident by Walter Van Tilburg Clark. Random House, 1940. The protypical western about lynching and mob justice.

The Road to Many a Wonder by David Wagoner. Farrar, Straus & Giroux, 1974. A young couple set off for the West and all that they've ever dreamed of. A funny and accurate vision of the West, too, in its own way.

Borderlands by Peter Carter. Farrar, Straus & Giroux, 1990. Ben Curtis joins a cattle drive in 1871, meets a black man he learns to respect, and loses his brother in a gunfight in this epic novel.

The Brave Cowboy by Edward Abbey. Dodd, Mead, 1956. A cowboy, an anachronism in our modern world, tries to help a friend break out of jail. Failing that, the cowboy flees, pursued by a lawman who won't give up.

Come Winter by Douglas Jones. Donald Hutter/Holt, 1989. In 1870, civilization is coming to northwestern Arkansas, courtesy of one man who sets out to control the entire county.

Darlin' Bill: A Love Story of the Wild West by Jerome Charyn. Arbor House 1981. Sally loves Darlin' Bill (Wild Bill Hickock), and with her schoolmaster husband, she roams the West pursuing her Darlin' Bill and meeting odd characters, such as George the hangman.

Fire on the Mountain by Edward Abbey. Dial, 1962. When the government takes over his property to use as a missile range, an old rancher fights back.

Shadow Catcher by Charles Fergus. Soho Press, 1991. In a 1913 official expedition to take photographs of the American Indians to please eastern whites, an unofficial young picture-taker catches the real dilemma of Indians and angers the Indian Bureau.

The White Man's Road by Benjamin Capps. HarperCollins, 1969. Young Indian males break loose from a stifling reservation to prove their manhood.

---

themselves a place to live, a way to earn their keep, and suitable companions. This means that teenagers can and do read many of the westerns written for a general adult audience.

Although some of the westerns specifically for young readers do not fit quite so clearly into the pattern of the romantic quest, they are interesting in providing readers with insights into some of the less known aspects of western history. For example, Kathryn Lasky's *The Bone Wars* is about teams of scientists competing for dinosaur fossils in the American West in the 1800s. Her powerful *Beyond the Divide*, told in journal form, is the story of Meribah Simon and her father, who in 1849 head west after Meribah's father is shunned for attending the funeral of a friend who had failed to observe Amish customs.

Young people growing up in single-parent or newly formed families may be interested in such books as Joan Lowry Nixon's *The Orphan Train Quartet*, which includes *A Family Apart, Caught in the Act, In the Face of Danger*, and *A Place to Belong*. The four stories are based on true accounts of homeless New York children sent to the frontier West for adoption. Patricia MacLachlan's *Sarah, Plain and Tall* is also about the forming of a new family. It's a children's story (a Newbery Award winner) of a mail-order bride who comes west to be the mother of Caleb and Anna. The 1991 television special starring Glenn Close was powerful enough to attract readers of all ages to the story.

Another appealing YA western is Pam Conrad's *Prairie Songs*, about a young doctor and his beautiful wife who are welcomed as newcomers to a Nebraska prairie town. Their joy turns to sorrow, however, as the young wife slips into madness. Liza K. Murrow's *West Against the Wind* is set during gold rush times. Abigail Parker and her family set out for California, in search of not gold but her missing father.

Animal Stories

Probably the first accomplishment romances that children read are stories in which animals play a part, e.g., Allan Eckert's *Incident at Hawk's Hill*, Fred Gipson's *Old Yeller*, Sterling North's *Rascal*, Marjorie Rawlings' *The Yearling*, and Wilson Rawls' *Where the Red Fern Grows*. In many such stories the animals are symbolically sacrificed as a symbol of the loss the young person undergoes in exchange for wisdom (e.g., the shooting by the soldiers of the wolf in *Dances with Wolves*).

Jean George's *Julie of the Wolves* shows Julie separated from her Eskimo foster family when she runs away from the retarded Daniel, who plans to make her his wife in fact as well as name. She sets out with the vague and unrealistic goal of finding her pen pal in San Francisco. As she gains wisdom and confidence, she decides to live in the old ways. Amaroq, the great wolf, lends "miraculous" help to her struggle for survival on the Arctic tundra. The climax comes when Julie learns that her father still lives and that she has arrived at his village. When she learns that he has married a "gussack" and now pilots planes for hunters, the disillusioned Julie grieves for the wolves and the other hunted animals and vows to return and live on the tundra. The temperature falls far below zero and the "ice thundered and boomed, roaring like drumbeats across the Arctic." Despite all that Julie does to save him, Tornait, Julie's golden plover, who has been her faithful companion, dies from the cold. Tornait is the last symbol of Julie's innocence, and as she mourns his death, she comes to accept the fact that the lives of both the wolf and the Eskimo are changing, and she points her boots towards her father and the life he now leads.

Through her quest, she comes to understand that her life must change, but, unexpectedly, she also learns a great deal about her native land and the animals who live there. Readers are optimistic that Julie will not forget what she has experienced and that she will have some part in protecting the land and animals, although perhaps not to the degree that she desires.

Fortunately, not all animals in YA stories are sacrificed. Some of them live long and happy lives, providing companionship and even inspiration to their owners (see Focus Box 4.3).

Accomplishment Stories with Religious Themes

Cynthia Rylant's *A Fine White Dust* exemplifies a subgenre of the accomplishment romance, one in which religion plays a major role. The book's title comes from the chalklike dust that gets on Pete's fingers when he handles the "little bitty pieces of broken ceramic" that used to be a cross he had painted in Vacation Bible School—back before he got so old that it wasn't cool to go anymore. His best friend is a confirmed atheist, and he has "half-washed Christians for parents." Nevertheless, the summer that Preacher Man comes to town, "something religious" begins itching Pete, something that going to church couldn't cure.

Rylant's skill in developing Pete's character and revealing the depths of his emotions when he is saved and wooed and then betrayed by the Preacher Man won for her a well-deserved Newbery Honor Award. The book is short, and the succinct titles of its twelve chapters could be used as a prototypical description of the accomplishment romance. It opens with "Dust" and a sense of ennui and ends with "Amen," when Pete finally decides that, "The Preacher Man is behind me. But God is still right there, in front." At last Pete can throw

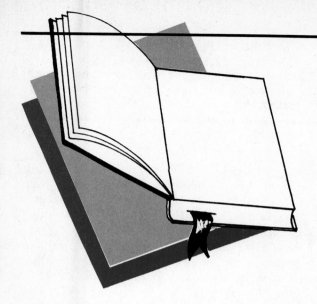

Accomplishment Stories Involving Animals

Black Star, Bright Dawn by Scott O'Dell. Houghton Mifflin, 1988. Bright Dawn helps her father train his dogs for the Iditarod sled race and ends up running it herself.

Call of the Wild by Jack London. Macmillan, 1903. This coming-of-age story is set in the excitement of the Alaskan goldrush, where both dogs and men were severely tested.

Darkling by K. M. Peyton. Delacorte, 1990. Jenny trains herself as well as the thoroughbred foal that her grandfather gave her.

Dawn Rider by Jan Hudson. Philomel, 1990. A young Indian girl finds a special place in her tribe by proving the worth of the horse that her tribe has stolen from the Snake Indians.

The Elephant War by Gillian Avery. Dell, 1980. Based on the sale of a beloved elephant from the London Zoo to the Barnum and Bailey circus, this refreshingly different story lets readers get acquainted with a spunky heroine as well as Victorian London.

Every Living Thing by Cynthia Rylant. Bradbury, 1985. In these twelve short stories people's lives are changed by their relationships with animals.

The Golden Pasture by Joyce Carol Thomas. Scholastic, 1988. Carlton Lee Jefferson spends the summer on his grandfather's ranch, where he trains a beautiful appaloosa horse.

The Last Wolf of Ireland by Elona Malterre. Clarion, 1990. Three hundred years ago the Irish set out to exterminate wolves, but young Devin defies the plan by hiding three pups.

On the Far Side of the Mountain by Jean Craighead George. E. P. Dutton, 1990. In this sequel to *My Side of the Mountain*, Sam Gribley gets involved in ecological issues.

Ride a Dark Horse by Lynn Hall. Morrow, 1987. Seventeen-year-old Gusty (translate that Gutsy) McGaw does much more than exercise horses in this combination mystery and animal story.

A Rumour of Otters by Deborah Savage. Houghton Mifflin, 1986. Alexa, who lives on a sheep ranch in New Zealand, sets out to find the otters that a Maori tribesman told her about.

Sniper   by Theodore Taylor. Harcourt Brace Jovanovich, 1989. Ben's parents leave him in charge of their wild animal preserve, never dreaming of the challenges he will face.

Taming the Star Runner   by S. E. Hinton. Delacorte, 1988. Fifteen-year-old Travis moves from a detention center to his uncle's horse ranch, where everyone hopes he will be rehabilitated.

---

away the cross that broke when he kicked his duffel bag in rage at learning that Preacher Man wasn't coming for him. In between are the chapters whose titles are almost an outline for a quest story, "The Hitchhiker," "The Saviour," "The Joy," "The Change," "The Telling," "The Invitation," "The Leaving," "The Wait," "Hell," "The Messenger," and "The Light."

Books that do what *A Fine White Dust* does (i.e., unabashedly explore religious themes) are relatively rare, partly because schools and libraries fear mixing church and state through spending tax dollars for religous books. Also, mainstream publishers fear cutting into potential sales by printing books with protagonists whose religious beliefs may offend some readers and make others uncomfortable. It's been easier for schools to include religious books with historical settings, such as Lloyd Douglas' *The Robe*, Scott O'Dell's *The Hawk That Dare Not Hunt by Day*, Elizabeth George Speare's *The Bronze Bow*, and Jessamyn West's *Friendly Persuasion*. Also accepted are books with contemporary settings that have proven themselves with adult readers, for example, Margaret Craven's *I Heard the Owl Call My Name*, Catherine Marshall's *A Man Called Peter*, and William Barrett's *Lilies of the Field*.

In lamenting the shortage of young adult books treating religious themes author Dean Hughes wrote:

> We need to be careful that, in effect, we do not say to young people that they *should* be most concerned about pimples and clothes and dates and football games—or even sex. Part of being human is addressing oneself to questions about justice, creation, morality, and the existence of divinity.[2]

In preparing for updating this textbook, we photocopied starred reviews and best-book lists from the last few years, clipped them apart, and filed these clippings in labeled envelopes. When we were finished, we were surprised at the almost empty envelope labeled *religion* compared to the brimming envelope labeled *supernatural/occult*. Books about devil worship or the occult are not the same thing as books about religion, but their popularity did make us wonder if, in today's intellectual and social climate, there's something slightly embarrassing about admitting to having faith. People may be more comfortable in joking about the mysteries of life or treating them with the kind of superior amusement that we reserve for horoscopes and ghost stories.

While there are some books focusing on religious themes (see Focus Box 4.4), what is more common is for an author to bring in religion as only a small

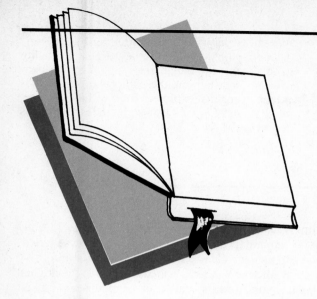

Accomplishment Stories with Religious Themes

The Chosen by Chaim Potok. Simon and Schuster, 1967. Potok's books, including *My Name Is Asher Lev* and *In the Beginning,* show what it is to come of age in a Hasidic Jewish community.

Cranes at Dusk by Hisako Matsubara. Dial, 1985. At the end of World War II, Saya's Shinto priest father defends her attending Christian church meetings because, "No religion is enough to answer all the questions."

David and Jonathan by Cynthia Voigt. Scholastic, 1992. Questions about religious and cultural differences grow into bigger questions about morality and life and death in this story of two boyhood friends growing up and apart.

God, the Universe, and Hot Fudge Sundaes by Norma Howe. Houghton Mifflin, 1984. Alfie learns that it's easier to face family problems and sadness when you have someone to love.

God's Radar by Fran Arrick. Bradbury, 1983. Roxie Cable and her family move to a small southern town and are faced with taking a new look at religion.

A Good Courage by Stephanie S. Tolan. Morrow, 1988. Tie-Dye's hippie mother drags him from one bad experience to another. When they end up in a commune run by a religious fanatic, Tie-Dye has to bring forth courage he didn't know he had.

I Heard the Owl Call My Name by Margaret Craven. Doubleday, 1973. A young vicar who is dying but doesn't know it serves his last two years with a remote Indian tribe in British Columbia.

I Will Call It Georgie's Blues by Suzanne Newton. Viking, 1983. It isn't easy for Neal and Georgie to be preacher's kids, especially when the preacher is as unbending as their father.

Is That You, Miss Blue? by M. E. Kerr. HarperCollins, 1975. Girls at a church-sponsored boarding school conspire to soften the blow for a teacher who is fired because her faith is unsettling to other faculty members.

Miriam   by Iris Rosofsky. HarperCollins, 1988. Miriam grows up in a traditional Jewish family, and when her brother dies at age thirteen her faith is tested.

A String of Chances   by Phyllis Reynolds Naylor. Atheneum, 1982. When a new baby dies, sixteen-year-old Evie faces some tough questions.

What I Really Think of You   by M. E. Kerr. HarperCollins, 1982. Despite their fathers being so different, the daughter of a small-town pentecostal preacher and the son of a big-time television evangelist explore what they have in common. Kerr's *Little Little* also includes references to evangelism.

---

part of a bigger story. In Jim Naughton's *My Brother Stealing Second,* Bobby reminisces about his family's church experiences before his brother was killed, and in Sue Ellen Bridgers' *Permanent Connections,* Rob finds comfort by visiting a little country church. Katherine Paterson, who has attended theological school and served as a missionary in China, includes both implicit and explicit religious references in her books, most directly in *Jacob Have I Loved* and *Bridge to Terabithia.* Madeleine L'Engle is devout, and along with some other writers of fantasy and science fiction, she includes religious overtones in her books (e.g., the struggle between good and evil in *A Wrinkle in Time*). The evil in Robert Cormier's *The Chocolate War* (see Chapter 3) is all the heavier because of the book's religious setting. Other books that include references to religious people and beliefs are Alice Childress' *Rainbow Jordan,* J. D. Salinger's *Franny & Zooey: Two Novellas,* Mary Stolz's *Land's End,* and Jill Paton-Walsh's *Unleaving.*

Of course religious publishing houses provide books focusing on religious themes, but these are not very useful to schools and libraries, because they are aimed so directly at believers of a particular faith, and sometimes in their zeal to convert potential believers, the authors write polemics against other groups. Nevertheless, teachers and librarians are advised to visit local religious bookstores to see what is offered, because some students may prefer to fill their independent reading assignments with books from these sources. Today's religious books range from biblical and western romances and adventures to self-help books and inspirational biographies. People who haven't taken a look at religious books over the past few years will probably be surprised at the slick covers and the upscale marketing techniques.

In relation to the accomplishment-romance, an especially troublesome group consists of books in which a misguided life is set right by an end-of-the-book conversion. Teachers hesitate to discuss the credibility of such stories, because they fear that in the process of building up literary sophistication, they may be tearing down religious faith. Nevertheless, teachers and librarians need to seek out and support those authors and publishers who treat religious motifs with honesty and respect and at the same time demand high literary quality. They also need to help parents and other critics realize that religious doubts are part of the maturation process and that reading about the doubts that others have or about imperfections in organized religion will not necessarily destroy one's own faith.

VE ROMANCE

The love-romance is slightly different from the accomplishment-romance or the adventure-romance, but it shares many of their characteristics. Love stories are symbolically associated with youth and springtime. An ordeal or a problem must be overcome which is followed by a happy ending. The "problem" is invariably the successful pairing of a likable young couple. An old definition of the love-romance pattern is, "Boy meets girl, boy loses girl, boy wins girl." This is a fairly accurate summary, except that with teenage literature it is the other way around. Most of the romances are told from the girl's point of view. She is the one who meets, loses, and finally wins a boy.

The tone of the love-romance is lighter than that of the adventure-romance. In a love story the protagonist neither risks nor gains as much as in an adventure.

Notwithstanding *Romeo and Juliet*, people seldom die, emotionally or physically, because of young love. For this reason the love-romance tends to be less serious in its message. Its power lies in its wish fulfillment. Women of all ages enjoy reading romances for the same reasons that people have always enjoyed either hearing or reading wish-fulfilling fantasies. The "Open Sesame" door to prosperity and the transformation of a cindermaid into a queen, a frog into a prince, and a Scrooge into a kindly old man are all examples of the same satisfying theme that is the key to the appeal of love-romances. In the teen romances an ugly duckling girl is transformed by the love of a boy into a swan. In her new role as swan she is not only popular and successful but happy.

Characteristics of Successful Love Stories

For the writer of a love story, probably no talent is more important than the ability to create believable characters. If readers do not feel that they know the boy and girl or the man and woman as individuals, then they can't identify with them and consequently won't care whether they make it or not. Another characteristic of the good love story is that it provides something beyond the simple pairing of two individuals. This something extra may be interesting historical details, introduction to a social issue, glimpses into the complexity of human nature, or any of the understandings and concepts that might be found in quality books or movies (see Focus Box 4.5).

Although most formula romances are aimed exclusively at a female audience comparable to the way that most pornography is aimed at a male audience, some writers are trying to write romances that will also be read by boys, even though they are not sports, adventure, or mystery stories. Hazel Rochman described such books as "domestic novels about boys in which heroes stay home and struggle with their feelings and their conscience rather than with tumultuous external events." Many such books are love stories, and as Rochman observed:

> The theme of so many girls' books—finding that you love the boy next door after all—has a new vitality from the male perspective, as in [Harry] Mazer's *I Love You, Stupid!* Sex is treated with honesty: in [Chris] Crutcher's *Running Loose*, after a long romantic buildup in which the couple drive and then ski to an isolated cabin for a weekend of lovemaking, the jock hero finds that he cannot perform. In [Richard] Peck's *Father Figure* and [Katie Letcher] Lyle's *Dark But Full of Diamonds*, the love for an older woman, in rivalry with the boy's own father, is movingly handled. . . .in *The Course of True Love Never Did Run Smooth*, [Marilyn] Singer's heroine finds strong and sexy a boy who is short, funny, and vulnerable.[3]

The most obvious difference between these boy-oriented romances and the larger body of love stories written from a girl's point of view is that their authors, who are mostly males, tend to put less emphasis on courtship and romance and more on sexuality. Rather than relying on discreet fadeouts, they

Love Stories with Something Extra

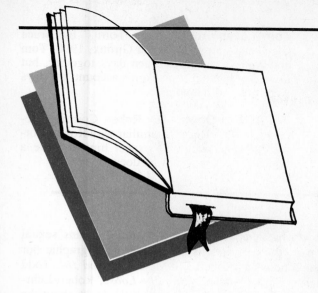

Alessandra in Love by Robert Kaplow. J. B. Lippincott, 1989. Even though fifteen-year-old Alessandra is witty and vivacious and—at least from her viewpoint—Wyn Reed is perfect for her, their romance is far from ideal.

Annie on My Mind by Nancy Garden. Farrar, Straus & Giroux, 1982. This book is unusual in showing the development of a tender and romantic lesbian relationship between two high school seniors.

Bingo Brown and the Language of Love by Betsy Byars. Viking, 1989. Sandwiched between *The Burning Questions of Bingo Brown* and *Bingo Brown, Gypsy Lover,* this book shows Melissa moving to Bixby, Oklahoma, and poor Bingo having to cook thirty-six dinners for his parents to pay his long-distance phone bills.

City Light by Harry Mazer. Scholastic, 1988. George is not a gracious loser when Julie tells him their romance is finished. But eventually, he gathers his dignity and his resources and is ready to forge ahead with Rosemary, a girl he meets through a computer bulletin board.

Cold Sassy Tree by Olive Ann Burns. Ticknor & Fields, 1984. Although this is the story of Will Tweedy growing up, it's also his grandfather's love story.

Daniel and Esther by Patrick Raymond. Macmillan, 1990. In 1936, Esther's anti-Fascist parents send her to a boarding school in England, hoping that she will be safe. There she and Daniel fall in love with each other, but when the war starts she must return to Vienna and Daniel is evacuated to the United States.

Forever by Judy Blume. Bradbury, 1975. Katherine and Michael become sexually involved, and although nobody gets punished, their love does not last forever.

Heartbeat by Norma Fox Mazer and Harry Mazer. Bantam, 1989. Tod plays matchmaker for his friend Amos but then finds he loves Hilary too.

If Beale Street Could Talk by James Baldwin. Doubleday, 1974. In this mature story told in frank, black English, pregnant Tish loves Fonny, who has been jailed on a false charge.

The Massacre at Fall Creek by Jessamyn West. Harcourt Brace Jovanovich, 1975. The year is 1824 and the place is Fall Creek, Indiana, where for the first time white men are being tried as criminals for killing Indians. A young couple plays a part in bringing at least some justice to the frontier.

The Silver Kiss by Annette Curtis Klause. Delacorte, 1990. Zoë's mother is dying of cancer and she's especially vulnerable when she meets the beautifully strange Simon, who turns out to be a 200-year-old vampire.

Teen Angel: And Other Stories of Young Love   by Marianne Gingher. Atheneum, 1988. This collection of ten short stories illustrates how differently young adults respond to love.

Temporary Times, Temporary Places   by Barbara Robinson. HarperCollins, 1982. In this dual story, readers see Janet's summer crush foiled by a case of poison ivy while Janet's aunt May adjusts to her own broken heart.

Tom Loves Anna Lo Clements. Farrar, Strau and Anna have only fil as readers can tell from ' were full and memorabl

We All Fall Down   b lacorte, 1991. Readers fa mier's books wouldn't typical love story, and I

---

allow their readers to know what happens, which so intercourse. For the most part, the descriptions are ne lovingly romantic, but in such books as Robert Lipsyte Strasser's *Workin' for Peanuts,* Chris Crutcher's *Runnii* man's *Juggling,* and Terry Davis' *Vision Quest,* there abundance of sexual feelings that the characters experie

As an antidote to the lopsidedness of books that are or overly sexy, some adult critics suggest offering book are as much friends as lovers. The romantic relationship story, and there is no indication of either partner exploit other, as often happens in exaggerated romances or ii oriented stories. As a ploy to attract male readers, sin confident that girls will read love stories, the narrator m may be a mix with alternate chapters coming from the Paul Zindel's *The Pigman* and M. E. Kerr's *I'll Love 1 Like Me.*

An example of a combination love and friendship : *The Girl of His Dreams.* Willis Pierce, the boy Mazer book, *The War on Villa Street,* has graduated from hi₃ by himself. He is a runner but too shy to compete or t(long, solitary runs he dreams about the girl he is sure t he meets Sophie, who takes care of the newsstand by works, she doesn't look or act like the girl of his dream has done such a good job of character development, t why the two are attracted to each other, and they end Sophie does: "She's happy, but the little bit of worry is bit of uncertainty."

The Formula Romance

The runaway popularity of formula love-romances writt agers and published as original paperbacks was the big

the early 1980s (see Chapter One, p. 31). Formula romances most often feature girls fifteen, sixteen, or seventeen years old with boyfriends who are slightly older. The target audience is supposedly girls between the ages of twelve and sixteen, although some ten- and eleven-year-olds are also finding them. The typical setting is a small town or suburb. There is no explicit sex or profanity. As one editor told us, "If there are problems, they have to be normal ones— no drugs, no sex, no alcohol, no bad parents, etc."

The kinds of problems featured are wish-fulfilling ones that most girls dream of coping with. For example, in Jill Ross Klevin's *That's My Girl,* ice skater Becky has to fight off getting ulcers while worrying about the upcoming Nationals, her chance at the Olympics. Her biggest worry is whether she will lose her boyfriend, who feels ignored. Janet Quin-Harkin's *California Girl* has an almost identical plot, except that Jennie is competing for the Olympics as a swimmer. In Rosemary Vernon's *The Popularity Plan,* Frannie is too shy to talk to boys, but her friends draw up a plan in which she is assigned certain ways to relate to a boy each day. Sure enough, she is soon asked for so many dates she has to buy a wall calendar to keep from getting mixed up. But by the end of the story she is happy to "give it all up" and settle for Ronnie, the boy she really liked all along.

Formula romances have many of the same qualities that publishers have developed for high-interest, low-vocabulary books. They are short books divided into short chapters. They have quick beginnings, more action than description, considerable use of dialogue, a straightforward point of view, and a reading level not much above fifth grade. And perhaps most important of all, the books are clearly labeled, so that readers know what they will be getting. As shown by the popularity of movie sequels, television serials, and reruns, and continuing columns in newspapers, although viewers and readers do not want to see or read precisely the same thing over and over again, they are comforted by knowing that a particular piece is going to be very similar to something they have previously enjoyed.

Some adults worry that teenage readers take the books seriously, that they fail to recognize them as fantasy, and that they therefore model their behavior and attitudes—and, more important, their expectations—after those portrayed in the romances. As one of our students wrote in her reading autobiography:

> Today when I read a romance, I just shake my head. Men do not ever act that way or say those things. I think teens should be exposed to some reading that is more realistic so they have some idea what to expect. I never knew what quite to expect. That was why I was so hurt by my first boyfriends and why I hurt them so bad.

A sampling of published quotations from critics illustrates a wider range of concern:

> Playing on the insecurities and self-doubt which plague most teen-aged girls, the Wildfire romances come just close enough to real life to be

convincing to young readers. But implicit in these hygienic stories are the old, damaging and limiting stereotypes from which we've struggled so hard to free ourselves and our children: that the real world is white and middle-class; that motherhood is women's only work; that a man is the ultimate prize and a woman is incomplete without one; and that in the battle for that prize, the weapons are good looks and charm, intelligence is a liability, and the enemy is the other woman.[4]

Absence is, in fact, at the heart of the criticism of these books. Third World people are absent, disabled people are absent, lesbians and gay men are absent, poor people are absent, elderly people are absent. . . .[5]

There is an eternal paradox here. We read such romantic stories as an escape from reality and yet they form our ideals of what reality should be. Hence that frustration, that vague sense of failure and disappointment when a night out at the disco doesn't turn out the way it does in the magazines.[6]

Although the formula romances have been promoted as "squeaky clean" and as an antidote to depressing problem novels, in reality many of them rely for their appeal on sexual titillation. A few years back, when we asked an editor about the white, see-through leotard that showed the skater's nipples on the cover of Jill Ross Klevin's *That's My Girl*, she blamed "the accident" on the bright lights necessary for a good photo. But a year later, the paperback cover of Bonnie and Paul Zindel's *A Star for the Latecomer* featured a young dancer whose nipples were also showing through a white leotard. Since this almost identical cover was a painting instead of a photograph, it could hardly have been an oversight. And we don't need Wilson Bryan Key, author of *Subliminal Seduction*, to identify the forbidden nature of such titles as *On Thin Ice, Against the Rules, Coming on Strong, Stolen Kisses, Playing House,* and *Anything to Win*—all reviewed in a single *SLJ* column.[7]

Defenders of the romances most often focus on their popularity and the fact that they are recreational reading freely chosen by young girls who otherwise would most likely be watching TV. Vermont Royster, writing in the *Wall Street Journal*, compared the romances to the reading of books his mother considered trash—Tom Swift, the Rover Boys, Detective Nick Carter, and Wild Bill Hickok. He acknowledged that the plotting was banal and monotonous and that writers could probably turn them out wholesale, but at least, "The spelling is correct and they do manage mostly to abide by the rules of English grammar." He welcomed the books as an aid in helping a generation of television-oriented kids acquire the habit of reading. Once they are hooked, "Call it an addiction if you will . . . young people can be led by good teachers to enlarge their reach."[8]

Teachers and librarians need to be especially careful in criticizing students' enjoyment of romances, because young readers are as sensitive as anyone else to hints that they are gullible and lacking in taste and sophistication. So rather than making fun of love romances, it is better to approach them from a positive angle, offering readers a wide variety of books, including ones that treat boy/girl relationships not as the only thing of importance, but as part of a bigger picture.

The Cyclical Effects of the Success of the Formula Romances

During the 1980s, the financial success of the teenage, formula romances undoubtedly influenced not only marketing practices, but also the decisions made by editors, authors, and publishers. *Love* became a popular word in book titles, even in books by authors well established prior to the popularity of the romances, and Betty Cavanna and Maureen Daly, authors of romances read by teenagers in the 1950s, were brought back to see if they could repeat their success.

A convention borrowed from the romances and now appearing in a much wider range of books is the glossing over of the part that sex plays in male/female relationships. In the romance, it's love at first sight, which must imply a physical attraction (i.e., a sexual attraction), yet the boys in many of the stories are portrayed as being almost platonically interested in the girl's thoughts and feelings rather than in her body. When Rainbow Jordan, the protagonist in Alice Childress' realistic book of the same name, learned that this wasn't the way it was in real life, she complained:

> True love is mostly featured in fairy tales. Sleepin' Beauty put off sex for a hundred years. When a prince finally did find her . . . he kiss her gently, then they gallop off on a pretty horse so they could enjoy the happy-ever-after. They never mentioned sex.

In their pseudo-attempt to be "squeaky clean," many of the formula romances encourage a kind of wish fulfillment that relates to the psychological ambivalence that young females feel about sexuality. On the one hand, they want to be loved, not only because it's emotionally satisfying but also because dating and courtship are glamorous and exciting. On the other hand, many of them are not yet ready for a sexual relationship and would be happy to have the dating and the cuddling without the complications of sex.

Barbara Wersba's *Fat: A Love Story* is a perfect illustration of how this kind of wish fulfillment has found its way into mainstream YA literature. (We are defining *mainstream books* as well-designed and publicized hardback books written by noted authors and released by prestigious publishers.) In Wersba's book, sixteen-year-old, overweight Rita gets a part-time job delivering cheesecakes for thirty-two-year-old Arnold Bromberg. She is a virgin; he isn't. She thinks she's in love with the wealthy and handsome Robert and that her friend Nicole is going to help her catch Robert. Instead, Nicole and Robert run off together, and in the last twenty pages of the book Rita is left to fall in love with Mr. Bromberg. When she tells him that she loves him "as a man," he is astonished, because he loves her too "passionately and deeply."

NAT HENTOFF
on Delayed Reactions

Writing for and to young readers is more grat-ifying than the other kinds of writing I do for one particular reason—young readers write back much more often than adult readers. They write with enthusiasm—both when they like something and even more so when they don't. Much of the time, a writer sends forth his work into the unknown, and the reactions, if any, remain unknown. But not when he or she aims his arrows, as it were, at those who are ten to seventeen or eighteen.

So, though I often fall behind in answering mail, I always answer young readers, usually within a day or two.

And I learn from those letters—not only about things I could have done better ("the father in that book wasn't a person at all—you didn't spend any time making him real!") but also about the readers themselves: what books and music they like, what

their teachers are like, w
that.

The most surprising a
got was from a young m
tarist, stranded in Hawa
Jazz Country years befor
changed his life. He kne
he was going to be a m

And that's what he b
road and now, years l
without a job in Hawaii.
for having written that bo
was send him some mo

It was a novel way to
and I did empathize wi
unable to see the mone
my book and his lack of

Still, he did make an i
obviously, I haven't forg

On the other hand,
west coast wrote me tha
quit being editor of her so
worn down by all the att
censor the paper. Then,
The Day They Came to .
turned her around. She
itor, she said, and fight
local affiliate to the Amer
to help her.

Then there is the long
er's reaction to one of my
a lecture I've given at a
a member of the faculty
a novel of mine he or s
and still remembers.

It's a good feeling. It
more books—if I can f
"traditional" these days
what's right and what's

Nat Hentoff's books include *Jazz Country*, HarperCollins, 1965; *I'm Really Dragged but Nothi* Schuster, 1968; *In the Country of Ourselves*, Simon and Schuster, 1971; *This School Is Drivin* and *The Day They Came to Arrest the Book*, Delacorte, 1982.

She sleeps on Mr. Bromberg's couch, he teaches her to drive his car, they adopt two kittens, he buys her new clothes, consoles her about her best friend's betrayal, counsels her about why she overeats, and plans and cooks their food so that she loses two pounds a week. During all of this, he insists that he won't have sex with her until she's eighteen.

> Oh, we made love at every possible opportunity, but it never ended in the bedroom. It ended in the kitchen—with us having a cup of tea. We loved each other, we were committed to each other, but Arnold would not take that final step.

Of course there's a happy ending. On Christmas Eve Rita gets Arnold to the church, where she performs a pretend wedding ceremony complete with dimestore rings, so that at last they can sleep together. On Christmas morning, Rita wakes up and looks at Arnold and sees her present, her past, and her future. She sees herself thin and grown up and married to Arnold for the rest of her life. In the old days, when realism was the undisputed king of YA books, such an unlikely plot would never have gotten past the desk of a literary agent, much less an editor, and on into the bookstores with two sequels: *Love Is the Crooked Thing* and *Beautiful Losers*.

Despite the reservations we have expressed about the popularity of the formula romances overwhelming and changing the rest of young adult literature, we will conclude by saying that the various types of accomplishment and adventure stories, including love-romances, are psychologically satisfying. More than any other genre, these stories match the particular stage of life that is young adulthood. Because of this match, and because the plots are straightforward and the reading levels are generally comfortable, these books are likely to remain popular for young adult leisure time reading.

NOTES

[1] Glenna Davis Sloan, *The Child as Critic* (Teachers College Press, 1975), p. 33.

[2] Dean Hughes, "Bait/Rebait: Books with Religious Themes," *English Journal* 70 (December 1981): 14–17.

[3] Hazel Rochman, "Bringing Boys' Books Home," *School Library Journal* 29 (August 1983): 26–27.

[4] Brett Harvey, "Wildfire: Tame but Deadly," *Interracial Books for Children Bulletin* 12 (1981).

[5] Sharon Wigutoff, "First Love: Morality Tales Thinly Veiled," *Interracial Books for Children Bulletin* 12:4 and 12:5 (1981): 17.

[6] Mary Harron, "Oh Boy! My Guy," (London) *Times Educational Supplement* (July 1, 1983): 22.

[7] Kathy Fritts, "Paperback Romance Series Roundup," *School Library Journal* 33 (January 1987): 86–88.

[8] Vermont Royster, "Thinking Things Over: The Reading Addiction," *Wall Street Journal* (June 24, 1981): 30.

OTHER TITLES MENTIONED IN THE TEXT OF CHAPTER FOUR

Barrett, William. *Lilies of the Field*. Doubleday, 1962.

Blume, Judy. *Are You There, God? It's Me, Margaret*. Bradbury, 1970.

Bridgers, Sue Ellen. *Permanent Connections*. HarperCollins, 1987.

Brooks, Bruce. *The Moves Make the Man*. HarperCollins, 1984.

Childress, Alice. *Rainbow Jordan*. Putnam, 1981.

Conrad, Pam. *Prairie Songs*. HarperCollins, 1985.

Cormier, Robert. *The Chocolate War*. Pantheon, 1974.

Craven, Margaret. *I Heard the Owl Call My Name*. Doubleday, 1973.

Crompton, Anne Eliot. *The Sorcerer*. Second Chance, 1982.

Crutcher, Chris. *The Crazy Horse Electric Game*. Greenwillow, 1987.

———. *Running Loose*. Greenwillow, 1983.

Davis, Terry. *Vision Quest*. Viking, 1979.

Douglas, Lloyd. *The Robe*. Houghton Mifflin, 1942.

Eckert, Allan W. *Incident at Hawk's Hill*. Little, Brown, 1971.

George, Jean. *Julie of the Wolves*. HarperCollins, 1972.

Gipson, Fred. *Old Yeller*. HarperCollins, 1964.

Green, Hannah. *I Never Promised You a Rose Garden*. Holt, 1964.

Guest, Judith. *Ordinary People*. Viking, 1976.

Hamilton, Virginia. *M. C. Higgins, the Great*. Macmillan, 1974.

Kerr, M. E. *I'll Love You When You're More Like Me*. HarperCollins, 1977.

Key, Wilson Bryan. *Subliminal Seduction*, NAL Penguin, 1974.

Klevin, Jill Ross. *That's My Girl*. Scholastic, 1981.

Lasky, Kathryn. *Beyond the Divide*. Macmillan, 1983.

———. *The Bone Wars*. Morrow, 1988.

Lehrman, Robert. *Juggling*. HarperCollins, 1982.

L'Engle, Madeleine. *A Wrinkle in Time*. Farrar, Straus & Giroux, 1962.

Lipsyte, Robert. *The Brave*. HarperCollins, 1991.

———. *The Contender*. HarperCollins, 1967.

———. *Jock and Jill*. HarperCollins, 1982.

Lyle, Katie Letcher. *Dark But Full of Diamonds*. Putnam, 1981.

MacLachlan, Patricia. *Sarah, Plain and Tall*. HarperCollins, 1985.

Marshall, Catherine. *A Man Called Peter*. McGraw-Hill, 1951.

Mason, Bobbie Ann. *In Country*. HarperCollins, 1985.

Mazer, Harry. *I Love You, Stupid!* HarperCollins, 1981.

———. *The Girl of His Dreams*. HarperCollins, 1987.

———. *The War on Villa Street*. Delacorte, 1978.

Murrow, Liza K. *West Against the Wind*. Holiday House, 1987.

Naughton, Jim. *My Brother Stealing Second*. HarperCollins, 1989.

Nixon, Joan Lowry. *The Orphan Train Quartet (A Family Apart, Caught in the Act, In the Face of Danger,* and *A Place to Belong)*. Bantam, late 1980s.

North, Sterling, *Rascal: A Memoir of a Better Era*. E. P. Dutton, 1963.

O'Dell, Scott, *The Hawk That Dare Not Hunt by Day*. Houghton Mifflin, 1975.

Paterson, Katherine. *Bridge to Terabithia*. Crowell, 1980.

———. *Jacob Have I Loved*. Crowell, 1980.

Paton-Walsh, Jill. *Unleaving*. Farrar, Straus & Giroux, 1976.

Peck, Richard. *Father Figure*. Viking, 1978.

Quin-Harkin, Janet. *California Girl*. Bantam, 1981.

Rawlings, Marjorie Kinnan. *The Yearling*. Scribner's, 1938.

Rawls, Wilson. *Where the Red Fern Grows*. Doubleday, 1961.

Rylant, Cynthia. *A Fine White Dust*. Bradbury, 1986.

Salinger, J. D. *The Catcher in the Rye*. Little, Brown, 1951.

———. *Franny & Zooey: Two Novellas*. Little, Brown, 1961.

Savage, Deborah. *A Rumour of Otters*. Houghton Mifflin, 1986.

Shaeffer, Jack. *Shane*. Houghton Mifflin, 1949.

Singer, Marilyn. *The Course of True Love Never Did Run Smooth*. HarperCollins, 1983.

Speare, Elizabeth George. *The Bronze Bow*. Houghton Mifflin, 1973.

Stolz, Mary. *Land's End*. HarperCollins, 1973.

Strasser, Todd. *Workin' for Peanuts*. Delacorte, 1983.

Tolkien, J. R. R. *The Lord of the Rings*. Houghton Mifflin, 1974.

Vernon, Rosemary. *The Popularity Plan*. Bantam, 1981.

Voigt, Cynthia. *Izzy, Willy-Nilly*. Atheneum, 1986.

Wersba, Barbara. *Beautiful Losers*. HarperCollins, 1988.

———. *Fat: A Love Story*. HarperCollins, 1987.

———. *Love Is the Crooked Thing*. HarperCollins, 1987.

West, Jessamyn. *Friendly Persuasion*. Harcourt Brace Jovanovich, 1956.

Wister, Owen. *The Virginian: A Horseman of the Plains*. Macmillan, 1902.

Zindel, Bonnie and Paul. *A Star for the Latecomer*. HarperCollins, 1980.

Zindel, Paul. *The Pigman*. HarperCollins, 1968.

For information on the availability of paperback editions of these titles, please consult the most recent edition of *Paperbound Books in Print*, published annually by R. R. Bowker Company.

SPORTS, ADVENTURE, MYSTERIES, AND THE SUPERNATURAL

Of Excitement and Suspense

All of us, save the most literal-minded, occasionally need to go outside ourselves, to dream old and new dreams about living in the fast lane or even on the edge. We need to dream about the strange and impossible, so that we can return refreshed to the mundane and ordinary. The books treated in this chapter—sports, adventures, mysteries, and the supernatural—provide the challenges and the vicarious thrills and danger we seem to crave.

These genres are usually considered to provide pleasure reading rather than reading that furthers intellectual development. For example, we recently heard an argument against a faculty member's promotion to full professor that was clinched by a condescending, "She reads mysteries!" The crux of the problem was that the woman reads mysteries instead of writing up her research; nevertheless, it was the accusation about mysteries that gave the committee the confidence to vote against her promotion.

Incidents such as this put those readers on the defensive who love to get goose bumps from a supernatural thriller or to read themselves to sleep with a good mystery. In reaction, they begin to make claims that are hard to substantiate—for example, they recommend mysteries set in different countries as a way to learn geography, they claim that horror stories are a good substitute for actual aggression, and they conjecture that by reading sports and survival stories young people can learn cooperation and team playing without suffering sprains and bruises. Such claims may be partially true, but they're exceedingly hard to prove. We'll be on safer ground if when we feel the need to defend the kinds of books in this chapter we include the simple fact that reading for pleasure is in itself a worthy activity. Getting something more is serendipity.

■ *THE CHALLENGE OF SPORTS*

Adults and young adults alike have been fascinated by sports and sports heroes as far back as the Olympic Games in ancient Greece. Today, spectator and participation sports are highly popular throughout the world. Millions of people jog, play tennis, swim, or golf. Even more watch basketball, football, or baseball on television. Others play in organized softball or soccer leagues sponsored by churches, city recreation departments, or private clubs. Sports play an incredibly important part in our lives and in our language (witness these clichés: *to be a team player, to quarterback* a situation, *to have an inside track, to make a close call,* and *to set the pace*). Given our national mania, most of us would be shocked if the current president of Cornell University repeated what his predecessor said in 1873 about a proposed football game with the University of Michigan: "I will not permit thirty men to travel 400 miles merely to agitate a bag of wind."

More than any other important facet of American life, sports are youth oriented. Athletes reach their peak in their teens or their twenties, and this leads to a powerful identification between sports heroes and young adults. It's a rare high school where there are no sports heroes. On the national level, where else but in sports and perhaps entertainment could young adults dream of the fame and adulation heaped upon tennis stars Jennifer Capriotti, Steffi Graf, and Michael Chang, and more recently, Olympic skater Kristi Yamaguchi?

Parents and schools encourage young people to engage in sports because, in addition to providing good physical exercise, sports are thought to be a way of teaching principles of competition while conflicts are played out within the security of the rules of the game. Games are considered a microcosm of the great American system of competition, which combines individual effort with team play and a common enemy to be bested. The competitive nature of sports is most easily seen when the foe is another team or another individual, but occasionally it's a record, someone else's or even the athlete's own, which is to be beaten. The drive to be best and the subsequent acclaim for the winner provides an impetus for superhuman efforts and the drama that makes for good literature.

The Wide World of Sports

In the introduction we referred to sports books as a genre. It would probably have been more accurate to have referred to "the topic of sports" because there are good, new sports books in almost every genre. (See Focus Box 5.1.) Nonfiction ranges from poetry, as in R. R. Knudson and May Swenson's *American Sports Poems,* to scientific information, as in Emily Isberg's *Peak Performance, Sports, Science, and the Body in Action,* which is based on a "Nova" public television program about interactions among computers, sports

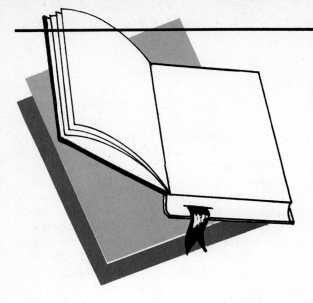

An Armful of Great Books About Sports

Bang the Drum Slowly by Mark Harris. Knopf, 1956. A fine pitcher and writer tells about the slow death of his friend from Hodgkin's disease. (fiction)

Extra Innings: Season in the Senior League by David Whitford. Edward Burlingame Books, 1991. A season with the league of ex-baseball players and managers in Florida.

Friends Till the End by Todd Strasser. Delacorte, 1981. Soccer star and all-round popular guy David Gilbert reluctantly visits Howie, who has leukemia, but they bond into a friendship that surprises both of them. (fiction)

God Save the Quarterback: American Football Goes to England by Michael Globetti. Random House, 1991. A season with the Birmingham (England) Bulls.

Grass Roots and Schoolyards: A High School Basketball Anthology edited by Nelson Campbell. Stephen Greene Press, 1988. This collection of magazine and newspaper columns features big-time—and small-town—high school basketball.

His Enemy, His Friend by John Tunis. Morrow, 1967. A boy sees his father killed as a hostage by Germans in World War II. After the war, a German team, including the man who ordered his father shot, comes to the small French town for a soccer game. (fiction)

How Life Imitates the World Series by Thomas Boswell. Doubleday, 1983. Boswell is one of the great baseball writers; see also his *Why Time Begins on Opening Day* (Doubleday, 1984).

The Natural by Bernard Malamud. Farrar, Straus & Giroux, 1952. The mythical novel about Roy Hobbs and his famous bat. Not Malamud at his best, but still fine. (fiction)

The Passing Game by Richard Blessing. Little, Brown, 1982. Craig Warren has potential greatness, but his playing is frightened and unsure. (fiction)

Shoeless Joe by W. P. Kinsella. Houghton Mifflin, 1982. A fan builds a baseball stadium for a legendary game with Shoeless Joe Jackson and other baseball immortals. See also *The Iowa Baseball Confederacy* (Houghton Mifflin, 1986) and a wonderful set of short stories, nominally about sports, *The Further Adventures of Slugger McBatt* (Houghton Mifflin, 1988). (fiction)

"Whatta-Gal": The Babe Didrickson Story by William Oscar Johnson and Nancy P. Williamson. Little, Brown, 1975. A biography of the all-American in track, field, golf, bowling, tennis, swimming, baseball, and more.

Yogi: It Ain't Over . . .   by Yogi Berra with Tom Horton. Mc-Graw Hill, 1989. The catcher–manager–language mangler who claims his favorite saying is, "If the world were perfect, it wouldn't be," writes a funny memoir.

---

medicine, steroids, and other technical developments. Fiction ranges from humorous spoofs, such as Paul Baczewski's *Just for Kicks,* to mysteries, such as Rosemary Wells' *When No One Was Looking.*

Most sports books have common elements: description of the activity or the game, with its rules and expectations; the training that's needed; the role of the spectators; the rewards to be expected; and the disappointments, which make the rewards that much better. The trend over the last several decades has been for the authors of fiction to focus on the toughening and the character-changing aspects of the sport rather than on inning after inning or quarter after quarter of a game. At the heart of contemporary sports fiction is an examination of the price of fame, the worth of the game, the transitory nature of glory, and the temptation, always doomed, to expect that temporary glory will be permanent.

Early sports writers for young people believed sincerely in the purity of sports. For example, at the turn of the last century, Ralph Henry Barbour, who devoutly believed in hard but fair play and the amateur spirit, dedicated his 1900 novel *For the Honor of the School,* "To That School, Wherever It May Be, Whose Athletics Are Purest." Dated though his fine novel now seems, Barbour was deadly serious in his belief that school spirit was inextricably coupled with athletic *and* academic excellence. He and other writers for young adults preached this doctrine until the 1940s.

In the 1950s and early 1960s, such writers as John F. Carson and H. D. Francis wrote excellent novels filled with heroes reeking of sweat. Today their kind of sports story goes for the most part unread and unwritten. Kindly old Pop Dugout, wily with his sports wisdom and remembered for his warm and genial backpatting, may never have been very real. Nevertheless, the sentimental fiction of the past had a charm that we have lost, and with it we have also lost many sports heroes for young readers.

Even as famous and prolific an author as John R. Tunis, a sportswriter for the *New York Evening Post* who published twenty-four novels for young people between 1938 and 1975, has been largely ignored. However, there's been a recent attempt to revive some of the old sports books with attractive new editions. Harcourt reissued Tunis' *Keystone Kids* and *Rookie of the Year,* and Morrow reissued a few of Zane Grey's sports stories, *The Shortstop* and *The Young Pitcher.* Morrow also put out new editions of several Tunis books, including his basketball story *Go Team, Go!* and his baseball story *Highpockets.* Tunis' *The Kid Comes Back* is about a young baseball player returning from World

War II with one leg shorter than the other. Before the war he was the "speediest man in the National League," and now the challenge is whether he can overcome the fear that is holding him back.

Sports Plus

In focusing on the dual issue of sports and personal development, Tunis' *The Kid Comes Back* was the forerunner of today's sports fiction, in which the people are as important as the game. Authors are using sports as a backdrop against which protagonists work out other problems.

Chris Crutcher is the most talented new writer to combine sports and personal development stories. *Running Loose*, his first novel, presents Louie Banks, who wants to play football, but not the way the unethical coach wants to play it. The novel is about football, fair play, and running, but it is also about love and death, caring and maturing.

Crutcher's *Stotan!* is about a swimming team and how it faces the serious illness of one of its members. In *The Crazy Horse Electric Game*, star athlete Willie Weaver suffers brain damage as the result of a water skiing accident. His beautifully coordinated body is left with a lurching walk, and when his parents' marriage goes awry he's left on his own to pull his shattered life together. Crutcher's recent *Athletic Shorts: Six Short Stories* features some of the characters from his other books. The succinctness of these stories might attract less ambitious readers and show them that sports fiction has more to offer than they thought.

Thomas Dygard explores social pressure as part of his sports stories. In *Halfback Tough*, Joe Atkins changes schools, and for lack of anything better to do goes out for football. When he succeeds, two of his "friends" from his old school come calling to help him remember that organized sports are for kids (it's more sophisticated to be a troublemaker). In *Tournament Upstart*, a tiny Ozark school moves up from the Class B to the Class A basketball tournament, but then their star player decides he's too good for this "hick" team. Dygard's *Forward Pass* has received more attention than his other books because the football coach for the Aldridge High Panthers takes the unusual approach of scouting out the girl athletes to find the pass receiver his team desperately needs.

Walter Dean Myers' *Hoops*, along with its sequel, *The Outside Shot*, is about a black youth trying to find his way out of poverty through basketball. Jim Naughton's *My Brother Stealing Second* is also about a young athlete who hopes to get away from a miserable mill town by going to college on a baseball scholarship. When he's killed in an automobile accident while driving back from the university, his younger brother, Bobby, is left to find out what happened and to tell the story of the family's recovery—not always a pretty picture. The book opens seven months after the accident, and Bobby explains how he eats breakfast every morning "mostly because Mom likes to make it, and because I let her down in so many other ways. She thinks eating breakfast together is a sign of our progress as a family." When the whistle from the mill blows, both parents go stiff; it takes a while for them to recover and get a conversation going, but they manage:

> The weird thing is that in about five minutes, they are back to normal. That's what pisses me off. It's like: *A quick shot of grief each morning leaves me free for the rest of the day.* As though it's an antiperspirant or something.

That's not Bobby's way. He prefers to wallow in his grief, to wrap himself in it like a cloak, but he can't stay wrapped in his cloak of grief and memories forever, and that's what makes an interesting story.

Robert Lehrman's *Juggling* (a soccer story) and Terry Davis' *Vision Quest* (a wrestling story) are unusual, because they honestly explore their young heroes' sexuality. *Vision Quest* is also unusual for its rare insight into amateur wrestling and the mysticism that often accompanies it. David Klass's *Wrestling with Honor* examines issues surrounding drug testing and personal freedom. Junior high students will be more interested in Matt Christopher's *Takedown*, in which a young wrestler's interest in the sport is mixed up with his desire to find his birth father, who he knows was a wrestler. A much lighter look at wrestling is Christi Killien's *Rusty Fertlanger, Lady's Man*. Rusty is a junior high student who wants to retain a low profile while he concentrates on developing his talents as a cartoonist. School rules dictate that everyone participate on an organized team. He chooses wrestling because he thinks it will be the least distracting. But as a lightweight, his first opponent is a girl, and it's not at all clear that he's going to be able to keep his low profile. Jerry Spinelli also zeroed in on the relatively new situation of girls wrestling in his humorous *There's a Girl in My Hammerlock*.

Like John R. Tunis, Robert Lipsyte is a professional sports writer who is also very good at writing for teenagers. Lipsyte does both fiction and nonfiction, and some interesting comparisons can be drawn between his nonfiction *Free to Be Muhammad Ali* and his novel *The Contender*, about a young black boxer from Harlem. The latter has grown increasingly popular since its publication in 1967. During the 1980s, Lipsyte devoted much of his energy to television, where he hosted the PBS late-night talk show *The Eleventh Hour*, but he is again writing for teenagers. His 1991 *The Brave* is advertised as a sequel to *The Contender*, but it's an unusual sequel because it has a new, young hero. He is George Harrison Bayer (named after his mother's favorite Beatle), but known as Sonny Bear. Sonny is a heavyweight boxer who runs away from his reservation home in upstate New York right into the arms of Alfred Brooks, the boxer from *The Contender*, who is now a New York City policeman.

A big part of the story is Sonny Bear's physical and emotional training both by the New York City policeman Alfred Brooks and by his great uncle Jake,

CHRIS CRUTCHER
on Writing Sports Fiction

Once again, I'm denying my label. *A writer of sports fiction.* Dan Jenkins writes great sports fiction. Frank Deford. *Those* guys know sports. They know how all the games are played at every level, have had beers with the greats. I, on the other hand, held down the far end of the bench on a high school basketball team that couldn't field enough players to cut me. As a hundred-sixty-pound lineman on my high school eight-man football team, my lone film highlight was a fifteen-second shot of my back as I lay in the grass after blowing a tackle my mother assured me she could have made. My NAIA college swim team, in our early years, considered it a success anytime as many swimmers got out of the water at the end of a race as dove in at the gun. *A writer of sports*

fiction? May the ghost of Clair Bee watch over us. Now *there* was a guy who wrote sports fiction.

True, sports is *in* my fiction. I love athletics. I love that human beings of any sex, color, sexual preference, size, or religious belief can find a challenge in athletics. I love that the full range of human emotion can be touched within the structure of agreed-upon rules, from a drive-way hoop to the Boston Garden. I love that no character I might create could be exempt from some athletic contest.

I hate it when an athlete or a coach shrouds his or her athletic triumphs in a cloak of patriotism. If sports are found wrapped in the American flag in one of my books, I unwrap them. I hate it even more when some class NFL athlete faces the camera in front of his locker after the Super Bowl to tell us Jesus Christ was probably the best gosh-darn wide receiver in the history of the world, or how God guided the ball into his hands amidst triple coverage in the end zone with no time on the clock. I like my athletics pure.

Athletics provides a rich background for my fiction because all the elements of good story-telling exist in a given contest. An exciting athletic encounter snatches me straightaway from the clutches of writer's block, breathes life into dying characters, tests the limits of their will, and mine. But I will be sad if I'm remembered only as a writer of sports fiction, because I hope that contests in the real world are as evident as those in the arena in my stories. When a character steps up for a hero's role in a Chris Crutcher story, I want him or her to be more than a jock who can take a hit, or nail a three-pointer, or swim to Guam. I want him or her tested in an arena with less evident boundaries—no half time, no lane ropes, no marked end zone.

Chris Crutcher's books include *Athletic Shorts,* 1991; *Chinese Handcuffs,* 1989; *Stotan!* 1986; and *The Crazy Horse Electric Game,* 1987, all Greenwillow.

who trains him in the old ways of the Running Braves, the Moscondagas, who in Jake's words:

> ... gave people hope, strength, Gave 'em the message, You don't have to feel bad about yourself, don't have to drink yourself to death, don't have to do everything the white man says. That's why the white man broke up the Running Braves.

Jake is clearly interested in training Sonny for more than boxing as he talks to him about getting control of the Hawk that is inside himself (i.e., the fear that he must turn into fury when he boxes and into wisdom and control when he's outside of the ring). Jake uses Native American metaphors that are mystical in nature, but midway through the book he drops the metaphors and comes right out and explains why he's working so hard to train Sonny:

> There's gonna be big troubles here someday. . . . White man's gonna figure out he can use this raggedy place. For gambling maybe, or to dump garbage. Laws are different on the Res. Gonna wave big money around. Moscondagas gonna be set against each other. Chiefs ain't strong enough to hold the Nation together. The People gonna need a brave.

Sports are a natural place for writers to look at interracial tensions because it's through sports that many young adults first come in contact with people outside of their own little groups. Good books that explore relationships between black and white athletes include Bruce Brooks' *The Moves Make the Man*, Frances A. Miller's *Losers and Winners*, and Cynthia Voigt's *The Runner*. Gary Soto uses sports as a common denominator in his stories about California Hispanics (e.g., the title story in *Baseball in April and Other Stories* and "Wrestling" in *A Summer Life*).

A. E. Cannon's *The Shadow Brothers* is about Marcus and Henry, who have been brothers ever since Henry came to Marcus' family as a seven-year-old foster child from the Navajo reservation. During their junior year in high school, Frank, a Hopi with "a chip on his soldier the size of a very large boulder," enrolls in their suburban high school. The three boys are runners, but their running is only the backdrop to the bigger story of Henry's growing awareness of being Navajo. Contrary to the school counselor's expectations that two "Indian boys" would become friends, Henry and Frank never hit it off. Nevertheless, Frank is partly responsible for Henry's growing awareness of his family background and his decision to return to the reservation. Henry told Marcus of his decision while they were running:

> I stopped dead in my tracks. Henry stopped too. He turned to face me. Neither of us said anything. We just stood there in the middle of the road staring at each other. Even though it was cool outside, I was covered with sweat, and so was Henry. Both of us were breathing hard.

Sports books are a natural place for authors to explore interracial tensions, as in Robert Lipsyte's *The Brave* (HarperCollins, 1991), Bruce Brooks' *The Moves Make the Man* (HarperCollins, 1984), and A. E. Cannon's *The Shadow Brothers* (Delacorte, 1992).

"I guess I just want you to tell me it's okay," said Henry, and he was pleading now, "even if you don't understand—"

"Well, you sure as hell got that one right!" I exploded. "The reservation instead of here?"

The boys spend a painful month avoiding the subject of Henry's leaving, but the day after school's out, Henry leaves just the same. Whether he will return for his senior year is left unanswered, and the books ends in midsummer with Marcus explaining:

I've started running at night now—just like Henry used to. Like Henry, I'm not the world's greatest letter writer, so this is my strange little way of keeping in touch with him. I run the same course we ran together at night. I run to the mouth of the canyon and back.

. . . When I run I like to think that Henry's running somewhere, too, late at night out in the desert, that rock-rimmed world of his where I don't belong. I hope that he's running straight and strong toward whatever it is he wants to find and that the ghost at his heels is gone.

On clear bright nights like this one I can see him in my mind's eye, running across the desert's red dirt with the moon in his eyes.

And the stars in his hair.

Girls in Sports

The April 15, 1992, issue of *The Chronicle of Higher Education* included several articles on the issue of gender and sports. On the happy side, one story showed a 100 percent increase in the numbers of women athletic directors at I-A universities (the number went from one to two). On the not-so-happy side was a story about a sex discrimination lawsuit filed by nine women at Brown University. They claimed that the university discriminates against women in its athletics program, most recently in its decision to eliminate varsity women's gymnastics and volleyball. Since 1990, three other schools (The University of New Hampshire, University of Oklahoma, and the College of William and Mary) reinstated teams under threats of similar suits charging the universities with violating Title IX of the Education Amendments of 1972, which requires institutions receiving federal aid to treat men and women equally. Another article reported on a House of Representatives panel investigating what the National Collegiate Athletic Association is doing to encourage gender equity in sports. Representative Cardiss Collins from Colorado noted that men receive more than two-thirds of athletic scholarship money, and men's sports receive more than three-quarters of the operation's funds. She added:

> If schools had special programs for male scientists, or if they designated two-thirds of their academic scholarships for men, we would be outraged. We should have similar outrage with respect to sports.[1]

Nevertheless, tremendous changes have occurred in relation to females and sports during the twenty years since Title IX was enacted. One of these changes has been the development of a body of sports literature for girls. And at least with young children, there are movements toward treating boys and girls the same as reflected in nonfiction, how-to books about, for example, soccer, tennis, running, swimming, and physical fitness. The successful magazine *Sports Illustrated for Kids* has many girl readers, and its publishing program includes books aimed at girls (e.g., *Steffi Graf* by Laura Hilgers). The fame and success of young women athletes has probably done more than anything else to inspire girls to take athletics seriously. A good book showing there's more than muscles involved is Pat Connolly's *Coaching Evelyn: Fast, Faster, Fastest Woman in the World*. Connolly, the first woman track-and-field coach at UCLA, now lives in Silver Spring, Maryland, where she coaches privately. This is her story of working with runner Evelyn Ashford, who won two gold medals at the 1984 Olympics and a silver and a gold in 1988. Nonfiction books about other successful athletes include *Mary Lou: Creating an Olympic Champion* by Mary Lou Retton and Bela Karolyi, *Martina* by Martina Navratilova with George Vecsey, and *Running Tide* by Joan Benoit with Sally Baker. Karen Stabiner's *Courting Fame: The Perilous Road to Women's Tennis Stardom* and John Feinstein's *Hard Courts: Real Life on the Profe$$ional Tennis Tours* are good for more mature readers.

Writer R. R. Knudson deserves considerable credit for opening the door to sports fiction for girls. In 1972, the same year that Title IX was passed, she published *Zanballer,* a fairly light problem novel about an athletic high school girl named Roxanne, but called Zan, and her friend Rinehart. By now, there are close to ten books about Zan and Rinehart, including *Zanboomer, Fox Running,* and *Rinehart Shouts.* Knudson was a precursor of things to come in choosing girls' sports as an appealing new topic and in bringing her same characters back for several different stories. However, the Zan books are not the typical series books, because they focus on different sports and bring in new characters to play important roles. Also, they're much more sophisticated than such series for young teens as Little, Brown's The Pink Parrots, about an all-girl baseball team; Fawcett's Silver Skates, about the boys and girls at Coach Mastroni's Lake Placid Skating School; Scholastic's The Gymnasts, about the girls on the Pinecones gymnastics team; and Fawcett's Perfect Ten, about three high school freshmen determined to become champion gymnasts.

It's ironic that the success of some of the books featuring girl athletes will contribute to making themselves obsolete. They grab readers' attention mainly by focusing on how unusual it is for a girl to be in a particular athletic situation. But once it becomes commonplace for girls to be physically competitive, such books as Jerry Spinelli's *There's a Girl in My Hammerlock,* Christi Killien's *Rusty Fertlanger, Lady's Man,* and Thomas Dygard's *Forward Pass* won't be as intriguing.

But there's still a long way to go, and it's probably a safe bet to say that in any high school or public library considerably more than half the money spent on sports-related books will be on books aimed at male readers. One of our students, Teri Rueth-Brandner, searched out some of the less well-known but appealing books about girl athletes (see her article, "Sports Fiction for Young Women: Not Enough of a Good Thing," in the June 1991 *Voice of Youth Advocates*). Among the titles she recommends are David Klass's *Different Season,* about a softball player who tries out for boys' baseball; Elizabeth Harlan's *Footfalls,* about a talented runner on the varsity track team who must learn to deal with her father's death; Tim Kennemore's *The Fortunate Few,* about a highly paid gymnast in England who sees the corruption that comes to big-time athletics; Robert McKay's *The Girl Who Wanted to Run the Boston Marathon,* about running and love; and Linnea A. Due's *High and Outside,* about a star softball pitcher with a drinking problem.

Rueth-Brandner's favorite novel is Tessa Duder's *In Lane Three, Alex Archer,* which tells the first-person story of fifteen-year-old Alexandra Archer. At the beginning of the book she is very close to representing New Zealand in the 1960 Rome Olympics. In the prologue she says:

I have always known that in another life I was—or will be—a dolphin. I'm silver and grey, the sleekest thing on fins, with a permanent smile on my face. I leap over and through the waves. I choose a passing yacht to dive under and hear the shouts of the children as I emerge triumphant close to the boat.

But she is drawn from her reverie by the realization that her toes are white with fright, her feet have turned to marble, and her arms feel like drunken windmills.

Duder's book, which received wide acclaim in New Zealand before being brought to the United States, is sports writing at its best. And although its setting is halfway around the world and a generation ago, it presents an appealing and believable heroine for the 1990s.

ADVENTURE STORIES

Adventure and survival stories can be more exciting than sports stories because adventure deals with real life, whereas sports involve only a game. "Once upon a time" is a magical phrase. Stated directly or implied, it opens every adventure tale and suggests action and excitement to follow. We may care about the people, but the action and violence are even more important. And the greatest of these is implied violence—something we fear may happen. The pace increases, so the action moves faster and faster, speeding us into the tale.

Robb White's *Deathwatch* epitomizes the elements of adventure novels—person versus person, person versus nature, person versus self, conflicts, tension, thrills, chills, and a hero frustrated at every turn by an inventive, devious, and cruel villain. The first paragraph forces us into the action and introduces the two actors:

> "There he is!" Madec whispered. "Keep still!" There had been a movement up on the ridge of the mountain. For a moment something had appeared between the two rock outcrops.
>
> "I didn't see any horns," Ben said.
>
> "Keep quiet!" Madec whispered fiercely.

We know from those few words that *Deathwatch* has something to do with hunting, although we have no reason yet to suspect that hunting will become an ominous metaphor. We recognize that the name *Madec* sounds harsh and seems vaguely related to the word *mad,* again without recognizing how prescient we are. Within the next few pages, we learn how carefully White has placed the clues before us. Ben crouches with his little .22 Hornet and watches Madec with his "beautifully made .385 Magnum Mauser action on a Winchester 70 stock with enough power to knock down an elephant—or turn a sleeping Gila monster into a splatter" and remembers that Madec had been willing to shoot anything that moved.

■ Madec huddled over his gun. There was an intensity in his eyes far beyond that of just hunting a sheep. It was the look of murder.

And murder is present. Before long, Madec takes a shot at a bighorn sheep, which turns out to be an old desert prospector—now quite dead—and he asks Ben to quash the incident and forget it ever happened. Ben refuses, and the book is off and running. So is Ben, running for his life, without gun, water, or food, amid hostile desert mountains and sand and a killing gun.

Madec personifies the maddened but crafty villain, able to read Ben's mind and forestall his attempts to get clothes, weapons, or water. We are almost certain Ben will win, but we wonder, because Madec is an extraordinary opponent. At each of Madec's devious turns to stop Ben from escaping, we doubt that sanity and virtue will win, just as we should in a good adventure novel. Ben changes from a calm, rational young man to a frightened, desperate animal and then into a cold, dangerous person who must think as Madec thinks to win out over the villain. Madec begins with all the power on his side—guns, water, food, and wealth. Given reality, we know that Madec must win, but given our sense of rightness and justice, we believe that he cannot be allowed to win. Ben has little interest in right or wrong after the first few pages. His interest is more elemental and believable—simple survival until he can escape.

The better adventure stories (see Table 5.1) provide believable characters, at the very least a likable and imperfect young protagonist, and a wily and dangerous antagonist (or villain). But because we are interested primarily in action, we are likely to be irritated by the intrusion of long descriptive or meditative passages. Writers must reveal characterization through the plot—what could happen, what might happen, and how these all tie together. We want surprises and turns of the screw. Heroes become entrapped, and the way to safety lies only through greater jeopardy.

The most significant literary device found in adventure stories is verisimilitude. With so much emphasis on danger, writers must provide realistic details to reassure us, despite our inner misgivings, that the tale is possible. We want to believe that the hero's frustrations and the cliff-hanging episodes really could have happened. Without that, the story is a cheat, and that we cannot tolerate. A love interest is possible but unlikely. A love may have been left behind, but none is involved in the tribulations. A girl and boy may flee together, and sex is possible (some writers would have us believe that sex is inevitable), but only as a momentary diversion.

Adventure stories are popular because boredom chafes at our souls and crowds out of our minds such practical concerns as safety and caution. But the human body—at least our own—reminds us all too quickly of risk. This may be why we prefer our adventures to come through books or, even better, through movies, where trick photography and special effects can make it easier for viewers to forget that losing is more common than winning.

Because the theme of going up against incredible odds and winning is so appealing, it's not surprising that adventure and survival stories appear in many

Table 5.1 **SUGGESTIONS FOR EVALUATING ADVENTURE STORIES**

A good adventure story has most of the positive qualities generally associated with good fiction. In addition it usually has:	A poor adventure story may have the negative qualities generally associated with poor fiction. It is particularly prone to have:
A likable protagonist with whom young readers can identify.	A protagonist who is too exaggerated or too stereotyped to be believable.
An adventure that readers can imagine happening to themselves.	Nothing really exciting about the adventure.
Efficient characterization.	Only stereotyped characters.
An interesting setting that enhances the story without getting in the way of the plot.	A long drawn-out conclusion after the climax has been reached.
Action that draws readers into the plot within the first page or so of the story.	

different genres. For example, in other chapters of this text we write about Steven Callahan's *Adrift: Seventy-six Days Lost at Sea* as a true personal experience; about Avi's sea yarn *The True Confessions of Charlotte Doyle* and J. H. Brennan's *Shiva: An Adventure of the Ice Age* as historical fiction; about Brock Cole's *The Goats* as a problem novel; about Robert C. O'Brien's *Z for Zachariah* as a dystopian look at the future; about Jean George's *Julie of the Wolves* as an accomplishment romance; and about Kathryn Lasky's *Beyond the Divide* as a western. What all these stories have in common is a young protagonist who goes against incredible odds and comes out a survivor.

Of the three basic conflicts, adventure tales usually center on person against person, although person against nature and person against self often become important as the tale unfolds and the protagonist faces frustration and possible failure. Person-against-nature stories are of two basic kinds: those in which someone is thrust into an adventure through an accident or an unforeseen set of circumstances and those in which people purposely challenge nature by going forth to explore unknown territory or to set a record of some kind. One of the most dramatic ways that people challenge nature is through mountain climbing. Recommended accounts include Sir Edmund Hillary's *Nothing Venture, Nothing Win* and Arlene Blum's *Annapurna: A Woman's Place*, which tells the story of thirteen women climbers, two of whom reached the top while two died. Elizabeth Arthur's *Beyond the Mountain* tells the story of Artemis Philips' seeking solace in the mountains of Nepal after her husband was killed in an avalanche. Elaine Brook and Julie Donnelly's *The Windhorse* shows how a mountaineer taught a blind woman to climb. Julie Tullis's *Clouds from Both Sides* is the biography of a woman who at forty-seven conquered K2 and died two days later. David Roberts' *Deborah: A Wilderness Narrative* tells of an attempted two-person climb of Mount Deborah in Alaska, while Tom Holzol and Audrey Salkeld's *First on Everest: The Mystery of Mallory and Irvine* explores the disappearance of George Mallory and Andrew Irvine, who in June of 1924 were seen for the last time 800 feet from the top of Mt. Everest.

Person-against-person stories include such spy thrillers as John Le Carré's *A Perfect Spy* and *The Spy Who Came In from the Cold* and William F. Buckley, Jr.'s *Operation Mongoose, R.I.P.* and *See You Later, Alligator*. The murder mysteries discussed later in this chapter also fall into this category, and so do some of our oldest legends (e.g., that of Robin Hood) and our newest science fiction (e.g., *Star Trek*). With either of these types of conflict, the satisfaction comes because the protagonist is able to win through overcoming his or her fears and weaknesses, which makes the stories also person against self.

Adventure Writers for Young Adults

Gary Paulsen is one of the best writers to come along for young readers in the last decade. In *Hatchet,* a young teen is the only passenger in a single-engine plane whose pilot suddenly dies. The boy panics and screams into the radio for help (there's no response) and then tries to fly the plane. It crashes into a remote Canadian lake and the boy must save himself from starvation as well as a multitude of other dangers with only the help of a hatchet and his wits. *Canyons* is another interesting survival story about two teenagers who live a century apart in canyons of the southwestern United States. Paulsen's *Voyage of the Frog* is set on a beautiful, strong, old sailboat that fourteen-year-old David inherits from his dearly loved Uncle Owen. When he takes the boat out to fulfill his uncle's request of having his ashes scattered at sea, David unexpectedly finds himself faced not just with grief but with a nine-day struggle to survive storms, sharks, and starvation. Paulsen's *The Crossing* is about Manuel Rustos, an orphaned teenager living on the mean streets of Juarez, Mexico. He makes a friend in Sergeant Locke, who crosses into Mexico from Fort Bliss to drink and forget the horrors of Vietnam. The Sergeant's tragic death opens the way for Manuel to run for the river and cross over into what he hopes will be a new life.

Another talented writer is Will Hobbs, who lives in rural Colorado and whose books reflect his interest in hiking, whitewater rafting, archeology, and natural history. *Bearstone,* about an American Indian boy sent to live with an old rancher whose wife has died, combines adventure with a story of growth and friendship. *Downriver,* the story of a group of boys and girls sent to an outdoor program designed to help troubled teenagers, comes closer to being a pure adventure. Jesse and her companions steal the counselor's van and rafts and drive to the Grand Canyon for whitewater rafting on their own.

One of the most intriguing adventure stories of recent years is Julian F. Thompson's *The Grounding of Group Six*. Some admittedly misfit teenagers, despised by their parents, who have paid to have them killed, survive the very special school where they have been sent. Thompson's novel works because

JULIAN F. THOMPSON
on Teenaged Kids

During the nearly thirty years that my "job" required me to be with teenaged kids, instead of people my own age, I got the feeling more than once that some people my own age—a former college classmate who had "made it big," for instance—had doubts about my . . . wisdom. Or perhaps my sanity, or "competitive fire."

Now that I write books about, and (mostly) for, that same constituency, I'm sometimes asked, by peers I don't know very well, if I've ever thought of writing a "real novel."

People who've been close to me, during both of these careers of mine, may have had their doubts about me, too. But they've known this, at least: I've always really loved what I was doing. "Young adults" (I never use that term except in quotes) delight me, and they always have.

But why? I hope you ask.

Not long ago, I got a two-page, hastily handwritten letter from a kid in Maine. With it came a copy of the eight-page, neatly word-processed, carefully reasoned, beautifully organized, copiously footnoted term paper she'd written about me and my books, for her eleventh-grade English class. The paper confirmed what her curious earlier letter had suggested: She was an academic star.

And much, much more. Here are two sentences from that scribbled second letter: "I think my English teacher liked it though, because now she plans to teach one of your novels next year. I hope she doesn't bump *Scarlet Letter* or *Grapes of Wrath,* though."

This kid and I have never met, but if we ever do, I know I'll like her. Already she's been great to me, in ways that characterize so many members of her age group.

First of all, she's given me a chance. She's read what books of mine she owns a "lot of times, something that I seldom do." She's let me be myself with her, and she's accepted me—though not without question. "Do you believe in the causes that you write about?" she asked in her first letter. Teenaged kids tend to be fair, I've found. They want to know about adults—who this one is, where he or she is coming from. They want to know if we are hypocrites or not. They want to find out if we understand where *they* are coming from.

And, second, she told me the entire truth and just assumed I'd not be hurt by it. I don't know if she realized *I* wouldn't want to see Hawthorne or Steinbeck "bumped" either, for the sake of me— but that's not the point. The point is that she blurted out the plain, un-proof-read truth, believing I could handle it. Earlier, she'd made it clear she liked and valued what I do; now she was letting me know she wasn't suspending her critical judgment altogether. Wonderful!

I hope she never changes much. At least in those respects. I know it's sort of silly, saying this, but teenaged kids . . . they so often give me *hope.*

Julian F. Thompson's books include *The Grounding of Group Six,* Avon, 1983; *A Band of Angels,* Scholastic, 1986; *Herb Seasoning,* Scholastic, 1990; and *Gypsyworld,* Henry Holt & Co., 1992.

he makes us care about these young people, because the novel is genuinely thrilling, and mostly because Thompson has a delightful, and sometimes morbid, sense of humor that makes the book often extraordinarily funny.

Colin Thiele's *Shadow Shark* is about two Australian cousins, Joe and Meg. Meg's dad hires his boat out to a professional shark hunter. Meg and Joe get to go along as cooks, but when the boat catches fire, the excitement of the hunt is forgotten and the two must combine all their abilities and resources to survive and to save Meg's father, who is injured and badly burned.

Otto Salassi approaches his adventure tales with tongue in cheek. *Jimmy D., Sidewinder, and Me* is about fifteen-year-old Duman Monk, who is now sitting in a jail cell writing to the judge in hopes of leniency when it comes to the sentencing. He explains how his deprived childhood and his adventures in hustling with the famous gambler led to his downfall. Salassi's *On the Ropes* is set in the early 1950s and begins with "Squint's Inheritance":

It's always a terrible thing when your mother dies, and I wish this story didn't have to begin where it does, with a funeral and all. But when your mother dies and you're almost alone in the world, well, that's a fact that makes a lot of other facts happen. One thing just stems from another.

From this innocent beginning, Squint is launched into a ten-year adventure with a rapscallion of a father whose creative show business resembles that of the Duke and the Dauphin in *Huckleberry Finn*.

MYSTERIES

Why are mysteries so popular? Basically, they are unrealistic and, as mystery writers cheerfully admit, have almost nothing to do with real-life detection by police or private agents. They demand deep suspension of our disbelief, yet the faithful gladly give it. Mysteries are mere games, but we love games. Some of us claim that we want to beat the detective to the murderer, but we rarely do, and when it happens we feel cheated.

The popularity of mystery movies (see Focus Box 5.2) and the number of hotels, ships, and individuals who sponsor parties in which a mock murder takes place, with the partygoers playing detectives, shows the entertainment value of mayhem, murder, and suspense. Because of the high entertainment value of mysteries and their relatively easy reading level, many mysteries published for a general audience find their way into the hands of teenagers.

Daniel's detection of the guilty Elders in "The Story of Susanna" in the *Apocrypha* may be the world's first detective story. However, the modern mystery begins with Edgar Allan Poe's "The Murders in the Rue Morgue," although "The Purloined Letter" (and Poe's detective, C. Auguste Dupin) is more satisfying today. Dime novel imitations of Poe soon appeared, notably Old Sleuth, Young Sleuth, Old King Brady, Cap Collier, and—best of them all—Nick Carter. The first detective novel was published in 1868—Wilkie Collins' *The Moonstone*. The world's greatest detective appeared nine years later when Sherlock Holmes (and his ever-faithful and usually befuddled Dr. Watson) moved out of Arthur Conan Doyle's *A Study in Scarlet* and into the affections of thousands of readers.

Holmes was followed by other distinctive detectives—brilliant and cocky, like Jacques Futrelle's Professor S. F. X. Van Deusen, or brilliant and humble, like G. K. Chesterton's Father Brown. Others followed and won their fans— Ellery Queen, Agatha Christie's Miss Marple and Hercule Poirot, Erle Stanley Gardner's Perry Mason, Dashiell Hammett's Sam Spade, and Raymond Chandler's Philip Marlowe. Where they left off, contemporary writers and detectives have picked up.

Writer and critic Hillary Waugh has said that the skeletons on which mysteries hang are "nothing more nor less than a series of ironclad rules." The rules are essential to present the puzzle properly and to ensure fair play. He lists them as follows:

Rule One: All clues discovered by the detective must be made available to the reader.

Rule Two: The murderer must be introduced early.

Rule Three: The crime must be significant.

Rule Four: There must be detection.

Rule Five: The number of suspects must be known and the murderer must be among them.

Rule Six: The reader, as part of the game of fair play, has the right to expect that nothing will be included in the book that does not relate to or in some way bear upon the puzzle.[2]

Types of Mysteries

The characteristics of the traditional murder mystery are well known and relatively fixed, although devotees are always interested in variations on the theme of murder. A mystery short story may settle for theft, but a novel, of course, demands murder. Accompanying crimes like blackmail or embezzlement may add to the delights of murder, but they never replace murder. The ultimate crime normally takes place a few chapters into the book, after readers have been introduced to major and minor characters, including the victim and those who might long for his death. The detective appears, clues are scattered, the investigation proceeds, the detective solves the case, the guilty are punished, the innocent are restored to their rightful place, and the world becomes right again.

Movies With Real Mysteries

And Then There Were None (1945, 98 min., black and white; Dir: René Clair; with Walter Huston and Louis Hayward) Ten people, all guilty of crimes but never convicted, are invited to a lonely island and murdered one by one.

The Big Sleep (1946, 114 min., black and white; Dir: Howard Hawks; with Humphrey Bogart and Lauren Bacall) Mix Philip Marlowe with a wealthy family and you may get murder. From Raymond Chandler's novel.

Charlie Chan in London (1934, 79 min., black and white; Dir: Eugene Forde; with Warner Oland) The detective saves a condemned man. Other fans believe *Charlie Chan in Panama* (1940, 67 min., black and white; Dir: Norman Foster; with Sidney Toler) is the best Chan mystery.

Chinatown (1974, 131 min., color; Dir: Roman Polanski; with Jack Nicholson, Faye Dunaway, and John Huston) Set in the 1930s and influenced by Chandler, an enigmatic detective falls for a femme fatale and finds murder.

The Kennel Murder Case (1933, 73 min., black and white; Dir: Michael Curtiz; with William Powell and Mary Astor) A suicide that Philo Vance thinks is a murder is connected to a fancy dog show. An ingenious mystery.

Laura (1944, 85 min., black and white; Dir: Otto Preminger; with Gene Tierney, Dana Andrews, and Clifton Webb) Vera Caspary's novel about a detective who falls in love with a corpse who doesn't stay dead.

The Maltese Falcon (1941, 100 min., black and white; Dir: John Huston; with Humphrey Bogart, Mary Astor, Sydney Greenstreet, and Peter Lorre) The search for the fabulous statue and the killer of Bogart's partner. From Dashiell Hammett's novel.

Murder, My Sweet (1944, 95 min., black and white; Dir: Edward Dmytryk; with Dick Powell and Claire Trevor) Philip Marlowe tries to find an ex-con's old girl friend and finds murder. From Raymond Chandler's *Farewell, My Lovely.*

Narrow Margin (1952, 70 min., black and white; Dir: Richard Fleischer; with Charles McGraw and Marie Winsor) A cop accompanies a gangster's wife on a train trip to a trial. Much better than the 1990 movie version.

The Penguin Pool Murder (1932, 70 min., black and white; Dir: George Archainbaud; with Edna May Oliver and James Gleason) A schoolteacher and a policeman team solve a murder in an aquarium. First of a brief mystery series about Hildegarde Withers.

The Spiral Staircase (1946, 83 min., black and white; Dir: Robert Siodmak; with Dorothy McGuire, George Brent, and Ethel Barrymore) A madman kills those who are handicapped, and McGuire plays a maid who is mute.

The Thin Man (1934, 93 min., black and white; Dir: W. S. Van Dyke; with William Powell and Myrna Loy) The death of an inventor working on a secret sets off the first of the "Thin Man" series. Great mystery-comedy.

Shannon Ocork has divided mysteries into the following six types.[3]

1. *The amateur detective*. At least in the older stories, the amateur detective was male (e.g., C. August Dupin or Sherlock Holmes and later Rex Stout's Nero Wolfe). These detectives are altruistic and usually optimistic. They are bright and see what others do not. Sometimes called traditional, golden-age, or classic mysteries (see some of them included in Focus Box 5.3), these flourished from the 1920s through the 1940s.

2. *The cozy mystery*. These stories are very close to the amateur detective stories. They are usually set in a small English village, although New England is increasingly popular. Agatha Christie, who began writing in the 1920s, is the most obvious writer of cozies. She scattered her best books throughout her life. Her 1939 *And Then There Were None* is her best book without a detective. Others include her 1950 *A Murder Is Announced,* a Miss Marple book, and her 1968 *By the Pricking of My Thumbs,* in which the usually tiresome Tommy and Tuppence Beresford stumble into a believable mystery.

3. *The puzzle*. These stories are exercises in ingenuity as we are led into an intricate murder, with the detective daring us to figure out the end of the story. Ellery Queen's early mysteries had a "Challenge to the Reader" about three or four chapters from the end, where the writer announced that we had all the clues Queen had and should be able to solve the mystery. Luckily, we rarely succeeded.

4. *The private detective*. These hard-boiled mysteries differ from other mysteries in significant ways. Private detectives lack altruistic motives. They enter cases for pay rather than for love of the chase or intellectual fondness for the puzzle. Working out of a cheerless office

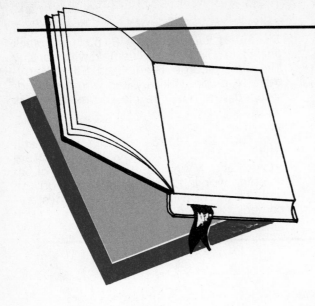

Old and New Mysteries Too Good to Miss

And Then There Were None by Agatha Christie. Dodd, Mead, 1939. Guilty people who escaped punishment are isolated and killed off one by one.

Buried for Pleasure by Edmund Crispin (Bruce Montgomery). Lippincott, 1949. A professor in England takes a holiday to run for political office, only to learn that death is easier to find than votes.

The Cherry Blossom by Robert Barnard. Scribner's, 1988. Scotland Yard's Perry Trethowan attends a romance writers' conference in Norway and learns they can be as petty and nasty—and murderous—as other people.

Eye of the Storm by Marcia Muller. Mysterious Press, 1989. Sharon McCone, private investigator for a law firm, visits her sister who's getting a bed-and-breakfast ready for business in the Sacramento delta. Then death comes visiting.

Farewell, My Lovely by Raymond Chandler. Knopf, 1940. Philip Marlowe is hired by a hulk of a man to find a beautiful woman. One of the great ones.

A Great Deliverance by Elizabeth George. Bantam, 1988. A priest finds Roberta Teys with an axe in her lap, sitting next to her decapitated father.

The Greek Coffin Mystery by Ellery Queen (Frederic Dannay and Manfred B. Lee). Little, Brown, 1932. An art dealer dies, as does a forger, and a great painting is stolen. Ellery Queen challenges the reader to solve the case before he does.

The Hound of the Baskervilles by Arthur Conan Doyle. 1902. Sherlock Holmes saves Sir Henry Baskerville from the legendary, ghostly hound on the moors of Dartmoor.

The Maltese Falcon by Dashiell Hammett. Knopf, 1930. Sam Spade and others search for a statue of a black bird worth $2 million.

A Murder Is Announced by Agatha Christie. Dodd, Mead, 1950. The best of all the Miss Marple mysteries. A murder is announced in an English village newspaper and the murder happens on schedule.

Murder on the Yellow Brick Road by Stuart Kaminsky. St. Martin's, 1977. The first Toby Peters story about a private investigator in the 1930s and 1940s. Here he investigates a killing on the set of *The Wizard of Oz*.

The Old Contemptibles by Martha Grimes. Little, Brown, 1991. Melrose Plant and Scotland Yard's Richard Jury work on a case in the Lake District in England involving a family with a history of unnatural deaths.

Phantom Lady by William Irish (Cornell Woolrich). Simon and Schuster, 1942. An innocent man is convicted of murder, and the woman who loves him sets out to find the murderer.

The Poison Oracle by Peter Dickinson. Pantheon, 1974. A classic locked-room mystery, but this locked room is in a zoo, and there is a witness to the murder, a chimpanzee.

An Unsuitable Job for a Woman by P. D. James. Scribner's, 1972. Cordelia Gray investigates a case officially called a suicide, but the victim's father believes it is murder.

When the Wind Blows by Cyril Hare (Henry Cecil). HarperCollins, 1950. A great concert violinist is killed with plenty of suspects waiting in the wings.

---

and around even less cheerful people, they are tired and cynical about the courts, the police, class distinctions, and life in general. Many are former police officers who left the force under a cloud. They have seen too much of the seamy world to feel hope for anything or anyone, and they know that detective work is hard and mostly routine and dull. With patience any bright person could do what they do. Not only does violence come with the territory, it is the territory. Moreover, we are surprised, even disappointed, if the violence isn't there.

5. *The police procedural.* Police procedurals are often the most believable mysteries, since the central characters are officers doing their mundane jobs and tracking down murderers with scientific methods and machines available only to the police. The books of Ed McBain are probably the most popular police procedurals today.

6. *The thriller.* These are usually spy thrillers. They may have bits of mystery tucked into them, but as in Ian Fleming's James Bond series, the mystery involves not so much who did it as how our hero can escape his latest impossible situation with even more than his usual derring-do.

Today's Popular Writers

Some of today's mystery writers (see Focus Box 5.3) may defy such neat classifications as the preceding, but certainly their books share the same characteristics. Sue Grafton is one of the hottest new writers, and her detective, Kinsey Millhone, is a great creation. Grafton's alphabetical series (e.g., *"A" Is for Alibi, "D" Is for Deadbeat, "H" Is for Homicide*) shows Millhone working as an insurance investigator in Santa Teresa (the name Ross Macdonald gave

Santa Barbara in his mysteries). Readers meet Kinsey Millhone in *"A" Is for Alibi:*

> My name is Kinsey Millhone. I'm a private investigator, licensed by the state of California. I'm thirty-two years old, twice divorced, no kids. The day before yesterday I killed someone and the fact weighs heavily on my mind. I'm a nice person and I have a lot of friends. My apartment is small but I like living in a cramped space. I've lived in trailers most of my life, but lately they've been getting too elaborate for my taste, so now I live in one room, a "bachelorette." I don't have houseplants. I spend a lot of time on the road and I don't like leaving things behind. Aside from the hazards of my profession, my life has always been ordinary, uneventful, and good. Killing someone feels odd to me and I haven't quite sorted it through. I've already given a statement to the police, which I initialed page by page and then signed. I filled out a similar report for the office files. The language in both documents is neutral, the terminology oblique, and neither says quite enough.

In this relatively short paragraph, Grafton lets us know who Kinsey Millhone is, not merely the obvious information but details that tell us about the real Millhone—her taste in apartments, her dislike for stuff she'll have to leave behind, the effect of her killing another human being, and her pawky wit ("The day before yesterday I killed someone and the fact weighs heavily on my mind").

In beginning her story this way, Grafton was following the advice of the Roman poet and critic Horace, who urged writers to begin *in medias res.* Ed McBain (Evan Hunter) uses a similar technique of opening in the middle of a story in his recent 87th Precinct novel, *Widows.* But notice how he can get more quickly into the plot because readers already know detective Steve Carella from earlier books.

> She'd been brutally stabbed and slashed more times than Carella chose to imagine. The knife seemed to have been a weapon of convenience, a small paring knife that evidently had been taken from the bartop where a bottle opener with a matching wooden handle sat beside a half-full pitcher of martinis, an ice bucket, and a whole lemon from which a narrow sliver of skin was missing.

No one writes police procedurals like Ed McBain. His books may be fiction, but they describe a very real world inhabited by policemen of the 87th Precinct in Isola (presumably New York City). Although they usually feature detective Steve Carella, they are mostly about the plodding, lackluster grind of police officers sifting through this and blundering through that to find out who has done what to whom. *Kiss* is about betrayal and bitterness. It focuses on Carella, who attends the trial of the man who killed his father. McBain also writes straight mysteries, which are not police procedurals and which feature Matthew Hope. *Three Blind Mice* is the latest book in this fine series.

Sara Paretsky is a newcomer to mystery writing. *Indemnity Only* introduces us to her V.I. Warshawski, private investigator, who is tough and drinks Johnny Walker Black Label. Proof that Warshawski is not typical of most private eyes comes in the first few lines of *Guardian Angel:*

> Hot kisses covered my face, dragging me from deep sleep to the rim of consciousness. I groaned and slid deeper under the covers, hoping to sink back into the well of dreams.

But it's not male passion that bothers V. I.; it's her dog, Peppy, wanting to be taken on a walk. Peppy is also due for puppies, and the old woman whose male dog impregnated Peppy has irritated many of her neighbors with her free-roaming canines. When the old woman winds up in the hospital with a broken hip, some neighbors take her dogs to be destroyed. V. I. is outraged at this nasty trick and sets out to right the wrong. When another person who lives in her building hires her to find a lost friend, Warshawski is off and running on the best of her cases thus far.

In the February 1992 *English Journal,* the editors published responses to the question, "Who is your favorite writer of detective fiction?" Tony Hillerman won by a margin of ten to one. One of the reasons for Hillerman's popularity is that he does such a good job of establishing atmosphere. He does what the fine mystery writer P. D. James[4] argues all writers must do—give a sense of place. For example, Hillerman begins *The Listening Woman* by letting us see, hear, and feel the world of the Indian Reservation:

> The southwest wind picked up turbulence around the San Francisco Peak, howled across the emptiness of the Moenkopi plateau, and made a thousand strange sounds in windows of the old Hopi villages at Shongopovi and Second Mesa. Two hundred vacant miles to the north and east, it sand-blasted the stone sculptures of Monument Valley Navajo Tribal park and whistled eastward across the maze of canyons on the Utah-Arizona border. Over the arid immensity of the Nokaito Bench it filled the blank blue sky with a rushing sound. At the hogan of Hosteen Tso, at 3:17 P.M., it gusted and eddied, and formed a dust devil, which crossed the wagon track and raced with a swirling roar across Margaret Cigaret's old Dodge pickup truck and past the Tso brush arbor.

Hillerman's place may not be our place, or a place we know, but it is a place we can recognize, and it is a place we will soon know.

Hillerman has come close to breaking the boundary of mystery writers and being accepted as a fine novelist without regard to a specific genre. His Navajo police novels began appearing in 1970 with *The Blessing Way,* in which we meet officer Joe Leaphorn's detection and the villain who uses Navajo religion to protect himself. The Indian lore and the religious aspects of the book are accurate, just as they are in later Hillerman novels, including *The Dance Hall of the Dead, The Listening Woman, The Ghostway,* and *The Skinwalkers.* Joe Leaphorn and Jim Chee, Hillerman's detectives, have the best of two worlds, the Anglo and the Indian. Although they are often confused about who and what they are, they always find that ultimately they are Indian.

In *Coyote Waits,* Hillerman's Leaphorn and Chee take on the shooting of Jim Chee's friend (a killing that Chee thinks he could have prevented) and differ about how the case should be handled. As their paths cross, Hillerman turns up fascinating minor characters and old legends about ghosts (including Butch Cassidy) and introduces us to a considerable body of knowledge about American Indian religious practices, the desert environment, and the 25,000 square miles that make up the Navajo Reservation. Hillerman respects and obviously admires his Navajo policemen, just as he does his readers. Sometimes his books are mysteries; more often they are police procedurals with a mystery attached. However, they always respect people with a particular way of life.

A bonus for fans of the Hillerman mysteries is the book *Hillerman Country,* a lovely and loving paean to the beauties of the Indian country in northern Arizona, western New Mexico, and southern Utah and Colorado. Hillerman's brother, Barney, took the photographs.

Two other writers who, along with Hillerman, have established themselves as benchmark writers against whom others are judged are Robert B. Parker and Dick Francis. In *Stardust,* Parker has his one-name Boston detective, Spenser, hired out as a guard to a TV star. He tries to make sense of her wacky, boozy life and keep her safe from whoever is stalking her. Francis is an ex-steeplechase jockey who put his knowledge of horse racing and the people who inhabit the racing world to effective use. In *Hot Money,* his twenty-sixth book, an amateur jockey and son of a rich man tries to learn who is out to kill his father.

One of the ways to keep mysteries from sounding all the same is to have unusual detectives solving unusual crimes. In Randy Russell's *Caught Looking,* an ex-con investigates a disappearing Cadillac and the murder of a baseball groupie. In Paul Bishop's *Chapel of the Ravens,* a world-class goalkeeper blinded in one eye turns writer/detective and is hired by a soccer team to discover who killed a goalie. In Walter Mosley's *Devil in a Blue Dress,* a black man, desperate for work in 1948, turns detective when he's asked to find a beautiful young blond for an unnamed client. In Sandra Scoppettone's *Everything You Have Is Mine,* a New York City lesbian detective is drawn into a date rape murder, at first disguised as a suicide. In David Willis McCullough's *Think on Death,* a young Protestant minister is drawn into investigating a murder, and in Veronica Black's *A Vow of Silence,* a nun is asked by her superior to investigate some odd happenings at another convent. Perhaps the most unusual of new detective stories is Walter Satterthwait's *Wilde West,* in which Oscar Wilde, while touring America, turns detective when he finds he's under suspicion for the murder of a red-headed prostitute.

Mysteries Written for Teenagers

Mysteries written specifically for teenagers (see Focus Box 5.4) will probably be shorter than the books described earlier. The protagonists (i.e., those who solve the crime) will be bright young people who see what others fail to see. The violence is more likely to be on the edges, or outside, of the story, and usually the person killed will be connected to the protagonist (e.g., a parent or other relative, a boyfriend or girlfriend, or perhaps an adult that the young person liked or admired). The young person recovers from the grief through doing the detective work.

Of mystery writers for young adults, two authors, Patricia Windsor and Jay Bennett, stand out. Patricia Windsor's *The Christmas Killer* is not her first book, but it is her finest atmospheric thriller. A Connecticut town is terrorized by a killer who begins with Nancy Emerson before Thanksgiving. Rose Potter starts having dreams in which the murdered girl appears and hints where her body can be found. The police question Rose's honesty and sanity, wonder if she's not involved in the killing, and finally realize that Rose may be in danger herself. Sections dealing with Rose's story and the murders of more young girls alternate with sections in which the deranged killer speaks about his lust for blood. He says:

> Killing is not a bad thing. Death is easeful, death is kind. I am friends with death. It cools the boiling blood. Blood is as red as a Christmas ribbon. Blood ties a body like a Christmas package. Blood is the color of Christmas berries, baubles, all things of joy. Why shouldn't I find joy in blood?

And he does. But in the last two paragraphs of the book, imprisoned as the killer is, we realize the story may not be over. He writes:

> Let a little time pass. I will send her a letter, tied up in my own blood and sealing wax. She will know me from my work. And she will think of me again.
>
> And, before long, I will escape this place, and I will be seeing her again.

Here's an eerie and scary book, just right for the night when a reader is home alone with the wind blowing and the house creaking.

Jay Bennett's novels rarely disappoint. *Deathman, Do Not Follow Me*, his first book, is less a mystery than a fascinating story of a loner. Later books have added to Bennett's reputation and brought him many young readers. *Say Hello to the Hit Man* is a marvelously suspenseful book about a young man who gets threatening phone calls from a gangland hit man. *Sing Me a Death Song* is a cliffhanger in which a young man is the only person who can save his mother's life.

Joan Lowery Nixon's *The Dark and Deadly Pool* concerns a young girl who

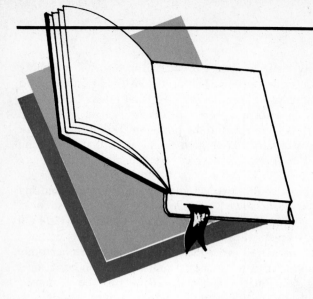

YA Mysteries

Accident by Todd Strasser. Delacorte, 1988. When his best friend is killed in a drunk-driving car crash, Matt suspects that the obvious guilty party is not guilty and sets out to learn the truth.

Die Softly by Christopher Pike. Archway Paperbacks, 1991. Herb gets to photograph the cheerleaders, including Alexa, girl of his dreams. He hides his camera in the girls' locker room and gets a terrific shot. Then a girl dies.

Fell by M. E. Kerr. HarperCollins, 1987; *Fell Back,* HarperCollins, 1989; and *Fell Down,* HarperCollins, 1991. Three psychological mysteries about John Fell, a fancy prep school, and deceptions.

Floating Illusion by Chelsea Quinn Yarbro. HarperCollins, 1986. A girl returning to Switzerland and school at the turn of the century finds that people aboard her cruise ship are being killed one after the other.

Guilt Trip by Stephen Schwandt. Atheneum, 1990. Eddie moves to Minneapolis to live with his aunt. He meets the rising young star of a local theater troupe and becomes involved in the mystery surrounding the death of the troupe's director.

Island of Ogres by Lensey Namioka. HarperCollins, 1989. A sixteenth-century mystery set on a Japanese island. A young samurai appears and finds an ineffectual local commander and strange nuns and other strange things.

Keeper of the Light by Jan O'Donnell Klaveness. Morrow, 1990. Ian returns to his grandmother's Cape Hatteras home to claim his inheritance only to find bitter local debate about her estate and her missing will.

Killing Mr. Griffin by Lois Duncan. Little, Brown, 1978. Susan may be brilliant, but she's also easily swayed when the charismatic Mark decides to kidnap the English teacher. Then the teacher dies.

Melusine by Lynne Reid Banks. HarperCollins, 1988. Roger and his family vacation at a French chateau and meet the owner's daughter, who has a secret—and a supernatural power.

Murder in a Pig's Eye by Lynn Hall. Harcourt Brace Jovanovich, 1990. A spoof of mysteries. Sixteen-year-old Bodie tries to solve a murder that never happened.

Nightmare by Willo Davis Roberts. Atheneum, 1989. A man falls from an overpass and the police call it suicide, but Nick doesn't believe it was that simple.

The Stalker   by Joan L. Nixon. Delacorte, 1985. Helped by a retired policeman, Jennifer sets out to prove that her best friend didn't kill her mother.

The Vandemark Mummy   by Cynthia Voigt. Atheneum, 1991. A young boy and his older sister are temporarily separated from their mother as the father takes a job as curator of Egyptian antiquities and runs into a mystery.

---

discovers a body floating in a pool, a typical ploy for Nixon, who usually pushes a young adult into a sudden crisis that leads to involvement in a murder.

T. Ernesto Bethancourt's series about slightly overweight and less than stunning Doris Fein, uncertain detective, is great fun for almost any reader. Teachers and librarians may mistake Doris Fein for Nancy Drew from the titles of books in the two series, but the confusion will end when readers get into any Doris Fein novel. Doris is fun; Nancy is a bore. Doris is possible; Nancy is not. *Doris Fein: Quartz Boyar* and *Doris Fein: Murder Is No Joke* are two exciting and amusing introductions to a delightful detective.

Lois Duncan's *Don't Look Behind You* is about a star tennis player whose mother is a successful author of children's books and whose father is a pilot—or so she thinks. But it turns out that he has really been working undercover for the FBI, and when her father testifies against a drug dealer, the family must go into the federal government's Witness Security Program.

Amy Ehrlich's *Where It Stops, Nobody Knows* is about a junior high student, Nina Lewis, who discovers that her mother isn't her real mother. Nina had been kidnapped as a baby, and this is why her "mother" decides to move every time that Nina gets settled in school. The plot is similar to the one in Caroline Cooney's *The Face on the Milk Carton*.

In Frances A. Miller's *The Truth Trap*, fifteen-year-old Matt McKendrick is accused of a murder he didn't commit. Matt learns a lot about human relationships in this popular book and its sequel, *Aren't You the One Who . . . ?* Sue Henry's *Murder on the Iditarod Trail* is as much an adventure story as a mystery, and in Robert R. McCammon's *Boy's Life*, a corpse tied to the steering wheel of a sunken car turns and stares at the young protagonist as if to plead for help.

STORIES OF THE SUPERNATURAL

We debated about placing this section on supernatural books in this chapter, with mysteries, or in the next chapter, with fantasy. What finally led us to leave it here was the simple fact that we have more space for it in this chapter. However, readers should realize that supernatural stories are as much akin to fantasy as to mysteries.

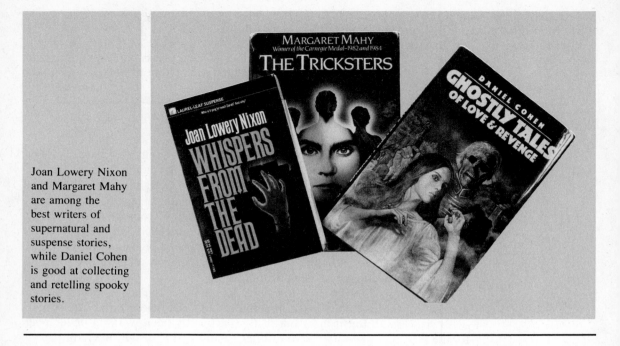

Joan Lowery Nixon and Margaret Mahy are among the best writers of supernatural and suspense stories, while Daniel Cohen is good at collecting and retelling spooky stories.

The supernatural has been an important part of our conscious fascination and our subconscious fear ever since humanity learned to communicate. That ambivalence may go back to prehistoric times, when shadows in a cave and light and dark mystified and frightened us. We have demanded answers to the unknown but have rarely found them, and so we have settled on myths and legends about superior and unseen beings. Such explanations are satisfying because when we are fighting the inexplicable, they make winning more pleasing and losing more acceptable.

Amidst all our modern knowledge and sophistication, we hold onto our fascination with the unknowable. We delight in chambers of horrors, tunnels of terror, and haunted houses. We claim to be rational beings, yet we read astrology charts. We mock the superstitions of others yet hold as pets one or two of our own, joking all the time when we toss salt over our shoulder, refuse to walk under a ladder, avoid black cats, and knock on wood. We follow customs without wondering why they came about. Black is assumed to be the appropriate dress for funerals since it is dark and gloomy and demonstrates solemnity. We may not know that black was worn at a time lost in history because spirits, sometimes malignant or perhaps indignant, were thought to linger near a corpse for a year. Wearing black made it more difficult for these evil spirits to see the living. As long as spirits were around, danger lurked. Hence, long mourning periods in black dress.

Greek and Roman literature abounds with supernatural elements. So does Elizabethan literature. Whether Shakespeare believed in ghosts or witches or things that go bump in the night is anyone's guess. Certainly, his audiences often did.

The Gothic novel of unexplained terror began with Horace Walpole's *The Castle of Otranto* in 1764. Success bred imitators, and Clara Reeves's *The Old English Baron* appeared in 1780; William Beckford's *Vathek* was published in 1786. The two greatest of the Gothics appeared in the 1790s: Ann Radcliffe's *The Mysteries of Udolpho* and Matthew Gregory Lewis' *The Monk*. Although Jane Austen did much to demolish the fad with *Northanger Abbey* in 1818, that posthumously published novel did not prevent Mary Shelley's 1818 *Franken-stein, or the Modern Prometheus,* the apotheosis of the genre, from winning admirers. The Romantic poets and prose writers continued to be half in love with the dark and the unknown, as much of Coleridge and Keats and the novels of the Brontë sisters illustrate.

Television never capitalized on the supernatural, perhaps because it is too literal a medium. Radio shows did far better, as anyone old enough to have enjoyed "Inner Sanctum" or "The Whistler" will testify. Horror movies (see Focus Box 5.5) have sometimes produced masterpieces of our internal struggles against the evil or the unknown (e.g., the episode with Michael Redgrave playing a schizophrenic ventriloquist in *Dead of Night*).

Supernatural novels have well-established ground rules. Settings are usually in an eerie or haunted house or in a place where a mysterious event occurred years ago. Some thrillers occur in more mundane places, perhaps a brownstone in New York City or a hotel shut down for the season, but readers know the mundane will remain calm only for a short time before frightening events begin and strange people come out to play. Darkness is usually essential, but not always physical darkness. The protagonist is oblivious to evil for a time but ultimately recognizes the pervasive power of the darkness of the soul. Sometimes the wife or husband sells out to evil and entices the spouse to join in a black mass. Rituals or ceremonies are essential. Family curses or pacts with the Devil have become commonplaces of the genre.

In the last edition of this textbook, Robert Westall observed that supernatural books break quite naturally into horror stories and ghost stories. The horror stories make the point that "the human organism is a frail thing of flesh subject to an infinity of abuse, and that it is painful and undignified for the human spirit to have to dwell in it." Such a depressing fact may be well worth saying, but not over and over again. And even the books by such ingenious and powerful writers as Poe and Lovecraft aren't something you would want to read if you were "on the way to build the Taj Mahal, or paint the Sistine Chapel ceiling, or even have a happy love affair."[5]

On the other hand, the ghost story is about the undying spirit, not the dying flesh. . . . [Ghosts] add an exciting fifth dimension to the often-boring four dimensions of real life. They make it possible for us to escape into the

Movies to Give You the Delights of Terror, Suspense, and the Supernatural

The Abominable Dr. Phibes (1971, 94 min., color; Dir: Robert Fuest; with Vincent Price) Scarred in a car crash that killed his wife, a mad doctor sets out to revenge his wife's death in a series of macabre murders.

The Body Snatchers (1945, 77 min., black and white, Dir: Robert Wise; with Boris Karloff and Bela Lugosi) From Robert Louis Stevenson's story, a doctor must work with evil men to get bodies for medical experiments.

The Bride of Frankenstein (1935, 75 min., black and white; Dir: James Whale; with Boris Karloff and Elsa Lanchester) The Monster gets a wife, which makes him more understandable and somehow more believable and almost human. Surprisingly funny, a true movie classic.

The Cat People (1942, 73 min., black and white; Dir: Jacques Tourneur; with Simone Simon) A shy woman lives in fear that an ancient curse will turn her into a killer. The sequel, *The Curse of the Cat People* (1944, 70 min., black and white; Dir: Guthrie von Fritsch), is equally good. Both are superior to the 1982 version.

Freaks (1932, 64 min., black and white; Dir: Tod Browning) A woman marries a carnival sideshow midget to get his money. When the other sideshow people discover what she's done, they take their awful revenge.

Ghost Breakers (1940, 82 min., black and white; Dir: George Marshall; with Bob Hope and Paulette Goddard) Goddard inherits a Cuban mansion filled with zombies and other spooky stuff. Better than most Hope films and genuinely scary.

The Haunting (1963, 112 min., black and white; Dir: Robert Wise; with Julie Harris and Clare Bloom) A group find the supernatural they're seeking in a ninety-year-old house. Based on Shirley Jackson's *The Haunting of Hill House*.

The Innocents (1961, 100 min., black and white; Dir: Jack Clayton; with Deborah Kerr) A governess, hired to take care of two children, is haunted by ghosts in a truly terrifying movie. Based on Henry James's *Turn of the Screw*. Kerr and the children are superb. A great movie on several levels.

M (1931, 99 min., black and white; Dir: Fritz Lang; with Peter Lorre) A child killer is a danger to both police and the underworld, and they combine to capture him.

The Mummy's Hand (1940, 67 min., black and white; Dir: Christy Cabanne; with Dick Foran and Peggy Moran) Archeologists find that an ancient princess they're searching for is guarded by a living mummy, Kharis.

Night of the Living Dead (1968, 96 min., black and white; Dir: George A. Romero) Made on less than a shoestring budget and with no actors that anyone would recognize, the story of flesh-eating zombies out to kill and eat seven people barricaded in a house is still terrifying.

Nosferatu (1922, 63 min., black and white; Dir: F. W. Murnau) The classic German silent film about Dracula. It's scary and eerie and has lost little of its power to shock and give viewers the shakes and the willies.

---

land of the impossible where, delightfully, anything can happen. They are also a comfort; a reassurance of our own immortality. I would adore to spend my first few years of death as a ghost, drifting round the world painlessly in the company of other friendly ghosts, seeing all the things I never got round to seeing in life because there were other boring earthbound things to be done.

He went on to explain that we need ghost stories:

In terms of love and the passing of time, we are all haunted houses, full of rooms we have shut off because of loss, or fear, or regret. To spend all our time wandering through such rooms would lead to madness. But to wander sometimes can be agonizingly sweet and rich. And never to dare to wander through them can make life a dusty boring hell.[6]

Annette Curtis Klause's *The Silver Kiss* is a good illustration of the genre. Nearly every night Zoë comes home to a dark and empty house. Her mother is in the hospital dying of cancer, and as early as page 2 readers get clues about supernatural elements. Zoë is almost as thin as her mother—"a sympathy death perhaps, she wondered half seriously. . . . Wouldn't it be ironic if she died, too, fading out suddenly when her look-alike went?" On page 3, Zoë remembers happier times with her mother, but even here there's a shadow: " 'You're a dark one,' her mother said sometimes with amused wonder. 'You're a mystery.' "

Zoë likes to walk in the neighborhood park and sit in front of the old-fashioned gazebo, where one night "a shadow crept inside, independent of natural shades." Then she saw his face:

■   He was young, more boy than man, slight and pale, made elfin by the moon. He noticed her and froze like a deer before the gun. They were trapped in each other's gaze. His eyes were dark, full of wilderness and stars. But his face was ashen. Almost as pale as his silver hair.

With a sudden ache she realized he was beautiful. The tears that prickled her eyes broke his bonds, and he fled, while she sat and cried for all things lost.

This was Zoë's first meeting with Simon, a 200-year-old vampire from Bristol, England. The story within a story where Simon explains how he became a vampire is a gem in its own right, and so is the end of the book when Zoë and Simon bid each other farewell.

As the popularity of books with supernatural themes has grown, more and more well-established authors are including supernatural elements in their books. For example, Cynthia Voigt's *Tree by Leaf* is set in the summer of 1920, when twelve-year-old Clothilde's disfigured father returns from World War I. As Clothilde faces frustration and despair, she undergoes a strange mystical experience that helps her grow.

Virginia Hamilton's *Sweet Whispers, Brother Rush* includes a wonderfully helpful uncle, who just happens to be a ghost. Mystical elements are also forces for good in Madeleine L'Engle's *A Ring of Endless Light* and Zoa Sherburne's *Why Have the Birds Stopped Singing?*

Robert Cormier stepped away from the harsh realism that supposedly is his trademark when he wrote *Fade,* a book that was inspired by an old family picture. Both the *Horn Book Magazine* and *Publishers Weekly* quoted Cormier as explaining that he had been fascinated by a photo in which one of his uncles didn't appear. "It always haunted me—why didn't my uncle appear? So I wrote a story to see what might have happened."

Fade begins in 1938, when a young French Canadian, Paul Moreaux, discovers that he has inherited a family gift/curse that comes to only one person in each generation, the ability to fade, to become invisible. At first, Paul is understandably intrigued by his new ability, but he learns soon enough that the power is more tragedy than blessing. Once after meeting a friend's sister and being smitten with love, Paul gives in to his own urges, becomes invisible, enters his friend's house, and watches horrified as his friend and the sister engage in incestuous lovemaking. Later, as he trembles from the cold of the night and the horror of what he has seen, Paul remembers a time when he had asked his Uncle Adelard about the fade.

■   "If the fade is a gift, then why are you so sad all the time?"
"Did I ever say it was a gift?" he replied.
"I thought a moment. "I guess not."
"What's the opposite of gift, Paul?"
"I don't know."
But now I knew. Or thought I knew.

The fifty years covered in *Fade* are believable, but oddly enough, Paul's supernatural gift/curse and what he does with it are more believable than the more mundane aspects of his life. Maybe that's because Cormier clearly was more interested in the supernatural parts of the book.

The sex and violence in *Fade* may prevent some readers from seeing what the book is about (i.e., that special powers are dual-edged and that we are susceptible to using our powers unwisely). We should be careful in asking God or the fates for what we most wish, since we might be cursed by having our wishes granted. Similar themes appear in Joyce Sweeney's *The Dream Collector* and in several of the light-hearted fantasy books for younger teens mentioned in Chapter Six.

The best of the humorous ghost stories are Richard Peck's Blossom Culp books, including *The Ghost Belonged to Me* and *Ghosts I Have Been*. Peck also relied on ghosts in *Voices After Midnight,* in which a family from California rents a 100-year-old townhouse for a short stay in New York. Chad, Luke, and their sister, Heidi, seek to find the truth about mysterious voices they hear and are drawn back to the great blizzard of 1888.

Among YA novelists specializing in supernatural themes, Lois Duncan has proved consistently popular. In *Summer of Fear,* Rachael Bryant's family is notified that relatives have died in a car crash, leaving a seventeen-year-old daughter, Julia, behind. The girl, who looks surprisingly mature, soon arrives and changes the lives of everyone around her. Rachael, the narrator, realizes, without knowing quite how or why, that Julia is different, somehow sinister, particularly because Julia has "the strangest eyes." The family dog Trickle clearly distrusts Julia (according to legend, animals have insight about the forces of evil). Trickle does not last long, but then neither does anyone who gets in Julia's way. Duncan's *Stranger with My Face* and *The Third Eye* were enjoyable, although not as powerful as *Summer of Fear* and the more recent *Locked in Time*.

With realistic stories American teenagers resist books from other countries, but with supernatural writing a "foreign" setting adds exotic details. Marie Gripe's *Agnes Cecelia* is a story of family secrets and resentments revealed through the supernatural powers found in an antique doll, but it's also a story of love and healing.

British novelist Robert Westall is the best YA writer in the field, but since his books are just beginning to appear in paperback in the United States, he is still finding his audience. Violence in *The Wind Eye* is powerfully implied as three youngsters find an old boat with strange designs, which they learn can take them back to St. Cuthbert's time and place. *The Watch House* carries on the theme of time shifts. A young girl's imagination is captured by an old crumbling watch house on the coast. *The Devil on the Road* is the best of Westall's supernatural tales. A university student on a holiday travels north and finds temporary employment as a caretaker of an old barn, once the home of a witch hanged 300 years before. *Break of Dark* is a fine series of chilling short stories, as is *The Haunting of Chas McGill and Other Stories. Rachel and the*

ROBERT WESTALL
on Growing Irrelevant

Do I grow irrelevant?

Eighteen years ago, when I wrote my first book, *The Machine Gunners,* I was practically drowning in a torrent of youth. My son was twelve, a disputatious, articulate twelve, who trusted me and let it all hang out, victories, defeats, lousy teachers, teenage skullduggery, the lot. I shared his TV with him, Top of the Pops, Star Trek. Daily, his friends piled through my back door to play their latest records. I was a full-time teacher, of boys from eleven to eighteen. The elevens clung to the hem of my jacket, whispering their anxieties. The eighteens left their shocking hippie magazines protruding from their briefcases, tempting me to appropriate and read them, and look suitably shocked. It was an almost sensuous pleasure to slip into my silent study at weekends and pop a sheet of paper into my typewriter. The teenage mind was as unthinkingly accessible as the air I breathed. As I said, I was practically drowning in their stream of consciousness.

Then came the first signs of trouble. My all-age school changed slowly into a Sixth Form College. As my youngest pupils became fourteen, sixteen, eighteen (and my son), the heroes of my books grew older with them. I even started a book in which the hero was a trainee accountant, and my editor asked warningly, "Are you sure you're still writing for children?"

For a while, I was saved by two nieces, aged eight and ten, who trusted me and let me into their world. But children die so quickly into adults. The eldest is now making her own living and cohabiting with a boyfriend. . . . And they were the last; after I left teaching six years ago. Now I meet one eighteen-year-old, at my writing group, once a fortnight, and all he does is convince me how far from the teen scene I now am.

Worse, since I lost contact, the teen world seems to have changed faster and faster. New experiences happen to them that will never happen to me now. The only person ever to offer *me* drugs was my doctor, and they were painkillers. My sex-life consists of long, deep, and meaningful conversations, putting the world right over a bottle of wine, with handsome, fascinating ladies who are waiting to become grandmothers. I stand in more danger of catching bubonic plague than of catching AIDS. Recently I had great difficulty measuring a wall with a young woman, because she understood feet and inches no better than I understood centimeters. I have lost all urge to make a lot of money, claw my way to the top, or trample on other people's faces doing so. I no longer care what my peer-group thinks. And in a country where one-quarter of the young are born shamelessly out of wedlock, and one-parent families are the majority, my own basic unit (which I am invariably tempted to employ in my books) of Mum, Dad, two kids, cat, dog, is steadily becoming as weird and quaint as the Addams Family.

Not that I have the slightest temptation to write about AIDS, drugs, or divorce; I was never a writer of problem-books. But my fictional young should be as sure-footed among such things (or as quickly dead) as an animal in its forest. They should think and speak differently, because they *know* such things without having to think about them; as Tolstoy's characters knew how to be Russian and Napoleonic.

What can I have to say that has the least relevance for the young today? And what can I do about it?

I suppose I could track down the young, as hunters track wild beasts; notebook at the ready for the latest item of slang and innuendo. I could ingratiatingly seek their company and their confidence. But the young have a perilously quick eye and very rude word for that kind of thing. It would be as unbecoming as draping my ample form in blue jeans and black leather. And when I used their little phrases in my next book, they would be six months out of date, and I would be told I'd never understood them in the first place.

There is, for me, of course, an easy refuge in the supernatural. The supernatural never dates, in spite of the efforts of Stephen King et al. to update it. The more obsolescent it is, the creepier. And the supernatural does allow you to write of old-fashioned things like love and hate, honor, desire, and retribution in a way that does not make the young curl their lips before the end of your first paragraph. Sin and repentance, Heaven and Hell are still fashionable in ghost stories. But the world is already too full, in my opinion, of those who bombard the young with sin and repentance in a general way, without ever getting down to the nuts and bolts of everyday reality, of the wet Monday morning when you haven't done your homework and your two best friends have ganged up and are laughing at you.

I am not yet ready to retire into being a well-paid provider of spooky titillation.

There remains one hope. The child that I was remains within me, as St. Augustine once wrote. That seventeen-year-old who built model aeroplanes, worried about keeping his place on the school football team, and slyly and shyly pursued the female of the species is as alive as he ever was, and has not forgotten a single horrible detail of *how* it was. As my editor said, I can write historical novels now without doing much research, and not put a foot wrong, because I was there and I saw it. I am as at home in 1940s and 1950s England as Tolstoy was in Napoleonic Russia.

But what use is that to the young of today? It has the value, I think, of comparison, of anthropology. When Margaret Mead wrote about growing up in Polynesia or New Guinea, we first read enthralled, and then, much more important, we turned and looked at our own lives with a fresh eye.

So, I offer you this strange creature, who really did play his guts out, for the honour of his school, believing (nearly) every word that his teachers and parents told him. Who believed in the essential goodness and fairness of the British Empire, who lived in a country where women could walk all night alone through London, without a thought of fear. Where a murder was a nine days' wonder; *any* murder. Where the word *rape* was never mentioned, where if a man offered you sweets or a lift in his car, he was only a bloke who liked kids. This strange outlandish creature had very few possessions of his own, even at the great age of eighteen, beyond an old bicycle and a secondhand tennis racket. But he had mother, father, grandmother, grandfather, aunts, and cousins, and living almost next door. And to him a forty-mile rail journey was an *enormous* adventure. And yet he had this odd gift for amusing himself and actually being happy.

Weird, huh? Almost science fiction?

But possibly invoking the question, "Why?"

If I keep that word on teenage lips, I shall die happy.

Robert Westall's books include *Ghost Abbey*, Scholastic, 1989; *Blitzcat*, Scholastic, 1989; *Echoes of War*, Farrar, Straus & Giroux, 1991; and *The Promise*, Scholastic, 1991.

Angel and Other Stories is particularly interesting for young writers, since one story, "Urn Burial," was later developed into a full-scale novel under the same title.

New Zealand's Margaret Mahy is certain to become better known as readers sample her offbeat fare, *The Tricksters, The Changeover,* and *The Haunting.* Mahy makes her readers care about her characters, which is no mean achievement, given the inherent strangeness of her plots.

Patricia Wrightson's *Balyet* is set in Australia. Jo accompanies Mrs. Willet, who cares for the sacred sites of an aboriginal tribe. But the two of them hadn't counted on the presence of Balyet, a young woman banished 1,000 years before, whose ghost wanders the hills, starved for friendship and affection.

In the last few years several YA authors have experimented with mystical elements in stories about Native Americans. Apparently, the Native American

The books shown here are more interesting because of mystical elements related to native American cultures.

settings or characters have an exotic appeal that serves as a foil to make the mystical themes more intriguing. Best known are Virginia Hamilton's 1976 *Arilla Sun Down* and Jamake Highwater's *Anpao: An American Indian Odyssey*, which was a Newbery Honor Book in 1978. Gary Paulsen has written several more recent books in which he lets the past flow into the present and future. The scene in *Dogsong* where Russel, a young Eskimo, sees the vision of his future self is especially powerful. Almost equally memorable is the relationship between the daughter of a New Mexico artist and an old Indian chief in *The Night the White Deer Died*. In *Canyons*, Paulsen writes about a contemporary white teenager who wants to earn a feeling of independence by living on his own in a southwestern canyon. He finds a skull and feels almost a compulsion to do the right thing for the Indian boy who lost his life a century ago when he entered the same canyon hoping to gain his manhood.

Such mystical elements appear in several genres; for example, Welwyn Wilton Katz's supernatural mystery, *False Face*, and Grace Chetwin's science fiction *Collidescope* in which an extraterrestrial cyborg (part human, part machine) named Hahn, a young Indian from precolonial times named Sky-Fire Trail, and a contemporary teenager named Frankie collide in space and time. Both James J. Alison's *Sing for a Gentle Rain* and Kevin Major's *Blood Red Ochre* are time travel stories bringing past and present young people together, while David Carkeet's *Quiver River* and Pamela F. Service's *Vision Quest* are problem novels in which young protagonists seek for understanding through explorations of Indian ways.

Teenagers make up a good portion of the readers of tales of exorcism and devil worship published for general adult audiences. William Blatty's *The Exorcist* and Ira Levin's *Rosemary's Baby* are standards. V. C. Andrews' books defy rational explanation, and their popularity is even more difficult to explain. Her tales of incest and general family ghoulishness and foolishness in *If There Be Thorns*, *Flowers in the Attic*, and *My Sweet Audrina* are mawkish and badly written, but no one can questions their popularity.

Leading all the writers in the field is Stephen King. A former high school English teacher, he frequently includes likable young people among his characters. And the fact that he writes about them without condescension is not lost on the audience. "The Langoliers" (from *Four Past Midnight*) is the story of a late night flight from Los Angeles to Boston. The plane goes through a time rip, and the only passengers who survive are the ten who happened to be sleeping. Fortunately, one of them is a pilot; otherwise there wouldn't have been much of a story to tell. There is also the blind Dinah, a young girl on her way to Boston for an operation on her eyes. She has such a superdeveloped sense of hearing that she is mistaken by the mad Craig Toomy, the ultimate Yuppie gone awry, as the chief Langolier. The character most closely filling the role of a young adult hero on a romantic quest is Albert Kaussner, a gifted violinist on his way to enroll in a Boston music conservatory. In his own mind he's not Albert or Al, but Ace Kaussner, "The Arizona Jew" and "The Fastest Hebrew West of the Mississippi."

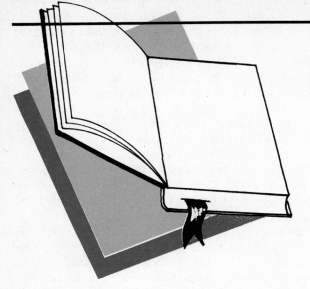

Young People and the Supernatural

The Changeover: A Supernatural Romance by Margaret Mahy. Atheneum/Margaret K. McElderry, 1984. Laura's little brother is under the spell of an evil demon and Laura sets out to use supernatural powers to rescue him.

The Cheerleader by Caroline Cooney. Scholastic, 1991. Althea wants to be popular even if it means making deals with a vampire.

Gypsies by Robert Charles Wilson. Doubleday/Foundation, 1989. Along with their psychic powers, Michael and his mother share danger as they flee for their lives.

King of the Cloud Forests by Michael Morpurgo. Viking Penguin, 1988. In the 1930s, when the Japanese invade China, fourteen-year-old Ashley Anderson escapes with his old family friend, Uncle Sung, but he is injured as the two cross the Himalayas into India. Rescue comes from the Yeti, mystical mountain people who think Ashley is a god.

The Lives of Christopher Chant by Diana Wynne Jones. Greenwillow, 1988. Fortunately for Christopher, he has nine lives. He'll need them all to get out of the trouble that his psychic powers bring to him and his parents.

Playing Beattie by Ruth Park. Atheneum, 1982. Set in Australia, this is the story of Abigail Kirk's disappointment in her parents and her accidental trip back into nineteenth-century Sydney.

Railway Ghosts and Highway Horrors by Daniel Cohen. Cobblehill, 1992. These scary stories come from popular folklore as well as from reports of unusual sightings and encounters near the scenes of accidents.

Stonewords: A Ghost Story by Pam Conrad. HarperCollins, 1990. Zoë comes to live with her grandparents and finds that she shares her name and her home with a ghost.

Those Who Hunt the Night by Barbara Hambly. Ballantine, 1988. A professor is hired by a vampire to do detective work on the mysterious deaths of fellow vampires.

Vampires: A Collection of Original Stories edited by Jane Yolen and Martin H. Greenberg. HarperCollins, 1991. These stories show that vampires are not restricted to spooky old houses or dark and stormy nights.

Wait Till Helen Comes: A Ghost Story by Mary Downing Hahn. Clarion, 1986. A seven-year-old, whose mother died in a fire, is drawn into a friendship with a child ghost.

Whispers from the Dead by Joan Lowery Nixon. Delacorte, 1989. A new home is supposed to be exciting and fun, but it's different in Sarah's new house, where she hears whispers of terrible things.

The journey turns out to be much more difficult than anything faced by Ace's mythical heroes of the Old West, and it even requires him to sacrifice his beloved violin. But at the end of the trip he is rewarded with his first love and the feeling of growth and confidence that comes with having passed a difficult test.

Stephen King's first book, *Carrie,* appeared in 1974 and sold well for a then unknown writer. From that point on, King maintained his place as *the* writer of the genre. Carrie is a young outsider, the daughter of religious fanatics, and the brunt of cruel jokes. She possesses the power of telekinesis, and she uses it to destroy the school, the students, and the town in a fit of justified rage. *Salem's Lot,* although better characterized, is something of a letdown after *Carrie,* as are *The Stand* and *The Shining,* which is possibly better known through its film version than as a novel. *Firestarter* is far better, with its portrait of an eight-year-old girl with the power to start fires merely by looking at an object. A government agency, "The Shop," learns about the child and launches a search for her. King effectively indicts this bureaucracy become evil. *Firestarter* may not be King's best book, but it is his most penetrating study of character and our country.

King's later books include *Different Seasons,* a collection of four novelettes; *Cujo,* a messy and disappointingly obvious horror tale of the lovable St. Bernard dog gone mad; and *Christine,* the story of a 1958 Plymouth Fury gone equally mad. *Pet Sematary* is an acknowledged variation of W. W. Jacobs' 1904 "The Monkey's Paw," which has a power that cannot be ignored, although it remains something of a prolonged ghastly joke. *The Tommyknockers* and *It* added a chill or two to King's repertoire, but little more.

Because young adults are curious and relatively open about exploring new ideas, the supernatural appeals to them (see Focus Box 5.6). Treading on spooky ground is a social experience—one not always approved of by censorious parents—and teenagers delight in rounding up friends to see a scary movie or discussing the possibilities of ghosts and goblins and worse horrors. This means that with or without approval from adults, supernatural stories are likely to remain popular with young readers.

NOTES

[1]"NCAA Officials Try to Counter Charges of Sex Bias in Sports," *The Chronicle of Higher Education* (April 15, 1992): A43.

[2]Hillary Waugh, "What Is a Mystery?" *The Basics of Writing and Selling Mysteries and Suspense: A Writer's Guide* 10 (1991): 6–8.

[3]Shannon Ocork, "What Type of Mystery Are You Writing?" *The Basics of Writing and Selling Mysteries and Suspense: A Writer's Guide* 10 (1991): 10–12.

[4]P. D. James, in Sylvia Burack, ed., *Writing Mystery and Crime Fiction* (Fiction, Inc., 1985), p. 93.

[5]Robert Westall, "On Nightmares for Money," *Literature for Today's Young Adults* (Scott, Foresman, 1989), p. 166.

[6]Westall, "On Nightmares for Money," p. 167.

OTHER TITLES MENTIONED IN THE TEXT OF CHAPTER FIVE

Alison, James J. *Sing for a Gentle Rain*. Atheneum, 1990.

Andrews, V. C. *Flowers in the Attic*. Simon & Schuster, 1979.

———. *If There Be Thorns*. Simon & Schuster, 1981.

———. *My Sweet Audrina*. Simon & Schuster, 1982.

Arthur, Elizabeth. *Beyond the Mountain*. Holt, Rinehart and Winston, 1983.

Avi. *The True Confessions of Charlotte Doyle*. Orchard, 1990.

Baczewski, Paul. *Just for Kicks*. Lippincott, 1990.

Bennett, Jay. *Deathman, Do Not Follow Me*. Hawthorne, 1968.

———. *Say Hello to the Hit Man*. Delacorte, 1976.

———. *Sing Me a Death Song*. Watts, 1990.

Benoit, Joan, with Sally Baker. *Running Tide*. Knopf, 1987.

Bethancourt, T. Ernesto. *Doris Fein: Murder Is No Joke*. Holiday House, 1982.

———. *Doris Fein: Quartz Boyar*. Holiday House, 1980.

Bishop, Paul. *Chapel of the Ravens*. Tor, 1991.

Black, Veronia. *A Vow of Silence*. St. Martin's, 1990.

Blatty, William. *The Exorcist*. HarperCollins, 1971.

Blum, Arlene. *Annapurna: A Woman's Place*. Sierra Club Books, 1980.

Brennan, J. H. *Shiva: An Adventure of the Ice Age*. Lippincott, 1989.

Brooks, Bruce. *The Moves Make the Man*. HarperCollins, 1984.

Buckley, William F. *Operation Mongoose, R.I.P.* Random House, 1987.

———. *See You Later, Alligator*. Doubleday, 1985.

Callahan, Steven. *Adrift: Seventy-six Days Lost at Sea*. Hughton Mifflin, 1986.

Cannon, A. E. *The Shadow Brothers*. Delacorte, 1990.

Carkeet, David. *Quiver River*. HarperCollins, 1991.

Chetwin, Grace. *Collidescope*. Bradbury, 1990.

Christie, Agatha. *By the Pricking of My Thumbs*. Dodd, Mead, 1968.

———. *A Murder Is Announced*. Dodd, Mead, 1950.

Cole, Brock. *The Goats*. Farrar, Straus & Giroux, 1987.

Connolly, Pat. *Coaching Evelyn: Fast, Faster, Fastest Woman in the World.* HarperCollins, 1991.

Christopher, Matt. *Takedown.* Little, Brown, 1990.

Cooney, Caroline. *The Face on the Milk Carton.* Bantam, 1990.

Cormier, Robert. *Fade.* Delacorte, 1988.

Crutcher, Chris. *Athletic Shorts: Six Short Stories.* Greenwillow, 1991.

———. *The Crazy Horse Electric Game.* Greenwillow, 1987.

———. *Running Loose.* Greenwillow, 1983.

———. *Stotan!* Greenwillow, 1986.

Davis, Terry. *Vision Quest.* Viking, 1979.

Due, Linnea A. *High and Outside.* HarperCollins, 1980.

Duder, Tessa. *In Lane Three, Alex Archer.* Houghton Miflin, 1989.

Duncan, Lois. *Don't Look Behind You.* Delacorte, 1989.

———. *Locked in Time.* Little, Brown, 1985.

———. *Summer of Fear.* Little, Brown, 1976.

———. *The Third Eye.* Little, Brown, 1984.

———. *Stranger with My Face.* Little, Brown, 1981.

Dygard, Thomas. *Forward Pass.* Morrow, 1989.

———. *Halfback Tough.* Morrow, 1986.

———. *Tournament Upstart.* Morrow, 1984.

Ehrlich, Amy. *Where It Stops, Nobody Knows.* Dial, 1988.

Feinstein, John. *Hard Courts: Real Life on the Profe$$ional Tennis Tours.* Villard Books, 1991.

Francis, Dick. *Hot Money.* Putnam, 1988.

George, Jean. *Julie of the Wolves.* HarperCollins, 1972.

Grafton, Sue. *"A" Is for Alibi.* Holt, 1982.

———. *"D" Is for Deadbeat.* Henry Holt, 1987.

———. *"H" Is for Homicide.* Henry Holt, 1991.

Grey, Zane. *The Shortstop.* Morrow, 1992 (originally published 1909).

———. *The Young Pitcher.* Morrow, 1992 (originally published 1911).

Gripe, Maria, translated by Rika Lesser. *Agnes Cecelia.* HarperCollins, 1990.

Hamilton, Virginia. *Arilla Sun Down.* Greenwillow, 1979.

———. *Sweet Whispers, Brother Rush.* Philomel, 1982.

Harlan, Elizabeth. *Footfalls.* Atheneum, 1982.

Henry, Sue. *Murder on the Iditarod Trail.* Atlantic Monthly, dist. by Little, Brown, 1991.

Highwater, Jamake. *Anpao: An American Indian Odyssey.* Lippincott, 1977.

Hilgers, Laura. *Steffi Graf.* Little, Brown/Sports Illustrated for Kids Books, 1990.

Hillary, Sir Edmund. *Nothing Venture, Nothing Win.* Coward McCann Geoghegan, 1975.

Hillerman, Tony. *The Blessing Way.* HarperCollins, 1970.

———. *Coyote Waits.* HarperCollins, 1990.

———. *The Dance Hall of the Dead.* HarperCollins, 1973.

———. *The Ghostway.* HarperCollins, 1985.

———. *The Listening Woman.* HarperCollins, 1978.

———. *The Skinwalkers.* HarperCollins, 1987.

Hillerman, Tony, and Barney Hillerman. *Hillerman Country.* HarperCollins, 1991.

Hobbs, Will. *Bearstone.* Atheneum, 1989.

———. *Downriver.* Atheneum, 1991.

Holzol, Tom and Audrey Salkeld. *First on Everest: The Mystery of Mallory and Irvine.* Henry Holt, 1986.

Isberg, Emily. *Peak Performance, Sports, Science, and the Body in Action.* Simon & Schuster, 1989.

Katz, Welwyn Wilton. *False Face.* Macmillan, 1988.

Kennemore, Tim. *The Fortunate Few.* Coward, 1981.

Killien, Christi. *Rusty Fertlanger, Lady's Man*. Houghton Mifflin, 1988.

King Stephen. *Carrie*. Doubleday, 1974.

_____. *Christine*. Viking, 1983.

_____. *Cujo*. Viking, 1981.

_____. *Different Seasons*. Viking, 1982.

_____. *Firestarter*. Viking, 1980.

_____. *Four Past Midnight*. Viking, 1990.

_____. *It*. Viking, 1986.

_____. *Pet Sematary*. Doubleday, 1983.

_____. *Salem's Lot*. Doubleday, 1975.

_____. *The Shining*. Doubleday, 1977.

_____. *The Stand*. Doubleday, 1978.

_____. *The Tommyknockers*. Putnam, 1987.

Klass, David. *Different Season*. Lodestar, 1988.

_____. *Wrestling with Honor*. Lodestar, 1989.

Klause, Annette Curtis. *The Silver Kiss*. Delacorte, 1990.

Knudson, R. R. *Fox Running*. HarperCollins, 1975.

_____. *Rinehart Shouts*. Farrar, Straus & Giroux, 1987.

_____. *Zanballer*. Delacorte, 1972.

_____. *Zanboomer*. HarperCollins, 1978.

Knudson, R. R., and May Swenson, compilers. *American Sports Poems*. Orchard Books, 1988.

Lasky, Kathryn. *Beyond the Divide*. Macmillan, 1983.

Le Carré, John. *A Perfect Spy*. Knopf, 1986.

_____. *The Spy Who Came in from the Cold*. Coward, McCann, 1963.

Lehrman, Robert. *Juggling*. HarperCollins, 1982.

L'Engle, Madeleine. *A Ring of Endless Light*. Farrar, Straus & Giroux, 1980.

Levin, Ira. *Rosemary's Baby*. Random House, 1967.

Lewis, Matthew Gregory. *The Monk*. Grove Weidenfeld, 1952 (originally published in 1797).

Lipsyte, Robert. *The Brave*. HarperCollins, 1991.

_____. *The Contender*. HarperCollins, 1967.

_____. *Free to Be Muhammed Ali*. HarperCollins, 1979.

Mahy, Margaret. *The Changeover: A Supernatural Romance*. Atheneum, 1984.

_____. *The Haunting*. Atheneum, 1982.

_____. *The Tricksters*. McElderry, 1987.

Major, Kevin. *Blood Red Ochre*. Delacorte, 1989.

McBain, Ed (Evan Hunter). *Kiss*. Morrow, 1992.

_____. *Three Blind Mice*. Little, Brown, 1990.

_____. *Widows*. Morrow, 1991.

McCammon, Robert R. *Boy's Life*. Pocket, 1991.

McCullough, David Willis. *Think on Death*. Viking, 1991.

McKay, Robert. *The Girl Who Wanted to Run the Boston Marathon*. Elsevier/Dutton, 1982.

Miller, Frances A. *Aren't You the One Who . . . ?* Macmillan, 1983.

_____. *Losers & Winners*. Ballantine/Fawcett, 1986.

_____. *The Truth Trap*. Ballantine/Fawcett, 1984.

Mosley, Walter. *Devil in a Blue Dress*. Norton, 1990.

Myers, Walter Dean. *Hoops*. Delacorte, 1981.

_____. *The Outside Shot*. Delacorte, 1984.

Navratilova, Martina, with George Vecsay. *Martina*. Knopf/Borzoi, 1985.

Naughton, Jim. *My Brother Stealing Second*. HarperCollins, 1989.

Nixon, Joan Lowery. *The Dark and Deadly Pool*. Delacorte, 1987.

O'Brien, Robert C. *Z for Zachariah*. Atheneum, 1975.

Paretsky, Sara. *Guardian Angel*. Delacorte, 1992.

_____. *Indemnity Only*. Delacorte, 1982.

Parker, Robert B. *Stardust*. Putnam, 1990.

Paulsen, Gary. *Canyons*. Delacorte, 1990.

_____. *The Crossing*. Orchard, 1987.

_____. *Dogsong*. Bradbury, 1985.

_____. *Hatchet*. Bradbury, 1987.

_____. *The Night the White Deer Died*. Delacorte, 1978.

_____. *Voyage of the Frog*. Orchard, 1989.

Peck, Richard. *The Ghost Belonged to Me*. Viking, 1975.

_____. *Ghosts I Have Been*. Viking, 1977.

_____. *Voices After Midnight*. Delacorte, 1989.

Retton, Mary Lou, and Bela Karolyi. *Mary Lou: Creating an Olympic Champion*. McGraw-Hill, 1986.

Roberts, David. *Deborah: A Wilderness Narrative*. Vanguard, 1970.

Russell, Randy. *Caught Looking*. Perfect Crime/Doubleday, 1992.

Salassi, Otto R. *Jimmy D., Sidewinder, and Me*. Greenwillow, 1987.

_____. *On the Ropes*. Greenwillow, 1981.

Satterthwait, Walter. *Wilde West*. St. Martin's, 1991.

Scoppettone, Sandra. *Everything You Have Is Mine*. Little, Brown, 1991.

Service, Pamela F. *Vision Quest*. Atheneum, 1989.

Sherburne, Zoa. *Why Have the Birds Stopped Singing?* Morrow, 1974.

Soto, Gary. *Baseball in April and Other Stories*. Harcourt Brace Jovanovich, 1990.

_____. *A Summer Life*. (University Press of New England, 1990), Dell, 1991.

Spinelli, Jerry. *There's a Girl in My Hammerlock*. Simon & Schuster, 1991.

Stabiner, Karen. *Courting Fame: The Perilous Road to Women's Tennis Stardom*. HarperCollins, 1986.

Sweeney, Joyce. *The Dream Collector*. Delacorte, 1989.

Thiele, Colin. *Shadow Shark*. HarperCollins, 1988.

Thompson, Julian F. *The Grounding of Group Six*. Avon, 1983.

Tullis, Julie. *Clouds from Both Sides*. Sierra Club Books, 1987.

Tunis, John R. *Go Team Go*. Morrow, 1991 (originally published 1954).

_____. *Highpockets*. Morrow, 1990 (originally published 1948).

_____. *Keystone Kids*. Harcourt Brace Jovanovich, 1990 (originally published 1943).

_____. *The Kid Comes Back,* edited by David Rather. Morrow, 1990 (originally published 1946).

_____. *Rookie of the Year*. Harcourt Brace Jovanovich, 1990 (originally published in 1944).

Voigt, Cynthia. *The Runner*. Atheneum, 1985.

_____. *Tree by Leaf*. Atheneum, 1988.

Wells, Rosemary. *When No One Was Looking*. Dial, 1980.

Westall, Robert. *Break of Dark*. Greenwillow, 1982.

_____. *The Devil on the Road*. Greenwillow, 1979.

_____. *The Haunting of Chas McGill and Other Stories*. Greenwillow, 1983.

_____. *Rachel and the Angel and Other Stories*. Greenwillow, 1988.

_____. *The Watch House*. Greenwillow, 1978.

_____. *The Wind Eye*. Greenwillow, 1977.

White, Rob, *Deathwatch*. Doubleday, 1972.

Windsor, Patricia. *The Christmas Killer*. Scholastic, 1991.

Wrightson, Patricia. *Balyet*. Margaret K. McElderry, 1989.

For information on the availability of paperback editions of these titles, please consult the most recent edition of *Paperbound Books in Print,* published annually by R. R. Bowker Company.

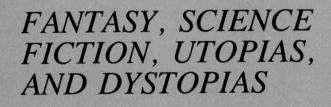

CHAPTER SIX

FANTASY, SCIENCE FICTION, UTOPIAS, AND DYSTOPIAS

Fantasy, science fiction, mythology, legends, and folktales are clearly related to each other and to humankind's deepest desires. A good illustration of this is the universal wish that people have to travel, to move their bodies easily and safely. Babies are thrilled when they learn to crawl, but this only increases their desire to move faster and more easily as they struggle to walk, run, navigate a bicycle, and finally drive a car or pilot a plane or a rocket.

Looking back at early stories, we can see how the concept of easy travel was incorporated into appealing stories. Various cultures took what they were the proudest of and, in an example of wish fulfillment, added the power of flight. The Greeks, who lived close to nature in a warm and hospitable climate, looked at the flight of birds and borrowed the idea of wings to create the flying horse Pegasus, which even today decorates Mobil gas stations. Their messenger god, Mercury, wore a winged helmet and winged sandals, as seen on today's symbol for Flowers by Wire. Germanic tribes were proud of their skill with leather and created a story about a magical pair of boots. Whoever wore the boots could travel with great speed, because each step was seven leagues long. Native Americans, who were proud of their skill with bows and arrows, have a story about a magical bow in which the bowsman is transported to wherever he shoots the arrow. And from Persia, the land of beautiful hand-woven rugs, we get stories about flying carpets.

We see the same phenomenon in today's industrialized countries. We are proud of our technology; hence, we mix it with our dreams. Stories based on the old dreams we call fantasy, but those based on the new technology we call science fiction. It's fun to compare old and new stories (see Focus Box 6.1), but it isn't always easy to draw a clear-cut line between fantasy and science fiction. Ursula Le Guin offered this explanation:

■ The basic concept of fantasy, of course, is this; you get to make up the rules, but then you've got to follow them. Science fiction refines the canon: you get to make up the rules, but within limits. A science-fiction story must not flout the evidence of science, must not, as Chip Delaney puts it, deny what is known to be known.[1]

Or, as Walter Wangerin, Jr., said in a lecture to a college audience:

■ Fantasy deals with the "immeasurable" while science fiction deals with the "measurable."[2]

No matter what the definition, the boundaries between science fiction and fantasy are fuzzy, so that more often than not the two genres are treated together (witness two important journals about these areas—*Science Fiction Chronicle: The Monthly Science Fiction and Fantasy Newsmagazine* and *The Magazine of Fantasy and Science Fiction*). Advertisements for the Science Fiction Book Club feature science fiction, fantasy, horror, the supernatural, and some selections that seem impossible to pigeonhole.[3] That comes as no surprise to members of the club, who probably read in more than one of these genres. And anyone who teaches or is around young people knows that in this area the books cross genre lines and age lines. Young adults read what adults read, and books that may have been published for young readers (e.g., Robin McKinley's Beauty or Lloyd Alexander's Prydain series) are now also read by adults.[4]

■ WHAT IS FANTASY?

Fantasy comes from a Greek word meaning "a making visible." Perhaps more than any other form of literature, fantasy is a way of refusing to accept the world as it is, a way of making experience visible so readers can see what could have been (and still might be), rather than merely what was or must be.

The appeal of fantasy may be, quite simply, that it is elemental. In that sense, its most comparable form of communication is music, which may be why so many composers have been influenced by it. Fantasy sings of our need for heroes, for goodness, and for success in our eternal fight against evil. Composers of works as dissimilar as Stravinsky's *Firebird* and Mahler's *Song of the Earth* and Strauss's *Thus Sprach Zarathustra* or *Ein Heldenleben* have sung that song. Writers sing similar songs when they tell stories of great heroes, usually of humble means and beginnings, seeking truth, finding ambiguities, and subduing evil, at least temporarily. And on its lighter side, musicians sing of beauty and love and dreams and dreamers, as in Mozart's *The Magic Flute* or Ravel's *Daphnis and Chloë* and Tchaikovsky's *Swan Lake*. Writers sing their lighter tales through stories about Beauty and the Beast, the happier and younger life of Arthur, and many of the old folktales and legends that are childhood favorites.

In the opinion of folklorist and fantasy writer J. R. R. Tolkien:

> Fantasy is a natural human activity. It certainly does not destroy or even insult Reason; and it does not blunt the appetite for, nor obscure the perception of, scientific verity. On the contrary, the keener and the clearer is the reason, the better fantasy it will make. If men were ever in a state in which they did not want to know or could not perceive truth (facts or evidence) then Fantasy would languish until they were cured.[5]

Ray Bradbury agrees that fantasy is elemental and essential:

> The ability to "fantasize" is the ability to survive. It's wonderful to speak about this subject because there have been so many wrong-headed people dealing with it. We're going through a terrible period of art, in literature and living, in psychiatry and psychology. The so-called realists are trying to drive us insane, and I refuse to be driven insane. . . . We survive by fantasizing. Take that away from us and the whole damned human race goes down the drain.[6]

Fantasy allows us—or even forces us—to become greater than we are, greater than we could hope to be. It confronts us with the major ambiguities and dualities of life—good and evil, light and dark, innocence and guilt, reality and appearance, heroism and cowardice, hard work and indolence, determination and vacillation, and order and anarchy. Fantasy presents all these, and it provides the means through which readers can consider both the polarities and the many shadings in between.

Conventions of Fantasy

The conventions of fantasy are well established. There must be a quest, larger and grander than the romantic quests discussed in Chapter Four. Heroes must prove worthy of their quest, although early in the story they may be fumbling or unsure about both themselves and their quests.

The trials encountered in the quest hasten maturity, and the striplings that readers first see soon prove wise and courageous. The young person might be alone or accompanied by friends. The purpose of the quest is to protect someone or some country from the powers of evil. The quest may be ordained, required, or occasionally, self-determined. The hero may briefly confuse good and evil, but the protagonist will ultimately recognize the distinction. When the obligatory battle comes between the powers of good and evil, the struggle may be prolonged and the outcome in doubt. But eventually good will prevail, although the victory is always transitory.

New Tellings of Old Stories

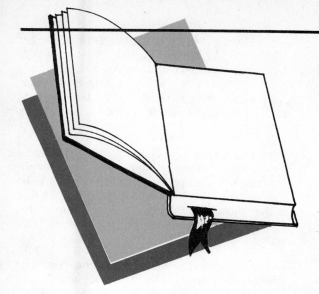

The Adventures of High John the Conqueror by Steve Sanfield, illustrated by John Ward. Orchard, 1989. Sixteen stories present the legend of High John, a black slave and folk hero, who tricks and teases his white masters and evokes laughter and admiration from both his fellow slaves and his owners.

Alan Garner's Book of British Fairy Tales by Alan Garner. Delacorte Press, 1985. A skilled writer retells some of his favorites.

In the Beginning: Creation Stories from Around the World by Virginia Hamilton, illustrated by Barry Moser. Harcourt Brace Jovanovich, 1988. Twenty-five stories from around the world show some surprising similarities.

Canterbury Tales by Geoffrey Chaucer, selected, translated from Middle English, and adapted by Barbara Cohen, illustrated by Trina Schart Hyman. Lothrop, 1988. Stories in this introductory version include "The Nun's Priest's Tale," "The Pardoner's Tale," "The Wife of Bath's Tale," and "The Franklin's Tale."

The Dawn Palace: The Story of Medea by H. M. Hoover. Dutton, 1988. Hoover's telling gives new insights into Medea's side of this old story.

The Macmillan Book of Greek Gods and Heroes by Alice Low, illustrated by Arvis Stewart. Macmillan, 1985. Included are three dozen myths and legends about Greek gods and heroes.

Merlin Dreams by Peter Dickinson, illustrated by Alan Lee. Delacorte, 1988. Dickinson writes about King Arthur's advisor not as a magician but as a tribal priest, a person with special knowledge and power.

Miriam's Well: Stories About Women in the Bible by Alice Bach and J. Cheryl Exum. Illustrated by Leo and Diane Dillon. Delacorte, 1991. In this companion book to *Moses' Ark: Stories from the Bible* (Delacorte, 1989), the authors, who are biblical scholars, provide notes at the end of each story explaining Hebrew word usages and their sources for additional information.

My Grandmother's Stories: A Collection of Jewish Folk Tales by Adele Geras, illustrated by Jael Jordan. Knopf, 1990. These old stories, including "A Phantom at the Wedding" and "The Market of Miseries," are told through the eyes of a young girl visiting her grandmother and listening to stories as the two work in the kitchen.

The Outlaws of Sherwood by Robin McKinley. Greenwillow, 1988. McKinley, a masterful storyteller, surprises readers with some of the twentieth-century ideas and attitudes that she gives her twelfth-century characters.

The People Could Fly: American Black Folk Tales retold by Virginia Hamilton, illustrated by Leo and Diane Dillon. Knopf, 1985. Hamilton divides her twenty-four tales into the categories of animals, supernatural, realistic and fanciful, and slave stories of freedom.

The Rainbow People by Laurence Yep. HarperCollins, 1989. Universal themes run through these twenty authentic Chinese folktales retold by a popular writer for young people.

Seasons of Splendour: Tales, Myths and Legends of India by Madhur Jaffrey, illustated by Michael Foreman. Atheneum, 1985. The author who grew up in India retells more than two dozen stories that she heard as a child. They are arranged around the religious festivals in the Hindu calendar.

They Dance in the Sky: Native American Star Myths by Jean Guard Monroe and Ray A. Williamson, illustrated by Edgar Steward. Houghton Mifflin, 1987. Just one tiny example of American Indian stories, these are centered around explanations of the patterns of the stars over North America.

Trail of Stones by Gwen Strauss, illustrated by Anthony Browne. Knopf, 1990. Through poetry and woodcut portraits, the author and artist take readers "into the woods" of the imagination as they show what might have happened to twelve fairy tale characters after the original fairy tales ended.

The Woman in the Moon and Other Tales of Forgotten Heroines by James Riordan, illustrated by Angela Barrett. Dial, 1985. A baker's dozen, these stories featuring girls and women as bold and clever central characters come from around the globe.

John Rowe Townsend, both a fine writer of YA novels and one of the most perceptive and honored critics of the field, maintained that the quest motif is a powerful analogy of life's pattern:

> ■ Life is a long journey, in the course of which one will assuredly have one's adventures, one's sorrows and joys, one's setbacks and triumphs, and perhaps, with luck and effort, the fulfillment of some major purpose.[7]

We all begin our quest, that long journey, seeking the good and being tempted by the evil that we know we must ultimately fight. We face obstacles and barriers throughout, hoping that we will find satisfaction and meaning during and after the quest. Our quests may not be as earthshaking as those of fantasy heroes, but our emotional and intellectual wrestling can shake our own personal worlds. In the December 1971 *Horn Book Magazine*, Lloyd Alexander wrote about this kind of comparison:

> ■ The fantasy hero is not only a doer of deeds, but he also operates within a framework of morality. His compassion is as great as his courage—greater, in fact. We might consider that his humane qualities, more than any other, are really what the hero is all about. I wonder if this reminds us of the best parts of ourselves?[8]

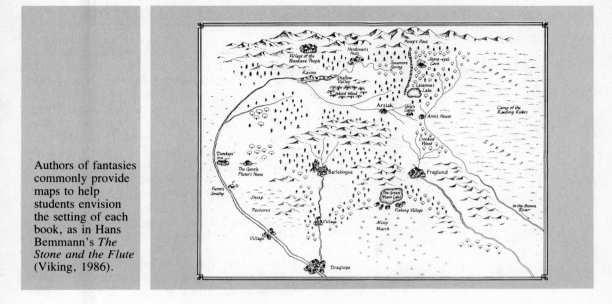

Authors of fantasies commonly provide maps to help students envision the setting of each book, as in Hans Bemmann's *The Stone and the Flute* (Viking, 1986).

Fears of Fantasy

Attacks on fantasy are common and predictable. Fantasy is said to be childishly simple reading. It's true there are simple fantasies, but most readers would consider these to be children's stories designed to whet young readers' appetites for "real fantasy." Anyone who has read Walter Wangerin, Jr.'s *The Book of the Dun Cow* or Evangeline Walton's Mabinogion series knows that fantasy is neither childish nor simple. Fantasies are often longer and more difficult than the typical book. They frequently demand close reading, filled as they are with strange beings and even stranger lands with mystical and moral overtones and ambiguities.

Fantasy has also been labeled escapist literature, and, of course, it is in several ways. Fantasy allows readers to escape the mundane and to revel in glorious adventures. For some readers (perhaps for all readers at certain times), escape is all that's demanded. For other readers, venturing on those seemingly endless quests, discovering all those incredible obstacles, and facing all those apparently tireless antagonists to defend the good and defeat the evil leads to more than mere reading to pass time. The escape from reality sends those readers back to their own limited and literal worlds to face many of the same problems they found in fantasy.

In the most illogical objection to fantasy (and a more common one than any of us could have predicted a few years ago), fantasy has been accused of being

WILLIAM SLEATOR
on Creating Readers

There is a pervasive attitude in the literary community that people who write for young adults are not "real" writers. Naturally I think this is baloney.

In the first place, people who write for young adults are, in a very real sense, *creating* readers. Adults who read have already developed the habit of reading for pleasure. But many teenagers have not. You can't just tell them that reading is the best entertainment there is, and that their lives will be vastly improved if they become addicted to reading. You have to prove it to them, by giving them books that they cannot put down. And that's where I come in.

My primary conscious preoccupation when writing is to tell a good story. Of course, like anyone who aims to be a quality writer, I work hard on style, on character development, on plot. But I'm also trying to write a riveting book. Things happen fast, the book has to be exciting, suspenseful, never a dull moment. There's no room for the padding that fills up so many 1100-page adult books. And that's one reason why it's so much fun to write for adolescents.

You also have to work very hard at establishing credibilty—teenagers are often more skeptical than adults. This is especially important when you are writing fantasy or science fiction. I always start my books in the real world, in a mundane situation—and let the weirdness creep in gradually. It's like a challenging puzzle—to trick the readers into believing that this crazy thing could really happen to them.

When I get letters from kids who tell me they usually don't like to read, but couldn't put down one of my books, I feel I have really succeeded. We are all doing a little to help create a new generation of readers, and that will certainly make the world a better place to live in.

The other nice thing about writing young adult books—if I dare to mention it—is that, because of public libraries and school libraries, you can make a living at it. The people I know who write adult books, who consider me to be second rate, all have full-time jobs to support their writing. And so, when they tell me that writing for young people is "good practice," I am laughing all the way to the bank.

William Sleator's books include *House of Stairs*, 1974; *Interstellar Pig*, 1984; *Strange Attractors*, 1989; and *The Spirit House*, 1991, all Dutton.

unreal, untrue, and imaginative (the term *imaginative* seems to have replaced *secular humanism* as one of today's leading bogeymen). To people who believe that using one's imagination leads to an inability to face reality and is somehow related to Satanism, fantasy probably seems dangerous. But fantasy is about reality, as explained nearly twenty years ago by Ursula Le Guin:

For fantasy is true, of course. It isn't factual, but it is true. Children know that. Adults know it too, and that is precisely why many of them are afraid of fantasy. They know that its truth challenges, even threatens, all that is false, phony, unnecessary, and trivial in the life they have let themselves be forced into living. They are afraid of dragons because they are afraid of freedom.

So I believe we should trust our children. Normal children do not confuse reality with fantasy—they confuse them much less often than we adults do (as a certain great fantasist pointed out in a story called "The Emperor's New Clothes"). Children know perfectly well that unicorns aren't real, but they also know that books about unicorns, if they are good books, are true books.[9]

Important Writers of Fantasy

As shown in Focus Box 6.2, contemporary authors are producing well-written fantasies that are receiving both critical and popular acclaim. But some still stand head and shoulders above the rest. For many fantasy enthusiasts, J. R. R. Tolkien is the yardstick against which all other writers are measured. *The Hobbit, or There and Back Again* began in 1933 as a series of stories Tolkien told his children about the strange little being known as Bilbo, the Hobbit. Even more famous is his trilogy, *The Lord of the Rings*. His love of language led him to create a language, Elfish, for his own amusement and for the book. Appendices to *The Lord of the Rings* are devoted to the history of Middle-Earth, its language, and its geography. An extension of Tolkien's work, *The Silmarillion*, led the *New York Times* bestseller list for several weeks in 1977, amazing for a fantasy, although the work proved disappointing to many Tolkien fans. Tolkien created many of the conventions of fantasy. For that alone he would be important. But his greatest importance lies in the excellence of *The Hobbit* and *The Lord of the Rings*, which can be (and for many people, are) read again and again for delight and insight.

Ursula Le Guin has dominated contemporary fantasy. Her early books, *The Left Hand of Darkness* and *The Dispossessed*, were mixtures of science fiction and fantasy, but her four finest books about Earthsea are superb fantasy. The setting of *A Wizard of Earthsea*, is of course, Earthsea, a world of vast oceans and multitudinous islands. Duny demonstrates early that he is capable of becoming a wizard, is given his true name, Ged, and learns the names of all things—word magic binds the worlds of fantasy and fairy tales together. Childishly showing off in a forbidden duel of sorcery at his school on Roke Island "where all high arts are taught," he uses his powers to call a woman from the dead and accidentally releases an evil Power, a Shadow that follows him thereafter. That capricious and childish act causes Ged to become deaf, blind, and mute for four weeks in a hot summer. The Archmage Gensher comes to Ged and says:

Recent Fantasy from Best Book Lists

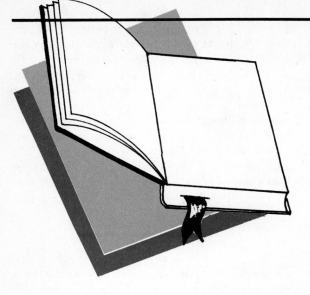

Dealing with Dragons by Patricia C. Wrede. Harcourt Brace Jovanovich, 1990. Cimorene, the youngest daughter of the king of Linderwall, is so bored with her typical princess life that she runs away to become a dragon's princess. All is well until she meets the wizard Zemenar and discovers his plot.

Letters from Atlantis by Robert Silverberg. Atheneum, 1990. Roy travels through time into the mind of a prince on the mythical island of Atlantis while his friend Lora travels to the same time period but finds herself in Ice Age Europe.

The Pearl of the Soul of the World by Meredith Ann Pierce. Little, Brown/Joy Street Books, 1990. In this final book of the Darkangel trilogy, Aeriel not only must rescue her husband from the White Witch, but also must save the land from the drought, which is one of the White Witch's plagues.

Ratha and Thistle-Chaser by Clare Bell. Margaret K. McElderry Books, 1990. Ratha is a young leader of the Named, a clan of intelligent cats, whose survival depends on its ability to break with tradition.

The Remarkable Journey of Prince Jen by Lloyd Alexander. Dutton, 1991. Prince Jen's journey is a prototype of the quest.

Afternoon of the Elves by Janet Taylor Lisle. Orchard Books, 1989. Nine-year-old Hillary and eleven-year-old Sara-Kate discover an elfin village through the hedges in Sara-Kate's unkempt backyard.

Black Unicorn by Tanith Lee, illustrated by Heather Cooper. Atheneum, 1991. Tanaquil makes herself a unicorn. When it comes to life, the two of them embark on a search for adventure.

Castle in the Air by Diana Wynne Jones. Greenwillow, 1990. In this follow-up to *Howl's Moving Castle* (Greenwillow, 1986), Abdullah embarks on all kinds of adventures when his flying carpet lands him in the garden of a beloved princess.

The Coachman Rat by David Henry Wilson. Carrol & Graf, 1989. This new version of Cinderella focuses on one of the rat coachmen. When midnight strikes, only his body turns back into a rat; he still feels and thinks like a human.

■ You have greater power inborn in you, and you used that power wrongly, not knowing how that spell affects the balance of light and dark, life and death, good and evil. And you were moved to do this by pride and by hate. Is it any wonder the result was ruin?

Ged completes his training and leaves a certified wizard, but with Ged goes the shadow, of what he knows not except that it is evil.

The remaining two-thirds of the novel consists of many adventures, but always, at the center of Ged's existence, is his quest for the meaning of the shadow. Ged ultimately recognizes that his quest is not to undo what he has done but to finish what he has started. On a lonely shore, Ged meets the shadow, and as if they were one—and they are—they speak the shadow's name, "Ged," and "Light and darkness met, and joined, and were one."

Vetch, Ged's friend, believes that Ged has been overcome by his foe, and he runs to help Ged. When Vetch finds Ged safe:

■ he began to see the truth, that Ged had neither lost nor won but, naming the shadow of his death with his own name, had made himself a whole: a man who, knowing his whole true self cannot be used or possessed by any other power other than himself, and whose life therefore is lived for life's sake and never in the service of ruin, or pain, or hatred, or the dark.

A short work less than 200 pages long, *A Wizard of Earthsea* is rich in characters and suspense and meaning. Ged's quest is an initiation rite that leads him to understand the nature of responsibility and who and what he is.

Ged reappears in *The Tombs of Atuan*, but the chief character is Tenar, dedicated from youth to the Powers of the Earth. In *The Farthest Shore*, Ged, now Archmage and the most powerful of wizards, accompanies a young man on a quest to seek out the evil that threatens to destroy the lands and the powers of the wizards. The evil is Cob, one of the living dead, who seeks the peace of death but cannot find it. Ged helps to find death for Cob, but it costs Ged dearly. Even that is not too much, for earlier Ged had told the young man:

■ You will die. You will not live forever. Nor will any man nor any thing. Nothing is immortal. But only to us is given to know that we must die. And that is a great gift: the gift of selfhood. For we have only what we know we must lose, what we are willing to lose.

Readers had long assumed that *The Farthest Shore* was the end. Then in 1990, *Tehanu: The Last Book of Earthsea* appeared, almost thirty years after the first Earthsea book. Characters from the previous books reappear, particularly Tenar and Ged. Many years after the last book, Tenar has married, raised two children of her own, and taken in a child, Therru, raped by her uncle who pushed her into a fire and left her emotionally and physically scarred. Soon thereafter Tenar is summoned to the deathbed of Ogion, an ancient wizard. The ancient man tells Tenar about Therru: "teach her all; they will fear her." Tenar nurses Ged back to life, and after some plot convolutions, evil is again defeated, for the time being, as Therru uses her power to call a dragon to aid her. This concluding book is in some ways the most beautiful of them all, and it pulls together all the themes of the other books—the values and dangers of power, the fear of the unknown, the need to live and to love, the need for hope, the perpetual need to fight evil. Contemporary readers will find in the book other messages they want to find—the importance of feminism, the horror of child abuse (and other kinds of human abuse), proof that Therru, and others like her, can find inner strength to fight and win. *Tehanu* is a rich book, a fitting end to Earthsea.

Anne McCaffrey's fantasy world is set on Pern. In her trilogy of *Dragonsong, Dragonsinger,* and *Dragondrums*, Pern is threatened every 200 years by shimmering, threadlike spores. Inhabitants protect themselves through the great Pern dragons, who destroy the threads as they fall. In *Dragonsong*, Menolly is forced by her father to give up music and her dream of becoming a Harper, although at the book's conclusion she is known to the Master Harper and is well on her way to a life of music. In the lesser second volume, Menolly trains to become a Harper and meets the sweet-voiced young boy Piemur. In this fantasy version of an old-fashioned school story, Menolly has trouble with envious students and faces demanding teachers. *Dragondrums* gets back on track in an exciting finale to the series. Pern is again threatened by the deadly Threadfall, and Piemur, whose voice has changed and made him doubt his future as a singer, is sent off as a drum apprentice and then is stranded along with a stolen firedragon. A bit rambling, *Dragondrums* is a satisfying portrait of a troubled boy who learns about responsibility and survival.

McCaffrey tells fine stories of adventures of young people in the throes of initiation rites, but rarely does she approach the complexity of thought or the mythic qualities of Le Guin's work, not even in *The White Dragon* or *Moreta: Dragon Lady of Pern*, satisfying fantasies though they are.

A recent German entry into the field of fantasy, Hans Bemmann's *The Stone and the Flute* is almost a prototype of the genre. Listener, the hero, loves music more than fighting; at seventeen, he receives a magic agent, and only a bit later he inherits a silver flute; and the remainder of his life clearly will be spent trying to understand the significance and power of these two things. There are, as is true with Le Guin's books and other good fantasies, multiple layers of meanings and ideas, riches piled on riches, each time surprising readers convinced that Bemmann could not surpass the last episode, the last insight. Although Bemmann is not young (he was born in 1922), this is a young book with a sense of adventure and power and compassion that sometimes seems reckless but ultimately is wise and reasoned.

Although most fantasies follow the basic conventions, they tend to fall into these categories: those set in new worlds, as with Le Guin and McCaffrey; those following myths from the Welsh *Mabinogion*; those celebrating Arthurian legends; those with one foot in contemporary reality and one foot in a fantasy world; those employing animals and often aiming moral barbs at humans; and those using fantasy to amuse. Obviously, some overlapping occurs in many fantasies.

Marion Zimmer Bradley's Darkover books are among the most popular of the fantasies set in a new world. Colonists from Earth come to the planet Darkover, with its one sun and four multicolored moons. Over 2,000 years, they lose contact with their home planet and evolve new cultures and new myths alongside the psi-gifted natives. *Darkover Landfall* is a good introduction to the series, although wherever fantasy buffs enter Darkover will likely serve equally well as a starting point. Darkover fans have written so extensively about Bradley's imaginary world that DAW books recently collected some of the best articles under the title *Red Sun of Darkover*, with an introduction by Bradley along with two Bradley articles about Darkover and thirteen contributions by fans elaborating on the magic and power and people of Darkover. For readers getting started on the Darkover books, *Red Sun* is especially helpful, since two pages prior to the title page list all the Darkover titles and, more important, briefly describe the Darkover world and the major plot developments.

Katherine Kurtz's Deryni series features a race of extrasensory-powered people in *Deryni Rising, Deryni Checkmate,* and *High Deryni.* Her Camber series takes place 200 years before the Deryni books.

Two satisfying writers of other-world fantasies for young adults are Patricia McKillip and Jane Yolen. McKillip creates a land of witches and magic and riddles in *The Forgotten Beasts of Eld* and later books, especially two recent books, *Moon-Flash* and *The Moon and the Face*, which are particularly exciting love stories. Perhaps a bit more traditional are Jane Yolen's trilogy of dragons, a young and unsure hero, and one of the most intriguing and strongest females in recent fiction in *Dragon's Blood, Heart's Blood,* and *A Sending of Dragons.*

Fantasy and the Mabinogion

The *Mabinogion* is a collection of medieval Welsh tales, first published in English in 1838–1849 by Lady Charlotte Guest. The eleven stories fall into three parts: the four branches of the Mabinogi (tales to instruct young bards) deal with Celtic legends and myths dealing with Pywll, prince of Dived; Branwen, daughter of Llyr; Manawyddan, son of Llyr; and Math, son of Mathonwy. There are also four independent tales and four Arthurian romances. Several writers have used the Mabinogi myths and legends as a basis for their books.

Lloyd Alexander's Prydain Chronicles consists of five volumes about Taran, the young Assistant Pig-Keeper. The opening book of this rich fantasy, *The Book of Three*, introduces the main characters, especially Taran, and sends him on his quest to save his land, Prydain, from evil. He seeks his own identity as well, for none know his heritage. Taran's early impatience is understandable but vexing to his master, Dalben, who counsels patience "for the time being."

"For the time being," Taran burst out. "I think it will always be for the time being, and it will be vegetables and horseshoes all my life."

"Tut," said Dalben, "there are worse things. Do you set yourself to be a glorious hero? Do you believe it is all flashing swords and galloping about on horses? As for being glorious. . . ."

"What of Prince Gwydion?" cried Taran. "Yes, I wish I might be like him."

"I fear," Dalben said, "that is entirely out of the question."

"But why?" Taran sprang to his feet. "I know if I had the chance. . . ."

"Why?" Dalben interrupted. "In some cases," he said, "we learn more by looking for the answer to a question and not finding it than we do from learning the answer itself."

Taran, youthful impetuousness and righteous indignation aglow, is bored by Dalben's thoughts and wants action, and that he finds soon enough in the books that follow: *The Black Cauldron*, *The Castle of Llyr*, *Taran Wanderer*, and *The High King*.

Far more difficult than Alexander and aimed at an older audience, Alan Garner's earlier books force his young protagonists to face the problem of good versus evil in *The Weirdstone of Brisingamen*, *The Moon of Gomrath*, and *Elidor*. Though Garner maintains they are less successful than his later work, the three books have proved popular in England, although they are less widely used in America. His two best works are *The Owl Service* and *Red Shift*, both complex—perhaps unduly so—and rewarding. *The Owl Service* has been praised by Mary Cadogan and Patricia Craig:

The Owl Service is perhaps the first really adult children's book; the first book, that is, in which childish sensibilities are not deferred to, in which the author has not felt that his audience needs, above all, to be protected.[10]

Based on the legend of Blodenweddin in "Math, son of Mathonwy" in the *Mabinogion*, *The Owl Service* tells of three young people who find a set of old dishes in an attic and learn that the pattern in the dishes is related to an old Welsh legend involving love and jealousy and hatred. *Red Shift* uses three parallel narratives about love—contemporary, seventeenth century, and second century—intertwining them to make connections about love and about our relationships with the past.

Among other writers who have used the *Mabinogion* as a basis for fantasy, Evangeline Walton (real name, Evangeline Walton Ensely) stands out. Her four-part series, *The Prince of Annwn: The First Branch of the Mabinogion*, *The Children of Llyr: The Second Branch of the Mabinogion*, *The Song of Rhiannon: The Third Branch of the Mabinogion*, and *The Virgin and the Swine: The Fourth Branch of the Mabinogion* (the last volume was reprinted in 1970 as *The Island of the Mighty: The Fourth Branch of the Mabinogion*) are among the best of direct retellings of the old Welsh legends. Walton's quartet is both mythology and ecology, for the author makes the earth a divinity that must not be despoiled by humanity. In an afterword to the first book, Walton writes:

 When we were superstitious enough to hold the earth sacred and worship her, we did nothing to endanger our future upon her, as we do now.

King Arthur and Other Myths in Fantasy

Arthurian legends have long been staples of fantasy. T. H. White's *The Once and Future King* (a source, for which it can hardly be blamed, for that most dismal of musicals, *Camelot*) is basic to any reading of fantasy. In four parts, *The Sword in the Stone*, *The Witch in the Wood*, *The Ill-Made Knight*, and *The Candle in the Wind*, White retells the story of Arthur—his boyhood, his prolonged education at the hands of Merlin, his seduction by Queen Morgause, his love for Guinivere and her affair with Lancelot, and Mordred's revenge and Arthur's fall. A later work, *The Book of Merlyn: The Unpublished Conclusion to The Once and Future King*, should, like most work left unpublished at an author's death, have been allowed to remain unpublished and largely unknown.

Among the shorter retellings of the legends, no one has surpassed the three-part series by Rosemary Sutcliff. *The Sword and the Circle: King Arthur and the Knights of the Round Table*, *The Light Beyond the Forest: The Quest for the Holy Grail*, and *The Road to Camlann: The Death of King Arthur* are masterfully written by a writer who loves the legends and has a firm grasp on the materials and the meanings.

Mary Stewart, author of several fine suspense novels, focuses more on Merlin than on Arthur in *The Crystal Cave*, *The Hollow Hills*, and *The Last Enchantment* and more on Mordred than on Arthur in the last book, *The Wicked Day*. Even better are Gillian Bradshaw's three books. *Hawk of May*, *Kingdom of Summer*, and *In Winter's Shadow* may puzzle a few readers at first—the author writes about Medraut instead of Mordred, Gwynhwyfar rather than Guinivere, Gwalchmai rather than Gawain—but readers who stay with the books will find them readable and most satisfying. Marion Zimmer Bradley's *The Mists of Avalon* takes a different approach, the conflict between the old religion of the Celtics, represented by Morgan Le Fay (here called Morgaine), and the new religion of Christianity, represented by Guinivere (here called Gwenhyfar).

Animal Fantasies

Animal stories aimed at instructing humans are as old as Aesop and as recent as yesterday's book review. Many students will come to high school having already enjoyed such books as E. B. White's *Charlotte's Web* and *Stuart Little*, Jane Langton's *The Fledgling*, Robert C. O'Brien's *Mrs. Frisby and the Rats of NIMH*, Kenneth Grahame's *The Wind in the Willows*, and Richard Adams' *Watership Down*.

They will be ready to go on and read Walter Wangerin, Jr.'s *The Book of the Dun Cow*, a delightfully funny theological thriller retelling the story of Chaunticleer the Rooster. Supposedly the leader for good against evil (the half-snake, half-cock—Cockatrice—and the black serpent—Wyrm), Chaunticleer is beset by doubts. He is aided by the humble dog, Mondo Cani, some hilariously pouting turkeys, and assorted other barnyard animals. Although this may sound cute, it is not, and the battle scenes are among the bloodiest, ugliest, and most realistic that readers are likely to find in fantasy. *The Book of Sorrows* was a disappointing sequel.

Clare Bell has written three books in a fine series about a race of superin-telligent cats related to saber-toothed tigers 25 million years ago. *Ratha's Creatures* describes the orderly society of the Named, the intelligent cats, and the band of the chaotic Un-Named, raiders and predators. Ratha tames fire and is exiled from the Named. In *Clan Ground*, Ratha is the clan leader of the Named and mistakenly allows Orange Eyes into the clan. In *Ratha and Thistle-Chaser*, Ratha must take her clan to the seacoast, where there is food and water for the clan's herd.

Many readers of fantasy associate the genre with high seriousness, but Peter Beagle stands out for treating a serious theme with a quiet wit and a sense of amusement in *A Fine and Private Place* and *The Last Unicorn*. The title of *A Fine and Private Place* comes from Andrew Marvell's "To His Coy Mistress":

> The Grave's a fine and private place,
> But none, I think, do there embrace.

The grave is also a lively and frequently funny place in Beagle's fantasy. A living human talks to a delightfully tough old raven. In *The Last Unicorn*, a lonely unicorn seeks the company of others of its kind, helped by the magician Schmendrick, who is incapable of telling any story without wild elaboration. Stopping at a town early in the quest, Schmendrick tells of his adventures:

> During the meal Schmendrick told stories of his life as an errant en-chanter, filling it with kings and dragons and noble ladies. He was not lying, merely organizing events more sensibly.

Tying Old and New Together

Writing for *School Library Journal*,[11] Audrey Eaglen suggests that we use modern versions of myths and legends to attract young readers to those stories that have stood the test of time in filling the deep intellectual and emotional needs of myth and story, as discussed by such philosophers as Joseph Campbell and Ayn Rand. She recommends Valerie Martin's *Mary Reilly* as a fascinating introduction to *Dr. Jekyll and Mr. Hyde*, and Annette Curtis Klause's *The Silver Kiss* (see Chapter Five) as a good introduction to *Dracula* and to *Frankenstein*.

She singles out Robin McKinley's *The Outlaws of Sherwood* (a retelling of *Robin Hood*) as most likely to pique the curiosity of teenagers enough to make them "take the plunge into Pyle's turn-of-the-century version with its glorious illustrations by Wyeth." McKinley's *The Blue Sword* and *The Hero and the Crown* are other successful book-length versions of traditional stories. Her *Beauty* is a retelling of the "Beauty and the Beast" legend, differing from earlier versions in a few significant details. McKinley's Beauty is strong and unafraid and loving. When her father tells her that he has been condemned to death by the Beast for stealing a rose, Beauty gladly agrees to change places with her father:

> "He cannot be so bad if he loves roses so much."
> "But he is a Beast," said Father helplessly.
> I saw that he was weakening, and wishing only to comfort him, I said, "Cannot a Beast be tamed?"

McKinley's version lacks the surrealistic quality of Jean Cocteau's magnificent film, but in most important ways her novel compares favorably with any other retelling, including the recent Disney film.

Another modern retelling that Eaglen recommends is H. M. Hoover's feminist retelling of *Medea* in *The Dawn Palace*:

> Medea is seen as something more than an insanely jealous murderer of her own children; the noble Jason, however, proves to be a hero with feet of clay. In a fascinating addendum, Hoover reveals that when Euripedes was presenting the play, the political situation of Greece was such that Medea's true story was suppressed. In its place, a story more aligned with the mis-ogynistic elders' view of male and female roles was created so that it could serve as propaganda for maintaining the sexual status quo. This section alone ought to make the reader want to go back to Euripedes' original, either in written form or in Judith Anderson's superb recording of the drama.

When the editors of *English Journal* asked for suggestions from teachers of books that could be used in the way that Eaglen wrote about,[12] they received several suggestions in which one or more of the books was a fantasy. Martha D. Rekrut, a Rhode Island teacher, told how she has had success using Robert C. O'Brien's *Z for Zachariah* as an introduction to John Hersey's *Hiroshima*. Lois Stover has used Robin Graham's true adventure *Dove* to get her ninth-grade students into reading *The Odyssey*. And Carolyn Lima has used Felice Holman's realistic *The Wild Children* as an introduction to George Orwell's *Animal Farm*.

WHAT IS SCIENCE FICTION?

In 1953, Robert A. Heinlein, one of science fiction's gurus, asked the question: "But what, under rational definition, is *science fiction*?" He went on to answer the question by defining the genre as speculative fiction based on the real world, with all its "established facts and natural laws." Although the result can be extremely fantastic in content, "it is not fantasy: it is legitimate—and often very tightly reasoned—speculation about the possibilities of the real world."[13]

Science fiction must adhere to natural law. A novel can use quite different laws of another planet, but those laws must be scientifically clear and consistent. We used to say that no dragons need apply for work in science fiction, but then Anthony Wolk pointed out that Anne McCaffrey's dragons have a biochemical foundation, arguably making Pern a science fiction world.[14] Being limited to real-world possibilities has rarely proved onerous to science fiction writers, many of whom are engineers or scientists or had their early training in the sciences.

There are other conventions, although none are as important as Heinlein's. Characters voyage into space and face all sorts of dangers. (Science fiction is, after all, more adventure than philosophy, although the latter is often present.) Other planets have intelligent and/or frightening life forms, although they may differ drastically from Earth's humans. Contemporary problems are projected hundreds or thousands of years into the future, and those new views of overpopulation, pollution, religious bickering, political machinations, and sexual disharmony often give readers a quite different perspective of our world and our problems today. Prophecies are not required in science fiction; nevertheless, some of the richest books of Isaac Asimov and Arthur C. Clarke have been prophetic. (Ray Bradbury, on the other hand, has said, "I don't try to predict the future—I try to prevent it.") Occasionally, a scientifically untenable premise may be used. On the August 15, 1983, "Nightcap" talk show on Arts Cable Television, Isaac Asimov said, "The best kind of sci-fi involves science." Then he agreed that, "Time travel is theoretically impossible, but I wouldn't want to give it up as a plot gimmick." Essentially, he was agreeing with Heinlein but adding that plot and excitement counted even more. The internal consistency and plausibility of a postulated imaginary society creates its own reality.

Ray Bradbury argues that the appeal of science fiction is understandable because science fiction is important literature, not merely popular stuff. Opening his essay on "Science Fiction: Why Bother?" he compares himself to a fourth-rate George Bernard Shaw who makes an outrageous statement and then tries to prove it. Bradbury says, "Science fiction is the most important fiction being written today." He adds that it is not "part of the Main Stream. It *is* the Main Stream."[15]

Carl Sagan, the Cornell University astronomer-author, has added his testimony, writing that it was science fiction that brought him to science. Kurt Vonnegut, Jr., also applauded science fiction through character Eliot Rosewater in *God Bless You, Mr. Rosewater, or Pearls Before Swine*. Stumbling into a

Every year science fiction fans gather at conventions to talk about their favorite characters, authors, and books.

convention of science fiction writers, Rosewater drunkenly tells them that he loves them because they are the only ones who:

> . . . know that life is a space voyage, and not a short one either, but one that'll last billions of years. You're the only ones with guts enough to really care about the future, who really notice what machines do to us, what wars do to us, what cities do to us, what big, simple ideas do to us, what tremendous misunderstandings, mistakes, accidents and catastrophes do to us.

He goes on to praise them for being "zany enough to agonize over time and distances without limit, over mysteries that will never die, over the fact that we are right now determining whether the space voyage for the next billion years or so is going to be Heaven or Hell."

Science fiction writer and scientist Arthur C. Clarke agrees with Rosewater on the admittedly limited but still impressive power of science fiction to scan the future. In his introduction to *Profiles of the Future*, Clarke writes:

> A critical—the adjective is important—reading of science-fiction is essential training for anyone wishing to look more than ten years ahead. The facts of the future can hardly be imagined *ab initio* by those who are unfamiliar with the fantasies of the past.

This claim may produce indignation, especially among those second-rate scientists who sometimes make fun of science-fiction (I have never known a first-rate one to do so—and I know several who write it). But the simple fact is that anyone with sufficient imagination to assess the future realistically would, inevitably be attracted to this form of literature. I do not for a moment suggest that more than one percent of science-fiction readers would be reliable prophets; but I do suggest that almost a hundred percent of reliable prophets will be science-fiction readers—or writers.[16]

Why does science fiction appeal to young adults and to adults? First and probably most important, it is exciting. Science fiction may have begun with the "rah-rah-we're-off-to-Venus-with-Buck-Rogers" kind of book, and although it has gone far beyond that, the thrill of adventure is still there in most science fiction. Science fiction writers refuse to write down to their audience (the highest praise they can give to their readers), and this is recognized and admired. Science fiction allows anyone to read imaginative fiction without feeling the material is kid stuff. Science fiction presents real heroes to readers who find their own

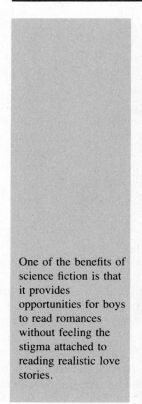

One of the benefits of science fiction is that it provides opportunities for boys to read romances without feeling the stigma attached to reading realistic love stories.

LAURENCE YEP
on Being an Outsider

Probably the reason that much of my writing has found its way to a teenage audience is that I'm always pursuring the theme of being an outsider—an alien—and many teenagers feel they're aliens. As a Chinese child growing up in a black neighborhood, I served as the all-purpose Asian. When we played war, I was the Japanese who got killed; then when the Korean War came along, I was a North Korean communist. This sense of being the odd-one-out is probably what made me relate to the Narnia and Oz books. They were about loneliness and kids in alien societies learning to adjust to foreign cultures. I could understand these a lot better than the stories in our readers where every house had a front lawn and no one's front door was ever locked. When I went to high school, I really began to feel like an outsider. I lost my grammar school friends because they all went into basketball while I went into science fiction. Then every morning I would get on a bus and ride into Chinatown, where I attended Catholic school. My family didn't speak Chinese, so I was put in the dumbbell Chinese class. I resented that, but what I resented more was that all the dirty jokes and the snide remarks were told in Chinese, so the Sisters wouldn't understand them. I couldn't understand them either.

At first it was only through science fiction that I could treat the theme of the outsider, but then I began to do historical fiction and finally contemporary fiction. *Sea Glass* is my most autobiographical novel, but I can't always write that close to home because it requires me to take a razor blade and cut through my defenses. I'm bleeding when I finish, and I have to take time off by writing fantasy or something only marginally related to my Chinese heritage, such as *The Mark Twain Murders.*

Laurence Yep's books include *Dragonwings*, HarperCollins, 1975; *Dragon Cauldron*, HarperCollins, 1991; *The Rainbow People*, HarperCollins, 1989; and *The Mark Twain Murders*, Macmillan, 1984.

world often devoid of anyone worth admiring, of heroes doing something brave, going to the ultimate frontiers, even pushing these frontiers further back, all of which are particularly important at a time when many young people wonder if any new frontiers exist. And as Laurence Yep points out in his statement above, science fiction provides a comfortable way to write and think about being different, being an outsider. And most important, science fiction writers see their readers as intellectually curious. This is praise of the highest order, and that is repaid by readers who often venerate the best of the science fiction writers.

Science fiction has its heritage of fine writers and important books (see Focus Box 6.3). Some critics maintain that the genre began with Mary Wollstonecraft Shelley's *Frankenstein, or The Modern Prometheus* in 1818. Others argue for Swift's *Gulliver's Travels* in 1726 or the much earlier Lucian's *The True History* in the second century A.D. No matter, for nearly everyone agrees that the first major and widely read writer was Jules Verne, whose *Journey to the Center of the Earth* in 1864 and *Twenty Thousand Leagues Under the Sea* in 1870 pleased readers on several continents. The first American science fiction came with Edgar Allan Poe's short story, "The Unparalleled Adventures of One Hans Pfaall," which appeared in the June 1835 issue of *Southern Literary Messenger* and was included in *Tales of the Grotesque and Arabesque* in 1840. Hans Pfaall's balloon trip to the moon in a nineteen-day voyage may be a hoax, but the early trappings of science fiction are there. Dime novels occasionally used science fiction, particularly in the "Frank Reade" series, as did some books from the Stratemeyer Literary Syndicate, particularly in the Tom Swift and Great Marvel series.

The development of modern science fiction began with Hugo H. Gernsback. (The Hugo Awards given each year for science fiction excellence honor his name.) An electrical engineer, in 1908 he began publishing *Modern Electrics*, the first magazine devoted to radio. In 1911, finding a few extra pages in his magazine, he began a serial about inventions and innovations in the future. Because it was successful, Gernsback used similar stories later. In 1926 he began *Amazing Stories*, and in 1929 he started *Science Wonder Stories*. His insistence on excessively literal and sterile scientific accuracy in stories made his work formula-ridden and repetitive, but he did offer a market for a type of science fiction story. Later magazines proved somewhat more liberal and willing to accept what then appeared offbeat, and many of today's major science fiction writers broke into print in those magazines.

After World War II, science fiction took great strides toward respectability as literature and prophecy, partly because science fiction writers had predicted both the atomic age and the computer revolution. Perhaps, because a long and deadly war was now over, people seemed more willing to consider alternatives and to reappraise society and to read literature that did both. The paperback revolution flourished, and science fiction became easily available to many readers.

Sure proof that science fiction had become academically respectable came in December 1959, when the prestigious and stuffy Modern Language Association began its science fiction journal, *Extrapolation*. Two other journals, *Foundation* (in England) and *Science-Fiction Studies* (in Canada), began publishing in the early 1970s. Colleges and secondary schools offered courses in the genre, and major publishers and significant magazines recognized and published science fiction. Radio, television, and movies (see Focus Box 6.4) introduced science fiction to millions of people not in the habit of reading for pleasure. A British radio show was especially influential in attracting readers to science fiction. Douglas Adams' quartet—*The Hitchhiker's Guide to the*

In Orbit with Solid Science Fiction Writers

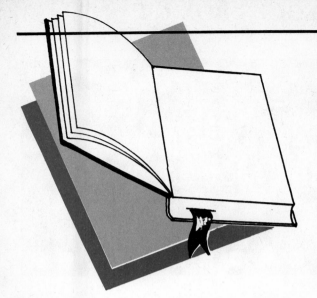

Isaac Asimov. Until his death in 1992, Asimov was the most prolific writer of our age. He also edited collections of science fiction short stories. His *Foundation* (Ballantine, 1984), *Second Foundation* (Ballantine, 1983), and *Foundation and Empire* (Ballantine, 1986) books describe a galactic empire and its decline.

Ray Bradbury. Bradbury's short stories are particularly good for introducing students to the genre. *The Martian Chronicles* (Doubleday, 1950) is really a collection of short stories; *Fahrenheit 451* (Ballantine, 1953) is a dystopian look at anti-intellectualism and censorship.

Orson Scott Card. The newest of the highly acclaimed writers, Card has won Hugo, Nebula, and Locus awards. In his Ender series (T. Doherty, 1985), Ender Wiggin first develops and then sets out to get rid of his miserable reputation when colonists on a planet discover a brutal, warlike, but intelligent species. (See also *Wyrms* [Arbor House, 1987].)

Arthur C. Clarke. One of the all-time great writers, Clarke's best book is usually considered to be *Childhood's End* (Houghton Mifflin, 1953), but he might best be introduced to teenagers but he might best be introduced to teenagers through his *Rendezvous with Rama* (Harcourt Brace Jovanovich, 1973). It is set in 2130 as humans investigate a hollow spaceship inhabited by robots.

Philip K. Dick. Dick's finest book, *Do Androids Dream of Electric Sheep?* (Doubleday, 1968), is set in a polluted future Earth in which androids become more and more human, and more and more dangerous.

Robert Heinlein. Best known for *A Stranger in a Strange Land* (Putnam, 1961), Heinlein has several books that appeal to young readers including, *Have Space Suit—Will Travel* (Scribner, 1958), *The Moon Is a Harsh Mistress* (Putnam, 1966), *Podkayne of Mars: Her Life and Times* (Putnam, 1963), and *Friday* (Holt, 1982).

Frank Herbert. Herbert's *Dune* (Chilton, 1965) is almost certainly the most influential science fiction book about religion. Several sequels, not quite as good, appeared over the next twenty years.

Walter H. Miller, Jr. Relished even by readers who say they hate science fiction, Miller's *A Canticle for Leibowitz* (Lippincott, 1959) is a powerful satire on religion and much more.

Science Fiction in the Movies

Aliens (1986, 137 min., color; Dir: James Cameron; with Sigourney Weaver) A return to a planet to destroy what spawns killer life forms. Better by far than the 1979 *Alien.*

E.T. the Extra-terrestrial (1982, 115 min., color; Dir: Steven Spielberg) A young boy befriends a young alien stranded on Earth.

Fahrenheit 451 (1967, 111 min., color; Dir: François Truffaut; with Julie Christie and Oskar Werner) Ray Bradbury's short novel about the place of the fireman in our lives and books and the future of humans.

Forbidden Planet (1956, 98 min., color; Dir: Fred McLeod Wilcox; with Walter Pidgeon and Leslie Nielsen) A retelling of Shakespeare's *The Tempest* as science fiction.

Invasion of the Body Snatchers (1956, 80 min., black and white; Dir: Don Siegel; with Kevin McCarthy) People begin acting strangely. Then pods with bodies suspiciously like other residents are found.

Metropolis (1926, 120 min., black and white; Dir: Fritz Lang) A dated yet fascinating view of a future world (but you do need to ignore the actors).

Plan 9 from Outer Space (1959, 79 min., black and white; Dir: Edward D. Wood, Jr.) Aliens plan to bring the dead to life and take over Earth. Many people, critics and ordinary viewers, believe this is the worst film ever made, but it's great fun to see if you don't take it seriously. (Who could?)

Slaughterhouse-Five (1972, 104 min., color; Dir: Roy Hill) Kurt Vonnegut's novel about a human who finds himself on another planet but who relives his World War II experiences.

Sleeper (1973, 88 min., color; Dir: Woody Allen; with Allen and Diane Keaton) A man frozen in 1973 is awakened 200 years later in a despotic world. The Miss America contest is hilarious in a wonderful sci-fi spoof.

Star Wars (1977, 121 min., color; Dir: George Lucas; with Mark Hamill, Carrie Fisher, and Harrison Ford) The modern film that made Saturday serial science fiction films respectable again—the excitement never lets up. *The Empire Strikes Back* (1980) and *The Return of the Jedi* (1983) look just fine on the small TV screen.

The Time Machine (1960, 103 min., color; Dir: George Pal; with Rod Taylor) Loosely based on H.G. Wells' social satire about the destiny of humans.

2001: A Space Odyssey (1968, 139 min., color; Dir: Stanley Kubrick) Space travel and machines and God and almost everything in between. A marvelous film that gets more and more rich with each viewing.

Village of the Damned (1960, 78 min., black and white; Dir: Wolf Rilla; with George Sanders) Residents of a small English village black out; later, the women bear eerie-eyed children. From John Wyndham's novel. A spooky and strange film deserving far more attention than it's received.

Galaxy; *The Restaurant at the End of the Universe*; *Life, The Universe, and Everything*; and *So Long, and Thanks for All the Fish*—began as BBC radio scripts, progressed to television scripts, and ultimately became highly successful novels spoofing science fiction and high tech. The first, far and away the best of the lot, begins as Arthur Dent's house is due for demolition to make way for a highway. He finds Ford Prefect, a somewhat strange friend and an apparently out-of-work actor, anxiously seeking a drink at a nearby pub. Ford seems hopelessly indifferent to Arthur's plight because, as he explains, the world will be destroyed in a few minutes to make way for a new galactic freeway. Soon the pair are safe aboard a Vogon Construction Fleet Battleship. Improbabilities arise out of more improbabilities, but readers get caught up in the wild and utterly unbelievable adventures, and the improbabilities are less important than the sheer enjoyment and humor.

Before readers can enjoy a spoof or parody of a genre, they have to know something about the original form. That Adams' books succeeded with teenagers as well as with adults shows how mainstream science fiction has become. As shown in Focus Box 6.5 best-book lists for young adults consistently include science fiction.

Science Fiction and Women

The March 1990 *English Journal* focused on science fiction and fantasy. One of the most interesting articles was Mitch Cox's on "Engendering Critical Literacy Through Science Fiction and Fantasy." He described the small group discussions taking place in his classroom:

In one group, two members were inviting their peers to explore metaphysical questions raised by Ursula K. Le Guin's *Lathe of Heaven* and Isaac Asimov's *End of Eternity*. . . . The second group was comparing and contrasting views of life after a nuclear holocaust [using] Pat Frank's *Alas,*

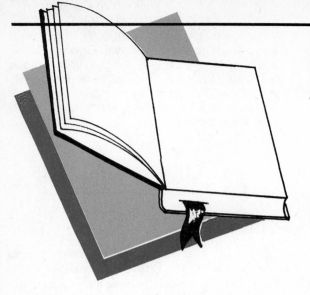

Recent Science Fiction from Best Book Lists

Alien Child by Pamela Sargent. Harper-Collins, 1988. Aliens raise the last of the human race, a boy and a girl, from frozen embryos. The question being asked is whether more embryos should be revived.

Born into Light by Paul Samuel Jacobs. Scholastic, 1988. Roger Westwood is an elderly man who tells what happened in his New England village at the turn of the century when an alien boy was found and taken in as part of the family.

Collidescope by Grace Chetwin. Bradbury, 1990. An extraterrestial cyborg (part human, part machine), a young Indian from precolonial times, and a contemporary teenager collide in space and time.

Dogsbody by Diana Wynne Jones. Greenwillow, 1988. The Dogstar, Sirius, is convicted of a crime and sent to earth in the body of a dog and given the task of finding the mysterious Zoi.

The Duplicate by William Sleator. E. P. Dutton, 1988. A machine that duplicates organic matter enables David to make a copy of himself. But then the duplicate decides to duplicate itself, which duplicates itself, and so on, into a whirlwind of problems.

Dydeetown World by F. Paul Wilson. Baen, 1989. In this science fiction novel for mystery lovers, Detective Sigmundo Dryer's client is a clone named Jean Harlow-C.

Invitation to the Game by Monica Hughes. Simon & Schuster, 1991. The year is 2154 and Lisse and seven classmates are confined in a DA (Designated Area) for the unemployed, where they begin playing a computer-simulated game that soon becomes all too real.

Jurassic Park by Michael Crichton. Knopf, 1991. Scientists get unexpected results when they use fossilized DNA to create dinosaurs for the world's most unusual theme park.

The Lives of Christopher Chant by Diana Wynne Jones. Greenwillow Books, 1988. Through his science experiments, Christopher lands himself and his absentminded parents in a heap of trouble.

Strange Attractors by William Sleator. Dutton, 1989. A scientist and his beautiful daughter from another universe mistakenly come to earth, where they act as "strange attractors." It's up to a high school scientist to keep them from upsetting the entire universe. Sleator's *Interstellar Pig* (Dutton, 1984) and *The Boy Who Reversed Himself* (Dutton, 1986) were also highly acclaimed.

2041 ed. by Jane Yolen. Delacorte, 1991. Twelve science fiction authors contributed to this collection of stories about the future.

Babylon, Walter Miller, Jr.'s *A Canticle for Leibowitz*, and Doris Lessing's *Shikasta*. . . . Students in a third group were discussing the role of the hero in T. H. White's *The Once and Future King*, Marion Zimmer Bradley's *The Mists of Avalon*, and C. J Cherryh's *Gate of Ivrel*.[17]

One of the matters this latter group was focusing on was the way Bradley and Cherryh, both females, reinterpreted the roles traditionally played by women in the Arthurian legends. Another set of books that Cox recommended for leading readers to examine how women have come to reevaluate the roles of the sexes in society is Joanna Russ's *The Female Man*, Ursula Le Guin's *The Left Hand of Darkness*, and Doris Lessing's *The Sirian Experiments*. Cox said that in addition to using such sets as these, he makes a conscious effort to include women writers and their works throughout his course.

Jane Donawerth made some interesting points in her article "Teaching Science Fiction by Women" in the same issue of *English Journal*. She pointed out that between 1818, when Mary Wollstonecraft Shelley published *Frankenstein, or the Modern Prometheus* and the depression days of the 1930s, women were among the chief writers dealing with technological utopias and other topics that foreshadowed science fiction.

But the times when such visions were welcomed did not last; at least in *Amazing Stories* and in *Wonder Stories*, the women virtually disappeared by the mid-1930s. I think that editorial policy, or simply civic pressure on the women, kept their stories from earning money that could go, instead, to a man supporting a family during the Depression.[18]

When women writers returned to the genre in the 1940s, they used masculine-sounding pen names, including Leslie F. Stone, C. L. Moore, Leigh Brackett, Andre Norton, A. M. Lightner, and J. Hunter Holly. Donawerth reported that in a panel discussion before the Science Fiction Research Association in Oxford, Ohio (June 24, 1984), Frederick Pohl, editor of *Galaxy* and *If*, hypothesized that "editors superstitiously believed that women's names on stories lowered sales to their adolescent male audience." But by the 1960s change was in the air.

- The Russians' launching of Sputnik had frightened Americans into a new emphasis on educating its children in science and technology.
- Such women as Naomi Mitchison, Ursula K. Le Guin, and Joanna Russ began writing under their own names and including female characters in their stories.
- Madeleine L'Engle made children's literature history by winning the 1963 Newbery Award for *A Wrinkle in Time*, a science fiction story.
- "Star Trek" which originally aired between September 8, 1966, and June 3, 1969, became a cult favorite, and its innumerable reruns brought science fiction to a whole new audience.

> ▪ The feminist movement demanded fair play for women and a critical look at the kinds of stereotyped roles that women had played in much of the science fiction of the last thirty years.

All these factors meant that women writers were ready to play a role in "the New Wave, the 1960s revolution in science-fiction writing that opened the genre to stylistic experimentation, to psychological characterization, and to less conservative themes such as sex, drugs, and critiques of war, imperialism, and the misuse of the ecosystem." Donawerth thinks that teaching science fiction by and about women counterbalances the old idea that science and technology are the exclusive domain of males. In addition, it leads students to an "awareness of important contemporary issues, such as changes in gender roles, alternative methods of childcare, and the importance of empathy and communication, rather than aggression, for resolving human problems."[19] See Focus Box 6.6 for her suggestions of short stories and books to teach while exploring such issues with both male and female readers.

UTOPIAS AND DYSTOPIAS

Utopias and dystopias are neither pure science fiction nor pure fantasy, but they share characteristics with both. Readers must suspend disbelief and buy into the author's vision, at least for the duration of the story. Like science fiction, utopian and dystopian books are usually set in the future, with technology having played a role in establishing the conditions out of which the story grows. But unlike science fiction and more like fantasy, once the situation is established, authors focus less on technology and more on sociological and psychological or emotional aspects of the story. A utopia is a place of happiness and prosperity; a dystopia is the opposite.

Two of the most interesting YA books published in the last few years fall into the category of dystopias. One is Bruce Brooks's *No Kidding*, which tells a serious story of a boy realizing that he can't, and in fact doesn't want to, make all the decisions for his alcoholic mother and his strange little brother. The story is set in a Washington, D.C., of the future, where 69 percent of the population is alcoholic and children are a treasured commodity because so many people have been made sterile by sitting in front of Cathode Ray Tubes. The story is about two young brothers, Sam and Ollie. Sam is rehabilitating his mother at the same time he attempts to direct and control the foster parents who want to adopt the younger Ollie. Sam is shocked when he finds out that even with all his help Ollie feels a need for something he doesn't have and regularly sneaks out at night to meet with a cultlike religious group.

Despite the grim plot, *No Kidding* is filled with some wonderful kidding about schools, social workers, educational jargon, and the wishful thinking that any problem can be corrected if only we can give it a name and obtain federal

Science Fiction with a Feminist Spin*

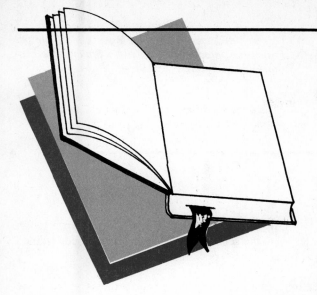

Barbary by Vonda McIntyre. Ace, 1988. When street-wise Barbary is brought to live on a space station with her dead mother's friend and his family, she brings along her cat, who ends up playing an important role.

The Day of the Drones by A. M. (Alice Martha) Lightner. Bantam, 1970. Lightner is a black author who did a reversal on the segregation issues of the 1960s in a postholocaust world in which whites are discriminated against because they used their technology to destroy the earth.

The Female Man by Joanna Russ. Bantam, 1975. One of the most important female utopias, Russ's book makes interesting reading alongside Marge Piercy's *Woman on the Edge of Time* (Fawcett, 1976) and Joan Slonczewski's *Door into Ocean* (Avon, 1976).

The Keeper of the Isis Light by Monica Hughes. Macmillan, 1984. Hughes writes specifically for teenagers, and in this book uses a doomed romance to explore prejudices surrounding physical differences.

The Left Hand of Darkness by Ursula K. Le Guin. Ace, 1969. The unusual setting is the planet Gethen, whose people are neither male nor female, neither asexual nor bisexual. *Dispossessed: An Ambiguous Utopia* (HarperCollins, 1974) and *The Eye of the Heron* (HarperCollins, 1978) also explore gender and ethnic restrictions.

Three Hundred Years Hence by Mary Griffith. Hall, 1975. Originally published in 1836, this utopian book portrays a Philadelphia of the future in which food is prepared communally and women own property and attend college.

"The Women Men Don't See," short story by James Tiptree, Jr. (really Alice Sheldon) in *Warm Worlds and Otherwise* (Ballantine, 1975). A mother and her daughter, passengers on a downed plane, decide to leave the pilot and the other passenger and take their chances with aliens.

Women of Wonder, Random, 1974, and *The New Women of Wonder*, Random, 1978, both edited by Pamela Sargent. Sargent's introduction to the first of these short story collections presents an excellent history of women writers of science fiction. Among the stories is Anne McCaffrey's 1961 "The Ship Who Sang" (also published as a novel), about a woman cyborg who becomes the center of the operating computer of a space ship.

Recommended background books for the teacher include Marion Zimmer Bradley's *The Keeper's Price* (DAW, 1980); Ursula Le Guin's *The*

Language of the Night edited by Susan Wood (Putnam, 1979); Sharon K. Yntema's *More than 100: Women Science Fiction Writers* (Crossing, 1988); Joanna Russ's *Magic Mommas, Trembling Sisters, Puritans & Perverts: Feminist Essays* (Crossing, 1985); Tom Staicar's *The Feminine Eye: Science Fiction and the Women Who Write It* (Frederick Ungar, 1982); and Natalie M. Rosinsky's *Feminist Futures: Contemporary Women's Speculative Fiction* (UMI Research P., 1984).

*Thanks to Jane Donawerth and her article in *English Journal*, March 1990.

funding. Sam goes to an AO (Alcoholic Offspring) school, where in a tough moment, the counselor confesses to the school nurse that she hasn't been trained as a generalist counselor, only as an AO specialist:

> I have *no* certification outside AO programs. My thesis was on the doctrinal interface between quantified behavior-analysis patterns and AOCLEP. Quantified! I am trained to deal with kids who are tested every week for theoretical knowledge of specific AO doctrine *and* behavioral adjustment in AO alignments. At my previous school a kid would come in and say "I aggressed on the math teacher's car in a third-level postdenial anger/pity syndrome, and I broke the windshield." I would say, "What's your denial factor?" and he would say "Eight," and I would say "Index of control achievement?" and he would say "Six," and I would know *exactly* what to do with him. . . . Now, what am I supposed to do with a kid who knows nothing except that he threw a rock at a car?

The other recent dystopian book is Peter Dickinson's *Eva*, a fascinating story about the daughter of a famous scientist devoting his life to working with chimpanzees. In this futuristic world, chimpanzees are relatively important because all the big animals have vanished. The scientist, his wife, his thirteen-year-old daughter Eva, and a chimpanzee named Kelly are coming home from an outing when they get in a wreck. Eva remembers nothing of the wreck but finds herself slowly waking up in a very controlled environment. Over several weeks she discovers that her mind has been planted in Kelly's body:

> You couldn't just invade a chimp body and take it over with your human mind, like a hero in a history book—you'd never get to be whole that way. Eva's human neurons might have copied themselves into Kelly's brain, but as Dad had said, that left a sort of connection, an interface, a borderland where human ended and chimp began. You couldn't live like that, with a frontier in you like a wall, keeping your selves apart. The only way to become whole was to pull the wall down, to let the other side back in, to let it invade in its turn, up into the human side, the neurons remembering

their old paths, twining themselves in among the human network until both sides made a single pattern. A new pattern, not Eva, not Kelly—both but one.

Basically, the rest of the book is about this process over the thirty years of Eva's life. The technology is fun to read about, but it's the psychological and the social aspects that leave readers pondering some unique facets of such issues as ecology, parent/child and male/female relationships, mass media advertising, medical ethics, and young adult suicide.

Utopias and dystopias are never likely to be popular with the masses because they usually lack excitement and fast-moving plots. Writers of adventure or fantasy or science fiction begin with a story (the more thrilling the better), and later, if ever, add a message. Writers of utopias and dystopias think first of the message and then devise a story to carry the weight of the message.

The books are usually about dissatisfaction with contemporary society. Many readers have no wish to think seriously about societal issues, much less to read about them. Readers who do not share the anger or irritation of utopian writers will easily miss the allusions needed to follow the story or find the message. For these reasons, utopian literature is likely to appeal only to more thoughtful and intellectual readers. Although these young adults may not share the anger of the writer, given their idealism, they probably share the writer's concerns about society and humanity.

The centuries-old fascination with utopias is suggested by the Greek origin of the word, which includes two meanings, "no place" and "good place." Most of us, in idle moments, dream of a perfect land, a perfect society, a place that would solve all our personal problems and, if we are altruistic enough, all the world's problems as well. In our nightmares, we also dream of the opposite, the dystopias, which are diseased or bad lands. But few of us do more than dream, which may explain why some people are so intrigued with authors who transfer their dreams to the printed page.

In his *Republic* in the fifth century B.C., Plato presented his vision of the ideal world, offering suggestions for educating the ruling class. With wise philosopher-kings, or so Plato maintains, the people would prosper, intellectual joys would flourish (along with censorship, for Plato would ban poets and dramatists from his perfect society), and the land would be permanently safe.

Later utopias were geared less to a ruling class and more to a society that would preserve its peace and create harmony and happiness for the people. Sir Thomas More's *Utopia* (1516) argued for mental equality of the sexes, simple laws understandable to all, and common ownership of everything. Whether More intended his book as a practical solution to society's problems is doubtful, but he probably did mean it as a criticism of contemporary English life. Utopias, after all, are personal and reflect an author's enthusiasm for (or abhorrence of) certain ideas. That was clearly true of two early utopias, Francis Bacon's *The New Atlantis* (1626) and Tommaso Campanella's *City in the Sun* (1623).

During the late 1800s, the popularity of such utopias as Samuel Butler's

Erewhon (1872) and *Erewhon Revisited* (1901), William Dean Howell's *A Traveler from Altruia* (1894), and Edward Bellamy's *Looking Backward* (1888) paralleled the popularity of people's real-life attempts to seek better lives through various utopian schemes. In the United States, utopian communities at places like Harmony, Pennsylvania; New Harmony, Indiana; Brook Farm, Massachusetts; Fruitlands, Massachusetts; Oneida, New York; Nauvoo, Illinois; and Corning, Iowa, were rarely more than temporarily satisfactory.

Utopian communities have been the setting for several novels. Elizabeth Howard's *Out of Step with the Dancers* shows a celibate Shaker community in 1853 through the eyes of Damaris as she accompanies her converted father to a strange new life. Religious pacifism in the face of the Civil War is the subject of Janet Hickman's *Zoar Blue*, about the German separatist community of Zoar, Ohio. Lynn Hall's excellent *Too Near the Sun* focuses on sixteen-year-old Armel Dupree and his Icarian community near Corning, Iowa. To the shame of his family, Armel's older brother has sought life in the outside world. Armel now wonders if he should follow his brother as he views an ideal community composed of less than ideal people.

The world outside and inside the community in Oneida, New York, where love is everywhere and sex is to be shared with all, proves something other than a heaven to the Berger family in Blossom Elfman's *The Strawberry Fields of Heaven*. Jane Yolen's *The Gift of Sarah Barker* is set in the Shaker village of New Vale. Taken there by her psychotic mother, Sarah learns that whatever happiness she can find with her beloved Abel, it cannot be in New Vale.

Yearning for the simpler life, where we dream of being part of something greater than ourselves, is natural. But for some young people, the search has led to religious groups less like communes and more like cults. Robert Coover explored the power and madness of a cult in *The Origin of the Brunists*. In that novel, a mining explosion kills ninety-seven people, but one survivor believes that God has saved him to proclaim the approaching end of the world. Two sound nonfiction works give insights about cults and why and how they are often so successful in attracting the most sincere young adults—Willa Appel's *Cults in America: Programmed for Paradise* and David G. Bromley and Anson D. Shupe, Jr.'s, *Strange Gods: The Great American Cult Scare*.

Dystopias are more dramatic and exaggerated than their counterparts, and for that reason are more successful in attracting young adults. Dystopias warn us of society's drift toward a particularly horrifying or sick world lying just over the horizon. They are sometimes misinterpreted as prophecies alone, but books like Aldous Huxley's *Brave New World* and George Orwell's *1984* and *Animal Farm* are part prophecy, part warning.

For many, the most obvious dystopia today is the postnuclear world some short—or distant—time ahead of us. Robert C. O'Brien's *Z for Zachariah* was an early young adult example of what many readers fear, being alone in a world that has gone mad and that may have no other human survivors or, perhaps worse yet, that has other survivors no longer quite human.

The theme has been common to several recent novels. Robert Swindell's

Brother in the Land presents a postnuclear world in which authorities seek to establish a new feudal society and a resistance group tries to fight back. Even less optimistic is Susan B. Weston's *Children of the Light*. Walter M. Miller and Martin Greenberg's excellent, if depressing, collection of twenty-one short stories about the world after the nuclear holocaust, *Beyond Armageddon*, should be available for readers who can stomach a truth that lies ahead of us *if* we choose not to alter our lives and our world.

Two books on this theme stand out. Louise Lawrence's *Children of the Dust* carries the nuclear holocaust through three generations, and James D. Forman's *Doomsday Plus Twelve* shows the inevitable struggle and war that must come again even after the nuclear holocaust. Neither Lawrence nor Forman are sanguine, but both are honest and write extremely well.

A theme that we'll probably see more of in future books is that of disasters caused by ecological carelessness. Thomas Baird's *Smart Rats* is a disturbing exploration of this theme. Everything is rationed, including children (one per family); the government is all-powerful, except when it comes to solving problems; contaminated areas are said to be harmless, and areas that the government doesn't want entered are said to be infested with killer rats, from which the book gets its title. Inspired by all the terrible things that are happening both inside and outside his family, seventeen-year-old Laddie Grayson connives his way into a forbidden area of the library and reads about the effects of various chemicals.

In this truly depressing book, Laddie keeps his theories to himself about an insecticide that his pregnant mother encountered, but he realizes what he must do. He also enrolls in a special school to become part of the "system." The question for readers is whether Laddie can remain inside the system without becoming corrupt.

To attract young adult readers, dystopian books have to have something extra, because with a few exceptions, young adults are optimistic and imaginative. Adults might read dystopian books on the premise that misery loves company, but teenagers have not lived long enough to lose their natural curiosity, nor have they been weighed down with adult problems, such as failing health, heavy family responsibilities, expenses surpassing income, and dreams gone bankrupt. So even when teenagers read dystopian books, they are likely to approach such books through rose-colored glasses, feeling grateful for the world as it usually is.

In honor of this optimism, we will close our discussion with a look at David Macaulay's *Motel of the Mysteries*, a wonderful spoof of scientific arrogance unmasked as wild guessing games. The book begins with the ominous description of the burial of the North American continent under tons of third- and fourth-class mail (caused by an accidental reduction in postal rates). Since the year 3850, scholars have wondered about the lost civilization, but it is left to forty-two-year-old Howard Carson to stumble and fall into a secret chamber. There he discovers a "gleaming secret seal" (DO NOT DISTURB) and a "plant that would not die." He enters the chamber and finds a body atop a "ceremonial

David Macaulay's
Motel of the Mysteries
is a spoof of scientific
arrogance.

platform near a statue of the "deity WATT" and a container, "ICE," designed
to "preserve, at least symbolically, the major internal organs of the deceased
for eternity." Later he enters the inner chamber and there finds another body
"in a highly polished white sarcophagus" behind translucent curtains. Near this
body is a "sacred urn" and a "sacred parchment" holder and the "sacred collar"
with a headband bearing a ceremonial chant, "Sanitized for Your Protection."
The drawing of Howard Carson playing savant and the many artifacts recovered
from the motel bedroom and bathroom add to the fun. Museum goers will
particularly enjoy the concluding section of the book devoted to "Souvenirs and
Quality Reproduction" from the Carson excavations now for sale.

The books we've talked about in this chapter—starting with the oldest stories
of humankind and moving on up through modern fantasy, science fiction, and
utopias and dystopias—start with life as we know it and attempt to stretch
readers' imaginations. All of us need to dream, not to waste our lives but to
enrich them. To dream is to recognize humanity's possibilities. In a world
hardly characterized by undue optimism, the genres treated here offer us challenges and hope, not the sappy sentimentalism of "everything always works
out for the best" (for it often does not) but realistic hope based on our noblest
dreams of surviving. If we go down, we do it knowing that we have cared and
dreamed and found something for which we are willing to struggle.

NOTES

[1] Ursula Le Guin, "On Teaching Science Fiction," in Jack Williamson, ed., *Teaching Science Fiction: Education for Tomorrow* (Oswick Press, 1980), p. 22.

[2] Walter Wangerin, Jr., in a lecture, "By Faith, Fantasy," quoted in John H. Timmerman's *Other Worlds: The Fantasy Genre* (Bowling Green University Popular Press, 1983), p. 21.

[3] The ad for the Science Fiction Book Club for March 1992 lists books as different as Isaac Asimov's *Complete Stories*; Roger Zelazny's *Prince of Chaos*; Lloyd Alexander's *The Prydain Chronicles*; Michael Crichton's *Jurassic Park*; Asimov's *Beginnings: The Story of Origins of Mankind, Life, the Earth, the Universe*; and *Great American Folklore*, all fine choices but with not much in common, except for their quality.

[4] This point, with many more examples, is made repeatedly by Leslie E. Owen in "Children's Science Fiction and Fantasy Grow Up," *Publishers Weekly* 232 (October 30, 1987): 32–37.

[5] J. R. R. Tolkien, *The Tolkien Reader* (Ballantine, 1966), pp. 74–75.

[6] Mary Harrington Hall, "A Conversation with Ray Bradbury and Chuck Jones," *Psychology Today* 1 (April 1969): 28–29.

[7] John Rowe Townsend, "Heights of Fantasy," in Gerard J. Senick, ed., *Children's Review*, Vol. 5 (Gale Research, 1983), p. 7.

[8] Lloyd Alexander, "High Fantasy and Heroic Romance," *Horn Book Magazine* 47 (December 1971): 483.

[9] Ursula Le Guin, "Why Are Americans So Afraid of Dragons?" *PNLA* (Pacific Northwest Library Association) *Quarterly* 38 (Winter 1974): 18.

[10] Mary Cadogan and Patricia Craig, *You're a Brick, Angela! A New Look at Girls' Fiction from 1839 to 1975* (Gollancz, 1976), p. 371.

[11] Audrey Eaglen, "Old Wine, New Bottles," *School Library Journal* 36 (September 1990): 171.

[12] "Using Adolescent Novels as Transitions to Literary Classics," *English Journal* 78 (March 1989): 82–83.

[13] Robert Heinlein, "Ray Guns and Rocket Ships," *Library Journal* 78 (July 1953): 1188.

[14] Anthony Wolk, "Challenge the Boundaries: An Overview of Science Fiction and Fantasy," *English Journal* 79 (March 1990): 26–31.

[15] Ray Bradbury, "Science Fiction: Why Bother?" *Teacher's Guide: Science Fiction* (Bantam, n.d.), p. 1.

[16] Arthur Clarke, *Profiles of the Future* (Holt, 1984), p. 9.

[17] Mitch Cox, "Engendering Critical Literacy Through Science Fiction and Fantasy," *English Journal* 79 (March 1990): 35–37.

[18] Jane Donawerth, "Teaching Science Fiction by Women," *English Journal* 79 (March 1990): 39–45.

[19] Donawerth, "Teaching Science Fiction by Women," p. 41.

■ OTHER TITLES MENTIONED IN THE TEXT OF CHAPTER SIX

Adams, Douglas. *The Hitchhiker's Guide to the Galaxy*. Harmony, 1979.

_____. *Life, the Universe, and Everything*. Harmony, 1982.

_____. *The Restaurant at the End of the Universe*. Harmony, 1980.

_____. *So Long, and Thanks for All the Fish*. Harmony, 1985.

Adams, Richard. *Watership Down*. Macmillan, 1974.

Alexander, Lloyd. *The Black Cauldron*. Holt, 1965.

_____. *The Book of Three*. Holt, 1964.

_____. *The Castle of Llyr*. Holt, 1966.

_____. *The High King*. Holt, 1968.

_____. *Taran Wanderer*. Holt, 1967.

Appel, Willa. *Cults in America: Programmed for Paradise*. Holt, 1983.

Asimov, Isaac. *End of Eternity*. Fawcett, 1978.

Baird, Thomas. *Smart Rats*. HarperCollins, 1990.

Beagle, Peter. *A Fine and Private Place*. Viking, 1960.

_____. *The Last Unicorn*. Viking, 1968.

Bell, Clare. *Clan Ground*. Atheneum, 1984.

_____. *Ratha's Creatures*. Atheneum, 1983.

_____. *Ratha and Thistle-Chaser*. McElderry-Macmillan, 1990.

Bemmann, Hans. *The Stone and the Flute*, translated by Anthea Bell. Viking, 1986 (originally published in Germany in 1983).

Bradley, Marion Zimmer. *The Best of Marion Zimmer Bradley*. DAW, 1988.

_____. *Darkover Landfall*. DAW Books, 1972.

_____. *The Mists of Avalon*. Knopf, 1983.

_____. *Red Sun of Darkover*. DAW Books, 1987.

_____. *Two to Conquer*. DAW Books, 1980.

Bradshaw, Gillian. *Hawk of May*. Simon & Schuster, 1982.

_____. *Kingdom of Summer*. Simon & Schuster, 1981.

_____. *In Winter's Shadow*. Simon & Schuster, 1982.

Bromley, David G., and Anson D. Shupe, Jr. *Strange Gods: The Great American Cult Scare*. Beacon Press, 1982.

Brooks, Bruce. *No Kidding*. HarperCollins, 1989.

Cherryh, C. J. *Gate of Ivrel*. DAW, 1976.

Clarke, Arthur C. *Profiles of the Future*. Holt, 1984.

Coover, Robert. *The Origin of the Brunists*. Viking, 1977.

Dickinson, Peter. *Eva*. Delacorte, 1989.

Elfman, Blossom. *The Strawberry Fields of Heaven*. Crown, 1983.

Forman, James D. *Doomsday Plus Twelve*. Scribner, 1984.

Frank, Pat. *Alas, Babylon*. Bantam, 1976.

Garner, Alan. *Elidor*. London: Collins, 1965.

_____. *The Moon of Gomrath*. London: Collins, 1963.

_____. *The Owl Service*. Walck, 1967.

_____. *Red Shift*. Macmillan, 1973.

_____. *The Weirdstone of Brisingamen*. London: Collins, 1960.

Graham, Robin. *Dove*. HarperCollins, 1972.

Grahame, Kenneth. *The Wind in the Willows* (originally published in 1908).

Hall, Lynn. *Too Near the Sun*. Follett, 1970.

Hersey, John. *Hiroshima*. Knopf, 1946.

Hickman, Janet. *Zoar Blue*. Macmillan, 1978.

Holman, Felice. *The Wild Children*. Scribner, 1983.

Hoover, H. M. *The Dawn Palace*. Dutton, 1988.

Howard, Elizabeth. *Out of Step with the Dancers*. Morrow, 1978.

Huxley, Aldous. *Brave New World*. HarperCollins, 1932.

Klause, Annette Curtis. *The Silver Kiss*. Delacorte, 1990.

Kurtz, Katherine. *Deryni Checkmate*. Ballantine, 1972.

———. *Deryni Rising. Ballantine, 1970.*

———. *High Deryni*. Ballantine, 1970.

———. *The Legacy of Lehr*. Walker, 1986.

Langton, Jane. *The Fledgling*. HarperCollins, 1980.

Lawrence, Louise. *Children of the Dust*. HarperCollins, 1980.

Le Guin, Ursula K. *The Dispossessed: An Ambiguous Utopia*. HarperCollins, 1974.

———. *The Farthest Shore*. Atheneum, 1972.

———. *Lathe of Heaven*. Bentley, 1971.

———. *The Left Hand of Darkness*. Ace, 1969.

———. *Tehanu: The Last Book of Earthsea*. Macmillan, 1990.

———. *The Tombs of Atuan*. Atheneum, 1972.

———. *The Wizard of Earthsea*. Parnassus, 1963.

L'Engle, Madeleine. *A Wrinkle in Time*. Farrar, Straus & Giroux, 1962.

Lessing, Doris. *Shikasta*. Knopf, 1979.

———. *The Sirian Experiments*. Knopf, 1981.

Macaulay, David. *Motel of the Mysteries*. Houghton Mifflin, 1979.

Martin, Valerie. *Mary Reilly*. Doubleday, 1990.

McCaffrey, Anne. *Dragondrums*. Atheneum, 1979.

———. *Dragonsinger*. Atheneum, 1977.

———. *Dragonsong*. Atheneum, 1976.

———. *Moreta: Dragon Lady of Pern*. Ballantine, 1983.

———. *The White Dragon*. Ballantine, 1978.

McKillip, Patricia. *The Forgotten Beasts of Eld*. Atheneum, 1974.

———. *The Moon and the Face*. Atheneum, 1985.

———. *Moon-Flash*. Atheneum, 1984.

McKinley, Robin. *Beauty: A Retelling of the Story of Beauty and the Beast*. HarperCollins, 1978.

———. *The Blue Sword*. Greenwillow, 1982.

———. *The Hero and the Crown*. Greenwillow, 1984.

———. *The Outlaws of Sherwood*. Greenwillow, 1988.

Miller, Walter H., Jr. *A Canticle for Leibowitz*. Lippincott, 1959.

Miller, Walter H., Jr., and Martin H. Greenberg. *Beyond Armageddon*. Fine, 1985.

O'Brien, Robert C. *Mrs. Frisby and the Rats of NIMH*. Atheneum, 1971.

———. *Z for Zachariah*. Atheneum, 1975.

Orwell, George. *Animal Farm*. Harcourt Brace Jovanovich, 1954.

———. *1984*. Harcourt Brace Jovanovich, 1940.

Russ, Joanna. *The Female Man*. Beacon, 1986.

Shupe, Anson D., Jr. *Strange Gods: The Great American Cult Scare*. Beacon Press, 1982.

Stewart, Mary. *The Crystal Cave*. Morrow, 1970.

———. *The Hollow Hills*. Morrow, 1973.

———. *The Last Enchantment*. Morrow, 1979.

———. *The Wicked Day*. Morrow, 1984.

Sutcliff, Rosemary. *The Light Beyond the Forest: The Quest for the Holy Grail*. Dutton, 1979.

———. *The Road to Camlann: The Death of King Arthur*. Dutton, 1982.

———. *The Sword and the Circle: King Arthur and the Knights of the Round Table*. Dutton, 1981.

Swindells, Robert. *Brother in the Land* . Holiday House, 1985.

Tolkien, J. R. R. *The Hobbit, or There and Back Again*. Houghton Mifflin, 1938.

———. *The Lord of the Rings*. Houghton Mifflin. Composed of three parts: *The Fellowship of the Rings*, 1954, rev. ed., 1967; *The Two Towers*, 1955, rev. ed., 1967; and *The Return of the King*, 1956, rev. ed., 1967.

———. *The Silmarillion*. Houghton Mifflin, 1983.

Vonnegut, Kurt, Jr. *God Bless You, Mr. Rosewater or Pearls Before Swine*. Holt, 1965.

Walton, Evangeline. *The Children of Llyr: The Second Branch of the Mabinogion*. Ballantine, 1971.

———. *The Island of the Mighty*. Ballantine, 1970 (first printed as *The Virgin and the Swine: The Fourth Branch of the Mabinogion*).

———. *The Prince of Annwn: The First Branch of the Mabinogion*. Ballantine, 1974.

———. *The Song of Rhiannon: The Third Branch of the Mabinogion*. Ballantine, 1972.

Wangerin, Walter, Jr. *The Book of the Dun Cow*. HarperCollins, 1978.

———. *The Book of Sorrows*. HarperCollins, 1985.

Weston, Susan B. *Children of the Light*. St. Martin's Press, 1986.

White, E. B. *Charlotte's Web*. HarperCollins, 1952.

———. *Stuart Little*. HarperCollins, 1945.

White, T. H. *The Book of Merlyn: The Unpublished Conclusion*. University of Texas Press, 1977.

———. *The Once and Future King*. Putnam's, 1958.

Yolen, Jane. *Dragon's Blood*. Delacorte, 1982.

———. *The Gift of Sarah Barker*. Viking, 1981.

———. *Heart's Blood*. Delacorte, 1984.

———. *A Sending of Dragons*. Delacorte, 1987.

For information on the availability of paperback editions of these titles, please consult the most recent edition of *Paperbound Books in Print,* published annually by R. R. Bowker Company.

CHAPTER SEVEN

HISTORY AND HISTORY MAKERS

Of People and Places

America has always viewed history in its own unique way. More than a century ago, Ralph Waldo Emerson described the great American tradition as "trampling on tradition," and Abraham Lincoln said that Americans had a "perfect rage for the new." Part of the reason was that as a young pluralistic country, America was united by its future rather than by its past. "Americans had their eyes focused on the horizon, and history was an impediment to progress." But by the beginning of the twentieth century, Americans were feeling more confident in their identity and were ready to begin looking back. For the first time, American history became a standard part of the school curriculum, thousands of towns erected statues of Abraham Lincoln and Ulysses S. Grant, and historical pageants flourished, including in the South, where Confederates began to look back with pride on their role in the Civil War.[1]

As interested as we may be in history, we are always more concerned about the present, and we find ourselves imposing present-day values on the past. In 1927, Henry Seidel Canby wrote, "Historical fiction, like history, is more likely to register an exact truth about the writer's present than the exact truth of the past."[2] In a recent book, *Mystic Chords of Memory*, historian Michael Kammen develops a similar point. *Time* magazine reviewer Richard Stengel praised Kammen for showing how "Throughout American history, facts have been transformed into myths and myths transformed into beliefs." Immigrants came to America to escape the past, but once they were settled here they contributed to a "kind of ethnic American syllogism: the first generation zealously preserves; the second generation zealously forgets; the third generation zealously rediscovers." Kammen wrote that after World War II, Americans were tied together by a sense of patriotism, but in the 1960s this was replaced by a decade of questioning. In the 1970s it turned to nostalgia (i.e., "history without guilt"), which continued in the 1980s with a "selective memory and a soothing amnesia." History became a growth industry, and under Reagan "public history was privatized, so that it was Coca Cola, not the U.S. government, that brought you the centennial of the Statue of Liberty."[3]

Despite the flaws that Kammen points out, the history "growth industry" has generally been positive for the education of young people. Commemorations of the 1976 bicentennial of the U.S. Declaration of Independence, the centennial of the Statue of Liberty, the bicentennial of the Bill of Rights, the fiftieth anniversary of the beginning of World War II, and the five-hundredth anniversary of Columbus' arrival in the New World have kept historical events in the public eye. The accuracy, completeness, and objectivity of commemorative events, television programs, movies, news and magazine articles, and books have of course varied, but most of us would agree that the attention has been good in arousing curiosity and in communicating an attitude that history is important.

Trade Books for History Study

Kammen's book focuses on people's predilection for comfortable myths (i.e., nostalgia), as opposed to factual history, but what he says isn't as true about history-related trade books for young people as it is about popular entertainment, such as *Gunsmoke*'s portrayal of the wild west, *Hogan's Heroes'* portrayal of World War II, and *The Waltons'* portrayal of American life in the early twentieth century. Moreover, it is not as true of trade books as it is of textbooks. Textbook writers often rely on comfortable myths, because to be adopted in a school district the books must go through so many committees and stages of approval that by the time they actually get to classrooms they are likely to be extremely bland. Or if a point of view is expressed, it's likely to be in support of the status quo. For example, a 1983 State of Texas mandate on textbook selection reads, "Positive aspects of the USA's history must be stressed in world history texts used in public schools." In commenting on this mandate, Betty Carter and Richard Abrahamson observed that "Those negatives—the sorry mistakes that have dotted our past and may well affect our future—are either left out, glossed over, or presented in a favorable light." For example, a history book prepared under this philosophy might present the Spanish-American War as "little more than a dramatic charge up San Juan Hill" and America's ignoring of Hitler's rise to power and his evil intentions as a "failure to communicate with Eastern Europe." Carter and Abrahamson warn that such distortions "turn the drama of history into a whitewash."[4]

Fortunately, the writers of history-related trade books are freer to pursue particular points of view because their books are going to be purchased individually or by libraries, which endorse, at least on paper, having a great variety of opinions and points of view. Also with trade books, writers have frequent chances to incorporate new attitudes and new findings, because individuals and libraries provide a steady market. And reviewers and other evaluators stand guard, so that over the last several years increasing emphasis has been given to the importance of authenticity and the use of primary sources. Nonfiction writer Brent Ashabranner, for example, has said that one of the things he's learned from reviewers is how seriously they feel about documentation. After his first few books were criticized, he has been much more careful with his bibliographies and has taken special pains to let readers know where he has gotten his information. He thinks extensive footnotes interrupt the flow of reading, and so he tries to put the information "into the text in a way that doesn't interfere with the prose but assures the reader that I didn't just make things up."[5]

Books created from letters and diaries reassure readers that they are reading authentic history, as in Barnard Edelman's *Dear America: Letters Home from Vietnam* and Annette Tapert's *Lines of Battle: Letters from American Servicemen, 1941–1945*. Relying on primary sources goes a long way toward keeping authors and subsequently their readers from wallowing in nostalgia. And today it's standard practice in history books for the author to include a foreword or afterword discussing his or her methods of research and giving suggestions for further reading. Milton Meltzer uses photos, letters, diaries, and speeches of people who were there to provide a personal-experience account of the Civil War in *Voices from the Civil War: A Documentary History of the Great American Conflict*.

Going back to Kammen's idea of history as a growth industry, interest in one area or one medium feeds interest and work in related areas. For example, in 1989, *The Civil War* series broadcast by PBS generated a new wave of interest in books and movies about the Civil War. An obvious follow-up was a large and expensive coffee table book, *The Civil War: An Illustrated History* by Geoffrey Ward, based on the filmscript and including many of the original letters. Dozens of other books also grew out of the project, either directly or indirectly. Among the follow-up books is *All for the Union: The Civil War Diary and Letters of Elisha Hunt Rhodes*, edited by Robert Hunt Rhodes and published in 1991 by Crown as an Orion book. The letters had already been edited and published in a small edition by one of the six great-grandchildren of Elisha Hunt Rhodes. When Ken Burns, producer of the PBS series, was doing research for the series, he ran across the volume and was so touched by the letters that he decided to use two common soldiers as the thread that would tie the series together. After the success of the PBS program, people were interested enough to want to read all of Rhodes's letters. Rhodes was nineteen when he joined the Union forces and twenty-three when he left. As Geoffrey C. Ward wrote in the foreword, the young soldier's observations were "fresh, vivid, understated, utterly free of the ornate and imitative style with which more learned veterans managed to put some distance between themselves and the ghastly sights they saw." An additional plus for young readers is the fact that Rhodes was still a teenager who had to get his widowed mother's permission

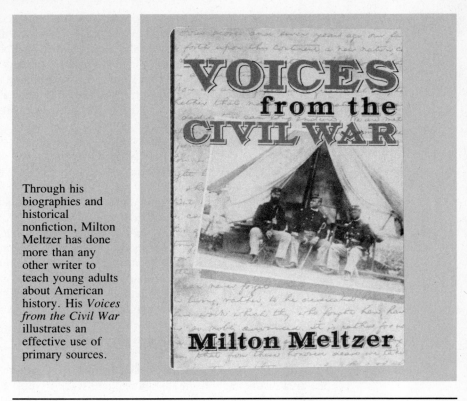

Through his biographies and historical nonfiction, Milton Meltzer has done more than any other writer to teach young adults about American history. His *Voices from the Civil War* illustrates an effective use of primary sources.

---

before he could join the Union forces. An earlier book that is also a fascinating account of a young soldier is David Herbert Donald's edited version of *Gone for a Soldier: The Civil War Memoirs of Alfred Bellard.*

The PBS series, which was broadcast a year earlier, undoubtedly increased interest in the movie *Glory,* a story of black Civil War soldiers. In turn, Clinton Cox, a prize-winning black journalist, capitalized on the interest engendered by the movie when he wrote *Undying Glory: The Story of the Massachusetts 54th Regiment,* published by Scholastic in 1991. But when a history teacher in our local high school showed *Glory,* a parent protested "because of the violence" and a major controversy erupted. The result was that the school board voted that no "R" rated movies were to be shown. Many of the townspeople who came to the public hearing to protest the board's recommendation suspected that the original discomfort over the movie *Glory* was not because of the violence, but because of the challenge the movie posed to several comfortable myths about African Americans.

Another example of a movie that challenges comfortable myths is Oliver Stone's *JFK,* which makes the case that Lee Harvey Oswald was a "patsy" rather than the person solely responsible for killing U.S. President John F. Kennedy. Moviegoers were accustomed to artists' changing stories to shape them into coherent dramas, as in such highly acclaimed movies as *Ghandi, Lawrence of Arabia,* and *All the President's Men.* But these movies kept the basic historical facts intact, whereas *JFK* claims that we didn't understand the facts and so need to take a second look. The film broke new ground in mixing real news photos and broadcasts with simulated ones and in filming parts of the staged motorcade with 8-mm. and 16-mm. film to make the re-creations blend in with the original homemade films used as evidence.

Dozens of newspaper and magazine articles debated such issues as whether the studio had an obligation to present the film as director "Oliver Stone's version of the truth," whether political and ethical questions were dwarfed by a profit motive, and whether, because John Kennedy's closest survivors are still alive, the studio should have exercised more control over the director. Interest in these questions led to debates over more general questions, including whether a historical film can be judged by the same journalistic standards as a news story and whether any filmmaker has a right to take a position and present it as the truth, much as Shakespeare did with his portrayal of Richard III.

As educators, we need to make students aware of such controversies. One way to do this is to demand that authors be careful to distinguish between what is known and what is only conjectured. We need to help students develop the skill to interpret the author's clues. A good book to start with, because of its format, is Dorothy and Thomas Hoobler's *The Fact or Fiction Files: Lost Civilizations.* On one side of the pages are the facts as they are known about such mysteries as Stonehenge and the carved heads on Easter Island. On the other side, the authors present hypotheses and conjectures.

William Loren Katz, in his *Breaking the Chains: African-American Slave Resistance*, spends a good deal of time discussing and refuting some of the myths and historical misrepresentations about slavery that have allowed people to believe that most slaves were satisfied with their lot.

Kathy Pelta, in her *Discovering Christopher Columbus: How History Is Invented,* uses her first two chapters to summarize undisputed facts about Columbus. In the rest of the book she discusses more controversial aspects of the story and shows where her information was found, what contradictory evidence exists, and how the facts of Columbus' life are still being discovered. The book is a how-to for historical research. Being centered on one timely event makes it both more interesting and easier to understand than it would be if the same principles were illustrated from different historical periods and happenings.

A commemoration as big as the celebration of the five-hundredth anniversary of Columbus' landing in the Americas provides an opportunity to see how different publishers approach historical nonfiction. Publishers begin years ahead to plan for this kind of big event. Some simply pull out old books, jazz them up a little, put on a new cover, and sit back, hoping to make a profit by capitalizing on the media hype. Others work hard to come up with something new and interesting that will contribute to, rather than just profit from, the event. It's the books in this latter group that will last and will not be tossed out like an old Christmas tree.

Books leading up to the celebration began appearing as early as 1988 and continued appearing all through 1992. The preference was heavily on the side of nonfiction. In keeping with today's penchant for visual as well as verbal appeal, virtually every book was fully illustrated, many with charts, maps, and historical drawings and woodcuts; others had photos and drawings. Some books were written by people who tried to retrace Columbus' voyage, others were annotated versions of his log, and still others focused on particular aspects of the journey, as with Gardner Soule's *Christopher Columbus: On the Green Sea of Darkness*, which dwells on the wildlife of the seas, including the sea birds that caused the crew to change its course away from Florida.

Putnam presented a reversal on the idea of Columbus "discovering" America by publishing Francine Jacobs' *The Tainos: The People Who Welcomed Columbus*. The book gives information about the inhabitants of the Caribbean who met Columbus and his men in 1492. It goes on to show how the Spaniard's arrival eventually resulted in the extinction of the Tainos.

In his *Columbus and the World Around Him,* Milton Meltzer clearly documents his conclusions and indicates where disagreements have occurred. He presents both good and bad sides of Columbus' character and actions. Like Pelta, Meltzer explains where he got his information and how he sorted, weighed, and analyzed it. An especially well-done book for adults, which could be appreciated by advanced young adults, is *America in 1492: The World of the Indian Peoples Before the Arrival of Columbus*, edited by noted scholar Alvin M. Josephy, Jr. Sixteen contributors, including N. Scott Momaday, Peter Iverson, Richard D. Daugherty, Joel Sherzer, and Vine Deloria, Jr., developed essays presenting the latest scholarship on such topics as religion, languages, arts, farming and other food sources, trading, and social organizations.

Holt invited six highly acclaimed authors to prepare pieces on different areas of the world to be published as *The World in 1492*. Jean Fritz writes about Europe; Jamake Highwater, about the Americas; Margaret Mahy, about Australia; Patricia and Fredrick McKissack, about Africa; and Katherine Paterson, about Asia. A book based on a similar idea of showing readers what else was happening in the year that Columbus sailed is Norman H. Finkelstein's *The Other 1492: Jewish Settlement in the New World*. He used 1492 as a reference to the year that Ferdinand and Isabella expelled all Jews from Spain. This eventually led to Jews immigrating to the New World, but the title may be a bit misleading because the emigration didn't occur until 150 years later.

The best way to show young readers that there are different opinions and different ways of looking at history is to encourage the use of several books on the same subject. When a topic is to be studied, instead of assigning all students to read the same book, bring in individual copies of various books, so that students can choose. Encourage them to trade with one another, to skim, and to read excerpts. Then after they have immersed themselves in their topic, they can make some kind of presentation to the class or work together on a culminating activity that illustrates the different viewpoints.

By making connections students can understand not just the *who, what,* and *when* of things, but also the *why.* For example, Malcolm C. MacPherson's *Time Bomb: Fermi, Heisenberg, and the Race for the Atomic Bomb* is a good companion book to Carl B. Feldbaum and Ronald J. Bee's *Looking the Tiger in the Eye: Confronting the Nuclear Threat.* The first book is the story of the intense personal competition between German physicist Werner Heisenberg and American physicist Enrico Fermi. Feldbaum and Bee's book gets its title from what J. Robert Oppenheimer, scientific director of the U.S. atomic bomb project, said almost a decade after he directed the first tests of an atomic bomb: "I believe that until we have looked this tiger in the eye, we shall be in the worst of all possible dangers, which is that we may back into him."

Another example of helping students draw connections is to introduce Dawn Lawson's *The Abraham Lincoln Brigade: Americans Fighting Fascism in the Spanish Civil War* by reading that old children's favorite, Munro Leaf's *The Story of Ferdinand,* with drawings by Robert Lawson. The book was published in 1936 as a protest against the Spanish Civil War. That tie-in and a brief discussion of the impact of the Spanish Civil War on such creative people as Ernest Hemingway and Pablo Picasso will prepare readers to get much more from *The Abraham Lincoln Brigade* than if they just picked it up at random.

One of the most useful contributions of teachers and librarians is to pull together groups of related books. For example, students can better appreciate Walter Dean Myers' *Malcolm X: By Any Means Necessary* if they also have access to other books about the history of African Americans. See Chapter Eleven on thematic units for further discussion of this point.

◼ *HISTORICAL FICTION*

Most of us read historical novels because we are curious about other times, places, and peoples; and we read them because, most important, we want adventure, suspense, and mystery. Movies as old as *Captain Blood, Gone with the Wind,* or *The Scarlet Pimpernel* continue to pique our interest, however ignorant we may be of the times and places described. Historical adventures remain readable much longer than contemporary, realistic stories (e.g., Sir Walter Scott's *Ivanhoe* [1819], Alexandre Dumas' *The Count of Monte Cristo* [1844], Mary Johnston's *To Have and to Hold* [1900], Rafael Sabatini's *Scaramouche* [1921], Helen Waddell's *Peter Abelard* [1933], Elizabeth Goudge's *Green Dolphin Street* [1944], and Margaret Walker's *Jubilee* [1966]).

As with any literary form, there are standards for judging historical novels. (See Table 7.1 for a summary.) They should be historically accurate and steeped in the sense of time and place. We should recognize totems and taboos, food,

Table 7.1   SUGGESTIONS FOR EVALUATING HISTORICAL FICTION

A good historical novel usually has:	**A poor historical novel may have:**
A setting that is integral to the story.	A story that could have happened any time or any place. The historical setting is for visual appeal and to compensate for a weak story.
An authentic rendition of the time, place, and people being featured.	
An author who is so thoroughly steeped in the history of the period that he or she can be comfortably creative without making mistakes.	Anachronisms in which the author illogically mixes up people, events, speaking styles, social values, or technological developments from different time periods.
Believable characters with whom young readers can identify.	Awkward narration and exposition as the author tries to teach history through characters' conversations.
Evidence that even across great time spans people share similar emotions.	Oversimplification of the historical issues and a stereotyping of the "bad" and the "good" guys.
References to well-known events or people, or other clues through which the reader can place the happenings in their correct historical framework.	Characters who fail to come alive as individuals having something in common with the readers. They are just stereotyped representatives of a particular period.
Readers who come away with the feeling that they know a time or place better. It is as if they have lived in it for at least a few hours.	

clothing, vocations, leisure activities, customs, smells, religions, literature—all that goes to make one time and one place unique from another. Enthusiasts will forgive no anachronism, no matter how slight. Historical novels should give a sense of history's continuity, a feeling of the flow of history from one time unto another that will, for good reason, be different from the period before. But as writers allow us to feel that flow of history, they should particularize their portraits of one time and one place. Historical novels should tell a lively story with a sense of impending danger, mystery, suspense, or romance.

Historical novels allow us—at their best they force us—to make connections and to realize that despair is as old and as new as hope, that loyalty and treachery, love and hatred, compassion and cruelty were and are inherent in humanity, whether it be in ancient Greece, Elizabethan England, or post–World War I Germany.

As with most writers, historical novelists may want to teach particular lessons. Christopher Collier, for example, makes no pretense about why he and his brother write about the American Revolution in their fine historical novels:

> ■   . . . the books I write with my brother are written with a didactic purpose—to teach about ideals and values that have been important in shaping the course of American history. This is in no way intended to denigrate the importance of the dramatic and literary elements of historical novels. Nothing will be taught, and certainly nothing learned, if no one reads the books.[6]

Among the best YA historical novels is Norma Farber's *Mercy Short: A Winter Journal, North Boston, 1692–93*. It is based on the true case of a young woman captured by Indians and then released. Cotton Mather ordered her to keep a journal to redeem her soul. Paul Fleischman's *Saturnalia* treats the same period. It gets its title from an ancient Roman custom of masters and slaves exchanging places. When plans are being made for a 1681 Saturnalia celebration in Boston, Fleischman shows the intertwining of lives of a tithingman, a printer, a printer's apprentice, a captured Narraganset Indian, a wigmaker, and the wigmaker's dishonest servant.

For years, British critics have called Rosemary Sutcliff the finest writer of British historical fiction for young people. From her finest early novel in 1954, *The Eagle of the Ninth*, through her 1990 *The Shining Company* she clearly has no peer in writing about early Britain. We need someone now to find a way to get American kids to read her books and savor them as most adult readers do. The books need to be promoted by excited librarians to the right young readers, those who care about history and a rattling good story and who are not put off by a period of time they know little about. Her 1990 *The Shining Company* may be even harder to sell than Sutcliff's earlier books about the Normans and the Saxons (e.g., *The Shield Ring* and *Dawn Wind*), because it is set in a more obscure time, seventh-century Britain. The source is *The Gododdin,* the earliest surviving North British poem.

When Prosper tries to save a white hart from a hunting party led by Prince Gorthyn, he expects punishment, but he finds that the prince admires his courage. Two years later, Prosper's offer to serve as the prince's shield bearer is accepted when Gorthyn obeys a royal command to be part of an army of 300 young men who will fight the invading Saxons.

For a year, the 300 men and their shield bearers prepare for battle until they have become as one, a brotherhood to save the king and his lands. The brotherhood is a noble ideal, but unfortunately its members are unable to handle some of the realities of the world, particularly treachery from a source they could never have suspected. So the 300 go into battle. One by one the heroes celebrated in *The Gododdin* die. And the battles that seemed so noble in the planning turn out to be bloody and awful in the execution, as wars of any sort— just or unjust—always become.

> We were no longer one fighting force, but splitting into smaller and smaller knots of desperate struggling men. . . . I do not know how many or how few we were by then, but the dull thunder of hooves on the soft ground was still behind us as we crashed into the shield mass, tearing great gaps into in, hurling it aside. . . . My sword hilt was slippery with blood, but the blood was not mine. A man came running low with his axe angled for Shadow's belly. I managed to wrench her aside at the last instant and cut him down and trample him into the ground. She reared up with a scream of fury, her forehooves lashing, and a man with a beard the colour of red coals went down to join him with his forehead smashed in. The last charge of the

Companions had become an ugly swirling soup of fire and mist and moonlight and snarling faces, the cries of men and the screams of stricken horses, the smell of blood and filth.

Sutcliff cares about people who make history, whether knaves or villains or, in this case, naive men who trusted their king and themselves beyond common sense.

Leon Garfield's world is the eighteenth century, with an occasional detour into early-nineteenth-century England. Beginning with *Jack Holborn* in 1965 and continuing with his more recent books, including *The Empty Sleeve*, Garfield set a standard for historical writing that few can match. Garfield's eighteenth century is the world of Fielding and Smollett, lusty and squalid and ugly and bustling and swollen, full of life and adventure and the certainty that being born an orphan may lead you ultimately to fame and fortune. Typically, eighteenth-century novels open with an orphan searching for identity. Garfield does not fear conventions, but his stories also play with reality versus illusion, daylight versus dreams, flesh versus fantasy. His ability to sketch out minor characters in a line or two and make them come alive is impressive. Of a man in *The Sound of Coaches*, he writes, "He was one of those gentlemen who affect great gallantry to all the fair sex except their wives." Of a prostitute, he writes, "A full face of beauty spots, with graveyard dust between." And of the protagonist we are told, "although jealousy was ordinarily foreign to Sam's nature, they did, on occasion, talk the same language." Garfield's epigrams are often most effective—for example, "Many a man is made good by being thought so."

Garfield's best book is *The Sound of Coaches*; it has an opening that catches the sights and feelings of the time:

Once upon a winter's night when the wind blew its guts out and a fishy piece of moon scuttled among the clouds, a coach came thundering down the long hill outside of Dorking. Its progress was wild and the coachman and his guard rocked from side to side as if the maddened vehicle was struggling to rid itself of them before going on to hell without the benefit of further advice. Even the passing landscape conspired to increase the terror of the journey, and the fleeting sight of a gibbet—its iron cage swinging desolately against the sky—turned the five passengers' thoughts towards the next world . . . of which destination there'd been no mention in Chichester where they'd booked their passage.

Once the five passengers, the coachman, and the guard (who is the coach-man's wife) reach Dorking, a young girl has a baby, dies, and leaves the orphan behind without any identity. The passengers, although at first annoyed by the irregularity of all that has happened, become parents of sorts to the baby, and the coachman and his wife raise the child. When Sam, our hero, grows up, he heads for London, searching for his father.

Wit, humor, and liveliness permeate Garfield's books. Perhaps the funniest are *The Strange Affair of Adelaide Harris* and its sequel, *The Night of the Comet.* In *Adelaide,* Bostock and Harris, two nasty pupils in Dr. Bunnion's Academy, become so entranced with stories of Spartan babies abandoned on mountaintops, there to be suckled by wolves, that they borrow Harris' baby sister to determine for themselves the truth of the old tales. Therein begins a wild comedy of errors and an even wilder series of coincidences and near duels and wild threats that hardly lets up until the last lines.

Scott O'Dell's books lag behind Garfield's and Sutcliff's but not by much. *The King's Fifth* is probably O'Dell's most convincing work, with its picture of sixteenth-century Spaniards and the moral strains put on anyone involved in the search for gold and fame. It is convincing, often disturbing, and, like most of O'Dell's historical novels, generally worth pursuing. Students coming to high school with a good reading background will probably already know O'Dell from his *Island of the Blue Dolphin* and *Sing Down the Moon*, both of which present original and positive portrayals of young Native American women suffering at the hands of white settlers in the middle to late 1800s.

O'Dell was a pioneer in featuring strong young women in these two books, but within the last couple of decades several good writers have followed his lead, so that good historical books about women and minorities are much easier to find. *The True Confessions of Charlotte Doyle* by Avi, a 1990 Newbery Honor Book, is illustrative. Although it isn't fantasy, this rollicking nineteenth-century sea yarn has to be read with a willing suspension of disbelief. The adventure begins in 1832, when thirteen-year-old Charlotte is brought to a British ship on which she is to sail to America to join her family. Her father's shipping company had called him home to Rhode Island in midwinter, and the family had gone with him while Charlotte stayed behind to finish her year at the Barrington School for Better Girls. She was to travel home during the summer on one of the company's ships. Two other families, who were to travel with her, are frightened away from the ship by something so terrible that even porters on the dock refuse to carry her luggage to the *Seahawk.*

Half the excitement is finding out the cause of the terror; the other half is seeing whether Charlotte can face it. Indeed she can, but not without some significant chills and thrills on the way. The story is enough to warm the hearts of feminists because, despite the accusation of murder, the trial, and the guilty verdict, Charlotte emerges as an exceptionally strong young woman ready to accept the challenge of the *Seahawk* all over again.

Phillip Pullman is a newcomer to the YA scene who has been described as a modern-day Charles Dickens. In his *The Ruby in the Smoke*, set in late Victorian London, orphaned but spunky Sally Lockhart searches for clues to her father's death and a mysterious lost ruby while evil old women and pirates and opium dealers thwart Sally at every turn. Pullman promises more than he can deliver in one novel, and so he continues the excitement and the good humor in *Shadow in the North*. The third book, *The Tiger in the Well*, gets more serious, when after the death of her lover, Sally is left with a child to protect from all sorts of mysterious threats.

Jan Hudson's *Sweetgrass* is a young woman's coming-of-age story set in the 1830s among the Blackfoot Indians of southern Canada and northern Montana. Fifteen-year-old Sweetgrass wants her father to arrange her marriage to Eagle-Sun, but he does not think she's old enough or strong enough yet. Eagle-Sun is from a different family group, and at the end of the summer, when the two families leave their shared camp to prepare for winter, neither one knows that before they meet the next summer, a smallpox epidemic will devastate their families. But in that terrible winter Sweetgrass saves her family, and no one can doubt that she has become a woman.

Joyce Hansen's *Which Way Freedom?* and *Out From This Place* are set during the Civil War. The protagonists are runaway slaves Obi and Easter. In *Which Way Freedom?* (a Coretta Scott King Honor Book), Obi serves in a black regiment of Union soldiers and is one of the few survivors of the Fort Pillow Massacre. In *Out From This Place*, Easter joins a group who works on an island plantation for pay. She learns to read and then faces the painful choice of whether to try to go to school or wait for Obi, who has promised to join her.

In Carolyn Reeder's *Shades of Gray*, Will Page is orphaned as a result of the Civil War and is sent to live with relatives that he can't respect because they had not joined the Confederate cause. Ann Rinaldi presents the Civil War from the perspective of Susan Chilmark, a young aristocratic girl who in *The Last Silk Dress* decides to help the Southern cause by collecting dresses from their neighbors to make a spy balloon. Events in both of these books cause the young protagonists to take a second look at cherished beliefs.

Ann Rinaldi tackled a more ambitious subject in *Wolf by the Ears*, a fictional story of Sally Hemmings' family. Sally was a mulatto slave in Thomas Jefferson's household, and some historians believe that Jefferson fathered several of her children. Rinaldi's book implies that this is true, but the question is never clearly answered, even though the protagonist, supposedly Jefferson's daughter, asks it often enough. The book's title comes from Jefferson's statement about slavery: "as it is, we have the wolf by the ears, and we can neither hold him, nor safely let him go. Justice is in one scale, and self-preservation the other." In a preface, Rinaldi cites her main source, Fawn M. Brodie's *Thomas Jefferson: An Intimate History*. She also explains that she wanted to write a book about alienation, because her own mother died when she was born, and "I never knew her family or even saw a picture of her until I was married. So there was always a part of me I could not acknowledge, a part of me I yearned to understand." This is why she was fascinated when she first heard of the Sally Hemmings' family, which included two boys who were thought to have run away, the young woman, Harriet, who is the protagonist of the book, and two younger brothers who apparently stayed on the plantation as slaves.

The book is an interesting illustration of the challenges faced by historical fiction writers, especially if they are writing for young readers. The more significant the themes in a book are, the stronger are people's preconceived ideas about them. It's quite unlikely that Rinaldi could please all of her readers, no matter how she portrayed such controversial topics as the treatment and education of slaves, mixed-bloods "passing" as white, and the commonness of slave women loving their masters and of masters impregnating slave women with or without love. Because of her audience, Rinaldi tiptoed around the issue of Jefferson's sexuality, even though it's at the heart of the plot. A common literary technique is to insert a love story as a counterbalance for whatever bad has happened to a woman. This is what Rinaldi does in having an educated, white liberal architect visit Monticello from Washington, D.C., and find Harriet attractive. He's a perfect gentleman and agrees to sponsor Harriet in Washington, D.C., where she will be a teacher until she decides whether or not she wants to marry him. Granted, this romantic element may be necessary to attract readers, but it's a kind of sugar coating that's likely to gag historians.

A similar kind of slanting or exaggeration so often appears in westerns that we chose to put that genre of historical novels in Chapter Four, under romances. But there are some historical novels set in the west that don't exactly fit into the typical mold of westerns. One such book is Kathryn Lasky's *The Bone Wars*, set in 1885, when teenagers Julian DeMott and Thaddeus Longsworth team up to uncover dinosaur remains in the Badlands of Montana. They face such obstacles as Indian wars, competition between opposing teams of paleontologists, and interference from army generals and government officials. Pam Conrad's *My Daniel* approaches the discovery of dinosaur bones from the perspective of an eighty-year-old grandmother who, when she was twelve, discovered with her brother a full dinosaur skeleton on a Nebraska farm. In *My Daniel*, she and her two grandchildren are visiting New York's Natural History Museum, where she will see the fully assembled dinosaur for the first time.

There's hardly a teenager alive who hasn't fantasized about saving his or her family from some dire circumstance, and so there's an inherent appeal to well-written stories set during the Depression, when a teenager's help proved crucial to a family. In Crystal Thrasher's *End of a Dark Road*, tenth-grader Seely plays that role when her father dies. George Ella Lyon's *Borrowed Children* is set in Depression-era Kentucky. When Mandy's mother has to stay in bed for six weeks after the birth of a new brother, Mandy stays home from school to take care of the family.

Books About War

It's becoming increasingly difficult to distinguish between fiction and nonfiction, and this is especially true in the writing of memoirs and reminiscences about war (see Focus Box 7.1). Struggling to survive in a war is not an adventure that people would choose either for themselves or for their children, but so many people of all ages have been forced into terrible circumstances that books on war—factual histories, journalistic nonfiction, autobiographic works, diaries,

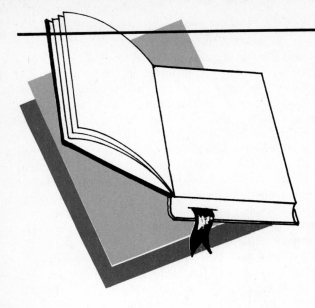

Reminiscences, Diaries, Memoirs, and Other Nonfiction About War

Flashbacks: On Returning to Vietnam by Morley Safer. Random House, 1990. One of our best-known journalists visits Vietnam, going to a hospital for amputees and visiting old soldiers with memories of the war.

At the Heart of the White Rose: Letters and Diaries of Hans and Sophie Scholl, edited by Inge Jens. HarperCollins, 1987. The White Rose was an underground group of students and teachers at Munich University who were opposed to Hitler.

Bloods: An Oral History of the Vietnam War by Black Veterans by Terry Wallace. Random House, 1984. Wallace interviewed twenty black veterans, who each tell a different story about the war and their lives after coming home.

The Cage by Ruth Minsky Sender. Macmillan, 1986. A slightly fictionalized account of the author's life in Poland and in a Nazi prison camp. *To Life* (Macmillan, 1988) continues the story from freedom to America.

The Diary of a Young Girl by Anne Frank. Doubleday, 1952. This warm self-study by a youngster makes the Holocaust personal and believable. Those wanting to go further may be interested in *The Diary of Anne Frank: The Critical Edition,* edited by David Barnouw and Gerrard van der Stroom (Doubleday, 1989). Other supplemental books include, *Anne Frank Remembered: The Story of the Woman Who Helped to Hide the Frank Family* by Miep Gies with Alison Leslie Gold (Simon & Schuster, 1987) and *The Last Seven Months of Anne Frank* by Willy Lindwer, translated from Dutch by Alison Meersschaert (Random House, 1991).

My Father, My Son by Elmo Zumwalt, Jr. and Elmo Zumwalt III (with John Pekkanen). Macmillan, 1986. Elmo Zumwalt, Jr. was the commander in Vietnam who ordered the use of Agent Orange. His son was serving under him, and the father now feels responsible for his son having cancer.

From That Place and Time: A Memoir, 1938–1947 by Lucy S. Dawidowicz. Norton, 1989. The historian remembers Polish Jewish friends from her student days, the Holocaust, and her work after World War II. Her *The War Against the Jews, 1933–1945* (Free Press, 1986) is also recommended as a scholarly *and* readable history.

The Things They Carried by Tim O'Brien. Houghton Mifflin, 1990. A collection of related short stories about Vietnam then and Vietnam now.

Touch Wood: A Girlhood in Occupied France by Renée Roth-Hano. Four Winds, 1988. When Germans threaten Jews in occupied France, Renée's parents send her to a convent in Normandy.

The Vietnam Photo Book by Mark Jury. Vintage, 1986 (orig. published in 1971). While on duty in Vietnam, Jury photographed and wrote stories about the individual men and women who were overlooked by television cameras.

---

and collections of letters and interviews—are among our most powerful. Old war movies abound on the late show (see Focus Box 7.2). Newspapers and magazines banner the headlines of this new or that old war, and television news programs barrage us with the latest atrocities.

We are continually preoccupied with war, perhaps because it is inherently frightening and evil, and in the minds of too many of us, horribly inevitable. The Bible is full of battles, but so are the *Iliad* and the *Odyssey*. War serves as background for *Antigone*, just as it does for *The Red Badge of Courage*. War has influenced artists and musicians, or it might be fairer to say that it has left its indelible mark on them.

Young adults are painfully aware of the nearness of war, although they may know little about its realities and even less about the details of past wars. Reading war literature, fiction or not, serves to acquaint young people with some of war's horrors and how easily people forget, or ignore, their humanity in the midst of war.

During World War II, Ernie Pyle was probably the American soldiers' favorite war correspondent, mostly because he took a genuine interest in people and demanded no special favors for being shot at. *Ernie's War: The Best of Ernie Pyle's World War II Dispatches* (edited by David Nichols) collects some of the work Pyle did in Great Britain, North Africa, Sicily, France, and the Pacific from 1940 until his death in 1945. Pyle wrote honestly without the trite theatrics of too many newspaper reporters. Writing about the death of Captain Henry T. Waskow, one of the most "beloved" men Pyle ever found in war, he told of Waskow's men coming in, gently, to see and honor the body, and Pyle ended the account this way:

Then a soldier came and stood beside the officer, and bent over, and he spoke to the dead captain, not in a whisper but awfully tenderly, and he said:

"I sure am sorry, sir."

Then the first man squatted down, and he reached down and took the dead hand, and he sat there for a full five minutes, holding the dead hand in his own and looking intently into the dead face, and he never uttered a sound all the time he sat there.

And finally he put the hand down, and then reached up and gently straight-

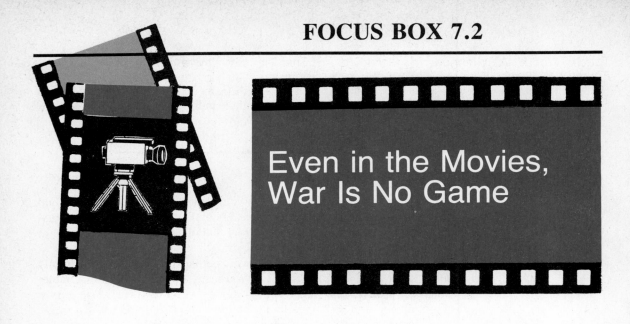

Even in the Movies, War Is No Game

All Quiet on the Western Front (1930, 105 min., black and white; Dir: Lewis Milestone; with Lew Ayres and Louis Wolheim) Young Germans flock to join the army to fight for glory. Based on Erich Maria Remarque's novel.

The Americanization of Emily (1964, 117 min., black and white; Dir: Arthur Hiller; with James Garner and Julie Andrews) Paddy Chayefsky's cynical script about the stupidity of war vs. the romanticized view that dying for one's country is good and noble.

Apocalypse Now (1979, 105 min., color; Dir: Francis Coppola; with Martin Sheen and Marlon Brando) An agent travels in Vietnam to kill another officer. Based on Joseph Conrad's *Heart of Darkness.*

Attack (1956, 107 min., black and white; Dir: Robert Altman; with Eddie Albert and Jack Palance) A study of cowardice and ineptness during the Battle of the Bulge in World War II.

Dr. Strangelove or: How I Learned to Stop Worrying and Love the Bomb (1964, 93 min., black and white; Dir: Stanley Kubrick; with Peter Sellers, George C. Scott, and Sterling Hayden) A black comedy about a true-blue American general who decides on his own to start World War III. Hysterically funny and terrifying all at once.

The Execution of Private Slovik (1974, 120 min., color; Dir: Lamont Johnson; with Martin Sheen) Based on William Bradford Huie's account of the only American executed for desertion during wartime since the Civil War.

Forbidden Games (1951, 87 min., black and white; Dir: René Clement) A young girl's parents are killed in World War II, and she is taken in by a peasant family. Their son and the girl form a deep bond that is shattered by the war. One of the world's most poignant war films.

Glory (1989, 122 min., color; Dir: Edward Zwick; with Denzel Washington and Matthew Broderick) The founding and fighting of the first black unit during the Civil War.

King and Country (1964, 90 min., black and white; Dir: Joseph Losey; with Dirk Bogarde and Tom Courtenay) An officer is assigned to defend a soldier accused of desertion during wartime.

The Men (1950, 85 min., black and white; Dir: Fred Zinnemann; with Marlon Brando) A soldier tries to adjust to life after a crippling injury.

Paths of Glory (1957, 86 min., black and white; Dir: Stanley Kubrick; with Kirk Douglas) During World War I, the stupidity and cupidity of the French top brass causes men to die pointlessly.

Platoon (1986, 120 min., color; Dir: Oliver Stone; with Willem Dafoe and Tom Berenger) Realistic film about life in the front lines in Vietnam.

The Red Badge of Courage (1951, 69 min., black and white; Dir: John Huston) Filming of Stephen Crane's classic story of war and courage.

---

ened the points of the captain's shirt collar, and then he sort of rearranged the tattered edges of his uniform around the wound. And then he got up and walked away down the road in the moonlight, all alone.

After that the rest of us went back into the cowshed, leaving the five dead men lying in a line, end to end, in the shadow of the low stone wall. We lay down on the straw in the cowshed, and pretty soon we were all asleep.

Few books about World War II, or any other war, succeed so well in creating a revulsion to the blood and messiness as does Farley Mowat's *And No Birds Sang*. After Mowat's company encountered and killed six truckloads of German soldiers, Mowat said:

It was not the dead that distressed me most—it was the German wounded. There were a great many of these, and most seemed to have been hard hit.

One ghastly vignette from that shambles haunts me still: the driver of a truck hanging over his steering wheel and hiccuping great gouts of cherry-pink foam through a smashed windscreen, to the accompaniment of a sound like a slush pump sucking air as his perforated lungs labored to expel his own heart's blood . . . in which he was slowly drowning.

Mowat's book is hardly the only honest account, but it reeks of death and lost dreams, and anyone wanting to know what war is like should not miss it.

Only a few years back, anyone wishing to read about the Holocaust would read Anne Frank's *Diary of a Young Girl*. Advanced students might find a few other sources, mostly historical, and the most mature students might view Alain Resnais' powerful short film, "Night and Fog." Today an outpouring of books about the Holocaust means that no one can pretend not to know about the happenings and the evils that went with it.

Most young adults will seek out books about young people caught in the Holocaust because they are better able to identify with people their own age or slightly older. A book that is similar to Anne Frank's *Diary* is Etty Hillesum's *An Interrupted Life: The Diaries of Etty Hillesum, 1941–1943*. Being twenty-seven years old, Hillesum probably knew precisely what her fate was to be. Her diary begins, "Here goes, then," and she writes of her love affairs, her graduate study at the University of Amsterdam, and her friends and ideas. She seems to have had little interest in politics until Jews were required to wear the yellow star. That jolted her, but she never sought to escape. In her last days, she volunteered to go with a group of condemned Jews to Westerbork Camp. She must have known that Westerbork was the usual first step to Auschwitz. Her journal complements Anne's *Diary*; Etty's irony and sophistication neatly counterpoint Anne's simplicity and innocence. *An Interrupted Life* is completed in *Letters from Westerbork*.

Hanna Volavkova's *I Never Saw Another Butterfly: Children's Drawings and Poems from Terezin Concentration Camp, 1942–1944* and Chana Byers Abells' *The Children We Remember* make for painful but necessary reading if we are to remember the lesson of the Holocaust. Milton Meltzer does his usual fine job of collection and reporting in *Never to Forget: The Jews of the Holocaust*. Ten years after he wrote that book, he returned to do a book about a much smaller number of people, *Rescue: The Story of How Gentiles Saved Jews in the Holocaust*. As he explained in the introduction:

> Now I have come to realize the great importance of recording not just the evidence of evil, but also the evidence of human nobility. Love, not hatred, is what the world needs. Rescue, not destruction. The stories in the book offer reason to hope. And hope is what we need, the way plants need sunlight.

The most shameful American action during World War II began in February 1942, when President Roosevelt ordered the forced evacuation of anyone of Japanese ancestry on the West Coast into detention camps scattered in desolate places inland. More than 120,000 people were deported for the remainder of the war. Jeanne Wakatsuki Houston and James D. Houston's *Farewell to Manzanar* describes the first author's life in a camp ringed by barbed wire and guard towers and with open latrines. That three-year ordeal destroyed the family's unity and left them with a burdening sense of personal inadequacy that took years to remove.

Another never-to-be-forgotten act of World War II was the dropping of the atomic bomb on Hiroshima. John Hersey's book *Hiroshima* lamenting that horror first appeared in the *New Yorker* in 1946. If anything, it is more important today than it was then. Rodney Barker's *The Hiroshima Maidens* is a follow-up to Hersey's *Hiroshima*, an account of the "Maidens Project," which helped to bring twenty-five disfigured women victims to the United States for treatment.

The war in Vietnam seemed for years to be the only war that would be ignored in print. Then a few years ago the dam broke, and now books on Vietnam make up a goodly portion of the world's war literature. Teacher Bill McCloud was trying to decide what to tell his junior high students about Vietnam, and so he wrote to people involved in the war to get their advice. The result is his book *What Should We Tell Our Children About Vietnam?* Responses came from more than 100 people as different as Garry Trudeau, Jimmy Carter, Pete Seeger, Kurt Vonnegut, Alexander Haig, Henry Kissinger, and Barry Goldwater. Another unusual book on Vietnam is Laura Palmer's *Shrapnel in the Heart: Letters and Remembrances from the Vietnam Veterans Memorial.* All items left at the Vietnam Memorial are saved by the U.S. Park Service, and from these letters, notes, and personal memorabilia Palmer chose deeply moving examples.

Recent and current wars are also finding their way into books. Brent Ashabranner's *Children of the Maya* and *Into a Strange Land* both include powerful accounts of young people whose lives have been drastically changed by wars.

Of the many books on war, there is no greater indictment of the absurdity and cruelty of war than Roger Rosenblatt's *Children of War*. Rosenblatt circled the globe seeking out children in Belfast, Israel, Cambodia, Hong Kong, and Lebanon whom he asked about themselves and what war had done to them. A nine-year-old girl in Cambodia had made a drawing, and after a year of help by an American psychologist, she was able to explain how the instrument in the drawing worked. Rosenblatt writes:

> The children harvesting rice include Peov. She is the largest of the three. Whenever a child refused to work, he was punished with the circular device. The soldiers would place it over the child's head. Three people would hold it steady by means of ropes. . . . A fourth would grab hold of the ring at the end of the other rope. . . . When the rope with the ring was pulled . . . the child would be decapitated. A portable guillotine.
>
> But it wasn't the soldiers who worked the device. It was the children.

War Fiction

In war stories authors are almost always more interested in what war does to humans than in a historic recounting of battles and campaigns and casualties. Memorable war books are likely to center on physical and psychological suffering. Death lurks on every doorstep, or it did once, and emotionally it still may for the characters. Often the war seems to happen in slow motion, the story focusing on one person engaged in one act. Or the reverse may be true, with events being telescoped to eliminate the trivial or nonessential to force

CYNTHIA VOIGT
on Learning and Knowing

I have a theory that the real difference between kids and adults is that kids expect themselves to be learning and adults expect themselves to know. This seems to me to be both a central and an essential difference.

If I expect myself to be learning, my attitude towards experiences, people, the whole side show, is characterized by questions and curiosity; probably more important, my understanding of who I am, myself, is that I am changing, growing, adding to myself. If I expect myself to know, then I stand before the world as a completed creature—and I am bound to be a disappointment to everybody concerned in the encounter. If I must know, in order to be a self I recognize and respect, the possibility for change diminishes. If I require the adults around me to know, I diminish them.

This may just be the difference between growing up and grown-up. Kids have it easy because there is no question that they are in process. Adults stand under the danger, or the temptation, of thinking that process ought to have been completed, or has been completed—which is, of course a fool's paradise. I don't know about the rest of the adults out there, but it seems to me I spend my time perpetually growing up, with no end in sight to the arduous and uneasy occupation—which strikes me, on the whole, as a good thing, and a beneficial thing. I don't envy kids, the young, and I don't regret the years I've got on them, but one of the things I cherish about teaching is that constant reminder, unspoken but clear, that learning, not knowing, is what it's about.

Cynthia Voigt's books include *Seventeen Against the Dealer*, 1989; *Homecoming*, 1981; *Izzy, Willy-Nilly*, 1986; and *On Fortune's Wheel*, all Atheneum.

readers (and sometimes characters) to see the realities and horrors of war more intensely. At one time we might have accepted romantic war stories, but a romanticized picture of war today would seem dishonest and offensive to most readers.

A fairly recent change in books for young readers is the inclusion of female characters in war stories. Lois Lowry won the 1990 Newbery Award for *Number the Stars*, the powerful story of ten-year-old Annemarie's part in helping her Danish family smuggle their Jewish neighbors to freedom. Other books treat emotional responses to war. Maureen Pople's *The Other Side of the Family* is a story of human relationships and what people want to believe about each other. During World War II, Katherine Tucker is sent from London to live with her mother's parents in Australia. But when Japanese submarines enter the

Sydney harbor, Katherine is sent inland to stay with her father's mother. She expects to find a wealthy woman, one who disowned her son because she was so disappointed in his choice of a bride. Instead, she finds an elderly woman so poor that she has to steal coal from the railroad tracks.

Theresa Nelson's *And One for All* is the story of seventh-grader Geraldine Brennan's personal war against grief and anger when her brother, Wing, is killed in Vietnam. Bobbie Ann Mason's *In Country,* about a girl's attempt to understand the war that killed the father she never knew, is a more sophisticated book for older readers, but it treats a similar theme.

Because there are now so many war-related books, writers are forced to go beyond the obvious. For example, Jiri Weil's *Mendelssohn on the Roof* (translated from Czech by Marie Winn) is a black comedy with lots of deaths and blood and laughs. Atop a Prague concert hall are several statues, among them one of Felix Mendelssohn. When Nazis discover that a Jew is so honored, they tell local authorities to remove it. The inept authorities have no idea which statue to knock down, and so begins the fun.

Entirely different in tone is Cynthia Voigt's *David and Jonathan*, about the changing relationship between two close friends when a cousin who survived the Holocaust comes to live with one of the families. He brings along his survivor guilt and all the baggage that came with the traumatic times.

Six War Novelists

Six novelists have written particularly effective war novels that young people enjoy (see Focus Box 7.3 for other recommended war fiction). Harry Mazer's *The Last Mission* is set toward the end of World War II. Jack Raab uses his older brother's identification to lie his way into the Air Force to destroy Hitler and save democracy, all by himself. That dream lasts only a short time before Jack learns that the Air Force involves more training and boredom than fighting. When Jack does go to war, his first twenty-four bombing raids go well, but on the last mission, his plane is hit, all his buddies die, and he is captured. When he returns home, the principal at his old school asks him to talk:

"I'm glad we won," he said. "We couldn't let Hitler keep going. We had to stop him. But most of all, I'm glad it's over." Had he said enough? There was a silence . . . a waiting silence. There was something more he had to say.

"I don't like war. I thought I'd like it before. But war is stupid. War is one stupid thing after another. I saw my best friend killed. His name was Chuckie O'Brien. My whole crew was killed." Now he was talking, it was coming out, all the things he'd thought about for so long. "A lot of people were killed. Millions of people. Ordinary people. Not only by Hitler. Not only on our side. War isn't like the movies. It's not fun and songs. It's not

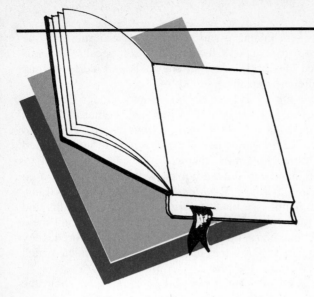

Recommended Fiction About War

All Quiet on the Western Front by Erich Maria Remarque. 1929. Paul and his comrades enlist for Germany in World War I out of patriotism and the thrill of the chase. They soon learn how unromantic, dull, and awful war can be.

Blitzcat by Robert Westall. Scholastic, 1989. The most unusual heroine in all the World War II stories is Lord Gort, a cat separated from her owner when he joins the British Royal Air Force.

Crutches by Peter Harling, translated from German by Elizabeth Crawford. Lothrop, 1988. When at the end of World War II Thomas and his mother become separated, it takes almost two years for him and "Crutches," a wounded German soldier, to find her.

The Magic We Do Here by Lawrence Rudner. Houghton Mifflin, 1988. A Polish Jew survives World War II by posing as a mute, slow-witted servant to a Nazi. He ultimately serves as witness to the horrors of the Nazi occupation.

My Brother Sam Is Dead by James L. and Christopher Collier. Four Winds, 1974. This is one of the most powerful of the Revolutionary War stories. Other Collier books about the same war include *The Bloody Country, The Winter Hero, Jump Ship to Freedom*, and *War Comes to Willy Freeman*, the latter two about former slaves involved in the war.

Pack of Wolves by Vasil Bykov, translated from Russian by Lynn Solotaroff. Crowell, 1981. The title refers to Nazi soldiers hunting down a small group of defenders on the Russian frontier, one of whom is a woman with a newborn baby.

Pocket Change by Kathryn Jensen. Bradbury, 1989. Josie's father begins having flashbacks about Vietnam and she comes to realize that old memories work their way to the surface like pocket change wears through cloth.

The Red Badge of Courage by Stephen Crane. 1895. Henry Fleming (usually called "the youth") is both inexperienced and terrified as he enters battle in the Civil War. Although he pretends to be brave and ready, when bloodshed begins he runs from the field and feels disgraced.

Shadow of the Wall by Christa Laird. Greenwillow, 1990. A thirteen-year-old boy living in the 1940 Warsaw Jewish ghetto helps orphans to survive.

The Sun Also Rises by Ernest Hemingway. 1926. Hemingway's greatest book is about what war does to emasculate people, physically and emotionally.

---

about heroes. It's about awful, sad things, like my friend Chuckie that I'm never going to see again." His voice faltered.

"I hope war never happens again," he said after a moment. "That's all I've got to say."

He sat down. He hardly heard the applause. The floor of the radio room was still slippery with Chuckie's blood. . . . Dave was still fumbling with his chute . . . the plane was still falling through the sky.

In *A Midnight Clear* by William Wharton (a pseudonym of a writer who refuses to identify himself publicly), six high-I.Q. soldiers in an intelligence and reconnaissance platoon are sent to determine whether any Germans are near a French chateau during World War II. The six play bridge, chess, and word games and refuse to admit they have anything to do with the war. Then the Germans show up, but instead of warfare, the Americans and the supposed enemy engage in a snowball fight. A meeting is arranged, they fraternize, sing Christmas carols, set up a Christmas tree, and peace reigns; then war starts up again and the killing resumes. Wharton's powerful story is as much about humanity's goals exceeding its abilities as it is about war.

English novelist Robert Westall writes about young people who refuse to stay outside the war in *The Machine Gunners* and its sequel, *Fathom Five*. The first novel is set in an English coastal town during 1940–1941. Rumors of a German invasion are rife, and Chas McGill wants to help win the war. Westall is superb at catching some of the humor of the time. Bombs drop, Chas's family heads for the shelter, but when his mother remembers insurance policies they must have with them, they turn back toward home.

A body fell through. It was Mrs. Spalding.

"Is she dead?" said Mrs. McGill.

"No, but she's got her knickers around her ankles," said Mr. McGill.

"Aah had tey hop aal the way," gasped Mrs. Spalding. "I was on the outside lav and I couldn't finish. The buggers blew the lav door off, and they've hit the Rex Cinema as well. Is there a spot of brandy?"

"Aah pulled the chain, Mam. It flushed all right." It was Colin, with a self-satisfied smirk on his face.

"You'll get the Victoria Cross for that," said Chas with a wild giggle.

WALTER DEAN MYERS
on Finding One's Identity

My earliest conscious identity was as my mother's darling boy. The memory of this period of warmth and intimacy with the woman who first gave me the gift of reading still brings me pleasure. My introduction to school changed my self-concept in important ways. I discovered that most of my classmates could not read, which surprised me. The first idea of being "bright" entered my thoughts. But I also became aware, painfully so, that the other children and my first-grade teacher had difficulty understanding me. I began speech therapy and began to layer my identity with that disability as well. Seeing my frustration in reading before a class, a teacher suggested that I write something to read instead of reading from a book. I began to write poems, which were praised by the teacher.

School, on the whole, was a joyous experience on the elementary level. I identified with the heroes we were given: George Washington, Thomas Jefferson, the wise Benjamin Franklin, and the brave Patrick Henry. We did plays in which we were colonists at Thanksgiving or threw tea into Boston Harbor. Unconscious of differences between myself and my white classmates, I was identifying as an American. But then one day I turned the page in our history books and encountered the concept of race. There was a picture of a small group of Africans, their heads down,

Walter Dean Myers' books include *Now Is Your Time*, HarperCollins, 1991; *Somewhere in the Darkness*, HarperCollins, 1992; *Scorpions*, HarperCollins, 1988; and *Fallen Angels*, Scholastic, 1988.

Chas and his friends locate a downed German plane, find the machine gun in working order, and hide it. When his school is hit by another plane a bit later, Chas steals sandbags to create a fortress, a safe place to display the machine gun. Then the rear gunner of the downed plane stumbles onto their fortress and becomes the boys' prisoner. The end of childish innocence comes when adults discover the fortress, the German is shot, and the young people are rounded up by their parents. *Fathom Five* is a rousing spy story set a little later in the war and is a story of Chas's lost love. Westall has amazing ability to portray the ambivalence of young people, the alienation they feel mixed with love and duty.

Howard Fast's *April Morning*, which has a Revolutionary War setting, has been favorably compared with *The Red Badge of Courage*. Fast's novel focuses

marching from a boat. They were identified not as Africans, of course but as "slaves."

From that day on, the identity of race—it was Negro in those days—dominated my identity. When we read *Huck Finn* I struggled against being Nigger Jim. I wanted to be the brave, adventuresome Huck. Unconsciously, I began to accept the values, or rather the lack of values, assigned to people of my race.

I began to reject the devalued race. If Negroes were physical, liked finger-popping music, and were never serious, then I would be intellectual, study classical music, and always be serious. In retrospect I was simply looking for those human values that the school ascribed to white Americans but neglected to give to black Americans.

The logical extension of my identity as an intellectual was the continuation of my education on the college level. The revelation that my parents would not be able to send me to college was devastating. It seemed perfectly logical for me to drop out of high school.

A gang and then the army gave me acceptable macho identities over the next few years, acceptable because I did not see alternatives. It certainly doesn't take much imagination for me to understand the lure of today's gangs.

After the army and a series of menial jobs, I started writing again. I wrote about things I knew—Harlem, basketball, gangs, the army. The values that I did not find in books as a child I was now putting into the books.

Two years ago I began writing a history book. In the book I wanted to talk about the Africans—Africans, not slaves—who had helped to create the United States. The book was a result of all of the experiences of my life, of my turning to books, of my racial conflicts, of my need to bring value to who I am.

I knew that my own family had been held on a plantation in what is now West Virginia. I delayed going to the plantation until the book was nearly finished, and I approached it with trepidation.

But I did not feel the pain that I expected and soon realized that in the years of writing, I had re-created a surety of identity that could not be threatened, not even by the shadow of enslavement.

This is what I want to do with my writing, to bring value to the young people who read my books, to allow them to discover their own identities without harmful value prejudices. In so doing I feel more value in my own existence. It's a good feeling.

---

on fifteen-year-old Adam Cooper, who is sure of the rightness of war until he is thrust into the midst of it and begins to wonder about the carnage and stupidity. In eight sections, which take readers from the afternoon of April 18, 1775, through the evening of April 19, *April Morning* explodes the family relationships of Adam and his father, his mother, his beloved granny, and the girl he loves. Adam survives by doing what has to be done, and he tries to make sense out of the horror, to understand what the war is all about. It is about him, whether he wants it to be or not.

James Forman's finest work, too little known, is *Ceremony of Innocence*. Hans and Sophie Scholl, brother and sister in Nazi Germany, print and distribute literature attacking Hitler. Arrested by the Gestapo, they are urged by friends to escape. A lawyer, who Hans suspects is a Nazi, encourages them to plead insanity. They refuse, endure the mock trial, are found guilty, and are taken away to be executed. Hans is the last to die by the guillotine.

Hans heard the sound of rollers, and at last there burst from his throat a cry, uttered in a great voice, a voice that combined anger, reproof, and an overwhelming conviction for which he was willing to die.

"Long live freedom!"

Then the greased blade fell. His teeth met through his tongue, and it was over.

The sixth book, Walter Dean Myers' *Fallen Angels*, is as different from the others as the Vietnam War was different from previous wars. The streets of Harlem are too hard for seventeen-year-old Richie Perry, and without really knowing what he is getting into, he joins the army. The story begins and ends with halfway-around-the-world plane trips, but the trips are different because coming home Richie is wounded and the back of the plane is filled with silver coffins. Many people think that this is Myers's best book (see Chapter Two for a full discussion).

AUTOBIOGRAPHIES AND PERSONAL EXPERIENCES

The Greeks enjoyed both their stories about the gods of Mount Olympus and the hero tales about the moral descendants of these gods. But the hero tales had an added attraction that helped listeners to identify with the protagonists. Unlike the gods, who live forever, the heroes had one human parent, which meant that they were mortal and could be killed. In any undertaking, the most that the gods could risk was their pride, but the heroes could lose their lives.

A comparison can be made to modern literature, with fiction resembling the stories about the gods. When we're reading fiction, we know that the author can always bring the protagonist out alive. But in true hero tales—that is, biographies—protagonists risk their lives, just as readers would have to do in the same situation. This adds an extra degree of credibility and intensity, because the reader thinks, "If this happened to someone else, then it might happen to me."

Personal Experiences with Illness and Death

This added intensity undoubtedly contributes to the popularity of true stories about people challenged with serious illness and death. Some parents, teachers, and librarians argue that such books are too morbid for healthy young people, but others remember that when they were young, they too were preoccupied with thoughts about death. It wasn't because they were unduly morbid or nigh unto death, but because death is an eternal mystery, as anyone who has read *Hamlet*, Dickinson's poetry, or Edgar Lee Masters' *Spoon River Anthology* knows full well.

Young adults, on the other hand, sometimes complain bitterly about the "morbid" or "sick" literature adults foist on them: *Macbeth*, Romantic poetry, "Thanatopsis," *Death of a Salesman, Oedipus Rex*, and "A Rose for Emily." In reality, both adults and young adults may be preoccupied with death, but they prefer to choose their own literature. And surely it could be argued that reading such literature helps young adults develop an appreciation of their own lives as well as a code of values to hold dear in the dread times to come.

Books about young people dying that have been popular for two decades or more include Doris Lund's *Eric*, about her son's losing battle with leukemia; John Gunther's *Death Be Not Proud*, about his son's slow death from a brain tumor; and three different versions of the story of Chicago Bears' runningback Brian Piccolo and his struggle with cancer. The favorite of this latter group is usually William Blinn's *Brian's Song*, created from the television movie, which is still shown in reruns. The movie plot came originally from a chapter in Gale Sayers' *I Am Third*, while Jeanne Morris wrote the most complete version of the story in *Brian Piccolo: A Short Season*. She and Piccolo worked together on the manuscript during his hospitalization.

Another favorite is Richard E. Peck's *Something for Joey*. Peck wrote the book based on the TV movie of the true story of John Cappelletti and his family's heart-rending but futile struggle to save John's little brother, Joey. In the year prior to the one in which Cappelletti won the Heisman trophy, Joey was diagnosed as having leukemia. The family struggled, thinking that if they could just keep Joey alive for five years, he would recover. They won their five-year battle but lost the war when Joey died the next year.

Knowing the popularity of these books, it should come as no surprise that many young readers would be interested in *Ryan White: My Own Story* by Ryan White and Ann Marie Cunningham. As a hemophiliac, Ryan received dozens of blood infusions. One of them was with AIDS-infected blood, and when he developed the disease he became a national symbol of both American prejudice and American caring. He died at age eighteen, shortly after the book was written. Not quite as dramatic is Elaine Landau's *We Have AIDS*, in which nine teenagers tell their stories. Interspersed between the stories, Landau provides factual information about AIDS and suggestions for further reading.

Some young adults prefer to pick up straightforward informational books focusing on death and/or illness, e.g., Jill Krementz' *How It Feels to Fight for Your Life* and *How It Feels When a Parent Dies*. Krementz presents full-page photos of the young people whose stories she tells through their own words. Elizabeth Richter's *Losing Someone You Love: When a Brother or Sister Dies* has a similar format; the book is based on seventeen young people who shared their firsthand experiences and feelings upon the death of a sibling.

Since readers identify with the young protagonists, it's, of course, satisfying when they win their struggle against an illness or a disability. Geri Jewell's autobiography, *Geri*, is the story of a young woman with cerebral palsy who succeeded in reaching her goal of becoming an acclaimed actress and comedienne. She also succeeded in writing an upbeat book showing the "hardness and usefulness of the disabled."

Samuel Abt's *LeMond: The Incredible Comeback of an American Hero* is the story of Greg LeMond, the first American to win the 2,000-mile Tour de France bicycle race. This was in 1986 and he became an instant hero, but then he was shot in a hunting accident and almost died. He was just getting his strength back in 1988 when he had to have his appendix removed. Everyone thought his career was finished, but in 1989 he surprised the world by crossing the finish line eight seconds ahead of the expected winner. Another amazing comeback story is told in *Second Ascent: The Story of Hugh Herr* by Alison Osius. At the age of seventeen, Hugh Herr was considered a world-class rock climber, but in 1982 he and a fellow climber were lost in a storm on Mt. Washington for three days. Although they were finally rescued, Herr's legs had to be amputated. He now climbs with artificial limbs and is involved in helping other amputees.

Two recent books by young cancer patients are wise and funny by turns. Although they will bring tears to their readers, that is clearly not their purpose. Matthew Lancaster's *Hang Toughf* is a solid little classic in which a ten-year-old author gives sound advice to other kids who have cancer. As he says, it's not fair, "but it happened, and you and I have to except it." And if your hair falls out, then "if your friends laugh at you, they're not very good friends." Eight-year-old Jason Gaes hated other books about kids with cancer because they always died, and he had cancer and he hadn't died, so he wrote *My Book for Kids with Cansur*, almost as good (and sometimes funnier) than *Hang Toughf*. Erma Bombeck tuned into the same theme with the help of young cancer patients for her book *I Want to Grow Hair, I Want to Grow Up, I Want to Go to Boise*.

Understandably, there aren't many personal experience stories about suicide. However, Sylvia Plath's *The Bell Jar* is a fictionalized autobiography about her life and her own death wish. Esther is preoccupied with the execution of the Rosenbergs, and throughout her story she reads constantly about death and suicide. At one point, Esther says, "I am an observer," and later she withdraws more and more from reality:

> I slunk down on the middle of my spine, my nose level with the rim of the window, and watched the houses of outer Boston glide by.
> As the houses grew more familiar, I slunk still lower.

Esther had dreamt of a wonderful career in exciting and glamorous New York City but now that she's in New York she's disillusioned.

> I was supposed to be having the time of my life. I was supposed to be the envy of thousands of other college girls just like me all over America. . . . Look what can happen in this country, they'd say. A girl lives in some out-of-the-way town for nineteen years . . . then gets a scholarship to college

and wins a prize here and a prize there and ends up steering New York like her own private car. *Only I wasn't steering anything, not even myself.*

More Upbeat Personal Experiences and Autobiographies

Most personal experience stories are not about death and illness; instead they are about adventures, successes, and experiences the writers feel so strongly about that they wish to share them with readers. Some are career stories, as with Bonnie Tiburzi's *Takeoff! The Story of America's First Woman Pilot for a Major Airline*, former surgeon-general C. Everett Koop's *Koop: The Memoirs of America's Family Doctor*, and test pilot Chuck Yeager's *Yeager: An Auto-biography*. Partly because of their fondness for animals, many young readers have appreciated Jane Goodall's *My Life with the Chimpanzees*. Other rec-ommended animal-related books include Diane Ackerman's *The Moon by Whale Light: And Other Adventures Among Bats, Penguins, Crocodilians and Whales*; R. D. Lawrence's *In Praise of Wolves* and *The North Runner*; and Candace Savage's *Wolves*.

Although Farley Mowat's books are not as upbeat, they make fascinating reading. In *A Whale for the Killing*, he thought he had found the perfect place to live until he discovered his neighbors were savages who took pleasure in killing a trapped whale. His angry prose also typifies *Never Cry Wolf* and *Sea of Slaughter*. He's less angry in his earlier *The Dog Who Wouldn't Be* and *Owls in the Family*.

Some authors are so skilled that they have told their own quite ordinary stories of growing up in such a way that young readers feel privileged to get acquainted with a new friend. Jim Wayne Miller named his book *Newfound* after Newfound, Tennessee, where the author and his brother, sister, and mother went to live after his parents divorced when he was in sixth grade. Annie Dillard's *An American Childhood* tells about growing up in the 1950s and 1960s. Tobias Wolff's *This Boy's Life* is set at about the same time, but in Seattle, where he grew up longing to be a "boy of dignity."

With autobiographies, we take it as a given that the writer is passionate about his or her subject, which can be either an advantage or a disadvantage. The disadvantage comes when authors' egos get in the way. For example, *Alicia: My Story* by Alicia Appleman-Jurman is a powerful account of one young woman's experience during the Holocaust. But looking back on the World War II memoir, some readers begin to wonder if the real Alicia could truly have been as brave as she's portrayed in the book.

Memory is a funny thing. In Lorene Cary's *Black Ice,* the story of a smart, black, high school junior from West Philadelphia who went as a scholarship student to the prestigious St. Paul's prep school in New Hampshire, Cary writes about returning to her old school as a teacher and later a trustee who watches and talks with students:

In this way I audit the layers of reminiscences, checking one against the other, mine against my schoolmates'. I trust the memory of my resentment of Sara's slender legs, the joy of perfect equipoise on the balance beam, the milky taste of Ricky's kisses. I trust the compassion a woman can feel for the girl she was. But it's also true that my memory is a card shark, reshuffling the deck to hide what I fear to know, unable to keep from fingering the ace at the bottom of the deck even when I'm doing nothing more than playing Fish in the daylight with children.

Later she writes:

I do not trust these memories. They are fossils, perfectly laid strata of adolescent fear and anger undisturbed by layers of forgiveness above.

Milton Meltzer said that when he wrote *Starting from Home*, he wanted it to be a kind of social history of his hometown of Worcester, Massachusetts:

I made several trips back to Worcester to look again at the places where I lived and had gone to school. I went to the library and used the files of the local press for many of the years I had been in junior and senior high school. I talked to people my own age who still live in the city. I also spent time interviewing my two brothers. My older brother had a fantastic memory for early childhood, and I interviewed him at great length about experiences we shared. I needed his perspective on various incidents to see how they matched mine. As often happens with personal testimony, we sometimes differed radically not only in our interpretation of what happened within the family but even on whether it happened to me or to him. I'd tell him a particular incident I was writing about from my childhood, and he'd tell me that I didn't do that, but he did, and I was stealing his life. In 1987 I wrote a book called *The Landscape of Memory*. Some of it goes into the phenomenon of memory and how faulty and unreliable it can be.[7]

The success of an autobiography depends greatly on the quality of the writing because there usually isn't a plot for readers to get excited about, nor are there the kinds of literary exaggeration that make for intriguing villains and heroes, as in some genres. Authors of books for young people have written a particularly good set of autobiographies (see Focus Box 2.1 on p. 55). We placed it early in this text in hopes of encouraging you to begin developing connections with the people behind the books you would be reading. Teachers and librarians can use authors' autobiographies to introduce students to writers who are very much alive and well. Although all the books are written by authors accustomed to writing for young people, they are not part of a planned series and so differ widely in reading levels and sophistication. For example, Nat Hentoff's *Boston Boy* is aimed at adult readers, whereas Richard Peck's *Anonymously Yours* is written for junior high or middle school students. With these extremes, and everything in between, students in a typically heterogeneous class can select the books that match their reading skills and levels of perseverance.

Many teenagers are more interested in reading partial biographies or accounts of personal experiences than they are in reading a full autobiography written toward the end of someone's long and productive life. Personal experience accounts encourage students in their own writing. They are also satisfying because in a relatively short space a complete story can be told, and it may have greater credibility when told in the first person by the one who actually experienced it. Intellectually, readers know that the writer isn't telling everything that happened and that he or she worked hard to select details and create a consistent tone. But emotionally, readers relax and imagine that they are the proverbial fly on the wall privy to the actual experience as well as to the subject's thoughts and emotions.

Another positive aspect is that personal experience stories are often written by relatively young people or by people looking back on experiences they had when they were young. For example, Robin Graham, author of *Dove*, was only sixteen and Steven Callahan, author of *Adrift: Seventy-six Days Lost at Sea*, was twenty-nine when they set sail on their respective adventures. Although Gregory Patent's *Shanghai Passage* is told from an adult perspective, it is about his experiences as a British schoolboy in Shanghai between the end of World War II and 1950 when his family succeeded in emigrating to America. And when personal experience books feature protagonists who are clearly adult, the adults are likely to be unencumbered by family responsibilities. Travel books enjoyed by mature young readers include Peter Matthiessen's *African Silences*, William Least Heat Moon's *Blue Highways: A Journey into America*, Charles Kuralt's *A Life on the Road*, Bruce Chatwin's *What Am I Doing Here?*, and Benedict Allen's *Who Goes Out in the Midday Sun?*

Whether to consider a book a personal experience or an autobiography is often a toss-up. For example, Maya Angelou's *I Know Why the Caged Bird Sings* and its three sequels are usually considered to be autobiographies because they move chronologically through Angelou's life, but it might be argued that they are personal experience stories because each book is about only a part of her life. There's also a crossover between personal experience accounts and the new journalism discussed in Chapter Eight. Many of the books listed there could be discussed in this chapter as personal experience accounts.

A Comparison of Two Personal Accomplishment Books

Although on the surface the two books we are comparing are very different, we want to show some of the similarities that make them communicate to young adults in the same way as do the adventure accomplishment romances discussed in Chapter Four. Gary Paulsen's *Woodsong* is an account of the seventeen days and nights in which he, a middle-aged man from Minnesota, ran the Alaskan Iditarod. Lorene Cary's *Black Ice*, mentioned earlier, recounts the author's experience in attending an exclusive New England prep school in 1972–1974 on an affirmative action scholarship. Few of us will have the experiences that these authors write about, but we all have felt some of their emotions, and so we are fascinated to read about them in these quite different contexts.

First, both authors admit their hopes of success, and the subsequent refining of these hopes. On day three of the race, when Paulsen and his dogs are starting to climb the Alaska Range, he begins to realize that his team is slow:

> . . . much slower than most other teams and I realize on this day that I will be very lucky to finish the race, let alone do well. Finishing is all I originally wanted, but the hot worm is always there—the thought that maybe your dogs are special and will prove themselves better than Rick's or Susan's or any of the other front-end runners. It is a futile dream, a strange thought to have, but it is there nonetheless.

Compare this to Cary's attitude about going to St. Paul:

> I was not afraid to go to St. Paul's School, although it was becoming clear to me from the solicitous white faces that people thought I was— or ought to be. I had no idea that wealth and privilege could confer real advantages beyond the obvious ones sprawled before us. Instead, I believed that rich white people were like poodles: overbred, inbred, degenerate. All the coddling and permissiveness would have a bad effect, I figured, now that they were up against those of us who'd lived a real life in the real world.

What Paulsen calls the "hot worm" of ambition, Cary refers to as the "greedy girl within." At graduation she is disappointed that she doesn't graduate with honors, but then the Rector's Award is announced and as the description of the winner begins to sound more and more like her:

> My ears perked up at "officer of the Sixth Form." That was one of us four sitting in pairs on either side of the aisle in the front row. . . . I shushed the greedy girl within. Starved for some special notice, she stood inside my skin jumping up and down. In the seconds while Mr. Oates read the list, I heard her clamor. I heard how deeply she had been hurt to receive nothing, nothing at all but a diploma. No honors, no cum laude, nothing. Nothing for me, nothing for my work? Not a farthing for my trouble? Nothing for the family who had traveled so far? Nothing to compensate for what they don't even know they have lost—my confidence, my trust? Not one little gift to give the people who have given up a daughter?

Both Paulsen and Cary have mystical experiences connected with nature and their own thoughts. Paulsen has his hallucinations and what he learns from both his dogs and wild animals. The title of Cary's book comes from the black ice that forms on the pond near St. Paul's, where she goes to contemplate the stories her grandfather used to tell, the stories that explain to her:

> . . . why the old people looked at us with such unforgiving eyes, why they pushed us away, but wouldn't let go. Without the stories, I'd have nothing to explain the cacophony in my head in the indigo New Hampshire night. I'd be back fifteen years old, sitting in the Art Building's common room, feeling the crazy panic again, hearing the white kids telling me to buck up because slavery's past, Jim Crow's dead and gone without a trace. Jump, Izzy.

Later she says, "St. Paul's gave me new words into which I must translate the old. But St. Paul's would keep me inside my black skin, that fine, fine membrane that was meant to hold my blood, not bind up my soul. The stories show me the way out."

Both Paulsen and Cary come as strangers, as outsiders, to their adventures. Near the end of Paulsen's book he is horrified when an Eskimo child runs out and stops his dogs. Paulsen grabs the youngster by his coat, perhaps saving his life by lifting him above the confused and snarling pack. When Paulsen asks the boy why he did such a thing, the boy responds that he wanted Paulsen to stay at his family's house that night so he could learn about dogsledding. Paulsen was amazed that an Eskimo, even a child, thought he could learn something from a man from Minnesota who was only pretending to know what he was doing.

Cary had a similar surprise when she began tutoring younger minority students at St. Paul's:

> When the girl left, I heard my own words. I had never said them before, never even thought them. I sat in my room grinning. More than anything I had said while I stood nervously trying to solicit discussion on blues lyrics, a half-hour with that girl and her no-thesis, no-introduction, no-proper-conclusion paper had shown me that I, too, had something to give to St. Paul's. I had come not just with my hat in my hand, a poorly shod scholarship girl, but as a sojourner bearing gifts, which were mine to give or withhold.

As the end of Cary's schooling approaches, her friend Anthony introduces her to the shot put, which she enjoys because it's like dance but without the bother of an audience:

> Inside the circle, from the crouch through the exploding sweep of the pivot, shot put felt more simple than I'd ever remembered childhood, and as powerful as I had hoped adulthood might be. For a while, it seemed as if the buggy, blue afternoons would stretch out indefinitely, as if in spring term of Sixth-Form year time acquired a half-life that kept graduation always coming, but never there.

This mixed emotion of finally getting into the experience and of wanting it to continue was described by Paulsen on the last day of the run:

> ■ As dark comes I can see the lights of the finish, of Nome, twenty or more miles ahead and when I realize what they are I stop the team.
>
> I do not want to go in and finish the race.
>
> I do not understand why, but I do not want to go in. I actually begin to walk up and take my leader and turn the dogs around and run back, back. . . .
>
> There is no sense to it but somehow it is because the race is something that doesn't seem like it can be done. Not really. You can talk about it and plan for it and train for it but it is not something you can do. . . . Not something that can be done. And yet you do it and then it becomes something you don't want to end—ever. You want the race, the exaltation, the joy and beauty of it to go on and on.

Readers of both books, and of many other personal experience accounts, can undoubtedly find more similarities than the ones we've pointed out here. Ones that come to mind but that we didn't have space to illustrate include the powerful metaphors both writers used to bring abstract concepts down to a manageable size; the different ways the authors showed their perseverance; the illustrations of such emotions as hope, frustration, and anger (either of humans or, in Paulsen's book, of animals), and the intensity that's a natural part of challenge.

■ BIOGRAPHIES

One reason biographies appeal to readers is that their authors have the best of two worlds. They can present the uniqueness and authenticity of one person's life and, at the same time, emotions and problems that all humans face. Traditionally, biographies—especially those for young readers—were written about heroic figures whose lives were thought worthy of emulation. Some biographies built their subjects up to almost godlike proportions, and the results were discouraging to young readers. People are well acquainted with their own weaknesses, and when they are told only about the strengths of their heroes, they conclude that heroes are of quite another breed. Today's biographies for young adults are likely to be written more objectively, providing a balance of both strengths and weaknesses. They demonstrate how the subject and the reader share similar emotions. Both have fears and insecurities and both succumb to temptations and vanities. After reading a good biography, the reader feels a kinship with the subject, not so much in spite of as because of the character's human frailties.

To say that a biography is written "objectively" does not mean that it is written without feeling. For biographies to ring true, the author must become so immersed in the subject's life that he or she can write with passion and commitment. This implies a point of view, not one imposed by an author who set out to prove a preconceived idea but a unifying force that guided the person's life and was discovered by the author through his or her research.

The Subjects of Biographies

Few of us will admit to selecting the biographies we are going to purchase and promote on the basis of how we feel about the subject, but that's like one of those old clichés, such as "Never judge a book by its cover," that is honored more in word than in deed. Someone could write a Ph.D. dissertation on how American's values have changed over the last thirty years as reflected by whose biographies were put on the shelves of libraries. In the early 1960s, readers at almost any library would find a predominance of biographies about white males who were inventors, statesmen, soldiers, and business leaders. During the 1970s, the imbalance became so obvious, particularly in school libraries, that educators and publishers took steps to correct the situation by preparing biographies about previously unsung heroes, including members of minority groups, women, handicapped individuals, and people whose contributions were not in military, political, or business spheres (see Focus Box 7.4 for some of these new counterbalancing biographies). Of course, there is still room for good books presenting new information on traditional heroes. Examples of such recent books include Tom D. Crouch's *The Bishop's Boys: A Life of Wilbur and Orville Wright,* Russell Freedman's *Franklin Delano Roosevelt,* and Rhoda Blumberg's *The Remarkable Voyages of Captain Cook* and *Commodore Perry in the Land of the Shogun.*

Collective biographies (i.e., one book presenting the stories of several individuals) have become increasingly popular because authors can write about individuals whose lives may not have been chronicled fully enough to provide information for an entire book. Authors usually bring together the stories of people who have something in common, such as a similarity of accomplishments or the same ethnic backgrounds. This is an efficient way to get information about previously ignored individuals into a library. Also, developing a unifying theme may be the best way to show a trend or connections among various subjects. For example, Russell Freedman's *Indian Chiefs,* the biographies of six western Indian chiefs during the 1800s, is a stronger condemnation of Anglo treatment of American Indians than it would have been had he told only one of the stories. Don Gallo's *Speaking for Ourselves: Autobiographical Sketches by Notable Authors of Books for Young Adults* does an excellent job of introducing teenagers to the fact that authors tend to be individualistic. Over eighty contemporary YA authors contributed two-page bibliographic statements—each telling a quite different story. William Drake's *The First Wave: Women Poets in America, 1915–1945* shows that many women were interested in literary endeavors through presenting accounts of twenty-seven highly acclaimed poets, including Marianne Moore,

Biographies to Fill in the Blanks

American Women: Their Lives in Their Words by Doreen Rappaport. Crowell, 1990. In tracing 350 years of women's history in the New World, Rappaport begins with an American Indian legend of creation in which "woman" plays an important role. Her concluding chapter, "What's Ahead?" is both a challenge and a prediction.

Anthony Burns: The Defeat and Triumph of a Fugitive Slave by Virginia Hamilton. Knopf, 1988. In 1854, a twenty-year-old slave named Anthony Burns escaped to Boston, and when his owner came to take him back to the South thousands of abolitionists rose to defend him in this foreshadowing of the Civil War. Hamilton's *Paul Robeson: The Life and Times of a Free Black Man* (HarperCollins, 1974) is also recommended.

Beyond the Myth: The Story of Joan of Arc by Polly Schoyer Brooks. Lippincott, 1990. Brooks relied heavily on general knowledge about the period as well as on the extraordinary trial record kept by the men who condemned Joan of Arc to bring a fresh look to this famous story.

The Elephant Man by Frederick Drimmer. Putnam, 1985. Here is the true story of the terribly deformed John Merrick, who lived in England between 1862 and 1890.

The First Wave: Women Poets in America, 1915–1945 by William Drake. Macmillan, 1991. Although this isn't a political book, it illustrates how women's roles were changing during the 1920s and through World War II.

Georgia O'Keeffe: The Wideness and Wonder of Her World by Beverly Gherman. Atheneum, 1986. Born in the 1880s, Georgia O'Keeffe became an independent and successful artist at a time when even the most artistic women were expected to be teachers while men became the artists.

In Kindling Flame: The Story of Hannah Senesh, 1921–1944 by Linda Atkinson. Lothrop, 1985. In 1941 Hannah Senesh felt safe in Palestine, but in 1944 she joined the British Army to return to Hungary as a freedom fighter. Her story shows the growth of pre–World War II anti-Semitism and the subsequent Holocaust.

Inspirations: Stories About Women Artists by Leslie Sills, illustrated by Ann Fay. Whitman, 1989. Sills tells the stories of four working artists, showing what they do and what they aspire to do.

Louisa May: The World and Works of Louisa May Alcott by Norma Johnston. Four Winds, 1991. Johnston did a good job of collecting and writing and gives credit to Louisa May's mother as well as her father in her development.

Margaret Bourke-White by Vicki Goldberg. HarperCollins, 1986. The courage and dedication of a Life magazine photographer who made us see truly what the world was like.

Nothing to Do But Stay: My Pioneer Mother by Carrie Young. University of Iowa Press, 1991. Young's essays show what life was like for her mother in South Dakota during the first third of this century.

Pioneer Women: Voices from the Kansas Frontier by Joanna L. Stratton. Simon & Schuster, 1981. Frontier women did more than sit atop covered wagons and wear sunbonnets.

Queen Eleanor, Independent Spirit of the Medieval World: A Biography of Eleanor of Aquitaine by Polly Schoyer Brooks. Lippincott, 1983. This is a readable introduction to medieval times and one of the first politically important women in history.

The Road from Home: The Story of an Armenian Girl by David Kherdian. Greenwillow, 1979. The author's mother was among the Armenians forced out of Turkey in 1915. She eventually came to America as a mail-order bride. Her story is continued in *Finding Home* (Greenwillow, 1981).

Rosa Parks: My Story by Rosa Parks with Jim Haskins. Dial, 1992. The woman who started the Montgomery bus boycott tells who she was and what she became.

The Triumph of Discovery: Women Scientists Who Won the Nobel Prize by Joan Dash. Messner, 1991. This four-part biography tells the stories of four of the nine women who in this century have received the Nobel Laureate in Science: Maria Goeppert-Mayer (1963), Rosalyn Yalow (1977), Barbara McClintock (1983), and Rita Levi-Montalcini (1986).

We Are Your Sisters: Black Women in the 19th Century by Dorothy Sterling. Norton, 1984. Primary sources (letters, speeches, newspaper clippings, etc.) are used to document the lives of both slave and free black women.

Woman in the Mists: The Story of Dian Fossey and the Mountain Gorillas of Africa by Farley Mowat. Warner, 1987. Fellow naturalist Farley Mowat drew on Fossey's journals and letters to re-create this moving story of Fossey's work with endangered gorillas in Africa.

Women Who Write by Lucinda Irwin Smith. Messner, 1989. Interviews with Nikki Giovanni and Joyce Carol Oates add interest to this overview of successful women authors. Smith concludes by offering advice to aspiring writers.

Edna St. Vincent Millay, and Amy Lowell. Jim Haskins' *One More River to Cross: The Stories of Twelve Black Americans* counters the stereotype that blacks have succeeded only as entertainers and athletes by including the stories of businesswoman C. J. Walker, explorer Matthew Henson, diplomat Ralph Bunche, congresswoman Shirley Chisolm, and astronaut Ronald McNair, while Peter Irons' *The Courage of Their Convictions: Sixteen Americans Who Fought Their Way to the Supreme Court* shows the variety of problems the justices are asked to solve.

Series of biographies are similar to collective biographies in that a central theme is chosen and then individual books are written that fit into the theme. However, the planning for series books is probably controlled as much by marketing as writing concerns. When publishers do series books, they can economize by using the same format and design. Also, a single advertising campaign works for several books. Librarians are often grateful for biographical series because such sets of books can fill gaps in a collection that a single title could not. And when librarians are pleased with the first one or two books in a series coming from a reputable publisher and a good editor, they can feel confident in ordering the forthcoming books.

For example, based on the quality of the writing in Marlka Drucker's *Frida Kahlo: Torment and Triumph in Her Life and Art* and Carolyn Balducci's *Margaret Fuller: A Life of Passion and Defiance*, many public and college and some high school libraries will be willing to order forthcoming books in the Barnard Biography Series. The books are being prepared under the sponsorship of Barnard College and published by Bantam with the explicit goal of expanding the "universe of heroic women." Columnist Anna Quindlen introduces the Margaret Fuller book by writing:

> I felt my first connection to Margaret Fuller when I was a girl yearning to grow into a newspaperwoman. At a time when a woman could exhibit neither her ankles nor her brains, Margaret Fuller was America's first female foreign correspondent, a reporter for the *New York Tribune* who covered England, France, and Italy. . . . Wherever she went, she was the first woman and almost the only one. To be admitted to these circles must have taken great courage and determination; to succeed must have taken great talent.

Silver Burdett and Lerner are publishers that specialize in biographies for junior and senior high libraries. The Achievers series from Lerner focuses on contemporary sports heroes—for example, Florence Griffith Joyner and Joe Montana. Their Lerner Biography series features more traditional heroes, such as Dwight Eisenhower and Douglas MacArthur. Silver Burdett has at least five series: Pioneers in Change, What Made Them Great, The American Dream: Business Leaders of the Twentieth Century, Alvin Josephy's Biography Series of American Indians, and Genius! The Artist and the Process. This last series includes books about playwright Arthur Miller, painter Pablo Picasso, architect Frank Lloyd Wright, poet Maya Angelou, dancer Mikhail Baryshnikov, and musician Duke Ellington.

Admittedly, many biographies, especially some of those prepared as parts of series, are prosaic, cut-and-paste accounts that present nothing new and are so boring that even reviewers resist reading them. They are purchased by librarians who also resist reading them. The result is that they go on library shelves to be checked out only under duress when teachers assign students to do a book report on a biography. The saddest part of this is that students who have been forced to read such books may consider all biographies boring and thus miss out on a whole genre.

Four of the authors discussed in the next chapter as star writers of nonfiction— Jean Fritz, James (Jim) Haskins, Albert Marrin, and Milton Meltzer—can be depended on to write biographies that will neither bore young readers nor fill their heads with false information. Fritz and Meltzer specialize in figures from American history, whereas Haskins specializes in minority figures and Marrin looks to the world for his subjects. Meltzer is the most prolific, having written biographies of Mary McLeod Bethune, Christopher Columbus, Benjamin Franklin, Martin Luther King, Jr., Dorothea Lange, Mark Twain, Thomas Jefferson, and George Washington.

Celebrity Biographies

Celebrity biographies, which are the ones that get in the news and so are likely to be requested from libraries, often present different problems for educators. One such problem goes back to Andy Warhol's statement that each of us will have "fifteen minutes of fame." The problem is that it takes more than fifteen minutes for a book to be written, published, and purchased, so schools and libraries are usually a step behind. By the time a biography of some new celebrity has gone through a rigorous selection procedure, the subject may no longer be of interest.

Coming to the rescue are the mass market paperbacks that are distributed through newsstands. Daniel and Susan Cohen have written several such books for Pocket Books' Archway Paperbacks; for example, *Going for the Gold: Medal Hopefuls for Winter '92* was published as "Your front-row seat to the 1992 Winter Olympics!" Although the cover and title made the book look like a collective biography, it was actually more of a source of information about each Olympic sport and a history of previous winners and "what to watch for," which included predictions about the 1992 hopefuls. Obviously, the book was intended to be short-lived, but the same authors will probably revise it again in four years, just as they did with the 1988 *Going for the Gold*.

Other similarly created and marketed Archway books by the Cohens include *Rock Video Superstars* and *Rock Video Superstars II*, *Wrestling Superstars* and *Wrestling Superstars II*, *Young and Famous: Hollywood's Newest Superstars* and *Beverly Hills 90210: Meet the Stars of Today's Hottest TV Series*. The Cohens' books are just one example. Other companies have similarly massmarketed books that can be purchased either from newsstands or, by those affiliated with schools and libraries, directly from the distributors who supply the newsstands.

Chances are that reviews of such books won't appear in professional journals, nor will librarians use them as the focus for professional book discussion groups. Nevertheless, such books may fill a need by providing youngsters with current information about people they admire. These paperback books cost about as much as a magazine and probably have about the same life expectancy. Rather than shelving them with regular biographies, librarians might consider placing them near the magazines or in a display indicating their timeliness. They aren't written to be long-lasting and so need not be given the same kind of treatment as other biographies.

A quite different problem involves celebrity biographies that are written for adults but read by young people, since some celebrities most admired by teenagers have life-styles and values that educators may not feel good about endorsing. Of course, the fact that we have a particular book in our library does not mean that we are endorsing everything the person does or believes in. But if children (or their parents) have been taught to read biographies with the intent of emulating the life of anyone judged worthy of having a book written about him or her, then we're going to have problems. For example, Wilt Chamberlain's *A View from Above* includes a chapter "On Sex and Love: What Rules the World" in which he writes:

> Does sex run the world? I think it does. . . . I *have always* believed there is more than one true love for a person. I also believe that lust is more a natural part of us than love, and that one can spend every waking moment falling in and out of lust. There are a few of us who are fortunate enough to be in a position to fulfill our lustful desires. I'm one of those lucky ones. So don't be shocked to hear that if I had to count my sexual encounters, I would be closing in on twenty thousand women. Yes, that's correct, *twenty thousand different ladies* [Chamberlain's emphasis]. At my age, that equals out to having sex with 1.2 women a day, every day since I was fifteen.

Chamberlain goes on in this vein for eighteen pages and then concludes with what he or his editors must have considered a conciliatory statement:

> Most men would think it a great achievement if they could make love to a thousand different women. But I've come to believe the greater achievement would be to make love to the same woman a thousand times.

As part of basketball star Magic Johnson's announcement that he was retiring from the Los Angeles Lakers because he had tested positive for the AIDS virus, Johnson said that during his career he "had accommodated as many women as possible." Johnson's purpose in making the statement was apparently to convince people that he had not acquired the disease through homosexual activities. The media picked up Johnson's statement and tied it in with Chamberlain's claim of 20,000 sex partners. Feminists were offended by the facts as well as by the tone of the men's comments and the ensuing media discussions. Martina Navratilova, for example, charged that "a woman making the same statement would have been castigated by the media."[8]

When it was discussed in our local newspaper, readers wrote letters to the editor in which they accused Chamberlain of everything from "jiving" his white readers to using an erroneous term when referring to the "ladies" he had been with. For adults to read Chamberlain's book and argue over these matters is all well and good, and in fact may help males and females to understand each other a little better. But chances of there being follow-up discussions among teenaged readers are slim, and even if an adult sponsors the reading of Chamberlain's book as a group or class project and then leads a discussion on it, young readers might be turned off by what they perceive as preaching. Discussions between teenagers and adults are always somewhat lopsided because adults have more knowledge and experience than teenagers. It takes a sensitive and skilled leader to keep teenagers from withdrawing mentally, if not physically, from serious discussions. If the young readers have more respect for the subject of the biography than for the discussion leader, the discussion leader must steer clear of lambasting the subject of the biography for having led a misguided life.

What does this mean for book selection? Assuming that most of us agree that in today's world we do not want to encourage young men to try setting records and keeping score on how many women they can "accommodate," what's our role? Do we buy and promote biographies only for people who have been dead long enough that we're fairly certain no ghosts will rise from their graves? We hope not. Besides, with revisionist history, even this time-honored approach isn't guaranteed. Another approach that we're not recommending is to buy only "safe" series books put out by educational publishers.

With a questionable book, it's usually better that teenagers have a chance to read the whole book rather than just get the smatterings of sexual titillation that appear in the media. One thing we can feel confident in suggesting is that when it comes to selecting books that you're unsure about, check out your initial reaction with others. Talk to colleagues, parents, and students. Perhaps it's the last group that is most important to include in discussions about book selection, because unless someone starts young people along such a line of thinking they may never understand that reading about someone's life doesn't necessarily mean emulating everything about that person. As librarian Mary Mueller observed:

> Our past and present are full of personages who lived outside traditional rules. They often used poor judgment or acted in a less-than-exemplary fashion. . . . How can we expect our students to really see the personality of Harry Truman without letting them see the tenacity, salty language, and temper that so characterized him?[9]

Books Exploiting Crime and Tragedy

It's easier to wholeheartedly condemn books that are written by criminals or psychopaths. In fact, the state of New York passed a law (declared unconstitutional in 1991) that outlawed anyone's making a profit from having committed a crime, with the intent of keeping criminals from getting rich by telling their stories to ghost writers or selling movie or television rights. At least informally the ruling was called the "Son of Sam" law "in honor of" the infamous New York killer David Berkowitz.

To the distress of many adults, popular reading choices for some teenagers are the very kinds of books that the Son of Sam law was supposed to discourage. We know that teenagers like to read about the extremes of society, and since they have free access to books written for the general public, we shouldn't be surprised when young people choose to read about people who are clearly *not* role models. Albert Marrin's *Stalin: Russia's Man of Steel, Hitler,* and *Napoleon and the Napoleonic Wars* are among the most highly praised biographies for young people, and adults don't seem nervous about children reading them. But this may relate to the fact that these people's roles in history seem fairly settled. The general public isn't nearly so sanguine when it comes to contemporary criminals, witness the media flap in the spring of 1992 about the marketing of baseball-type collectors' cards featuring criminals, including the Wisconsin serial killer Jeffrey Dahmer.

Helter Skelter: The True Story of the Manson Murders by Vincent Bugliosi and Curt Gentry was very popular during the late 1970s and early 1980s, and psychologists hastened to explain to worried teachers and parents that reading about someone does not necessarily mean that the reader wants to follow in that person's footsteps. Curiosity, more than hero worship, is at play. As humans, we are drawn to examining and pondering our dual natures. We peer into the evil nature of something truly horrible in the same way that we peer into a great chasm or over the ledge of a skyscraper. We have no intention of falling or jumping over, yet the fact that some people have fallen or jumped in similar situations makes us shudder, because we recognize the possibility.

Should we expect young people to be any different from their parents in being fascinated by the horrors of the world? The flourishing business that tabloid newspapers do attests to the fact that people are intrigued by those who have done terrible things. On television, documentary-dramas of real events garner huge audiences. After much inner turmoil, the networks decided against doing a dramatized version of David Berkowitz, the "Son of Sam" killer, because, as Brandon Stoddard, president of the ABC motion pictures unit, explained, even though merely labeling a TV film a true story can add millions to a network's audience, to tell Berkowitz' story "would have been incredibly exploitative. He was a very sick man. . . . When you try to examine the psyche of an individual who is that abnormal, it is difficult to find insights that are useful to the average American."[10]

Antihero biographies feature characters who are less than successful, but they differ from the stories of out-and-out villains such as Charles Manson or David Berkowitz in that the authors are hoping to provide the kinds of insights that Stoddard argued would be missing from the Berkowitz story. Antiheroes are meek, humble, and confused people trying to understand life. They make mistakes, including very severe mistakes, yet the author writes about them with sympathy, as in Norman Mailer's *The Executioner's Song,* the story of Gary Gilmore's crime spree in Spanish Fork, Utah, and his subsequent execution in the Utah State Prison. He is in no way held up as a role model or as having a life that any reader would want, yet readers come away with some understanding of his thinking and his psyche.

The Debunking Biography

The debunking biography is another fairly recent trend in which a popular hero, or perhaps an institution, is taken down from a pedestal. Although such books are certainly "antihero," they differ from true examples of the literary meaning of the term in that the subject of a debunking biography is not written about with sympathy. Among the most famous of recent debunking biographies was Kitty Kelley's controversial biography of Nancy Reagan. Probably few young adults read it because politics and the Reagans are not part of their sphere of interest. They would have been much more likely to read all or parts of the spring 1992 blockbuster *Diana: Her True Story* written by Andrew Morton. *The Sunday Times* of London paid $462,500 to print prepublication excerpts, which in turn were paraphrased and discussed by much of the world's press. The result was that many more people read excerpts and news stories about the book than read the book itself, which wasn't so much a debunking of Princess Diana as it was of her husband, Prince Charles, and the institution of British royalty.

Sports heroes and movie stars are prime subjects for debunking biographies that will attract young readers. For example, some young adults were attracted to the antiparent theme in Christina Crawford's *Mommie Dearest,* which debunked actress Joan Crawford for the way she played her real-life role of mother. Jim Bouton's *Ball Four: My Life and Hard Times Throwing the Knuckleball in the Big Leagues* was a debunking of professional baseball, and Samuel Wilson Fussell's *Muscle: Confessions of an Unlikely Body Builder* debunked weight-lifting. Books like these serve as antidotes for gullibility and excessive hero worship. Not to read debunking books is to miss one facet of humanity, but to read only debunking books is to produce only debunkers, and that we already have in sufficient number.

Connections Between History and Biography

We borrowed the title for this chapter from an "Up for Discussion" piece in *School Library Journal* entitled "History and History Makers: Give YAs the Whole Picture."[11] Mary Mueller, librarian at Rolla Junior High School in Missouri, was recommending biographies and histories as mutually complementary because individuals are shaped by the times and circumstances of their lives, which they in turn influence and shape for themselves as well as for those around them and those who will follow. In making a plea for librarians to be assertive in recommending biographies alongside history books, she pointed out how few books about the 1960s, the civil rights movement, and the Vietnam War include information about the "rich, complex character of Lyndon Johnson, a man who greatly influenced all three and who is extremely important to any understanding of these happenings and the era in which they occurred." She also argued for updating the 900s sections in our libraries, noting that in times of shrinking budgets we hesitate to weed out historical books and feel more justified in spending money for a new computer book than for a biography of someone who lived 200 years ago.

We'll end this chapter with the same plea that Mueller made, which is that there are so many changes in attitudes and outlooks, "to say nothing of revisionists' theories," that history and biography sections need just as much loving care and attention—including weeding, replacing, and promoting—as do any other sections of a library.

NOTES

[1]Richard Stengel, "Books: American Myth 101," *Time* Magazine (December 23, 1991) 78.

[2]Henry Seidel Canby, "What Is Truth?" *Saturday Review of Literature* 4 (December 31, 1927): 481.

[3]Stengel, "Books," p. 78.

[4]Betty Carter and Richard F. Abrahamson, *From Delight to Wisdom: Nonfiction for Young Adults* (Oryx Press, 1990), p.180.

[5]Carter and Abrahamson, "A Conversation with Brent Ashabranner," in *From Delight to Wisdom: Nonfiction for Young Adults* (Oryx Press, 1990), p. 101.

[6]Christopher Collier, "Criteria for Historical Novels," *School Library Journal* 29 (August 1982): 32.

[7]Carter and Abrahamson, "A Conversation with Milton Meltzer," in *From Delight to Wisdom: Nonfiction for Young Adults* (Oryx Press, 1990), p.55.

[8]Dennis Love, "Lifestyles: War of Sexes Raged," *The Arizona Republic,* December 29, 1991.

[9]Mary E. Mueller, "Up for Discussion: History and History Makers: Give YAs the Whole Picture." *School Library Journal* 37 (November 1991): 55–56.

[10]Sally Bedell, "Is TV Exploiting Tragedy?" *TV Guide,* June 16–22, 1979, p. 6.

[11]Mueller, "Up for Discussion," pp. 55–56.

OTHER TITLES MENTIONED IN THE TEXT OF CHAPTER SEVEN

Abells, Chana Byers. *The Children We Remember*. Greenwillow, 1986.

Abt, Samuel. *LeMond: The Incredible Comeback of an America Hero*. Random House, 1990.

Ackerman, Diane. *The Moon by Whale Light: And Other Adventures Among Bats, Penguins, Crocodilians, and Whales*. Random House, 1991.

Angelou, Maya. *I Know Why the Caged Bird Sings*. Random House, 1970.

Applebaum-Jurman, Alicia. *Alicia: My Story*. Bantam, 1988.

Ashabranner, Brent. *Children of the Maya: A Guatemalan Indian Odyssey*. Putnam, 1986.

———. *Into a Strange Land: Unaccompanied Refugee Youth in America*. Putnam, 1987.

Avi. *The True Confessions of Charlotte Doyle*. Orchard, 1990.

Balducci, Carolyn Feleppa. *Margaret Fuller: A Life of Passion and Defiance*. Barnard Biography Series. Bantam, 1991.

Barker, Rodney, *The Hiroshima Maidens*. Viking, 1985.

Blinn, William. *Brian's Song*. Bantam, 1972.

Blumberg, Rhoda. *Commodore Perry in the Land of the Shogun*. Lothrop, 1985.

———. *The Remarkable Voyages of Captain Cook*. Bradbury, 1991.

Bombeck, Erma. *I Want to Grow Hair, I Want to Grow Up, I Want to Go to Boise: Children Surviving Cancer*. HarperCollins, 1989.

Bouton, Jim, edited by Leonard Shecter. *Ball Four: My Life and Hard Times Throwing the Knuckleball in the Big Leagues*. World, 1970.

Brodie, Fawn M. *Thomas Jefferson: An Intimate History*. Norton, 1974.

Bugliosi, Vincent, and Curt Gentry. *Helter Skelter: The True Story of the Manson Murders*. Norton, 1974.

Callahan, Stephen. *Adrift: Seventy-six Days Lost at Sea*. Thorndike, 1986.

Cary, Lorene, *Black Ice*. Knopf, 1991.

Chamberlain, Wilt. *A View from Above*. Villard, 1991.

Chatwin, Bruce. *What Am I Doing Here?* Viking, 1989.

Cohen, Daniel and Susan. *Beverly Hills 90210: Meet the Stars of Today's Hottest TV Series*. Pocket Books Archway, 1991.

_____. *Going for the Gold: Medal Hopefuls for Winter '92*. Pocket Books, 1991.

_____. *Rock Video Superstars*. Pocket Books, 1985.

_____. *Rock Video Superstars II*. Pocket Books, 1987.

_____. *Wrestling Superstars*. Pocket Books, 1985.

_____. *Wrestling Superstars II*. Pocket Books, 1986.

_____. *Young and Famous: Hollywood's Newest Superstars*. Pocket Books, 1987.

Conrad, Pam. *My Daniel*. HarperCollins, 1989.

Cox, Clinton. *Undying Glory: The Story of the Massachusetts 54th Regiment*. Scholastic, 1991.

Crawford, Christina. *Mommie Dearest*. Morrow, 1978.

Crouch, Tom D. *The Bishop's Boys: A Life of Wilbur and Orville Wright*. Norton, 1989.

Dillard, Annie. *An American Childhood*. HarperCollins, 1987.

Donald, David Herbert, ed. *Gone for a Soldier: The Civil War Memoirs of Private Alfred Bellard*. Little, Brown, 1975.

Drake, William. *The First Wave: Women Poets in America, 1915–1945*. Macmillan, 1987.

Drucker, Malka. *Frida Kahlo: Torment and Triumph in Her Life and Art*. Barnard Biography Series. Bantam, 1991.

Edelman, Barnard, ed. *Dear America: Letters Home from Vietnam*. Norton, 1985.

Farber, Norma. *Mercy Short: A Winter Journal, North Boston, 1692–93*. Dutton, 1982.

Fast, Howard. *April Morning*. Crown, 1961.

Feldbaum, Carl B., and Ronald J. Bee. *Looking the Tiger in the Eye: Confronting the Nuclear Threat*. HarperCollins, 1988.

Finkelstein, Norman H. *The Other 1492: Jewish Settlement in the New World*. Scribner, 1989.

Fleischman, Paul. *Saturnalia*. HarperCollins, 1990.

Forman, James. *Ceremony of Innocence*. Hawthorne, 1970.

Frank, Anne. *Diary of a Young Girl*. Doubleday, 1952.

Freedman, Russell. *Indian Chiefs*. Holiday, 1986.

_____. *Franklin Delano Roosevelt*. Clarion, 1990.

Fritz, Jean et al. *The World in 1492*. Holt, 1992.

Fussell, Samuel Wilson. *Muscle: Confessions of an Unlikely Body Builder*. Poseidon, 1991.

Gaes, Jason. *My Book for Kids with Cansur*. Melius and Peterson, 1987.

Gallo, Donald R., ed. *Speaking for Ourselves: Autobiographical Sketches by Notable Authors for Books for Young Adults*. National Council of Teachers of English, 1990.

Garfield, Leon. *The Empty Sleeve*. Delacorte, 1988.

_____. *Jack Holborn*. Pantheon, 1965.

_____. *The Night of the Comet*. Delacorte, 1979.

_____. *The Sound of Coaches*. Viking, 1974.

_____. *The Strange Affair of Adelaide Harris*. Pantheon, 1971.

Goodall, Jane, *My Life with the Chimpanzees*. Pocket Books, 1988.

Graham, Robin. *Dove*. HarperCollins, 1972.

Gunther, John. *Death Be Not Proud*. HarperCollins, 1949.

Hansen, Joyce. *Out from This Place*. Walker, 1988.

————. *Which Way Freedom?* Walker, 1986.

Haskins, Jim. *One More River to Cross: The Stories of Twelve Black Americans*. Scholastic, 1992.

Hentoff, Nat. *Boston Boy*. Knopf, 1986.

Hersey, John. *Hiroshima*. Knopf, 1946.

Hillesum, Etty. *An Interrupted Life: The Diaries of Etty Hillesum, 1941–1943*. Pantheon, 1984.

————. *Letters from Westerbork*. Pantheon, 1986.

Hoobler, Dorothy and Thomas. *The Fact or Fiction Files: Lost Civilizations*. Walker, 1992.

Houston, Jeanne Wakatsuki, and James D. Houston. *Farewell to Manzanar*. Houghton Mifflin, 1973.

Hudson, Jan. *Sweetgrass*. Philomel, 1989.

Irons, Peter. *The Courage of Their Convictions: Sixteen Americans Who Fought Their Way to the Supreme Court*. Free Press, 1988.

Jacobs, Francine. *The Tainos: The People Who Welcomed Columbus*. Putnam, 1992.

Jewell, Geri, with Stewart Winer. *Geri*. Morrow, 1984.

Josephy, Alvin M., Jr. *America in 1492: The World of the Indian Peoples Before the Arrival of Columbus*. Knopf, 1992.

Kammen, Michael. *Mystic Chords of Memory*. Knopf, 1991.

Katz, William Loren. *Breaking the Chains: African-American Slave Resistance*. Atheneum, 1990.

Koop, C. Everett. *Koop: The Memoirs of America's Family Doctor*. Random House, 1991.

Krementz, Jill. *How It Feels to Fight for Your Life*. Little, Brown, 1989.

————. *How It Feels When a Parent Dies*. Knopf, 1981.

Kuralt, Charles. *A Life on the Road*. Putnam, 1985.

Lancaster, Matthew. *Hang Toughf*. Paulist, 1985.

Landau, Elaine. *We Have AIDS*. Franklin Watts, 1990.

Lasky, Kathryn. *The Bone Wars*. Morrow, 1988.

Lawrence, R. D. *In Praise of Wolves*. Holt, 1986.

Lawson, Dawn. *The Abraham Lincoln Brigade: Americans Fighting Fascism in the Spanish Civil War*. Crowell, 1989.

Leaf, Munro. *The Story of Ferdinand*. Viking, 1936.

Least Heat Moon, William. *Blue Highways: A Journey into America*. Little, Brown, 1982.

Lowry, Lois. *Number the Stars*. Houghton Mifflin, 1989.

Lund, Doris. *Eric*. Lippincott, 1974.

Lyon, George Ella. *Borrowed Children*. Orchard, 1988.

MacPherson, Malcolm C. *Time Bomb: Fermi, Heisenberg and the Race for the Atomic Bomb*. Dutton, 1986.

Mailer, Norman. *The Executioner's Song*. Little, 1979.

Marrin, Albert. *Hitler*. Viking, 1987.

————. *Napoleon and the Napoleonic Wars*. Viking, 1991.

————. *Stalin: Russia's Man of Steel*. Viking, 1988.

Mason, Bobbie Ann. *In Country*. HarperCollins, 1985.

Masters, Edgar Lee. *Spoon River Anthology*. Macmillan, 1962.

Matthiessen, Peter. *African Silences*. Random House, 1991.

Mazer, Harry. *The Last Mission*. Delacorte, 1979.

McCloud, Bill. *What Should We Tell Our Children About Vietnam?* University of Oklahoma Press, 1989.

Meltzer, Milton. *Columbus and the World Around Him.* Watts, 1990.

————. *The Landscape of Memory.* Viking, 1987.

————. *Never to Forget: The Jews of the Holocaust.* HarperCollins, 1976.

————. *Rescue: The Story of How Gentiles Saved Jews in the Holocaust.* HarperCollins, 1988.

————. *Starting from Home: A Writer's Beginning.* Viking, 1989.

————. *Voices from the Civil War: A Documentary History of the Great American Conflict.* Crowell, 1989.

Miller, Jim Wayne. *Newfound.* Orchard/Richard Jackson, 1989.

Morris, Jeannie. *Brian Piccolo: A Short Season.* Rand McNally, 1971.

Morton, Andrew. *Diana: Her True Story.* Simon & Schuster, 1992.

Mowat, Farley. *The Dog Who Wouldn't Be.* Little, Brown, 1957.

————. *Never Cry Wolf.* Little, Brown, 1963.

————. *And No Birds Sang.* Little, Brown, 1980.

————. *Owls in the Family.* Little, Brown, 1961.

————. *Sea of Slaughter.* Atlantic, 1985.

————. *A Whale for the Killing.* Little, Brown, 1972.

Myers, Walter Dean. *Fallen Angels.* Scholastic, 1988.

————. *Malcolm X: By Any Means Necessary.* Scholastic, 1993.

Nelson, Theresa. *And One for All.* Orchard, 1989.

North, Sterling. *Rascal: A Memoir of a Better Era.* Dutton, 1963.

O'Dell, Scott. *Island of the Blue Dolphins.* Houghton Mifflin, 1960.

————. *The King's Fifth.* Houghton Mifflin, 1966.

————. *Sing Down the Moon.* Houghton Mifflin, 1970.

Osius, Alison. *Second Ascent: The Story of Hugh Herr.* Stackpole, 1991.

Palmer, Laura. *Shrapnel in the Heart: Letters and Remembrances from the Vietnam Veterans Memorial.* Random House, 1987.

Patent, Gregory. *Shanghai Passage.* Clarion, 1990.

Paulsen, Gary. *Woodsong.* Bradbury, 1990.

Peck, Richard. *Anonymously Yours.* Julian Messner, 1991.

Peck Richard E. *Something for Joey.* Bantam, 1978.

Pelta, Kathy. *Discovering Christopher Columbus: How History Is Invented.* Lerner, 1991.

Plath, Sylvia. *The Bell Jar.* HarperCollins, 1971.

Pople, Maureen. *The Other Side of the Family.* Holt, 1988.

Pullman, Phillip. *The Ruby in the Smoke.* Knopf, 1987.

————. *Shadow in the North.* Knopf, 1988.

————. *The Tiger in the Well.* Knopf, 1990.

Pyle, Ernie. *Ernie's War: The Best of Ernie Pyle's World War II Dispatches.* David Nichols, ed. Random House, 1986.

Reeder, Carolyn. *Shades of Gray.* Macmillan, 1989.

Rhodes, Robert Hunt, ed. *All for the Union: The Civil War Diary and Letters of Elisha Hunt Rhodes.* Crown Books, 1991 (orig. published in 1985).

Richter, Elizabeth. *Losing Someone You Love: When a Brother or Sister Dies.* Putnam, 1986.

Rinaldi, Ann. *The Last Silk Dress.* Holiday House, 1988.

————. *Wolf by the Ears.* Scholastic, 1991.

Rosenblatt, Roger. *Children of War.* Doubleday, 1983.

Sayers, Gale. *I Am Third.* Viking, 1970.

Soule, Gardner. *Christopher Columbus: On the Green Sea of Darkness*. Watts, 1988.

Sutcliff, Rosemary. *Dawn Wind*. Walck, 1961.

————. *The Eagle of the Ninth*. Walck, 1954.

————. *The Shield Ring*. Oxford University Press, 1957.

————. *The Shining Company*. Farrar, 1990.

Tapert, Annette, ed. *Lines of Battle: Letters from American Servicemen, 1941–1945*. Times Books, 1987.

Thrasher, Crystal. *End of a Dark Road*. Macmillan, 1982.

Tiburzi, Bonnie. *Takeoff! The Story of America's First Woman Pilot for a Major Airline*. Crown, 1984.

Voigt, Cynthia. *David and Jonathan*. Scholastic, 1992.

Volavkova, Hanna, ed. *I Never Saw Another Butterfly: Children's Drawings and Poems from Terezin Concentration Camp, 1941–1944*. Schocken, 1978.

Ward, Geoffrey. *The Civil War: An Illustrated History*. Knopf, 1990.

Weil, Jiri, translated by Marie Winn. *Mendelssohn on the Roof*. Farrar, Straus & Giroux, 1991.

Westall, Robert. *Fathom Five*. Greenwillow, 1979.

————. *The Machine Gunners*. Greenwillow, 1976.

Wharton, William. *A Midnight Clear*. Knopf, 1982.

White, Ryan, and Ann Marie Cunningham. *Ryan White: My Own Story*. Dial, 1991.

Wolff, Tobias. *This Boy's Life*. Atlantic Monthly Press, 1989.

Yeager, Chuck, with Leo Janos. *Yeager: An Autobiography*. Bantam, 1985.

For information on the availability of paperback editions of these titles, please consult the most recent edition of *Paperbound Books in Print*, published annually by R. R. Bowker Company.

NONFICTION BOOKS
Of Interesting Information

There's a movement afoot to find a replacement term for *nonfiction,* because as any lexicographer knows, defining something by what it is not (i.e., "not a novel or a short story") is an inefficient way to tell what something is. Another objection to the term is that the use of *non* gives it negative connotations. People want to replace it with something more positive sounding, such as *information books,* but we predict that, at least for the immediate future, *nonfiction* will remain an overall cover term, with other terms coming into use for more specific sets of books.

Over the past decade, increased attention and respect have been given to the role of nonfiction as a freely chosen reading interest for young people. For example, the American Library Association made history by awarding its coveted 1988 Newbery Medal to Russell Freedman's *Lincoln: A Photobiography.* Milton Meltzer, who has long championed the cause of nonfiction, applauded by saying:

> ■ It was a terrific thing to do, but it took fifty years to do it. The few books they gave prizes to before, that were called nonfiction, really were not. Instead, they were books written in the outmoded vein of biography that was highly fictionalized, had invented dialogue, and sometimes concocted scenes. That's all changed today, but it took a long time.[1]

A couple of years later, the National Council of Teachers of English began giving the Orbis Pictus Award for outstanding nonfiction, named in honor of the first picture book for children, which was prepared in 1657 by John Amos Comenius. He used woodcuts for the book entitled *Orbis Pictus: The World of Sensible Things Drawn; that is the Nomenclature of all Fundamental Things in the World and Actions in Life Reduced to Ocular Demonstration.* It's fairly safe to say that today we've reduced both the length of our book titles and the scope of their contents. Nevertheless, one could make some interesting comparisons between Comenius' 1657 book and David Macaulay's 1988 *The Way Things Work: From Levers to Lasers, Cars to Computers—A Visual Guide to the World of Machines.*

Another indication of the increased respect being given to nonfiction books is the publication in 1990 of *Nonfiction for Young Adults: From Delight to Wisdom* by Betty Carter and Richard F. Abrahamson (Oryx Press). In their introductory chapter, they cite twenty-two research studies. Among the reported findings are the following:

- An interest in reading nonfiction emerges at about the fourth grade and grows during adolescence.
- Interest in reading nonfiction crosses ability levels; one study showed that nonfiction made up 34 percent of the leisure reading of academically able teenagers and 54 percent of the control group's leisure reading.
- Nonfiction makes up a much larger proportion of boys' reading than of girls' reading.
- One study categorized the seven most popular types of nonfiction as cartoon and comic books, weird but true stories, rock stars, ghosts, magic, stories about famous people, and explorations of the unknown.
- Remedial readers prefer informative nonfiction and read "primarily to learn new things."
- Students choose nonfiction for a wide range of reasons often unrelated to school curricular matters, as shown by the fact that computer-related books are popular in schools with no computers and books on the Ku Klux Klan are frequently checked out in junior highs where recent American history is not studied.
- When students gave reasons for reading particular books, it became clear that the purpose of the reading is guided more by the student than by the type of book. One boy read books on subjects he already knew about because it made him feel smart; others preferred how-to books, so that they could interact with the author while learning to draw, care for a pet, program a computer, make a paper airplane, and so on; and still others preferred *The Guiness Book of World Records.* But even here purposes differed. Some read the book to discover amazing facts, but others read it to imagine themselves undergoing strange experiences.

NARRATIVE OR STORYTELLING IN NONFICTION

When E. L. Doctorow, the author of *Ragtime,* accepted the National Book Critics Circle Award, he said, "There is no more fiction or nonfiction—only narrative." The blending of fiction and nonfiction means that today it is harder than it was a few decades ago to make a clear-cut distinction between novels and informational books based on real events. How closely fiction and nonfiction have blended together in the minds of teachers was shown by a survey in which 300 English teachers responded to a request to list ten adolescent novels and ten adult novels worthy of being recommended to teenagers for reading. Among twenty nonfiction titles recommended as novels were Piers Paul Read's *Alive,* James Herriot's *All Creatures Great and Small,* Robin Graham's *Dove,* Peter Maas's *Serpico,* Doris Lund's *Eric,* Alvin Toffler's *Future Shock,* Maya Angelou's *I Know Why the Caged Bird Sings,* Dee Brown's *Bury My Heart at Wounded Knee,* Claude Brown's *Manchild in the Promised Land,* Eldridge Cleaver's *Soul on Ice,* and John H. Griffin's *Black Like Me.*

The blending has occurred from both directions. On one side are the nonfiction writers who use the techniques of fiction, including suspense, careful plotting and characterization, and literary devices, such as symbolism and metaphor. On the other side are the novelists who collect data as an investigative reporter would. Here at Arizona State University, our faculty in creative writing have waged a campaign to convince the administration that they need research assistants just as much as do faculty members in history or chemistry. In *Midnight Hour Encores* Bruce Brooks acknowledged thirty-two individuals for talking to him "about music in relentless detail," and at the beginning of *Izzy, Willy-Nilly* Cynthia Voigt acknowledged help from medical personnel who taught her about physical and mental aspects of amputation. When Richard Peck wrote *Are You in the House Alone?* he gathered current statistics on rape and then fashioned his story around the most typical case—that is, a young girl in a familiar setting being raped by someone she knows, who is not prosecuted for the crime.

These books are fiction in the sense that fictional names are used and that they combine bits and pieces of many individual stories. Nevertheless, in another sense, these stories are more real and actually present a more honest portrayal than some pieces labeled nonfiction that are true accounts of bizarre or strange happenings.

The question of what is true (nonfiction) and what is untrue (fiction) might be compared to the question of what we mean by *real,* which Margery Williams asks in her children's classic *The Velveteen Rabbit.* She answers that when something has lived a long time and is well loved and well worn through use, it becomes real. According to this definition, Louisa May Alcott's *Little Women* is real. A mental image of the warm, supportive family portrayed in the book is a real part of the psyches of literally millions of readers around the world who believe that the book is a true presentation of the Alcott family. Actually, the genteel poverty that Alcott wrote about is a far cry from the facts. It was

THE PEOPLE BEHIND THE BOOKS

MILTON MELTZER
on Fiction and Nonfiction

During many years of writing nonfiction about social issues, I've often used the devices of fiction
to multiply the power of facts by evoking from
readers their sense of concern, even of construc-
tive anger. I've wanted to help them to see the
weaknesses of our world, its inequality, its injustice, that leave so many poor, so many ignored,
abused, betrayed. To obtain any betterment of
such lives people need to care, need to respect
these "others," and to respect themselves and
their own ability to bring about social change by
making democracy work to its fullest capacity. So
I investigate thoroughly whatever interests me—
it could be poverty, crime, terrorism, racism, slavery, war, politics, the Holocaust—and with the
facts gathered from the greatest variety of sources
I can unearth, try to make the issue real to the
reader. I think I've used almost every technique
fiction writers call on (except to invent the facts)
in order to draw the readers in, deepen their feeling for people whose lives may be remote from
their own, and enrich their understanding of forces
that shape the outcome of all our lives. In the end,
I believe it is not a question of what is fiction and
what is fact, but of what is true and what is false.
Fiction can lie about reality; so can nonfiction. And
both can tell the truth.

Milton Meltzer's books include *The Bill of Rights: How We Got It and What It Means,* Crowell, 1990; *Columbus and the World Around Him,* Watts, 1990; *Voices from the Civil War,* Crowell, 1989; and *Starting from Home: A Writer's Beginnings,* Viking, 1988.

not so much a question of the Alcott girls not having matching gloves on their
hands as it was a question of their not having food on the table. We can say,
then, that the "reality" of *Little Women* exists quite apart from verifiable facts.

Literature—fiction and nonfiction—is more than a simple recounting or re-
playing of the life that surrounds the writer. It is a distillation and a crystalli-
zation. Only when an author skillfully chooses descriptive details and develops
believable dialogue does an account of an actual event become real to the reader.
Certainly Alex Haley's *Roots* became real to millions of television viewers as
well as to millions of readers, yet the book contains many fictional elements
in both subject matter and presentation. It is these elements that make the book
stand out as "literature," whereas the histories of other families are little more
than dreary records read on special occasions by dutiful family members.

Haley's book is successful for many reasons, but among the most important is that he was a master at selecting the incidents and details he wanted to include. Good writers of nonfiction do not simply record everything they know or can uncover. For example, with Haley's book, people's imaginations were captured by the fact that on September 29, 1967, he "stood on the dock in Annapolis where his great-great-great-great-great-grandfather was taken ashore on September 29, 1767," and sold as a slave to a Virginia owner. From this point, Haley set out to trace backward the six generations that connected him to a sixteen-year-old "prince" newly arrived from Africa.

What the public might not stop to consider as they read about this dramatic incident is that it is setting the stage for only a small portion of Haley's "roots." In 1767 there were people living all around the world in all kinds of situations whose bloodlines were related to Haley's. In the generation in which Haley started his story with the young couple, Omoro and Binta Kinte, and the birth of their first son, Kunta, there were 256 parents giving birth to 128 children, each one of whom is also a great-great-great-great-great-grandfather or grandmother to Alex Haley. The point is that even though Haley was writing nonfiction, he had an almost unlimited range of possibilities from which to choose, and he made his choices with the instinct of a storyteller rather than a clerk.

Because of the mass media, today's readers are so accustomed to strange facts and hard-to-believe stories that they have begun consistently to ask such questions as, "Is it true?" "Is that for real?" and, "Honestly?" This emphasis on "truth" has put some writers of fiction in a peculiar situation, witness the strange case of Clifford Irving, the novelist who in the 1970s served a jail term for claiming that his story about an eccentric billionaire was a biography of Howard Hughes.

Alfred Slote, an author of sports stories, reported a less dramatic case to the fourth annual conference of the Children's Literature Association. He told how his publishers decided to illustrate his books with photographs rather than drawings in an attempt to make his fiction look like sports nonfiction, which sells better. Slote is a photographer as well as a writer, so he offered to take the pictures and was surprised at how his writing became influenced by whether or not he would be able to get an actual photograph. He concluded by asking whether he could build castles in the sky if he had to produce a photograph of each one.

Several authors are probably asking themselves similar questions. The public wants "true" stories yet expects them to be as well crafted and as exciting as the best of fiction. Beatrice Sparks, who seven years after the publication of the "anonymous" *Go Ask Alice,* came forward and announced herself on the covers of two other books (*Voices* and *Jay's Journal*) as the "author who brought you *Go Ask Alice,*" said that she published the story, which was "based on" a girl's actual diary, anonymously to make it seem more authentic. She thought that having the story appear to come directly from a young girl who died of an overdose would make its anti-drug message more acceptable to the target audience.[2]

The New Journalism

Several factors have contributed to the development of what Truman Capote called the "most avant-garde form of writing existent today." He coined the term *nonfiction novel* for *In Cold Blood*, an account of an especially brutal murder and the susbsequent trial. Tom Wolfe prefers the term *new journalism* and wrote a book by that name in which he proposes that it is the dominant form of writing in contemporary America. Other terms that are used include *creative nonfiction, literary journalism, journalistic fiction,* and *advocacy journalism*. Although its roots were growing right along with journalism in general, it did not really begin to flower until the 1950s and 1960s. Part of the reason for its development is the increased educational level of the American public. Newspaper readers and television viewers, including young adults, are not satisfied with simplistic explanations. They want enough background information that they can feel confident in coming to their own conclusions.

Our affluence, combined with modern technology, helps make the new journalism possible. Compare similar incidents that happened 126 years apart. In 1846 a group of travelers who came to be known as the Donner party were trapped in the high Sierras by an early snow. They had to stay there all winter without food except for the flesh of their dead companions. After they were rescued, word of their ordeal gradually trickled back east, so that for years

Table 8.1 SUGGESTIONS FOR EVALUATING JOURNALISTIC FICTION

A good piece of journalistic fiction usually has:
An authentic story that is individual and unique but also representative of human experience as a whole.

Information that is accurate and carefully researched. This is extremely important because, with most of these stories, readers will have heard news accounts and will lose faith in the story if there are inconsistencies.

A central thesis that has grown out of the author's research.

Enough development to show the relationship between the characters' actions and what happens. People's motives are explored, and cause and effect are tied together.

An author with all the writing skills of a good novelist so that, for example, the characters reveal themselves through their speech and actions, rather than through the author's descriptions.

A dramatic style of writing that draws readers into the story.

A poor piece of journalistic fiction may have:
A stacking of the evidence to prove a sensational idea. The author set out not to find the truth but to collect evidence on only one side of an issue.

A trite or worn subject that is not worthy of booklength attention from either writer or reader.

Evidence of sloppy research and little or no documentation of sources.

Conversations and other accessory literary devices that contradict straight news accounts.

Inclusion of extraneous information that does not help the story build toward a central idea or thesis.

A pedestrian style of writing that lacks drama.

afterward sensationalized accounts were being made up by newspaper reporters who had no chance actually to come to the scene or interview the survivors.

In 1972 a planeload of Uruguayan travelers crashed in the Andes mountains. As in the Donner party, some people knew each other before the trip, but others were strangers. During the terrible weeks of waiting to be rescued they all got to know each other and to develop intense relationships revolving around leadership roles and roles of rebellion and/or giving up. They endured unspeakable hardships. Many died; those who lived did so because they ate the flesh of those who died. But in this situation, the people were rescued by helicopters after two of the men made their way out of the mountains. Word of their two-and-a-half-month ordeal was flashed around the world, and by the time the sixteen survivors, mostly members of a rugby team, had been flown back to Uruguay, reporters from many nations were there. A press conference was held, and the journalists were told about the cannibalism.

This was the second surprise in the story. The first had been their survival. The drama of the situation naturally fired imaginations all around the world. Lippincott suggested to author Piers Paul Read that this was the kind of story that would make a good book. He went to Uruguay, where he stayed for several months interviewing survivors, rescuers, family, and friends of both the deceased and the survivors, and the government officials who had been in charge of the search. More than a year later, Lippincott published *Alive: The Story of the Andes Survivors,* which was on the *New York Times* best-seller list for seven months, was recently made into a movie, and will probably continue to be read by young adults for the next several years, both in and out of school.

The fact that the survivors were in their early twenties undoubtedly helps teenagers to identify with the story, but so do the literary techniques that Read used. He focused on certain individuals, presenting miniature character sketches of some and fully developed portraits of others. The setting was crucial to the story, and he described it vividly. He was also careful to write so that the natural suspense of the situation came through. His tone was consistent throughout the book. He admired the survivors but did not shy away from showing the negative aspects of human nature when it is sorely tried. In a foreword he said that the only liberty he allowed himself was the creation of dialogue between the characters, although, whenever possible, he relied on diaries and remembered comments and quarrels, as well as his acquaintance with the speaking styles of the survivors.

The influence of the new journalism is seen in many aspects of books promoted for young readers. When Jean Fritz wrote *Homesick: My Own Story,* she did not call it an autobiography. In the foreword she explained:

> When I started to write about my childhood in China, I found that my memory came out in lumps. Although I could for the most part arrange them in the proper sequence, I discovered that my preoccupation with time and literal accuracy was squeezing the life out of what I had to say. So I decided to forget about sequence and just get on with it. . . . letting the events fall

as they would into the shape of a story, lacing them together with fictional bits, adding a piece here and there when memory didn't give me all I needed. . . . So although this book takes place within two years—from October 1925 to September 1927—the events are drawn from the entire period of my childhood, but they are all, except in minor details, basically true. The people are real people; the places are dear to me. But most important, the form I have used has given me the freedom to re-create the emotions that I remember so vividly. Strictly speaking, I have to call this book *fiction,* but it does not feel like fiction to me. It is my story, told as truly as I can tell it.

What "new journalism" books have in common is a combination of factual information and emotional appeal. They are stories of real people with whom readers can identify. Technically, they might be classified as biography, history, drama, essay, or personal experience, but regardless of classification, they are among those books that are likely to serve young adults as a bridge between childhood and adult reading. They have this power because of the straightforward, noncondescending manner of writing that is characteristic of good journalism.

Nonfiction best-sellers often outsell fiction best-sellers, and television producers know they can add millions of viewers if they advertise a program

Nonfiction books usually have shorter life spans and are aimed at more specific audiences than are fiction titles. Nevertheless, over the last two decades, nonfiction sales have increased continuously for leisure reading.

as "a documentary" rather than "a drama." Popular movies are done in "non-fiction" style (e.g., *Hoffa,* about Jimmy Hoffa's rise and fall as a leader in the trucker's union and the mysteries surrounding his disappearance, and *A League of Their Own,* about the women baseball players recently inducted into Baseball's Hall of Fame for keeping the sport alive during World War II). A recent article in *Time* magazine under the title of "The Cops and the Cameras" showed how real-life accounts of police action are now more popular than the old *Starsky and Hutch* type of show. Reporter Richard Zoglin wrote:

> But as fictional cop shows have become an endangered species in prime time, real-life law enforcers are multiplying. *Cops,* Fox's cinema verité look at police on their day-to-day rounds, is going strong in its fourth season; a week ago, it scored its highest ratings ever. ABC's *American Detective* provides a somewhat slicker (punched up with narration and dramatic music) glimpse of real cops in action. CBS's *Top Cops* and ABC's *FBI: The Untold Stories* use re-creations to celebrate the exploits of law enforcers, while CBS's *Rescue 911* recounts heroic deeds by police, paramedic and other emergency personnel.[3]

He went on to discuss the benefits and the drawbacks of having film crews accompany real police on their rounds. He also talked about the interactive nature of crime shows in which, "The FBI and other law-enforcement agencies enlist TV's help in tracking down fugitives through shows like *America's Most Wanted* and *Unsolved Mysteries*."

And even the success of the tabloids depends on their nonfiction format. The majority of readers don't really believe all those stories about Elvis Presley still being alive or about women giving birth to aliens or apricot pits curing cancer; yet for the fun of it they're willing to give themselves over to a momentary suspension of disbelief—something we used to talk about only in relation to fairy tales.

The Evaluation of Nonfiction

Evaluating nonfiction for young readers is more complicated than evaluating fiction because

1. People select informational books primarily on the basis of the subject matter, and since there is such a variety in subjects, people's choices vary tremendously, resulting in a lack of consensus on what is "the best."
2. Informative books on such topics as computers and car repair become dated more quickly than fiction books. Students preparing to take the SAT tests, wanting advice on handling money, or planning for a career need the most recent information. The constant turnover of informative books leaves us with few touchstone examples.

3. The transitory nature of informative nonfiction books discourages teachers and critics from giving them serious consideration as instructional materials. And although well-written personal experience narratives have longer life spans, people who have made up their minds that they aren't interested in nonfiction find it easy to ignore all nonfiction.
4. Reviewers and prize givers may not feel competent to judge the technical or other specialized information presented in many informative books. Also, many reviewers, especially those working with educational journals, come from an English-teaching tradition, and they tend to focus on books that would be used in conjunction with literature rather than biology, home economics, social studies, industrial arts, history, or business classes.
5. In evaluating nonfiction, there is no generally agreed-upon theory of criticism or criteria for judgment.

We suggest that the evaluation situation can be improved by readers looking at fiction and nonfiction in similar ways. Replace looking at plot and characterization with looking at the intended audience and the content of the book. (What is it about? What information does it present?) Then look at the appropriateness and success with which each of the following is established. Examining a nonfiction book carefully enough to be able to describe the setting, theme, tone, and style will give you insights into how well it is written and packaged.

Setting

Informative books have settings or scopes. For example, they may be historical, or restricted to regional interests, or have a very limited scope. In evaluating the setting and/or the scope of a book, one needs to ask whether the author set realistic goals, considering the reading level of the intended audience and the amount of space and back-up graphics available.

Theme

Informational books also have themes or purposes that are closely tied to the author's point of view. Authors may write in hopes of persuading someone to a particular belief or to inspire thoughtfulness, respect, or even curiosity. Some authors shout out their themes, others are more subtle. You need to consider consistency as you evaluate the theme. Did the author build on a consistent theme throughout the book?

Tone

The manner in which an author achieves a desired goal—whether it is to persuade, inform, inspire, or amuse—sets the tone of a book. Is it hard-sell, strident, one-sided, humorous, loving, sympathetic, adulatory, scholarly, pedantic, energetic, or leisurely? Authors of informative books for children used to take a leisurely approach as they tried to entice children into becoming interested in their subject. But today's young readers are just as busy as their parents and most likely go to informative books for quick information rather than leisure time entertainment. A boy who wants to repair a bicycle doesn't want to start out by reading about the Wright brothers and their bicycle shop before getting to the part on how gears and brakes work.

Style

The best informative books also have style. As author Jane Langton said when she was asked to serve as a judge, the good books "exude some kind of passion or love or caring . . . and they have the potential for leaving a mark on the readers, changing them in some way."[4] George A. Woods, former children's editor of the *New York Times Book Review,* said that he selected the informational books to be featured in his review mostly on his own "gut-level" reactions to what was "new or far better than what we have had before." He looked for a majesty of language and uniqueness and for books that would add to children's understanding by making them eyewitnesses to history.[5] A problem in examining an author's style is that each book must be judged according to the purpose the author had in mind. From book to book, purposes are so different that it is like the old problem of comparing apples and oranges. Some books will be successful simply because they are different—more like a mango than an apple or an orange.

David Macaulay's *Unbuilding* is such a book. Technically, it should probably be classed as fiction because it's the make-believe story of an Arab oil magnate who purchases the Empire State Building and has it dismantled and crated up for shipment to his Arab desert to be reconstructed as his company's office building. In the fictional part of the book, Macaulay makes snide jokes about big money, historical preservationists, and people's gullibility. The nonfiction, informative side of the book lies in the accuracy of the detailed architectural drawings, which show how the building was created.

Cutaways and double-page spreads emphasize the building's beauty as well as the magnificent accomplishment of its 1930s construction. From a purely informational stand, Macaulay could have used the same drawings and entitled the book something like *Construction of the Empire State Building*. That's really what readers learn, but the effect of the clever reversal—turning the book into what one reviewer called an "urban fairly-tale"—was to take it out of the "ordinary" category and to make it a book that in Jane Langton's words exudes "some kind of passion or love or caring."

Contemporary Influences on the Publishing of Informational Books

Prior to the 1950s what was published for young readers was in the main either fiction (novels or short stories), poetry, or textbook material to be used in school. No one thought that young readers would be interested in factual books unless they were forced to study them as part of their schoolwork. But then the Russians launched Sputnik, and Americans were sincerely frightened that Russia was scientifically and technologically ahead. In 1961, Congress passed the National Defense Education Act, which gave millions of dollars to school libraries for the purchase of science and math books. These books were to be supplements to the curriculum, which students would read independently. Publishers competed to create informative books that would qualify for purchase under the Act and would attract young readers.

The rise in the popularity of nonfiction has paralleled the information explosion and the rise in the power and influence of the mass media. Today there is simply more information to be shared between reader and writer. Television, radio, movies, newspapers, and magazines all communicate the same kinds of information as do books, but people expect more from books because the other media are limited in the amount of space and time that they can devote to any one topic. Moreover, whatever is produced by the mass media must be of interest to a *mass* audience, whereas individual readers select books. Of course publishers want masses of individual readers to select their books. Nevertheless, there is more room for experimentation and controversial ideas in books than in the kinds of media that are supported by advertisers and that therefore must aim to attract the largest possible audience.

As the most pervasive of the media, television has a tremendous influence on book publishing. For example, obvious TV tie-ins include Carl Sagan's *Cosmos,* based on his television series, and Robert McCrum's *The Story of English* and Jim Arnosky's *Drawing from Nature,* both written as companion books to PBS series of the same names. Less obvious TV tie-ins include books about those current events that are discussed enough on television that authors are inspired to do research to answer the questions that cursory news reports don't have time or space to probe (see Focus Box 8.1).

The influence of television on format and design is hard to prove, but there's an obvious difference between the majority of informative books coming out today and those that were published twenty years ago. More of the current books are illustrated with numerous photographs, many in color, and they are organized and laid out in chunks of information, so that readers can browse, skim, and take rest breaks—comparable to taking time out for commercials.

The best example is provided by the Eyewitness books distributed by Knopf. Their wonderfully clear photographs have been described as a museum between the covers of a book and an appealing alternative to encyclopedias. Among the titles that have found their way to various best-book lists are *Bird, Butterfly & Moth, Dinosaur, Mammal, Music, Plant, Rocks & Minerals, Seashore, Shell, Skeleton,* and *Tree.*

The Need for Scientific Literacy

At the 1988 meeting of the Conference on College Composition and Communication in St. Louis, science writer Jon Franklin spoke on a panel entitled "Nonfiction: The Genre of a Technological Age." Formerly a science writer for the *Evening Sun* in Baltimore and now a teacher of journalism at the University

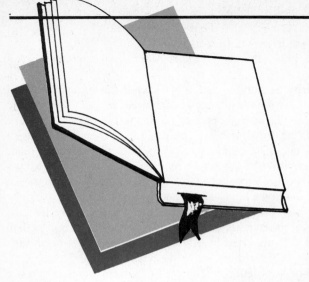

Going Behind the News—Social Issues

Ain't Gonna Study War No More: The Story of America's Peace Seekers by Milton Meltzer. HarperCollins, 1985. Meltzer has done more than any other author to gather information on current issues and present it so that students will want to read it. His *Poverty in America* (Morrow, 1986) and *The American Promise: Voices of a Changing Nation 1945–Present* (Bantam, 1990) are also recommended.

An Ancient Heritage: The Arab-American Minority by Brent Ashabranner, photos by Paul S. Conklin. HarperCollins, 1991. This is an easy-to-read introduction to the wide variety of Americans tracing their ancestry or their own births to the Middle East.

The Bill of Rights: How We Got It and What It Means by Milton Meltzer. Crowell, 1990. Probably the most interesting part of Meltzer's well-written book is the last section, where he discusses events and legal decisions in which the amendments have played a part.

The Greenhouse Effect: Life on a Warmer Planet by Rebecca Johnson. Lerner, 1990. The strengths of this book include its beautiful photos, clear explanations of how computers make predictions, and sensible guidance on mitigating the effects of global warming.

The Kid's Guide to Social Action by Barbara Lewis. Free Spirit, 1991. Lewis' guide to procedures and tactics includes true accounts of young people making a difference when their communities set out to solve such problems as how to dispose of hazardous waste, beautify streets and sidewalks, build a community library, and provide housing for the homeless.

Neighbors at Odds: U.S. Policy in Latin America by Elaine Pascoe. Watts, 1990. Readers will come away with a new appreciation of the challenges that face the United States in relating to its very close neighbors.

Panama Canal: Gateway to the World by Judith St. George. Putnam, 1989. St. George explores the difficulties involved in building the Panama Canal, which was as much a fulfillment of a dream for its generation of engineers as landing on the moon was for the next generation of engineers and scientists.

Rachel and Her Children: Homeless Families in America by Jonathan Kozol. Crown, 1988. Kozol used the families housed in the Martinique Hotel in New York to illustrate the tremendous problem facing many Americans.

Should Drugs Be Legalized? by Susan Neiburg Terkel. Watts, 1990. In chronicling the history of drugs in the United States, Terkel gives both sides of the controversy while being careful to distinguish between advocating the legalization of drugs and advocating their use.

Taking on the Press: Constitutional Rights in Conflict by Melvyn Zerman. Crowell, 1986. Zerman's thoughtful discussion shows that the concept of freedom of the press isn't as clearcut as most people think.

Teenage Soldiers, Adult Wars, edited by Roger Rosen and Patra McSharry. Icarus World Issues Series, 1991. The underlying theme of this collection of essays and stories is the conflict between individual choice and authority. Young soldiers from Afghanistan to Northern Ireland report their experiences and feelings as they fought in the battles started by adults.

Who's to Know? Information, the Media, and Public Awareness by Ann E. Weiss. Houghton Mifflin, 1990. Both government and industry have reasons for controlling information, and as conglomerates take over ownership of mass media in the United States, there is a tendency for more information to be controlled.

---

of Maryland in College Park, Franklin's topic was "Literary Structure: A Growing Force in Science Journalism." He pointed out how in the past decade, more than half the winners of the Pulitzer Prize in nonfiction had been science books, and how the increasingly important role of scientific writing in newspapers and magazines is changing basic concepts of journalism. The upside-down pyramid, in which the key points are stated first and the details are filled in later, so that an editor can cut the story whenever the available space is filled, does not work for science writing because it results in oversimplification. Science stories have to be written inductively, building from the small to the large points, because most of the scientific developments and concepts that are in the news are too complex for readers to understand unless they get the supporting details first.

Just as journalists are having to learn new ways to write, Franklin says that readers are going to have to learn new ways to read. He made a persuasive plea for teachers to focus more attention on helping students learn to read and feel comfortable with scientific writing. He claims that if people feel uncomfortable with scientific writing, they are likely to resent and reject scientific concepts (witness the controversy over creationism and evolution).

Franklin worries about the development of a new kind of elitism based on scientific literacy. He gave examples of science stories that were acceptable as books but not as newspaper features because only a few hundred people in any metropolitan area were prepared to read and understand the concepts. Book publishers face the challenge of finding this relatively small number of scientifically literate people across the nation and marketing their books to them. Franklin's proposal to keep the gap from widening between the scientifically literate and those who reject all science is two-pronged. On the one hand, science writers have to work harder to find organizational patterns and literary techniques that will make their material understandable and interesting. On the other hand, schools must bring the reading of technological and scientific information into the curriculum with the goal of preparing students to balance their lifetime reading.

LAURENCE PRINGLE
on Trying to Be Fair

Environmental problems worry young adults. Some of them express their concern in letters to legislators and corporations; they try to convince school administrators to buy recycled paper.

These idealistic young people may be somewhat naive, and vulnerable to one-sided arguments, whether from the petroleum industry or from an environmental group. People who write about natural resource issues for teenagers have a responsibility to fairly present all sides of an issue, and to show the gray as well as the black and white. Notice I didn't say they have to be objective. As I wrote in a 1979 essay, this would be an extraordinary achievement, "considering that everyone involved in the controversies, including Nobel laureate scientists, is being subjective and biased."

Writers who tackle environmental problems (or other social issues) face an ethical dilemma, because anyone who is well informed on an issue is not neutral. Whether you call it bias or point of view, you have to keep it in check. But "kept in check" doesn't mean absent. There are ways for a writer to express his or her leanings. Sometimes it is as simple as quoting a spokesperson whose very words are a self-indictment. And then there is the last page or two of chapters and books, a place to sum up and leave closing thoughts. Here, too, a writer must be fair, but anyone who wants to know how I *really* feel about an issue can find some clues in that neighborhood.

The main goal, however, is to help kids understand the issues so they can make their own decisions. One key to achieving this goal is encouraging young adults to have a healthy skepticism on controversial issues. The sharpest skepticism is aimed at economic and political interests and at extremists at both ends of the spectrum.

The self-interest of pesticide manufacturers, the auto industry, the nuclear power enterprise, and so on, is so blatant that it is tempting to see environmental issues in simple "good guy–bad guy" terms. Resist the temptation. Authors should help readers realize that "good guys" as well as "bad guys" select, omit, and exaggerate information to argue their cause. Some environmental groups deserve more respect than others. Fortunately, several major ones have scientists on their staffs, base their political actions on the best evidence available, and have strong credibility.

Most books for young people about environmental issues, mine included, are somewhat slanted. Their authors have value systems that tilt their writing in the direction of saving the earth's biodiversity and other precious resources, of improving the overall quality of life, of taking into account the well-being of future generations. This puts me and many other authors in opposition to people more concerned with short-term profits, or getting re-elected.

We bend over backwards and sometimes have to hold our noses—an awkward writing position—trying to be fair. However, for the sake of the idealistic young people reading the books, I hope our feelings, our values, yes, our biases, always come through.

Laurence Pringle's books include *Rain of Troubles: The Science and Politics of Acid Rain,* Macmillan, 1988; *Nuclear Energy: Troubled Past, Uncertain Future,* Macmillan, 1989; *Global Warming,* Arcade, 1990; and *Living Treasure: Saving Earth's Threatened Biodiversity,* Morrow, 1991.

Books to Support and Extend the School Curriculum

Informational books purchased by school libraries are usually referred to as "books to support the curriculum," but a more accurate description would probably be "books to extend the curriculum." For the most part, these books do not help students who are doing poorly in class. Instead, they provide challenges for successful students to go further than their classmates. They also serve as models for research, and they go beyond the obvious facts to present information that is too complicated, too detailed, too obscure, or too controversial to be included in textbooks. A legitimate complaint often voiced about history books is that they focus on war and violence and leave out life as it is lived by most people. Another complaint is that they leave out the experiences of women and minorities. Well-written and well-illustrated tradebooks serve as a counterbalance to these omissions.

The various focus boxes presented throughout this chapter and this text present only a sampling of the many books available as companion reading, or even replacement reading, for typical textbooks. In selecting academically oriented books, librarians should remember that teenagers most often pick up such books to find specific information. They want the material to be streamlined and to the point. They also want it to be indexed and organized in such a way that they can easily refer back to something or can look up facts without reading the whole book. And since young readers lack the kind of background knowledge that most adults have, it is especially important that the basic information come first, so that they won't be confused by unclear references.

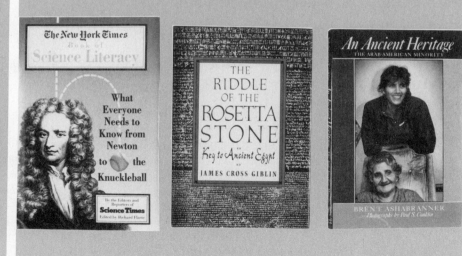

Examples of the many excellent trade books being published as curricular support in science, language, and social studies classes, respectively, are *The New York Times Book of Science Literacy,* Random House, 1991; James Cross Giblin's *The Riddle of the Rosetta Stone,* Crowell, 1990; and Brent Ashabranner's *An Ancient Heritage: The Arab-American Minority,* HarperCollins, 1991.

Table 8.2   *SUGGESTIONS FOR EVALUATING INFORMATIVE NONFICTION*

A good piece of informative writing usually has:
A subject of interest to young readers, written about with zest. Information that is up-to-date and accurate.

New information, or information organized in such a way as to present a different point of view than in previously available books.

A reading level, vocabulary, and tone of writing that are at a consistent level appropriate to the intended audience.

An organization in which basic information is presented first so that chapters and sections build on each other.

An index and other aids to help readers look up facts if they want to return to the book for specific information or to glean ideas and facts without reading the entire book.

Adequate documentation of the sources of information, including some original sources.

Information to help interested students locate further readings on the subject.

In how-to-books, clear and accurate directions including complete lists of the equipment and supplies needed in a project.

Illustrations that add interest as well as clarity to the text.

A competent author with expertise in the subject matter.

A poor piece of informative writing may have:
Obsolete or inaccurate information and/or illustrations. Even one such occurrence causes the reader to lose faith in the rest of the book.

Evidence of cutting-and-pasting in which the author merely reorganized previously prepared material without developing anything new in content or viewpoint.

Inconsistencies in style or content, for example, college level vocabulary but a childish or cute style of writing.

An awkward mix of fiction and nonfiction techniques through which the author unsuccessfully tries to slip information in as an unnoticed part of the story.

A reflection of out-of-date or socially unfair attitudes, for example, a history book that presents only the history of white upper-class males with a title and introduction that give the impression that it is a comprehensive history of the time period being covered.

A biased presentation in which only one side of a controversial issue is presented with little or no acknowledgement that many people hold different viewpoints.

In how-to books, frustrating directions, that oversimplify and/or set up unrealistic expectations so that the reader is disappointed in the result.

Preparing for College and Careers

In an *English Journal* article,[6] Richard F. Abrahamson and Betty Carter noted that for academic teenagers books about college are the number 1 nonfiction choice. It's important to bring such books to the attention of high school students early because the actual application process takes eighteen months and its success or failure may depend on what classes one took in the freshman year of high school. General college preparation books include *The Fiske Guide to Colleges 1992* (a new edition comes out each year) by Edward B. Fiske, education editor of *The New York Times*, and Ellen Rosenberg's *College Life: A Down-to-Earth Guide*. More specialized books include *The Black College Career Guide* put together by Massey-Young Communications, *America's Lowest Cost Colleges* put together by Brandon Books, and *The Other Route into College: Alternative Admission* by Stacy Needle. The Princeton Review series has several books under the general title of *Cracking the System*; for example, *Cracking the System: The SAT & PSAT*.

The work ethic may be more important to Americans than to some other people because of our frontier heritage and the value that was put on hard work. Folklorists point out that only frontier cultures such as those of the United States, Canada, and Australia have stories about such work heroes as John Henry, Paul Bunyan, Pecos Bill, and Old Stormalong. In other cultures, it is common for folk heroes to be tricky individuals who manage to get out of work, but in the United States people are accorded social standing in relation to the jobs they hold, rather than their ancestry, religion, or wealth. Even the children of wealthy families prepare for and usually pursue a career because work is considered an essential part of a meaningful life (see Focus Box 8.2).

The work heroes of today are individuals whose jobs may be quite ordinary but who have found personal fulfillment through what they do. Readers are interested first in the person as a whole and second in the job as it relates to the person. Today's readers want real people, not the old-fashioned Cherry Ames kind of career book.

Presenting related stories of several individuals is a common approach. Young readers also want a here-and-now immediacy in career books, so they like to read financial success stories about teenagers. However, adults need to help young readers be realistic about the wish fulfillment inherent in such a book as Gloria D. Miklowitz and Madeleine Yates's *The Young Tycoons: Ten Success*

College and career books are among the most popular in high school libaries.

Aspiring to Successful Careers

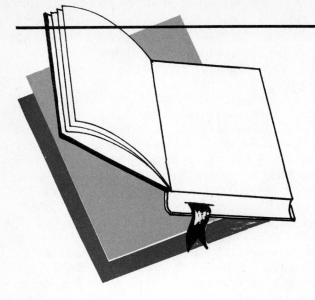

All Creatures Great and Small by James Herriot. St. Martin's, 1972. In this and the sequels *All Things Bright and Beautiful, All Things Wise and Wonderful,* and *The Lord God Made Them All,* Herriot shows the human side of being in the animal business.

The Amateur Naturalist by Gerald Durrell and Lee Durrell. Knopf, 1983. Readers will learn what it means to study nature from two members of a family famous for its scientific work.

Artists of Handcrafted Furniture at Work by Maxine B. Rosenberg, photos by George Ancona. Lothrop, 1988. Four artists reveal how they began working with wood and how they feel toward making art that becomes part of people's lives.

Behind the Front Page by David S. Broder. Simon & Schuster, 1988. Here's a book for students who aspire to become another Woodward or Bernstein.

But What If I Don't Want to Go to College? by Harlow G. Unger. Facts on File, 1991. Picking a vocational school, passing the GED, and comparing wages from different jobs are among the topics discussed in this guide.

Cartoons and Cartooning by Harvey Weiss. Houghton Mifflin, 1990. "A few bright ideas, a little imagination, and a sense of humor" are more important than drawing skill, says this author, who is himself a successful cartoonist.

Circus Dreams: The Making of a Circus Artist by Kathleen Cushman and Montana Miller, photographs by Michael Carroll. Little, Brown, 1990. After graduating from high school in Massachusetts, Montana Miller enrolled as the first American in the National Center for Circus Arts in France. This photo essay records her first year in circus college.

The New York Times Career Planner by Elizabeth M. Fowler. Times Books, 1987. Mature teens will browse through this book, which is mostly taken from the author's newspaper "Careers" column.

A Not Entirely Benign Procedure: Four Years as a Medical Student by Perri Elizabeth Klass. Putnam, 1987. High school students will hope that by the time they get to medical school, practices will have changed at least a little.

Nothing but the Best: The Struggle for Perfection at the Juilliard School by Judith Kogan. Random House, 1987. This behind-the-scenes look at what it takes to become a concert musician shatters the myth that it's always wonderful to be "the best."

Ramona: Behind the Scenes of a Television Show   by Elaine Scott. Morrow, 1988. The production of Beverly Cleary's *Ramona Quimby* was used as the illustration of what's involved in producing a television show.

Sketching Outdoors in Autumn   by Jim Arnosky. Lothrop, 1988. Arnosky is an artist and naturalist who has done several books illustrating both his techniques and the pleasure he gets from transferring nature's work to his sketch pad.

So You Want to Be a Star! A Teenager's Guide to Breaking into Show Business   by Randi Reisfeld. Archway Paperbacks, 1990. The author is a magazine editor and uses a magazine style to give advice interspersed with success stories of Paula Abdul, New Kids on the Block, Tiffany, and Jason Hervey.

The TV and Movie Business: An Encyclopedia of Careers, Technologies, and Practices   by Harvey Rachlin. Harmony/Crown, 1991. Written for the general adult audience, this book will probably be skimmed rather than read cover to cover by teenagers.

Stories. This book makes financial success look so easy that readers will think that with a little effort they too can become rich overnight. If it doesn't happen they are likely to lose faith in the printed word, and more important, in themselves or their parents, who are unable to provide start-up funds or helpful contacts.

Career-related books are extremely important to young adults because they must make decisions that will strongly influence not only how they will earn a living but also what life-styles they will have. Teachers and librarians should make a special effort to bring books of this type to the attention of all students. The more knowledge they have, the better able they will be to make the kind of far-reaching decisions that society demands of its young adults.

Nonfiction to Help Teenagers Learn Who They Are and Where They Fit

When young adult librarian and critic Patty Campbell spoke at an American Library Association annual meeting, she pointed out that teenagers are so wrapped up in what the psychologists have labeled the "adolescent identity crisis" that they have neither the time for nor the interest in sitting down and reading about the world in general. What they are looking for are books that will help them decide on who they are and where they fit into the scheme of things. Informative books they judge to be helpful include sex education books, some physical and mental health books of the *I'm Okay, You're Okay* type, selected how-to books, and biographies or true accounts of experiences teenagers can imagine themselves or their acquaintances having. Nearly all the other information books published for teenagers are read under duress—only because teachers assign reports and research papers. In this section, we will discuss some of the types of books that Campbell said teenagers read to help them figure where they fit in. Noticeably absent are the true accounts of experiences that teenagers imagine themselves living. (See Chapter Seven for such biographies.)

From the very beginning of life, babies are testing their limits. They want to know how much they can eat, how far they can reach, how loudly they can scream, and how much their parents will let them get away with. As the years go by and they grow into teenagers, they become more subtle and more sophisticated, but they are still interested in testing limits. The difference is that with young adults, their sphere of interest is now so much broader that it includes the whole world and even beyond. There is no way that they can personally test all the limits in which they are interested. Some would be too dangerous, some are mutually exclusive, some would take too long, and some cannot be entered into voluntarily. Because of these and other considerations, teenagers (as well as many adults) turn to books that present the extremes of life's experiences. Whatever is the biggest, the best, or the most bizarre is of interest. That is the basis for the popularity of the *Guiness Book of World Records* and similar books. An additional appeal of books presenting miscellaneous information is that they provide instant entertainment. Someone with only a minute or two can open Lila Perl's *Don't Sing Before Breakfast, Don't Sleep in the Moonlight: Everyday Superstitions and How They Began* and read a complete discourse. The same is true for the question-and-answer format of the Reader's Digest *ABC's of the Bible: Intriguing Questions and Answers About the Greatest Book Ever Written.*

Succinctness and easy accessibility are also selling points to use when encouraging teenagers to dip into collections of essays. For example, students who have enjoyed Robert Cormier's fiction might look on his *I Have Words to Spend: Reflections of a Small-Town Editor* as a chance to share thoughts with the kind of uncle or grandfather they wish they had been lucky enough to have. The book contains over 80 newspaper columns chosen by Cormier's wife, Constance Senay Cormier, from those he wrote for the *Fitchburg Sentinel and Enterprise* between 1969 and 1977 and for the *St. Anthony Messenger* between 1972 and 1980. Teenagers can also enjoy Russell Baker's, Erma Bombeck's, and Andy Rooney's collections. It's ironic that the kind of writing high school students are most often assigned is the personal essay, yet they are seldom encouraged to read contemporary examples.

Part of understanding where one fits into the world comes through the challenge of learning how to do things—that is, testing one's abilities to make something or develop a skill (see Focus Box 8.3). The topics for how-to books are almost unlimited. They range from something as simple as how to embroider your jeans to the moderately complex task of making your own shoes to the very complex task of building your own solar energy house. (Some libraries have given up stocking books on automobile and motorcycle repair because readers find them so useful that they don't bring them back.)

How-to books are seldom best-sellers, simply because they are so specialized that they appeal to fairly limited audiences. Authors of how-to books need to be extremely good writers. Even one ambiguous sentence can cause problems.

A Sample of How-To Books

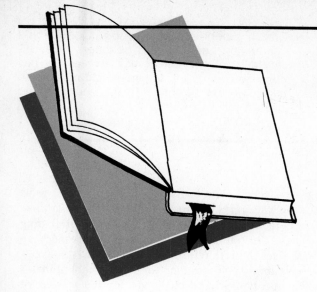

All-Terrain Bicycling by Charles Coombs. Holt, 1987. Coombs includes safety tips as well as information on the selection and care of an all-terrain bike.

Baby-Sitting Safe and Sound by Dorothy R. O'Connell. Ballantine/Fawcett, 1990. This small handbook has advice about the health and safety of the children as well as advice on how to deal with their parents.

Bird on Basketball: How-to Strategies from the Great Celtics Champion by Larry Bird with John Bischoff. Addison-Wesley, 1986. Larry Bird teaches readers both techniques (e.g., how to dribble and how to play defense) and personal philosophy.

Dinosaur Dig by Kathryn Lasky, illustrated by Christopher G. Knight. Greenwillow, 1990. Lasky's family traveled to the Montana Badlands, where they spent a summer digging for dinosaur bones.

Draw Fifty series by Lee J. Ames. Doubleday. Ames has been doing his guides to sketching for nearly twenty years. Titles include *Draw Fifty Boats, Ships, Trucks & Trains* (1987), *Draw Fifty Famous Faces* (1978), and *Draw Fifty Beasties: And Yugglies & Turnover Uglies & Things That Go Bump in the Night* (1988).

Exploring the Sky: 100 Projects for Beginning Astronomers by Richard Moeschl. Chicago Review Press, 1988. The projects in this book center around subjects as easy to understand as a sun dial to something as complicated as the big-bang theory.

Go for It: Get Organized by Sara Gilbert. Morrow, 1990. Gilbert gives help in establishing priorities, simplifying tasks, setting and reaching goals, and dividing those goals between the "have to's" and the "want to's."

The Great Ancestor Hunt: The Fun of Finding Out Who You Are by Lila Perl. Clarion, 1989. Perl shows how doing genealogy isn't just finding out about one's ancestors; it's also relating to one's family as part of "history in the making."

Perfect Put-Downs and Instant Insults by Joseph Rosenbloom. Sterling, 1988. It's debatable whether teenagers need a how-to book in this particular category, but at least it's fun to read.

Science Experiments You Can Eat by Vicki Cobb. HarperCollins, 1989. Cobb aims her books, which make science fun, at a junior high audience. With Kathy Darling, she has also done *Bet You Can! Science Possibilities to Fool You* (Greenwillow, 1990).

Smart Spending: A Young Consumer's Guide by Lois Schmitt. Scribner, 1989. Included is information on how to read the fine print, do comparison shopping, and make credible complaints. Common scams and tricks are also described.

Directions that are hard to understand, failure to list all the supplies and tools that will be needed, and come-on statements that make projects look easier than they are set the stage for frustration. If there is no index to aid readers in finding what they need to know, or if the illustrations are inaccurate, then readers are apt to lose interest in the project and to lose faith in such books.

In some cases, how-to books may open the door for high school students who have never really gotten into books. The challenge for the teacher or librarian is to let students know about the range of available how-to books. Once students learn of a book about one of their interests, perhaps through a display, a booktalk, a school newspaper article, a give-away bibliography, or a recommendation from a friend, they are likely to find their way into a library. If they find what they want, they will most likely return. And when motivated by a desire to accomplish something, students are often able to read above their school-tested reading levels. One reason is that how-to books incorporate principles of programmed learning in immediately rewarding good readers by helping them succeed.

With sports books, obviously the first thing a reader looks for is the particular sport, consequently, authors choose titles that practically shout to potential readers. The sports books that stand out from the crowd usually have a believable and likable personality behind them. They are inspirational as much as instructive, but one thing to watch for in a how-to sports book is whether costs are mentioned. It is almost cruel for an author to write a glowing account of a child star in tennis, gymnastics, skating, swimming, or dancing and leave young readers with the impression that all it takes is hard work. Those readers whose parents do not have time or money for transportation, lessons, entry fees, equipment, and clothes should be let in on the secret that there's more to how you play the game than meets the eye.

Self-help Books—Mental and Physical

A kind of how-to book that deserves its own category is that of self-help (i.e., managing one's own life so as to be successful right now as well as in the future). This includes taking care of one's body (see Focus Box 8.4). When young people go to the shelves of libraries in search of books about health, it is most often in search of an answer to a specific problem; for example:

Can I get AIDS from French kissing?

Do I have diabetes?

Why do I feel like crying all the time?

How serious is Herpes?

Am I pregnant?

What's mononucleosis?

How serious is scoliosis?

Is being fat really unhealthy?

What causes pimples?

What happens if someone has Hodgkin's disease?

My mother has breast cancer. Is she going to die?

Is anorexia nervosa just in a person's head?

Why does my grandfather say such strange things? Will I be like that when I'm old?

What will happen if I have V.D. and don't go to the doctor?

If a book on the body is to attract readers who aren't looking for specific answers, the book needs to have some distinctive quality. It might be an especially appealing format, a specialized approach, or the amazing photographs in the books of Lennart Nilsson, including *Behold Man* and *A Child Is Born,* which make the books attractive to readers of all ages. *Going Vegetarian: A Guide for Teenagers* by Sada Fretz is the kind of sensible, well-written book that any age reader could profit from. The author chose to aim her book at teenagers because their growing bodies have certain nutritional needs, so they may be in more danger than adults if they do not understand the intricacies of balancing their diets.

A decade ago, dozens of books on drugs were being published, but the flood has slowed to a trickle, probably because there's not much left to say. In selecting books on drugs, adults should remember that most teenagers think and know more about drugs than do teachers and librarians, and this results in a credibility gap. We therefore need to be especially careful to provide realistic books. Back in the 1970s, Peter G. Hammond, writing in *School Library Journal,* said that after the National Coordinating Council on Drug Education, of which he was executive director, had studied some 1,000 books and pamphlets and 300 drug abuse education films, they reached the following conclusion:

You can trust most contemporary pieces of drug information to be valid and relevant about as much as you can trust the drug sold by your friendly street pusher to be potent, safe, and unadulterated. In both cases vested

Physical and Emotional Well-being

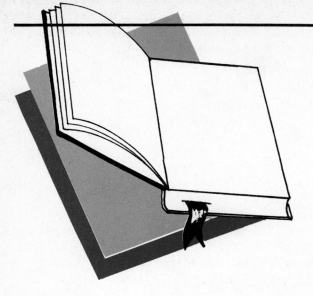

Adoption: The Facts, Feelings, and Issues of a Double Heritage by Jeanne DuPrau. Messner, 1990 (original 1981). Anecdotes and case histories are scattered through the seven chapters, which include a thorough discussion of whether children should be given access to their adoption records.

The American Medical Association Handbook of First Aid and Emergency Care: A Comprehensive, Step-by-Step Guide to Dealing with Injuries, Illnesses, and Medical Emergencies. Random House, 1990. Numerous sketches, a clear organization, boldface headings, and a complete index make this 332-page reference book easy to use.

Child Abuse: An American Epidemic by Elaine Landau. Messner, 1985. Causes and effects of emotional, sexual, and physical abuse are discussed, with the goal of finding solutions to a severe problem.

Everything You Need to Know About an Alcoholic Parent by Nancy Shuker. Rosen, 1989. The focus here is on feelings and the point of view of the young person rather than on alcoholism and its causes. Straightforward advice includes do's and don't's.

Good Sports: Plain Talk About Health and Fitness for Teens by Nissa Simon. Crowell, 1990. Simon includes basic concepts of fitness and training as well as information on how to deal with risks and injuries.

How It Feels to Fight for Your Life by Jill Krementz. Little, Brown, 1989. Interesting photos are printed alongside these interviews with young people from a variety of backgrounds, all of whom are suffering from serious illnesses.

How It Feels When Parents Divorce by Jill Krementz. Knopf, 1984. As in the companion volumes, *How It Feels to Be Adopted* (Knopf, 1982) and *How It Feels When a Parent Dies* (Knopf, 1981), the photos make it seem like those being interviewed are talking directly to readers.

The Kids' Book About Death and Dying: By and for Kids edited by Eric Rofes. Little, Brown, 1985. In this companion volume to *The Kids' Book of Divorce* (Random House, 1982), young people talk openly about their feelings in relation to what they have experienced.

Losing Someone You Love: When a Brother or Sister Dies by Elizabeth Richter. Putnam, 1986. These interviews with fifteen teenagers may be too painful to read at the moment of loss, but they can be a help in the healing process and in enabling readers in general to empathize with others' losses.

Make the Most of a Good Thing: You! by Diana Shaw. Little, Brown, 1987. Shaw's optimistic approach in this self-help book gives a pleasant immediacy to her advice.

Talking About Stepfamilies by Maxine B. Rosenberg. Bradbury, 1990. One out of five teenagers live in a stepfamily, and these stories of sixteen such individuals are meant to help others cope with the multitude of changes that occur when families are restructured.

Teenage Suicide by Sandra Gardner, with Gary Rosenberg, M.D. Messner, 1990. Case studies of young people who were saved from suicide attempts are supplemented by a chapter on self-destructive behavior, addresses of sources for help, and suggested further reading.

Teenagers Face to Face with Cancer by Karen Gravelle and Bertram A. John. Messner, 1986. Emotions and facts are woven together in these stories of sixteen teenage cancer patients.

What You Can Believe About Drugs: An Honest and Unhysterical Guide for Teens by Susan Cohen and Daniel Cohen. M. Evans, 1988. Narcotics, cocaine, marijuana, cigarettes, caffeine, and steroids are discussed, along with the political and emotional factors that influence how Americans respond to drugs.

When Living Hurts by Sol Gordon. Union of American Hebrew Congregations, 1985. This well-written antisuicide book is intended for depressed teenagers and their families and friends.

Zen and the Art of Motorcycle Maintenance: An Inquiry into Values by Robert M. Pirsig. Morrow, 1974. The quality of the writing makes this more than a book on mental well-being.

---

interests abound: scientists and drug educators can be just as irrational about the dangers and benefits of drugs as can those who promote these chemicals to the youth culture.[7]

In the late 1960s and early 1970s there was a blitz of information on drugs, but Hammond says that information and education are not the same thing. One of the problems has been that everyone wants a pat answer, a quick-and-easy solution to a very complex problem. Sociologists and anthropologists know it is a temptation when studying any new culture to want to simplify matters by lumping everything together into one clear-cut picture. Such a one-dimensional presentation would make the drug culture much easier to comprehend, but the real situation isn't that simple.

Richie by Thomas Thompson is a true story of the George Diener family and what happens when their teenage son begins taking puffs of his friends' marijuana cigarettes and then goes on to barbiturates. When Richie is on drugs, he becomes aggressive and earns both a police record and his father's hatred. In the midst of one bitter quarrel after Richie had had two automobile accidents in the same afternoon, George Diener shoots and kills his son. At the trial he is acquitted. The concluding pages of the book make a vivid statement about both drugs and the generation gap.

As shown in Focus Box 8.4, publishers have released a variety of self-help books focusing on mental and emotional health. Probably the mental health book most appreciated by young adults is Robert M. Pirsig's *Zen and the Art of Motorcycle Maintenance: An Inquiry into Values*. This is a gently persuasive book about the Zen approach to working on the "motorcycle that is yourself." The narrative that holds it all together is an account of a cross-country motorcycle trip that Pirsig took with his eleven-year-old son.

Sex Education Books

The exploration of sexual matters in books for young readers (see Focus Box 8.5) is an especially sensitive area for the following reasons:

1. Young adults are physically mature, but they probably have had little intellectual and emotional preparation for making sex-related decisions.
2. Parents are anxious to protect their children from making sex-related decisions that might prove harmful.
3. Old restraints and patterns of behavior and attitudes are being questioned, so that there is no clear-cut model to follow.
4. Sex is such an important part of American culture and the mass media that young people are forced to think about and take stands on such controversial issues as homosexuality, premarital sex, violence in relation to sex, and the role of sex in love and family relationships.
5. Talking about sexual attitudes and beliefs with their teenage children may make parents uncomfortable, especially if the father and the mother have different views. This means that many young people must get their information outside of the home.

A few recently written books focus specifically on AIDS, but generally information about sexually transmitted diseases (STD) is incorporated into overall treatments that cover emotional as well as physical aspects of sexual activity. No single book can ever satisfy all readers, and this is true of those dealing with sex education. An entire collection must be evaluated and books provided for a wide range of interests, attitudes, beliefs, and life-styles. Those who criticize libraries for including books that present teenage sexual activity as the norm have a justified complaint if the library does not also have sex education books that present, or even promote, abstinence as a normal route for young people.

Certainly the authors of sex education books do not intend to promote promiscuity, but the fact that topics are being treated "nonjudgmentally" may give some readers that impression. This is similar to the quandary that the authors of one sex education book found themselves in when they did a chapter on abortion. They felt compelled to explain that simply because they were including such a chapter did not mean they were advocating it as the right or best or most liberated decision. Instead, they chose to give it considerable space because the information had been unavailable in past years.

Materials dealing with sex are judged quite differently from those on less controversial topics. For example, in most subject areas books are given plus

Sex Education

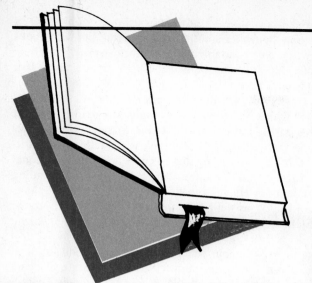

AIDS: Distinguishing Between Fact and Opinion, Juniors Opposing Viewpoints. Greenhaven Press. For younger teens or reluctant readers, this is much like *AIDS* (also Greenhaven, 1989) for older teens, in using charts, cartoons, graphs, and photos to present facts and debunk myths.

Boys and Sex and Girls and Sex by Wardell B. Pomeroy. Delacorte, 1991. The third editions of these companion books have been "revised for the '90s." They're comprehensive and written in a straightforward style. They end with a chapter entitled "I Forgot to Ask," which answers forty or so questions that teens commonly have.

Changing Bodies, Changing Lives, 2nd edition, by Ruth Bell and others. Random House, 1987. The people who put together *Our Bodies, Ourselves* worked on this successful book aimed at young males and females. It takes a holistic approach to sex education.

Lynda Madaras Talks to Teens About AIDS. Newmarket, distributed by Harper-Collins, 1988. The goal of this straightforward book is to help teenagers protect themselves from AIDS and to understand what it does to those who have it.

Risky Times: How to Be AIDS-Smart and Stay Healthy. by Jeanne Blake. Workman, 1990. Included are the latest research findings, along with stories about young people who have AIDS and about people who have contributed their time and talents to help AIDS sufferers.

Safe, Strong, and Streetwise by Helen Benedict. Little, Brown, 1987. The world view presented in this guide to self-protection is a far cry from that presented in teen romances.

Sex Stuff for Kids 7–17: A Book of Practical Information and Ideas for Kids by Carole S. Marsh. Parents and Teachers, 1988. Marsh uses an informal, almost flip, style to present serious information on reproduction, contraception, AIDS, and pregnancy.

Talk Sex by Sue Johanson. Penguin Books, 1989. As a nurse and sex educator, Sue Johanson has answered thousands of teenagers' questions, both in person and in weekly radio and TV shows. She uses the same question–answer format to discuss a wide range of topics.

What Do I Do Now? Talking About Teenage Pregnancy by Susan Kuklin. Putnam, 1991. Medical workers explain the options to the pregnant young women whose stories are told.

When Someone You Know Is Gay by Susan Cohen and Daniel Cohen. M. Evans, 1989. Historical and scientific information is supplemented by interviews with gay teens.

marks if they succeed in getting the reader emotionally involved, but with books about sex, many readers feel more comfortable with straightforward, "plumbing manuals"—the less emotional involvement the better. Other readers argue that it's the emotional part that young people need to learn.

Another example of how differently teachers, librarians, and critics treat sex-related materials is the way in which we ignore pornography as a reading interest of teenagers, especially boys. Most of us pretend not to know about pornography so that we won't have to analyze and evaluate it or talk with students about it. One of the few mentions of this kind of reading that has appeared in professional literature was a mid-1970s survey made by Julie Alm of the spare-time reading interests of high school students in Hawaii. In this survey, fourteen students listed *The Sensuous Woman* by "J" as their favorite book. This was the same number that listed John Steinbeck's *The Pearl*, John Knowles's *A Separate Peace*, and the Bible.

Tone is extra important in books about sex because people come to such books with their own ideas about appropriateness. (When one of our graduate students looked at Peter Mayle's cartoon style books *Where Did I Come From?*, *What's Happening to Me?*, and *Will I Like It?*, he was appalled and said he'd rather make fun of the American flag than of sex.) Another thing to watch for when selecting sex education books is whether sex is portrayed from only one viewpoint, either male or female. For example, Mayle's *Where Did I Come From?* reinforces the traditional active-man/passive-woman stance. Although defenders will point out that Mayle's book is simplified so as to be readable by very young children, critics argue that because young children are so impressionable, it's more important than ever that readers do not come away thinking that sexual intercourse is something done *to* women *by* men.

The design and format of all books, but especially of books about such a sensitive subject as sex, send out their own messages. For example, the cover of Ruth Bell's *Changing Bodies, Changing Lives* has five snapshots on it, only one of which is of a boy and girl, and instead of looking "romantic," they look playful. The other shots are of group activities with teens not necessarily paired off but obviously enjoying each other's company. The effect is to make sexuality seem like a normal, pleasant part of growing up.

Some authors write separate books for boys and for girls, which is a debatable practice. In no other area, except perhaps athletics, is there such purposeful separation between boys and girls. Starting in the fourth grade, girls are taken off to see their first movie on menstruation and boys are left in the room to be given a talk by the coach. Some people believe that this kind of separation is appropriate and, in fact, has advantages similar to the check-and-balance system practiced by the separate branches of the federal government. However, others believe that since sex is something participated in by males and females together, they should be taught the same set of rules. The idea is that if men and women started out with the same set of rules, they would not have so much trouble communicating and establishing fulfilling lifelong relationships.

Because there are relatively few books on the subject of homosexuality and

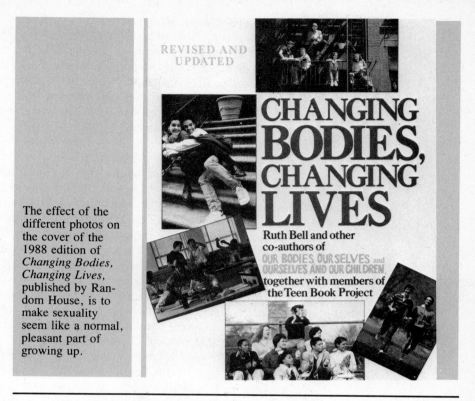

The effect of the different photos on the cover of the 1988 edition of *Changing Bodies, Changing Lives,* published by Random House, is to make sexuality seem like a normal, pleasant part of growing up.

because students hesitate to read what there is, each book takes on disproportionate importance. Morton Hunt, who wrote the well-received *Young Person's Guide to Love,* was criticized by John Cunningham for Hunt's later book, *Gay: What You Should Know About Homosexuality.* Cunningham pointed out that, although it is common for sex education books to have a conversational style using the second-person pronoun *you,* Hunt consistently used the third-person pronoun *them* showing that he did not intend "to put the gay reader at ease or to suggest that the book might be directed to gays."[8] Because he was dissatisfied with Hunt's book, as well as with others on the topic, Cunningham worked with Frances Hanckel to write *A Way of Love, A Way of Life: A Young Person's Introduction to What It Means to Be Gay.* Some of the chapter titles give the flavor of the book: "Sticks and Stones: Understanding Names and Terms About Homosexuality," "How to Tell If You're Gay," "Feeling Bad About It; Feeling Good About It," "Sex Isn't All Good News," and "A Dozen Gay Lives."

Another issue that students may hesitate to read about is that of child abuse, but they can hardly avoid being aware of the issue because of the way it is discussed on television and radio and in newspapers and magazines. A decade ago, the topic was seldom mentioned either in public or private. For example, if Beverly Cleary had published her autobiography *A Girl from Yamhill* in 1978, instead of 1988, she probably wouldn't have included the sexual encounter with her Uncle Joe. But it's probably healthy for such an incident to be included as part of a larger story rather than as something that a reader would have to search out. Of course there are books for readers who are looking for the topic (e.g., Elaine Landau's *Child Abuse: An American Epidemic*, Helen Benedict's *Safe, Strong, and Streetwise*, and Lynn B. Daugherty's *Why Me? Help for Victims of Child Sexual Abuse [Even If They Are Adults Now]*).

When helping young adults make reading decisions in this area, we need to consider the reader's purpose. If the reader wants basic information, then nonfiction is far superior, because it can present a wider range of information in a clear and unambiguous way. But if the reader desires to understand the emotional and physical aspects of one particular relationship, an honest piece of fiction usually does a better job. The important thing for adults to remember is that they should provide both kinds of material in conjunction with a listening ear and a willingness to discuss questions.

Because the subject of sex is such a sensitive and personal one, this is probably the area most in need of open discussion and exchanges of ideas. Schools and libraries need to seek community help in developing policies. Family values must be respected, but honest and accurate information must also be available for those who seek it. Charting a course along this delicate line is more than any one individual should be expected to do. People need to get together to work out the philosophy and policy that best fits their particular situation. But this cannot be done in ignorance. The general public may get away with objecting to or endorsing ideas and books that they have never really explored or read, but a professional working with books is obligated to find and study the latest, most authentic information and to bring that information to those who are helping to shape policies and practices. Such policies and practices will differ from group to group and from person to person. The more you understand about such differences, the better able you will be to participate in book selection, discussion, and sometimes, defense.

■ *AUTHORS OF NONFICTION FOR YA'S*

Some nonfiction authors are so productive that it makes one wonder if they have something like the Stratemeyer Syndicate helping them write their books. What's more likely is that they approach the task like journalists doing research for newspaper features. They write on current topics and bring together other people's research, making it accessible to teenagers. Elaine Landau is one such writer whose listings in the 1991–1992 *Books in Print* took up more than a column and included these YA books published in 1990 and 1991: *Chemical & Biological Warfare, Child Abuse: An American Epidemic, Dyslexia, Lyme Disease, Nazi War Criminals, Teenage Violence, We Have AIDS, We Survived*

LEE J. AMES
on An Unexpected Reward

Do I "write" books for Young Adults? I'm not sure that's a proper description of what I do. Eighteen years ago, while employed as an artist-in-residence at Doubleday, my editor, Bill Hall, suggested I write a book. "Lee, I have an idea. Since we've temporarily run out of artwork for you, you might fill the time writing a book . . . on drawing."

After spending every spare moment of my life until then as a total graphics person, advertising artist, fine artist, cartoonist, designer, animation in-betweener, I hardly felt qualified to "write"! But I made the effort and produced forty-eight, min-

imum text, maximum art pages, entitled *Draw Draw Draw*. Surprise! A modest success.

Then it was back to the drawing board for a decade. When another slack period occurred, I thought, "Wouldn't it be neat to author a second book?" Doubleday agreed and we put together *Draw 50 Animals.* That was in 1974. We have since produced twenty-one *Draw 50* titles. Except for brief introductions and occasional labels, these books are virtually without text.

In a recent interview included in the book *Nonfiction for Young Adults: From Delight to Wisdom,* by Betty Carter and Richard Abrahamson, the first question to me was prefaced with, "In a recent study of nonfiction books circulated in junior high libraries, drawing books were the most circulated kind of nonfiction, and your books were the most checked out of all the drawing titles."

Believe me, I am thrilled, happy as a lark, pleased as punch, and spend fifteen minutes each day jumping with joy (joy, not Joy)! Yet, if you've checked out the Draw 50s, you know I am decidedly not a "writer."

What is most meaningful to me is what I've learned from librarians and letters from my readers. In this era of visual entertainment and education, my nonthreatening, textless books (and others like them) have brought many kids and young adults back into using the libraries and liking books. That's the fantastic, very unexpected, but heartwarming reward that came my way. Although unintentionally, how nice to know I've helped bring many young people back to books, back to reading.

Lee J. Ames's books include *Draw Fifty Beasties: And Yugglies & Turnover Uglies & Things That Go Bump in the Night,* 1988; *Draw Fifty Sharks, Whales and Other Sea Creatures,* 1989; *Draw Fifty Horses,* 1984; and *Draw Fifty Cats,* 1986, all Doubleday.

The Holocaust, and *Weight: A Teenage Concern.* Earlier books still in print included ones on such topics as adolescent prostitutes, homosexuality, sexually transmitted diseases, anorexia, and surrogate mothers.

Not all educators appreciate the kind of work that Landau does because they think it would be better training to have students go directly to the magazine and journal articles that Landau goes to for her information. The argument is similar to the one that college teachers of freshman composition have over whether it's best to use a source book when students do research papers or to have students go only to primary sources. There's something to be said for both sides. However, teachers and librarians should at least be aware of the issue and should help students go beyond relying on any one book when they are researching controversial issues.

Alvin and Virginia Silverstein are also extremely productive authors; they focus largely on health-related science. Some of their recent books include *Cancer: Can It Be Stopped?; Genes, Medicine, and You; Glasses & Contact Lenses: Your Guide to Eyes, Eyewear, and Eyecare; The Story of Your Foot; Wonders of Speech; Overcoming Acne: The How and Why of Healthy Skin Care; So You Think You're Fat?; The Addictions Handbook;* and *Lyme Disease, The Great Imitator: How to Prevent and Cure It.*

Isaac Asimov was another prolific author for readers of all ages. Young adults will most likely recognize his name in connection with science fiction, but he was also praised for his informative books in which he made complex scientific concepts understandable for young people.

Jim Arnosky's name consistently appears on lists of books frequently checked out from libraries. He is a naturalist with a refreshing optimism, who thinks that the first part of a better tomorrow is the awakening to our problems today. His books got a big plug when PBS commissioned him to do a Drawing from Nature series. Titles that are popular with teenagers include *Drawing from Nature, Sketching Outdoors in Spring* (also in summer, autumn, and winter), *Secrets of a Wildlife Watcher, Drawing Life in Motion,* and *Fish in a Flash: A Personal Guide to Spin-Fishing.*

A couple of highly acclaimed writers of children's nonfiction, James Cross Giblin and Leonard Everett Fisher, do their books mainly for middle school and junior high students (grades 3–7). But some of them can be used at higher levels. We had college students in an Introduction to Linguistics class who appreciated Giblin's well-written and beautifully illustrated *The Riddle of the Rosetta Stone: Key to Ancient Egypt* (see Focus Box 8.6). And we've seen high school students' eyes light up when Fisher's books, with their beautiful illustrations, were included with other history books. Fisher started out as an illustrator (he has more than 200 books to his credit) but has gone on to write, design, and illustrate his own books. With historical topics he often supplements his own work with maps, drawings, photographs, and paintings from the period. Recent books that provide a good balance in high school history classes include *The Oregon Trail, The Wailing Wall, Monticello,* and *The White House.*

Some Nonfiction Stars

As the role of nonfiction has become increasingly recognized in the young adult market, a group of significant authors has emerged. In addition to presenting

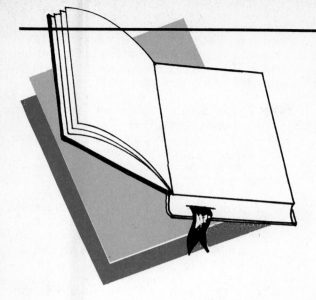

A Sampling of Nonfiction Trade Books for Language Arts Classes

Anguished English by Richard Lederer. Wyrick & Co., 1987; Dell, 1989. Teachers recommended reading aloud these truly funny errors gleaned from unpublished writings. To get the full pleasure they advise spending just a few minutes a day with either this book or Lederer's *Get Thee to a Punnery* (Dell, 1990).

The Art of Fiction: Notes on Craft for Young Writers by John Gardner. Knopf, 1984. A highly respected writer both instructs and inspires those hoping to follow in his footsteps.

Books: From Writer to Reader, revised, by Howard Greenfield. Crown, 1989. This account of the writing, editing, printing, and binding of books needed revising because within the last decade word processors have dramatically changed the way authors write.

Dr. Grammar's Writes from Wrongs by Dr. Grammar (Richard Francis Tracz). Vintage, 1991. After a twenty-one-page introduction, the author presents his material in a question-and-answer format arranged into four sections: grammar, usage, mechanics, and punctuation.

The Henry Holt Encyclopedia of Word and Phrase Origins by Robert Hendrickson. Holt, 1990. "Political plum," "can't cut the mustard," and "Break a leg!" are among the phrases whose histories are given in this book meant for skimming.

The Land of Narnia by Brian Sibley. HarperCollins, 1990. Sibley's fully illustrated book is a combination of biography and literary criticism aimed at teenagers who have fond memories of C. S. Lewis' *Chronicles of Narnia.*

Melba Toast, Bowie's Knife and Caesar's Wife: A Dictionary of Eponyms by Martin Manser. Avon, 1990. Paragraph-length histories are given for over 1,000 words that came into English from someone's name.

Mother Tongue: English and How It Got That Way by Bill Bryson. Morrow, 1990. Advanced students will enjoy this best-selling history of the English language, including the tracing of vulgarities and slang.

Quest for a King: Searching for the Real King Arthur by Catherine M. Andronik. Atheneum, 1989. Andronik discusses medieval legends artifacts, recent theories, and archaeology along with beliefs and hopes that King Arthur really lived.

The Random House Thesaurus of Slang by Esther Lewis and Albert E. Lewis. Random House, 1988. Over 150,000 uncensored slang terms are grouped under 12,000 standard words with similar meanings.

The Riddle of the Rosetta Stone: Key to Ancient Egypt by James Cross Giblin. Crowell, 1990. Giblin tells the story of the stone slab covered with writing that Napoleon's soldiers found in Egypt in 1799. The writing was in three different languages and eventually enabled linguists to decipher one of the world's first writing systems.

Signs of the Apes, Songs of the Whales: Adventures in Human-Animal Communication by George Harrar and Linda Harrar. Simon & Schuster, 1989. Based on the Nova public television series, this book tells how Washoe the chimp, Koko the gorilla, and two dolphins in Hawaii named Phoenix and Akeakamai have been taught to "speak."

Talk About English: How Words Travel and Change by Janet Klausner. Crowell, 1990. This well-done history prepared for young readers includes the standard history of English plus chapters on relationships among words, the meanings of names, and how words change.

The Truth About Unicorns by James Cross Giblin. HarperCollins, 1991. Giblin's book is of interest in language arts classes not only because there are many myths and legends about unicorns, but also because it can serve as a model for research.

What's Your Story? A Young Person's Guide to Writing Fiction by Marion Dane Bauer. Houghton Mifflin, 1992. This popular writer for young adults applied her talents to writing an excellent guide for aspiring authors.

In Your Own Words: A Beginner's Guide to Writing, revised edition by Sylvia Cassedy. Crowell, 1990. Cassedy provides general guidance on being observant and creative and then applies this advice to the writing of several different kinds of fiction, nonfiction, and poetry.

---

solid information, these authors can usually be trusted to provide that something extra that comes when a writer is truly involved in the subject and puts heart and soul into a book. We are not claiming that the following five authors, introduced in alphabetical order, are the only ones about whom this could be said, but we are willing to say that these five (along with Milton Meltzer, see p. 303, and Laurence Pringle, see p. 314) are among a growing body of nonfiction writers who prepare their books with the same kind of care and feeling that goes into the best fiction writing.

Brent Ashabranner At the 1991 National Council of Teachers of English Convention in Seattle, it was heartwarming to see the long lines of teachers wanting Ashabranner to autograph copies of his books. He's been a writer ever since he won a *Scholastic Magazine* contest in high school, but only after he retired in 1980 did he start writing full time for young people. Ashabranner had an international career working in several countries for the U.S. Agency for International Development. He also directed the U.S. Peace Corps in Nigeria and India and later served as

Deputy Director of the Peace Corps in Washington, D.C. Upon his retirement, he had planned on becoming a full-time writer of fiction, but then a professional photographer and good friend, Paul Conklin, came to him with the idea of doing a book about the Cheyenne Indians. Ashabranner went with Conklin to talk with members of the Sweet Medicine tribe. The book *Morning Star, Black Sun: The Northern Cheyenne Indians and America's Energy Crisis* was the result of their collaboration. The most striking fact to emerge from Ashabranner's conversations with the young Indians was "how much they wanted to retain their culture and yet how much they wanted to succeed in the dominant culture of today."[9] Ashabranner later explored that theme in *To Live in Two Worlds: American Indian Youth Today* and in *Into a Strange Land: Unaccompanied Refugee Youth in America.* Probably because of his years of living in other countries, he's especially interested in helping young readers reach beyond their immediate horizons and develop empathy for others. His *Always to Remember: The Story of the Vietnam Veterans Memorial* is about conflict resolution as much as it is about the memorial. And to varying degrees, most of his books show some kind of conflict, as in *Children of the Maya: A Guatemalan Indian Odyssey, Gavriel and Jemal: Two Boys of Jerusalem, The New Americans: Changing Patterns in U.S. Immigration, Dark Harvest: Migrant Farm Workers in America,* and *The Vanishing Border: A Photographic Journey Along Our Frontier with Mexico.* He sometimes works with his daughters Melissa and Jennifer. (The latter is a photographer.) He plans to write approximately two books a year, not all of them about conflict. His *People Who Make a Difference* is about unsung heroes, and *Crazy About German Shepherds* is about his favorite breed of dog.

Jean Fritz

Children's literature people may be surprised at our claiming Jean Fritz as a writer for adolescents, because she has written many more books for children than for adolescents. Only since she wrote, *Homesick: My Own Story,* published by Putnam in 1982, has she done the longer kind of book considered appropriate for teenagers. Before then, she did mostly historical biographies for children. But even if she never wrote books specifically for teenagers, her influence would have been felt, because as Jim Roginski stated:

> Jean Fritz has done one thing few authors can ever hope to accomplish: she has irrefutably changed an entire style of writing for children. Up until she started writing biographies for children, the genre was, with few exceptions, essentially a dull and lifeless one. Historical scenes were re-created, often without attention to accurate detail. Dialogues were invented, sometimes in contemporary jargon, thus negating the impact of an historical biography. Facts were frequently distorted and distilled to the point of futility. It was her attention to detail, her refusal to romanticize a person or event, and her impeccable searching out of diaries, journals, and letters to re-create the past that has brought Jean to the forefront of biographical writing for children.[10]

Fritz's autobiographical *Homesick* was relished by both young and old readers, who had come to love the witty author for having changed their attitudes about history through such prize-winning picture books as *Why Don't You Get a Horse, Sam Adams?; And Then What Happened, Paul Revere?; Where Do You Think You're Going, Christopher Columbus?;* and *Where Was Patrick Henry on the 29th of May?* Since then, Fritz has used her same compelling and thorough approach to write *China Homecoming,* the story of her return to China in 1984 and *China's Long March: 6,000 Miles of Danger,* the story of the men and women in the Chinese Communist Red Army who in 1934–1935 marched across China to the northwest frontier to escape from Chiang Kai-shek. She has also done two highly acclaimed biographies, much fuller than her earlier "question biographies," a genre that she says she's tired of.[11] They are *The Great Little Madison* and *Bully for You, Teddy Roosevelt,* recommended for grades 5–8.

James (Jim) Haskins As with many other authors of nonfiction, James Haskins writes both for children and young adults. He's been a stockbroker, a high school teacher in New York, and a faculty member at several colleges, including Staten Island Community College, Manhattanville College, Indiana University, and Purdue. In 1979 he published an adult book, *Diary of a Harlem Schoolteacher.* For young adults, his main contribution has been to recognize the need for biographies and other books about minorities. But unlike so many of us who bemoan the lack of a particular kind of book, Haskins set out to put his pencil (more likely his word processor) where his mouth was. Since the mid-1970s he has consistently prepared books on black heroes and black history as well as on such topics as rights for people with disabilities, the American labor movement, and women leaders in other countries (e.g., Corazon Aquino and Indira Gandhi). Among his many books for YAs still in print in 1991 were *Black Dance in America: A History Through Its People, Black Music in America: A History Through Its People, Black Theatre in America, Nat King Cole, The Sports Great Magic Johnson, Outward Dreams: Black Inventors and Their Inventions,* and *Against All Opposition: Black Explorers in America.* With some of his subjects, he's done separate books for different age groups, including a children's and a YA book on Diana Ross and a YA and adult book on Lena Horne.

Patricia Lauber Patricia Lauber is another author who has done many books for children but is now doing books that are appreciated by teenagers as well as adults. After graduating from Wellesley, she went to work as a writer for *Look* magazine and then took a job with *Junior Scholastic* magazine, where she discovered that she liked writing for children. She especially enjoyed writing about animals and gradually became more and more interested in science writing, eventually becoming editor-in-chief of *Science World.* She has always been known as a careful and interesting writer, and although her style of writing may not have changed tremendously in the last few years, her books appeal to a wider range of readers for two reasons. Television and other news stories have made people more interested in science as it relates to current events. Improvements in technology have allowed publishers to accompany her text with gorgeous full-color photos. Although the official age level on Lauber's *Volcano: The Eruption and Healing of Mt. St. Helens* is listed as grades 3–5, we saw people of all ages picking it up to admire the photos and at least skim the words. Publishers of her more recent books recognized them as picture books for all ages and listed them as either "gr. 4–up" or "gr. 5–up." They include *Summer of Fire: Yellowstone, 1988; Seeing Earth from Space, Journey to the Planets*, revised ed.; and *Voyagers from Space: Meteors and Meteorites*.

Albert Marrin   Albert Marrin earned a Ph.D. in history from Columbia University in 1968 and shortly thereafter began publishing history-related books. We first took notice of his books in 1985 when his *1812: The War Nobody Won* was chosen as a *Boston-Globe Horn Book* Honor Book for Nonfiction. Since then his books have consistently appeared on best-book lists. *School Library Journal* praised his *Stalin: Russia's Man of Steel* as a "commanding narrative that conveys the terror that Stalin caused." *SLJ* also gave a starred review to *Napoleon and the Napoleonic Wars* and praised his *The Spanish-American War* for delineating "how American jingoists, expansionists, 'big navy' advocates, yellow journal-ists, and filibusterers maneuvered the nation into taking part in the easy defeat of an outgunned Spanish fleet," in what diplomat John Hay called "A splendid little war!" Mary Mueller, also writing in *SLJ*, recommended Marrin's *Struggle for a Continent: The French and Indian Wars* and *The War for Independence* as good introductions to the early years of America. She said that his two biographies, *Hitler* and *Stalin,* could "add greatly to an understanding of how evil the two men actually were, and his look at their monstrous behavior is both fascinating and repelling."[12]

This chapter has only skimmed the topic of nonfiction for young adults, which in the last few years has changed and developed more than any other genre. Contributing factors to the changes include the information explosion, new publishing technologies, the introduction of fascinating topics through the mass media, and the existence of topics of worldwide interest, including ecology and changing political structures. Nonfiction deserves a greater proportion of our attention, if only because it is receiving a greater proportion of young people's attention. Students may graduate from high school without ever reading a science fiction novel, a romance, or even a mystery, but no student graduates without coming into contact with nonfiction. If these contacts are positive ones, then there's a much better chance that the student will go on as an adult to relate to books and seek them out whenever information is needed.

■ NOTES

[1]"A Conversation with Milton Meltzer," in *Nonfiction for Young Adults: From Delight to Wisdom* by Betty Carter and Richard F. Abrahamson (Oryx Press, 1990), pp. 53–54.

[2]Alleen Pace Nilsen, "The House That Alice Built: An Interview with the Author Who Brought You *Go Ask Alice*," *School Library Journal* 25 (October 1979): 109–112.

[3]Richard Zoglin, "The Cops and the Cameras," *Time*, April 6, 1992, pp. 62–63.

[4]Milton Meltzer, "Where Do All the Prizes Go? The Case for Nonfiction," *Horn Book Magazine* 52 (February 1975): 23.

[5]George A. Woods, personal correspondence to Alleen Pace Nilsen, Summer 1978.

[6]Richard F. Abrahamson and Betty Carter, "Of Survival, School, Wars, and Dreams: Nonfiction That Belongs in English Classes," *English Journal* 76 (February 1987): 104–109.

[7]Peter G. Hammond, "Turning Off: The Abuse of Drug Information," *School Library Journal* 19 (April 1973): 17–21.

[8]John Cunningham, "Growing Up Gay Male," *Voice of Youth Advocates* 1 (June 1978): 11–16.

[9]"A Conversation with Brent Ashabranner" in *Nonfiction for Young Adults: From Delight to Wisdom* by Betty Carter and Richard F. Abrahamson (Oryx Press, 1990), p. 97.

[10]Jim Roginski, "Prelude to the Interview" with Jean Fritz in *Behind the Covers: Interviews with Authors and Illustrators of Books for Children and Young Adults* (Libraries Unlimited, 1985), p. 73.

[11]Roginski, "Prelude to the Interview," p. 78.

[12]Mary E. Mueller, "History and History Makers: Give YAs the Whole Picture," *School Library Journal* 37 (November 1991): 55–56.

■ OTHER TITLES MENTIONED IN THE TEXT OF CHAPTER EIGHT

Alcott, Louisa May. *Little Women*, 1868.

America's Lowest Cost Colleges. Brandon Books, Distributed by NAR Productions, P. O. box 233, Barryville, NY 12719.

Angelou, Maya. *I Know Why the Caged Bird Sings*. Random House, 1970.

Anonymous. *Go Ask Alice*. Prentice-Hall, 1971.

Arnosky. Jim. *Drawing from Nature*. Lothrop, 1987.

———. *Drawing Life in Motion*. Morrow, 1991.

———. *Fish in a Flash: A Personal Guide to Spin-Fishing*. Bradbury, 1991.

———. *Secrets of a Wildlife Watcher*. Lothrop, 1983.

———. *Sketching Outdoors in Spring* (also *Summer, Winter,* and *Autumn*). Lothrop, 1987.

Ashabranner, Brent. *Always to Remember: The Story of the Vietnam Veterans Memorial*. Putnam, 1988.

———. *Children of the Maya: A Guatemalan Indian Odyssey*. Putnam, 1986.

———. *Crazy About German Shepherds*. Dutton, 1990.

———. *Dark Harvest: Migrant Farm Workers in America*. Putnam, 1985.

————. *Gavriel and Jemal: Two Boys of Jerusalem*. Putnam, 1984.

————. *Into a Strange Land: Unaccompanied Refugee Youth in America*. Putnam, 1989.

————. *To Live in Two Worlds: American Indian Youth Today*. Dodd, Mead, 1984.

————. *The New Americans: Changing Patterns in U.S. Immigration*. Putnam, 1983.

————. *People Who Make a Difference*. Dutton, 1989.

————. *The Vanishing Border: A Photographic Journey Along Our Frontier with Mexico*. Putnam, 1986.

Bell, Ruth. *Changing Bodies, Changing Lives*. Random House, 1987.

Benedict, Helen. *Safe, Strong, and Streetwise*. Little, Brown, 1987.

The Black College Career Guide. Massey-Young Communications, 33 E. 78th St., Covington, KY 41011.

Brooks, Bruce. *Midnight Hour Encores*. HarperCollins, 1986.

Brown, Claude. *Manchild in the Promised Land*. Macmillan, 1965.

Brown, Dee. *Bury My Heart at Wounded Knee: An Indian History of the American West*. Holt, 1971.

Capote, Truman. *In Cold Blood*. Random House, 1966.

Cleary, Beverly, *A Girl from Yamhill: A Memoir*. Morrow, 1988.

Cleaver, Eldridge. *Soul on Ice*. McGraw-Hill, 1968.

Conklin, Paul. with Brent Ashabranner. *Morning Star, Black Sun: The Northern Cheyenne Indians and America's Energy Crisis*. Putnam, 1982.

Cormier, Robert, *I Have Words to Spend: Reflections of a Small-Town Editor,* edited by Constance Senay Cormier. Delacorte, 1991.

Daughtery, Lynn B. *Why Me? Help for Victims of Child Sexual Abuse (Even If They Are Adults Now)*. Mother Courage, 1985.

Doctorow, E. L. *Ragtime*. Random House, 1975.

Eyewitness series. Knopf, late 1980s to the present.

Fisher, Leonard Everett. *Monticello*. Holiday House, 1988.

————. *The Oregon Trail*. Holiday House, 1990.

————. *The Wailing Wall*. Macmillan, 1989.

————. *The White House*. Holiday House, 1989.

Fiske, Edward B. *The Fiske Guide to Colleges 1992*. Random House, 1991.

Freedman, Russell. *Lincoln: A Photobiography*. Clarion, 1987.

Fretz, Sada. *Going Vegetarian: A Guide for Teenagers*. Morrow, 1983.

Fritz, Jean. *Bully for You, Teddy Roosevelt*. Putnam, 1991.

————. *China Homecoming*. Putnam, 1985.

————. *China's Long March: 6,000 Miles of Danger*. Putnam, 1988.

————. *The Great Little Madison*. Putnam, 1989.

————. *Homesick: My Own Story*. Putnam, 1982.

————. *And Then What Happened, Paul Revere?* Putnam, 1973.

————. *Where Do You Think You're Going, Christopher Columbus?* Putnam, 1981.

————. *Where Was Patrick Henry on the 29th of May?* Putnam, 1982.

————. *Why Don't You Get a Horse, Sam Adams?* Putnam, 1982.

Graham, Robin. *Dove*. HarperCollins, 1972.

Giblin, James Cross. *The Riddle of the Rosetta Stone: Key to Ancient Egypt*. Crowell, 1990.

Griffin, John H. *Black Like Me*. Houghton Mifflin, 1977.

Hanckel, Frances, and John Cunningham. *A Way of Love, A Way of Life: A Young*

Person's Introduction to What It Means to Be Gay. Lothrop, 1979.

Haley, Alex. *Roots.* Doubleday, 1976.

Harris, Thomas A. *I'm Ok—You're Ok: A Practical Guide to Transactional Analysis.* HarperCollins, 1969.

Haskins, James. *Against All Opposition: Black Explorers in America.* Walker, 1991.

———. *Black Dance in America: A History Through Its People.* Crowell, 1990.

———. *Black Music in America: A History Through Its People.* Crowell, 1987.

———. *Black Theatre in America.* HarperCollins, 1991.

———. *Diary of a Harlem Schoolteacher.* Grove Press, 1970.

———. *Nat King Cole.* Scarborough House, 1979.

———. *Outward Dreams: Black Inventors and Their Inventions.* Walker, 1991.

———. *The Sports Great, Magic Johnson.* Enslow, 1989.

Herriot, James. *All Creatures Great and Small.* St. Martin's, 1972.

Hunt, Morton. *Gay: What You Should Know About Homosexuality.* Farrar, Straus & Giroux, 1977.

———. *A Young Person's Guide to Love.* Farrar, Straus & Giroux, 1977.

Hyde, Margaret O. *Sexual Abuse: Let's Talk about It.* Westminster, 1987.

"J." *The Sensuous Woman.* Lyle Stuart, 1970.

Landau, Elaine. *Chemical & Biological Warfare.* Dutton, 1991.

———. *Child Abuse: An American Epidemic.* Messner, 1990.

———. *Dyslexia.* Watts, 1991.

———. *Lyme Disease.* Watts, 1990.

———. *Nazi War Criminals.* Watts, 1990.

———. *Teenage Violence.* Messner, 1990.

———. *We Have AIDS.* Watts, 1990.

———. *We Survived the Holocaust.* Watts, 1991.

———. *Weight: A Teenage Concern.* Dutton, 1991.

Lauber, Patricia. *Journey to the Planets,* revised ed. Crown, 1987.

———. *Seeing Earth from Space.* Orchard/Watts, 1990.

———. *Summer of Fire: Yellowstone, 1988.* Orchard/Watts, 199.

———. *Volcano: The Eruption and Healing of Mt. St. Helens.* Bradbury, 1986.

———. *Voyagers from Space: Meteors and Meteorites.* HarperCollins, 1989.

Lund, Doris. *Eric.* HarperCollins, 1974.

Maas, Peter. *Serpico,* Viking, 1973.

Macaulay, David. *The Way Things Work: From Levers to Lasers, Cars to Computers—A Visual Guide to the World of Machines,* illustrated by the author. Houghton Mifflin, 1988.

———. *Unbuilding.* Houghton Mifflin, 1980.

Marrin, Albert. *1812: The War Nobody Won.* Atheneum, 1985.

———. *Hitler.* Viking, 1987.

———. *Napoleon and the Napoleonic Wars.* Viking, 1991.

———. *The Spanish-American War.* Atheneum, 1991.

———. *Stalin: Russia's Man of Steel.* Viking, 1988.

———. *Struggle for a Continent: The French and Indian Wars.* Atheneum, 1987.

———. *The War for Independence.* Atheneum, 1988.

Mayle, Peter. *What's Happening to Me?* Lyle Stuart, 1975.

———. *Where Did I Come From?* Lyle Stuart, 1973.

———. *Will I Like It?* Corwin, 1977.

McCrum, Robert et al. *The Story of English.* Viking, 1986.

McFarlan, Donald. *The Guiness Book of World Records 1990–91.* Bantam, 1991.

Miklowitz, Gloria D. and Madeleine Yates. *The Young Tycoons: Ten Success Stories.* Harcourt Brace Jovanovich, 1981.

Mowat, Farley. *Never Cry Wolf*. Little, Brown, 1963.

Needle, Stacy. *The Other Route into College: Alternative Admission*. Random House, 1991.

Nilsson, Lennart. *A Child Is Born*. La Leche, 1983.

———. *Behold Man*. Little, Brown, 1974.

Peck, Richard. *Are You in the House Alone?* Viking, 1976.

Perl, Lila. *Don't Sing Before Breakfast, Don't Sleep in the Moonlight: Everyday Superstitions and How They Began*. Clarion, 1988.

Pirsis, Robert M. *Zen and the Art of Motorcycle Maintenance: An Inquiry into Values*. Morrow, 1974.

Read, Piers Paul. *Alive*. Lippincott, 1974.

Reader's Digest. *ABCs of the Bible: Intriguing Questions and Answers About the Greatest Book Ever Written*. Reader's Digest, 1990.

Robinson, Adam and John Katzman. *Cracking the System: The SAT & PSAT* (Princeton Review Series). Villard Books/Random House, 1986.

Rosenberg, Ellen. *College Life: A Down-to-Earth Guide*. Penguin, 1992.

Ryden, Hope. *God's Dog*. Viking, 1979.

Sagan, Carl. *Cosmos*. Random House, 1983.

Silverstein, Alvin and Virginia. *The Addictions Handbook*. Enslow, 1991.

———. *Cancer: Can It Be Stopped?* HarperCollins, 1987.

———. *Genes, Medicine, and You*. Enslow, 1988.

———. *Glasses & Contact Lenses: Your Guide to Eyes, Eyewear, and Eyecare*. HarperCollins, 1988.

———. *Lyme Disease, the Great Imitator: How to Prevent and Cure It*. Avstar, 1990.

———. *Overcoming Acne: The How and Why of Healthy Skin Care*. Morrow, 1990.

———. *So You Think You're Fat?* HarperCollins, 1991.

———. *The Story of Your Foot*. Putnam, 1987.

———. *Wonders of Speech*. Morrow, 1988.

Sparks, Beatrice. *Jay's Journal*. Times Books, 1979.

———. *Voices*. Times Books, 1978.

Toffler, Alvin. *Future Shock*. Random House, 1970.

Voigt, Cynthia, *Izzy, Willy-Nilly*. Macmillan, 1986.

Williams, Margery. *The Velveteen Rabbit*. 1992.

For information on the availability of paperback editions of these titles, please consult the most recent edition of *Paperbound Books in Print*, published annually by R. R. Bowker Company.

POETRY, SHORT STORIES, DRAMA, AND HUMOR

Of Lines and Laughs

The poetry, drama, humor, and to a lesser extent, short stories that young adults enjoy belong less exclusively to them than do their reading choices in other genres. If one examines typical anthologies studied in high school literature classes, the plays that students read have been produced for general adult audiences and the short stories have been published in such magazines as the *New Yorker* or the *Saturday Evening Post*. Teenagers often find themselves laughing at the same humorous stories that make their parents laugh. The lyrics of popular songs, which are one form of poetry, are sung by people from ages eight to eighty, and when we examined the card catalogues of three different libraries to see how the books on the Honor Sampling were purchased and shelved, the only book we found in three different areas of the same library—children's, young adults', and adults'—was a poetry collection, *Reflections on a Gift of Watermelon Pickle*.

One of the reasons these genres tend to transcend age divisions may be that they are social. Rather than being enjoyed in solitude, as is a good mystery or a sad problem novel, poetry is better when it's read aloud (note the popularity of poetry readings). Mentally disturbed people laugh when they are alone, but normal people laugh more when they are with others. And the experience of watching a dramatic presentation is noticeably different for a member of a large, enthusiastic audience from what it is when one is alone, listening to a cassette tape or watching a televised production. And in the days before mass media magazines turned away from fiction, regular family entertainment consisted of reading aloud the short stories that arrived in weekly or monthly magazines.

◼ POETRY

◼ I saw the gooseflesh on my skin. I did not know what made it. I was not cold. Had a ghost passed over? No, it was the poetry. . . . I wanted to cry; I felt very odd. I had fallen into a new way of being happy.[1]

This is how Sylvia Plath described her introduction to poetry when her mother was reading to her from Matthew Arnold's "Forsaken Merman." Not all of us remember the first time that we were touched by the power of language; nevertheless, most book lovers have experienced something similar even if we aren't as articulate as was Sylvia Plath in describing it.

Almost everything we've said about literature in general could also be said about poetry. Poets use the same literary devices discussed in Chapter Two, but they do it more succinctly. One of the characteristics of poetry is its compactness. Poets do with words something similar to what manufacturers do with dehydrated food. They shrink bulky thoughts down to packageable sizes, which they expect consumers to fill out by adding their own thoughts, ideas, memories, and images. This is why reading poetry is harder work than reading prose, but it can also be more rewarding because the reader is more involved.

Readers' appreciation for poetry develops in much the same way as their appreciation for prose. They begin with an unconscious delight in sounds—the repetition and rhythm of nursery rhymes, songs, and television commercials. Then they go on to the fun of riddles, puns, playground chants, and autograph rhymes. Researchers in children's language development have found that children often do not understand the dual meanings of the words that are keys to particular jokes or riddles, yet they take pleasure in hearing the joke patterns, and when they learn enough about the world to catch on to the double meanings of what they are saying, their pleasure is increased. In a study where children were asked to select from a long list those words that went well together, the younger children—those in the primary grades—matched *cocoon* with *baboon* and *monsoon*. In contrast, the older children used meaning as their basis for selection. To go with *cocoon*, they chose *moth* and *butterfly*. This doesn't mean that the sounds of words were no longer important; it simply means that as the children matured and knew more about the world, they could rely on more than sound.

Something similar can be observed in children's appreciation of poetry. Although it may be the sounds of the nursery rhymes that first appeal to them, very soon they get involved in such simple plots as those found in "This Little Piggie Went to Market," "Ring Around the Rosie," and "Pat-a-Cake, Pat-a-Cake." By the time children are in the middle grades their favorite poems are those that tell stories (e.g., Robert Browning's "The Pied Piper of Hamelin," Henry Wadsworth Longfellow's "Hiawatha's Childhood" and "The Midnight Ride of Paul Revere," Robert Service's "The Cremation of Sam McGee," James

PAUL B. JANECZKO
on Collecting Poems

If you've ever read a book of poetry and noticed poems that touched you more than others, you've taken the first step toward creating a poetry anthology. I look for poems that strike me. These are the ones I save, copying and filing in subject/topic folders. After the poems have sat in the folders for a time, I read through them again to refresh my memory of the poems I've saved. It also helps me make connections, to see similarities and differences in the poems that may help me place them with other poems.

An anthologist must break ground, so I need to go beyond the poems that I discover in journals and books. One new source I found is the poets themselves. Since I worked on *Poetspeak: In Their Work, About Their Work*, I've stayed in touch with a long list of poets who are eager to send me new poems and spread the word to other poets. Now, when I'm thinking about a new anthology, I can generate computer postcards stating my needs and mail them to all the poets on my mailing list.

Stacks of poems, however, do not an anthology make. Poems must connect with other poems. Some associations are obvious, but I look for connections that may not be apparent at first reading. I want readers to think about why poems are where they are. I want to bring order to the collection, an order that will give the timid, inexperienced reader of poetry a gentle nudge in a helpful direction. I discovered while working on *Dont Forget to Fly* that groups of two to six poems work better for me than larger groups. Small groupings, however, make the anthology more difficult to organize because I must not only connect the poems in each section, but I must also connect the sections.

When I've decided on the poems for a new collection, I let them rest for a few months. Then I tinker with the book, fine-tune it by cutting out some poems, changing the order, perhaps adding a poem or two to make the book flow more effortlessly. Even though I realize that few people read an anthology from cover to cover as they would a novel, I try to make sure that my collections are carefully "plotted" from first poem to last.

Why collect poems? Long before I created my first anthology in 1977, I was hooked on poetry, believing the words of James Dickey, "What you have to realize. . . , if you love poetry is that poetry is just naturally the greatest goddamn thing that ever was in the whole universe. If you love it, there's no substitute for it." And if you love it, you have to pass it on.

Paul Janeczko's edited collections include *Preposterous: Poems of Youth*, Orchard, 1991; *The Place My Words Are Looking For*, Bradbury, 1990; and *The Music of What Happens*, Orchard, 1988. He is the author of *Brickyard Summer*, Orchard, 1989.

Whitcomb Riley's "The Gobble-Uns'll Get You if You Don't Watch Out," and Edgar Allan Poe's "The Raven").

Capitalizing on this interest in story, publishers continue to produce new editions beautifully designed to attract junior and senior high school readers. For example, in the last few years Trina Schart Hyman illustrated a new translation by Barbara Cohen of Chaucer's *Canterbury Tales*; Barry Moser drew fresh and funny new illustrations for Ernest Lawrence Thayer's *Casey at the Bat,* and Neil Waldman did beautiful watercolor illustrations for Alfred Noyes's *The Highwayman*. Cynthia Rylant told a modern story in *Soda Jerk*. The setting is Maxwell's Drugstore, where the narrator works the soda fountain and shares his observations through poetry.

After learning to appreciate stories in poems, young readers go on to take pleasure in recognizing kinship with a poet, finding someone who expresses a feeling or makes an observation that the reader has come close to but hasn't quite been able to put into words. Much of the "Pop" poetry that English teachers consider trite or overdone is appreciated by young readers in this stage. We know a creative writing teacher who criticized a student-written poem as being overly sentimental by writing on the paper, "This sounds like Rod McKuen." The student was thrilled at being compared to McKuen, and the teacher didn't have the heart to explain that she had not intended the remark as a compliment.

Progressing from this stage, readers begin to identify with the poet as a writer. They understand and appreciate the skill with which the poet has achieved the desired effect. This understanding brings extra pleasure, which is why English teachers are interested in helping students arrive at this level of poetic appreciation, but the teacher who tries to get there too fast runs the risk of leaving students behind.

Poet Eve Merriam believed that something like this has happened to most of the upper-grade students who are turned off to poetry. They were made to feel dumb because they didn't catch on to every nuance of meaning or sound that their teacher saw, which was an experience they don't wish to repeat. When working with students like this, librarians, public speaking or drama teachers, and others who work with teenagers outside of English classrooms have an advantage, because students can more easily believe that the poetry is being shared for pleasure rather than for some esoteric teaching goal. Fortunately, more English teachers are realizing the damage that can be done by too early and too intensive a concentration on "literary" aspects of poetry. They are providing students with a variety of poems and encouraging them to read first for pleasure and second for literary analysis. They let students start where they are in their appreciation of poetry, whether it's the humorous poems of Shel Silverstein in his *Where the Sidewalk Ends* and *The Light in the Attic*, the religious poems selected by Nancy Larrick in her *Tambourines! Tambourines to Glory! Prayers and Poems,* the wordplay poems of Eve Merriam in her *Rainbow Writing* and *Out Loud*, the almost militant poems in Maya Angelou's *And Still I Rise*, or the almost classic poems in Edna St. Vincent Millay's *Poems Selected for Young People*.

Poetry Written or Collected Specifically for Young Adults

We did not include poetry in the first edition of this book because we didn't think that people wrote poetry specifically for teenagers. Such poets as David McCord and Aileen Fisher search for topics especially appealing to and appropriate for children, but we didn't know anyone who did this for young adults. Then in 1982, Mel Glenn published *Class Dismissed! High School Poems*, which was chosen for several best-book lists. So were the later sequels, *Class Dismissed II: More High School Poems; Back to Class;* and *My Friend's Got This Problem, Mr. Candler: High School Poems.* Here is poetry with all the characteristics of the modern YA problem novel. Young protagonists from a variety of racial and socioeconomic backgrounds use candid, first-person speech to discuss intense situations, ranging from having a crush on a teacher to quitting school, getting caught shoplifting, and being stabbed. The titles of the poems

Mel Glenn was the first writer to succeed in adapting the subjects and mode of realistic problem novels to poetry. In *My Friend's Got This Problem, Mr. Candler* (Clarion, 1991), each poem is written in the voice of a student talking to a high school guidance counselor.

are kids' names, and most poems are illustrated with a photograph. Although Glenn wrote the poems himself, the design of the book gives the impression that the kids in the photographs are the poets. The publishers probably wanted to capitalize on the current popularity of "folk poetry," that is, the writing and sharing of original poems.

Although writing poetry specifically for a young adult audience is a recent development, collecting poems with special appeal to teenagers and packaging them for the high school market has a much longer history. A book that nearly thirty years ago proved the potential success of this kind of venture was *Reflections on a Gift of Watermelon Pickle,* published first by Scott, Foresman in 1966 and later reprinted in various formats and issued on a record. Editors Steve Dunning, Edward Lueders, and Hugh L. Smith selected the poems by getting the reactions of teenagers to both well-known and new poems gleaned from hundreds of poetry magazines. But there was more to their success than just the individual poems. The title, taken from the concluding poem, is intriguing, and the spacious design with its watermelon green cover and reddish-pink endpapers make the book memorable.

Over the last decade, Paul Janeczko, a high school English teacher in Auburn, Maine (see his statement on p. 344), has consistently edited well-received anthologies with many of the same characteristics as the *Watermelon Pickle* book (i.e., an intriguing title, spacious and attractive designs, poems that have been tested for their appeal to young readers, and an organization that leads readers from one poem to the next).

His first collection, *Postcard Poems,* is filled with poems short enough to send to a friend on a postcard—for example, W. S. Merwin's "Separation":

> *Your absence has gone through me*
> *Like thread through a needle.*
> *Everything I do is stitched with its color.*[2]

and Ralph Waldo Emerson's "Poet":

> *To clothe the fiery thought*
> *In simple words succeeds,*
> *For still the draft of genius is*
> *To mask a King in weeds.*

Most of his books have a cyclical organization with between two and five poems on similar subjects. For example, in *Dont Forget to Fly,* Constance Sharp's "I Show the Daffodils to the Retarded Kids" is grouped with Joyce Carol Oates's "Children Not Kept at Home" and Theodore Roethke's "My Dim-Wit Cousin." In all, there are forty groupings with subjects ranging from suicide to dressmaker's dummies, swimming, and Sunday. In *Strings: A Gathering of Family Poems,* Janeczko uses a similar kind of organization but goes through members of the family: wives, husbands, grandparents, and so on, and through places with special meanings for families, such as kitchens (with a "slice of sun and a song"), as well as one where a 1940s child playing under the table hears the radio announcer, "We interrupt this broadcast . . ." and has his head filled with thoughts of Hitler, Roosevelt, and Joe Louis. Instead of thinking of poems as puzzles, Janeczko wants teachers to think of them as language experiences.

With most poetry collections the anthologizer selects a topic and then finds either a goodly number of poems or a number of good poems (depending on the standards of the anthologist) on a similar topic. Limiting themselves to either a particular topic or a particular poet gives anthologists a way to get a handle on what could be an overwhelming job of selection. Although such a limitation makes designing and naming a book easier, it handicaps the anthologist by restricting the raw material from which selections can be made. Some of the best poems treat unique experiences or explore hidden sides of life. They are appealing simply because they are on topics that are usually ignored.

Poetry appeals to the senses—sight as well as sound—and because of this, reading shouldn't be rushed. Books of poems need to be designed to give readers room to breathe. A book jam-packed with poems exudes a sense of urgency, a need to speed-read. Such books are good reference tools for someone wanting to find a particular poem, but they aren't books that readers—teenage or adult—are likely to pick up for pleasure-time browsing.

Current interests and trends are just as likely to influence the reception of poetry as the reception of fiction. (See Focus Box 9.1 for the variety of themes being explored in anthologies—for example, ecology, ethnic diversity, love, and hobbies.) Because readers come to poetry not so much for information as for a change of pace, a bit of pleasure through wordplay, a sudden recognition or insight, a recollection from childhood, or a time of emotional intensity, the design of the book needs to invite readers in.

Even though the age range that can read and enjoy poetry is usually much wider than that for prose, there is still a subtle dividing line between children's and young adult poetry. Teenagers will be amused by humorous poetry prepared for children, but they are likely to feel slightly insulted if offered serious children's poetry. It's comparable to their being offended if they are taken to the children's department of a store to buy their clothes, although by themselves they might wander into a children's department to buy a stuffed animal. The freedom of choice is what's at issue, and book people need to realize that if a collection of poems is going to be marketed basically to high schools, the designers should be aware of their audience's feeling that they have passed through childhood and are now young adults.

Helen Plotz is a good anthologist who has put together several collections for Crowell, Macmillan, and Greenwillow. These books (e.g., *Imagination's Other Place: Poems of Science and Mathematics* and *Eye's Delight: Poems of Art and Architecture*) find their way into many young adult collections. However, some of her titles stand between the poems and a young adult audience. One example is the title *Saturday's Children: Poems of Work*. It makes an appropriate allusion to the old nursery rhyme about Monday's child being fair of face, Tuesday's child full of grace, and so on, but without encouragement from a forceful teacher or librarian, not many young adults will pick up a book

Recommended Collections of Poetry

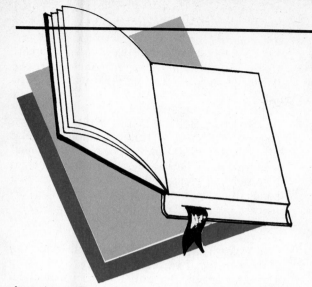

etry" as well as for those "who might be seized with that rare and undiagnosed compulsion to paste a favourite poem on the wall."

American Sports Poems, edited by R. R. Knudson and May Swenson. Orchard, 1988. Poets as good as Grace Butcher, Tess Gallagher, John Updike, Anne Sexton, and Robert Francis treat both common and unusual sports.

The Concise Columbia Book of Poetry, edited by William Harmon. Columbia University Press, 1990. This collection won starred reviews for the appealing idea of including the 100 most frequently anthologized poems. Notes on the poems, helpful indexes, and brief biographies of the poets make it an exceptionally useful book.

The Dream Keeper and Other Poems by Langston Hughes. Knopf/Borzoi, 1986. This is a new edition of the landmark book first published in 1932.

Earth, Air, Fire & Water: Poems Selected by Frances McCullough, Revised Edition. HarperCollins, 1989. McCullough says she chose these poems from all kinds of poets on all kinds of subjects because of "what might be called their specific gravity: the pull they exert on their readers." McCullough also edited the well-received *Love Is Like the Lion's Tooth* (HarperCollins, 1984).

Life Doesn't Frighten Me At All, compiled by John Agard. Henry Holt, 1990. Agard chose his poems for teenagers "with an allergy to po-

Mindscapes: Poems for the Real World, edited by Richard Peck. Dell, 1990. Before Richard Peck became a YA writer, he was an English teacher with a wide and fine taste in poetry. His *Sounds and Silences* (Dell, 1990) is also a good collection.

Neighborhood Odes by Gary Soto, illustrated by DaVid Diaz. Harcourt Brace Jovanovich, 1992. Soto's poems celebrate the everyday events of the Hispanic neighborhood in Los Angeles where he grew up.

Now Sheba Sings the Song by Maya Angelou. Dial, 1987. Beautifully done portraits of black women accompany Angelou's poems. Other not-to-be-missed Angelou books of poetry include *I Shall Not Be Moved,* 1990; *And Still I Rise,* 1978; *Oh Pray My Wings Are Gonna Fit Me Well,* 1975; and *Just Give a Cool Drink of Water 'fore I Die,* 1971, all Random House.

Preposterous: Poems of Youth, edited by Paul Janeczko. Orchard, 1991. Buy, rent, borrow, or steal any book edited by Janeczko. He's an American treasure. Other titles, all published by Bradbury, include *Dont Forget to Fly,* 1981; *Going Over to Your Place: Poems for Each Other,* 1987; *Pocket Poems: Selected for a Journey,* 1985; *Postcard Poems: A Collection of Poetry for Sharing,* 1979; and *Strings: A Gathering of Family Poems,* 1984.

Rainbow Writing by Eve Merriam. Atheneum, 1976. Merriam relies on wordplay and fresh images to make her poetry fun for readers. *Out Loud* (Atheneum, 1973), *The Inner City Mother Goose* (Simon & Schuster, 1969), and *If Only I Could Tell You: Poems for Young Lovers and Dreamers* (Knopf, 1969) are other Merriam titles.

Rhythm Road: Poems to Move To, selected by Lillian Morrison. Lothrop, 1988. Each of the eighty-eight poems relates to some kind of movement, most commonly in sports or dance, but also in science, technology, and thought.

Six American Poets, edited by Joel Conarroe. Random House, 1991. Here's a healthy sampling of Walt Whitman, Emily Dickinson, Wallace Stevens, William Carlos Williams, Robert Frost, and Langston Hughes.

Some Haystacks Don't Even Have Any Needle: And Other Complete Modern Poems, Lothrop, 1969, edited by Steve Dunning and Hugh L. Smith. This sequel to *Reflections on a Gift of Watermelon Pickle and Other Modern Verse* is still popular after thirty years.

Tambourines! Tambourines to Glory! Prayers and Poems, selected by Nancy Larrick. Westminster, 1982. A popular anthologizer collects poems about religious experiences. Her other successful collections include *Room for Me and*

a Mountain Lion: Poetry of Open Space (Evans, 1974), *Bring Me All of Your Dreams* (Evans, 1980), and *Crazy to Be Alive in Such a Strange World: Poems About People* (Evans, 1977).

Time Is the Longest Distance: An Anthology of Poems Selected by Ruth Gordon. HarperCollins, 1991. This collection of poetic thoughts related to time would be good to read alongside Jean Theisman's *The Rain Catchers,* in which the grandmother removes the minute hands of all her clocks. Gordon's *Under All Silences: Shades of Love* (HarperCollins, 1987) is also a highly acclaimed anthology.

The Voice That Is Great Within Us: American Poetry of the Twentieth Century, edited by Hayden Carruth. Bantam, 1983. This excellent collection of modern poetry features poets from Robert Frost to Joel Sloman.

Waltzing on Water, edited by Norma Fox Mazer and Marjorie Lewis. Dell, 1989. The poets include Sharon Olds, May Swenson, Linda Pastan, Marge Piercy, and Muriel Rukeyser.

We Animals: Poems of Our World, edited by Nadya Aisenberg. Sierra Club, distributed by Random House, 1989. The bond between humans and animals is explored in poetry by Wendell Berry, Theodore Roethke, Robert Frost, Ted Hughes, Maxine Kumin, Czeslaw Milosz, Marianne Moore, and others.

---

whose five-word title includes three words that have negative connotations for most teenagers: *children, poems,* and *work.* Another example is *Gladly Learn and Gladly Teach: Poems of the School Experience,* which exudes a middle-aged, schoolmarm fussiness.

Humorous Poetry

Too many young adults, hardly enamored of poetry to begin with, assume that *poetry* and *humor* are mutually exclusive terms. Such books as Paul Fleischman's *Joyful Noise: Poems for Two Voices*, Piet Hein's *Grooks*, and Alvin Schwartz's *And the Green Grass Grew All Around: Folk Poetry from Everyone* should help dispel that notion, even though some people would prefer to call the folk poetry collected by Alvin Schwartz "verse" rather than "poetry." We'll talk here about some of the humor in poetry that's a little harder to find. Teenagers will appreciate it, but they will need a teacher or librarian to search it out and bring it to their attention.

Don Marquis' *archy and mehitabel* is a prime example. archy (he never uses capitals) is a gigantic cockroach with guts, a born writer with desperate drive. After approaching the typewriter, he

would climb painfully upon the framework of the machine and cast himself with all his force upon a key, head downward, and his weight and the impact of the blow were just sufficient to operate the machine, one slow letter after another. He could not work the capital letters, and he had a great deal of difficulty operating the mechanism that shifts the paper so that a fresh line may be started. We never saw a cockroach work so hard or perspire so freely in all our lives before. After about an hour of this frightfully difficult literary labor he fell to the floor exhausted, and we saw him creep feebly into a nest of the poems which are always there in profusion.

So Marquis discovers archy's first literary effort, and he follows with other poems, all of them funny, although they are well over fifty years old: "the song of mehitabel," "the cockroach who had been to hell," "aesop revised by archy," "pete the parrot and shakespeare," and "freddy the rat perished."

Because death is the most feared of life's universal experiences, we can't leave it alone. We keep poking at it as we do with a sore tooth, probably hoping that we will be surprised to find that it no longer hurts. The succinctness of poetry is ideal for mentally poking at death, because we can make a quick jab and then back off, as with the humorous lines that sometimes appear on gravestones. Fritz Spiegl's *A Small Book of Grave Humor* has several examples that are funny to many readers and at least strange to those who cannot regard anything about death as amusing. Humor about death goes back to the Greeks. In the mammoth collection of odds-and-ends verses called *Poems from the Greek Anthology*, translated by Dudley Fitts, there are both conventional and unconventional epitaphs. A few are bitter, whereas others are satiric and amusing; for example:

On Marcus the Physician
Yesterday Dr. Marcus went to see a statue of Zeus.
Though Zeus,
*   and though marble,*
We're burying the statue today.

On Envious Diophon

Diophon was crucified:
But seeing beside him another on a loftier cross,
He died of envy.

Mark Twain makes great fun of bad poetry about death in *Adventures of Huckleberry Finn*. He is thought to have been inspired by Julia Moore, "The Sweet Singer of Michigan," who never lost an opportunity to write about the dead and the bereaved. Granted that she wrote in dead seriousness, her poetry can now be read only as amusing, or odd, verse. One of her major works concerned a little girl named Libbie:

One morning in April, a short time ago,
    Libbie was alive and gay;
Her savior called her, she had to go,
    Ere the close of that pleasant day,
While eating dinner, this dear little child
    Was choked on a piece of beef.
Doctors came, tried their skill awhile,
    But none could give relief.

A contemporary of Julia Moore, Howard Heber Clark, who tilled the same poetic field, may have helped to kill obituary verse with this tribute to little Willie:

Willie had a purple monkey climbing on a yellow stick,
And when he sucked the paint all off it made him deathly sick,
And in his latest hours he clasped that monkey in his hand,
And bade good-bye to earth and went into a better land.

Oh! no more he'll shoot his sister with his little wooden gun;
And no more he'll twist the pussy's tail and make her yowl, for fun.
The pussy's tail now stands out straight; the gun is laid aside;
The monkey doesn't jump around since little Willie died.[3]

Although Clark's little Willie was presumably not meant for our laughter, a series of poems about another little Willie (sometimes called little Billy) deliberately provoked laughter. Harry Graham, an English soldier in the Coldstream Guard who wrote under the penname Col. D. Streamer, produced an enduring and much-quoted masterpiece of 1902 with his *Ruthless Rhymes for Heartless Homes* with poems like these:

Billy, in one of his nice, new sashes,
Fell in the fire and was burned to ashes.
Now, although the room grows chilly,
I haven't the heart to poke poor Billy.

Making toast at the fireside,
Nurse fell in the grate and died;

And what makes it ten times worse,
All the toast was burnt with nurse.

Father heard his children scream,
So he threw them in the stream,
Saying, as he drowned the third,
"Children should be seen, not heard."

So popular were these sadistic poems that papers printed new catastrophes by imitators, most—but not all—about Little Willie and his latest nastiness, and the form of poetry became known as "Little Willie" poems.[4] A few of the most popular imitations were these:

Willie poisoned Auntie's tea.
Auntie died in agony.
Uncle came and looked quite vexed.
"Really, Will," he said, "what next?"

Dr. Jones fell in the well,
And died without a moan.
He should have tended to the sick
And left the well alone.

Little Willie, mean as hell,
Drowned his sister in the well.
Mother said, while drawing water,
"Gee, it's hard to raise a daughter."

Poetry for Sophisticated Readers

Moving from the ridiculous to the sublime, well-read, sophisticated young adults are ready to read and enjoy the same poetry that educated adults enjoy, but a few guiding principles might help teachers and librarians smooth the path to what they consider appropriate appreciation of the best poetry.

1. Young adults, who haven't been around as long as adults and therefore haven't had the time to pick up as much background information, will be more likely to understand the allusions of contemporary poets than those of historical poets. We are not recommending that anyone try to limit the poetry that young adults are exposed to, but we do think that they should first be offered the works of such modern poets as the following:

Maya Angelou	Donald Hall
James Dickey	Ted Hughes
Nikki Giovanni	Randall Jarrell

Donald Justice	Marge Piercey
X. J. Kennedy	Theodore Roethke
Ted Koozer	Anne Sexton
Maxine Kumin	Karl Shapiro
Denise Levertov	William Stafford
Eve Merriam	May Swenson
Joyce Carol Oates	Robert Penn Warren
Linda Pastan	Paul Zimmer

2. The power of literature is that it helps people transcend the circumstances that they happened to be born into, and so we highly recommend that students be offered poetry representing cultures and times different from their own. But adults who work with young readers should realize that they will probably need to make a conscious effort to help even bright and sophisticated students transcend cultural barriers. Reading independently, young adults will be better able to relate to poets who are presenting their own cultures. For example, an American teenager will be better able to picture the Boston that Anne Sexton wrote about in "The Wedding Night" and the allusions both to Walt Whitman and to American life-styles that Allen Ginsberg wrote about in "A Supermarket in California" than will an Australian or British teenager. Likewise, an American Indian teenager might be more ready to appreciate poetic renditions of ceremonial chants than will be a child from white, middle-class suburbia. And the minority child who has grown up being forced to think about racial differences is in a better position than other readers to relate to Imamu Amiri Baraka's (LeRoi Jones) "Poem for Half White College Students" and Nikki Giovanni's "Ego Tripping." Part of the role of the teacher is to help young people feel comfortable as they read poetry that takes them beyond their own circles of experience.

3. It helps to ease students into literary criticism through a biographical approach. Successful high school students are accustomed to reading biographies, but they probably haven't had much experience with literary criticism. Fortunately, most biographies of poets—whether they are book length, as is Neil Baldwin's *To All Gentleness, William Carlos Williams: The Doctor Poet;* chapter length, as in Jean Gould's *American Women Poets: Pioneers of Modern Poetry;* or only a few paragraphs, as in Paul Janeczko's *Poetspeak*—include substantial doses of *explication de texte* that can serve as an introduction to literary criticism.

4. Since prose is much more like everyday language than poetry, young people usually find it easier to read. Adults can help students bridge

this gap by bringing to their attention poetry written by authors whose prose works they already feel comfortable with. For example, someone who has read Alice Walker's *The Color Purple* will probably be ready to appreciate the poems in her *Good Night Willie Lee, I'll See You in the Morning*. In a similar way, Ray Bradbury's science fiction fans may want to read his fifty-plus poems in *When Elephants Last in the Dooryard Bloomed,* and students who have read Maya Angelou's autobiographical *I Know Why the Caged Bird Sings, Singin' and Swingin' and Gettin' Merry Like Christmas,* and *The Heart of a Woman* will probably be interested in her poetry. And young readers who liked Cynthia Rylant's *A Kindness, Missing May,* or *A Couple of Kooks: And Other Stories About Love* will probably enjoy her *Soda Jerk*, in which a boy working at Maxwell's soda fountain shares his observations through poetry and her autobiographical poems in *Waiting to Waltz: A Childhood.*

The Writing and Reading Connection

Today hundreds of small poetry magazines are published in the United States, and many of these include poems written by high school and college students. A class assignment that we have given for several years is to ask our college students to collect examples they like of ten different kinds of poems. One of the categories is an original, unpublished poem written by either the student or a roommate, friend, or family member. No student has ever complained about not being able to find a friendly poet willing to share.

Poets are looking for audiences. After a poetry reading on our campus by a nationally known poet, a man in the audience stood up to complain that he had been told by the editor of the local newspaper, who kept rejecting his poems, that there were too many people writing poems today. The poet looked thoughtful for a moment and then responded, "No, there just aren't enough people reading poems."

Poetry lovers all over are working to change this state of affairs, and among these poetry lovers are librarians who sponsor writing groups (see Focus Box 9.2) and subscribe to and display both large and small poetry magazines as well as publications from neighboring schools and poetry anthologies from national presses. Such librarians help share the good news that poetry-loving adults, who are eager to recruit young readers as poetry lovers, make an extra effort to design books that are particularly inviting because of their spaciousness and high-quality design and layout. In addition, these librarians serve as a support and confidence builder for teachers who themselves have not had good experiences with poetry and so are hesitant to venture beyond whatever comes in their prescribed textbooks.

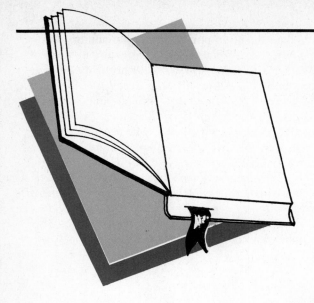

Books to Help Students Write Poetry

poetry that begins with making lists. A thirty-minute audiocassette comes with the book that includes 200 examples of list poems.

50 Contemporary Poets: The Creative Process, edited by Alberta T. Turner. David McKay, 1977. Turner asked many poets to talk out in print the creative process of one of their poems. Among the poets are Linda Pastan, Donald Justice, Nancy Willard, Norman Dubie, Robert Francis, and Maxine Kumin.

A Fire in My Hands: A Book of Poems by Gary Soto. Scholastic, 1991. Soto's poems are about simple, everyday events. Each of the poems is accompanied by an explanatory comment, and his assumption is that his readers will also be interested in writing poems: "Poems should feed into other poems—a needle passing a stitch through cloth."

Gonna Bake Me a Rainbow Poem: A Student Guide to Writing Poetry by Peter Sears. Scholastic, 1990. The poems used for illustrating the points made in this entertaining guidebook came from winners in the Scholastic Writing Awards program.

The List Poem: A Guide to Teaching and Writing Catalog Verse by Larry Fagin. Teachers and Writers Collaborative, 1991. Fagin explains the concept and the history of creating

Listening to the Bells: Learning to Read Poetry by Writing Poetry by Florence Grossman. Boynton/Cook, 1991. Aimed at middle school kids, Grossman explores honesty in reading and writing poetry.

The Place My Words Are Looking For, edited by Paul Janeczko. Bradbury, 1990. Thirty-nine American poets talk about what they think poetry is and how to get started writing it. They use their own poems to illustrate the pleasures of expressing thoughts and feelings through words.

Poem-Making: Ways to Begin Writing Poetry by Myra Cohn Livingston. Harper-Collins, 1991. Written for junior high students, Livingston's book could be used by teachers of any age student to get ideas and examples of voice, sound, rhythm, figurative language, and special forms of poetry.

Poetspeak: In Their Work, About Their Work, edited by Paul Janeczko. Bradbury, 1983. Over sixty poets contributed notes about the writing of poetry or about why and how they wrote the particular poem published in this collection.

Sleeping on the Wing: An Anthology of Modern Poetry with Essays on Reading and Writing   by Kenneth Koch and Kate Farrell. Random House, 1991. The philosophy of this book is expressed in the statement, "A logical place to start reading poetry is with modern poetry—since that is the poetry of our own time. It is also a good place for people who are writing now to find inspiration for their own poems."

Teaching Poetry Writing to Adolescents   by Joseph I. Tsujimoto. National Council of Teachers of English, 1988. Excellent examples of stu-dent poetry are included in this book about getting kids to write better poetry and become better readers of poetry.

Wishes, Lies, and Dreams: Teaching Children to Write Poetry,   Second Edition, by Kenneth Koch. Chelsea House, 1980. In this book, and in *Rose, Where Did You Get That Red?* (Random House, 1974), Koch presents poetry ideas and patterns along with samples of poems written by students in the New York Public Schools, where Koch has been a poet in residence.

 ## SHORT STORIES

Short stories fit into today's penchant for hurry-up ideas, condensations, and instant gratification. But a short story is more than a *Readers' Digest* version of a novel, because from the beginning it is planned to fit into less space. Short stories are uniquely appropriate to young readers for the following reasons:

1. Short stories have a limited number of characters.
2. Their plots are usually straightforward.
3. The development is most often direct and to the point.
4. In a classroom, students can read fifteen short stories in the time it takes to read one or two novels. Through reading the larger number of short stories, they can meet a greater variety of viewpoints and representatives of different ethnic groups and cultures.
5. The best of modern American authors have written short stories, which means that students can experience high-quality writing in pieces that are short enough for comfortable reading.

Because of these advantages, short stories have always had a place in high school English classes. (See Chapter Eleven for a discussion.) The collections we will talk about here are those being prepared not as textbooks but as free-choice reading for teenagers. Chris Crutcher's *Athletic Shorts* has an especially attractive and marketable book jacket—a gorgeously painted pair of boxer shorts with the brand name tag reading "6 Short Stories." Alice Bach and J. Cheryl Exum's *Miriam's Well: Stories About Women in the Bible* imaginatively fills the need felt by lots of Bible readers to hear from such women as Sarah, Miriam, Leah, Rachel, the wife of Job, the wife of Lot, and even Delilah. Gary Soto's *Baseball in April: And Other Stories* brings accounts of young Hispanics to a wide reading audience, and Joyce Carol Thomas' *A Gathering of Flowers: Stories About Being Young in America* brings together stories from several unique groups within the United States. Lori M. Carlson and Cynthia L. Ventura edited *Where Angels Glide at Dawn: New Stories from Latin America*, which is designed to bring teenagers the same kind of pleasure and knowledge that American adults have discovered over the last twenty years as they have begun reading the diverse literature of Latin America.

Don Gallo, as much as anyone, deserves credit for promoting the writing of short stories by some of today's best young adult authors. He invited such well-known YA authors as Sue Ellen Bridgers, Richard Peck, Bette Greene, Robert Lipsyte, Kevin Major, Ouida Sebestyen, and Rosa Guy to contribute unpublished short stories to a collection that Delacorte published in 1984 under the title of *Sixteen*. The nastiest and funniest story is Richard Peck's "Priscilla and the Wimps." Almost equally memorable are Norma Fox Mazer's "I, Hungry Hannah Cassandra Glen," Robert Cormier's "In the Heat," and M. E. Kerr's "Do You Want My Opinion?" Later volumes, entitled *Visions* and *Connections*, contain stories that are sometimes funny, sometimes macabre, sometimes sad, but almost always surprising and effective. Many of the stories deserve to be read aloud and/or talked about.

Gallo had a good idea in asking those authors for short stories, because YA novels and short stories share many characteristics. In fact, thirty years ago many of the stories now published as YA novels would have appeared in magazines as long short stories. M. E. Kerr began her career writing short stories about teenagers for *Compact* and *Ladies Home Journal*, and at least two of the other contributors to Gallo's collections had already published their own collections of short stories. Norma Fox Mazer's 1976 *Dear Bill, Remember Me: And Other Stories* is on the Honor List (see Chapter One), and her 1982 *Summer Girls, Love Boys* was almost as popular. Robert Cormier has published dozens of short stories, and in 1980 he published *Eight Plus One*, an anthology of his stories judged most appealing to the young adults who like his novels. He added background information about how each story developed.

At a session on "The Resurgence of the Short Story" at the 1987 National Council of Teachers of English convention, teacher Bob Seney from Houston, Texas, recommended more than two dozen collections of short stories and showed how they represented realistic fiction, science fiction, fantasy, humor, animal stories, folklore, and myth. Students who are hung up on a particular kind of book can usually be enticed to try at least a short story in another genre. And even within the same genre, they can be encouraged to select more challenging books. For example, he recommended Ellen Conford's *If This Is Love, I'll Take Spaghetti* and Barbara Girion's *A Very Brief Season* as good transitions from formula romances. Although he advised teachers not to overanalyze short stories, he suggested using them for reading aloud in class to introduce a topic for discussion or writing, to illustrate a point, or to fill out a thematic unit.

Short stories are also good for readers' theater and dramatization, and they can be used to give students enough experience with literary concepts, so that they can learn the meanings of literary terms from actual experience rather than from memorizing definitions.

Successful collections of short stories resemble successful collections of poetry in that the design and format of the book are important in attracting readers. Also helpful are clear-cut titles when the most important thing about a book is its subject (e.g., *James Herriot's Dog Stories; Roger Caras' Treasury of Great Cat Stories;* Bruce Coville's *Herds of Thunder, Manes of Gold: A Collection of Horse Stories and Poems;* and Jane Yolen and Martin H. Greenberg's *Vampires: A Collection of Original Stories*). A book whose appeal is less specific needs an intriguing title and a theme that will hold the collection together. But even with a unifying theme, there needs to be balance, so that the stories aren't all the same. Peter Sieruta's *Heartbeats* was praised by so many reviewers that it is included on the 1989 Honor List (see Chapter One). Nevertheless, the stories are about characters so much the same that they tend to run together in readers' minds. A *School Library Journal* reviewer praised Isaac Asimov's *Young Monsters* for avoiding this problem:

> The editors have done a masterful job of arranging the stories to alleviate tension. For example, the grisly "Disturb Not My Slumbering Fair" by Chelsea Quinn Yarbro, which features Diedre, a zombie who feasts on the dead ("It would be so good to sip the marrow from his bones, to nibble the butter-soft convolutions of his brain") is followed by Richard Parker's "The Wheelbarrow Boy," a humorous study of a teacher who changes an unruly student into a wheelbarrow—and then can't change him back.[5]

Of course, collectors of other people's stories have more flexibility than writers who use only their own stories, but Cynthia Rylant's *A Couple of Kooks: And Other Stories About Love*, Martha Brooks's *Paradise Cafe and Other Stories*, and Nancy White Carlstrom's *Light: Stories of a Small Kindness* have stories different enough that readers won't get confused or bored.

Prepackaged collections of stories are convenient, but you may also wish to collect your own. Useful reference tools for finding publication information are the *Chicorel Index to Short Stories in Anthologies and Collections*, which includes information on publications up until 1977, and the *Short Story Index*, published at frequent intervals by the H. W. Wilson Company. It includes information on magazine publications from 1953 to the present.

In conclusion, short stories are as varied in style and subject matter as are novels, and because of their brevity they are especially appealing to young readers. We are fortunate that today's publishers have recognized the appeal of short stories to teenagers and are marketing collections for independent reading as well as for class use.

◼ *DRAMA*

Most of the plays currently produced on high school stages had their beginnings on Broadway several decades ago and were brought into the schools within a few years after their New York successes (e.g., Moss Hart and George S. Kaufman's 1936 *You Can't Take It with You*, Thornton Wilder's 1938 *Our Town*, Joseph Kesselring's 1941 *Arsenic and Old Lace*, Rodgers and Hammerstein's 1943 *Oklahoma!*, and Jay Thompson et al.'s 1959 *Once Upon a Mattress*). These plays are still being produced because as one critic observed, the seven words you can't say on the radio have now become the seven words you must say on Broadway. Lowell Swortzell agreed that today's Broadway scripts "scarcely can be made required reading for high school students." He explains:

> ◼ David Mamet's *American Buffalo* (called by the *New York Times* the best American play of the decade) and his Pulitzer Prize winning *Glengarry Glen Ross* together present the moral corruption of contemporary life in what one critic described as a "violent vision of the dog-eat-dog jungle of urban American capitalism." Mamet is the master of demythologizing the American dream of success through characters doomed by self-hatred and paranoia who sputter the stage's most nervous and scatological language. Sam Shephard is another Pulitzer Prize winner whose *Fool for Love* deals with a possible incestuous love affair between a half brother and half sister who literally bounce off the walls in a violent physical struggle for power over one another. Harvey Fierstein's 1983 Tony Award winning *Torch Song Trilogy* depicts a drag queen, the world of gay bars, and the complexity of homosexual relationships.[6]

Not all Broadway plays are this grim (see Focus Box 9.3), and Swortzell did recommend some recent plays for high school reading, including August Wilson's *Fences*, about the loss of dreams by a black family in the 1950s, and Neil Simon's trilogy: *Brighton Beach Memoirs*, *Biloxi Blues*, and *Broadway Bound*. He also suggested that commercial success doesn't necessarily correlate with a good reading experience. Three plays that had short runs are still good for reading: Woody Allen's autobiographical *The Floating Lightbulb*; William Gibson's *Monday After the Miracle*, a continuation of the story of Annie Sullivan and Helen Keller; and Ted Talley's *Terry Nova*, about British explorer Captain Robert Scott's ill-fated exploration of the South Pole (all available from the Drama Book Shop, Inc.; 723 Seventh Avenue; New York, NY 10019).

On the good-news side of this story is the fact that within the last five to ten years a significant cadre of plays written specifically for young adult audiences has been developing. In a previous edition of this textbook, we said that one of the reasons there weren't many plays written for teenagers was that they

ROBERT CORMIER
on Telling Movies

A group of English teachers at a recent conference were startled when I told them that movies have had as great an influence on my writing as all the books I have read. They were startled because I had just finished telling them that I read incessantly and voraciously, and visit a library almost every day of my life. Yet I paid homage to the movies and, not so incidentally, to my mother.

As a young wife and mother of three children—she would eventually give birth to eight children—my mother loved to read, but she also loved movies with a passion. Then a crisis occurred in her life, details of which have no place here. The result was a promise that she would never go to the movies again. She is now ninety years old and has kept that promise with rare exceptions.

My mother gave up movies at the threshold of that golden age—the thirties and forties when wonderful stories flashed on the screens of darkened theaters and stars like Bette Davis and Humphrey Bogart and James Cagney and Joan Crawford were as familiar to us as members of our families, yet utterly unreachable. This was the era of the double feature in movie palaces with plush seats and chandeliers and velvet curtains that rose and fell with a kind of majesty.

What stories those movies told! Special effects were crude, and technicolor was reserved for spectacles. But the stories—romantic, comic, often tragic, sometimes nonsensical—held us in their thrall, and we'd emerge late in the afternoon dazzled, not only by the sunshine but by the glow of the movies we'd just seen.

At home, I would tell my mother what I had seen at the theater that day. I remember following her from room to room, describing each scene, *acting out* each scene, supplying dialogue and description as she dusted the furniture, washed the dishes, swept the floor, or mended socks.

I did all of this unselfconsciously, barely aware that I was recreating entire movies, from opening sequences to dramatic climaxes. All the while she listened raptly, reacting visibly, *ohhing* and *ahhing*, tears sometimes glistening in her eyes.

What an education that was for me although I did not know it at the time.

The books I read and loved in those days—from Thomas Wolfe's gargantuan efforts to Hemingway's deceptively simple prose—fed my hunger to be a writer. But recreating those movies for my mother taught me vital lessons in plotting and story structure, narration and pacing, and dialogue.

If I am successful today as a storyteller (and I regard myself as a storyteller above all else), I owe much of it to the movies—and to my mother.

Robert Cormier's books include *We All Fall Down*, Delacorte, 1991; *I Have Words to Spend*, Delacorte, 1991; *Fade*, Delacorte, 1988; and *The Chocolate War*, Pantheon, 1974.

A Few Excellent Paperback Anthologies of Plays for Class Use

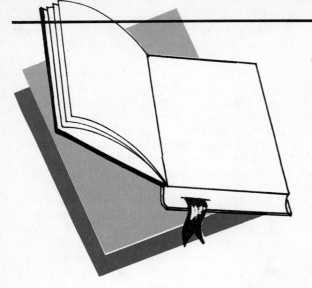

The Bedford Introduction to Drama, edited by Lee A Jacobs. Gedford Press, 1989. This extraordinary college drama anthology includes thirty-one plays, ranging from Aristophanes' *Lysistrata* to Henrik Ibsen's *Hedda Gabler*, Bertolt Brecht's *Mother Courage* and Athol Fugard's *"Master Harold" . . . And the Boys*; in addition, it has valuable material on history and criticism for teachers' use.

Eight Great Comedies, edited by Sylvan Barnet et al. Mentor/NAL, 1958. Included are classics like Aristophanes' *Clouds*, Shakespeare's *Twelfth Night*, and Gay's *The Beggar's Opera*.

Eight Great Tragedies, edited by Sylvan Barnet et al., Mentor/NAL, 1957. Among the classics are Sophocles' *Oedipus the King*, Shakespeare's *King Lear*, and O'Neill's *Desire Under the Elms.*

Famous American Plays of the 1920s, edited by Kenneth Macgowan. Dell, 1959. Six plays include Philip Barry's *Holiday* and Elmer Rice's *Street Scene.*

Famous American Plays of the 1930s, edited by Harold Clurman. Dell, 1959. Five plays include John Steinbeck's *Of Mice and Men* and Clifford Odets' *Awake and Sing.*

Famous American Plays of the 1940s, edited by Henry Hewes. Dell, 1967. Five plays include Maxwell Anderson's *Lost in the Stars* and Arthur Miller's *All My Sons.*

Famous American Plays of the 1950s, edited by Lee Strasberg. Dell, 1967. Included are Tennessee Williams' *Camino Real* and Edward Albee's *The Zoo Story.*

Famous American Plays of the 1960s, edited by Harold Clurman. Dell, 1972. Included are Joseph Heller's *We Bombed in New Haven* and Robert Lowell's *Benito Cereno.*

Famous American Plays of the 1970s, edited by Ted Hoffman. Dell, 1981. Six plays include Sam Shepard's *Buried Child* and David Rabe's *The Basic Training of Pavlo Hummel.*

Famous American Plays of the 1980s, edited by Robert Marx. Dell, 1991. Five plays include Sam Shepard's *Fool for Love* and August Wilson's *Ma Rainey's Black Bottom.*

Greek Drama, edited by Moses Hadas. Bantam, 1965. Nine classic plays include Sophocles' *Antigone* and Euripedes' *Medea.*

Plays By and About Women by Victoria Sullivan and James Hatch. Vintage, 1973. Eight plays include Clare Boothe's *The Women,* Doris Lessing's *Play with a Tiger,* and Alice Childress' *Wine in the Wilderness.*

Plays from the Contemporary American Theatre, edited by Brooks McNamara. Mentor/NAL, 1988. Eight plays include August Wilson's *Ma Rainey's Black Bottom,* Benth Henley's *Crimes of the Heart,* and David Rabe's *Streamers.*

Stages of Drama: Classical to Contemporary Masterpieces of the Theatre, Second Edition. St. Martin's Press, 1991. Although planned for college classes, high school teachers will find much that they can use in addition to the thirty-three plays that range from Euripedes' *The Bacchae* to Henrik Ibsen's *A Doll's House,* Bertolt Brecht's *Life of Galileo,* and Vaclav Havel's *Temptation.*

---

weren't the ones buying tickets to Broadway plays or flying to London on theater tours; hence, playwrights weren't motivated to write for teenagers.

It's still true that young people don't have the money to go on theater tours, but they make up a healthy portion of television and movie audiences, so that most of us have grown accustomed to seeing teenagers as the main characters on both big and little screens. The carryover effect is that talented writers are now writing serious plays designed for young people to either read or perform. But be warned that these are not the kinds of nondescript plays that were found in books for high school students a generation ago. In an *English Journal* article, "Toward a Young Adult Drama," Rick E. Amidon described them as "works which question fitting in, popularity, sex, drugs, making choices, taking chances." He labeled Jerome McDonough the "father of young adult drama" because of his dozen "powerful, practical-to-produce, and effective plays for the young adult stage." His plays differ from those typically produced at high schools in that they are shorter (fifty to seventy minutes long), they deal with topics dear to the hearts of teenagers, most of the casts are flexible, so the plays can be adapted to how many actors are available, and they have contemporary settings. One of his plays, *Faugh* (pronounced "Fawg"), gets its name from the *F*ine *A*rts *U*nder-*G*raduate *H*ousing. As described by Amidon, the residents of F.A.U.G.H. are

> a mismatched group of teens and former teens: Nikky has been a student for nine years and still has no intentions of ordering graduation invitations; Herbert believes his computer has fallen in love with him because love notes keep appearing on his monitor; and a menagerie of others provide the type of complex, yet comic educational environment young adults (and not so young adults) praised in such films as *The Big Chill, The Breakfast Club,* and *Pretty in Pink.*[7]

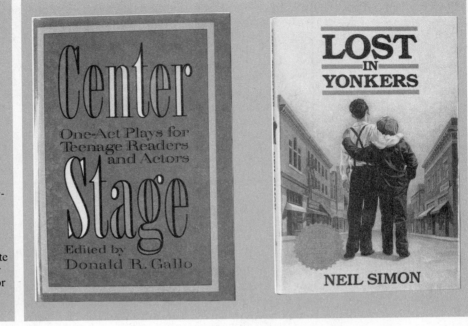

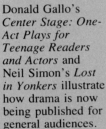

Donald Gallo's *Center Stage: One-Act Plays for Teenage Readers and Actors* and Neil Simon's *Lost in Yonkers* illustrate how drama is now being published for general audiences.

Another McDonough play, *Juvie*, is about young suspects brought to a juvenile detention center and acting out their crime so that the audience sees both their aggression and their guilt and remorse. McDonough has also written *Addict*, *Limbo*, *Plots*, and *Stages*.

Hindi Brooks, who has been a writer for television's *Fame* and *Eight is Enough*, has written a play entitled *Wising Up!* set in a group home for teenagers. The characters in another of his plays, *Making It!*, attend a performing arts high school, where the idea of "making it" as a performer is an analogy for making it in the world. Amidon concluded about McDonough and Brooks that, "Their passion to communicate through these young adult plays, recording the conflicts with drugs, crime, family, relationships, school, race, and peer-pressure, and consciously to offer promise and reconciliation, rather than continual chaos, makes these plays significant."[8] (McDonough's and Brooks's plays are available from I. E. Clark in Schulenberg, Texas.)

In an *English Journal* article, Anthony L. Manna complained that for English teachers and librarians, drama is the "hidden genre." He had examined several recent best-of-the-year lists compiled by such publications as *Booklist*, *School Library Journal*, and the *New York Times Book Review* and found only one play listed, Paul Zindel's *Let Me Hear You Whisper*. To prove that the exclusion wasn't because good drama isn't being written, he went on to recommend more than a dozen contemporary plays that would be excellent for reading in either junior or senior high school classrooms.[9]

In thinking about Manna's point and trying to figure out why drama has been the "hidden genre" for young adults, we came up with the following reasons:

1. Students often have trouble visualizing what they'd see if the play were being performed. Plays are meant to be seen, not read silently or even aloud in class. Settings need to be visualized. Stage directions are often puzzling and distracting.

2. Characters are revealed through dialogue. It's the way students learn about the feelings and personalities of the characters. That slows down the reading and makes drama into drudgery for many students. The cast of characters prior to the opening of the text requires kids to look back and forth, first to the text, then to the dramatis personae, and finally back to the text to find out who's talking.

3. Plays require active reading, giving the characters voices and personalities. Unlike fiction or narrative poems, there's no narrator to give opinions or insights or a point of view.

4. Kids aren't used to reading plays aloud, and they often sound silly (usually deliberately so) when they're assigned parts. They need to read the entire play first to determine motivations and the play's mood or point. The best way to get any class ready to do a play would be to see it first, preferably done by a first-rate cast. That's unlikely, though teachers near a big city with a repertory might just be lucky one year. If not that, most high schools have drama clubs or classes eager to show off before other students. They might illustrate an act or two of a play the class will read. And there are always videotapes of plays that have been filmed. Leonard Maltin's *TV Movies and Video Guide* is published yearly by Signet/New American Library, and it indicates after plot summaries whether the film is available in video.

5. It's difficult to keep kids awake when only a few kids are reading in class and no one is really listening, not even those reading parts. How can we do plays and keep our kids' interest—or ours, for that matter?

These complications mean that without help and encouragement from their teachers, few teenagers will read drama. The criteria for choosing plays for reading aloud are different from those for performing. When we were editing the *English Journal*, we invited teachers to tell us about plays they had successfully used for classroom reading. (See "Our Readers Write," October, 1984). Four out of the twenty-four teachers who responded suggested Reginald Rose's three-act television play *Twelve Angry Men*. It is the story of a jury making a decision on the future of a nineteen-year-old boy charged with murdering his father. Three out of the four teachers commented to the effect that they and their students affectionately called the play "Twelve Angry People," since girls as well as boys were assigned parts. The following excerpts taken from the teachers' descriptions not only show why this particular play is successful in class but also can serve as guides when predicting the potential of other scripts for reading either in classes or in interest groups sponsored by libraries or drama departments.

- It calls for twelve continual parts, enough to satisfy all students who like to read aloud.
- It teaches practical lessons of value to students' lives.
- It may serve as a springboard for research and further discussion on how the judicial system works.
- It creates a forum for students to prove the psychology of group dynamics and peer behavior.
- It sparks student excitement from the beginning and sustains it throughout.
- It can be read in two and a half class sessions.
- The "business" is minimal and can be easily carried out as students read from scripts.
- Pertinent questions can be asked when the jury recesses after Acts I and II.
- The setting is a hot, stuffy jury room—just like our classroom at the end of the year.
- Students are attracted to the realism, and they can relate to a motherless slum youth of nineteen.
- The excellent characterization allows students to discover a kaleidoscope of lifelike personalities.

Some of the other suggestions and the teachers' reasons follow, supplemented by suggestions from the December 1990 *English Journal* "Booksearch" column that was devoted to "Drama of the '80s":

Robert Bolt's *A Man for All Seasons*. Baker (also French), 1960. It's good for its portrayal of one of the most famous periods of English history and for its exploration of a hero. Interesting comparisons can be drawn to works treating heroes of noble birth, as in *Antigone* and *Hamlet,* and heroes of ordinary birth, as in *Death of a Salesman* and *The Stranger*.

Lucille Fletcher's *Sorry, Wrong Number* in *Fifteen American One-Act Plays*, edited by Paul Kozelka. Pocket Books, 1971. Since it's a radio play written to be heard and not seen, it is ideal for reading aloud.

Athol Fugard's *"Master Harold"* . . . *and the Boys*. Penguin, 1982. This powerful one-act play asks students to examine the psychological effects of racism on whites.

William Gibson's *The Miracle Worker*. Baker (also French), 1951. Students love the poignancy of the story of Helen Keller and Annie Sullivan, but it is also a good illustration of flashbacks, foreshadowing, symbolism, and dramatic license when compared to such biographies as Nella Braddy's *Annie Sullivan Macy* and Helen Keller's *The Story of My Life*.

A. R. Gurney, Jr.'s *What I Did Last Summer*. Dramatists, 1983. As Anna tells fourteen-year-old Charlie in this play about the last summer of World War II, "All choices are important. They tell you who you are."

Tim Kelly's *Les Misérables*. Dramatists, 1987. With eleventh and twelfth graders, the boys like action, the girls like romance, and they all like music. So here's a play that answers everyone's needs.

Jerome Lawrence and Robert E. Lee's *Inherit the Wind*. Dramatists, 1955. Based on the Scopes trial, this play is especially interesting in relation to current controversies over creationism versus evolution. The lines are easy to read aloud, and there is a good balance between sharp wit and high drama.

Mark Medoff's *Children of a Lesser God*. Dramatists, 1980. Especially since the success of the movie, students appreciate this Tony Award-winning play about a deaf young woman and her relationship with a hearing teacher.

John Patrick's *The Teahouse of the August Moon*. Dramatists, 1953. The way it lightheartedly pokes fun at American customs and values is refreshing.

Rod Serling's *A Storm in Summer* in *Great Television Plays, Vol. 2,* edited by Ned E. Hoopes and Patricia Neale Gordon. Dell, 1975. Students like the way it relates an encounter between a ten-year-old Harlem boy and a bitter, sarcastic Jewish delicatessen owner in upstate New York.

Alfred Uhry's *Driving Miss Daisy*. Dramatists, 1988. The impressive film serves as a backdrop for reading this play that helps students learn what is involved in a lasting friendship.

Gore Vidal's *Visit to a Small Planet,* in *Visit to a Small Planet and Other Television Plays* by Gore Vidal. Little, Brown, 1956. Because this play was written for television, the action is easy to visualize and the stage directions simple enough to discuss as an important aspect of the drama itself.

Paul Zindel's *The Effect of Gamma Rays on Man-in-the-Moon Marigolds*. Dramatists, 1970. This moving story of the damaging forms that parent/child love can take brought Paul Zindel to the attention of the literary world.

Play scripts are sold through distributors, most of whom will happily send free catalogues to teachers who request them. A typical script price for a full-length play is $4.50, whereas a typical royalty charge is $40 for the initial production and $30 for each subsequent production. Teachers wanting scripts for in-class reading rather than for production should so note at the time of ordering so that no royalty is charged. If the play is to be produced, whether admission is charged or not, the producer should pay the fee when the scripts are ordered. A royalty contract will be mailed along with the scripts. Two of the largest distributors are Samuel French (7623 Sunset Blvd.; Hollywood, CA 90046) and Dramatists Play Service, Inc. (440 Park Avenue S.; New York, NY 10016). Anchorage Press (P.O. Box 8067; New Orleans, LA 70182) is recommended for children's and teenage drama, and Contemporary Drama Service (Box 7710-5; Colorado Springs, CO 80933) is good for spoofs and for television scripts.

Three guides are especially useful to teachers. *The Crown Guide to the World's Great Plays, from Ancient Greece to Modern Times*, Second Edition, edited by Joseph T. Shipley, has the most detailed plot summaries (e.g., the one for *Waiting for Godot* runs to slightly more than three lengthy pages). Theodore J. Shank's *A Digest of 500 Plays: Plot Outlines and Production Notes* has briefer summaries (e.g., *Godot* is about one-third of a page), but the book is excellent on production matters. The third edition of the National Council of Teachers of English *Guide to Play Selection* has even briefer summaries (*Godot* gets eight lines) but includes many more plays.

Books that are helpful in introducing students to performance with something less daunting than a whole play include *The Actor's Book of Contemporary Stage Monologues* edited by Nina Shengold, *100 Monologues: An Audition Sourcebook for New Dramatists* edited by Laura Harrington, *Scenes and Monologues from the New American Theatre* edited by Frank Pike and Thomas G. Dunn, and *Sometimes I Wake Up in the Middle of the Night*, monologues written by students of the Walden Theatre Conservatory.

Since 1985, teenage writers have competed with their own one-act plays. Wendy Lamb edits the winning plays which are published by Dell, e.g., *Hey Little Walter: And Other Prize-Winning Plays from the 1989 and 1990 Young Playwrights Festivals* and *Sparks in the Park and Other Prize-Winning Plays from the 1987 and 1988 Young Playwrights Festivals*.

HUMOR IN YOUNG ADULT LITERATURE

Rafael Sabatini began his first novel, *Scaramouche*, with a one-sentence characterization of his hero: "He was born with a gift of laughter and a sense that the world was mad." The ability to laugh at ourselves and the madness of the world is nature's gift to a perpetually beleaguered humanity. The need seems even more desperate today, although probably every previous generation could have made the same claim, so we laugh at almost everything and anything. At a time when taxes, death, and sex are serious matters indeed, they are also the staples of humor. We are pleased when we find something, anything, to laugh at. We are even more pleased when we discover someone who consistently makes us laugh. As Steve Allen reminds us:

Without laughter, life on our planet would be intolerable. So important is laughter to us that humanity highly rewards members of one of the most unusual professions on earth, those who make a living by inducing laughter in others. This is very strange if you stop to think of it; that otherwise sane and responsible citizens should devote their professional energies to causing others to make sharp, explosive barking-like exhalations.[10]

Given their enforced world of school and an ever-demanding society, young people need laughter every bit as much as adults, maybe even more so. What do young people find funny? Lance M. Gentile and Merna M. McMillen's article, "Humor and the Reading Program," offers a starting point. Their stages of children's and young adult's interest in humor, somewhat supplemented, are as follows:

- *Ages 10–11.* Literal humor, slapstick (e.g., "The Three Stooges"), laughing at accidents (banana-peel humor) and misbehavior, sometimes mildly lewd jokes (usually called "dirty jokes"), and grossness.
- *Ages 12–13.* Practical jokes, teasing, goofs, sarcasm, more lewd jokes, joke riddles, sick jokes, elephant jokes, grape jokes, tongue twisters, knock-knock jokes, moron jokes, TV blooper shows, and grossness piled upon grossness.
- *Ages 14–15.* More and more lewd jokes (some approaching a mature recognition of the humor inherent in sex); humor aimed at schools, parents, and adults in authority; "Mork and Mindy" and their ilk; and grossness piled upon even greater grossness. Young adults may still prefer their own humor to their parents' humor, but they are increasingly catching on to adult humor and may prefer it to their own.
- *Ages 16 and up.* More subtle humor, satire and parody now acceptable and maybe even preferable, witticisms (rather than last year's half-witticisms, which they now detest in their younger brothers and sisters). Adult humor is increasingly part of their repertoire, partly because they are anxious to appear sophisticated, partly because they *are* growing up.[11]

Despite what must seem obvious truth to good teachers and librarians—that a sense of humor is essential for survival of educators and students—some deadly serious people wonder if this (or any other time, presumably) is the time for levity. The answer is, of course, yes—this is the time (and so is any other time). And many young people may be surprised to find that they laugh at the same things their parents and grandparents laughed at in the movies (see Focus Box 9.4).

Ellen Conford apparently ran into one of those humorless individuals at a librarians' meeting. During a question–answer session, Conford was asked if there was any subject she felt she couldn't treat humorously. She answered, "Cancer and abortion. Other than those two, I can make jokes about almost anything." Another person, a man, asked about the nuclear holocaust, specifically what was Conford doing about it.

Time for the Giggles—It's Comedy Tonight

The Bank Dick (1940, 74 min., black and white; Dir: Eddie Cline; with W. C. Fields) A ne'er-do-well accidentally foils a bank robbery and is made a guard. Then the real robbers appear. Maybe Fields's best movie.

Bringing Up Baby (1938, 102 min., black and white; Dir: Howard Hawks; with Katharine Hepburn and Cary Grant) The epitome of screwball comedies. A wacky socialite captures a paleontologist with the help of a leopard.

The Court Jester (1956, 101 min., color; Dir: Norman Panama; with Danny Kaye and Glynis Johns) Our hero pretends to be a jester to save the royal baby. Almost no let-up of laughs or derring-do. One of the great comedies.

The General (1927, 74 min., black and white; Dir: Buster Keaton) Keaton's funniest film. A man anxious to enlist in the Confederate army is turned down to keep him at the switch of his railway engine. When Union forces come near, he becomes a hero. *Sherlock, Jr.* (1924, 45 min., black and white) is another Keaton film masterpiece. He plays a movie projectionist who walks into a screen and becomes part of the story.

Kind Hearts and Coronets (1949, 104 min., black and white; Dir: Robert Hamer; with Dennis Price and Alec Guinness) An impoverished young man related to titled wealth sets out to kill whoever in the family stands in his way to the title. The victims are all played by Guinness. Funny black comedy.

Modern Times (1936, 83 min., black and white; Dir: Charlie Chaplin) His last silent film was an attack on machines misused by greedy men and social ills of all sorts. Perhaps his funniest film, certainly one of his best.

A Night at the Opera (1935, 92 min., black and white; Dir: Sam Wood) The Marx brothers take on opera and everyone wins but the ever-present and ever-befuddled Margaret Dumont. *Duck Soup* (1933, 70 min., black and white; Dir: Leo McCarey) is their other satirical masterpiece.

The Pink Panther Strikes Again (1976, 103 min., color; Dir: Blake Edwards; with Peter Sellers and Herbert Lom) Inspector Clouseau's superior goes insane (all inadvertently caused by Clouseau) and sets out to conquer the world. The other funny Pink Panther film is *A Shot in the Dark* (1964).

Take the Money and Run (1969, 85 min., color; Dir: Woody Allen) Not Allen at his most subtle but at his funniest. He plays an incredibly inept bank robber, always on the run, always trying, always failing.

Way Out West (1937, 65 min., black and white; Dir: James W. Horne; with Stan Laurel and Oliver Hardy) The boys go west to deliver a mine deed. A gem, but their short films are funnier than most of their features. "Big Business" (1929) may be, as lots of us think, the funniest film ever made, with the boys trying to sell Christmas trees in July.

Young Frankenstein (1974, 105 min., color; Dir: Mel Brooks; with Gene Wilder and Peter Boyle) Brooks's affectionate spoof of *Frankenstein* and *Bride of Frankenstein* with a much stranger housekeeper, an even stranger monster, a weird servant, and two wild and strange women who love young Frankenstein. Funny and loving and even a bit scary once in awhile.

"Don't you think," he went on, "that it's your responsibility as a writer for young people to alert them about the dangers of the arms race?"

"No!" I said, horrified.

"But if their own authors don't tell them, who will?"

"Dan Rather," I said. "Peter Jennings. Tom Brokaw. Any kid with ears already knows about the possibility of being incinerated in three seconds. And they know they have no power to do anything to save themselves. You want me to scare them some more?

"Not me!" [12]

Conford added that there are already talented YA authors who can treat the world seriously, but there are all too few who can make young people laugh. She's right.

Maybe English teachers assume that life is too serious to be treated any other way in school. Certainly there's very little humor in literary anthologies. These anthologies, especially those used in secondary schools, imply that literature is too sacred for humor. That would have seemed odd to Mark Twain, who (an oversight?) has found his way into more American literature anthologies than any other author. Maybe the problem is that high school English teachers got their training in such oh-so-serious-literature classes that they don't know where to turn for humor.

Mass Media and Humor

Actually, humor is all around us—in advertisements, television, movies, and newspapers (see Focus Box 9.5). The comic strips might be one place to start looking. Jeff McNelly's "Shoe," Berke Breathed's "Outland," Gary Larson's "The Far Side," and Bill Watterson's "Calvin and Hobbes" are imaginative and

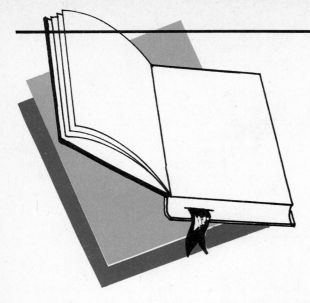

Folk Humor, Comics, Nonfiction, and Miscellaneous Humor

The Art of Hanna Barbera: Fifty Years of Creativity by Ted Sennett. Viking, 1989. Biographical chapters on Joe Barbera and Bill Hanna are followed by information and full-color reproductions of Tom and Jerry, the Flintstones, Yogi Bear, Scooby-Doo, Quick Draw McGraw, Huckleberry Hound, the Jetsons, and the Smurfs.

Bloom County Babylon: Five Years of Basic Naughtiness by Berke Breathed. Little, Brown, 1986. Bill the Cat, Opus (the penguin), Oliver Wendell Jones, Milo Bloom, and other weird people participate in the most inspired satire and sheer lunacy on today's comic pages.

Bugs Bunny: Fifty Years and Only One Grey Hare by Joe Adamson. Holt, 1990. Published in honor of Bugs Bunny's fiftieth-anniversary, this oversized and expensive coffee-table book is fun to browse.

Curses! Boiled Again! The Hottest Urban Legends Going by Jan Harold Brunvand. Norton, 1989. Along with *The Vanishing Hitchhiker: American Urban Legends and Their Meanings* (Norton, 1981) and *The Choking Dob-*erman: And Other "New" Urban Legends (Norton, 1984), this is a scholarly but very readable account of what anthropologists have been able to learn about some of the most popular of the urban legends.

Lake Wobegon Days by Garrison Keillor. Viking, 1985. In this book and in *Happy to Be Here* (Atheneum, 1982), Keillor presents the funny sketches and stories that made his National Public Radio "A Prairie Home Companion" so popular.

Scary Stories 3: More Tales to Chill Your Bones by Alvin Schwartz. Illustrations by Stephen Gammell. HarperCollins, 1991. Schwartz has done many folklore collections, but *Scary Stories to Tell in the Dark* (HarperCollins, 1981) and *More Scary Stories to Tell in the Dark* (HarperCollins, 1984) proved to be so popular that they are apparently being turned into a series.

Southern Fried Rat and Other Gruesome Tales by Daniel Cohen. Avon Flare, 1989. Cohen has popularized some of the same urban legends that appear in Brunvand's and Schwartz's more carefully documented collections.

The Stinky Cheese Man and Other Fairly Stupid Tales by Jon Scieszka, illustrated by Lane Smith. Viking, 1992. Although *School Library Journal* reviewed this for grades two to six, we found that even our college students loved these hilarious parodies of old folktales.

There Are Alligators in Our Sewers and Other American Credos by Paul Dickson and Joseph C. Goulden. Delacorte, 1983. Josh Billings' quote, "The trouble with most folks isn't so much their ignorance, as knowing so many things that ain't so," begins this collection of superstitions and common folk wisdom organized under forty different categories.

often satiric and extremely funny. If comics have to be justified, the insecure teacher could point out that both McNelly and Breathed have won Pulitzer prizes. Old-time radio, particularly the work of Paul Rhymer and "Vic and Sade," might be worth considering, especially since James Thurber thought Rhymer was a genius, but then so do Jean Shepherd and Ray Bradbury.

Newspaper columnists are another source of humor. Teenagers, along with their parents, check out the condition of the world by reading the letters written to Ann Landers and to her sister, Abigail Van Buren ("Dear Abby"). Some of them also read Erma Bombeck's, Andy Rooney's, and Art Buchwald's columns and books. They identify with the frustrations that these writers, especially Bombeck and Rooney, express about everyday events.

A relatively new genre in American humor is urban legends, or FOAF tales, because they are told by a *Friend Of A Friend*. These stories are parodies of weird and unusual news items; in fact, many of them find their way into newspapers as serious stories. And although they are filled with fascinating details that add to their credibility, exact names and addresses are never given. However, this does not stop most people from insisting that the stories really happened. Jan Harold Brunvand, a University of Utah folklorist and author of two of the most popular books—*The Vanishing Hitchhiker: American Urban Legends and Their Meaning* and *The Choking Doberman: And Other "New" Urban Legends*—explained that people keep asking him how he knows the stories that he collects didn't really happen. These questioners often claim that they have

access to some indisputable evidence of the truth of one. I usually reply, "If you know that one of them is true, then please get me the proof; I'd be delighted to have it." Frequently it is some classic automobile story floating around in oral tradition, like "The Killer in the Backseat" or "The Death Car," that people are absolutely sure "really happened."

So these people try very hard to remember who told them, and exactly when it was, and where they were living at the time that a fine sports car was advertised for sale by a wronged wife at an extraordinarily low price; or when someone accidentally was sold an experimental car with a carburetor that got 200 miles per gallon; or when a jealous husband filled an unfamiliar new car parked in his driveway with wet cement.[13]

Brunvand said that these people "always conclude eventually that they cannot unearth any firsthand information on the stories they thought were true or locate anyone else who can vouch for them." Instead they "have for verification not personal experience, nor even a friend's own experience, but only an unnamed, elusive, but somehow readily trusted anonymous individual, a friend of a friend."

Scholars who study the tales say that the reason we are so quick to believe them and pass them on to our friends is that they speak to fears we have, which is what Alvin Schwartz capitalized on in his *Scary Stories* collections. Some of the fears are the old-fashioned, cold-blooded-murder type; others focus on technology that we aren't sure we trust (e.g., cars, computers, and microwaves). Some of them center on our fears of new immigrants and customs we don't understand, or on how vulnerable we are and how dependent on big business. For example, Daniel Cohen starts his Avon Flare book *Southern Fried Rat and Other Gruesome Tales* with a story of Jim and Karen picking up a snack after a movie. The restaurant is so crowded that Jim wants to go someplace else, but Karen is so hungry that she suggests they get a carry-out order and eat in the car. Jim worries about dropping greasy crumbs on the upholstery of his car, but Karen is so hungry that she tears into the order. Pretty soon she slows down and remarks that it doesn't taste right, then she says it doesn't feel right either and asks Jim to turn on the light. To their horror, they discover that sticking out of the extra crispy coating is a three-inch tail. Karen had been eating a fried rat.

Karen went into shock. Jim felt pretty sick too, but he managed to drive to the hospital, where Karen had her stomach pumped. Karen's family threatened to sue. The fried chicken chain paid them a huge amount of money to keep quiet about what happened, so the case never got to court, and it was never written up in the papers. Of course, the chicken people deny that it ever happened.

In some ways FOAF tales are like the old folktales and nursery rhymes that were told to frighten children into good behavior (e.g., "Humpty Dumpty" warned against climbing on walls, "Little Red Riding Hood" warned them to be wary of strangers, "The Three Bears" told them not to enter houses uninvited, and "Hansel and Gretel" cautioned against wandering off alone into deep forests). The moral that could be tacked onto most of today's stories is something like, "If you were doing what you were supposed to be doing, this wouldn't have happened." For example, if you hadn't left your car unlocked, the killer wouldn't have hidden in the back seat; if the man hadn't been unfaithful to his wife, she wouldn't have sold his car so cheap; if the young couple hadn't been parking in a lonely lover's lane, the man with the hooked arm would never have tried to get into their car; and if Karen hadn't been gobbling her food, she would have noticed the rat tail.

No one likes to be preached at, but since the message in urban legends is hidden under the amusement and the irony, listeners don't recognize the stories as cautionary tales. Besides, there's something satisfying about seeing that these misfortunes are happening to someone else instead of to us. At one of the WHIM (Western Humor and Irony Membership) conferences held at ASU, Max Shulman explained that if readers are inspired by something he's written to say, "I know someone like that," they'll laugh. But if what he writes, makes them say, "Oh, no, that's me!" they won't laugh. The success of urban legends illustrates his point because most of us can easily see the fatal flaw, the little mistake, that someone in the story made. We know we're too smart for that, so we laugh.

Serious but Funny YA Novels

If you ask teenagers for examples of humor they have enjoyed, they are much more likely to give you the names of television shows, movies, or comedians than of young adult novels. Nevertheless, there's a fresh breeze blowing across the landscape, which Roger Sutton remarked on in the November 1990 *School Library Journal*. Under the heading "Hard Times at Sweet Valley," he showed how in *Friend Against Friend* (Sweet Valley High #69) a heavy-handed social consciousness was creeping in. He found this ironic because mainstream YA fiction is turning to lighter treatments of serious subjects. As an example, he compared how earnestly Sandra Scoppetone had to defend her 1974 *Trying Hard to Hear You* (a story about a girl discovering that her best friend and her boyfriend are gay) with how lightheartedly Ron Koertge could treat the subject of homosexuality in his 1988 *The Arizona Kid*. In the latter book, Billy spends the summer on an Arizona ranch and comes to terms with the fact that his uncle is gay. Sutton wrote:

> Laugh at a gay person? Or at divorce?—Brock Cole's *Celine* (1989), about two children of divorce, is funny; so is Bruce Brooks' *No Kidding* (1989), a novel about children of alcoholics. All three of these books also have moments of almost unbearable pain, none of it resolved by a simple matter of "adjustment."[14]

He concluded that although these books lack the dogged explanations of the problem novel, "they more than compensate with their respect for the reader's imagination and sense of humor."

A book that could be added to this list of serious but funny books is Robert Lipsyte's *The Chemo Kid*. Fred Bauer is just drifting along "like a Styrofoam burger box floating in the storm drains of life," but then he gets cancer.

Admittedly, there's not much humor in that, but when readers go to the hospital with Fred's girlfriend Mara, they get to meet fellow patient Vandal, who stomps onto the terrace, where poor Fred is trying to explain to Mara that he's probably going to lose his hair, that he'll probably get sores in his mouth, and turn either a puffed-up yellow or green. Just as he's beginning to suspect that he's some kind of a sadist because he's "enjoying the widening of her eyes, the quivering of her lips," Vandal arrives:

> He was wearing heavy black boots, black jeans, and a black leather motorcycle jacket without sleeves. He had a plastic chemo bag draped on each shoulder as if they were some kind of gang insignia. Tubes snaked out of the chemo bags into the needles in his forearms. "Weed?" He shook a cigarette out of a pack and held it out to Mara.
> "No, thanks." She frowned. "Should you be smoking?"
> "Should be smoking reefer."
> I said, "There's no smoking on this floor."
> "Whatsa matter, 'fraid you'll get cancer?" He laughed through his nose. "Frai-dee."

During this minor skirmish over whether or not smoking is allowed, Vandal taps his cigarette on the back of his hand and casually explains, "I call it C City. Folks are dyin' to get in, dyin' to get out."

Vandal, who's embarrassed when his family visits the hospital and calls him "Vincent," plays a key role in the story. He's the one who comes up with Fred's nickname of "The Chemo Kid," and he's the one who later on brings his buddies out to Fred's suburban community to help with Mara's environmental project. When Fred's old friends are embarrassed at Vandal's flip reference to "The Chemo Kid" as the "World's ugliest superhero," Fred lets it pass. "There are some things you just can't explain, like tumor humor. It's a location joke. You have to be there."

Other Funny YA Novels

Although critics do not place Paula Danziger's novels in the pantheon of YA fiction, Danziger is among the most popular writers for young teens. Her novels are, admittedly, loaded with puns and jokes and one-liners and visual humor, but they are far more than mere collections of laughs. *Can You Sue Your Parents for Malpractice?* and *The Divorce Express* remain favorites with junior high school students because they do not talk down to their readers and because they do not pretend that here are easy answers to any problems. Danziger's inability to develop characters, particularly adults, and her willingness to toss glib comments around as if they were profound may annoy adults, but her humor is exactly what her readers want.

More successful by far for a slightly older audience is T. Ernesto Bethancourt's *The Dog Days of Arthur Cane*. Reduced to the simple plot of a young man who irritates an African student and is thereby turned into a mongrel dog, the novel sounds simple-minded, but it is not. Arthur wakes up one morning, finds that he is a quite different self, and tries to resolve the immediate problems (and eventually must solve some long-range problems or die).

Thinking that a drink of water would help, I went back into the bathroom. I looked up at a sink that seemed ten feet high. I could see my glass up there, but no way to reach it. But being a good sized dog, I could get up on my hind legs and get my head into the sink. After falling down a few times, I got my front paws hooked over the edge of the sink and my hind feet braced. The only problem was that the water wasn't running, and I couldn't turn it on.

And later, still unsatisfied:

My thirst was worse now, if that was possible. And there was the john, with cool water in it. But I still couldn't bring myself to drink any.

And even later, even more unsatisfied:

I won't lie to you about what I ended up doing. By the way, that blue stuff doesn't taste bad at all. Kind of like raunchy Kool-Aid.

And all this in the first chapter.

M. E. Kerr is consistently funny, although her novels are essentially serious studies of young people caught up in emotional quandaries. Kerr looks wryly at her young characters, but she never lacks compassion for them or her readers. *Dinky Hocker Shoots Smack,* her first novel and the only one not told in first person, is filtered through the consciousness of fifteen-year-old library habituè Tucker Woolf, whose sketches remind his mother of a "depressing Bosch." In advertising for a home for his cat Nader (named after Ralph Nader), Tucker meets Dinky, whose mother suffers for the ills of the world and ignores Dinky; Dinky's cousin Natalia, who is emotionally troubled and talks in rhymes; and P. John Knight, whose left-wing father has made P. John become right wing with a vengeance. Kerr's humor in this book, as in later ones, does not arise from one-liners or obvious jokes but from the characters themselves. She drops references to Nader, Bosch, Dostoevsky, and the Bible, among others. She assumes young adults can think and feel and laugh.

Her best and funniest book is *If I Love You, Am I Trapped Forever?* Alan Bennett, the narrator, lives in upstate New York with a grandfather and a mother deserted by Alan's father years before. Alan describes himself early in the book as "The most popular boy at Cayuta High. Very handsome. Very cool.

Dynamite." His life and his love life with Leah are perfect in every way until Duncan Stein moves to town, and slowly Alan's life and world crumble. Whatever else Doomed (Alan's nickname for Duncan) is, he is atypical. No basketball, no school clubs, no going steady, nothing that makes him identifiable to Alan. But Doomed does gain notoriety with his underground newspaper, *Remote*, and creates a dating fad at Cayuta High—going steady is out and one-time-only dates become the in thing.

Alan's puzzlement is obvious and understandable. Doomed plays by no rules Alan knows, nor is Doomed interested in Alan's friendship. When Alan and Doomed walk together from homeroom to English class, they have a short and pointed conversation:

> We were studying Alfred Lord Tennyson's poem "In Memoriam" that week. The poem was a tribute to his friend, Arthur Hallan, who died suddenly of influenza when he was just twenty-two.
>
> I said something to Doomed then about trying to make friends with him, and then I said, "Well, I guess we'll never be known as Tennyson and Hallam, will we, Stein?"
>
> Stein said, "Croak and find out, why don't you?"
>
> How hostile can you get?

The funniest YA novels are two English imports. Sue Townsend's *The Secret Diary of Adrian Mole, Aged 13¾* and *The Growing Pains of Adrian Mole*. Both are about young Adrian, who tells his diary of the horrors of growing up in a family where the mother does not love the father, where no one (especially the BBC) fully appreciates the value of his sensitive writings, where his beloved Pandora does not long for his caresses as much as Adrian longs to caress her, and where things almost never go right and almost always go wrong.

Townsend understands Adrian and young people generally. Adrian often sounds naive, sometimes he sounds foolish, but he is never ridiculed, although he may look ridiculous, sometimes even in his own eyes. Adrian tells all—or what he thinks is all—in his diary, but he has almost no objectivity about his world, and often the readers can be far more objective about Adrian's life and world. Above all, Adrian is honest. He does not lie to himself or us, the readers of his diary. He may be misguided or dead wrong or hopelessly unaware of adult duplicities at times, but his honesty is fixed and admirable. Late in *The Secret Diary* Adrian's form (school class) is preparing for a trip to the British Museum:

> Wednesday, September 16th—Our form is going to the British Museum on Friday. Pandora and I are going to sit together on the coach. She is bringing her *Guardian* from home so that we can have some privacy.
>
> Thursday, September 17th—Had a lecture on the British Museum from Ms. Fosington-Gore. She said it was a "fascinating treasure house of personkind's achievements." Nobody listened to the lecture. Everyone was watching the way she felt her left breast whenever she got excited.

Others do not always understand or appreciate Adrian's wish to crowd all of life's experiences into a few months. When Adrian asks Pandora to show him one of her nipples, she writes him this letter:

> ▪ Adrian
>
> I am writing to terminate our relationship. Our love was once a spiritual thing. We were united in our appreciation of art and literature, but Adrian you have changed. You have become morbidly fixated with my body. Your request to look at my left nipple last night finally convinced me that we must part.
>
> Do not contact me.
>
> Pandora Braithwaite
>
> P.S. If I were you I would seek professional psychiatric help for your hypochondria and your sex mania. Anthony Perkins, who played the maniac in *Psycho,* was in analysis for ten years, so there is no need to be ashamed.

Later, we see Adrian at his most incisive:

> ▪ My mother has decided that sugar is the cause of all the evil in the world, and has banned it from the house.
>
> She smoked two cigarettes while she informed me of her decision.

Richard Peck's several novels about Blossom Culp and ghosts and funny things that may go bump in the night are all fine, as is Benjamin Lee's *It Can't Be Helped,* a delightful English novel about an inept but charming young would-be radical. Robert Kaplow's *Alex Icicle: A Romance in Ten Torrid Chapters* is a delightful spoof of books and styles. Almost as funny are his *Alessandra in Love* and *Two in the City.* And Barbara Robinson's *The Best Christmas Pageant Ever* has become a popular read-aloud for the holiday season.

Gentle, Almost Nostalgic Humor

In the last fifteen years, several books of humor have appeared that are mildly mocking but clearly do not mean to hurt anyone, unless it is the authors as they reminisce on their ill-spent youth. Librarians and teachers will recognize that the type derives from Stephen Leacock, as in "My Financial Career," and Paul Rhymer, who wrote so many warm and funny scripts for "Vic and Sade."

Garrison Keillor's "A Prairie Home Companion" on National Public Radio was consistently funny and warm about the people in the fictitious town of Lake Wobegon, Minnesota. The advertisements were amusing (Ralph's Pretty Good Grocery Store and Powdermilk Biscuits, "made from the whole wheat that gives shy persons the strength to do what needs to be done"), and Keillor's quiet charm made Lake Wobegon ("the town that time forgot and the decades cannot improve") come alive. Keillor's humor comes across in the pages of *Lake Wobegon Days* and *Happy to Be Here: Stories and Comic Pieces*, especially in a brief play, "Shy Rights: Why Not Pretty Soon," which gently spoofs the noisier arguments advanced by other minority groups for their rights.

Better known—and for some young adults one of their peak reading experiences—is the work of Jean Shepherd. Although Shepherd enthusiasts are fond of *In God We Trust, All Others Pay Cash; A Fistful of Fig Newtons;* and *The Ferrari in the Bedroom*, most readers agree that his funniest book is *Wanda Hickey's Night of Golden Memories and Other Disasters*. Shepherd is clearly fond of his characters. Although he certainly uncovers some of life's absurdities, there is no bitterness in his work. Shepherd relishes the golden memories, slightly painful and slightly exaggerated, of his own youth and his own youthful dreams.

The title story in *Wanda Hickey's Night* . . . begins as Shepherd remembers back on his junior prom, renting a white jacket formal, polishing up the old Ford V-8 convertible, and vainly pushing himself to ask Daphne Bigelow for the big date. ("Each time, I broke out in a fevered sweat and chickened out at the last instant.") In desperation, he asks the ever-present, ever-available Wanda Hickey to double-date with a friend.

Off to the Cherrywood Country Club to dance to Mickey Isley and his Magic Music Makers, our hero discovers that he soon develops a bad case of the sweats, which soon leads to an even worse case of rash. Outside and ready for the big drink at the Red Rooster Roadhouse, he discovers that he has left the convertible top down and that rain has poured into the car; the foursome, miserable and wet, drive off.

But the roadhouse proves no oasis of sanity. Proving his masculinity and sophistication, he orders triple shots of bourbon on the rocks and drinks up:

> Down it went—a screaming 90 proof rocket searing savagely down my gullet. For an instant, I sat stunned, unable to comprehend what had happened. Eyes watering copiously, I had the brief urge to sneeze, but my throat seemed to be paralyzed.

All during this, Wanda coos into his ears, "Isn't this romantic? Isn't this the most wonderful night in all our lives?"

Our hero, sure that the liquor had done its worst, proceeds to eat a meal of lamb chops, turnips, mashed potatoes, cole slaw, and strawberry shortcake, almost immediately followed by a trip to the restroom, where he sees his meal a second time. Later he takes Wanda home, but he cannot bring himself to kiss her when he smells sauerkraut on her breath. He returns home to a sardonic, if mildly sympathetic, father who reassures his son that his head will "stop banging" in a couple of days. An exhausted and strangely satisfied young man falls into bed.

Nora Ephron's *Crazy Salad* is stronger fare than either Keillor's or Shepherd's books, but many young women laugh as they read "A Few Words About Breasts" and "On Never Having Been a Prom Queen."

Some Gentle Satires

One of the more widely used handbooks of literature opens its definitions of satire this way:

> A literary manner which blends a critical attitude with humor and wit to the end that human institutions of humanity itself may be improved. The true satirist is conscious of the frailty of institutions of man's devising and attempts through laughter not so much to tear them down as to inspire a remodeling.[15]

Roger Sutton asked Richard Peck how he thought kids responded to satire, and Peck answered:

> Not well. I had to write a letter back to a class who had written to me about *Secrets of the Shopping Mall* saying that they understood the first part but then it got weird. Well, it was meant to get weird, and I said to them, "Please ask your teacher to tell you what satire is." They weren't ready for it, but of course nobody's ready until he's done some reading. . . . I think maybe satirizing the shopping mall was a problem. I could have satirized the school or the family. But the mall is their setting of choice and almost neutral ground.[16]

Some teachers and librarians assume that satire must be vicious or biting in tone and content, but some effective satires are gentle, even loving.

Jean Merrill's *The Pushcart War* is a classic among children's and young adult books, a gentle and most effective satire of war and human cupidity. Supposedly written in 1996, ten years after the end of the brief "Pushcart War," the novel is presented as straight, factual history, allowing the reader to see the humor, nobility, and nastiness of humans as the war unfolds. The war begins as a truckdriver drives over and demolishes a pushcart, propelling its owner into a pickle barrel. Soon the pushcart owners band together to fight back and the war is on. Noble figures like General Anna (formerly Old Anna), Maxie Hammerman, Morris the Florist, and Frank the Flower walk across history, as do bad guys like Albert P. Mack (usually known as Mack, the truckdriver), Big Moe, Louis Livergreen, and Mayor Emmett P. Cudd. *The Pushcart War* is funny, wise, learned, and utterly delightful for almost any reader, young adult or adult.

Several writers, all of whom have written for the *New Yorker*, offer young adults the chance to sample somewhat more sophisticated, although still reasonably gentle, satire. James Thurber's gentleness may be more apparent than real, but many of his sketches and short stories have proved popular to the young. Nostalgic pieces like "The Night the Bed Fell" and "University Days" are accessible to young people, and "Fables for Our Time"—especially "The Shrike and the Chipmunk," "The Owl Who Thought He Was God," and "The

Unicorn in the Garden"—are popular with many teenagers. His rewriting of history in "If Grant Had Been Drinking at Appomattox" is funny *if* readers know history, just as "The Macbeth Murder Mystery" is funny *if* readers know the play. Thurber's three best short stories are, unhappily, often beyond the emotional understanding of young adults, but if readers can handle them, "The Secret Life of Walter Mitty," "The Catbird Seat," and "The Greatest Man in the World" are among the finest, most sophisticated, and least gentle satires.

E. B. White is far more gentle and likable than Thurber, although his adult material has less immediate appeal to the young. *The Second Tree from the Corner* is, simply put, one of the great works in American literature, and why it goes largely unknown among so many teachers and librarians is one of life's great mysteries. White's poetry in that book is clever and amusing (especially "The Red Cow Is Dead" and "Song of the Queen Bee") and "The Retort Transcendental" is a wonderful parody of Thoreau taken too far. The finest short stories are "The Decline of Sport," a relatively funny satire on the inevitable decline in sports, and "The Morning of the Day They Did It," a less than amusing satire on the end of the world.

S. J. Perelman was once a writer for the Marx brothers, and titles for several of his sketches in *The Most of S. J. Perelman* and *The Last Laugh* suggest the wackiness of Marx brothers comedies (e.g., "Waiting for Santy," "Farewell, My Lovely Appetizer," "Rancors Aweigh," and "To Yearn Is Subhuman, to Forestall Divine"). Young people fascinated by comic word play will love Perelman. Others are hereby warned.

Woody Allen is a favorite of young people, although many probably have trouble following his verbal play. His movies, especially *Annie Hall* and *Take the Money and Run,* are filled with wackiness and wisdom, more often than not strangely mixed, but Allen's books are far wittier and have far better one-liners than his films. *Getting Even* is typical Allen wit, which assumes readers know Freud, Hasidic Jews, what college catalogues read like, and more. *Without Feathers* and *Side Effects* assume intelligent and sophisticated readers. Allen is fascinated by God and death, and his books have wisdom and some wacky wit about both.

Black Humor and Satire

So-called black humor uses irony and fantasy to ridicule the absurdities and bleakness of the human situation. Often savagely satirical, black humor virtually forces readers to laugh at the despair they feel when they are confronted with war, bureaucracies, social control, obsessive love (and obsessiveness generally), illogical political talk and propaganda, television, advertising, the bomb, and psychiatrists. If black humor has an obvious weakness, which is happily ignored by most readers, it is an obsession with the theme that arises out of situations to illustrate the theme, rather than the more traditional method of beginning with a human situation involving believable characters and letting them escape.

Of the many writers plowing this field, two have proved popular with young people who enjoy iconoclastic literature. Ken Kesey's *One Flew Over the Cuckoo's Nest* concerns Randal Patrick McMurphy's confinement to a mental hospital because he refuses to knuckle under to authority. He changes the lives of and brings hope to other patients despite the attempts of Nurse Ratchet to bring peace and conformity to the ward.

Even more popular is Joseph Heller's savage attack on war and wartime stupidity in *Catch-22*. Captain John Yossarian, bombardier in the 25th Squadron, based on a Mediterranean island near the end of World War II, wants no part of any more missions. He believes that if he can convince everyone that he is crazy, he will be freed of all combat duty. But Doc Daneeka points out a catch:

> "You mean there's a catch?"
> "Sure there's a catch," Doc Daneeka replied. "Catch-22. Anyone who wants to get out of combat duty isn't really crazy."
>
> There was only one catch and that was Catch-22, which specified that a concern for one's own safety in the face of dangers that were real and immediate was the process of a rational mind. Orr was crazy and could be grounded. All he had to do was ask; and as soon as he did, he would no longer be crazy and would have to fly more missions. Orr would be crazy to fly more missions and sane if he didn't, but if he was sane he had to fly them. If he flew them he was crazy and didn't have to; but if he didn't want to he was sane and had to. Yossarian was moved very deeply by the absolute simplicity of this clause of Catch-22 and let out a respectful whistle.
>
> "That's some catch, that Catch-22," he observed.
> "It's the best there is," Doc Daneeka agreed.

Heller's novel preceded the Vietnam War and the peace movement by several years, but because the book so perfectly pointed out the absurdity of a pointless war, *Catch-22* became something of a rallying point for protesters, just as it still rallies those who wonder about the military mind and bureaucracies gone mad in wartime.

The Ultimate in Humor

For some young adults, and for far more adults, the finest of all humorists is P. G. Wodehouse. This English writer of nearly 100 novels created a fantasy world permanently locked somewhere vaguely in the 1920s and 1930s and featuring some highly unbelievable characters. But other writers as different politically and socially as Evelyn Waugh and George Orwell and Rudyard Kipling ardently admired Wodehouse and thought him a genius. So he is.

Wodehouse's best-known creations are the feeble-brained Bertie Wooster and his brilliant and snobbish butler, Jeeves. Readers who begin with some of the Jeeves short stories in *Very Good, Jeeves* or *Carry On, Jeeves* may be puzzled by the comic opera world they find, but they will discover wit, charm, and fun in abundance. Readers may then be prepared to move on to the Jeeves novels (e.g., *The Inimitable Jeeves; The Mating Season; Jeeves and the Feudal Spirit; Stiff Upper Lip, Jeeves;* and *Much Obliged, Jeeves).*

Wodehouse enthusiasts may differ on the stories or novels they consider the funniest (some would vote for "Mulliner's Buck-U-Uppo" in *Meet Mr. Mulliner,* and others would argue for "Uncle Fred Flits By" in *Young Men in Spats*), but almost anyone who has sampled Wodehouse will stay for other items on the menu.

The range of humor available to young adults is incredible. Mockery, heroism, naiveté, cynicism, stupidity, cruelty, mayhem, death, the quest, madness, nastiness, sexuality, insults, viciousness, innocence, tears, the macabre, bitterness, and laughter, laughter, laughter in abundance are easily found to meet the tastes of any reader. And these smiling readers will be forever grateful to whoever gave them a nudge toward what brought them happiness.

◼ NOTES

[1] Quoted by Frances McCullough in her introduction to *Earth, Air, Fire and Water* from Charles Newman, *The Art of Sylvia Plath*. Indiana University Press, 1970.

[2] W. S. Merwin, "Separation," in *The Moving Target* (Atheneum, 1963).

[3] Walter Blair's edition of *The Sweet Singer of Michigan* (Pascal Covici, 1928) is excellent on Clark and Moore. A deliciously funny article by Bradley Hayden, "In Memoriam Humor: Julia Moore and the Western Michigan Poets," *English Journal* 72 (September 1983):22–28, is a fine introduction to these wonderful nonpoets.

[4] More anonymous "Little Willie" poems can be found in Clement Wood's *Poet's Handbook,* (Greenberg, 1940).

[5] Carolyn Gabbard Fugate, "Review of *Young Monsters*," *School Library Journal* 31 (May 1985):98.

[6] Lowell Swortzell, "Broadway Bound? Or Beyond?" *English Journal* 76 (September, 1987):52.

[7] Rick E. Amidon, "Toward a Young Adult Drama," *English Journal* 76 (September, 1987):59.

[8] Amidon, 59.

[9] Anthony L. Manna, "Curtains Up on Contemporary Plays," *English Journal* 73 (October, 1984):51–54.

[10] Steve Allen, *Funny People* (Stein & Day, 1981), p. 1.

[11] Lance M. Gentile and Merna M. McMillan, "Humor and the Reading Program," *Journal of Reading* 21 (January 1978):343–50.

[12] Ellen Conford, "I Want to Make Them Laugh," *ALAN Review* 14 (Fall 1986):21.

[13] Jan Harold Brunvand, *The Choking Doberman and Other "New" Urban Legends* (Norton, 1984), p. 50.

[14] Roger Sutton, "In the YA Corner: Hard Times at Sweet Valley High," *School Library Journal* 35 (November 1990):50.

[15] Willard Flint Thrall and Addison Hibbard, *A Handbook to Literature,* revised by C. Hugh Holman (Odyssey, 1960), p. 436.

[16] Roger Sutton, "A Conversation with Richard Peck," *School Library Journal* 35 (June 1990):36.

◼ OTHER TITLES MENTIONED IN THE TEXT OF CHAPTER NINE

Allen, Woody. *Getting Even*. Random House, 1971.

———. *Side Effects*. Random House, 1980.

———. *Without Feathers*. Random House, 1975.

Angelou, Maya. *The Heart of a Woman*. Random House, 1981.

———. *I Know Why the Caged Bird Sings*. Random House, 1970.

———. *Singin' and Swingin' and Gettin' Merry Like Christmas*. Random House, 1976.

———. *And Still I Rise*.

Asimov, Isaac et al., eds. *Young Monsters*. HarperCollins, 1985.

Bach, Alice, and J. Cheryl Exum. *Miriam's Well: Stories about Women in the Bible*. Delacorte, 1991.

Baldwin, Neil. *To All Gentleness, William Carlos Williams, The Doctor Poet*. Atheneum, 1984.

Bethancourt, T. Ernesto. *The Dog Days of Arthur Cane*. Holiday House, 1976.

Bradbury, Ray. *When Elephants Last in the Dooryard Bloomed*. Knopf, 1973.

Brooks, Bruce, *No Kidding*, HarperCollins, 1989.

Caras, Roger. *Roger Caras' Treasury of Great Cat Stories*. Dutton, 1987.

Carlson, Lori M., and Cynthia L. Ventura, eds. *Where Angels Glide at Dawn: New Stories from Latin America*. J. B. Lippincott, 1990.

Chaucer, Geoffrey. *Canterbury Tales,* translated by Barbara Cohen, illustrated by Trina Schart Hyman. Lothrop, 1988.

Chicorel, Marietta, ed., *Chicorel Index to Short Stories,* 2 volumes, American Library Publishing Co., 1977.

Cole, Brock. *Celine*. Farrar, Straus & Giroux, 1989.

Conford, Ellen. *If This Is Love, I'll Take Spaghetti*. Four Winds, 1983.

Cormier, Robert. *Eight Plus One*. Pantheon, 1980.

Coville, Bruce, comp. *Herds of Thunder, Manes of Gold: A Collection of Horse Stories and Poems,* illus. by Ted Lewin. Doubleday, 1989.

Crutcher, Chris. *Athletic Shorts*. Greenwillow, 1991.

Danzinger, Paula. *Can You Sue Your Parents for Malpractice?* Delacorte, 1979.

————. *The Divorce Express*. Delacorte, 1982.

Dunning, Stephen, and others, eds. *Reflections on a Gift of Watermelon Pickle and Other Modern Verse*. Scott, Foresman, 1966.

Ephron, Nora. *Crazy Salad*. Knopf, 1975.

Fitts, Dudley, ed. and trans. *Poems from the Greek Anthology in English Paraphrase*. New Directions, 1956.

Fleischman, Paul. *Joyful Noise: Poems for Two Voices*. HarperCollins, 1988.

Gallo, Donald R. *Center Stage: One-Act Plays for Teenage Readers and Actors*. HarperCollins, 1990.

Gallo, Donald R., ed. *Connections: Short Stories by Outstanding Writers for Young Adults*. Delacorte, 1989.

————. *Sixteen*. Delacorte, 1984.

————. *Visions*. Delacorte, 1988.

Girion, Barbara. *A Very Brief Season*. Macmillan, 1984.

Glenn, Mel. *Back to Class*. Clarion, 1988.

————. *Class Dismissed: High School Poems*. Clarion, 1982.

————. *Class Dismissed II: More High School Poems*. Clarion, 1986.

————. *My Friend's Got This Problem, Mr. Candler: High School Poems*. Clarion, 1991.

Gould, Jean. *American Women Poets: Pioneers of Modern Poetry*. Dodd, Mead, 1980.

Graham, Harry. *Ruthless Rhymes for Heartless Homes*. R. H. Russell, 1902.

Guide to Play Selection, Third Edition. National Council of Teachers of English, 1975.

Harrington, Laura. *100 Monologues: An Audition Sourcebook for New Dramatists*. Mentor, 1989.

Hein, Piet. *Grooks*. Doubleday, 1969.

Heller, Joseph. *Catch-22*. Simon & Schuster, 1961.

Herriot, James. *James Herriot's Dog Stories*. St. Martin's, 1987.

Janeczko, Paul. *Brickyard Summer*. Orchard, 1989.

————, compiler. *Dont Forget to Fly*. Bradbury, 1981.

————, compiler. *The Music of What Happens: Poems that Tell Stories*. Orchard, 1988.

Kaplow, Robert. *Alessandra in Love*. Lippincott, 1989.

————. *Alex Icicle: A Romance in Ten Torrid Chapters*. Houghton Mifflin, 1984.

————. *Two in the City*. Houghton Mifflin, 1979.

Keillor, Garrison. *Happy to Be Here: Stories and Comic Pieces.* Atheneum, 1982.

———. *Lake Wobegon Days.* Viking, 1985.

Kerr, M. E. *Dinky Hocker Shoots Smack.* HarperCollins, 1972.

———. *If I Love You, Am I Trapped Forever?* HarperCollins, 1973.

Kesey, Ken. *One Flew Over the Cuckoo's Nest.* Viking, 1962.

Koertge, Ron. *The Arizona Kid.* Little, Brown, 1988.

Lamb, Wendy. *Hey Little Walter: And Other Prize-Winning Plays from the 1989 and 1990 Young Playwrights Festivals.* Dell, 1991.

———. *Sparks in the Park and Other Prize-Winning Plays from the 1987 and 1988 Young Playwrights Festivals.* Dell, 1989.

Lee, Benjamin. *It Can't Be Helped.* Farrar, Straus & Giroux, 1979.

Lipsyte, Robert. *The Chemo Kid.* HarperCollins, 1992.

Marquis, Don. *archy and mehitabel.* Doubleday, 1927.

Mazer, Norma Fox. *Dear Bill, Remember Me? and Other Stories.* Delacorte, 1976.

———. *Summer Girls, Love Boys.* Delacorte, 1982.

Merriam, Eve. *Out Loud.* Atheneum, 1973.

———. *Rainbow Writing.* Atheneum, 1976.

Merrill, Jean. *The Pushcart War.* W. R. Scott, 1964.

Millay, Edna St. Vincent. *Poems Selected for Young People.* HarperCollins, 1979.

Noyes, Alfred. *The Highwayman,* illustrated by Neil Waldman. Harcourt, Brace Jovanovich, 1990.

Peck, Richard. *Secrets of the Shopping Mall.* Delacorte, 1979.

Perelman, S. J. *The Last Laugh.* Simon & Schuster, 1981.

———. *The Most of S. J. Perelman.* Simon & Schuster, 1958.

Pike, Frank and Thomas G. Dunn. *Scenes and Monologues from the New American Theatre.* Mentor, 1988.

Plotz, Helen, ed. *Eye's Delight: Poems of Art and Architecture.* Greenwillow, 1983.

———. *Gladly Learn and Gladly Teach: Poems of the School Experience.* Greenwillow, 1981.

———. *Imagination's Other Place: Poems of Science and Mathematics.* Crowell, 1955.

———. *Saturday's Children: Poems of Work.* Greenwillow, 1982.

Robinson, Barbara. *The Best Christmas Pageant Ever.* HarperCollins, 1972.

Rylant, Cynthia. *A Couple of Kooks and Other Stories About Love.* Orchard, 1990.

———. *A Kindness.* Orchard, 1988.

———. *Missing May.* Orchard, 1992.

———. *Soda Jerk.* Orchard, 1990.

———. *Waiting to Waltz.* Bradbury, 1984.

Schwartz, Alvin, collector. *And the Green Grass Grew All Around: Folk Poetry from Everyone.* HarperCollins, 1992.

Scoppetone, Sandra. *Trying Hard to Hear You.* HarperCollins, 1974.

Shank, Theodore J. *A Digest of 500 Plays: Plot Outlines and Production Notes.* Crowell Collier, 1963.

Shengold, Nina, ed. *The Actor's Book of Contemporary Stage Monologues.* Penguin, 1987.

Shepherd, Jean. *A Fistful of Fig Newtons.* Doubleday, 1982.

———. *The Ferrari in the Bedroom.* Dodd, Mead, 1973.

———. *In God We Trust, All Others Pay Cash.* Doubleday, 1976.

———. *Wanda Hickey's Night of Golden Memories and Other Disasters.* Doubleday, 1971.

Shipley, Joseph T., ed. *The Crown Guide to the World's Great Plays, from Ancient Greece to Modern Times,* Second Edition. Crown, 1984.

Sieruta, Peter. *Heartbeats.* HarperCollins, 1989.

Simon, Neil. *Lost in Yonkers.* Random House, 1991.

Soto, Gary. *Baseball in April: And Other Stories*. Harcourt Brace Jovanovich, 1990.

Spiegl, Fritz, ed. *A Small Book of Grave Humor*. Arco, 1973.

Thayer, Ernest Lawrence. *Casey at the Bat*, illustrated by Barry Moser, introduced by Donald Hall. Godine, 1988.

Thomas, Joyce Carol, ed. *A Gathering of Flowers: Stories About Being Young in America*. HarperCollins, 1990.

Townsend, Sue. *The Growing Pains of Adrian Mole*. Grove Press, 1986, first published in England in 1982.

_____. *The Secret Diary of Adrian Mole, Aged 13¾*. Grove Press, 1986, first published in England in 1982.

Twain, Mark. *Adventures of Huckleberry Finn*, 1884.

Walden Theatre Conservatory. *Sometimes I Wake Up in the Middle of the Night*. Dramatic Publishing, 1986.

Walker, Alice. *The Color Purple*. Harcourt Brace Jovanovich, 1982.

_____. *Good Night Willie Lee, I'll See You in the Morning*. Dial, 1979.

White, E. B. *The Second Tree from the Corner*. HarperCollins, 1954.

Wilson, H. W., Company. *Short Story Index*. Published every few years since 1955.

Wodehouse, P. G. *Carry On, Jeeves*. 1925; Penguin, 1975.

_____. *The Inimitable Jeeves*. 1931; Penguin, 1975.

_____. *Jeeves and the Feudal Spirit*. 1954; Penguin, 1975.

_____. *The Mating Season*. 1949; HarperCollins, 1983.

_____. *Meet Mr. Mulliner*. 1927; Penguin, 1981.

_____. *Much Obliged, Jeeves*. 1971; Penguin, 1982.

_____. *Stiff Upper Lip*. 1963; HarperCollins, 1983.

_____. *Very Good, Jeeves*. 1930; Penguin, 1975.

_____. *Young Man in Spats*. 1922; Penguin, 1981.

Yolen, Jane, and Martin H. Greenberg, eds. *Vampires: A Collection of Original Stories*. HarperCollins, 1991.

For information on the availability of paperback editions of these titles, please consult the most recent edition of *Paperbound Books in Print*, published annually by R. R. Bowker Company.

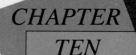

EVALUATING, PROMOTING, AND USING YOUNG ADULT BOOKS

Chances are that you are studying adolescent literature because you expect to work, or are already working, in a situation that calls for you to bring young adults in touch with books. This chapter begins with a section on evaluation, including the evaluation of literature for and about minorities, followed by discussions centered around common professional roles for adults who work with books and young readers: librarians, reading teachers, social studies teachers, parents, and counselors or youth workers. (See Chapter Eleven for information for English teachers.) These areas were chosen to give focus and organization to the information, but it should be realized that there is considerable overlap. Everyone working with young readers and books needs to be skilled in suggesting the right book for the right student or at least pointing someone in the right direction. When two people are talking about a book they both enjoyed, there is no way to divide the conversation into such discrete categories as literary analysis, personal feelings, sociological implications, and evaluation of potential popularity. Librarians will find themselves discussing books as if they were classroom teachers. Teachers can adopt some of the promotional techniques that librarians use, and librarians can use some book discussion tactics that teachers use. In short, the organization of this chapter may make it appear that librarians work with young readers and books quite differently from teachers or counselors. But in reality, nearly all adults who work with young readers and books have much the same goals and share many of the same approaches.

All of us will meet wide-ranging differences in abilities and personalities, which implies great differences in interests. Those interests demand an alert and prepared adult who is aware of them, who can uncover them, and who is familiar with an enormous number of titles to meet them. To an inexperienced person, the information about books that a librarian or teacher can call forth seems magical, but developing that repertoire takes time, patience, and hard work. Reading many young adult books comes with the territory for the professional, but so does reading professional books, magazines of all sorts, several newspapers, adult books, and much, much more. The professional likes to read (or would not be working with books), so that makes the job easier and more fun, but the professional reads beyond the areas that are personally enjoyable. For example, whether a professional likes science fiction or not, he or she must know titles of new science fiction. When young adults ask a teacher or librarian for another book like *The Martian Chronicles* (or *Forever* or *The Hitchhiker's Guide to the Galaxy* or *Crossings* or *The Color Purple*), they pay that person a sublime compliment. Woe unto the teacher or librarian who says, "I'm sorry, but I don't know anything about science fiction," or "Why don't you broaden your reading background just a bit?" Such a response kills interest and will probably turn kids away from reading.

In any given group, a teacher or librarian might find students like the following (and gradations in-between): Alice reads nothing at all (she did once but now that she has become a woman she has put away childish things); Brenda reads nothing because her reading skills are so poor she is virtually illiterate; Candy read a book once, her first book all the way through, and she hated it; Del reads magazines and an occasional sports biography if he's in an intellectual mood; Emily reads Sweet Valley High romances; Fred reads all kinds of books as long as they're science fiction; George reads a few books but always classics ("He's going to college," his mother says proudly); Howie reads only religious books and has already warned the teacher about the Satanic powers in *Lord of the Flies,* scheduled for class reading in two weeks; Imogene reads anything that is popular—Harold Robbins, best-sellers, novelizations of movies and television specials; Jon reads classics, football stories, mysteries, and everything else and refuses to be pigeonholed; Jean reads from the Great Books list and anything else a college suggests for its prospective students; and Lynn reads all the time, perhaps too much (she's bright but socially immature).

Serving the needs of such a diverse group is far from easy, but when the job is well done, it's a valuable contribution.

EVALUATING YOUNG ADULT LITERATURE

The role of the evaluator of books for young adults is more important than ever because new marketing practices have brought about such changes as the following:

- Many original paperbacks are marketed more like magazines than books.

- Lifespans for books, whether hardback or paperback, are shorter.
- Media tie-ins and covers are designed to inspire impulse buying directly by teenagers.
- Many more books are being produced and marketed in series or sets.

The fact that more books than ever are being published and that publishers are opting for shorter life spans for all books increases the workload for those who evaluate and recommend books. With so many ephemeral books around, there's a greater need for knowledgeable people to find and promote the excellent ones. And it's ironic that when there are more books to choose from, most schools and libraries have less money to spend. Also, book prices have increased more than budgets, so that if a purchasing mistake is made, especially with a series or a set of books, a proportionately larger bite is taken out of school, library, and personal budgets.

In response to these factors, professional reviewers are beginning to be more assertive in praising books they think deserve to be singled out and in criticizing those that they think are inferior. For example, in 1991, *School Library Journal* began publishing a *Star Track* supplement, which each six months reprints the reviews of the books that received stars. The August 1991 issue included the ninety starred reviews (only eighteen of which were for junior high and up) that had been among the 1,663 reviews appearing in the *Journal* between January and June of 1991.

The Horn Book Guide to Children's and Young Adult Books, also appearing twice a year since its 1990 inception, is different in format, but it is undoubtedly inspired by the same desire to separate the wheat from the chaff. *Horn Book* editors began operating in 1924 on the assumption that their business was to promote reading and to encourage parents and institutions to buy good books. So rather than writing negative criticism, they simply did not review books that they thought were of poor or mediocre quality. But in today's climate, such subtlety goes unnoticed, so in their semiannual *Guide,* which is made up of annotations rather than reviews, the editors group the books in categories from best to worst: 1 = Outstanding, 2 = Superior, 3 = Average to Above Average, 4 = Below Average, 5 = Marginal, and 6 = Not Recommended.

Writing About Books

If you devote your professional life to working with young people and books, chances are that at some level you will be involved in evaluating books and helping to decide about which ones receive prizes and get starred reviews and which ones are ignored or receive "Not Recommended" labels. Teachers and librarians working with books for young people have more opportunity to be among the decision makers than do those working with books for adults. This is because fewer than two dozen people in the United States are full-time reviewers of juvenile books. The bulk of the reviewing is done by teachers and

KATHERINE PATERSON
on Comfort and Calm

During the period when my youngest was sweating out the wait for college acceptance, I came upon her in the living room reading. Now that was not in itself extraordinary. Mary has been a reader since she was five. But the book my intelligent eighteen-year-old was absorbed in was *Charlotte's Web*, which she first met when she was about three. She looked up at me, her eyes shining. "This is a great book," she said.

When adults talk about books for young adults, I wish they'd remember how hard it is to be an adolescent—how many life-shaping decisions must be made at a time when most people are not ready to make them. Parents and teachers may try to encourage and reassure, but I have found that my children often return to the stories they loved when they were young to help them get through rough periods.

Books for young adults should include mind and heart stretchers like the classics. Can I ever forget what *Tale of Two Cities* and *Cry the Beloved Country* meant to me as a teenager? Surely they will include books like those of Sue Ellen Bridgers and Robert Cormier with which young people will more readily identify. But for comfort, for reassembling the identities that seemed to have come unstuck, what about a fresh look at *Charlotte's Web, Where the Wild Things Are*, or *Tuck Everlasting*?

It might be fun, as well as instructive, to have students write about or discuss their favorite childhood book. A lot can be learned about story structure by examining children's books, and a side benefit for the students may be a few hours of calm amidst the general turbulence of their lives.

Katherine Paterson's books include *Lyddie*, Lodestar, 1991; *Bridge to Terabithia*, Crowell, 1977; *The Great Gilly Hopkins*, Crowell, 1978; and *Jacob Have I Loved*, Crowell, 1980.

librarians who evaluate books both as part of their assigned workloads and as a professionally related hobby. Whether or not you wish to be one of these reviewers, you need to know what's involved, so that you will understand how these people's work can help you in selecting the books that are best for your purposes. The sheer number of books published each year makes it necessary that book lovers share the reading responsibilities and pool their information through written evaluations.

Evaluation underlies nearly all writing about books. Even when someone is simply making notes to serve as a reminder of the contents of a book, that person is making an evaluation and concluding that the book is worth remembering. Three concerns run throughout the evaluation of young adult literature:

1. What different types of writing meet specific needs, and how can they do it best?
2. Should reviews of young adult books be less promotional and more critical?
3. Is the writing and scholarship in the field aimed too much at the uses of literature rather than at the analysis of the literature itself?

Writing Note Cards

The type of writing most often done by teachers and librarians is the making of note cards or—in this day of word processors—typing half-sheet descriptions. College students in young adult and children's literature classes sometimes look on this activity as little more than a teacher-imposed duty that they will be only too glad to leave behind once the class is finished. But making notes will probably be a lifelong activity for anyone who works professionally with books. Note cards form a continuous record of the books someone has read and can personally recommend. Teachers and librarians use the cards to jog their memories when they compile book lists, when students ask for "a good book," and when they plan teaching units and promotional activities.

The comments on note cards vary according to the needs of the writer. Most people include the publisher and date, a short summary of the story, the characters' names and the other details that make this book different, and a brief evaluation. The writer might also add a few comments suggesting future uses of the book.

For example, if the book were Alice Childress' *A Hero Ain't Nothin' But a Sandwich,* a librarian might write the card in the form of a booktalk, including information about the movie. An English teacher might note that it would be a good book for illustrating the literary principle of point of view. A reading teacher might note that it is short and easy reading except for the use of black dialect, which would probably cause problems for less skilled readers. A youth worker might make a note about the potential of the book as a catalyst to get kids talking about what they think adults should do in situations like Benjie's and whether or not the responsibility belongs to Benjie rather than to those around him. In a community where books are judged as appropriate for school study on the basis of their topic and such things as "perfect" grammar and happy endings, someone might note that it would be desirable to share the book with other professionals and adult friends of the library in order to develop community support for its use. Positive reviews and honors won might also be helpful information. The sample card that follows was prepared by a student in an adolescent literature class who was planning to be an English teacher.

Writing Annotations

Annotations are similar to note cards, but they are usually written for someone else to see rather than for the writer's own use. And since they are usually part of an annotated bibliography or list where space is at a premium, writers must make efficient use of every word. Communicating the plot and tone of a book as well as a recommendation in only one or two interesting sentences is challenging, but no one wants to read lists of characters and plot summaries all starting with "This book. . . ." That annotations can be intriguing as well as communicative is shown by the following two samples for Virginia Hamilton's *Sweet Whispers, Brother Rush*. To save space, the bibliographical information given on the lists is not reprinted here.

Poetic, many-layered novel of 14-year-old Teresa's devotion to her retarded and doomed brother Dab. A strong story of hope and power of love.
School Library Journal, December, 1982

Fourteen-year-old Tree learns a lot about her family and the interconnections between their past and present tragedies from Brother Rush, her uncle's ghost.

Booklist, March 15, 1983

Notice how both writers communicated the age of the protagonist, the fact that it was a family story, and, through the use of *doomed* and *tragedies*, that it

A Hero Ain't Nothin' But a Sandwich by Alice Childress. Coward, McCann & Geoghegan, 1973, Avon paperback.

The best part of this drug-related book is that it shows people really trying. A family rallies around thirteen-year-old Benjie. The dad is just living with the family, but he proves himself to be a real father. The story is told from several viewpoints--one chapter at a time. This makes it good for showing that not all people who live in a ghetto feel and act the same. It's open-ended with the reader being left to wonder whether or not Benjie shows up for drug counseling. Realistic, black dialogue adds to the authenticity. I liked it. Could be used as a read-aloud introduction to a unit on drugs.

was a fairly serious book. The writers also hinted at mystery and intrigue, the first one through "Poetic, many-layered . . . hope and the power of love" and the second one through the reference to "Brother Rush, her uncle's ghost."

Writing Reviews

A problem in reviewing juvenile books is that more books are published than can be reviewed in the media. (See Appendix A for major reviewing sources for young adult books.) In addition to these, dozens of national publications carry occasional review articles, and many library systems sponsor reviewing groups whose work is published either locally or through such nationally distributed publications as *Book Waves,* from the Bay Area (northern California) Young Adult Librarians, and *Books for the Teen Age,* from the Young Adult Services Office of the New York Public Library. And some teachers of children's and young adult literature work with their students to write regular review columns for local newspapers.

When publishers send out their new books, review editors glance through them and select the ones to forward to reviewers. Because the editor doesn't anticipate reviewing all books, it's likely that the publisher who can afford to send out the most copies will get the most reviews, as will the author whose name is already recognized. The fact that juvenile books are reviewed mostly by librarians and teachers working on a part-time basis slows down the reviewing process, especially if they take time to incorporate the opinions of young readers. With adult books, reviews often come out prior to or simultaneously with the publication of the book, but with juvenile titles it's not uncommon to see reviews appearing a full year or more after the book was released.

Although young adult books get off to a slower start than adult books, once they are launched they may well last longer. Teachers work them into classroom units, librarians promote them, and paperback book clubs keep selling them for years. Children continue to grow older and to advance in their reading skill and taste, so that every year a whole new set of students is ready to read *A Separate Peace, The Catcher in the Rye,* and even *The Outsiders*. As a result, reviews, articles, and papers continue to cover particular titles years after their original publication dates.

The field of juvenile reviewing is sometimes criticized for being too laudatory because the reviews are written by book lovers who are anxious to "sell" literature. Also, those editors who have room for only a limited number of reviews devote their space to the books they think are the best, so of course they are complimentary.

People generally evaluate books on the basis of either literary quality, reader interest, potential popularity, or what the book is teaching (i.e., its social and political philosophy). Evaluators should make clear their primary emphasis lest readers misunderstand them. For example, a critic may review a book positively because of its literary quality, but a reader will interpret the positive review as a prediction of popularity. The book is purchased and put on the shelf, where it is ignored by teenagers. Consequently, the purchaser feels cheated and loses confidence in the reviewing source.

In an attempt to resolve that kind of conflict, when Mary K. Chelton and Dorothy M. Broderick founded *VOYA* (*Voice of Youth Advocates*), they devised the evaluation code shown in Table 10.1. Each review is preceded by a *Q* number, indicating *quality,* and a *P* number, indicating *popularity.* They suggest that a fringe benefit to using such a clearly outlined code is that it helps librarians analyze their buying patterns. Those who lean heavily toward either quality or popularity will see their biases and be able to strike a more appropriate balance.

A quite different set of criteria from either popularity or literary quality is that of social or political values. The Council on Interracial Books for Children has been very open about its belief that books should "become a tool for the conscious promotion of human values that lead to greater human liberation."[1] The organization provides checklists for reviewers to use in examining books for racism, sexism, elitism, materialism, individualism, ageism, conformity, escapism, positive vs. negative images of females and minorities, cultural authenticity, and the level of inspiration toward positive action. It is expected that reviews in the *Interracial Books for Children Bulletin* will focus on such matters.

However, most reviewers—whether or not they realize it—are influenced by their personal feelings toward how a book treats social issues. For example, Sue Ellen Bridgers' *Notes for Another Life* was highly recommended and praised in *Horn Book Magazine,* the *New York Times Book Review,* and the *Bulletin of the Center for Children's Books,* but when Janet French reviewed the book for *School Library Journal* she wrote:

> The blurb suggests that this is "a family chronicle for all ages." It would have been more accurate to describe it as a propaganda vehicle for female domesticity. Good women subordinate their talents and yearnings to the home and their children; all other paths lead to havoc. For a riveting story of four deserted children, lead readers instead to Cynthia Voigt's marvelous upbeat *Homecoming.*[2]

Table 10.1   *VOYA EVALUATION CODE*

Quality	Popularity
5Q: Hard to imagine it being better written.	5P: Every young adult was dying to read it yesterday.
4Q: Better than most, marred only by occasional lapses.	4P: Broad general young adult interest.
3Q: Readable without serious defects.	3P: Will appeal without pushing.
2Q: A little better editing or work by the author would have made it 3Q.	2P: For the young adult reader with a special interest in the subject.
1Q: Hard to understand how it got published.	1P: No young adult will read unless forced to for assignments.

This review was written in such a way that readers can easily recognize that the reviewer's opinion was shaped by her disagreement with the plot. For a reviewer to use this as the basis for a negative recommendation is perfectly justifiable *if* the situation is made clear. The problem comes when reviewers reject books on the basis of such social issues but don't admit to themselves, much less to their readers, that their feelings have been influenced by whether a story sharpens or dulls whatever personal ax they happen to be grinding at the moment.

There are as many reviewing styles as there are journals and individual reviewers. But nearly all reviews contain complete bibliographical information, including number of pages and prices, perhaps a cataloguing number, the intended age level, a summary statement of the contents, and some hint of the quality of the book as evaluated by the reviewer. A few years ago an issue of *Top of the News* (the ALA publication now called *Journal of Youth Services in Libraries*) had as its feature topic "Reviews, Reviewing, and the Review Media." Editor Audrey Eaglen solicited answers to the question, "What makes a good review?"[3] Here are excerpts from some of the responses:

An intelligent review . . . is never obsequious, if it is favorable. It is never flip, if it is unfavorable. It never quotes from the front flap.

Rosemary Wells, author

Are there any clever devices or intriguing aspects of the book which could be used to pique the interest of a group and "sell" the book. Also I need to be alerted to potentially controversial issues, be it strong language, explicit sex, violence, or whatever, not so I can avoid buying the book, but so I can plan and prepare and thereby deal with a conflict should it arise.

Katherine Haylman, school librarian

How attractive is the cover? While we might feel that no one should judge a book by its cover, the truth is that everyone does.

Dorothy Broderick, editor and educator

I want a clear-cut commitment as to recommendation or nonrecommendation. I don't have the time to read every book published, and I'm hoping that some literate person will help me decide where to invest my reading hours.

Walter Dean Myers, author

Does the book have magic for YA's? Are there format faults, for example, does the size and shape make it look like a baby book? Is the word *children* used anywhere on the dust jacket? And if there is going to be a film or television tie-in, who are the stars and when will it be released?

Patty Campbell, author and critic

The reviewer must decide what information is most important for the book being reviewed and for the audience for which the review is being written. Writing reviews is a skill that improves with practice and effort. A good way to begin developing this skill is to study several reviews of the same book as they appear in different publications. Note the essentials that seem to be the same in each review and then compare the information that is different. See if you can explain the differences in light of the source's reading audience.

For the person reading reviews, one of the biggest problems is that they all run together and begin to sound the same. To keep this from happening, reviewers need to approach their task with the same creative spirit with which authors write books. They need to think of new ways of putting across the point that a book is highly recommended or that it has some unique quality that readers should watch for, as in these two excerpts of reviews that were written by authors reviewing books written by other authors. Granted, authors probably have had more practice in working with words, and therefore their skill is greater than that of most reviewers, but they probably also try harder because they know how important it is to do something to make a review stand out, to give the reader something by which to remember the book.

The first excerpt is taken from a review of Alice Childress' *Rainbow Jordan*, written by Anne Tyler for the *New York Times Book Review*:

> Rainbow is so appealing that she could carry this book on her own, but she doesn't have to. There's Miss Josie, who gives us her clearer view to balance what Rainbow tells us. . . . And there's the mother herself—short-tempered, inconsistent, sometimes physically abusive, not much of a mother at all, really. Seen through Rainbow's adoring eyes, she's at least someone we can understand ("Life is complicated," Rainbow says, "I love her even now while I'm putting her down.") In fact, Rainbow's story moves us not because of her random beatings or financial hardships, but because Rainbow needs her mother so desperately that she will endlessly rationalize, condone, overlook, forgive. She is a heartbreakingly sturdy character, and *Rainbow Jordan* is a beautiful book.[4]

Katherine Paterson made these comments about Virginia Hamilton's *Sweet Whispers, Brother Rush* as part of an article she wrote for the *New York Times Book Review:*

> There are those who say that Virginia Hamilton is a great writer but that her books are hard to get into. This one is not. It fairly reaches off the first page to grab you, and once it's got you, it sets you spinning deeper into its story. Needless to say, this is not a conventional ghost story. In fact, the function of the ghost in this book is to provide 14-year-old Tree Pratt with a place from which to view her world. . . . In this book everyone we meet, including the ghost, is wonderfully human. . . . The language too is of Miss Hamilton's own special kind, which uses the speech forms of the young to enhance rather than restrict the music of the book.[5]

Writing Scholarly and Pedagogical Articles

A fourth kind of writing about young adult books is made up of articles or papers that go into more depth than is possible in reviews. Since most reviewers of juvenile books have little hope of coming out with a "scoop" or of being the first one to pass judgment on a new book, they focus on deeper treatments or on tying several books together. Dorothy Matthews analyzed the writing about adolescent literature that appeared in professional journals over a five-year period.[6] She categorized the writing into three types. First were those articles that focus on the subjective responses of readers to particular books, such as reader surveys, lists of popular titles, and reviews written from the point of view of how the book is likely to affect young readers. Articles of this kind are primarily descriptive.

The second type was also descriptive and consisted of pedagogical articles giving teachers lists of books that fit together for teaching units, ideas for book promotion, and techniques for teaching reading, social studies, or English. They may include brief comments on the literary qualities of the novels, but, again, the writer's primary intention is to be informative.

The third kind of writing was that restricted to the books themselves. It is in this group that Matthews thinks hope lies for developing a body of lasting scholarly knowledge that will be taken seriously by the academic community. These papers include discussions of adolescent literature as a genre, historical background of the field, relationships between authors and their work, patterns that appear in YA novels, and themes and underlying issues. More of this kind of literary analysis is being done as authors write books serious enough to support it. Examples of some of these articles are included in Appendix B, "Some Outstanding Books and Articles About Young Adult Literature."

Twayne Publishers paved the way for some serious extended criticism of young adult literature when they inaugurated a Young Adult Authors subset in their United States Authors series. As of 1992, thirteen books had been completed under such titles as *Presenting Judy Blume, Presenting Sue Ellen Bridgers, Presenting Robert Cormier,* and so on. Rosa Guy, S. E. Hinton, M. E. Kerr, Norma Klein, Norma Fox Mazer, Walter Dean Myers, Zibby Oneal, Richard Peck, William Sleator, and Paul Zindel are among the authors so far written about. The same company has also begun to examine specific genres, with the first title being *Presenting Young Adult Horror Fiction* by Cosette Kies.

Also, a look into a recent edition of *Dissertation Abstracts International* will show an increasing number of dissertations being written on young adult literature. However, the majority of topics deal more with social or pedagogical issues than with literary ones.

Fairly new journals that support the growing body of literary criticism about books for young readers include *Children's Literature in Education: An International Quarterly, Children's Literature, ALAN Review,* and VOYA (*Voice of Youth Advocates*). Within the last fifteen years, these journals have joined the other well-established journals listed in Appendix A.

In summary, writing about young adult books falls into four categories: note cards for personal use, annotations, reviews, and scholarly or pedagogical writing. Most of you will be involved in the first kind, that is, making note cards for your own use. But some of you will also be making annotations, writing reviews, and doing scholarly or pedagogical analyses. This latter kind of writing and critiquing can be especially intriguing because significant changes have occurred within recent years and relatively few scholars have worked with young adult literature. This means there is ample opportunity for original research and observation, whether from the viewpoint of a literary scholar, a teacher, a librarian, or a counselor or youth worker. The field as a whole will grow strong as a result of serious and competent criticism and analysis.

DECIDING ON THE LITERARY CANON

Educators are finding themselves in the midst of a lively debate over what books should be taught in America's classrooms. An oversimplification of the issue is to say that on one side are those who believe in acculturation or assimilation. They think that if we all read approximately the same books, we will come away with similar values and attitudes and hence be a more united society. On the other side are those who believe in diversity and want individuals and groups to find their own values, attitudes, and ways of life reflected in the literature they read. This latter group views the traditional literary canon as racist and sexist with its promotion in schools serving to keep minorities and women "in their place."

Katha Pollitt, contributing editor of *The Nation,* made some interesting observations when she wrote that, "In a country of real readers a debate like the current one over the canon would not be taking place." She described an imaginary country where children grow up watching their parents read and going with them to well-supported public libraries where they all borrow books and read and read and read. At the heart of every school is an attractive and well-used library, and in classrooms children have lively discussions about books they have read together, but they also read lots of books on their own, so that years later they don't remember whether "they read *Jane Eyre* at home and Judy Blume in class, or the other way around."[7]

Pollitt wrote that in her imaginary country of "real readers—voluntary, active, self-determined readers," a discussion of which books should be studied in school would be nothing more than a parlor game. It might even add to the aura of writers not to be included on school-assigned reading lists because this would mean that their books were "in one way or another too heady, too daring, too exciting to be ground up into institutional fodder for teenagers." The

See Appendix A
for books and
periodicals
designed to assist
teachers and
librarians in filling
their professional
roles.

alternative would be millions of readers freely choosing millions of books, each book becoming just a tiny part of a lifetime of reading. Pollitt concluded her piece with the sad statement that at the root of the current debate over the canon is the assumption that the only books that will be read are those that are assigned in school: "Becoming a textbook is a book's only chance: all sides take that for granted." She wonders why those educated scholars and critics who are currently debating this issue and must be readers themselves have conspired to keep secret two facts that they surely must know:

> ... if you read only twenty-five, or fifty, or a hundred books, you can't understand them, however well chosen they are. And ... if you don't have an independent reading life—and very few students do—you won't *like* reading the books on the list and will forget them the minute you finish them.[8]

Pollitt's argument sheds a different light on the question of the literary canon and puts even more of a burden on those of us who have as our professional responsibility the development of life-long readers. We are the ones who should be raising our voices to explain the limitations of expecting children to read just what's assigned in class. We are also the ones with the responsibility of helping students develop into the kinds of committed and enthusiastic readers that Pollitt described in her imaginary country.

But in the meantime, we also have an obligation to become knowledgeable about the issues that underlie the current debate over the literary canon and to assist schools and libraries in making informed choices with the resources they have. We, as authors of this textbook, have already committed ourselves to the idea of an expanded canon (and no doubt you, as a reader, have as well). Note that some of the harshest critics of adolescent literature are those in favor of promoting only the traditional canon; others tolerate adolescent literature only because they view it as a means to the desired end of leading students to appreciate "real" literature.

At the 1991 National Council of Teachers of English convention in Seattle, Washington, Rudolfo Anaya, author of *Bless Me, Ultima* and a professor of creative writing at the University of New Mexico, predicted that the biggest literary change that will occur in the 1990s will be the incorporation of minority literature into the mainstream. He did not mean just the inclusion on booklists of the names of authors who are members of minority groups, but also the incorporation of new styles and ideas into the writing of nonminority authors.

Anaya explained that Mexican-Americans have a different world view. When he was in college, he loved literature and read the standard literary canon with enthusiasm and respect, but when he went to write his own stories he couldn't use Hemingway or Milton as models. He could create plots like theirs, but then he was at a standstill because nowhere in the literary canon did he find people like the ones he knew. His Spanish-speaking family has lived in eastern New

Mexico for more than 100 years. The harsh but strangely beautiful landscape and the spirit of the Pecos River had permeated his life, as had stories of *La Grande,* the wise old woman who had safely pulled him from his mother's body even though the umbilical cord was wrapped around his neck. There were also stories of *La Llorona,* a woman who had gone insane and murdered her children and whose tortured cries traveled on the wind around the corners of his childhood home. All his life, such dramatic dreams and stories were woven in and out of reality, but nowhere in the literature that he studied in school did he find such stories. When he wrote one—*Bless Me, Ultima*—and sent it to all the big publishers, not one of them recognized it as "literature," although when it was finally published it won the Premio Quinto Sol Award for the best novel written by a Chicano in 1972 and has since become increasingly well known.

Anaya worked on the book for seven years, during which he felt he was "writing in a vacuum. I had no Chicano models to read and follow, no fellow writers to turn to for help. Even Faulkner, with his penchant for the fantastic world of the South, could not help me in Mexican/Indian New Mexico. I would have to build from what I knew best." He went on to explain:

> Those realizations we later see so clearly actually come in small steps, and that's how it was for me. I began to discover that the lyric talent I possessed, as the poet I once aspired to be, could be used in writing fiction. The oral tradition which so enriched my imagination as a child could lend its rhythm to my narrative. Plot techniques learned in Saturday afternoon movies and comic books could help as much as the grand design of the classics I had read. Everything was valuable, nothing was lost.[9]

Anaya's observations about not having models to follow and being forced to create a new narrative style in order to tell a story coming from his own experience relates to the frustration that teachers and librarians often express when they go to look for young adult novels about minority characters. The problem is that they are looking for the same kinds of coming-of-age stories that are typical in mainstream YA literature, except they want the characters to have brown skin and "different" names. The absence of such books, especially such books written by Indian authors, is in itself part of the cultural difference. It's a safe observation to say that the more closely a book with an American Indian protagonist resembles what we have described in Chapter One as a typical YA book, the greater is the chance that the author is not Indian and that the Indian protagonist is of mixed parentage or is living apart from the native culture.

As discussed in Chapter Five (see pp. 206–207), several recent YA books contain mystical elements tied in with American Indian themes. These books are an interesting example of how Anaya's prediction that ethnic writing will become incorporated into the mainstream is already coming true. However, we should warn that not everyone will be pleased to see this kind of incorporation, because they will view the books as contaminated or impure. The authors have used old legends and beliefs for their own purposes, interweaving them with contemporary situations and ideas. Also, the authors are not American Indians.

However, being in the blood line of a particular group does not guarantee acceptance by the group. For example, most high school teachers think they are contributing to an awareness of cultural diversity and the enlargement of the literary canon by leading students to read Maxine Hong Kingston's *Woman Warrior*. But noted Chinese writer Frank Chin criticizes Kingston, along with Amy Tan for *The Joy Luck Club* and David Henry Hwang for his plays, *F. O. B.* and *M. Butterfly*. He accuses these writers of "boldly faking" Chinese fairy tales and childhood literature. Then he goes on to ask and answer the question of why the most popular "Chinese" works in America are consistent with each other but inconsistent with Chinese culture and beliefs:

> That's easy: (1) all the authors are Christian, (2) the only form of literature written by Chinese Americans that major publishers will publish (other than the cookbook) is autobiography, an exclusively Christian form [based on confession]; and (3) they all write to the specifications of the Christian stereotype of Asia being as opposite morally from the West as it is geographically.[10]

Chin's comments are in an essay, "Come All Ye Asian American Writers," that is used as an introduction to an anthology entitled *The Big Aiiieeeee!*, apparently put together for use in college classes. The 619-page book is too intimidating for most high school students, but they could appreciate many of the individual stories, poems, and essays. The book's title comes "from the pushers of white American culture" who in movies, television, radio, and comic books "pictured the yellow man as something that when wounded, sad, or angry, or swearing, or wondering, whined, shouted, or screamed, 'Aiieeeee!' "

We are citing *The Big Aiiieeeee!* as an illustration of the complexities involved in the whole matter of ethnic differences. As Chin goes on to state his case, he brings in religion and gender differences as well as differences caused by race, history, social class, and politics. In answer to the kind of criticism he offers, Kingston has explained:

> Sinologists have criticized me for not knowing myths and for distorting them; pirates [those who illegally translate her books for publication in Taiwan and China] correct my myths, revising them to make them conform to some traditional Chinese version. They don't understand that myths have to change, be useful or be forgotten. Like the people who carry them across oceans, the myths become American. The myths I write are new, American. That's why they often appear as cartoons and Kung Fu movies. I take the power I need from whatever myth. Thus Fa Mu Lan has the words cut into her back; in traditional story, it is the man, Ngak Fei the Patriot, whose parents cut vows on his back. I mean to take his power for women.[11]

Knowledge of these opposing viewpoints should not frighten teachers back into the comforts of the established canon; instead it should help teachers prepare for meeting the challenges involved in going beyond the "tried and true."

Teaching Ethnic Literature

Most educators feel a duty to bring ethnic-based literature to young people in hopes of increasing general understanding (see Focus Boxes 1.3, 1.4, 2.2, and 2.3, pp. 26, 28, 64, and 66). Besides that lofty goal, here are some additional reasons for making special efforts to bring ethnic books to young people:

- Young readers can identify with characters who straddle two worlds because they have similar experiences in going between the worlds of adulthood and childhood.
- Motifs that commonly appear in ethnic-based stories—including loneliness, fear of rejection, generational differences, and troubles in fitting into the larger society—are meaningful to teenagers.
- Nearly all teenagers feel that their families are somehow different, and so they can identify with young protagonists from minority families.
- Living in harmony with nature is a common theme, especially in American Indian literature, that appeals to today's ecology-minded youth.
- As movies, TV programs, mass media books, and magazines inundate teens with stories and photos of people who are "all alike," readers find it refreshing to read about people who are different and in some ways exotic.
- Myths and legends that are often brought into ethnic-based literature satisfy some deep-down psychological and aesthetic needs that are not met with contemporary realism or with the romanticism masked as realism that currently makes up the body of fiction provided for young adults.

As pointed out by Alecia Baker and Randee Brown, who talked about several of the above points at the 1991 National Council of Teachers of English convention in Seattle, Washington, the role of adults is more important in relation to ethnic than to mainstream literature for young people because ethnic literature needs to be "taught," whereas with many of the books mentioned in other sections of this text it's enough just to make students aware of their existence. Doing this for ethnic books is harder because many are published by small presses, which means they are not advertised in glossy catalogs or reviewed in as many professional journals. And if a library subscribes to an ordering service, ethnic books from small presses probably won't be among the ones preselected by the service.

One of the most important concepts that needs to be taught is that there are large differences among people typically identified as a group. The October

1991 *National Geographic* magazine had America before Columbus as its feature topic and included the fact that there are more than 300 different tribes now living in the United States. When Europeans first came to the American continent there were more than thirty distinct nations speaking perhaps 1,000 different languages. During the past 500 years, these people have had such common experiences as losing their lands, being forced to move to reservations, and having to adapt their beliefs and life-styles to a technological society. These experiences may have affected their attitudes in similar ways, but still it is a gross overgeneralization to write about American Indians as if they were one people holding the same religious and cultural views. Obviously, in a single class it would be impossible to study dozens of different Indian tribes, and so a compromise solution might be to study the history and folklore of those tribes who lived, or are living, in the same geographical area as the students. With this approach, it is important for students to realize that they are looking at only one small part of a bigger group, and that if they studied a different group they would learn equally interesting but different facts.

A similar point could be made about the thoughtlessness of lumping all Asian Americans together. The Chinese and Japanese, the two groups who have been in the United States the longest, come from countries with a long history of hostility toward each other. And a refugee from Vietnam or Cambodia has very little in common with someone whose ancestors came to California in the 1850s. Likewise, Puerto Ricans in New York have quite a different background from southwestern Mexican-Americans. And even in the Southwest, people whose families have lived there from the days before Anglo settlers arrived resent being lumped together with people who just came over the border from Mexico.

Students need to be taught about the history of any ethnic group whose literature they are reading. We shouldn't assume that students are informed about their own groups, nor should we embarrass students by assigning them to particular groups or asking them to serve as "representatives." The reason we need to teach about the histories of groups whose literature is being read is that without knowing the history, readers won't be able to understand or appreciate the bitterness that finds its way into some ethnic literature. Knowing a group's history will also help students understand why some members of ethnic groups resent books written about their group members by outsiders. And readers who get impatient with Hispanic authors for including words and phrases in Spanish will probably be a little more tolerant if they realize that today's generation of Mexican-American authors went to school in the days before bilingual education. In their early childhood, many of them heard nothing but Spanish and were amazed to arrive at English-speaking schools where they would be punished for speaking the only language they had ever known. They want monolingual readers to experience just a bit of the discomfort they felt so keenly.

Understanding the work history of minorities, many of whom performed hard physical labor as long as there was daylight and then "camped out" with fellow workers, will help students appreciate oral traditions. Similar to the way that

Rudolfo Anaya broke new literary ground with his *Bless Me, Ultima,* many other minority writers are breaking new ground by changing the format of stories and translating them from an oral tradition into a written form. An example is Laurence Yep's *The Rainbow People* and *Tongues of Jade,* which are his retellings of stories collected by Jon Lee in Oakland's Chinatown in the 1930s and later by Wolfram Eberhard in San Francisco's Chinatown.

When we talk about oral traditions, we should tie them into today's storytelling, which is very much alive through television talk shows, kids telling stories at slumber parties and summer camp, workers entertaining each other during their breaks, and just plain old gossip. A contemporary favorite is the urban legends (see Focus Box 9.5, p. 372) in which people tell each other incredible stories about events they believe actually happened. With these examples, the stories that are told are short, mostly anecdotes and jokes. That's because storytellers aren't going to memorize whole novels to tell out loud, nor would anyone's friends want to sit and listen to something that long.

Before printing presses, typewriters, word processors, movies, radio, and television, people had more of an incentive to remember and tell the stories that communicated the traditions and values of a society. And even today, oral traditions play an important role for groups that do not have access to this kind of technology or whose stories are not part of popular culture mass media. Many minority writers are the first of their group to experiment in translating oral stories into written and printed formats. This is one of the reasons that the first publications to come from particular groups are more likely to be poetry and short stories than novels.

Another reason that short pieces will be written and printed sooner than long ones relates to life-styles. Following a recent speech, Gary Soto was asked why so much of Hispanic literature is in the form of poetry and short stories. He gave the very practical answer that writing a poem is faster than writing a novel. During the protest movements of the late 1960s and early 1970s he could write a poem in the morning and use it at a rally that evening. He added that minority group members are mostly working people with families to support. Few minority writers have the luxury of working full time as writers, and so the idea of writing a novel is all the more daunting when it has to be squeezed into the few hours a week that can be stolen from family and employment responsibilities.

Young adult literature has more well-known books by and about African-Americans than any of the other minority groups. This is partly because English is the native language of most blacks and because a generation ago the ice was broken for black writers by such luminaries as Langston Hughes and Ralph Ellison. Also, the civil rights movement of the 1960s brought to publishers' attention the obvious inequity of such large school districts as Detroit, Chicago, and Harlem using textbooks and other school materials that focus almost exclusively on Caucasians while the majority of the students belong to minority groups. A similar awareness is now developing for Asians, Hispanics, American Indians, and to a lesser extent immigrants from the Middle East.

We'll conclude this section with a plea for all those working with books and young adults to continue seeking out and promoting the use of minority literature. Educators have shied away from working with minority literature because:

1. They didn't study it when they were in school and so they feel less prepared than when teaching mainstream literature.
2. They fear censorship both because of prejudice against minorities and because of the fact that some minority writers use language considered inappropriate for schoolbooks.
3. Minority literature is harder to find, especially minority literature that has been given a "seal of approval" by the education establishment (i.e., positive reviews and suggestions for teaching).
4. Ethnic identification is such a sensitive topic that teachers fear that when they are discussing a piece of literature either they or their students may say something that will offend some students or hurt their feelings.

Being a professional means that you do not shy away from responsibilities just because they are challenging. Instead you prepare, so that you can be successful—at least most of the time—in the work you have chosen for your career.

USING YA LITERATURE IN THE LIBRARY

When discussing public libraries, it is often assumed that every library has a young adult librarian and a special section serving teenagers. Although this may be the ideal arrangement, there are certainly many libraries where this has never been the practice and many others where shrinking budgets are making young adult librarians an endangered species. A fairly common approach is for libraries to enlarge their children's sections to serve slightly older children (up to age fifteen or sixteen) while sending everyone else to the adult division. Some of the problems with such an arrangement, cited in a *Voice of Youth Advocates* article ("Whose Job Is It Anyway?"[12]), are the following:

- Teenagers enter a children's section reluctantly, and their size, voices, and active natures intimidate the children who are there.
- The purpose of young adult services is to provide a transition from the children's collection to the resources of the total library, and when a librarian accompanies a teenager looking for something into the larger adult collection there's no one left to serve the children.
- It's difficult for the same person who runs programs for preschoolers, prepares story hours for older children, and reviews hundreds of children's books to switch gears to the fads and multiple interests of teenagers.

- YA librarians deal not only with "safe" YA books, but also with adult materials of interest to young adults. These are often controversial and are likely to prove more problematic to a children's librarian whose training has engendered different perceptions and attitudes.
- Without "sponsorship" by knowledgeable young adult librarians, there may not be enough circulation for serious, high-quality books, which will result in a greater reliance on popular taste (e.g., formula romances and series books).

Certainly these worries are valid, and we all need to do what we can to persuade decision makers that young adult librarians serve an important role. But if the choice is between closing a library two days a week and having separate librarians for children and teenagers, most library boards will vote to keep the library open. This dictates more flexibility and more challenge for the librarian who serves both age groups. Parents who have both teenagers and young children will vouch for the differences between the two, yet they manage somehow. Many librarians will have to do the same. We hope this textbook will help.

Matching Books with Readers

Most people working with books and young readers have come to accept the idea that there is no such thing as one sacred list of books that every student should read. The best that can be hoped for are agreeable matches between particular books and particular students. To bring such matches about, adults need to be acquainted with a wide range of books and with individual students. A commonly used technique in getting to know students is to ask them what books they have previously enjoyed and then to suggest something similar or something by the same author. An alternative is to ask young readers to describe the book they would most like if an author were going to write just for them, and then to suggest three or four books that contain elements they have mentioned.

Other people use written forms of reader interest surveys in which students write down their hobbies, the kinds of classes they are taking, what they want to do for a career, what books they have read, and the kinds of stories they most enjoy. The problem with such forms is that they are usually filled out and then stored in a drawer. No one has time to interpret them. However, one of our students who is a junior high librarian designed a reader interest survey for her students. She added their reading test scores and programmed her library computer with 100 of the best books she had read. All her students received individual computer printouts suggesting six books that they would probably like and that would be within their reading level.

Similar commercial programs are becoming available, but what made this program successful was that the librarian had read and personally reacted to each book that she listed in the program. The individualized printouts served as conversation starters from which one-to-one relationships developed. Although she worked hard to initiate the project, she considered it worth the effort because once the machinery was set in order, it could be done for hundreds of students almost as easily as for thirty and she could continue to update it with the new books she was reading.

The key to being able to recommend the right book to the right student is for adults to have such a large and varied reading background that they can personally act as a computer. Skilled teachers and librarians program their minds to draw relationships between what students tell or ask and what they remember about particular books. Experience sharpens this skill, and those librarians who make an effort consistently to read a few new books every month increase their repertoire of books rapidly. As an aid to memory, many people keep a card file of the books they read. They glance through it every few weeks to remind themselves of all the books they know. They also use it as a handy reference when a title or an author slips their minds.

Booktalks

With all their other responsibilities, few librarians have as much opportunity as they would like to guide individual reading on a one-to-one basis. The next-best thing is to give presentations or booktalks to groups. A booktalk is a short introduction to a book, which usually includes one or two paragraphs read from the book. Booktalks are comparable to movie previews or teasers in presenting the characters and a hint of the plot, but they never reveal the ending. Joni Bodart has described booktalking as a kind of storytelling that resembles an unfinished murder mystery in being "enticing. It is a come-on. It is entertaining. And it is fun, for both the listener and the booktalker."[13]

The simplest kind of booktalk may last only sixty seconds. In giving it, the booktalker must let listeners know what to expect. For example, it would be unfair to present only the funniest moments in a serious book—a reader might check it out expecting a comedy. If a book is a love story, then some clue should be given, but care needs to be taken because emotional scenes read out loud and out of context can sound silly. The cover of a book often reveals its tone, which is one of the reasons for holding up a book while it is being discussed or for showing slides if a presentation is being given to a large audience.

Booktalks need to be carefully prepared ahead of time. It takes both concentration and skill to select the "heart" of a story. People who try to ad-lib have the advantage of sounding spontaneous, but they also run the risk of using up all their time telling about one or two books or of getting bogged down in telling the whole story, which would defeat the purpose. Most young readers do not want to hear a ten- or fifteen-minute talk on one book, unless it is dramatic and used as a change of pace along with several shorter booktalks. And even with short booktalks, people's minds begin to wander after they've

HAZEL ROCHMAN
on Booktalking

Reading is a private experience. So how do you promote it without getting between the reader and the book?

When I love a book and want to share the pleasure with others, it's hard not to over-booktalk. As much as possible I try to keep myself out of the way, I want to say just enough to get the audience hooked, and then I leave reader and story alone together. There's always that tension: How can I get them to read this great book, and how can I not spoil it for them? And this applies not only to giving away the end of the story, but to all the surprises along the way in character, plot, and situation. When they come to a great scene, I don't want them to hear my voice.

Booktalking is like storytelling in that I want to draw kids immediately into the world of the book—its story, people, place, voice, ideas. The big difference in storytelling is that a booktalk is just a lure, a hook, to get the audience to read the book. That's one reason why I read aloud from the book rather than memorizing or paraphrasing. Reading aloud is the least intrusive way to talk about the story in the author's own voice. Of course, I choose the passage carefully, I make sure it's worth reading aloud, I mark it carefully (usually with a yellow

listened for ten or fifteen minutes. The ideal approach is for the teacher or librarian to give booktalks frequently, but in short chunks.

However, this may not be practical if the person giving the booktalk is a visitor (e.g., a public librarian coming to a school to encourage students to sign up for library cards and begin to use the public library). In situations like this, the librarian can arrive in class with a cart full of books ready to be checked out. A half-hour or so can be devoted to the booktalks, with the rest of the time saved for questions and answers, browsing, sign-up, and check-out. In cases like this it's good to have a printed bibliography or bookmark to leave with students for later use in the library.

Until recently, this kind of school visit from public librarians was standard practice in Mesa, Arizona. When the library suffered budget cuts so that these visits were no longer possible, the young adult librarians still made the effort by videotaping booktalks and sending the videos out, along with bibliographies, to some of the teachers who had come to depend on their services.

paper sticker) so that I can find the quote without fumbling around, and I keep it short.

I don't want to mislead, it's not fair to present *Wuthering Heights* as if it's a YA romance. They might check it out, but they won't trust me next time and I'll have made reading a disappointing experience.

I try not to sensationalize, to read aloud scenes of violence or titillation. It's easy to get attention that way, but it's exploitative. On the other hand I don't avoid controversial material. The very impersonality of the booktalk—the fact that I'm talking in general to a group—means that I can introduce a variety of topics, from gay love to abortion, without invading anyone's privacy.

There are things to learn about booktalking. We've all felt our eyes glaze over as a friend gives a blow-by-blow account of a beloved book or a movie. I have to select, prepare, and practice. But I think it's important not to get hung up on details of technique: on writing out and memorizing and practicing and videotaping my gestures and my presentation. I haven't got time for that

unless I'm going to do the same perfect booktalk over and over again. It's much more important to spend the time reading so that I have all kinds of books to share with all kinds of readers.

Pleasure in reading comes from comfort, from affirmation of the familiar world—what writer Margaret Atwood calls "hot water bottles and thumb-sucking" kind of reading. We all enjoy that kind of escape reading. But there's also pleasure in books that unsettle us, books that disturb us while they entertain, moving us deeply into a new way of seeing ourselves. Kafka said a book must "wound and stab us"; it must "affect us like a disaster . . . . A book must be the axe for the frozen sea inside us." I try not to condescend to teenagers, not to aim everything at some vague idea of a reluctant reader. Young people continually surprise me with their openness to all kinds of reading. Take poetry: those who like rap and rock and MTV are open to the pleasures of rhythmic, deeply felt words and surprising imagery, more open than many adults who assume that poetry is something esoteric and removed from daily life. I try not to stand in the way.

Hazel Rochman is assistant editor of *Booklist* and a reviewer for the "Books for Youth" section. She compiled the anthology *Somehow Tenderness Survives: Stories of Southern Africa*, HarperCollins, 1988, and prepared a video and book on booktalking, *Tales of Love and Terror*, for the American Library Association, 1987.

This kind of group presentation has the advantage of introducing students to the librarian, which is especially important with public librarians. When students go to the library already feeling acquainted, they are more at ease in initiating a one-to-one relationship, a valuable part of reading guidance. It also gives students more freedom in choosing books that really appeal to them. For example, if a student asks a librarian to recommend a good book, the librarian probably will not have time to tell the student about more than two or three books. The student usually feels obligated to take one of these books whether or not it sounds appealing. But when the librarian presents ten to fifteen different titles, students can choose from a much larger offering. This also enables students to learn about and to select books that might cause them embarrassment if they were recommended on a personal basis. For example, if a girl is suspected of having lesbian leanings, it may not help the situation for the librarian to hand her Nancy Garden's *Annie on My Mind*. But if this were included among several books introduced to the class and the student chose it herself, then it might fill a real need. And the fact that the librarian talks about it, showing that she has read it, opens the door for the girl to initiate a conversation if she so desires.

Another advantage to group presentations is that they are obviously more efficient. For example, if a social studies class is beginning a unit on World War II in which everyone in the class is required to read a novel having something to do with the war and also write a small research paper, it makes sense for the librarian to give the basic information in one group presentation. Being efficient in the beginning will enable the librarian to spend time with individual students who have specific questions rather than making an almost identical presentation to thirty individuals. Table 10.2 gives some suggestions taken from an article by Mary K. Chelton, "Booktalking: You Can Do It."

Table 10.2   DO'S AND DON'T'S FOR BOOKTALKING

Do	Don't
1. Do prepare well. Either memorize your talks or practice them so much that you can easily maintain eye contact.	1. Don't introduce books that you haven't read or books that you wouldn't personally recommend to a good friend as interesting.
2. Do organize your books so that you can show them as you talk. To keep from getting confused, you might clip a note card with your talk on it to the back of each book.	2. Don't "gush" over the books. If it's a good book and you have done an adequate job of selecting what to tell, then it will sell itself.
3. When presenting excerpts, do make sure they are representative of the tone and style of the book.	3. Don't tell the whole story. When listeners beg for the ending, hand them the book. Your purpose is to get them to read.
4. Even though you might sometimes like to focus on one or two themes, do be sure, over the months you meet with any group, that you present a wide variety of books. Include informative books that young readers would probably like to know about but might be too embarrassed to ask for.	4. Don't categorize books as to who should read them, for example, "This is a book you girls will like"; or show by the books you have brought to a particular school that you expect only Asian Americans to read about Asian Americans and only American Indians to read about American Indians, and so forth.
5. Do experiment with different formats, for example, a short movie, some poetry, or one longer presentation along with your regular booktalks.	5. Don't give literary criticisms. You have already evaluated the books for your own purposes and if you did not think they were good, you would not be presenting them.
6. Do keep a record of which books you have introduced to which groups. This can be part of your evaluation when you compare before and after circulation figures on the titles you have talked about. Also, good record keeping will help you not to repeat yourself with a group.	
7. Do be assertive in letting teachers know what you will and will not do. Perhaps distribute a printed policy statement explaining such things as how much lead time you need, the fact that the teacher is to remain with the group, and how willing you are to make the necessary preparation to do booktalks on requested themes or topics.	

Other helpful sources for promoting books (see Focus Box 10.1) include an American Library Association book and videotape featuring Hazel Rochman and entitled "Tales of Love and Terror: Booktalking the Classics, Old and New," Joni Bodart's *Booktalk! Booktalking and School Visiting for Young Adult Audiences,* and the *Wilson Library Bulletin Booktalker,* a newsletter published five times a year as a pull-out section to the *Wilson Library Bulletin.* Joni Richards Bodart edits the newsletter, which is made up mainly of talks about books recommended for readers from the middle grades through high school. The talks are between 200 and 400 words long and will save you preparation time, but we don't advise using these booktalks without at least skimming each book you decide to introduce, so that you will know a little more about it than what's in the suggested write-up.

Displays

Making displays is another effective way to promote books. Most young adults have some common needs, although they might not admit them or even be aware of them. The sensitive adult who knows books can quietly alert students to titles and authors that might prove worthwhile. It can be done simply; indeed, the simpler and less obvious, the better—perhaps nothing more than a sign that says "Like to watch Oprah Winfrey?—You'll Love These" (personal experiences and social issues books, although not identified in just that way), or "Did You Cry Over *Gone with the Wind?*" (books about love problems and divorce).

None of these simple gimmicks involves much work, but what's more important is that they do their job without the librarian seeming pushy or nosy. No book report is required and no one will know whether John checks out Howard Fast's *April Morning* because his father recently died or because he likes American history.

When it comes to promoting books, librarians should not be ashamed to borrow ideas from the world of commerce. After all, we are competing directly for students' time and interest and indirectly for a share of the library budget and the taxpayers' dollars. Attractive, professional-looking displays and bulletin boards give evidence that things are happening in the library (or the classroom), and they help patrons develop positive attitudes toward books and reading. Even if there is no artwork connected with a display, it can encourage reading simply by showing the front covers.

Preparing displays can bring the same kind of personal satisfaction that comes from creatively decorating a room or painting a picture. People who have negative feelings about making displays have probably had experiences in which the results did not adequately compensate for the amount of time and effort expended. One way to correct this imbalance is to follow some general principles that help to increase the returns on a display while cutting down on the work.

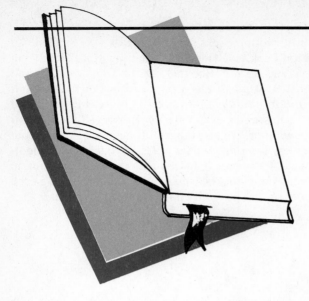

Resources to Help in Promoting Books

for today's series books, but the majority of the annotations are for older, individual titles.

Connecting Young Adults and Libraries: A How-to-Do-It Manual by Patrick Jones. Neal-Schuman Publishers, 1992. Designed to increase the chances of success for educated, intelligent people who find themselves filling the role of young adult librarian even though they've not had specific training.

Courtly Love in the Shopping Mall: Humanities Programming for Young Adults by Evelyn Shaevel and Peggy O'Donnell, edited by Susan Goldberg and Rolly Kent. American Library Association, 1991, 146 pp., $17.50. The authors received a grant to promote the consideration of humanities topics by young adults. They share their experience in hopes of encouraging other librarians to offer similar programs.

Happily Ever After: A Guide to Reading Interests in Romance Fiction by Kristin Ramsdell. Libraries Unlimited, 1987, 203 pp., $33. Designed to help with the question, "Can you recommend a good love story," these annotated bibliographies are organized into subgenres, including Romantic Mysteries and Sagas, Contemporary, Historical, Gay, Inspirational, and Young Adult Romance. Brief identifications are given

More Books Appeal: Keep Young Teens in the Library by Karen Cornell Gomberg. McFarland, 1990, 152 pp., $14.95. In a continuation of the kinds of activities that she suggested in her earlier *Books Appeal: Get Teenagers into the School Library* (McFarland, 1987), Gomberg presents over 200 plans for library activities. Topics include Publicity, Fun with Book Lists, Quiet Mental Games, Reference Books, and Fiction Crossword Puzzles.

Seniorplots: A Book Talk Guide for Use with Readers Ages 15–18 by John T. Gillespie and Corinne J. Naden. R. R. Bowker, 1989, 386 pp., $29.95. In addition to suggestions of excerpts that will make good booktalks, Gillespie and Naden present a summary of each featured book, a paragraph about the book's theme, and suggestions of ten or more books relating to it. Earlier books in the same series include *Junior Plots, More Junior Plots,* and *Juniorplots 3*.

Tales of Love and Terror: Booktalking the Classics, Old and New (book and videotape) by Hazel Rochman. American Library Association, 1987. One of Rochman's points is that the archetypes and patterns of the old myths are given a new life in some of our best contemporary YA literature.

The WLB Booktalker newsletter, edited by Joni Richards Bodart and published as a pull-out section of the *Wilson Library Bulletin* five times a year; also available separately for $9.95. Each issue contains approximately sixty booktalks, many written by subscribers, along with news and encouragement about booktalking. To order, send check or money order to Customer Services; the H. W. Wilson Company; 950 University Avenue; Bronx, New York 10452.

The Young Adult Program Idea Booklet, compiled by the YA Task Force of the Children's and Young Adult Services Section, Wisconsin Library Association, 1991. Librarians throughout Wisconsin contributed descriptions of programs held in their libraries. Necessary preparations are described along with an evaluation of each program's success. To order, send $14.25 (which includes shipping costs) to the Wisconsin Library Association; 4785 Hayes Rd.; Madison, WI 53704-7364.

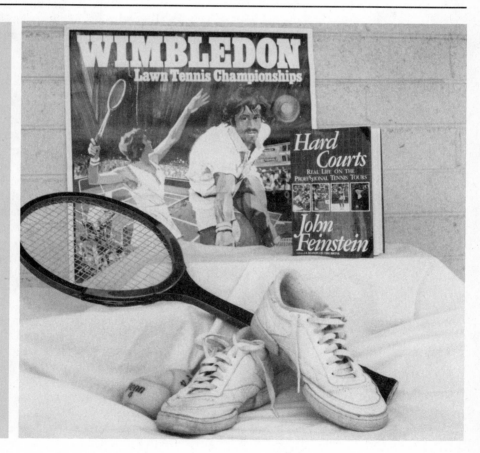

Using real items in displays is an easy and effective way to attract attention.

1. Go window shopping in the best stores—the ones that appeal to the young adults that you are wooing—and when you see a display that you like, adapt its features to your own purposes.
2. Promote more than one book and have multiple copies available. Enthusiasm wanes if people have to put their names on a list and wait. Use color photocopies of the book jackets, so that as the books are checked out, your display won't look skimpy.
3. Tie the displays into current happenings. For example, when its time for the band concert, feature the books in Focus Box 10.2 alongside a poster advertising the concert.
4. Use displays to get people into the library. Offer free bibliographies and announce their availability through local media.
5. Put your displays in high-traffic areas where everyone, not just those who already use the young adult collection, will see them.
6. Use interchangeable parts, so that it isn't necessary to start from scratch each time. Stained fruit baskets and crates from grocery stores, leaning boards with screwed-in hooks for holding books, and boxes covered with drapes are all good ways to get variety and height into a display. Plain backgrounds are better than figured ones to focus attention on the books.
7. Take advantage of modern technology (e.g., buy stick-on letters and use your computer and your desk-top publishing skills to prepare attractive bibliographies and signs).

The changing location of portable displays is in itself an attention getter. A portable display can be as small as a foot-square board set in the middle of a table or as large as a camper's tent set up in the middle of a room and surrounded by books about camping, hiking, backpacking, ecology, and nature foods. If space is a problem, small bulletin boards can be hung from the ceiling or stood against pillars or walls. They can do double duty (e.g., dividing the children's section from the young adult section or separating a reading corner with its casual furniture from the desks and tables set aside for study).

It's a good idea to give students a sense of ownership over the displays by involving them as much as possible. Art teachers are usually happy to work with librarians to have a place where student work can be attractively displayed alongside such art-related books as Louise Plummer's *My Name is Sus5an Smith. The 5 Is Silent*; Gary Paulsen's *The Monument*; Brock Cole's *Celine*; and Zibby Oneal's *In Summer Light*. Snapshots of students with their pets will add interest to a display under the headings of "The Comforts and Delights of Owning a Dog," and "The Comforts and Delights of Being Owned by a Cat." For the dog display put out all the good dog books you can find. We recommend Terry Kay's *To Dance with the White Dog*; James Street's *Good-bye My Lady*; Jeanne Schinto's *The Literary Dog: Great Contemporary Dog Stories*; Michael J. Rosen's *The Company of Dogs*; J. R. Ackerley's *My Dog Tulip*; Fred Gipson's *Old Yeller* and *Savage Sam*; Wilson Rawl's *Where the Red Fern Grows*,

A Few Notes About Music

Bernstein: A Biography by Joan Peyser. Beech Tree, 1987. The life of the flamboyant and popular conductor and composer who was one of the few musicians to move easily among all sorts of music and people.

George Gershwin by Edward Jablonski. Doubleday, 1987. Jablonski may be more interested in Gershwin's music than in his life, but then so are most of us, both his show tunes and his serious music.

Is That It? by Bob Geldof with Pau Vallely. Weidenfeld and Nicholson, 1987. A rock singer with the Boomtown Rats grew up not just to worry about the world's starving masses but to do something—the Band Aid record in 1984 and the Live Aid concert in 1985.

Jaqueline du Pré: A Life by Carol Easton. Summit, 1989. From her middle teens through her late twenties, du Pré was a highly regarded cellist. That stopped when she learned she had multiple sclerosis.

Midnight Hour Encores by Bruce Brooks. HarperCollins, 1986. Sixteen-year-old Sib plays the cello better than any other sixteen-year-old in the world, and she uses her talent to get her single-parent father to take her to a musical audition in California, where as a bonus she plans on meeting her mother. (Fiction.)

Nadja on My Way by Nadja Salerno-Sonnenberg. Crown, 1989. This young violinist shows that both dedication and luck are necessary to achieve the kind of success that musicians dream of.

Paper Doll by Elizabeth Feuer. Farrar, Straus & Giroux, 1990. Seventeen-year-old Leslie Marx is a talented violinist who lost both legs in an accident. Her parents treat her as though she's a child and aren't ready for her interests to go beyond playing the violin. (Fiction.)

Second Fiddle: A Sizzle and Splat Mystery by Ronald Kidd. Lodestar, 1988. In this lighthearted mystery for junior high readers, Prudence Szyznowski and Arthur Hadley Reavis Pauling II team up to discover who's trying to foil their plan to save the Pirelli Youth Orchestra. (Fiction.)

And a Voice to Sing with: A Memoir by Joan Baez. Summit, 1987. Baez writes a sometimes irritating, sometimes delightfully bitchy, recounting of her controversial politics and her singing.

Elizabeth Yates's *The Seventh One*, and *Roger Caras' Treasury of Great Dog Stories*. For the cat display, we especially recommend Robert Westall's *Blitzcat* and *Yaxley's Cat*, Derek Tangye's *A Cat Is Waiting*, Cleveland Amory's *The Cat Who Came for Christmas* and its sequel *The Cat and the Curmudgeon*, Lilian Jackson Braun's *The Cat Who Could Read Backwards*, Peter Gethers' *The Cat Who Went to Paris*, Doris Lessing's *Particularly Cats . . . and Rufus*, A. N. Wilson's *Stray*, Rita Mae Brown and Sneaky Pie Brown's *Wish You Were Here*, and Roger Caras' *Treasury of Great Cat Stories*.

Occasionally, students working as library interns or helpers will enjoy the challenge of doing displays all by themselves, bringing in trash for a display on recycling or ecology or bringing in an overstuffed chair and a footstool as the focal point for a display of leisure-time books. Whatever is interesting and different is the key to tying books in with real life. An ordinary object—a kitchen sink, a pan full of dirty dishes, or a torn and dirty football jersey—is out of the ordinary when it appears on a bulletin board or a display table. Also, don't overlook the possibility of putting up posters such as those offered by the American Library Association or tying commercial posters in with books. Remember the part that the poster message, "Don't disturb the universe," played in Cormier's *The Chocolate War*.

Programs

Stores have special sales and events to get people into the marketplace, where they will be tempted to buy something. In the same way, ambitious librarians put on young adult programs to do something special for those who regularly use the library and, at the same time, to bring nonusers into the library. Opinions are divided on whether or not programs should be designed to promote the use of library materials and on whether they should be educational rather than recreational. Without getting into a discussion of both viewpoints or a complete description of how to set up young adult programs, we can offer some advice from people whose libraries have been especially active in arranging programs:

1. Take a survey, or better, talk with your teenage clientele to see what their interests and desires are.
2. Avoid duplicating the kinds of activities that students do in school and in conjunction with other community agencies.
3. Include young adults in planning and putting on programs. The library can be a showcase for young adult talent.
4. Work with existing youth service agencies to cosponsor events, or plan them in conjunction with school programs so as to have the beginning of an audience and the nucleus of a support group.
5. Do a good job of publicizing the event. The publicity may influence people unable to come, so they will feel more inclined to visit the library at some other time.

A customer looks over American Library Association posters with YA appeal. They were on display at an ALA convention booth.

6. Have a casual setting planned for a relatively small group, with extra chairs available in case more people come than you expect. Bustling around at the last minute to set up extra chairs gives an aura of success that is more desirable than having row upon row of empty chairs.

Among the kinds of programs commonly held are film programs, outdoor music concerts featuring local teenage bands, talent shows in a coffeehouse setting, chess tournaments, and showings of original movies or videos. Workshops are held in computer programming, photography, creative writing, bicycle repair, and crafts. Another kind of program features guest speakers. In public libraries these are often on subjects that schools tend to shy away from, such as self-defense and rape prevention, drug and birth control information, and introductions to various hotlines and other agencies that help young adults.

Large-scale workshops are sometimes held in libraries to which various schools bring their students. For example, in a town with three high schools, one big day on choosing careers may be planned at the community library. Guest speakers who could not give up three days of their time may be willing to make a single appearance, and special exhibits and displays can be set up once rather than three times.

Regardless of the topic or format of a program, librarians should view programs as opportunities to encourage library visitors to become regular book users. The following practices will help:

1. Hold the program so that it is in or very near the young adult book section. If this is impractical, try routing traffic past the YA area or past displays of YA books.
2. Pass out miniature bibliographies, perhaps printed on a bookmark or in some other easy-to-carry format.
3. Schedule the program to end at least a half-hour before the library closes, so that participants can browse and sign up for library cards.
4. Place paperback book racks where they are as tempting as the displays that grocery and discount stores crowd into checkout areas.
5. For ten or fifteen minutes at the start of the program, while waiting for late-comers to straggle in, do a welcome and warm-up by giving a few booktalks related to the subject of the evening.

Some libraries have had success with book discussion groups in which teen-agers serve as readers and critics. These usually work best if their evaluations can be shared, for example, on a bulletin board, in a teen opinion magazine, through a display of books they recommend, in a monthly column in a local

A mixture of regularly scheduled events and special programs keeps library patrons aware of the young adult section of the library.

newspaper, or through the periodic printing and distribution of annotated lists of favorites.

When an author is invited to speak, it is the host librarian's responsibility to begin several weeks in advance to be sure that people are reading the author's books. English and reading teachers should be notified so that they can devote some class time to the author's work. A panel of students who especially enjoyed the author's work might be set up to interact with the author at the end of the formal presentation. Another way to involve students, and perhaps teachers, would be to invite three or four to have lunch or dinner with the guest author. (Check this out first, since some speakers prefer to be left alone to gather their thoughts before making a presentation.) If you are setting up an author's visit, it is usually best that you first write the publisher of the author's most recent book. State how much money, if any, you have available. Sometimes publishers pay for an author's transportation, but you will usually need to pay at least for food and housing and, if possible, to offer an honorarium. If you have no money, say so immediately, and then be patient, flexible, and grateful for whomever you get. An author might be scheduled to speak in or near your area and might then come to you as an extra. Also it is highly possible that there are young adult authors living in your own state. The Children's Book Council (67 Irving Place; New York, NY 10003) has a geographical listing of authors. However, it should be considered only a beginning, as not all authors are listed with them.

Magazines

Magazines and their place in school and library collections have changed considerably since the days when girls read *Seventeen* and boys read the joke page in *Boy's Life* and looked at the pictures in *National Geographic*. Popular adult magazines such as *People, U.S. News and World Report, Sports Illustrated, Cosmopolitan,* and *Life* are staples in teenagers' reading habits, but there are also several dozen magazines devoted specifically to teenagers (see Focus Box 10.3 for recommendations).

As with adult magazines, there are now magazines for every taste—even a few that will please teachers—but what's important for educators to realize is that many students who won't pick up books are eager to read the latest magazines in their areas of interest. With many of the teen magazines, poor readers can feel their first success with the printed word, because much of the information is communicated through easy-to-read layouts and photographs. Also, the material, which is presented in short, digestible chunks, is of prime interest to teens. Some of the magazines will be read by both boys and girls, but because of the abundance of advertising money for cosmetics and fashions, many magazines are purposely designed to appeal only to females. Others, such as *Hot Rod, Muscular Development,* and *Street Motorcycling at Its Best,* will be financed by advertisements for products usually purchased by males.

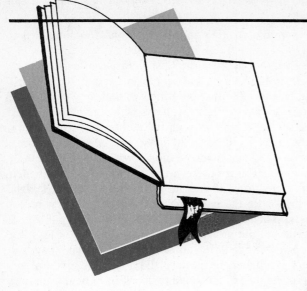

Magazines for YA's— Beyond the Ordinary*

Beckett Baseball Card Monthly. A leading authority on sports card collecting, James Beckett's name makes this an attractive choice for the growing audience of young collectors. ISSN 0886-0599, $19.95 per year. Order from Statabase Inc., 4887 Alpha Rd., Suite 200 Dallas, TX 75244.

Bop. Everything a young girl wants in a music fan magazine—plenty of color photos and posters, quizzes, contests, gossip, pen pals, and reader mail. ISSN 8750-7242, $16.95 per year. Order from Laufer Publishing; 3500 W. Olive Ave., Suite 850; Burbank, CA 91505.

Car and Driver. The ultimate magazine for car enthusiasts, *Car and Driver* includes complete coverage and plenty of photos of the newest and hottest cars. ISSN 0008-6002, $14.98 per year. Order from Hachette Magazines; 1633 Broadway; New York, NY 10009.

Cracked. It's hard to imagine a humor magazine that aims lower than *Mad,* but this one does by aspiring to be at the sophomoric/silly level. ISSN 0883-7561, $14.40 for eight issues a year. Order from Globe Communications Corp.; 441 Lexington Ave.; New York, NY 10017.

Dragon. The official magazine for the Dungeons and Dragons set, this is full of game tips, news, and wonderful illustrations. ISSN 0279-6848, $30 per year. Order from TSR, Inc.; Box 111; Lake Geneva, WI 53144.

Merlyn's Pen: The National Magazine of Student Writing. Editors select the top 3 percent of student contributions to publish in this well-received literary magazine. ISSN 0882-2050, $18.95 for four issues during the school year. Order from Merlyn's Pen; Dept. EJ; P.O. Box 1058; East Greenwich, RI 02818.

News for You. Aimed at adults and teens learning to read, *News for You* has a tabloid format with articles of high interest written for those with a low reading vocabulary. ISSN 0884-3910, $11.04 per year. Order from New Readers Press; 1320 Jamesville Avenue; Syracuse, NY 13210.

Nintendo Power. One of many magazines devoted to the video game audience, this one consists of product information, game tips, and how-to instruction. ISSN 10412-9551, $16.22 per year for six issues. Order from Box 97043; Redmond, WA 97043.

Sassy. Nothing else like it, although because of it *Teen, Seventeen,* and *YM (Young Miss)* look and read a whole lot different. This groundbreaking publication has articles and features "in tune" with its mostly female readership. At the time of this writing, a male version named *Dirt* was being launched. ISSN 0162-8917, $14.97 per year. Order from Sassy Publishers; 230 Park Avenue; New York, NY 10169.

Thrasher.   The absolute skater's bible, *Thrasher* includes skating news, tons of ads, photos, and product information. It also focuses on alternative music. ISSN 0889-0692, $18.50 per year. Order from High Speed Productions; Box 884570; San Francisco, CA 94188.

WWF Magazine.   This is the slickest of all the wrestling magazines with 100 percent hype and a ten-page merchandise catalog in each issue. Although it's another cog in the promotion's money-making machine, it's lots of fun. ISSN 8756-7792, $20 per year. Order from Titan Sports, Inc.; P.O. Box 420174; Palm Coast, FL 33142.

*Thanks to Patrick Jones, Manager of the Tecumseh Branch Library in Fort Wayne, Indiana, for compiling this list and to Nel Ward, Librarian at Central High School in Phoenix, Arizona, and Diane Tucillo, YA librarian at the Mesa, Arizona, Public Library for helping with it. Unless noted otherwise, all magazines are monthly. Quoted prices were in effect during the spring of 1992.

But just as important is the fact that there's no limit to the challenges that good students can find in magazines. A much higher percentage of adult Americans read magazines rather than books, and yet in school we give people little help in introducing them to magazines or in picking out the ones they will get the most from.

It is almost as if kids find magazines in spite of teachers, not because of them. We would do well to change our attitudes and look upon magazines as taking up where books leave off in presenting up-to-date information on a wide variety of topics chosen to be especially interesting to young adults. We need to make special efforts to teach the skills necessary to do research in all kinds of modern periodicals. As pointed out in Chapter Eight, many contemporary writers of informative books for teenagers get most of their information from magazines and journals. If teenagers can learn to get such information themselves, then they won't be limited to reading only about those topics and viewpoints chosen by someone else as "appropriate" for teens.

Using YA Books in the Reading Classroom

Now that many individual teachers, schools, and school districts have adopted a whole language approach to teaching reading, writing, and speaking skills to children, the role of trade books as opposed to textbooks and exercise sheets has become much more acceptable in teaching reading. Under the best circumstances, students come to high school having read many books and being eager to read many more. And under the worst circumstances (i.e., when students arrive in high school unable to read or not wanting to read), the idea of teaching them with genuine literature instead of with workbooks and exercises will be at least familiar to most colleagues and administrators.

Including a section on reading in this text is in some sense superfluous because this whole book is devoted to teaching and promoting reading, but the interests and responsibilities of teachers of reading differ in some ways from those of English teachers or of librarians. One difference is that, except for remedial programs, teaching reading as an academic discipline in the high schools is a fairly recent development. The assumption used to be that normal students had received enough formal instruction in reading by the time they completed elementary school. They were then turned over to English teachers who taught mostly literature, grammar, and composition. Certainly English teachers worked with reading skills, but they were not the primary focus. Today more and more states are passing laws setting minimal reading standards for high school graduation, and this has meant that reading has become almost a regular part of the high school curriculum. In some schools, all ninth-graders now take a reading class; in other schools, such a class is reserved for those who test one or two years below grade level. Depending on how long it takes them to pass the test, students may take basic reading classes for several semesters.

Reluctant Readers

In the teaching profession the reluctant reader is nearly always stereotyped as a boy from the wrong side of town, someone S. E. Hinton would describe as an outsider, a greaser. Actually, reluctant readers come in both male and female varieties and from all social and I.Q. levels. Many of them have fairly good reading skills; they simply don't like to read. Others are poor readers partly because they get so little practice. What these students have in common is that they have been disappointed in their past reading. The rewards of reading—what they received either emotionally or intellectually—have not come up to their expectations, which were based on how hard they worked to read the material. They have therefore come away feeling cheated.

The reading profession has recognized this problem and has attempted to solve it by lowering the price the student has to pay (i.e., by devising reading materials that demand less effort from the student). These are the controlled vocabulary books commonly known as "high-low books," meaning high interest, low vocabulary. They are moderately successful. One problem is that there isn't enough variety to appeal to everyone. A disproportionate number of them have been written to the stereotyped target audience of the young male from a gang. The authors are rarely creative artists; they are educators who have many priorities that come before telling a good story. An alternative approach to encourage reluctant readers is to make the rewards greater rather than to reduce the effort. This is where the best adolescent literature comes into the picture. The rewards are often high enough to fully recompense supposedly reluctant teenage readers. And once these readers enjoy the satisfaction of receiving what they consider full pay for their work, they are happy to play the reading game.

Young adult literature has a good chance of succeeding with the reluctant reader for the following reasons:

1. It is written specifically to be interesting to teenagers. It is geared to their age level and their interests.
2. It is usually shorter and more simply written than adult material, yet it has no stigma attached to it. It isn't written down to anyone, nor does it look like a reading textbook.
3. There is so much of it (almost 800 new books published every year) that individual readers have a good chance of finding books that appeal to them.
4. As would be expected, since they are the creations of some of the best contemporary writers, the stories are more dramatic, better written, and easier to get involved in than the controlled vocabulary books.
5. The language used in good adolescent literature is much more like the language that students are accustomed to hearing. In this day of mass media communication, a student who does not read widely may still have a fairly high degree of literary and language sophistication gained from watching television and movies.

Taking all this into account, some types of adolescent literature will still be enjoyed more than others by reluctant readers. In general, reluctant readers want the same things from the books they read that the rest of us want, but they want them faster and in less space. If it's information they are looking for, they want it to be right there. If they are reading a book for thrills and chills, they want it to be really scary. If they're reading for humor, they want it to be really funny. And if they're not sure about committing themselves for a large chunk of time, they want books in which they can get a feeling of accomplishment from reading short sections or even paragraphs. This helps explain the continuing popularity of the *Guinness Book of World Records*.

Booklist publishes an annual "High-Interest/Low-Reading-Level Booklist" compiled by a Young Adult Library Services Association committee. Single copies in leaflet format can be ordered from *Booklist* (American Library Association; 50 E. Huron St., Chicago, IL 60611) for fifty cents and a stamped, self-addressed envelope. The list is divided into three different reading levels figured on the Fry Readability Scale, none of which are above grade 6. The committee considers "titles intended for the young adult that are written using controlled vocabulary, short sentences, short paragraphs, simplicity of plot, and uncomplicated dialogue." Selection criteria include a sense of timeliness, maturity of format, and appeal of content. Fiction must include "believability of character and plot as well as realistic dialogue." (Also, look at the February 15, 1992, *Booklist* for Frances A. Miller's "Books to Read When You Hate to Read: Recommended by Reluctant YA Readers in Grades 7–12.")

The National Council of Teachers of English publishes every few years, as one of its Bibliography series, *High Interest—Easy Reading: A Booklist for Junior and Senior High School Students*. William McBride was chair of the committee that chose the books for the most recent edition, published in 1990.

The NCTE book is cumulative, covering recommended titles from several years with an emphasis on fiction.

Free Reading Classes

The push for higher reading scores has opened the high school curriculum to reading classes for all students, not just those with low reading scores. For example, most high schools offer study skills courses in which skimming, speed reading, and selecting main ideas are taught. Some high schools also offer a class in free reading. Such classes have been taught since the 1930s, and were especially popular in the 1970s, when high schools offered a range of electives, including free reading courses under such titles as Individualized Reading, Paperback Power, Contemporary Reading, and Personalized Reading. Some schools still offer such classes, but with the back-to-the-basics swing that occurred in the 1980s today's free reading is more likely to be incorporated into a six-week unit or a twice-a-week program worked in as part of more standard English or reading classes.

The thinking behind the organization of such classes is that one of the chief reasons that out-of-school reading drops off so dramatically when children leave elementary school is that the social and work schedules of high school students leave them little time for reading. In free reading courses students read any books they choose. A classroom library is usually provided containing multiple copies of popular YA and adult titles. Teachers usually send a note of explanation to parents that includes the statement that the choice of books is up to the student and his or her parents. Nearly all class time is reserved for reading, with the exception of a couple of days near the beginning, when either the teacher or the librarian gives booktalks to help the students choose books. Once the class gets started, students both formally and informally recommend "good books" to each other.

When students finish a book, they hold a conference with the teacher, who preferably has also read the book. The purpose of the conference is not to test whether the student has really read the book, but to encourage thinking about the book and the author's intentions. These student/teacher conferences also give teachers opportunities to suggest other books, with the goal of helping young readers make progress in advancing their reading skills and their reading tastes. It's crucial to the success of such conferences that teachers be familiar with a large number of popular books and that they respect the reading of such books and are genuinely interested in what students have to say about them. The class is doomed to failure if teachers view it as a kind of focused study hall in which their job is to do little more than keep control and keep kids reading. It's also doomed to failure if students view it as a "cake" class, and for this reason teachers are fairly stringent as they devise various systems for giving credit. Students keep records of the number of books (or number of pages) read, they assist the teacher in judging the difficulty of the material, they mark their improvement over the semester (perhaps shown by a test score or by the number of pages the student reads in a class period), and the teacher grades the students on their preparation for the individual conferences.

Various studies summarized by Dick Abrahamson and Eleanor Tyson in "What Every English Teacher Should Know About Free Reading"[14] have shown:

- Free reading is enjoyed by both students and teachers.
- Over a semester, students pick a variety of books, ranging from easy to difficult and from recent to classic.
- Reading skills improve, with some of this improvement undoubtedly related to attitude change.
- Students taught through free-reading are more likely to read as adults and to foster reading activities with their children.
- Individual conferences help literature come alive for students.
- The conferences also help to break down barriers between students and teachers.
- Good teachers employ the concept of reading ladders (e.g., helping a girl move from a Sweet Dreams romance to a Norma Fox Mazer or an M. E. Kerr book and on to *Gone with the Wind* and *Jane Eyre*).

With so many benefits, why isn't the course taught more often? Part of the reason is an image problem. Someone serious about teaching or proposing to teach this kind of a class should probably refer to it as *individualized* rather than *free* reading. *Free reading* smacks of free love and the permissiveness of the 1970s. Although the connotations of such a course title might attract students, these same connotations fly in the face of those who believe "You get what you pay for." Besides, the course is already suspect because of its avowal of quantity over quality, what some have called "reading by the pound," and its emphasis on pleasure for students. More people than we care to think about are sure that if students are having a good time they can't also be learning.

Another problem is that the teacher's role is practically invisible. Being able to listen to students while working ever so subtly to suggest books that will raise levels of reading and improve skills without discouraging young readers takes a knowledge of hundreds of books plus tact and considerable talent in communication. Yet this teaching occurs in private sessions between two people. One of our favorite graduate students is a high school reading teacher who teaches an individualized reading class along with some of the more traditional remedial reading classes. She laughs in frustration about her principal's visits to her individualized reading class. After popping his head into her room on several different occasions and seeing the kids reading and her talking with a student at her desk, he sent her a note requesting that she let him know "when you are going to be teaching," so that he could come and observe.

She's still trying to educate him about the type of class she's teaching. It is not for the dysfunctional or disabled reader. It is for the average, or above-average, student who simply needs a chance to read and discuss books. In effect, it is one last try on the part of the school to instill in young people the habit of reading for pleasure. The student who lacks the skills for this kind of reading class or for a more standard class in literature needs expert help from a professional reading teacher. Preparing teachers for that kind of role is beyond the scope of this book.

In the Social Studies Class

Social studies teachers have always recognized the importance of biographies and of the kind of historical books featured in Chapter Seven, but they may not be as aware of the many books, both fiction and nonfiction, that are available to help them teach students about contemporary social issues. For example, John McPhee's *Encounters with the Archdruid* explores the clash between a man who loves dams and David Brower, one of today's most charismatic and irritating conservationists. Barry Holstun is a writer who cares to see *and* feel as shown by his *River Notes*, which tells what the river is and what it says and does to us. In *Desert Solitaire*, Edward Abbey shares thoughts about his life and his fellow citizens as he worked in a national park. In *The Journey Home: Some Words in Defense of the American West*, Abbey presents a collection of odds and ends that become an autobiography and a statement of his fears for, and his feelings about, the West.

See Chapter Eight for other nonfiction books treating topics of interest to teenagers. Besides the big topic of ecology, social issue books focus on several major themes. Books on issues related to sex ask questions about pornography, rape, abuse, abortion, and prostitution. Books related to medicine ask questions about failures in the health care system and ethical questions about transplants, surrogate parenting, euthanasia, animal rights, and experiments on humans. Books on government ask questions about individual rights as opposed to the welfare of the group. Such questions range from whether the state has a right to require motorcycle helmets and seat belts to whether it should legislate drugs and sexual preference. A topic of particular interest to young adults is that of who declares wars versus who fights wars. Jim Murphy took a historical approach to this question in his *The Boys' War: Confederate and Union Soldiers Talk About the Civil War*, whereas Robert Rosen and Patra McSharry took a contemporary approach. They collected stories and essays from young soldiers fighting in South America, Afghanistan, and Northern Ireland for their *Teenage Soldiers, Adult Wars*.

Social studies teachers miss a powerful resource if they fail to bring fiction into their classes. For example, Philip Pullman's *The Broken Bridge* can give readers empathy for the added complications that children of multiracial marriages experience in figuring out their identity. The story is set in a contemporary Welsh village, where sixteen-year-old Ginny, whose deceased mother was a Haitian artist, tries to sort out her feelings when a white half-brother comes to live with her and her English father. Norma Fox Mazer's *Silver* makes the problem of sexual abuse real through the story of Sarabeth moving to a new town and finding a group of friends, one of whom is being molested by an uncle.

One of the great values and pleasures of literature is that it frees us to travel vicariously to other times and places. Movies, television, and photographs allow people to see other places, but literature has the added dimension of allowing the reader to share the thoughts of another person. One never feels like a stranger in a country whose literature one has read. In today's jet age, distances are rapidly shrinking, so that it is more important than ever that people realize that members of the human race, regardless of where or how they live, have more similarities than differences.

Historical fiction (see Chapter Seven), contemporary fiction set in other countries (see Focus Box 2.4, p. 86), fiction about members of ethnic groups (see Focus Boxes 1.3, 1.4, 2.2, and 2.3, pp. 26, 28, 64, and 66), and well-written informative books should all be part of high school social studies classes. When Laurence Yep wrote *Dragonwings,* he fictionalized the true story of a Chinese immigrant in California who made a flying machine in 1909 that flew for twenty minutes. Yep explained in an afterword that very little was actually known about the man because "Like the other Chinese who came to America, he remains a shadowy figure. Of the hundreds of thousands of Chinese who flocked to these shores we know next to nothing." What Yep wanted to do with his story was to change at least a few of these people from "statistical fodder" into real people with "fears and hopes, joys and sorrows like the rest of us."

This is what good literature can do for any mass of social facts, figures, and statistics. Katherine Paterson's *Lyddie* does it for Lowell, Massachusetts, in 1840; there thirteen-year-old Lyddie Worthen goes to work in a fabric mill in hopes of earning enough money to save her family's farm. And Uri Orlev's *The Man from the Other Side* does it for Warsaw, Poland, during World War II, when Marek helps his Polish stepfather smuggle food and guns through the underground sewers to the Jewish ghetto.

Turning facts into believable stories that touch readers' emotions is the biggest contribution of fiction to the social studies class. However, it is important for readers to realize that many different books need to be read because each book presents a limited perspective. Stereotypes exist in people's minds for two reasons. One is that the same attitudes are repeated over and over, so that they become a predominant image. Another is that an individual may have had only one exposure to a particular race, group, or country. For example, readers of Chaim Potok's *The Chosen* don't learn everything about Hasidic Jews, but they know a lot more than they did before they read the book, and their interest may have been piqued, so that they will continue to watch for information and to read other books.

Nearly everyone agrees that by reading widely and sharing their findings, social studies class members can lead each other to go beyond stereotypes. However, for this to happen on more than an ad hoc or serendipitous basis, the teacher needs to identify clear-cut goals and then seek help from professional sources and other teachers and librarians in drawing up a selective list of books to be offered to students.

PARENTS AND YOUNG ADULT LITERATURE

"Tell me a story."

"Read just one more!"

"Can we go to the library today?"

Such requests are among the pleasant memories that parents have of their young children. These memories become even more cherished when parents look at these same children, now teenagers rushing off to part-time jobs or after-school sports, or spending so much time with friends that they no longer seem to have time to do required school assignments, much less read a book.

When parents ask us what they can do to encourage their teenage children to read, we find it easier to tell them what *not* to do, because we've observed at least three clear-cut roads to failure.

1. Don't nag. There's simply no way to force young adults to read, much less to enjoy it.
2. If you choose to read the books your teenagers are reading, don't do it as a censor or with the intent of checking up on your child or your child's school.
3. Don't suggest books to your teenager with the only purpose being to teach moral lessons.

Lest we appear unduly pessimistic, we hasten to add that we have also seen some genuinely rewarding reading partnerships between teenagers and their parents. These successful partnerships have resembled the kind of reading-based friendships that adults have with each other. Mutual respect is involved, and the partners take turns making suggestions of what will be good to read. Conversations about characters, plots, authors, and subject matter come up naturally, with no one asking teacher-type questions and no one feeling pressured to talk about what he or she has just read.

Teenagers enjoy being in a helping role (i.e., being experts whose opinions are valued). Some of the best partnerships we've seen have been between our students whose teenage children have volunteered to read and share their opinions on the books they've seen their mothers reading (sorry we can't remember any fathers in this role although we have known fathers who do read and serve as examples).

A key to enticing young people to read is simply to have lots of books and magazines available. But they need to be available for genuine browsing and reading by everyone in the family, not purchased and planted in a manner that will appear phoney to the teenager. A teenager who has never seen his or her parents read for pleasure will surely be suspicious when parents suddenly become avid readers on the day after parent/teacher conferences.

Perhaps a more important benefit than modeling behavior is that when parents read some of the best new books (the Honor Sampling is a good starting place), they gain an understanding of what is involved in being a teenager today. Parents who have read some of the realistic problem novels will have things to discuss with their children whether or not the children have read the books. And even when children aren't interested in heart-to-heart discussions, parents will be more understanding if they've read about the kinds of turmoil that teenagers face in struggling to become emotionally independent. In our own classes, and we understand the same is true for others teaching young adult literature, we are getting an increasing number of adult students who are there simply because they enjoy reading and talking about the young adult fiction that was not being written when they were teenagers. Those who are parents of teenagers consider it serendipitous if their teenagers also get interested and begin reading the same books.

A more structured approach is for parents to work with youth groups and church groups or to volunteer as a friend of either the public library or the school library. These kinds of activities provide parents with extra opportunities to involve young people in sharing reading experiences. In such situations, it's often a benefit to have other young people involved and for parents to trade off, so that they aren't always the leader for the particular group in which their child is a member.

In Clarifying Human Relations and Values

Workers with church and civic youth groups, teachers of classes in human relations, and professional counselors working with young adults have all found that adolescent literature can be a useful tool in the work they do. When we talk about using books to help students understand their own and other people's feelings and behavior, we sometimes use the term *bibliotherapy*. But it is a word that goes in and out of fashion, at least in reference to the informal kind of work that most teachers and librarians do with young adults. Its technical meaning is the use of books by professionally trained psychologists and psychiatrists in working with people who are mentally ill. It is because of this association with illness that many "book" people reject the term. Their reasoning is that if a young adult is mentally ill and in need of some kind of therapy, then the therapy should be coming from someone trained in that field rather than from someone trained in the book business or in teaching and guiding normal and healthy young adults.

However, most people agree that normal and healthy young adults can benefit psychologically from reading and talking about the problems of fictional characters. They get the kinds of insights that are reflected in the following comments collected from students by Ina Ewing, a teacher at Maryvale High School in Arizona:

The book [Judy Blume's] *Forever* shows a girl making a hard decision. Every girl has to make that decision at one time or other and so Kathy is like a lot of girls I know. My friends don't talk about it though, so it's good to read about someone else's decision. I think it helps.

[in reference to John Neufeld's *Lisa, Bright and Dark*] I never realized that even kids our age have big enough problems to go crazy. I always thought the ones who went nuts were the ones who were taking dope. I would sure try to help a friend of mine though who thought she was going crazy. It must be scary.

[In reference to Paul Zindel's *The Pigman*] When my grandma died my grandpa came to live with us. It was a big bother because I had to move into a room with my brother. Now I'm glad that he has a place to stay so he won't be so lonely.

[In reference to Ann Head's *Mr. and Mrs. Bo Jo Jones*] I liked the way the book told the side of a couple that makes it when they get married. Most books tell you that if a girl and guy have to get married, it won't last. Even though they had their share of problems, they made their marriage work in the end. It shows that sometimes pregnancy occurs because love is strong in spite of everything else.[15]

All teenagers have problems of one type or another, and simply finding out that other people have them too provides some comfort. We are reassured to know that our fears and doubts have been experienced by others. We feel more confident when we read about people successfully coping with problems that we may have in the future. Notice that of the four student comments given here, only one refers to an actual event. The others are conjectures about things that might happen.

David A. Williams, a communications professor at the University of Arizona, said in a newspaper interview that he would die happy if he could "prove that a positive correlation exists between the rise in anxiety in the country and the decline of pleasure reading." Research done during the 1950s and 1960s has shown that anxiety is directly related to a poor concept of oneself. "It seems to me," he said, "that the human being's major concern in life is to determine what it means to be a human being." The paradox is that before people can see themselves, they have to get outside of themselves and look at the whole spectrum of human experience to see where they fit in. "When we are feeling anxious it is usually because we have a narrow perspective which sees only what it wants to see." Someone who is anxiety-ridden, paranoiac, or resentful selects experiences from life to validate those feelings. For people like this, reading can put things back into perspective. "When we read about others who have suffered similar anxieties, we don't feel so cut off and, although the world doesn't change, we change the way we look at it."[16]

Books put things back into perspective because they talk about the human experience in ways that bring readers back to an awareness of their commonality with other human beings and that open up avenues of communication that successful discussion leaders tap into.

However, it is important for adults to be careful in guiding students to read and talk about personal problems. No one should be forced to participate in such a discussion, nor should a special effort be made to relate stories to the exact problem that a group member is having. In fact, it would probably be best to avoid matching up particular problems with particular students. When someone is in the midst of a crisis, chances are good that he or she does not want to read and talk about someone else in a similar predicament. As a general rule, one will probably get the most from such a discussion before and/or after— rather than during—a time of actual crisis.

Such discussions are usually held in clubs, church groups, classes on preparation for marriage and human relations, and counseling and support group meetings at crisis centers and various institutions to which young people are sent. Since membership in these groups changes from meeting to meeting and there are no pressures for participants to do outside reading as "homework," a leader will probably be disappointed or frustrated if the discussion is planned around the expectation that everyone will have read the book. A more realistic plan is for the leader to give a summary of the book and a ten- to twenty-minute prepared reading of the part that best delineates the problem or the topic for discussion. Using fairly well-known books, including ones that have been made into movies, will increase the chances of participation. Using popular books will also make it easier for students whose appetites have been whetted to find the book and read it on their own.

In an adult group of professionals, the same purpose would be accomplished by reading a case study that would then be discussed. But case studies are written for trained adults who know how to fill in the missing details and how to interpret the symptoms. Teenagers are not psychologists, nor are they social workers or philosophers. Literature may be as close as they will ever come to discussing the kinds of problems dealt with in these fields. And the oral presentation of a well-written fictional account has the advantage of being entertaining and emotionally moving in ways that factual case studies could not be.

What follows the oral presentation can be extremely varied, depending on the nature of the group, the leader's personality, and what the purpose or the goal of the discussion is. The literature provides the group—both teenagers and adults—with a common experience presented through the neutral (as far as the group is concerned) eyes of the author. This common experience can then serve as the focus for discussion. Pressures and tensions are relieved because everyone is talking in the third person about the characters in the book, although in reality many of the comments will be about first-person problems.

M. E. KERR
on Cover Art II

I am still dismayed by the cover art of both hardcover and softcover publications of my books . . . and it is no comfort to hear that eventually with more hard/soft contracts there will be but one cover.

Only foreign publishers seem to understand that one does not have to "talk down" to kids. I have seen everything from Red Grooms' "City Boy," as a cover for *Fell* (L'Ecole Des Loisirs) to a marvellous, almost surrealistic interpretation of *Gentlehands* (Fluwelen Vingers) for Lemniscaat, Dutch.

Here in the states all YA books look alike, with illustrations that seem to be in a time tunnel of the forties and fifties slick magazine era. They are not art, nor even an attempt to be sophisticated graphic art. Compare them with the jacket art of album covers (reduced for CD's), the stylized presentations on MTV, even video sleeves for popular movies, and these photogenic young people seem more like a page from the Crew or Bean catalogs advertising sweaters and pants.

They sit up on the book racks, one looking as dull as another, no single publishing house distinguishing itself with any attempt at something provocative, daring, new . . . like the very kids they sell to, afraid to go out looking different from the others.

The Powers That Be tell me it's a matter of money, but the artists reply no, it's a matter of taste . . . and "they" don't want creative work: they want just that look they all have.

So they have it. Occasionally, they rise above it for mystery or horror. One editor told me the reason their paperback horror covers are better is because a decision was made never to show a young female being menaced, so the artists had to be more inventive.

But mostly, it boggles the mind to see one cover after the other, same poses, same expressions, the same, the same . . . And meanwhile there are educators, publishers, and media folk assembling to ask themselves yet again why kids have to be goaded into reading.

What the publishers ought to be doing is thanking their lucky stars there are concerned teachers and librarians out there pushing the books and the idea of reading, for they (the publishers) are doing nothing to enhance their product. The writer, who cares the most, is usually barely tolerated in any discussion of packaging. At any rate, none of us seems to be able to lift the curse of the catalog look from YA covers.

M. E. Kerr's books include *Fell Back*, 1989; *Night Kites*, 1987; *Dinky Hocker Shoots Smack*, 1972; and *If I Love You, Am I Trapped Forever?*, 1973, all HarperCollins.

The theory developed by Lawrence Kohlberg and his associates at Harvard University during the 1960s about how people solve moral problems is relevant. According to Kohlberg's findings, moral judgment is not something that can be intellectually taught. Rather, it develops with experience and age, in a predictable sequence. Longitudinal studies conducted in many different cultures have shown that young people between the ages of ten and twenty-five go through six stages of development in their attempts to solve moral problems. People sometimes become fixated at one of these stages (e.g., an adult operating at the second stage, that of immediate reciprocity, which can be linked to a you-be-nice-to-me-and-I'll-be-nice-to-you approach). Typically, however, people continue to progress through the stages, which are grouped into three levels. Table 10.3 shows these levels and stages. The table is taken from one of the few articles that has been written on the relationship between books and the behaviors involved in moral judgment, "Moral Development and Literature for Adolescents" by Peter Scharf.

In Scharf's article he makes the point that the way a reader responds to a particular story will depend on the stage of moral judgment that he or she has reached. For example, at age thirteen a reader is apt to respond to Dostoevsky's *Crime and Punishment* as a mystery, but at age twenty the same reader would be more likely to look at it as a complex study of human morals. Great literature has an impact at almost any age, but students respond the most to that which fits the particular level at which they are struggling to make sense of the world. At the beginning levels (early teens), readers are reassured to read books in which there are definite rules and clear-cut examples of right and wrong. As readers move into the conventional or middle levels, they are interested in literature that focuses on social expectations. According to Scharf, this literature

stimulates a sense of moral conventionality by praising "appropriate" social attitudes. Often protagonists will represent heroic values which are

Table 10.3   CLASSIFICATION OF MORAL JUDGMENT INTO LEVELS AND STAGES OF DEVELOPMENT

Levels	Stages of Development
Level I. Preconventional	Stage 1: Obedience and punishment orientation
	Stage 2: Naively egoistic orientation
Level II. Conventional	Stage 3: Good-boy orientation
	Stage 4: Authority and social-order maintaining orientation
Level III. Postconventional	Stage 5: Contractual legalistic orientation
	Stage 6: Conscience or principle orientation

Source: Adapted from Lawrence Kohlberg, "Stage and Sequence: The Cognitive Developmental Approach to Socialization," from *Handbook of Socialization Theory and Research,* edited by David Goslin. Copyright © 1969 by David A. Goslin. Reprinted by permission.

reflected and emulated by young readers. Villains are often portrayed as "unfeeling" or "cruel" in often one-dimensional, somewhat stereotyped ways. Good literature of this type presents a coherent moral universe in which good and evil are polarized and defined. . . . While this type of literature may seem "corny" or "sentimental" to adults, it is a necessary stage toward the learning of more complex personal moral philosophies.[17]

As students become confident at this level and feel that they understand the expectations of society, they begin tentatively to explore and question these expectations. Many young people reject the conventional moral order and seek to set up or to find a more satisfactory social order. Scharf wrote:

> Needless to say, this questioning is disturbing to many adults, including librarians. They fail to see that such a rejection of conventional societal truth is a critical step in the adolescent's defining for himself an autonomous value base.[18]

Because many young adults are in the stage of rebellion and questioning, Holden Caulfield in Salinger's *The Catcher in the Rye* speaks forcefully to them. As people mature, they gradually pass through this stage of rebellion and are not so concerned with society and its expectations. Instead they develop an internal system by which they make moral judgments. This final stage is distinct from both early adolescent conformity and the relativism and nihilism of middle adolescence. Scharf thinks that books and libraries have a unique role in pro-

Table 10.4   THE POWERS AND LIMITATIONS OF YA LITERATURE

What literature can do:	What literature cannot do:
1. It can provide a common experience or a way in which a teenager and an adult can focus their attention on the same subject.	1. It cannot cure someone's emotional illness.
2. It can then serve as a discussion topic and a way to relieve embarrassment by enabling people to talk in the third person about problems with which they are concerned.	2. It cannot guarantee that readers will behave in socially approved ways.
3. It can give young readers confidence that, should they meet particular problems, they will be able to solve them.	3. It cannot directly solve readers' problems.
4. It can increase a young person's understanding of the world and the many ways that individuals find their places in it.	
5. It can comfort and reassure young adult readers by showing them that they are not the only ones who have fears and doubts.	
6. It can give adults as well as teenagers insights into adolescent psychology and values.	

viding readers with the range of material that they need to reflect upon in developing their inner values.

In conclusion, literature can in no way solve someone's problems. But it can serve as a stimulus to thought, and it can open channels of communication. It can serve as a conversation topic while rapport and understanding grow between an adult and a teenager or among the members of a group. And reading widely about all kinds of problems and all kinds of solutions will help to keep young people involved in thinking about moral issues.

Table 10.4 shows what young adult literature can and cannot do when it is used as a tool to teach about human relations and values.

This chapter has shown that using and promoting books with young readers is a shared opportunity and responsibility. It belongs not only to librarians and English and reading teachers but to everyone who works closely with young people and wants to understand them better. It can serve as a medium through which to open communication with young adults about their concerns.

NOTES

[1]*Human and Anti-Human Values* (Council on Interracial Books for Children, 1976), p. 4.

[2]Janet French, "Review of *Homecoming*," *School Library Journal* 28 (September 1981): 133.

[3]Audrey Eaglen, "What Makes a Good Review," *Top of the News* 35 (Winter 1979): 146–152.

[4]Anne Tyler, "Looking for Mom," *New York Times Book Review*, April 26, 1981, p. 52.

[5]Katherine Paterson, "Family Visons," *New York Times Book Review*, November 14, 1982, p. 41.

[6]Dorothy Mathews, "Writing about Adolescent Literature: Current Approaches and Future Directions," *Arizona English Bulletin* 18 (April 1976): 216–19.

[7]Katha Pollitt, "Why We Read: Canon to the Right of Me . . . ," *The Nation*, September 23, 1991, reprinted in *The Chronicle of Higher Education*, October 23, 1991.

[8]Pollitt.

[9]*Rudolfo Anaya Autobiography as Written in 1985*. Copyright 1991 Rudolfo Anaya (TQS Publications; P.O. Box 9275; Berkeley, CA 94709), pp. 16–17.

[10]*The Big Aiiieeeee!: An Anthology of Chinese American and Japanese American Literature*, edited by Jeffery Paul Chan, Frank Chin, Lawson Fusao Inada, and Shawn Wong (New American Library, 1991), p. 8.

[11]Maxine Hong Kingston, "Personal Statement," in *Approaches to Teaching Kingston's THE WOMAN WARRIOR*, edited by Shirley Geok-lin Lim (Modern Language Association, 1991), p. 24.

[12]Dorothy M. Broderick, "Whose Job Is It Anyway?" *VOYA* 6 (February 1984): 320–26.

[13]Joni Bodart, *Booktalk! Booktalking and School Visiting for Young Adult Audiences* (H. W. Wilson, 1980), p. 2–3.

[14]Dick Abrahamson and Eleanor Tyson, "What Every English Teacher Should Know About Free Reading," *The ALAN Review* 14 (Fall 1986): 54–58, 69.

[15]Ina Ewing, "The Psychological Benefits of Young Adult Literature," unpublished paper, Arizona State University Department of Educational Technology and Library Science, spring semester, 1978.

[16]"Feeling Uptight, Anxious? Try Reading, UA Prof Says," *Tempe Daily News*, December 15, 1977.

[17]Peter Scharf, "Moral Development and Literature for Adolescents," *Top of the News* 33 (Winter 1977): 131–36.

[18]Scharf, 131–36.

OTHER TITLES MENTIONED IN THE TEXT OF CHAPTER TEN

Abbey, Edward. *The Journey Home: Some Words in Defense of the American West*. Dutton, 1977.

Ackerley, J. R. *My Dog Tulip*. Poseidon, 1986.

Adams, Douglas. *The Hitchhiker's Guide to the Galaxy*. Crown, 1980.

Amory, Cleveland. *The Cat Who Came for Christmas*. Little, Brown, 1987.

———. *The Cat and the Curmudgeon*. Little, Brown, 1990.

Anaya, Rudolfo. *Bless Me, Ultima*. TQS Publications, 1972.

Blume, Judy. *Forever*. Bradbury, 1975.

Bradbury, Ray. *The Martian Chronicles*. Doubleday, 1958.

Braun, Lilian Jackson. *The Cat Who Could Read Backwards*. Dutton, 1966.

Bridgers, Sue Ellen. *Notes for Another Life*. Knopf, 1981.

Brown, Rita Mae and Sneaky Pie Brown. *Wish You Were Here*. Bantam, 1990.

Campbell, Patricia J. *Presenting Robert Cormier, Updated Edition*. G. K. Hall/Twayne, 1989.

Caras, Roger. *Treasury of Great Dog Stories*. Dutton, 1987.

———. *Treasury of Great Cat Stories*. Dutton, 1987.

Chan, Jeffery Paul, Frank Chin, Lawson Fusao Inada, and Shawn Wong, eds. *The Big Aiiieeeee!: An Anthology of Chinese American and Japanese American Literature*. Meridian, 1991.

Cole, Brock. *Celine*. Farrar, Straus & Giroux, 1989.

Childress, Alice. *A Hero Ain't Nothin' But a Sandwich*. Putnam, 1973.

———. *Rainbow Jordan*. Putnam, 1981.

Cormier, Robert. *The Chocolate War*. Pantheon, 1974.

Dostoevsky, Feodor. *Crime and Punishment*. 1866.

Fast, Howard. *April Morning*. Crown, 1961.

Garden, Nancy. *Annie on My Mind*. Farrar, Straus & Giroux, 1982.

Gethers, Peter. *The Cat Who Went to Paris*. Crown, 1991.

Gipson, Fred. *Old Yeller*. HarperCollins, 1956.

———. *Savage Sam*. HarperCollins, 1962.

Golding, William. *Lord of the Flies*. Putnam, 1955.

Hamilton, Virginia. *Sweet Whispers, Brother Rush*. Putnam, 1982.

Head, Ann. *Mr. and Mrs. Bo Jo Jones*. Putnam, 1967.

Hinton, S. E. *The Outsiders*. Viking, 1967.

Hipple, Ted. *Presenting Sue Ellen Bridgers*. G. K. Hall/Twayne, 1990.

Kay, Terry. *To Dance with the White Dog*. Peachtree, 1991.

Kies, Cosette. *Presenting Young Adult Horror Fiction*. Twayne, 1991.

Kingston, Maxine Hong. *The Woman Warrior: Memoirs of a Girlhood Among Ghosts*. Knopf, 1976.

Knowles, John. *A Separate Peace*. Macmillan, 1960.

Lessing, Doris. *Particularly Cats . . . and Rufus*. Knopf, 1991.

Mazer, Norma Fox. *Silver*. Morrow, 1988.

McBride, William G. ed. *High Interest—Easy Reading: A Booklist for Junior and Senior High School Students,* 6th ed. National Council of Teachers of English, 1990.

McFarlan, Donald. *The Guinness Book of World Records 1990–91*. Bantam, 1991.

McPhee, John. *Encounters with the Archdruid*. Farrar, Strauss & Giroux, 1971.

Mitchell, Margaret. *Gone with the Wind*. Macmillan, 1936.

Murphy, Jim. *The Boys' War: Confederate and Union Soldiers Talk About the Civil War*. Clarion, 1990.

Neufeld, John. *Lisa, Bright and Dark*. Phillips, 1969.

Oneal, Zibby. *In Summer Light*. Viking, 1985.

Orlev, Uri. *The Man from the Other Side*. Houghton, 1991.

Paterson, Katherine. *Lyddie*. Dutton, 1991.

Paulsen, Gary. *The Monument*. Delacorte, 1991.

Potok, Chaim. *The Chosen*. Simon & Schuster, 1967.

Plummer, Louise. *My Name Is Sus5an Smith. The 5 is Silent*. Delacorte, 1991.

Pullman, Philip. *The Broken Bridge*. Knopf, 1992.

Rawls, Wilson. *Where the Red Fern Grows*. Doubleday, 1961.

Rosen, Michael J., ed. *The Company of Dogs*. Doubleday, 1990.

Salinger, J. D. *The Catcher in the Rye*. Little, Brown, 1951.

Schinto, Jeanne, ed. *The Literary Dog: Great Contemporary Dog Stories*. Atlantic Monthly Press, 1990.

Steele, Daniele. *Crossings*. Delacorte, 1982.

Street, James. *Good-bye, My Lady*. Lippincott, 1954.

Tan, Amy. *The Joy Luck Club*. Putnam, 1989.

Tangye, Derek. *A Cat Is Waiting*. Michael Joseph, 1977.

Voigt, Cynthia. *Homecoming*. Atheneum, 1981.

Walker, Alice. *The Color Purple*. Harcourt Brace Jovanovich, 1982.

Weidt, Maryann N. *Presenting Judy Blume*. G. K. Hall/Twayne, 1989.

Westall, Robert. *Blitzcat*. Scholastic, 1989.

———. *Yaxley's Cat*. Scholastic, 1992.

Wilson, A. N. *Stray*. Orchard, 1989.

Yates, Elizabeth. *The Seventh One*. Walker, 1978.

Yep, Laurence. *Dragonwings*. HarperCollins, 1976.

———. *The Rainbow People*. HarperCollins, 1989.

———. Tongues of Jade. HarperCollins, 1991.

Zindel, Paul. *The Pigman*. HarperCollins, 1968.

For information on the availability of paperback editions of these titles, please consult the most recent edition of *Paperbound Books in Print*, published annually by R. R. Bowker Company.

LITERATURE IN THE ENGLISH CLASS
A Few Words About Teaching

Our goal throughout this text has been to prepare users to bring young people and books together in a variety of settings, including traditional, modern, and alternative schools; public and school libraries; and wherever young people are found. In Chapter Ten we offered general information on evaluating and promoting books as well as specific guidance for librarians, reading and social studies teachers, parents, and workers with church and other youth groups. We hope that Chapter Seven ("History and History Makers") and Chapter Eight ("Nonfiction Books") give teachers the preparation they need to incorporate trade books into interdisciplinary units organized for team teaching and block scheduling of such classes as social studies and language arts. We also hope that the discussions of books throughout Part Two give teachers the background knowledge to succeed in selecting books if they have chosen to use a whole-language approach. And we hope that those fortunate enough to be using this book in a class will be able to participate in discussions and small group activities that can serve as models for cooperative learning in high school classes. In Chapter Nine we looked at some of the same materials we are treating in this chapter (i.e., poetry, short stories, and drama), but there we approached the genres more from a free reading than from a teaching standpoint. We hope that the two treatments complement each other.

We recognize that there is no single best way to teach and that environments, students, and goals vary tremendously from school to school and from parent to parent. Nevertheless, some methods of teaching literature to young people have proved that they work for large numbers of teachers and their students. Thus, in response to requests from previous users of this textbook, we devote this chapter to a discussion of standard approaches to the teaching of literature in high school and to tying that teaching in with books written specifically for young adults.

THE ROLE OF LITERATURE

Most parents and critics accept that literature has a place in secondary English classes, although they differ on whether it belongs there because it extends reading skills begun in elementary school, encourages young people to do something better than play video games and watch TV, or exposes young people to the classics of the Western world. Some believe that reading for pleasure is its own justification, but others regard literature as a frill, an insignificant part of English class, compared to composition or grammar.

Over the years teachers have also disagreed on the place of literature, some arguing that the classics are the only legitimate concern of English teachers. Others believe that some modern books may be used as aids in getting young people to the classics, and still others believe that the time devoted to reading is too short, too precious, to allow for anything but the best books. That point of view was recently espoused by Janet Daley in the *London Times Educational Supplement* as she explained:

> Schools have a particular responsibility for teaching historical literature because it is—redeemingly—alien to children's everyday lives. It is one of the duties of education (as opposed to training) to offer an escape route from whatever limiting and stultifying forces threaten to entrap children's minds. It is just *because* the past is another country that we need guidance on the journey. The proper teaching of historical literature is all about how to adjust to one's expectations of language and society in order to understand authors whose worlds were so unlike our own. What does it matter if it involves some tedium learning to read Chaucer, or coping with the rural dialects of Thomas Hardy? Most things that are worth knowing take some effort to acquire.[1]

She went on to argue against the view that children know what is best for them. Instead, she wrote, "It is education's task to stretch the bounds of their understanding, not to give in to the prejudices which arise from their ignorance."

Many American teachers would applaud these sentiments. However, other teachers believe that literature exists to be enjoyed. They agree with the classical philosophy of Horace that literature should *please and instruct*. Although they wouldn't dispute that literature can be used profitably for other purposes, these teachers begin by assuming that literature is fun, whether the fun of something

Nearly all English teachers feel more comfortable when their students choose to read the kinds of books this boy is looking at. What they disagree on is how to get students to this stage.

as lighthearted as a Little Willie poem or the fun of something as satisfying as one of Plato's dialogues.

Even before 1900, Samuel Thurber, a leading English teacher in New England, said that the "primal law of all literature teaching" is that it "should be interesting."[2] and Franklin T. Baker, one of the early leaders of the National Council of Teachers of English (NCTE), wrote in 1915 that teachers of literature differed from teachers in other disciplines because "we speak of literature as primarily a thing to be enjoyed. Other departments treat their subjects as primarily to be learned."[3]

If enjoyment is a subversive word to many English teachers, the word *fun* is even more subversive. When an English teacher asked his department chair for advice twenty-two years ago on preparing a study guide, he was told, "Don't use the word *fun*. Teachers are suspicious of anything in school being *fun*."[4] More recently, Theodore Hipple, NCTE leader and Executive Secretary of the Assembly on Literature for Adolescents of NCTE (ALAN), wrote in his English methods text:

First of all, the study of literature can be—and should be—fun. There are some teachers for whom fun and education seem to be incompatible terms; fun in the classroom and learning are mutually exclusive. It is such teachers whom we can hold at least partly responsible for an adult population that regards the one-dimensional characters of television series as better evening companions than Huck Finn or Hamlet.[5]

PRINCIPLES OF TEACHING ENGLISH

We believe in five principles about English teachers and the teaching of literature. The remainder of this chapter illustrates these five principles and their implications. We have developed these principles from our own experiences as well as from the writings and thoughts of many others (see Focus Box 11.1).

1. *English teachers must never forget that literature should be both entertaining and challenging.* Teachers need to alert kids to literature that the teachers find satisfying and fun. Teachers need to find ways of getting literature to students so they will find challenge and satisfaction—perhaps in talking about individual works in many genres, perhaps in a genre unit, a thematic unit, or free reading. Is this easy to do? No, not always, but it might convince a few students that teachers care about reading and kids. If the literature doesn't provide entertainment and challenge, English teachers have failed. And even when a teacher succeeds with one piece of literature and one student, winning is only temporary, as all English teachers know.

2. *English teachers must know a wide range of literature.* Teachers should know classics of English and American literature, of course; they should also know American popular literature and YA literature and something about European literature (e.g., Norwegian drama or French short stories or Russian novels). They should know women writers and ethnic writers, especially, but not exclusively from our country, and they should have some acquaintance with Oriental literature. What they don't know about literature, they will learn. That demands that English teachers read all sorts of literature—the great, the new, the popular, the demanding, the puzzling. And why do they read? Because they are readers themselves and because they are always looking for books that might work with students. One of life's joys for English teachers, and its greatest annoyance, is that they view every poem, every film, every newspaper article, every football game, every everything for its potential use in class.

3. *English teachers ought to know enough about dramatic techniques and oral interpretation to be comfortable reading aloud to students.* We need teachers eager and able to read material to students that just might interest, intrigue, amuse, or excite them, material that might make young people aware of new or old books or writers or techniques or

ideas. Outside of speech or drama classes, no classes require so much oral performance from teachers as English classes. Poetry must be read aloud. Drama demands it. And reading fiction aloud is half the fun of teaching short stories. If students are to learn how to read poetry or drama, it will come from English teachers comfortable with their own oral reading. One added benefit is that common devices in literature, such as metaphor or irony or ambiguity, are often more apparent when heard rather than read. Obviously, the availability of poetry or fiction on tapes or CDs means other voices can be heard, but that does not mean the teacher's voice should be silent. Granted, Ian McKellen's voice reading Shakespeare exceeds the grasp of us mortals, but McKellen isn't there to explain why he read a passage from *Richard III* or *Macbeth* or *Othello* as he did. English teachers are there to explain why they chose to read a particular passage and why they read it as they did.

4. *English teachers need to remember the distance in education and sophistication between them and their students.* No matter what the rapport between them, it's almost equally easy for teachers to overestimate as to underestimate their students, although experienced teachers would surely prefer the first error to the second. Choosing material for an entire class is never easy and often seems impossible. Some materials—say a *New Yorker* short story or a T. S. Eliot poem or a Harold Pinter play—assume a sophistication that high school students often do not have, although sometimes their glibness in class will temporarily fool a neophyte. On rare occasions, a class is ready for the Pinter, but while waiting for that class, it's tempting for teachers to choose material that will challenge no one and that no one will greatly enjoy. Selecting literature for fifteen, thirty-five, or forty-five students is almost inevitably an exercise in frustration and failure. That comes with the territory, but it's no excuse for not trying to meet all students' needs with that one fabulous, never-to-be-forgotten classroom novel, or poem, short story, or play.

Experienced English teachers know this, but most parents and other citizens do not. Teachers should try to let others in on the secret. For most outsiders, how the English teacher selects what poems are to be used from the class anthology or what paperback novel will be read by the entire class is an arcane mystery. English teachers might consider explaining the process, even though the unraveled mystery might be dull:

"How did you decide to use *The Scarlet Letter* this year, Mr. Jones?"

"Well, there are only eight novels with class sets available to the juniors and everything had already been checked out except *The Scarlet Letter* and *Giants in the Earth,* and I've never had any luck with that."

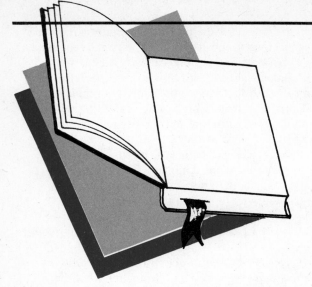

Using Literature in Secondary Schools

reader-response theory and how it works in literature is a bit too whimsical at times but mostly fun and profit.

Literature As Exploration, 4th ed., by Louise Rosenblatt. Modern Language Association, 1976. One of the most readable and pedagogically valuable books in the field, this is the basis of reader response theory and practice.

Literature Study in the High Schools, 3rd ed., by Dwight L. Burton. Holt, 1970. From the late 1950s until the 1970s, this was *the* book that turned librarians and English teachers on to adolescent literature.

The New Hooked-On Books, Tenth Anniversary Edition by Daniel Fader. Berkley, 1976. Fader popularized the use of paperbacks with kids and shocked lots of teachers.

Reader Response in the Classroom: Evoking and Interpreting Meaning in Literature by Nicholas Karolides. Longman, 1992. Contains wonderful articles on reader response.

Readers, Texts, Teachers, edited by Bill Corcoran and Emrys Evans. Boynton/Cook, 1987. An excellent collection of articles on using literature.

Reading and Response, edited by Michael Hayhoe and Stephen Parker. Open University Press, 1990. The articles focus on classroom applications of reader-response theory.

Reading Their World: The Young Adult Novel in the Classroom, edited by Virginia Mon-

Adolescent Literature as a Complement to the Classics, edited by Joan Kaywell. Christopher-Gordan, 1992. Leading scholars in young adult literature have contributed original essays tying specific pieces of young adult literature with often-taught literature, including the poetry of Shelley, *The Adventures of Huckleberry Finn*, *Death of a Salesman*, *Catcher in the Rye*, *The Scarlet Letter*, and *The Great Gatsby*.

Authors' Insights: Turning Teenagers into Readers and Writers, edited by Don R. Gallo. Boynton/Cook, 1992. Authors of adolescent literature wrote these articles aimed at English teachers.

The Effective Teaching of English by Robert Protherough, Judith Atkinson, and John Fawcett. Longman, 1989. The best text today on teaching English.

Enhancing Aesthetic Reading and Response by Richard M. Anderson and Gregory Rubano. National Council of Teachers of English, 1991. This is good on theory, excellent on practice.

How Porcupines Make Love II: Teaching a Response-Centered Literature Curriculum by Alan C. Purves. Longman, 1990. Purves'

seau and Gary Salvner. Boynton/Cook, 1992. Contributors include Sandy Asher, Sue Ellen Bridgers, Don Gallo, Pat Kelly, Richard Peck, and Bobbi Samuels.

Researching Response to Literature and the Teaching of Literature: Points of Departure, edited by Charles R. Cooper. Ablex, 1985. Cooper gathered research on literature and teaching literature.

Response and Analysis: Teaching Literature in Junior and Senior High School by Robert E. Probst. Boynton/Cook, 1988. With its brilliant theory and practical suggestions, this book is certain to be a classic in the field.

Teaching Literature for Examinations by Robert Protherough. Open University Press, 1986. A case study by Terry Gifford, "Teaching Garner's *Red Shift* for an Alternative A-Level," is a model of how to prepare to use a tough book. See also Protherough's *Developing Response to Fiction* (Open University Press, 1983).

Teaching Literature in Middle and Secondary Grades by John S. Simmons and H. Edward Deluzain. Allyn & Bacon, 1992. Down-to-earth and highly recommended.

Teaching Literature in the Secondary School by Richard W. Beach and James D. Marshall. Harcourt Brace Jovanovich, 1991. Backed by good, sound theory, the authors touch on almost anything an English teacher would want to know about teaching literature.

Teaching Literature, Nine to Fourteen by Michael Benton and Geoff Fox. Oxford University Press, 1985. Here are helpful suggestions for teaching all genres to almost all kids.

Transactions with Literature: A Fifty-Year Perspective, edited by Edmund J. Farrell and James R. Squire. National Council of Teachers of English, 1990. NCTE sponsored this collection of papers about Louise Rosenblatt's influence on teaching literature during the last fifty years.

Understanding Unreliable Narrators: Reading Between the Lines in the Literature Classroom by Michael W. Smith. National Council of Teachers of English, 1991. Smith shows how students learn better when they are encouraged to bring their own real-world values and beliefs to their reading.

Not very exciting, perhaps, but honest, and most parents can accept honesty.

5. *Finally, English teachers should teach and use only literature they enjoy.* Teachers shouldn't be expected to fake enthusiasm or interest. If a teacher doesn't like Robert Frost's poetry or Stephen Crane's *The Red Badge of Courage,* the teacher has no business using Frost or Crane. It's permissible for both teachers and young people not to like a work or an author, assuming of course the teacher has read and responsibly considered the author or work in question (we can be a bit more charitable toward students on this point). If teachers don't like highly regarded modern works like Raymond Carver's short stories or Athol Fugard's *"Master Harold"* . . . *and the Boys* or May Swenson's poetry, they shouldn't teach them. There are too many stories and

plays and poems out there that teachers will presumably be enthusiastic about. (Obviously this point follows our second point, that teachers are incurable, wide readers.)

None of this implies that teachers cannot change their minds about literature or writers, just as teachers know that occasionally it's great fun and profitable to work with literature about which they feel ambivalent. Nor does this imply that students should be discouraged from reading and talking about works the teacher has no great enthusiasm for.

Our five principles for teaching literature extend to works in the curriculum guide as well as the literary canon of great books. It is not being unduly critical of the manner in which many literature curriculum guides are developed to note that they are created by human beings with certain strengths and weaknesses, and they are fallible. As long as they are taken as guides, teachers can be helped, particularly beginning teachers. But when curriculum guides are taken as biblical edicts, absurdity reigns and their value disappears.

Assuming teachers have a wide knowledge of literature, they can find a variety of works of equal quality to teach. What is gained from a bored teacher presenting Poe's poetry to an equally bored class? It is much better to assume that in the four years of high school these students will have one English teacher who likes Poe. And if it doesn't happen? There are worse disasters we can imagine. And what if no teacher wants to teach Shakespeare? We cannot imagine an English department so devoid of taste or ability, but if one exists, it's surely preferable that students leave school ignorant of Shakespeare than that they be bored by him.

Forcing teachers to teach something they do not like encourages classroom dishonesty. Teachers spout trite and obvious interpretations of literature taken from the teacher's guide, and students regurgitate on tests what they neither care about nor understand. Such dishonesty inevitably breeds boredom with literature and contempt for learning.

Literature that a teacher thinks worth teaching, however defined, ought to encourage honest teaching and honest responses from kids. As Louise Rosenblatt has pointed out again and again:

> No one else can read a literary work for us. The benefits of literature can emerge only from creative activity on the part of the reader himself. He responds to the little black marks on the page, or to the sounds of the words in his ear, and he "makes something of them." The verbal symbols enable him to draw on his past experiences with what the words point to in life and literature.[6]

Allowing young people to respond to literature slows down the teacher and the lesson because thinking takes time and brainpower. Time is also required for building trust, especially for students who are accustomed to memorizing and spitting back whatever the teacher has said. Some students simply don't believe that a teacher really wants their opinions. Students have to be convinced that responding honestly to literature is worth the trouble and hard work. An invitation to what appears to be an intellectual coup d'état doesn't come easily from a teacher, nor does the acceptance come easily from students.

USING YA LITERATURE IN ENGLISH CLASSES

One of the reasons we endorse YA lit for English classes is that students can believe a teacher who asks for their honest response to a book that features a contemporary young person facing a problem that students have been more likely to face than has their teacher. YA lit is often recommended as a bridge to appreciating literary techniques, but its role in developing the trust needed for a response-centered approach to literature may be even more important.

Teachers who believe in the value of YA literature for either of these purposes sometimes forget that many English teachers still make fun of YA books. To us, the criticisms often seem irrational and defensive, almost as if the books threatened teachers and their worlds. Nevertheless, YA converts need to be aware of the following protestations. We cannot resist offering some counter-arguments, even though we realize we're preaching to the choir.

1. *No one around here knows anything about it. If it was really worth knowing we'd have heard about it.* It's been around quite a long time now, and since the publication of books by S. E. Hinton, Paul Zindel, Robert Lipsyte, Norma Fox Mazer, Harry Mazer, Robert Cormier, Rosa Guy, Gary Paulsen, and many more, lots of people have heard about it. In any case, the statement is a rationalization for learning nothing new. Ignorance isn't an impressive justification for anything.

2. *Adolescent literature has no heritage and no respectability.* It has a heritage going back more than 130 years. Some people respect it, but few will respect anything they haven't read.

3. *We teach only the greatest of literature, and that automatically eliminates adolescent lit from our consideration. Why should we demean ourselves or our students—and their parents—by stooping to something inferior?* We wonder how the greatest of literature was chosen for this curriculum. Were these great books chosen from a list supplied by a college teacher or by some independent body? How great are they for high school students? And how long has it been since the teacher read any adolescent books? Some students—and not just the slowest—get little pleasure from reading. We believe it is the English teacher's responsibility to help students find pleasure in reading. We wonder whether this program will do that.

4. *We can't afford thirty or forty copies of something we don't know. That's why we don't use adolescent books.* Maybe you ought to read some of the books. That may tell you whether you'd want to use a class set, and it might suggest that individual titles are better than a set of anything.

5. *Kids have to grow up and take themselves and their work seriously. I do. We expect them to. That takes care of adolescent literature as far as this school is concerned.* We take our work and our kids seriously too. We'd also like them to enjoy some of their reading. Bruce Brooks's and Sue Ellen Bridgers' books contain plenty of serious stuff, but they also provide the joy of discovering similarities between readers and characters.

6. *Adolescent literature has no permanence. Something is popular today and something else is popular tomorrow. Great literature is timeless and unchanging. How can we be expected to keep track of ephemera?* What a wonderful justification for reading nothing new. Yes, new books come out all the time. Some new books have a chance to escape the dustheap. Some don't. Most adolescent books don't last, but Alcott's *Little Women* and Twain's *Huckleberry Finn* have been around a long time. Also, consider that S. E. Hinton's *The Outsiders* and Robert Lipsyte's *The Contender* are both twenty-five years old. Paul Zindel's *The Pigman* is twenty-four years old. Will they last? That's anyone's guess. We would put money on a bet that some of Robert Cormier's and Katherine Paterson's books will last. For that matter, we can think of a dozen other YA writers who seem likely to last.

7. *Why have kids spend time in class reading something they can easily read on their own? Shouldn't class time be spent on books that are challenging, books that kids won't find on their own, books that will make kids stretch intellectually?* Some of those kids may not find those books as challenging as Cormier's *After the First Death* or Alan Garner's *The Owl Service* or Alice Childress' *A Hero Ain't Nothin' But a Sandwich,* and those three titles, among many more, are challenging emotionally and intellectually. Besides, what is there about *The Pearl* or *Silas Marner* or *The Old Man and the Sea* that makes their difficulties worth stretching for? The painful truth is that many young people don't find reading enjoyable, and even though they may not find *Silas Marner* on their own, they also won't find Zindel's *The Pigman* or Voigt's *Homecoming,* which might come closer to reaching them.

8. *Isn't adolescent literature formula literature?* Yes, sometimes, but mostly, no. *Formula* is a dirty word—*archetype* has more positive connotations. It's impressive to hear someone talk about Dostoevsky's grand inevitability in *Crime and Punishment*. It's not so impressive to

hear someone talk about the total predictability of a Nancy Drew mystery. There's nevertheless an uncomfortable similarity between the two comments, if not the two books. And then we mustn't forget that there's YA lit and YA lit. Surely a teacher could be justified in using Cormier's *I Am the Cheese* or Paula Fox's *One-Eyed Cat* in a discussion of archetypes.

9. *Isn't it silly and simple-minded stuff about dating and trivia like that?* Sometimes, yes. Most of the time, no. How long has it been since you read Virginia Hamilton, Jill Paton-Walsh, Cynthia Voigt, or Zibby Oneal?

10. *Isn't it mostly about depressing problems—like suicide, death, abortion, pregnancy? Hasn't it been censored a lot?* Yes, it can be serious and some of it has been censored, but see the thoughtful comment on this that follows.

Observations by Elaine Simpson and Dorothy Broderick speak more effectively than we can to the last three objections. Simpson addresses her remarks to those librarians and others who for years criticized junior novels for their innocence and their pat answers that instilled false conceptions and failed to deal with fundamental problems:

Then juvenile authors and editors began giving us such books as *Go Ask Alice*; *Run Softly, Run Fast*; *Admission to the Feast*; *Run, Shelley, Run*; *The Chocolate War*. I could go on and on naming both fiction and nonfiction.

And what happened? All too many of these same people who had been asking for an honest story about serious teenage problems began protesting: language like *that* in a book for young people? Are rape, abortion, homosexuality, unwed mothers, suicide, drugs, unsympathetic portrayals of parents, and violence appropriate for junior novels? Are young people ready for such explicit realism? Would you want your daughter to read one?[7]

Dorothy Broderick focused on the charge most often expressed by ultraconservatives, "namely, that young adult books are not uplifting. Why, oh why, cry these critics, do the authors have to deal with such depressing subjects. Why can't we go back to the good old days?" Broderick's answer:

As one who has spent six decades on this planet, let me tell you an important fact: *there were no good old days*. Every problem confronted in a young adult novel today not only existed during my childhood and adolescence, but was known to most of us. There were drunks in families, there were wife abusers, there were child molesters, divorce, certainly death and dying, mental illness, pre-marital pregnancy, and, yes, abortions if you were among the elite. In high school, one of my classmates went home one day

NORMA FOX MAZER
on Respect

I doubt there is a children's book writer extant who hasn't been asked when s/he is going to write a "real" book. A "real" book is, of course, a book for adults. Presumably a grownup book, certainly a book read by people whose hormones have settled down. The question implies that any "adult" book carries more status and is "realer" and therefore worthier than any book written for children.

Why is this so? Isn't it because anything associated with children is diminished, discounted, depreciated? Children are seen as lesser, less than. Children are considered not quite "real." We Americans may love our children, but it's quite clear we don't respect them. They are not seen as completed or finished; this makes them "kids" but not people. Children don't have rights, as other citizens do. They "belong" to their parents. "Cute," "adorable," and "silly" are words used often for kids. We constantly tell them to shut up, grow up, remind them that they're "almost thirteen" or "al-

most sixteen," thereby letting them know that being a child is something like having a disease. The only cure is to outlive it and become healthy: i.e., older, an adult.

As a society, we don't put our children first. Our maternal death rate is the highest in the Western World. Twenty percent of our children live in poverty. We mouth the idea that our children are our most valuable resource, but as a nation we don't act on it. Too many chidren are beaten and abused, are torn between their fighting parents, kidnapped as though they were packages rather than people.

But let's not even talk about that kind of stuff, that dangerous, deranged, bizarre, clouded area of life. Let's talk about a couple of "normal" things. That those who stay home with their small children, who "don't work" (that's the way we say it, despite the evidence in front of our eyes), are neither given much respect nor paid. That those who work with children are overworked, underpaid, and undervalued. (In Syracuse, New York, pay for preschool teachers is less than that for garbagemen.)

Reading over what I've written, I see it's depressing. What's worse, I don't know how to end it. No upbeat moral. So let me tell you about a letter I received today. It began, "Hi. My name is Lene Mapp. I live in Abilene Texas. . . ." She talked to me for two pages, asked if Harry would send her a book and enclosed a picture and three poems. "My life," she wrote, "is just like I, Trissy, except I went off into a (sic) all white section of town. . . . You don't know how releived (sic) I was to know someone knew what I was going through."

There, of course, is my ending. My reminder that what I do *is* serious stuff and that writing for kids—the hell with the grownup, "adult" world—is very serious stuff not only to those of us who do it, but to those we do it for—the kids, themselves.

Norma Fox Mazer's books include *After the Rain*, Morrow, 1987; *Silver*, 1988; *Downtown*, Morrow, 1984; and with Harry Mazer, *Heartbeat*, Bantam, 1989.

to find his father had hung himself in the garage; a couple of weeks later he went home to find his mother had done the same thing.[8]

Adolescent literature has a place in the literature program because it appeals to young people. Why? YA novels are short, or at least shorter than most modern novels or classics studied in schools. It's easy for teachers to dismiss that point, but it's not a point that young people ignore. YA books are easier to read (or so they seem at first reading) than most adult or classic novels. They're about young people the age of the readers and concerned with real issues and problems facing adolescents, particularly the readers (and that's often not true of adult books or classics). They look like they might be fun to read. The dust jackets may bother some adults, but they may also appeal to the young. The photos or paintings on YA paperbacks are calculated to grab readers just as are the photos and paintings on adult novels. But with YA books there's also a blurb showing, for example, that the book is about a kid who has this wonderful brother who's dying of AIDS, or it's about a girl whose grandmother is senile, or a boy and a girl enmeshed in a love affair against their parents' wishes. With such come-ons, who will be surprised when young people grab YA titles. The last reason for their popularity with many young people is that the books are often perceived to be unacceptable to traditional teachers, that is, they're forbidden fruit.

What makes YA books so unattractive to some teachers? Besides the reasons listed earlier, Robert C. Small, Jr., adds an unpleasant final reason. He writes that the goal of most literature programs is to designate the teacher as literary expert and translator of books to lowly students who seem to have no role at all, other than to be recipients of the largesse of the expert-translator-teacher.[9] When young people read adolescent books, they are the experts, and they may need to serve as translators to adults who wish to understand the adolescent books.

What makes YA books so attractive to other English teachers is the fact that for an imaginative teacher, YA books have so many uses. An individual title can be studied by the whole class, although that's comparatively rare. They can be paired with adult books, classics or not, as Patricia Lee Gauch suggested.[10] They work beautifully in free reading and thematic units. Their possibilities extend as far as the teachers' imaginations, for they provide what other good novels do along with an almost guaranteed adolescent interest. Richard Jackson, editor-in-chief at Bradbury Press, made it clear why Bradbury will continue to print them and why YA novels appeal to young people and English teachers when he wrote:

Bradbury will continue to publish YA fiction because I like it and believe in a story's potential to touch the life of a teenager—a creature of so many moods, who deserves enough stories for each of them. Ideally, YA literature should illuminate rather than educate, raise questions rather than trot out answers. And it should entertain. Though society changes from one generation to another, its rites of passage remain quite fixed. Literature for young adults will endure because the impulse to record and reconsider those rites strikes us all. We can't resist it—and though they may not admit the fact, adolescents do hear us.[11]

One of Jackson's points deserves a brief comment. One aspect of older and less sophisticated YA novels was the temptation of authors to answer questions that had been raised. In too many of these superficial novels, the questions were simple, the answers simplistic, and a hard-sell education in middle-class morality was provided:

Q: What happens if I give in to my boyfriend?
A: You get pregnant or you feel gobs of guilt.

Q: Is sex pleasurable?
A: Only if you're married.

Q: Will my mother forgive me if I go to the senior all-night dance?
A: Yes, it will hurt her, but she will forgive you. But would you want your daughter in twenty years to do that to you?

Judy Blume, easily the most popular writer for young women, retains her popularity for several reasons, but one is that she doesn't provide neat, easy answers. Sex doesn't solve all problems. Death isn't easily forgotten. Love doesn't last, but then nothing necessarily does. These lessons may not be as warm and comforting as the old trite answers of earlier YA novels, but readers recognize and respect honesty, and that is the hallmark of Blume—and the mass of YA writers today.

Anyone looking for good lists of YA books could hardly do better than to skim through issues of *Booklist*. See especially the August 1990 issue for a summary of "Young Adult Special Lists and Features." Sample titles showing the kind of features the *Booklist* editors prepare include "Playing the Game: Sports Fiction," "Life in the Balance: Suspense and Survival," and "Growing Up Black" (also Female, Hispanic, Jewish, Native American). Frances A. Miller's "Books to Read When You Hate to Read: Recommended by Reluctant YA Readers in Grades 7–12" is excellent for helping teachers with hard-to-reach students. Of the thirty-seven books listed, nineteen were published for adolescents, including golden, surefire titles such as Lois Duncan's *I Know What You Did Last Summer*, S. E. Hinton's *The Outsiders* and *That Was Then, This is Now*, Harry Mazer's *The Last Mission*, Richard Peck's *Remembering the Good Times*, Theodore Taylor's *The Cay*, Cynthia Voigt's *Homecoming*, and Zindel's *The Pigman*.[12]

A Word About Genres

We've found an exercise helpful on the first day of adolescent literature class. We ask students to assume the following:

> ■ You're home at night, there's nothing worth watching on TV, you don't feel like going out, so you prowl around in your books, trying to find something worth reading for enjoyment, for relaxation. You're not reading to prepare for a class, you're not reading to save the culture of the Western world, you're reading for the fun of it. Assume that there are lots of books around you, particularly (1) biographies and autobiographies, (2) drama, (3) novels, (4) poetry, and (5) short stories.
>
> On a sheet of paper, indicate what would be your first choice of genre if you were to do your reading right now, your second choice, your third, your fourth, and finally your last choice.

Simple, but students sometimes have trouble. They want to announce that their choices right then are not the permanent choices they'd make in some vague future time. They often want to let us know their reason for marking one genre particularly low, and they sometimes whisper on leaving that they ranked the genres the way "they ought to be ranked" rather than as the students enjoyed them. Inevitably, we have to announce, half-jokingly, that there are no right answers.

We pick up the slips of paper and tabulate the results, although we do not hand out the results until several weeks later, when we begin to talk about different genres and how we might present them to students. We usually begin with short stories, partly because it's an easier genre to talk about than poetry (or at least students think it's easier) and because it's a good time to talk about the exercise of that first day. We have never had a class—of the more than three classes per year for twenty years—that did not collectively agree that the two favored genres for relaxed, enjoyable reading were novels and short stories (in that order). Novels come out considerably ahead of short stories, and short stories are even farther ahead of whatever comes in third, usually biographies/autobiographies or drama. Poetry is almost always a dismal last.

Robert Protherough, Judith Atkinson, and John Fawcett similarly concluded in their English methods text that with kids' reading interests as they left the primary grades, "Fiction is the overwhelmingly preferred reading matter (over 90 per cent of primary children say they like reading stories and over three-quarters of the voluntary reading of secondary students consists of narratives) and provides the strongest incentive to read."[13]

We pretend to no scientific exactness in this exercise, but students are often surprised by the results. It is obvious that fiction (short stories or novels) is more popular than the other genres. The fact that poetry, drama, and biographies/autobiographies are all older genres than novels or short stories comes up

See Focus Box 11.1 for a partial listing of the many excellent books that English teachers will find helpful.

later and in many ways is even more sobering to some English majors. In keeping with the popularity of nonfiction that Betty Carter and Richard Abrahamson reported on in their book *From Delight to Wisdom: Nonfiction for Young Adults* (see Chapter Eight), perhaps the next time we do this exercise with a class we should add the category of nonfiction to see how many students in our hypothetical situation would turn to an informative book or an article in a magazine or a newspaper.

Teaching Short Stories

As our students tell us year after year, everyone loves a story, except, of course, the one you assigned yesterday to be discussed today. Your English class unanimously voted "dumb," "made no sense to me," or "it looked like it wasn't worth reading, so I never got around to it."

English teachers want students to enjoy and maybe even profit from reading short stories, but some preparation is necessary. Kids are not born with genes labeled "How to Read Short Stories Perceptively." Teachers need to provide help. Robert Scholes advised:

> Our job is not to produce "readings" for our students but to give them the tools for producing their own. Our job is *not* to intimidate students with our own superior textbook production; it is to show them the codes on which all textbook production depends, and to encourage their own textual practice.[14]

It is the job of English teachers to determine what those codes are with each genre and to suggest ways for students to enter imaginative works. Tempting as simple solutions have been to curriculum designers, Scholes does not mean that students should be required to master a vocabulary list of "Thirty Magic Literary Terms That Will Change Your Life and Make You the Reader You Have Always Longed to Be." There's a place for learning about *verisimilitude, point of view, unreliable narrator, sprung rhythm, synecdoche, foreshadowing, Petrarchan sonnet,* and *carpe diem* if and when the terms enlighten students, but never as a series of terms in an intellectual vacuum.

Finding out about the codes that make one piece of literature succeed while another one fails will force teachers to consider how they went about getting into a short story, for example, and how they get into a story that's new to them. There is no single way of getting at any literary work, and several approaches may need to be tried. Students may come to class having already learned to listen, to take assiduous notes on what the teacher says is important, and to play all this back at test time, but none of that has very much to do with reading.

And in many ways, a careful reading of a work by student A produces a different work from an equally careful reading by student B or student C. The words in John Updike's "A & P" do not change from reader to reader, but the feelings of the readers based on past experience and present morality yield a slightly different story with each reader, and sometimes a greatly different story. Louise Rosenblatt wrote:

> A novel or a play remains merely inkspots on paper until a reader transforms them into a set of meaningful symbols. The literary work exists in the live circuit set up between reader and text: the reader infuses intellectual and emotional meanings into the patterns of verbal symbols, and those

symbols channel his thoughts and feelings. Out of this complex process emerges a more or less organized imaginative experience.[15]

One adolescent literature class suggested these six steps as ways of helping ninth-graders break the code in reading a short story.

1. Speed-read the story to get some sense of what it's about and who the characters are.
2. Back up and read the story again slowly.
3. Isolate your problems in reading the story (dialect, structure, conflicting characters, etc.).
4. Read the first sentence (and the first paragraph). What do they tell you about the setting, characters, or tension?
5. Predict from the first paragraph what's likely to follow.
6. Read the story aloud.

Whatever merits these six points might have for college students, most experienced teachers assume that high school students are unlikely to read the story more than one time (if that) outside of class. But once students learn with the help of a teacher how literary codes can be broken, they may sometimes read more carefully, depending on how interesting they find the story. Points 4 through 6 have merit if teachers lead the class in following through.

What can we safely say to our classes about virtually all short stories? We can tell students that all fiction is based on conflict, and we might begin by exploring with them different kinds of conflict. We can say, with some confidence, that the title of the story usually is significant. One of the problems young readers have with Updike's "A & P," once they're willing to get beyond the usual remark that "nothing happens," is understanding what the title means, since many A & P (taken from the name of the Great Atlantic and Pacific Tea Company) grocery stores seem to have gone the way of all flesh. Students rarely have a clear idea of what this store symbolized in many communities, which was something quite different from a Safeway or a Vons, for example. We doubt that our students are incredibly richer for knowing about the A & P and its place in Updike's fictional community, but it's essential for understanding something about the story and who the characters are.

We can tell students that first-person narrators are similar to readers in many ways—fallible mortals likely to make mistakes in judging people or letting their emotions get in the way. Students are sometimes puzzled when we raise this point, but it's essential, since readers tend to take the narrator's word for almost anything. But narrators make mistakes, and some of them are beauts. Dr. Watson is a wonderful narrator for the Sherlock Holmes stories, since, like us, he is puzzled by the thinking machine he rooms with. Watson's slowness permits us to catch up, and his blunders may bring down Holmes's wrath just as they allow us to see many sides of both characters.

When Huckleberry Finn goes to a circus in Chapter XXII, he watches the carryings on of the clowns and the ringmaster and all the women horseback riders "dressed in clothes that cost millions of dollars, and just littered with diamonds." Later, Huck gets nervous when a drunk is allowed to ride the horses and is amazed when the drunk turns out to be a rider in the circus.

Then the ringmaster he see how he had been fooled, and he *was* the sickest ringmaster you ever see, I reckon. Why, it was one of his own men! He had got up that joke all out of his own head and never let on to nobody. Well, I felt sheepish enough to be took in, but I wouldn't 'a' been in that ringmaster's place, not for a thousand dollars.

One of our students was convinced that Huck may have been right and that the ringmaster truly had been taken in, but we have more faith in Twain's artistry and the significant fact that this brief episode takes place between the abortive lynching of Colonel Sherburn and the dismal first dramatic performance of the duke and the king.

The fallible narrator may be even more important, if more subtle, in Updike's "A & P." Sammy quits his job at an A & P when his boss (a family friend) tells some young women that they are inappropriately dressed. Sammy makes the grand gesture at least in part to impress the girls, who leave without witnessing Sammy's nobility. He describes the act as, "The sad part of the story, at least my family says it's sad, but I don't think it's so sad myself." A few seconds after Sammy's spur-of-the-moment gallantry, the store manager tells Sammy that he (Sammy) doesn't want to do this. And Sammy says something presumably profound about himself and other young romantics, "it seems to me that once you begin a gesture it's fatal not to go through with it." The manager tells Sammy, "You'll feel this the rest of your life," and Sammy adds, "I know that's true, too." More mature students who enjoy talking about the story—and it is slow moving and meditative and unlikely to appeal to younger students—will see an eternal romantic doomed to gestures all his life. Readers may put different amounts of faith in Sammy's words, concluding that like Huck, he doesn't lie, but he may not recognize the truth.

We can also tell students how important those first words are in most short stories. It's the author's opportunity to grab the audience, and some readers (at least outside school) may decide to drop the story and the author based on those words. Most students rush through the first lines. In class we can force them to slow down by reading aloud the first lines over and over.

William Saroyan begins "Seventeen" with these words:

Sam Wolinsky was seventeen, and a month had passed since he had begun to shave; now he was in love. And he wanted to do something. A feeling of violence was in him, and he was thinking of himself as something enormous in the world. He felt drunk with strength that had accumulated from the first moment of his life to the moment he was now living, and he felt almost insane because of the strength. Death was nothing. It could not matter if he died; feeling as he did, it could not matter. All that mattered was this moment, Wolinsky in love, alive, walking down Ventura Avenue, in America, Wolinsky of the universe, the Crazy Polak with the broken nose.

What do these words tell, literally? We know the age of a character, and although we can't be sure he's the central character, common sense and the brevity of short stories make it likely that he is. He's developing facial hair (or he wants it to appear and he shaves to make that happen). He's in love, but he feels violent (are those emotions connected? Should they be?). Note all those tough, ugly words—*violence, enormous* (or is that sexual?), *drunk with strength, insane, death, died, the crazy Polak,* and *broken nose.* It's the juxtaposition of *in love* and *alive* and *death* that disturbs us as we read. One paragraph does not a short story make, and there's more to follow, but much can often be found in those first few lines. This story and Updike's "A & P" are published in Robert Gold's fine collection, *Point of Departure,* one of many excellent paperback anthologies designed for teaching short stories (see Focus Box 11.2).

Sometimes (the most obvious example is Shirley Jackson's "The Lottery"), the first line lulls readers into a mood that proves totally wrong, and as the words roll by we begin to suspect something is amiss. If the writer has played fair, as Jackson has, and the readers later discover that they misread the clues, a surprisingly fine story can emerge. If the writer has played false and deliberately misled the reader, as O. Henry sometimes did and as many romance writers do, then we have a story providing no more than momentary amusement.

The questions English teachers pose for students should be carefully thought out and played with. Experienced teachers need not develop and practice the questions before class, but the ideas must be something worth talking about, something of significance. They can range from memory questions about details to questions asking students to generalize from the story to major human concerns. Whatever the questions, if they are to be worthwhile to students or teachers, they must be worth talking about, not mere chitchat to take up fifty-five minutes of class.

Many teachers ask students to keep journals and to respond to a question or a comment on the board for the first five or ten minutes of class. This activity serves several purposes, including quieting students, turning their attention to the story, and focusing on an issue in the story (probably a key aspect). It allows or forces students to consider what they will say later in class when the question or comment is posed again. Journals also provide an opportunity for students to outline preliminary ideas for papers that may be developed later.

The first few moments of class discussion are often taken up with simple recall questions, reassuring to students and setting up details in the story that may have significance later on. One schema developed and recommended by Edward J. Gordon and Dwight L. Burton[16] suggests how teachers can move from concrete to abstract, as in the following example based on questions our students devised for teaching Nadine Gordimer's "A Company of Laughing Faces" (again in Gold's *Point of Departure*). (Gordimer's short story is set at a beach resort in South Africa. A young girl has been brought there by her

Some Teachable Paperback Anthologies of Short Stories

American Short Story Masterpieces, edited by Raymond Carver and Tom Jenks. Dell, 1987. Included in this most exciting new collection are Flannery O'Connor's "A Good Man Is Hard to Find," Ursula Le Guin's "Ile Forest," Bernard Malamud's "The Magic Barrel," Joyce Carol Oates's "Where Are You Going, Where Have You Been?" and James Baldwin's "Sonny's Blues."

Fifty Great American Short Stories, edited by Milton Crane. Bantam, 1965. Classic stories include Irwin Shaw's "The Girls in Their Summer Dresses," Fitz-James O'Brien's "What Was It?" Mary E. Wilkins Freeman's "A New England Nun," Theodore Dreiser's "The Phoebe," Conrad Aiken's "Silent Snow, Secret Snow," and James Agee's "A Mother's Tale."

Fifty Great Short Stories, edited by Milton Crane. Bantam, 1952. Favorites are John Steinbeck's "The Chrysanthemums," James Thurber's "The Catbird Seat," John Collier's "The Chaser," J. D. Salinger's "To Esme with Love and Squalor," Katherine Mansfield's "The Garden Party," and Shirley Jackson's "The Lottery."

Great American Short Stories, edited by Wallace and Mary Stegner. Dell, 1957. This fine and safe collection includes William Daniel Steele's "The Man Who Saw Through Heaven," Henry James's "The Real Thing," and Walter van Tilburg Clark's "The Wind and the Snow of Winter."

Mid-Century, edited by Orville Prescott. Pocket Books, 1958. One of the better collections, *Mid-Century* contains such offbeat stories as Shirley Ann Grau's "The Black Prince," Frank Rooney's "Cyclists' Raid," Dorothy M. Johnson's "Lost Sister," Louis Auchincloss' "The Trial of Mr. M," and Joseph Whitehill's "The Day of the Last Rock Fight."

New Women and New Fiction: Short Stories Since the Sixties, edited by Susan Cahill. Mentor, NAL, 1986. Provocative and helpful new stories include Toni Cade Bambaras' "My Man Bovanne," Fay Weldon's "Alopecia," Anne Tyler's "Teenage Wasteland," Bobbie Ann Mason's "Shiloh," and fifteen other stories.

Point of Departure: 19 Stories of Youth and Discovery, edited by Robert S. Gold. Dell, 1967. Stories include John Updike's "A & P" and "Tomorrow and Tomorrow and So Forth," Bernard Malamud's "A Summer's Reading," William Saroyan's "Seventeen," and Nadine Gordimer's "A Company of Laughing Faces."

Points of View,   edited by James Moffett and Kenneth R. McElheny. Mentor/NAL, 1965. The most unusually structured of all these anthologies, it may be the most teachable. Included are William Carlos Williams' "The Use of Force," Nikolai Gogol's "The Diary of a Madman," Joseph Conrad's "The Idiots," and Ivan Turgenev's "The Tryst."

Short Stories: An Anthology of the Shortest Stories,   edited by Irving Howe and Ilana Wiener Howe. Bantam, 1982. The Howes selected lots of too-little-known, very-short stories that are great for class use, including Ernest Hemingway's "A Clean, Well-Lighted Place," James Thurber's "If Grant Had Been Drinking at Appomattox," Paula Fox's "News from the World," and Luisa Valenzuela's "The Censors."

Short Story Masterpieces,   edited by Robert Penn Warren and Albert Erskine. Dell, 1954.

Contains Joseph Conrad's "An Outpost of Progress," F. Scott Fitzgerald's "Winter Dreams," D. H. Lawrence's "The Horse Dealer's Daughter," Irwin Shaw's "The Eighty-Yard Run," Saki's "The Open Window," Somerset Maugham's "The Outstation," and more.

A Short Wait Between Trains: An Anthology of War Short Stories,   edited by Robert Benard. Dell, 1991. The title comes from Robert McLaughlin's story. Others include Kay Boyle's "Defeat," Ralph Ellison's "Flying Home," Bernard Malamud's "The German Refugee," and Ernest Hemingway's "In Another Country."

Sixteen,   edited by Donald R. Gallo. Dell, 1984. The best of Gallo's collections, this one contains several teachable stories. Almost as good are *Connections* (Delacorte, 1989) and *Visions* (Delacorte, 1988).

---

demanding mother to spend Christmas holidays with "nice" people. The girl is almost raped, finds the nice people dull and not all that nice, and finds a friend in a little boy who later drowns.)

1. *Questions requiring students to remember facts:*
   a. Describe the setting of the story.
   b. Describe the protagonist and the other major characters.
   c. What new things had Kathy's mother bought for her?
   d. List the major events in the story.
2. *Questions requiring students to prove or disprove a generalization made by someone else.*
   a. Although the story is set in a South African resort, I think it could have happened at any resort frequented by the upper middle class. Do you agree or disagree? What differences were there between this holiday and that of American college students going to Florida beaches during spring break? Are these differences crucial to the story?
   b. Some readers have interpreted this story as saying that Kathy was a conformist. Do you agree? In what ways was she a conformist? In what ways was she different?
   c. One interpretation is that the nameless young man in the story

represents the anonymous crowds of young people at the resort. Do you agree or disagree? On what evidence?

    d. When Kathy put on her new clothes, the author said that the "disguise worked perfectly." Was Kathy in "disguise" any more than the others? Support your answer with evidence from the story as well as from your own experiences.

3. *Questions requiring students to derive their own generalizations.*
    a. What kind of relationship did Mrs. Hack and Kathy have?
    b. What is Kathy's perception of being young? Who has shaped that perception? Do the events in the story change her perception?
    c. Why doesn't the author give the "young man" a name?
    d. Why does the author contrast the constant activity of the other young people with Kathy's stillness?

4. *Questions requiring students to generalize about the relation of the total work to human experience:*
    a. What did Kathy mean when she said that the sight in the lagoon was the "one truth and the one beauty" in her holiday?
    b. Compare Kathy's relationship with the nameless young man to that of the Bute boy. What is the author saying by showing these two different relationships?
    c. Relate the different parts of the story to Kathy's development in life.
    d. What is the significance of the statement, "The only need she [Kathy] had these days, it seemed, was to be where the gang was; then the question of what to do and how to feel solved itself." Is Kathy satisfied with the answer the gang provides for her? Why or why not?

5. *Questions requiring students to carry generalizations derived from the work into their own lives:*
    a. Have you been in a situation similar to the one experienced by Kathy? How did it make you feel?
    b. What kinds of security do you get from a group? How hard is it to break away?
    c. Have you seen parents like Kathy's mother? What are some ways that young people defend themselves from well-meaning parents who don't understand the situation?

Probably the most important part of a discussion—and unfortunately the most often ignored—is the summing up. In too many classes, the bell rings in the midst of a discussion and students rush away without gathering their thoughts. Such "fly-away" endings cause students to lose respect for class discussions. If they think the teacher is just filling in time until the bell rings, they won't put forth their best efforts. The successful teacher keeps an eye on the clock and saves at least a couple of minutes to draw things together before students are distracted from the topic at hand. Also, good teachers continually work to develop skill in summarizing throughout a discussion. They draw attention to those points that the class basically agrees upon, they praise insightful comments that help the rest of the class see something they might have missed, they search out reasons for disagreement, and they lead students to see connections between the present discussion and previous ones about similar themes or topics.

Determining what short stories (or poems or plays) belong in what grades is one of life's little puzzlements, probably of interest only to English teachers. Updike's "A & P" has been taught as early as ninth grade, but that seems a bit premature. Gordimer's "A Company of Laughing Faces" has been taught as early as tenth grade, and possibly earlier. Both are frequently taught in college, sometimes in the freshmen year, sometimes in graduate school.

We provide next our guesses of where a few favorite short stories belong in secondary school. These are stories we recommend for teaching; see Chapter Nine for stories recommended for independent reading. Obviously, many others should be added each year. (See Focus Box 11.2 for publication information on the anthologies that are cited.)

Seventh Grade

James Agee's "A Mother's Tale." 1952. A youngster tries to convince his mother and others that danger awaits. (Found in Crane's *Fifty Great American Short Stories.*)

Stephen Vincent Benet's "By the Waters of Babylon." 1937. The end of civilization is upon us with a frightening twist at the end. (Found in Crane's *Fifty Great American Short Stories.*)

Norma Fox Mazer's "I Hungry Hannah Cassandra Glen . . ." 1984. Being hungry is powerful motivation for going to a funeral. (Found in Gallo's *Sixteen.*)

Todd Strasser's "On the Bridge." 1987. A boy learns the truth, and it hurts. (Found in Gallo's *Visions.*)

Eighth Grade

Robert Cormier's "In the Heat." 1984. In the midst of anything, there is death. (Found in Gallo's *Sixteen.*)

William Melvin Kelley's "A Good Long Sidewalk." 1964. A young black shovels a snowy sidewalk and finds out about racial prejudice. (Found in Gold's *Point of Departure.*)

Daniel Keye's "Flowers for Algernon." 1959. An experiment changes a retarded man into a genius and back. (Found in Moffett's *Points of View.*)

Richard Peck's "Priscilla and the Wimps." 1984. A bully tyrannizes the school until Priscilla appears. (Found in Gallo's *Sixteen.*)

Ninth Grade

Jack London's "To Build a Fire." 1908. A man learns that the Yukon is unforgiving. (Found in Crane's *Fifty Great American Short Stories*.)

John Steinbeck's "Flight." 1938. A boy accidently kills a man and must flee. (Found in Warren's *Short Story Masterpieces*.)

James Thurber's "The Catbird Seat." 1942. A timid man finds it is possible to gain power. (Found in Stegners' *Great American Short Stories*.)

Joseph Whitehill's "The Day of the Last Rock Fight." 1954. A school tradition becomes a tragedy. (Found in Prescott's *Mid-Century*.)

Tenth Grade

William Faulkner's "Barn Burning." 1939. A boy's father is tried as a barn burner. (Found in Warren's *Short Story Masterpieces*.)

Bernard Malamud's "A Summer's Reading." 1958. A boy who's hardly been noticed makes a grand gesture. (Found in Gold's *Point of Departure*.).

Mauro Senesi's "A Dog for Rock." 1966. The leader of a pack of boys finds affection and loses power. (Found in *Atlantic* for November 1966. More difficult to find than the other stories but worth the effort.)

Eleventh Grade

F. Scott Fitzgerald's "Winter Dreams." 1926. The prototypical Fitzgerald hero falls desperately in love with the prototypical Fitzgerald heroine. (Found in Warren's *Short Story Masterpieces*.)

Katherine Mansfield's "The Garden Party." 1922. In the midst of parties there is death. (Found in Crane's *Fifty Great American Short Stories*.)

Joyce Carol Oates's "Where Are You Going, Where Have You Been?" A flame comes to the moth's door. (Found in Carver's *American Short Story Masterpieces*.)

Irwin Shaw's "The Eighty Yard Run." 1942. A football hero marries a cheerleader, and she grows up. (Found in Warren's *Short Story Masterpieces*.)

Twelfth Grade

John Collier's "The Chaser." 1940. A young man desperately in love gets what he asks for, then. . . . (Found in Gold's *Point of Departure*.)

Nadine Gordimer's "A Company of Laughing Faces." 1960. A girl who doesn't fit in finds a dead boy and chooses not to tell anyone. (Found in Gold's *Point of Departure*.)

Henry James's "The Real Thing." 1893. Appearance versus reality. (Found in Stegners' *Great American Short Stories*.)

Robert McLaughlin's "A Short Wait Between Trains." In World War II, black soldiers waiting for a meal see German prisoners of war treated far better than they are. (It's the undated title story in Benard's collection.)

John Updike's "A & P." 1962. A young man makes a gesture, but the right audience doesn't see him. (Found in Gold's *Point of Departure.*)

Using Novels in English Class

The practice of assigning one novel to be read by an entire class is popular with teachers, partly because it's reassuring to know what's on the agenda for the next few days or, in some classes, even the next few weeks. And after struggling with grammar and composition, where class members' abilities are obviously at great distances from each other, it's a treat for the teacher and the students to all join in reading the same book.

Although many teachers assume that having specific novels read by the entire class has always been a standard part of the English curriculum, the practice is not universally accepted. Some teachers argue that whatever can be learned by studying a common novel can be just as easily learned by studying several short stories. But others say that short stories neither allow for a long-term immersion in a created world nor provide complex character development taking place over a period of a character's lifetime.

One of the problems in using novels is the expense of acquiring a set of novels of your choice (e.g., Bernard Malamud's *The Assistant,* Robin McKinley's *The Hero and the Crown,* or Mary Shelley's *Frankenstein or the Modern Prometheus*) rather than inheriting whatever is left in the English department closet. Another problem is the length of time it takes for students to read the novel (rarely less than a week and more likely two). Adults have been known to stop reading when boredom sets in, but no such benediction comes to kids when they're reading a book for a class. More than sixty years ago, Howard Francis Seely wondered about our attraction to novels.

Just why is it deemed imperative that a whole class read the same novels at the same time, anyway? I haven't heard a sound answer yet. . . . The burden of most of these answers can be recapitulated briefly. A frequent one is that reading one book permits class discussion (which discussion, however, more often than not turns out to be the answering of factual questions chiefly of a trifling nature). . . . A third answer indicates reading this one particular book in this particular class will enlighten the pupils to the structure of the novel as a literary form (which it won't, and which would be of doubtful immediate or ultimate value even if it did). . . . Perhaps the most frequent (and likely the most futile) argument of all is this: If Johnny hasn't read *The Talisman* in the ninth grade with his group, what will happen to him when he comes to *The Spy* in the tenth? That question is generally hurled at me with an air of utter, crushing finality. I can only faintly ask, "Well, just what *would*?" With that I'm given up as hopeless.[17]

A few years later, a teacher from England worried about teaching the novel on other grounds:

> Once the novelty has worn off a book, the child's interest in it can very easily flag. We have only to consider our own reading to realise the truth of this. Even the best novel rarely occupies us more than a few evenings. It is curious that teachers (or those who control teachers) should so often expect the restless mind of the child to possess a greater staying power in this respect than they possess themselves. There is no reason why every book should be studied to the bitter end.[18]

English teachers who wish to use novels for common reading obviously need to choose books they believe will appeal to young people. Never choose something because it's reputedly a classic and therefore will somehow be magically good for students. Never choose a work just because it's modern, therefore relevant. Teachers should selfishly choose a book they like because they may be one of a small group still reading the book after a few days. On the other hand, teachers should avoid choosing a work they love—novel, short story, play, or especially a poem—because some student is certain to attack the beloved, and murderous thoughts will rule the teachers' hearts.

Do not choose a book solely because it has won an award. Some teachers and librarians assume that an award-winning book is quality literature, and generally there's merit in that, but winners are chosen by humans, not gods, and humans make mistakes, some of them wondrous to behold. For years, the Newbery Award was vastly overrated by librarians and teachers and anathema to many young people. The winner was chosen not because it appealed to young people but because adults convinced themselves that the prize winners were books kids would read if they had any taste. That explains, if not justifies, the selection of some early Newberys, e.g., the wonderfully atmospheric and terribly slow-moving *Waterless Mountain* by Laura Adams Armer. It's almost plotless and doomed to be ignored by any but the most sensitive readers. Recent committees have been more inclined to consider reader appeal along with other criteria.

But anyone who has been part of a committee charged with choosing a book award knows that books are removed from final consideration for reasons having nothing to do with literary merit or adolescent appeal. Controversial books, such as those with more than marginal profanity or mild sex, frighten committees, and compromise is inevitable.[19] A mediocre book by a usually excellent author may win an award if many people believe the author should have won

LYNN HALL
on the Letters We Get

One aspect of the author profession that most of us are unprepared for, I think, is how to respond to the letters we get.

At first I was so thrilled to get reader letters that I was ready to adopt every child who wrote. That wears off. It wears off quite quickly these days, under the flood of teacher-forced letters, the ones that start out, "Dear Mr. Hall, Our teacher says we have to write to a author. You're it." Or, "I didn't like that book our teacher made us read. It had too much horses in it and I don't like horses."

Especially daunting are the ones that arrive, usually some time in June, saying, "If you don't answer this before next week I'll get an F on my project."

Letters from adults can be terrific, and most are. Not all. I received one recently from a parent, incensed at my filthy language in a YA novel her fifteen-year-old daughter was reading. She said, "When I got to the obscenity on page 74 I just took that book away from my daughter!" Of course I immediately ran to check page 74 and found that my protagonist, a seventeen-year-old working in a racing stable, had said "Good Lord." Good Lord.

Another recent letter was from a witch coven in Oregon. Yes. On coven letterhead. It berated my use of the term "warlock," for a male witch, in my book *Dagmar Schultz and the Powers of Darkness*. Apparently warlock is a pejorative term. I didn't know that. Silly me.

Most letters are great, and a few have led to lasting friendships. Given this opportunity, though, I'd like to toss out a few suggestions to teachers, regarding letters to authors as classroom assignments.

I think it's a fine idea from the teachers' and students' viewpoint, so long as everyone bears in mind that this assignment also becomes an assignment for the author. If we don't answer every letter personally we're rotten human beings; if we do, we sometimes are swamped! Take the number of children in a classroom, multiply it by all the third- through seventh-grade classes in the country, divide by the number of well-known authors, and you begin to get the picture. One of the greatest gifts an author can receive is a letter of genuine appreciation for our books which doesn't require a reply.

Another problem is that often the return addresses are illegible or forgotten, or are school addresses on letters which don't get forwarded to us (publishers are sometimes slow) until after the end of the school year.

Sometimes too, not often but sometimes, the letters are quite rude. "Our teacher made us read your book, I didn't like it," etc., and I've occasionally thought that teachers might check the letters, not only for spelling and sentence structure, but for politeness, thoughtfulness. The concept of a child's careless remarks hurting someone else's feelings could well be taught in these instances, along with the language skills.

I live alone in an isolated rural area, and I love it, but it does mean that much of my social life comes to me through the mailbox. Reader letters can be a delightful part of that social life, and although they sometimes become a chore to answer, I'd feel terrible if they ever stopped coming.

Lynn Hall's books include *The Secret Life of Dagmar Schultz*, Scribner's, 1988; *Halsey's Pride*, Scribner's, 1990; *The Tormentors*, Harcourt, 1990; and *Murder in a Pig's Eye*, Harcourt, 1990.

last year, while an excellent book by a new and unknown author may go unnoticed. This is as true of awards for adults as for young people; the Pulitzer, for example, and Nobel winners have frequently been controversial and debated for years.

Some teachers do not have to worry about selecting the novel they are going to teach because choices are established by school or district curricula. Among the most widely used titles are John Steinbeck's *Of Mice and Men,* Harper Lee's *To Kill a Mockingbird,* Mark Twain's *Adventures of Huckleberry Finn,* William Golding's *Lord of the Flies,* and Robert Cormier's *The Chocolate War.* All five are understandably popular with teachers and students, and all five are among the most widely censored books in public schools.

Those interested in finding suggestions on what novels work well in classrooms should skim through back issues of the *English Journal* or their state NCTE affiliate journals, like New York's *English Record,* the *Arizona English Bulletin, California English,* the *Connecticut English Journal,* and the *Virginia English Bulletin.* Successful English teachers understandably love to tell about the ones that didn't get away. Exceptionally helpful questions and ideas about using novels can be found in articles by Geoff Fox[20] and Richard Peck.[21]

A practice that appeals to some English teachers is to focus on themes rather than to assign one novel. The teacher divides a class of thirty or forty students into small groups of five to seven people and selects five to ten titles with a closely related theme for each small group. The members each read one or more of the books. During their small group discussions of the theme, readers talk about how the theme was developed in their books. Later in a class discussion each small group presents its theme, why the theme was significant, and what their books had to say about that theme.

There are several obvious advantages to this approach. Shy students fearful of talking in class may be willing to talk in a small group, and it is certainly easier for other class members to encourage the timid. In a class of thirty to forty, students rarely have enough time to get across their ideas. Small groups not only encourage participation but almost demand that everyone talks. But teachers need to remember that young people don't automatically know how to take part in a small group. Teachers need to give guidance and set up specific tasks. Worthwhile discussion is no accident.

Two other advantages to reading books in small groups deserve mention. It's often easier to find five or ten copies of a book than thirty copies, and it may be wise to try a novel in a small group before you consider it for an entire class. Using five or seven novels for small groups also allows students to choose books that match their individual abilities and maturity levels. And books that might cause public relations problems or attempted censorship if they are required reading for an entire class can be examined and studied by small groups whose members will decide for themselves whether or not they wish to read a particular title.

Using Poetry in English Class

In our college classes, we begin our study of poetry by talking about the results of our first-day exercise and listening to our students' comments. Only rarely do they feel they need to explain their fondness for novels, but they usually need somehow to justify their attitudes toward poetry, probably because they have been taught to kneel before the altar of poetry before they have been given a chance to enjoy it.

They usually begin by telling us how significant poetry is, how many great poets they have read, and how much they enjoyed poetry when they were children, especially Dr. Seuss. A few tack on Shel Silverstein's work, which they read to their children. But when we ask students to write down the titles of a few poems they have enjoyed as adults, they glance upward, presumably to supplicate the almighty, or they stare out the windows, where life is real.

Then we begin talking about what happened to the fondness for poetry they felt as children and the discomfort they now feel as adults. The following five comments pop up over and over, semester after semester. The comments are almost identical to what we've also heard from high school students when we've talked with them about poetry. We realize the statements are slanted because they come from students searching their memories for bad experiences to explain their negative feelings toward poetry. But in spite of the lack of objectivity, we are repeating them here in hopes that they will have instructional value for teachers hoping to be more successful.

1. Their high school teachers seemed unenthusiastic about poetry, "just going through the motions." Some teachers taught a unit on poetry to "get rid of it all at once," others seemed afraid of poetry or at least uncertain of what to do with it.

2. Some teachers substituted a flood of technical terms for the poetry they might have taught. The effect was to inundate students who had to memorize the terms but saw no connection between the terms and poetry or anything else. One teacher reportedly said, "Until you understand these terms, you won't be able to understand the poetry we'll read later." The student who reported this said she could not remember that they ever got around to reading poetry. Another student remembers being required to write a poem with one metaphor, at least two similes, and one example of personification. That exercise and two or three poems was the poetry unit for the entire year.

3. Some of our students' teachers talked about how terribly compact poetry is, how terribly slow-moving it is, and how terribly significant it is. They did not seem to talk about how terribly interesting it can be.

4. Many teachers worried about the difficult language and the allusions in poetry and took great delight in expounding and expanding on these, often referring to graduate seminars they had taken that had made clear these arcane matters. Most of our students said that they too had taken

some of those graduate courses but saw no reason that their secondary students had to know about them.

5. Students remembered playing constant guessing games on the meaning or morals of various poems. Teachers asked students for their ideas but took little interest in what students said. Occasionally, a student would guess the right answer, but more often, the teacher would be the one to announce the right meaning or moral.

To be fair, we must also report that a number of our students, although always a minority, remember their teachers with affection and their teaching of poetry with respect and admiration. Those teachers clearly honored their students and got respect by giving it. They listened to students, even when they disagreed, and they did not force their reading of a poem down anyone's throat. They chose poetry for adolescent appeal *and* literary merit, the former always outweighing the latter. These uncommon teachers were exactly what we hope our students will become—teachers who love poetry, who choose poetry they believe kids will enjoy, who are excited about poetry of many kinds, and who recognize that successful literature in class is literature that works for students today, not at some vague time in the future.

Books about teaching literature inevitably give suggestions on teaching this or that genre, but readers can almost palpably sense the urgency of suggestions for teaching poetry. See Focus Box 9.2, page 356, for ways to combine the reading and writing of poetry. Other good books on teaching poetry include Louise Rosenblatt's seminal *The Reader, the Text, the Poem: The Transactional Theory of the Literary Work*; Patrick Dias and Michael Hayhoe's *Developing Response to Poetry*; and Stephen Dunning's *Teaching Literature to Adolescents: Poetry*.

Richard Beach and James Marshall's first suggestion is "Never teach a poem you don't like."[22] That is virtually what Stephen Dunning lists as his first and second principles for teaching poetry: "The teacher who is not himself a reader of poetry must not pretend to teach poetry," and, "The teacher of poetry must teach only those poems for which he can engender real enthusiasm."[23] These suggestions or principles are much like the first premise listed by Geoff Fox and Brian Merrick: "Poetry is to be experienced before it is to be analyzed."[24] And in a recent worry about the state of poetry in our country, Dana Gioia wrote,

Poetry teachers, especially at the high school and undergraduate levels, should spend less time on analysis and more on performance. . . . Poems should be memorized, recited, and performed. The sheer joy of art must be emphasized. The pleasure of performance is what first attracts children to poetry, the sensual excitement of speaking and hearing the words of the poem. Performance was also the teaching technique that kept poetry alive for centuries. Maybe it holds the key to poetry's future.[25]

Something like a six-point consensus about teaching poetry emerges from these writers and from articles on teaching poetry in the *English Journal*.

1. As English teachers read aloud the poems they personally enjoy, they should show their enthusiasm. James Squire wrote, "With many poems, good reading aloud is all that is needed in the way of classroom treatment."[26] And as Robert Boynton and Maynard Mack note in the first words of their *Introduction to the Poem*, "Poetry is first and foremost a performer's art. Its life is in the spoken language, in the application of normal speech sounds and rhythms to gain varied and subtle ends. To enjoy it, you must speak and hear it. . . ."[27]

2. Teachers should know lots of poems. That does not mean they have to use them all, particularly those remote from adolescent life. Luckily, good collections of poetry are not hard to find (see Focus Box 9.1 on p. 349).

3. Teachers should focus on the poem, not explanations or critical comments or theories or the mechanics/techniques of the poem. Performance and enjoyment should precede analysis. In too many classes, analysis is all that counts.

4. Teachers should avoid units on poetry. Poems deserve to be used in class often, perhaps even daily. Thematic units that bring poems in touch with short stories or plays work well. Dropping a funny poem or two into class just for the fun of it works if the poems are within the grasp of kids. Teachers worthy of the name know how to choose poems that stand the best chance of bringing kids to poetry.

5. Students occasionally, or regularly, should help to select the poems for reading and discussion.

6. Poetry classes exist primarily for one reason—to bring the poems to the kids. That demands time to consider and wonder and revisit the poems. Time is essential, not to see how many poems can be knocked off in a class period but to allow us to hear poems again and again in our minds. (We observed one teacher, who must have hated poetry, set a local record by killing thirty-six Emily Dickinson poems in less than a class period.)

Young people sometimes maintain that they don't like love poems, but that usually means they don't care for love poems by writers of the Romantic period or love poems outside the ken of the young. Anyone who's been around a school corridor for a few minutes knows full well that young people care about love. Another claim is that teenagers don't like nature poems. This can usually be translated to mean they didn't care for Emerson's feeble efforts or, again, the Romantic writers. Kids care about nature. They love going on hikes and picnics and hunting and fishing, and there's lots of good poetry that taps into those interests.

In Chapter Nine we talked about poetry that works with young people, particularly collections by Mel Glenn and Paul Janeczko and humorous poetry.

Although there's no such thing as a surefire poem for every occasion and all teachers, some poems come close to being successful more often than not. For example, many young people go through an Edgar Allan Poe phase and go around reciting "Annabel Lee" or "The Raven" or that most esoteric poem for the young, "Ulalume." Robert Frost's narrative poetry usually works well, especially "Home Burial."

Three inexpensive and easily found paperback anthologies are loaded with poems that work with many audiences. Richard Peck's *Sounds and Silences: Poetry for Now,* revised edition (Dell, 1990), contains Theodore Roetke's "My Papa's Waltz," May Swenson's "Southbound on the Freeway," W. H. Auden's "The Unknown Citizen," Robinson Jeffers' "Hurt Hawks," e. e. cummings' "next to of course god america i," and poems by Langston Hughes, Robert Francis, Countee Cullen, Denise Levertov, W. D. Snodgrass, and more. Peck's other collection, *Mindscapes: Poems for the Real World,* revised edition (Dell, 1990), is almost as good, containing A. E. Housman's "To an Athlete Dying Young," William Carlos Williams' "Tract," David Wagoner's "Staying Alive," John Updike's "Ex-Basketball Player," and poems by Robert Hayden, Kenneth Fearing, Donald Hall, Charles Bukowski, David Ignatow, May Swenson, Galway Kinnell, Donald Justice, and William Stafford. Add to these two a slim anthology of women's poems, Norma Fox Mazer and Marjorie Lewis' *Waltzing on Water* (Dell, 1989) with Maxine Kumin's "The Fairest One of All," Linda Pastan's "It Is Raining on the House of Anne Frank," May Swenson's "How Everything Happens (Based on the Study of the Wave)," and lots more. With these three books, plus poems gleaned from teachers' reading in *Harpers,* the *New Yorker, Atlantic,* and to the surprise of some, recent issues of *English Journal,* any teacher can easily have more than 100 poems worth reading and using in class.

It's often downright scary to try out a poem that neither teacher nor students know. Pat Mora's "1910," from her collection *Chants* is a good choice.[28] It tells a sad, maybe even frightening, story. Minority students who have been stepped on by shopowners would appreciate the pathos and dignity and terror. And almost any poem by Marge Piercy would provoke discussion. "What's That Smell in the Kitchen?" and "I Am a Light You Could Read By," from *Circles on the Water: Selected Poems by Marge Piercy* work particularly well with sophisticated students.

Students often delight in sports poems. Most teachers know Robert Francis' "Pitcher" and "Base Stealer." Fewer know *Aethlon: The Journal of Sports Literature,*[29] which carries poetry, some of it great fun indeed. Two poems in the spring 1991 issue could provide enjoyment and profit in any English class.

Double Vision
by Barbara Smith
You who are sports have no use for words,
Flexing eyebrows and fingers at Dickinson and Poe,
Sneering at bowling pins and degrading dance

And you who are words hunch squint-eyed in libraries,
Call them illiterate apes, their brains in their muscles,
And give them F's in English
While we few who are both enjoy double vision,
Watch footballs write sonnets on yard-line stripes,
Hear limericks in left-handed hooks on the hoop,
Rhyme couplets as tennis balls clear the net,
And see each gold medal as a Pulitzer Prize.

A Friend Sends Me Old Baseball Cards in a Book of Poetry
by Edwin Romond

for Don Colburn

In the 50's they stuck to flat bubblegum
but today I open a gift book of poems
and they float like butterflies into my lap.
The book speaks the somber stuff of living
and dying, all its lines broken
from cover to cover. But these faces grin
forever young from mounds and dugouts,
their eyes bright with the life of baseball.
So I prop them on my shelves
against the hardbacks of literature
and consider how half these men have died,
the rest live gray and chunky into their sixties,
maybe grieving the game that faded
to lunatic contracts and plastic grass.
Do they ever limp across dens to search
for themselves on cards like these?
They're warm as snapshots of elderly uncles
who'd play catch with me until dark.
I love how they grin from my tiers of books;
I love how I feel as I smile back.

One of the delights, and challenges, of working with modern poetry is that students (and teachers) have no source to turn to for determining the meaning or worth of the poems. Comments on a T. S. Eliot poem are easy to come by, and a glance at criticism will tell us whether this poem is major Eliot or minor Eliot. We hardly need to read the poem to comment on it, to determine its place in the canon, or to chase down all those wonderful symbols and allusions. In fact, we need not think at all. But without a critic-god, a journal article, or *Cliffs Notes* to determine the worth or meaning of a modern poem, teachers and students must fall back on honest responses to the poem. Years ago, Luella Cook, one of the great people in English education, warned teachers about the dishonesty of canned responses to literature, and although she referred to students alone, her warning might be extended to teachers as well.

The problem of teaching literature realistically faced, then, becomes one of widening the range of responses to literature, of guiding reading experience so that reaction to books will be vivid, sharp, compelling, provocative. The great tragedy of the English classroom is not that students may have the "wrong" reactions—that is, veer from accepted judgment—but that they will have no original reaction at all, or only the most obvious ones, or that they will mimic the accepted evaluations of criticism.[30]

More than fifty years later, a Texas high school teacher wrote that he wanted his students to reject:

. . . the possibility of responding to a piece of literature by repeating what they have heard a teacher or someone else say about that piece of literature. I want to stress to students that responding to poetry is not repeating a response that someone else has made.[31]

Instead, it is thinking of the unique meaning that the poem has for the individual who is doing the responding. The problem lies first in finding literature that students will want to respond to and second in listening to the students when they do respond. It sounds so simple, doesn't it?

Using Shakespearean Drama in English Class

If, as we noted in Chapter Nine, drama presents problems to the English teacher, Shakespeare presents many more problems (see Focus Box 11.3). Teachers may be unsure of what to do with all those iambic pentameter lines and all those mystifying plots about obscure kings they hardly recognize and kids recognize not at all. What with the archaic or obsolete language, boys playing girls, soliloquies and obscure allusions, and rumors that *Romeo and Juliet* has been banned because of "suggestive scenes," as one censor blushingly said, it's not surprising that some teachers take the easy way out and ignore Shakespeare. That's a shame. Shakespeare was great fun for his contemporaries, and he can be great fun if teachers and students will relax and enjoy his plays. That means, as we've said in Chapter Nine on modern plays, Shakespeare ought to be seen before he's read.

Luckily, many of Shakespeare's plays have been adapted for the screen. That is not to say, as many purists argue, that the movie is nothing more than a filmed play (see Focus Box 11.4). Laurence Olivier's *Hamlet* is a Freudian psychological thriller. Mel Gibson's *Hamlet* is younger and angrier. Neither is like Nicol Williamson's reading. These are full-blown films with all the pos-

Books About Shakespeare and Other Drama

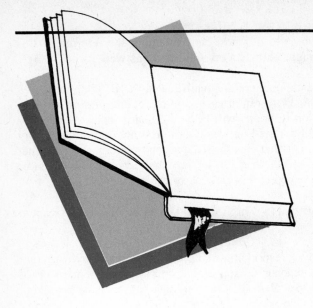

Shakespeare: The Essential Reference to His Plays, His Poems, His Life and Times, and More by Boyce Charles. Roundtable Press/Dell, 1991. The formidable title promises much and delivers even more. Plays, theatrical history, textual matter, sources, themes, characters in plays, actors, directors, critics, and much more are treated in this splendid, essential book.

Shakespeare's Bawdy: A Literary and Psychological Essay and a Comprehensive Glossary by Eric Partridge. Dutton, 1948. Routledge, Chapman and Hall issued a 1991 edition of this essential book that keeps readers and teachers from making fools of themselves in talking about Shakespeare and his language.

Teaching Drama: A Mind of Many Wonders by Norah Morgan and Juliana Saxton. Heinemann, 1987. Seven chapters explore the many faces (and problems) of dramatizing a play.

Beginning Readers Theatre: A Primer for Classroom Performance by Gerald Lee Ratliff. Speech Communication Association, 1981. Here's a good statement of what readers theater is and how it works.

Drama in English Teaching by Tricia Evans. Croom Helm, 1984. Drama as Evans sees it is not a frill in English class but an essential element of the entire English curriculum.

Organizing and Managing the High School Theatre Program by James R. Opelt. Allyn & Bacon, 1991. A good guide for both beginners and old stagehands.

Play Directing: Analysis, Communication, and Style, 3rd ed., by Francis Hodge. Prentice-Hall, 1988. Hodge's insights will be useful for reading as well as directing plays.

Shakespeare Alive! by Joseph Papp and Elizabeth Kirkland. Bantam, 1988. A brief introduction to Shakespeare and his plays, times, and stage, for the beginner.

Teaching Literature to Adolescents: Plays by Alan B. Howes. Scott, Foresman, 1968. An interview with Arthur Miller is coupled with many ideas about teaching drama.

Teaching Young Playwrights by Gerald Chapman. Heinemann, 1990. Chapman presents the simplicity and complexity of playwrighting for young children to teenagers.

Unlocking Shakespeare's Language: Help for the Teacher and Student by Randal Robinson. National Council of Teachers of English, 1989. Learning about Shakespeare's language and syntax for understanding and acting.

FOCUS BOX 11.4

The Many Varieties of Shakespeare on Film

If you're in the mood for *Macbeth*, you can choose Orson Welles' very Scottish production (1948, 89 min., black and white; with Welles as Macbeth); Roman Polanski's stylish piece (1971, 140 min., color, with Jon Finch as Macbeth); or Akira Kurosawa's Japanese wonder, *Throne of Blood* (1957, 108 min., black and white with Toshiro Mifune).

If you'd prefer *Hamlet*, you can choose from Laurence Olivier's psychoanalytic version (1948, 153 min., black and white; starring Olivier); Tony Richardson's wilder production (1969, 114 min., color; starring Nicol Wiliamson); or the recent Franco Zeffirelli version (1990, 135 min., color; starring Mel Gibson).

If you feel like *Romeo and Juliet*, you can watch Renato Castellani's underrated and ignored version (1954, 140 min., color; with Laurence Harvey and Susan Shentall as the lovers) or Franco Zeffirelli's much-used production (1968, 138 min., color; with Leonard Whiting and Olivia Hussey playing the young, if dull, lovers—but this film does have John McEnery, and that makes up for almost anything). You could, if you were in a different mood, watch the Royal Ballet of England do the *Romeo and Juliet* ballet, with the glorious

Prokofiev music (1966, 126 min., color), but the photography isn't all that glorious.

If you care to cry for lost glory, *Othello* awaits in two productions, with Stuart Burge (1965, 166 min., color; with Laurence Olivier, Frank Finlay, and Maggie Smith) or the old Orson Welles version (1952, 92 min., black and white; with Welles and Michael Mac-Liammoir).

If *King Lear* is what you must have, Peter Brook's production has Paul Scofield (1971, 137 min., black and white), while Akira Kurosawa's magnificent Japanese version, *Ran* (1985, 161 min., color), is too little known (and it ought to be seen, long as it is, by all of us).

If you care to see British pageantry and glory and hear glorious poetry, watch either of two fine versions of *Henry V*. Laurence Olivier's production is the older but it's still fine (1945, 137 min., color). Kenneth Branagh's recent version is equally worth seeing (1989, 137 min., color).

If you're looking for sheer and erratic genius, look at Orson Welles's *Chimes at Midnight* (1967, 115 min., black and white), with Welles playing Falstaff in a film made up of parts of *Richard II, Henry IV* (Parts I and II), *Henry V*, and *The Merry Wives of Windsor*.

If you want to know what it was like to tour the provinces of India with a Shakespearean company, watch *Shakespeare Wallah* (1965, 115 min., black and white; with Felicity Kendal, the nicest reason for watching anything).

And if you want to see the purest villain of them all, *Richard III* is always an actor's dream. Until something else comes along, Laurence Olivier's production will do just fine (1955, 155 min., color).

---

sibilities that film has and the stage lacks, but the stage has advantages over the screen, and they should be brought to students' attention too.

Purists who doubt that Shakespeare's plays should be sullied by being filmed grow fewer and fewer by the year. More than thirty years ago, Margaret Farrand Thorp argued that the kind of audience that Shakespeare wrote for would today be reached through the screen rather than the theater.

> Shakespeare's plays were written for the stage so why should we try to present them in any other medium? Simply because today William Shakespeare is rapidly dwindling into a closet dramatist. Poll a freshman class in even the best of our eastern colleges, ask any group of young people under thirty how many Shakespearean plays they have seen in the flesh. You will be appalled at the answers: one or two, perhaps at best; again and again it will be none. . . . If Shakespeare is to remain a national heritage . . . we must transfer him somehow to the motion picture screen.[32]

Going beyond watching and listening, students need to act out Shakespeare, not merely mouth his words as they sit in class. Most students won't believe they can act Shakespeare, but they can, with a little help, a little encouragement, and a little rehearsal time.

For a number of years we've had our adolescent literature classes work with, as opposed to work over, *Macbeth,* which most of them have already done in other classes. We divide the class into five groups, each assigned to perform one act, and we announce that our wondrous production of *Macbeth* will be due for viewing three periods later. That leaves part of one period for each group to decide what it will do for its ten- to thirteen-minute production of its act and two meetings for rehearsals. It is as certain as a flu epidemic at test time that a few naysayers will announce that it cannot be done. But we notice that even they decide in a few minutes to get down to work.

And so the two class periods pass by and the production takes place. True, there are giggles galore as simple props fail and the best-laid plans go wildly astray. True, the fight scene in the last act doesn't quite work out, although both Macbeth and Macduff get a few moments' exercise and we all laugh. Yes, those who didn't want to be the weird sisters learn how much fun hokey drama can be. Yes, we enjoy ourselves, even the few invited guests (more often than not, small children whose mothers couldn't get a babysitter).

A few actors turn out to be excruciating and awful, usually a Macbeth who, we hope, has learned that bombast is not acting. Most are competent, and a very few learn that they have undiscovered talent. Our next class meeting is taken up with awards for the best this or that in the productions. Then we ask our players what they got out of doing *Macbeth*. After a few ribald or disparaging comments, they seem to agree they had fun. Some say that they had never been in a play before and that they had been nervous, knew they would never be able to act and would probably ruin the play, but they didn't. We've sent only a few professional actors to Broadway, but that was never our aim. We wanted students to have the enjoyment and satisfaction of acting, something that had been denied them.

They had tried a forbidding assignment, and instead of its being awful, it was worthwhile and fun. They also agreed that it was something they wished they had done in their high school days, something they planned to do with their own classes.

We hope they do. It's important to get across to classes that acting isn't all that esoteric, that it can be satisfying, but that students have to get up to do it. Students cannot be allowed to sit in class, straight row after row, mumbling through lines while others fall asleep. *Macbeth* done that way has only a few major roles: Macbeth, Lady Macbeth, Duncan, and Banquo. Our most recent production had five Macbeths (actually seven, since two acts split his part), four Lady Macbeths, three Macduffs, three Banquos, and almost an infinity of weird sisters.

Occasionally, a student asks us why we do *Macbeth* rather than another play, perhaps a Greek classic or a modern play. The answer is easy. Our students study *Macbeth* in Shakespeare class and have the text. We can hardly assume any common text other than Shakespeare. More to the point, *Macbeth* is in virtually all high school literary texts at some grade or other, so whatever other plays their students may read, *Macbeth* is almost certain to be one of them.

Drama in the classroom need not stop with *Macbeth*. *Romeo and Juliet, Hamlet,* and *Julius Caesar* are deservedly widely used, although *Othello, Twelfth Night,* and *Richard III* deserve the occasional chance. *King Lear, Coriolanus, Anthony and Cleopatra,* and *The Tempest* might be worth a try in an especially bright group. And there's always *Oedipus Rex* and *Antigone* to do, or *Medea* or *Electra* or *Everyman* or *Dr. Faustus*. The wonderful thing about working with plays in secondary school is that there's always a favorite play you've never done, and there are always new English classes coming up.

A Short Note on Films in the English Class

In 1913 Robert W. Neal wrote a three-page note in the *English Journal* about a medium that was already controversial.[33] Movies had been damned from the

The availability of videos has changed the English classroom almost as much as it has changed home entertainment.

pulpit, and librarians were understandably opposed to them, as they had been to another major time-waster, the dime novel. But Neal did not come to attack. He announced that movies were "here to stay and we shall have to make the best of them." He added that if the teacher were "to turn the moving picture to his own purposes, the teacher of course must be reasonably familiar with it." Neal suggested that teachers should read a book on the technique of the "photo-play" and read a periodical on the medium. So much for the image of the stuffy English teacher in 1913.

But English teachers proved stand-offish about the movies if Samuel Rosenkranz's 1931 comment is to be believed:

> We continue to teach our standards of evaluation in the drama and to ignore the cinema, and our pupils continue to patronize the cinema and to ignore the drama. We refuse to recognize the fact that they are going to the picture shows, and that we must adapt our literature and composition courses in such a manner that adequate recognition is given to the fact that there are some genuine needs to be met.[34]

Some teachers must have listened because eight years later, Hardy Finch could brag that English teachers kept up with the times, for "Over two hundred schools throughout the United States are now engaged in the production of films."[35]

The heyday of short and feature-length films in English classes came during the revolutionary 1960s and 1970s, when the most popular reading of many English teachers was not the *English Journal* but *Media and Methods*. Under the direction of Anthony Prete and Frank McLaughlin, *M & M* was possibly the most exciting professional magazine in our history. During those glorious days of yore, English teachers prided themselves on knowing and using short and long films.

Many of these same films are still available because they were purchased by university film cooperatives. Books discussing their rich uses (see Focus Box 11.5) are also available in libraries if not in bookstores. The following are a few excellent short films that English teachers can profitably use.

"A Chairy Tale," 10 min., black and white. Norman McLaren, the genius of the National Film Board of Canada, made this symbolic and funny film using a technique he invented, pixillation (making cartoon movements with human characters) about the world of a man and his chair.

"The Hand," 19 min., color. Jiri Trinka's 1962 Czech film is about a simple potter who comes under the control of a mysterious and dictatorial gloved hand.

"Hangman," 12 min., color. Here is an animated version of Maurice Ogden's poem about the divide-and-conquer methods of a totalitarian regime.

"Nahanni," 19 min., color. "Nahanni" tells the true story of Albert Faille and his drive to reach the headwaters of the Nahanni River in Canada and all the gold rumored to be there.

"Neighbors," 10 min., color. McLaren uses his pixillation technique to illustrate how peace so easily becomes war.

"Night and Fog," 31 min., both black and white and color. Alain Resnais' quiet and dramatic film about German concentration camps is a must-see.

"Occurrence at Owl Creek Bridge," 27 min., black and white. Robert Enrico's film of Ambrose Bierce's Civil War story was a Cannes winner.

"One-Eyed Men Are Kings," 15 min., color. In one of the funniest films made, a man is forced to walk his mother's dog and play a blind man.

"Sticky My Fingers, Fleet My Feet," 23 min., color. A middle-aged man plays his last touch football game in this whimsical and sad but mostly hysterical movie.

"Toys," 7 min. color. Kids stare at war toys in a department store, and when the toys come alive, blood flows.

In "A Revolution Reshapes Movies," an article about VCRs in the January 7, 1990, *New York Times,* Vincent Canby wrote,

Nothing that happened in the 1980's compares to the Videocassette Revolution, sometimes known as the VCR, a term also used to designate

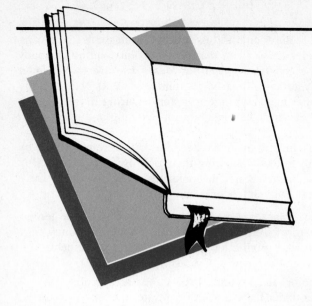

Some Handy Dandy Books About Film

The American Short Story, edited by Calvin Skaggs. Dell, 1977. Here are texts of nine short stories selected for filming on the "American Short Story" series along with screenplays, scenes, or interviews. *The American Short Story,* Volume 2 (Dell, 1980) does the same thing for eight more short stories.

The Celluloid Curriculum: How to Use Movies in the Classroom by Richard A. Maynard. Hayden, 1971. Over twenty years old, this book is still helpful to any English teacher who cares about movies.

Discovery in Film by Robert Heyer and Anthony Meyer. Paulist Press, 1969. The authors comment perceptively on many short films.

Films Deliver: Teaching Creatively with Films, edited by Anthony Schillaci and John M. Culkin. Citation Press, 1970. This is a good collection of articles and criticism on using film, especially short films in classrooms.

5001 Nights at the Movies, rev. ed., by Pauline Kael. Holt, 1984. Kael's long plot summaries are invaluable for film studies.

From Fiction to Film: Ambrose Bierce's "An Occurrence at Owl Creek Bridge," edited by Gerald R. Barrett and Thomas L. Erskine. Dickenson, 1973. Texts of both the short story and the film are presented shot by shot.

Good Looking: Film Studies, Short Films, and Filmmaking, edited by David Sohn. North American Publishing, 1976. Sohn gleaned the best of seven years of *Media and Methods.* He also wrote *Film: The Creative Eye,* commenting on films distributed by Pyramid, which includes short films as great as Saul Bass's, "Why Man Creates."

Guide to Short Films by Jeffrey Schrank. Hayden, 1979. Schrank provides excellent coverage of many short films.

Halliwell's Filmgoer's and Video Viewer's Companion, 9th ed., by Leslie Halliwell. HarperCollins, 1990. A basic tool for anyone who cares about films.

The Liveliest Art: A Panoramic History of the Movies by Arthur Knight. New American Library, 1957. Just what the title says.

Novels into Films by George Bluestone. University of California Press, 1968. Here's the first significant study of what happens to a work when it's translated into film.

Reading the Movies: Twelve Great Films on Video and How to Teach Them by William V. Constanzo. National Council of Teachers of English, 1992. Films include *Citizen Kane, The Graduate, The Grapes of Wrath*, and *Singin' in the Rain*.

Short Story/Short Film by Fred H. Marcus. Prentice-Hall, 1977. Included among the texts of short stories and their film versions are Melville's "Bartleby" and Saki's "The Open Window."

The TV and Movie Business: An Encyclopedia of Careers, Technologies, and Practices by Harvey Rachlin. Harmony, 1991. The book almost fulfills the breadth of the title—a compliment to a book that succinctly tells us about the mundane and the arcane. If you've been curious what a *grip* is or a *gaffer* or what a *best boy* is, here's the place to look.

Understanding the Film by Ron Johnson and Jan Bone. National Textbook, 1976. This book is an introduction to film language, scripts, evaluation, and more.

---

the appliance on which cassettes are played. The VCR is turning the business of movies upside down and even affecting the kinds of movies we see. Movies will never be the same.

Doubtless Canby is right, but he missed how the VCR is changing the English classroom in many schools. Teachers can now have at their fingertips most of the great movies of the world to use in conjunction with the original source, a novel or play, or with other materials in a thematic unit. For example, they can easily get comedies like *Singin' in the Rain, Bringing Up Baby,* and *The Court Jester* (see Focus Box 9.4 p. 370), and films with ideas such as those in *Rashomon* and *The Night of the Hunter*.

With the VCR, teachers can use films in ways not even foreseen in the happy teaching-film world of the 1960s and 1970s. For example, teachers fascinated by what happens to a novel that is dramatized for Broadway and later filmed can now follow those intramedia transformations with their students. One of the most interesting examples is Carson McCullers' *The Member of the Wedding,* published as a short novel in 1946. McCullers dramatized the story, which succeeded on Broadway and can be found in a Dell paperback, *Famous American Plays of the 1940s*. Later it was filmed with Ethel Waters, Julie Harris, and Brandon de Wilde.

Arthur Miller's *Death of a Salesman* starred Lee J. Cobb on Broadway, and although Cobb did not appear in the film, he and a fine cast (including Mildred Dunnock) recorded the play (Dustin Hoffman played Bernard). In a tightly budgeted film in 1951, Frederic March was excellent—although no Lee J. Cobb. And in 1985, Dustin Hoffman appeared in an easily found TV version.

One of the more interesting transformations occurred with a short story, "Rashomon," by a Japanese writer, Ryunosuke Akutagawa. Akira Kurosawa, the great Japanese film director, used the story, along with another by Akutagawa, "In the Grove," to make his 1950 film, *Rashomon*. Fourteen years later, Martin Ritt directed his version of Kurosawa's film, locating it in Mexico and starring Paul Newman, Claire Bloom, and Laurence Harvey. The short stories about the nature of truth are quiet and perceptive. Kurosawa's film is one of the world's greatest films, whereas Ritt's movie is usually treated as a joke. Used in conjunction with the stories and Kurosawa's film, Ritt's work may lack majesty, but it is not without interest (and it's almost certainly more immediately accessible for many of our students).

Unhappily, and predictably, objections have been heard to the use of films in English classes. Charlotte Larson's article in the winter 1992 issue of *Arizona English Bulletin* details her use of *The Great Santini* in a junior high unit on the family. For the several years she had used the unit and the film, Larson had warned the parents of her students about the language. When a parent of a recent student objected, the administration followed the path of least resistance and banned the film. For once, however, there's a happy ending. Supported by many of her students and their parents, Larson appealed the decision and won her case.

A more predictable end came to other teachers, as reported by Marie Hardenbrook in the same issue of the *Arizona English Bulletin*. History teachers had been using *Glory,* the brilliant film about black Civil War soldiers, rated "R" partly for its language and partly for its violence. At a school board meeting where one board member alleged that some teachers were "visiting their local rental stores Sunday night for Monday morning's lesson plan," teachers and education lost when the board decided to ban all "R"-rated movies from class use.

Using Thematic Units in the English Class

Peter Elbow's recent reflections on the 1987 English Coalition Conference are entitled *What Is English?*[36] For years, scholars have asked that question, not to be cute but to determine what goes into that thing called English. English is so broad that the running joke is that if something doesn't belong anywhere and no one else wants it, it ends up in the English curriculum.

The joke isn't all that funny. This was especially true in 1991, when a local school recognized the importance of AIDS instruction and the administration decided it belonged in the English curriculum. Why? (1) English classes included all the kids, and (2) English teachers had never turned down any such request before. To the surprise of both the administration and other teachers, the English teachers finally said no to something.

Part of the reason that thematic units have become popular in English classes is that they provide a way to bind together a number of apparently dissimilar elements, including literature, language, media, and popular culture. But first we need to distinguish the *thematic unit* from two other kinds of units. The *project unit* has a clear end product, with all the steps that lead up to that end. For example, the production of a class play ends when the play is put on, a class-published slang dictionary ends when the booklet is put together and handed out, and reading and talking about a novel ends with the last discussion and the test. A *subject-centered* unit consists of a body of information the teacher feels is important for the class. For example, units on the history of the language, the rise of drama to Shakespeare's time, or "Our Friend, the Introductory Adverbial Clause" (the latter is not made up—we saw it in action, if that's the right word). These units have no clear-cut ending, barring the test, but they do have generally clear limits of what's to be included.

The *thematic unit* is different in that it binds together many elements of English while centering on a theme or motif that runs through a body of literature. For example, a question most of us have asked ourselves is, "Why do some people want to manipulate others?" This question is also asked in Aldous Huxley's *Brave New World,* George Orwell's *1984,* Shakespeare's *Othello* and *King Lear,* F. Scott Fitzgerald's *The Great Gatsby,* Henrik Ibsen's *An Enemy of the People,* Robert Cormier's *Fade,* M. E. Kerr's *If I Love You, Am I Trapped Forever?* and Sophocles' *Antigone.*

Is this a theme deserving the four or five weeks' time that the usual thematic unit takes? Here are four criteria against which to stack such a question:

1. The theme needs to appeal to kids. If it's too easy or too hard or too boring, the teacher will lose the students' interest and attention.
2. The theme needs to be worth doing—in other words, intellectually and emotionally respectable for these particular kids at this particular time of their development and at this particular time of the year.
3. There must be lots of easily located literature on the theme.
4. The theme needs to appeal to the teacher; if the teacher isn't excited about it, the kids won't be either.

Assuming that the theme meets these four requirements, the teacher must begin a search for literature on the theme that students will enjoy and be challenged by, composition topics (written and spoken) worth using and related to the theme, films (short and feature-length) related to the theme and worth viewing, and spelling and vocabulary lists related to the theme. That means the teacher will need to determine the following:

1. A list of sensible objectives (or learning outcomes, if you prefer) for this *specific* unit (not English classwork in general) that both kids and their parents will understand.
2. A work of some length (usually a short novel or a play) to open the unit and make clear to students what the unit aims at. Such a work isn't essential, but it's customary and usually helpful.
3. A body of short works (poetry and short stories and essays) to be used throughout the unit because they are related to the theme.
4. A series of composition assignments (usually two or three written assignments and two or three oral assignments) on the theme.
5. A list of vocabulary words, perhaps twenty to thirty or so, to be talked about and tested five at a time.

6. A list of spelling words, perhaps twenty to thirty or so, to be talked about and tested about five at a time.

7. A way of beginning the unit that will grab students' attention and interest while focusing on the theme. Obviously, teachers can (and do) begin thematic units with a "Hey, kids, how would you like to talk about _____?" or a "Hey, kids, we're going to turn to something entirely different now, a unit on _____," but surely there's a slightly more fascinating way. A short film or the teacher reading aloud a short story (or a recent news clipping) might work.

8. A way of wrapping up the unit that will tie all the strands together. Tests, the All-American way to wrap anything up, are always possible. Some classes find panel discussions useful, some might profit from a student evaluation of the unit and the literature read, and others might benefit from some creative art project or a dramatization.

9. The problems that the unit—and students—may encounter and how the teacher will work through them. Perhaps it's time to incorporate peer editing into the class, and if this unit is as good a time as any other to introduce kids to peer evaluation and editing, then the teacher needs to plan on preparing class members to work in small groups. Perhaps the short book chosen to get the unit started (e.g., Monica Hughes's *Hunter in the Dark*) has some vocabulary problems, or Nathaniel Hawthorne's short story "Young Goodman Brown" may present problems getting the kids to understand Colonial life and religion. These and similar problems need to be worked through and solutions found.

Two exceptionally helpful articles on developing thematic units are Richard S. Alm's "What Is a Good Unit?"[37] and John H. Bushman and Sandra K. Jones's "Getting It All Together . . . Thematically."[38] Thematic units can range from complex and sophisticated topics for college-bound kids to simple topics that are appropriate for junior high. For example, a thematic unit on "Our Ability to Endure," which centers on the theme of survival and power, is a topic of immediate interest to eighth- and ninth-graders. It could open with words from William Faulkner's much-anthologized Nobel Award speech and move to one of these as common reading and the remainder as supplementary reading: Avi's *The True Confessions of Charlotte Doyle,* Alice Childress' *Rainbow Jordan,* Robert Cormier's *After the First Death,* James Forman's *Ceremony of Innocence,* Anne Frank's *The Diary of a Young Girl,* Harry Mazer's *The Last Mission,* or Robb White's *Deathwatch.*

A more intellectually and emotionally complex thematic unit on "Redemption" might begin with reading and discussing Katherine Mansfield's "The Garden Party" in Crane's *Fifty Great Short Stories* (see Focus Box 11.2) or Nadine Gordimer's "A Company of Laughing Faces" in Gold's *Point of Departure* (see Focus Box 11.2). This might be followed by the entire class reading Bernard Malamud's *The Assistant,* and sometime during the unit each student might be asked to read at least one supplementary work on some phase of redemption, for example, classics like Dante's *The Divine Comedy*, Dostoevsky's *Crime and Punishment*, Goethe's *Faust*, Shakespeare's *King Lear* or *Hamlet*, Sophocles' *Oedipus Rex* or *Antigone*, and almost any other Greek drama or the major works of Joseph Conrad, Thomas Hardy, Nathaniel Hawthorne, and Herman Melville. Modern fiction applicable to the same theme includes Hal Borland's *When the Legends Die*, F. Scott Fitzgerald's *The Great Gatsby*, Ursula K. Le Guin's *Wizard of Earthsea*, Peter Matthiessen's *At Play in the Fields of the Lord*, John Steinbeck's *Of Mice and Men*, Frank Waters' *The Man Who Killed the Deer*, and the major works of Arthur Miller, Graham Greene, and Thornton Wilder. Young adult fiction that could fit into the unit includes Fran Arrick's *Tunnel Vision*, Judy Blume's *Tiger Eyes*, Robert Cormier's *After the First Death*, Robert Lipsyte's *The Contender*, Margaret Mahy's *Memory*, Paul Zindel's *The Pigman*, and the novels of S. E. Hinton.

We once had a student come to the office and announce that he wanted to learn everything that a good high school English teacher needed to know. He wondered where he should begin, and we suggested he start with literature. He agreed and wondered yet again where he should begin. We mentioned that good English teachers know the classics. After we cleared up the confusion that we weren't talking about Steinbeck, not yet, we turned to Aeschylus, Sophocles, Euripedes, and Aristophanes, none of whom he knew. Since he begged that we move on to the eighteenth century, where he claimed he knew the novel, we moved onward and upward only to hear his complaint when we brought up writers like John Gay, William Blake, or Richard Brinsley Sheridan. A day or so later, we pointed out that good English teachers not only know English and American literature, of course, but also know Third World literature and German, Japanese, Norwegian, and Russian literature, and more.

Somewhere as we rounded Russian literature, our earnest student gave up. After this catalogue of what he needed to know, he asked one last question before he disappeared from the office, "How can anyone learn all that?"

The answer, which he obviously didn't want to hear, was that thousands of good people do it all the time, not in a few hasty weeks but in a lifetime. They are called English teachers.

■ NOTES

1. Janet Daley, "Don't Close History Books," *Times Educational Supplement,* January 11, 1991, p. 19.

2. Samuel Thurber, "English Literature in the Schools," *Academy* 6 (December 1891): 487.

3. Franklin T. Baker, "High School Reading: Compulsory or Volunteer," *English Journal* 4 (January 1915): 3.

4. Bud Church, "If It's Fun, Is It Bad?" *Media and Methods* 6 (January 1970): 41.

5. Theodore W. Hipple, *Teaching English in Secondary Schools* (Macmillan, 1973), p. 55.

6. Louise M. Rosenblatt. *Literature As Exploration,* 4th ed. (Modern Language Association, 1983), pp. 278–279.

7. Elaine Simpson, "Reason, Not Emotion," *Top of the News* 31 (April 1975): 302.

8. Dorothy Broderick, "Serving Young Adults: Why We Do What We Do," *Voice of Youth Advocates* 12 (October 1989): 204.

9. Robert C. Small, "Teaching the Junior Novel," *English Journal* 61 (February 1972): 222.

10. Patricia Lee Gauch, " 'Good Stuff' in Adolescent Literature," *Top of the News* 40 (Winter 1984): 129.

11. Richard W. Jackson, *CBC Features* 39 (October 1984–July 1985): 5. A publication of the Children's Book Council.

12. *Booklist* 88 (February 15, 1992): 1100–1101.

13. Robert Protherough, Judith Atkinson, and John Fawcett, *The Effective Teaching of English* (Longman, 1989), p. 38.

14. Robert Scholes, *Textual Power: Literary Theory and the Teaching of English* (Yale University Press, 1985), pp. 24–25.

15. Rosenblatt, p. 25.

16. Edward J. Gordon, "Levels of Teaching and Testing," *English Journal* 44 (September 1955): 330–334; Dwight L. Burton, "Well, Where Are We in Teaching Literature?" *English Journal* 63 (February 1974): 28–33.

17. Howard Francis Seely, "Our Novel Stock-in-Trade," *English Journal* 18 (November 1929): 724–725.

18. G. F. Lamb, "The Reading Habit," *Tomorrow* (England) 2 (July 1934): 10.

19. Three informative articles that comment on books that didn't win awards (or weren't nominated), although the books are popular today and deserve careful attention: Joni Bodart's "The Also-Rans; or 'What Happened to the Ones That Didn't Get Eight Votes?'" *Top of the News* 38 (Fall 1981): 70–73, and Pam Spencer's "Winners in Their Own Right," *School Library Journal* 36 (July 1990): 23–27, and "Part II," *School Library Journal* 38 (March 1992): 163–167.

20. Geoff Fox, "Twenty-four Things to Do with a Book," in Anthony Adams, ed., *New Directions in English Teaching* (Palmer Press, 1982), pp. 219–222.

21. Richard Peck, "Ten Questions to Ask About a Novel," *ALAN Newsletter* 5 (Spring 1978): 1, 7.

22. Richard W. Beach and James D. Marshall, *Teaching Literature in the Secondary School* (Harcourt Brace Jovanovich, 1991), p. 384.

23. Stephen Dunning, *Teaching Literature to Adolescents: Poetry* (Scott, Foresman, 1966), pp. 12–34.

24. Geoff Fox and Brian Merrick, "Thirty-six Things to Do with a Poem," *Children's Literature in Education* 12 (Spring 1981): 51.

25. Dana Gioia, "Can Poetry Matter?" *Atlantic* 267 (May 1991): 106.

[26]James R. Squire, ed., *Response to Literature* (NCTE, 1968), p. 70.

[27]Robert W. Boynton and Maynard Mack, from the introduction to *Introduction to the Poem* (Boynton/Cook, 1985).

[28]Pat Mora's article, "A Letter to Gabriela, a Young Writer," *English Journal* 79 (September 1990): 40–42 is a good introduction to the poet.

[29]Barbara Smith, "Double Vision," *Aethlon: The Journal of Sports Literature* 8 (Spring 1991): 139, and Edwin Romond, "A Friend Sends Me Old Baseball Cards in a Book of Poetry," *Aethlon: The Journal of Sports Literature* 8 (Spring 1991): 135.

[30]Luella B. Cook, "Reading for Experience," *English Journal* 25 (April 1936): 280.

[31]Bill Martin, "Response to Poetry: Making Use of Differences," *English Record* 42: 2 (1992): 23.

[32]Margaret Farrand Thorp, "Shakespeare and the Movies," *Shakespeare Quarterly* 9 (Summer 1958): 357–358.

[33]Robert W. Neal, "Making the Devil Useful," *English Journal* 2 (December 1913): 658–660.

[34]Samuel Rosenkranz, "English at the Cinema," *English Journal* 20 (December 1931): 824.

[35]Hardy R. Finch, "Film Production in the School—A Survey," *English Journal* 28 (May 1939): 365.

[36]Peter Elbow, *What Is English?* (Modern Language Association 1990).

[37]Richard S. Alm, "What Is a Good Unit in English?" *English Journal* 49 (September 1960): 395–399.

[38]John H. Bushman and Sandra K. Jones, "Getting It All Together . . . Thematically," *English Journal* 64 (May 1975): 54–60.

OTHER TITLES MENTIONED IN THE TEXT OF CHAPTER ELEVEN

Alcott, Louisa May. *Little Women*. 1868.

Angelou, Maya, *I Know Why the Caged Bird Sings*. Random House, 1970.

Armer, Laura Adams. *Waterless Mountain*. Longman, 1931.

Arrick, Fran. *Tunnel Vision*. Bradbury, 1980.

Avi. *The True Confessions of Charlotte Doyle*, Orchard, 1990.

Beckman Gunnel. *Admission to the Feast*. Holt, 1972.

Blume, Judy, *Tiger Eyes*. Bradbury, 1981.

Borland, Hal. *When the Legends Die*. Lippincott, 1963.

Childress, Alice. *A Hero Ain't Nothin' But a Sandwich*. Coward, McCann, 1973.

_____. *Rainbow Jordan*. Putnam, 1981.

Clark, Walter van Tilburg. *The Ox-Bow Incident*. Random House, 1940.

Cormier, Robert. *After the First Death*. Pantheon, 1979.

_____. *The Chocolate War*. Pantheon, 1974.

_____. *Fade*. Delacorte, 1988.

_____. *I Am the Cheese*. Knopf, 1977.

Crane, Stephen. *The Red Badge of Courage*. 1895.

Dante. *The Divine Comedy*. 1321.

Dias, Patrick, and Michael Hayhoe. *Developing Response to Poetry*. Open University Press, 1988.

Dostoevsky, Fyodor. *Crime and Punishment*. 1866.

Duncan, Lois. *I Know What You Did Last Summer*. Little, Brown, 1973.

Dunning, Stephen. *Teaching Literature to Adolescents: Poetry*. Scott, Foresman, 1966.

Eliot, George, *Silas Marner*. 1861.

Fitzgerald, F. Scott. *The Great Gatsby*. Scribner, 1925.

Forman, James. *Ceremony of Innocence*. Hawthorn, 1970.

Fox, Paula. *One-Eyed Cat*. Bradbury, 1984.

Frank Anne. *The Diary of a Young Girl*. Doubleday, 1952.

Fugard, Athol. *"Master Harold"* . . . *and the Boys*. Knopf, 1982.

Garner, Alan. *The Owl Service*. William Collins, 1967.

Go Ask Alice. Prentice-Hall, 1971.

Goethe, Johann Wolfgang von. *Faust*. 1808, 1832.

Golding, William. *Lord of the Flies*. Coward, McCann, 1954.

Hawthorne, Nathaniel. *The Scarlet Letter*. 1850.

Hemingway, Ernest. *The Old Man and the Sea*. Scribner, 1952.

Hinton, S. E. *The Outsiders*. Viking, 1967.

———. *That Was Then, This Is Now*. Viking, 1971.

Hughes, Monica. *Hunter in the Dark*. Atheneum, 1982.

Ibsen, Henrik. *A Doll's House*. 1879.

———. *An Enemy of the People*. 1882.

Kerr, M. E. *Gentlehands*. HarperCollins, 1978.

———. *If I Love You, Am I Trapped Forever?* HarperCollins, 1973.

Lee, Harper. *To Kill a Mockingbird*. Lippincott, 1960.

Le Guin, Ursula K. *Wizard of Earthsea*. Parnassus, 1968.

Lipsyte, Robert. *The Contender*. HarperCollins, 1967.

Mahy, Margaret. *Memory*. McElderry, 1988.

Malamud, Bernard. *The Assistant*. Farrar, Strauss & Giroux, 1957.

Matthiessen, Peter. *At Play in the Fields of the Lord*. Random House, 1965.

Mazer, Harry. *The Last Mission*. Delacorte, 1979.

McKinley Robin. *The Hero and the Crown*. Greenwillow, 1984.

Mora, Pat. *Chants*. Arte Publico Press, 1985.

Peck, Richard. *Remembering the Good Times*. Delacorte, 1985.

Piercy, Marge. *Circles on the Water: Selected Poems by Marge Piercy*. Knopf, 1990.

Rôlvaag, O. E. *Giants in the Earth*. HarperCollins, 1927.

Rosenblatt, Louise. *The Reader, the Text, the Poem: The Transactional Theory of the Literary Work*. Southern Illinois University Press, 1978.

Samuels, Gertrude. *Run, Shelley, Run!* Crowell, 1974.

Shakespeare, William. *Hamlet*. c. 1601.

———. *King Lear*. c. 1605.

Shelley, Mary. *Frankenstein or the Modern Prometheus*. 1818.

Sophocles. *Antigone*. Fifth century B.C.

———. *Oedipus Rex*. Fifth century B.C.

Steinbeck, John. *The Pearl*. Viking, 1948.

———. *Of Mice and Men*. Viking, 1937.

Taylor, Mildred. *Roll of Thunder. Hear My Cry*. Dial, 1976.

Taylor, Theodore. *The Cay*. Doubleday, 1969.

Twain, Mark. *Adventures of Huckleberry Finn*. 1884.

Voigt, Cynthia. *Homecoming*. Macmillan, 1981.

Waters, Frank. *The Man Who Killed the Deer*. Farrar, Straus & Giroux, 1942.

Wersba, Barbara. *Run Softly, Go Fast*. Atheneum, 1970.

White, Robb. *Deathwatch*. Doubleday, 1972.

Wiesel, Elie. *Night*. Farrar, Straus & Giroux, 1960.

Zindel, Paul. *The Pigman*. HarperCollins, 1968.

For information on the availability of paperback editions of these titles, please consult the most recent edition of *Paperbound Books in Print*, published annually by R. R. Bowker Company.

CHAPTER TWELVE

CENSORSHIP: OF WORRYING AND WONDERING

Most teachers and librarians are aware that stories about censorship pervade newspapers and magazines. They know that only a few months after publication of *The Satanic Verses* in late 1989, Salman Rushdie's book had been banned in many countries, and that because the Ayatollah Khomeini had determined that the book was blasphemous, Rushdie's life was to be forfeited. At about the same time, Senator Jesse Helms, a politician slightly less powerful than Khomeini, decided that Robert Mapplethorpe's homoerotic art was deeply offensive, particularly because government funds had paid for the Mapplethorphe exhibition. Thereafter, Helms was out to change guidelines for grants from the National Endowment for the Arts to prevent similar horrors.

The Rev. Donald Wildman was ever vigilant in watching that the film and television industry did not lead us further into the land of filth and corruption. And other would-be censors were scoring, or attempting to score. In August 1990, after a seventeen-day trial, a British heavy-metal band was held not responsible for the deaths of two young men. The band was accused of having subliminal messages in their album "Stained Glass" that led to the suicides of Raymond Belknap and James Vance. Slightly more than a week later, the owner of a Florida record store was convicted of obscenity charges for selling a recording by the rap group 2 Live Crew.

Occasionally, although not as often as most of us would like, the attacks were so silly that the newspaper reports made censors sound foolish and gave many a small chuckle. In Mesa, Arizona, in late July 1990, a mother of two looked closely at the cover of Disney's videocassette of *The Little Mermaid* and found a castle tower that was clearly a phallic symbol. She called a local grocery chain, which pulled the video from its stores. Sanity returned when Disney executives admitted they were upset by the furor but refused to change the cover and the grocery stores went back to selling foodstuffs. And a bill that would have required people to speak kindly about fruits and vegetables in Colorado died after the governor refused to sign it. Steve Acquafresca, an apple grower who had noticed the bad press given to Washington apple growers over their use of chemicals to make the fruit look more attractive, argued that the bill was needed to keep people from bad-mouthing produce. More people were amused than convinced by his arguments.

But far more common than tidbits of humor about censors are grim stories about censors and their fights to purify us all. School texts are rarely safe, as attacks across the country on the Holt, Rinehart and Winston elementary series *Impressions* prove. Conservative parents in northern California, sometimes representing groups like Citizens for Excellence in Education or the Traditional Values Coalition, maintained that the series (1) did not sufficiently emphasize good, old-fashioned American culture and values; (2) focused on occult and Satanic materials; and (3) removed traditional and classic stories in favor of the new and ephemeral. Other parents across the country attended school board meetings and lambasted the series, maintaining the stories were violent, scary, Satanic, and generally inappropriate for children. Although the series was retained in almost all the several dozen attacks, opposing parents vowed to keep up the fight.

Teachers and librarians know that attacks on books and book banning are here to stay and are deadly serious, increasingly so in the last decade. Colin Campbell's words of ten years ago still ring true:

> A censorial spirit is at work in the United States, and for the past year or so it has focused more and more on books. Efforts to remove certain titles from school and public libraries, from paperback racks and bookstores, from the eyes of adults as well as children, have increased measurably.[1]

BEST-CASE VS. WORST-CASE SCENARIOS

We do not define everyone who questions or objects to a book as a censor. Most parents are sincerely concerned about the welfare of their children, but making a special effort to go to school to make a complaint is likely to make them feel resentful or nervous or angry. If taking time from work were not enough reason to feel irritated, many parents have a built-in love–hate ambivalence toward schools. They may have had a miserable time with a teacher when they were young. They may worry about being talked down to by a much younger teacher or librarian. They may wonder if anyone will take them or their complaint seriously. These factors conspire, so that when the parents arrive at the school or the library, they exude hostility and are mistaken for aggressive censors rather than concerned parents.

Keeping this possibility of mistaken identity in mind, educators need to be considerate and reasonable and to listen more than they talk, at least for the first few minutes. Once objectors calm down and recognize that the teacher or librarian might possibly be human, then and only then will the educator learn what is really troubling the parents. Everyone may learn, sometimes to the listener's surprise, that no one wants to ban anything, but parents do wonder *why* the teacher is using the book or *why* the librarian recommended it to their child. They may want their child to read something else but agree that they have no wish to control the reading of anyone else. This is the situation that we identify as a best-case scenario. The problem is easier to handle (not always easy, but certainly *easier*).

In such cases, teachers and librarians should remember that the announced objection may not always be the real objection. Censors have been known to attack Huxley's *Brave New World* or Orwell's *1984* for their sexual references when the real objection was to the frightening political attitudes the author displayed (or was thought to display). It's human nature to fear things we don't understand, hence the discomfort that many parents feel over the recent popularity of scary, supernatural books. An attack on the language in John Howard Griffin's *Black Like Me* may be only a subterfuge for a censor's hatred of blacks

The rising popularity of occult and supernatural books contributes to many parents' general uneasiness about what their children are reading. Shown here are *Vampires: A Collection of Original Stories* edited by Jane Yolen and Martin H. Greenberg and *Scary Stories 3: More Tales to Chill Your Bones* collected by Alvin Schwartz (both HarperCollins, 1991).

(and any minority group), whereas an attack on an oblique reference to masturbation in Judy Blume's *Deenie* may in reality be a protest against the liberal attitudes that pervade all of her books.

The underlying reasons for objections to particular books often are more significant than teachers or librarians may suspect. Sometimes the complaining parents don't even realize why a particular author or book makes them feel uncomfortable. This is why it's so important for parents to talk and for educators to listen sincerely. Parents who are worried about the moral climate facing their children are painfully aware that they have little power to change the material on television, nor can they successfully fight the movies offered by local theaters or do away with local "adult" bookstores. Whom, then, can they fight? What can they change? An easy answer is to go to school and protect at least that little corner of their children's lives.

Thoughts of inflation and recession, fears of sexually transmitted diseases, threats of global warming and the depletion of the earth's resources, and faltering communication and affection among family members depress many of us most of the time. Under the worst-case scenario, we see these parental fears and worries being exploited for political gain. Parents are courted and brought into political action groups advocating censorship. The selling point of such groups is that there is little we can do to attack the gigantic problems spurred on by who knows what or whom. Either we give up or, in the case of censors, we strike back at the only vulnerable element in most communities, the schools. And why not attack schools, what with the rising militancy of teachers and the massive public criticism of schools' performances on SAT or ACT tests? Why not indeed? And so the censors attack.

These individuals and groups—as opposed to sincere parents wanting what's best for their own children—are the objectors we define as censors. Their desire is not to talk and reason, but to condemn, and as educators we feel a strong obligation to uncover their motives and to counter their claims.

The American Library Association has been on record against censorship since the 1920s, but its strongest statement first appeared in 1939 as the Library Bill of Rights. The document has periodically been tightened and strengthened, and the latest version can be found in the *Intellectual Freedom Manual,* 3rd ed. The entire *Intellectual Freedom Manual* is filled with provocative ideas and helpful suggestions and should be required reading for librarians and English teachers alike. The National Council of Teachers of English was a bit late entering the battle, but the first edition in 1962 of *The Students' Right to Read* set forth NCTE's position and contained a widely used form for complaints, "Citizen's Request for Reconsideration of a Book." The 1972 edition expanded and updated the earlier edition. In 1982, the complaint form was amended to read "Citizen's Request for Reconsideration of a Work," and a complementary publication, *The Students' Right to Know* by Lee Burress and Edward B. Jenkinson, elaborated on NCTE's position toward education and censorship.

A BRIEF HISTORY OF CENSORSHIP

Some English teachers and librarians apparently believe the censorship of young adult reading began with the publication of J. D. Salinger's *The Catcher in the Rye*. But censorship goes far back in history. Plato believed in censorship. In *The Republic,* he argued that banishing poets and dramatists from his perfect state was essential for the moral good of the young. Writers often told lies about the gods, he maintained, but even when their stories were true, writers sometimes made the gods appear responsible for the evils and misfortunes of mortals. Plato reasoned that fiction was potentially emotionally disturbing to the young. Plato's call for moral censorship to protect the young is echoed by many censors today.

In *The Leviathan* in 1615, Thomas Hobbes justified the other basic case for censorship. Humanity was, in Hobbes's view, inherently selfish, venal, brutish, and contentious. Strife was inevitably humanity's fate unless the state established and enforced order. Hobbes acknowledged the right of subjects to refuse to obey a ruler's orders if he did not protect his people, but in all cases the sovereign had not merely the right but the duty to censor anything for the good of the state.

Between Plato and Hobbes and thereafter, history offers a multitude of examples of censorship for moral or political good—the Emperor Chi Huang Ti burned Confucius' *Analects* in 211 B.C.; Julius Caesar burned much of the Library of Alexandria in 48–47 B.C.; English officials publicly burned copies of William Tyndale's translation of the Bible in 1525; the Catholic Index of Forbidden Works was published in 1555; Prime Minister Walpole forced passage of a Licensing Act in 1737, which required that every English play be examined and approved before production, and on and on and on.

America's premier censor, although hardly its last, appeared in the early 1870s. Anthony Comstock came from a religious family, and before he was eighteen, he had raided a saloon to drive out the devil and the drinkers. In June 1871, Comstock was so outraged by repeated violations of Sunday Closing Laws by saloons in his neighborhood that he reported them to the police. They ignored him, which taught him a good lesson about the futility of fighting city hall alone. Armed with the Lord's help and his own determination, Comstock secured the help of three prominent men and founded the Society for the Suppression of Vice in New York in 1872, and he was off and running. The following year he went to Washington, D.C., to urge passage of a federal statute against obscenity and abortion and contraceptive devices. That same year, he was commissioned a Special Agent of the Postmaster General, all without salary until 1906.

With the new law and Comstock's zeal and energy, he confiscated and destroyed "bad" literature and imprisoned evil authors and publishers almost beyond belief. By 1914, he had caused the arraignment of 3,697 people with 2,740 convicted or pleading guilty, total fines of $237,134.30, and prison sentences totaling 565 years, 11 months, and 20 days. In his last year of life, 1915, Comstock added another 176 arrests and 140 convictions. He also caused fifteen suicides.[2]

His most famous book was *Traps for the Young* (1883). By traps, Comstock meant the devil's work for young people—light literature, newspaper advertisements, saloons, literature obtained through the mail, quack medicine, contraceptives, gambling, playing pool, free love and anyone who advocated it, and artistic works (fine arts, classics of literature, photographic reproductions of art). Comstock was convinced that any young person who shot pool or smoked or chewed tobacco or drank alcohol or read dime novels or did anything else he disapproved of (and that catalogue was long indeed) was doomed to hell and to a life of crime and degradation.

Librarians, as may be seen in "Fiction and Libraries" in Chapter Thirteen (p. 553), were more frequently pro-censorship than anti-censorship. As Arthur E. Bostwick wrote in 1910:

> In the exercise of his duties in book selection it is unavoidable that the librarian should act in some degree as a censor of literature. It has been pointed out that no library can buy every title that is published, and that we should discriminate by picking out what is best instead of by excluding what is bad.[3]

Mark Twain's encounters with late-nineteenth-century censors are described in Chapter Thirteen, but he was hardly the only major writer of his time to come under attack. Stephen Crane's *The Red Badge of Courage* was attacked for lacking integrity and being inaccurate. At the sixth session of the American Library Association in 1896, a discussion of *The Red Badge of Courage* and whether it should be included in a list of ALA-recommended books brought forth comments that revealed more about the critics than about the book:

> Mr. Larned: "What of Crane's *Red Badge of Courage?*"
> A. L. Peck: "It abounds in profanity. I never could see why it should be given into the hands of a boy."
> G. M. Jones: "This *Red Badge of Courage* is a very good illustration of the weakness of the criticism of our literary papers. The critics in our literary papers are praising this book as being a true picture of war. The fact is, I imagine, that the criticisms are written by young men who know nothing about war, just as Mr. Crane himself knows nothing about war. Gen. McClurg, of Chicago, and Col. Nourse, of Massachusetts, both say that the story is not true to the life of the soldier. An article in the *Independent,* or perhaps the *Outlook,* says that no such profanity as given in the book was common in the army among the soldiers. Mr. Crane has since published two other books on New York life which are simply vulgar books. I consider the *Red Badge of Courage* a vulgar book, and nothing but vulgar."[4]

It is more difficult to know how much censorship occurred in English classes of the nineteenth century since the major journal for English teachers, the *English Journal*, did not begin until 1912, but a few items may suggest that English teachers endured or perhaps encouraged censorship at the time. Until 1864, Oberlin College would not allow Shakespeare to be studied in mixed classes. That Shakespeare was apparently of questionable value can be seen by an editorial in 1893 lauding students of Oakland High School who objected to using an unexpurgated edition of *Hamlet:*

> All honor to the modest and sensible youths and maidens of the Oakland High School who revolted against studying an unexpurgated edition of *Hamlet!* The indecencies of Shakespeare in the complete edition are brutal. They are more than indelicacies, they are indecencies. They are no part of Shakespeare's thought, have no connection with the play, and can be eliminated with as little jar as could the oaths of a modern slugger. Indeed, Shakespeare's vulgarity was, to all intents and purposes, profanity, scattered promiscuously through the lines with no more meaning than so many oaths.[5]

An editorial writer in 1890 quoted from a contemporary account in the *Congregationalist* about books some young people had been reading.

> In this series of papers we purposely avoid all mention of some thoroughly bad books chosen by our young friends. We remember hearing the principal of a young ladies' seminary, in trying to express her strong disapproval of a certain book, say impulsively to the pupils, "I think I should expel a girl if I found her reading such a work." Before the week closed no less than three copies were in surreptitious circulation. There is something in human nature which craves that which is prohibited. Just so surely as we gave the titles of books worthy of condemnation, some youth would thirst instantly for a knowledge of their contents.[6]

Would that present-day censors could recognize what this critic obviously recognized, that merely mentioning an objectionable title creates new readers by the hundreds.

And one last incident a few years later: An English teacher reported on her use of *Treasure Island* with a junior high school class. Of the students who were enthusiastic, one student well on her way to becoming a literary snob wrote:

> *Treasure Island* should be read, firstly, because it is by a famous author, secondly, most people like it and, thirdly, because it is considered a classic.

Two other students objected. A boy wrote:

■ I like a cleaner story. In this story there is too much bloodshed, drinking, and swearing.

A girl, however, pointed out the evil nature of the story and the nefarious and inevitable consequences of reading Stevenson's awful book:

■ This story full of murder, fighting, and wiping blood off of knives is not suitable for boys and girls to read and if these kinds of books were not written there would not be so many boys go wrong. I don't think there should be any more books written like it, because it don't learn you anything and nowadays we should read books that do us some good.[7]

A modern censor could not have said it better.

■ AND WHAT IS THE STATE OF CLASSROOM AND LIBRARY CENSORSHIP TODAY?

Censorship was hardly a major concern of English teachers or school librarians (although it certainly was for public librarians) before the 1960s. Prior to World War II, it rarely surfaced in schools, although John Steinbeck's *The Grapes of Wrath* and *Of Mice and Men* caused some furor in newspapers, and when students began to read the books, the furor reached the schools. After World War II, Norman Mailer's *The Naked and the Dead* and J. D. Salinger's *The Catcher in the Rye* and other books "indicative of a permissive, lax, immoral society," as one censor noted, caught the eyes of adults and young adults alike. Granted, most objections were aimed at the writers and bookstores that stocked them, but teachers were now aware that they needed to be more careful about books they allowed students to read for extra credit or book reports. Two events changed the mild worry into genuine concern.

Paperback books seemed to offer little of intellectual or pedagogical value to teachers before World War II. Even after the war, many teachers blithely assumed paperbacks had not changed, and given the often lurid covers, teachers seemed to have a point, although it was more superficial than real. Administrators and parents continued to object even after the Bible, Plato's *Dialogues,* and *Four Tragedies of Shakespeare* proved to teachers and librarians that paperbacks had merit. Students discovered even earlier that paperbacks were handy to stick in a purse or back pocket, and paperback titles were appealing, not stodgy, as were most textbooks. So paperbacks came to schools, censors notwithstanding, and these cheap and ubiquitous books created problems galore for teachers.

Perhaps as important, young adult books prior to the late 1960s were generally safe, pure, and simplistic, devoid of the reality that younger people daily faced. Sports and going to the prom and getting the car for the big Friday night date loomed large as the major problems of young adult life in too many of these novels. Young people read them for fun, knowing that they were nothing more than escape reading with little relationship to reality or to anything of significance. Then in 1967, Ann Head's *Mr. and Mrs. Bo Jo Jones* and S. E. Hinton's *The Outsiders* appeared, and young adult literature changed and could not go back to the good-old-pure days. Paul Zindel's *The Pigman* followed in 1968, and although all YA books that followed were hardly great or honest, a surprising number were. English teachers and librarians who had accepted the possiblity of censorship with adult authors popular with the young—Steinbeck, Fitzgerald, Heller, Hemingway, for example—now learned that the once safe young adult novel was no longer safe, and censorship attacks soon began. Head's and Hinton's and Zindel's books were denounced, but so were young adult novels as good as Robert Lipsyte's *The Contender* (1967), A. E. Johnson's *A Blues I Can Whistle* (1969), John Donovan's *I'll Get There. It Better Be Worth the Trip* (1969), and Jean Renvoize's *A Wild Thing* (1971)—and that was merely the beginning.

Comments about censorship of all kinds appear with almost nauseating regularity in the daily press as is shown by this collection of articles.

Surveys of the state of censorship since 1963 indicate that censorship is either getting worse or fewer teachers and librarians are willing to lie quietly while the censor trods over them. Lee Burress' pioneer study "How Censorship Affects the School," in October 1963, was only the first of these surveys. Nyla H. Ahrens' doctoral study in 1965 was the first national survey. State surveys of Arizona censorship conditions appeared in the February 1969 and February 1975 *Arizona English Bulletin*. National studies appeared ever more often: L. B. Woods's "The Most Censored Materials in the U.S.," in the November 1, 1978, *Library Journal*; Burress' "A Brief Report of the 1977 NCTE Survey," in James Davis' *Dealing with Censorship*; and the much anticipated and disappointing *Limiting What Students Shall Read,* in 1981. The 1982 survey of high school librarians by Burress found that 34 percent of the librarians reported a challenge to at least one book as compared to 30 percent in his 1977 survey. A survey of Canadian censorship by David Jenkinson published in the February 1986 *Canadian Library Journal* provided no optimism about censors. Two surveys by Donelson—one in the March 1985 *School Library Journal* of censorship for the previous thirteen years and comparing conclusions from six previous surveys, and another in the October–November 1990 *High School Journal* summarizing the censorship incidents in the *Newsletter on Intellectual Freedom* from 1952 through 1989—provide little comfort to teachers or librarians.

But surveys make for dull reading and convey all too little about the individual teacher or librarian besieged by censors. Reports of a few incidents below from 1990 onward in newspapers or the *Newsletter on Intellectual Freedom* may suggest some of the emotional and pedagogical dilemmas faced by real people, who are too often alone and without allies, not even their fellow professionals.

1. *February 1990, Tempe, Arizona.* When the Tempe High School drama teacher decided to do *Little Shop of Horrors* for the school musical, a few parents objected. One mother said that the play's man-eating plant was an assault on the tradition of "wholesome family fare." She admitted she had not read the script, but she was sure there was something wrong about it. "I just think it's really in bad taste." Later, when she learned there was no connection between the musical and the picture she'd confused it with, *The Rocky Horror Picture Show,* she said, "Maybe I'm getting excited about something I shouldn't be."[8]

2. *April 1990, Idaho.* A teacher assigned *My Name Is Asher Lev* to her twelfth-grade English class. A day later, a student handed the book back to her teacher. The student explained, "My family and I don't believe in Israel and we hate Jews. My family wants me to read something else."[9]

3. *May 1990, Culver City and Empire, California.* Two school districts banned a new edition of "Little Red Riding Hood" in which Red

carried a bottle of wine for Granny. An assistant superintendent said, "It gave the younger ones the wrong impression about alcohol."[10]

4. *May–June, 1990. Illinois, California, Kentucky.* T-shirts bearing the likeness and philosophy of Bart Simpson were attacked in several schools when students wore the T-shirts with the words, "I'm Bart Simpson. Who the hell are you?" or "Underachiever: And proud of it, man." Some educators worried about the bad language or attitude being modeled. Others worried that given the problems of the world today, Bart was small potatoes, as were educators worried about such trivia.[11]

5. *September 1990, Rohnert Park, California.* A parent objected to a book assigned in senior literature classes, Margaret Atwood's *The Handmaid's Tale,* as too explicit. The parent said, "In school, if my daughter was caught passing a note like that, there is no doubt they would call me, have me down at the school and tell me there's something wrong with my daughter."[12]

6. *September–October 1990, Baldwin, Michigan.* June Jordan's collection of poetry, *Living Room,* was banned from the local high school library allegedly because the book had "profanity" and "racial slurs." One book banner said, "This is a moral issue. It doesn't need to be on our shelves. Our children are exposed to enough of this on the streets."[13]

7. *November–December 1990, Harwinton, Connecticut.* A couple told the school board that "some real-life situations are not suitable for children," among them masturbation, swearing, and death. They cited five objectionable novels—Robert Cormier's *The Chocolate War,* Bette Greene's *Summer of My German Soldier,* Katherine Paterson's *Bridge to Terabithia,* Robert Newton Peck's *A Day No Pigs Would Die,* and Paul Zindel's *The Pigman.* The mother said, "Schools are there to enlighten children, not discourage them. . . . I don't think controversial or offensive books should be taught in class."[14]

8. *December 1990, Plano, Texas.* The school board entertained a debate on whether the *Adventures of Huckleberry Finn* should be allowed on the reading lists of seventh- and eighth-graders.[15]

9. *December 1990, Commerce, Texas.* A parent asked school officials to take all "romance" books from the high school library because there was too much sexual material, particularly in Liz Hamlin's *I Remember Valentine* and Norma Klein's *Angel Face.* "These books appear to be romance books, but they also appear, by my standards, to be pornographic."[16]

10. *January–April 1991, Greenville, South Carolina.* One school trustee said that his Christianity was "on the line" with some parents when the school board voted (4–2) to allow five books to be used in classrooms—James Collier's *My Brother Sam Is Dead,* Pat Conroy's

The Water Is Wide, Judith Guest's *Second Heaven,* and John Steinbeck's *East of Eden* and *The Grapes of Wrath.*[17]

11. *March 1991, Dover, Delaware.* An eighth-grade history teacher filed suit to force the school district to allow showing an R-rated film, *Glory,* after the school superintendent banned the showing of R-rated films in the district.[18]

12. *April 1991, Hollywood, Florida.* When a principal removed a student painting from the school's art fair, students objected. Although the administrator claimed he had no idea his action would be controversial, he added, "but sometimes as a principal you're put in a position to make a decision. As you're aware, a Superior Court ruling allows principals to censor."[19]

13. *April 1991, Carroll Township, Pennsylvania.* Two black teachers requested that Steinbeck's *Of Mice and Men* be removed from the curriculum because the novel has words offensive to blacks.[20]

14. *August 1991, Quincy, Massachusetts.* The mayor asked local theater owners not to show the film *Boyz 'N the Hood* after the city's acting chief of police said the film "is of no value and is nothing but trouble." Luckily enough for the chief, owners of both theaters didn't intend to show the film anyway. One owner volunteered, "It's basically a family neighborhood theater, and we wouldn't play anything controversial like that. . . . "[21]

15. *August 1991, Charleston, West Virginia.* Middle-class parents objected to S. E. Hinton's *Rumble Fish* and *That Was Then, This Is Now* because the books were too frank. One parent said, "The words and subject matter are such that I don't think seventh-graders should be exposed to it. At that age group, they're going to be zeroing in on that instead of the message."[22]

16. *September 1991, San Ramon, California.* Two novels about homosexuality (Nancy Garden's *Annie on My Mind* and Frank Mosca's *All American Boys*) were donated to high school libraries by the Bay Area Network of Gay and Lesbian Educators. The vice-principals at two schools removed the books to "examine them," and that was the end of those books.[23]

17. *September 1991, Tempe, Arizona.* After a few parents objected to the showing of the R-rated film *Glory,* the school board voted not to allow the showing of R-rated films in classrooms. This was particularly intriguing, because no formal complaint against *Glory* or any other film was ever filed. One of the three voting against use of R-rated films explained, "The time we have with students is precious. We should use that time to expose them to only the best and the brightest things. We don't have time to show R-rated films." One of two voting to allow some R-rated films rebutted, "I believe that we should expose kids to what's bright and beautiful, but I also believe

we should produce kids that can survive in the world, and reality is not always that bright and beautiful."[24]

18. *February 1992, O'Fallon, Illinois.* An Air Force master-sergeant objected to the word *nigger* in *The Adventures of Tom Sawyer* and asked that the book be banned from the curriculum. His objection closed with these words about the book, "May it hopefully only sit in the library and rot."[25]

SOME ASSUMPTIONS ABOUT CENSORSHIP AND CENSORS

Given the censorship attacks of the last twenty-plus years, we can make the following assumptions about censorship.

First, any work is potentially censorable by someone, someplace, sometime, for some reason. Nothing is permanently safe from censorship, not even books most teachers and librarians would regard as far removed from censorial eyes—not *Hamlet* or *Julius Caesar* or *Silas Marner* or *Treasure Island,* or anything else.

Second, the newer the work, the more likely it is to come under attack.

Third, censorship is capricious and arbitrary. Two teachers bearing much the same reputation and credentials and years of experience and using the same work will not necessarily be equally free from attack (or equally likely to be attacked). Some schools in conservative areas go free from censorship problems even though teachers may use controversial books. Other schools in relatively liberal areas may come under the censor's gun.

Fourth, censorship spreads a ripple of fear. The closer the censorship, the greater the likelihood of its effect on other teachers. And if the newspaper coverage of the incident has been extensive, the greater the likelihood that schools many miles away will feel the effect. Administrators may gently (or loudly) let their teachers know it is time to be traditional or safe in whatever the teachers choose for the coming year.

Fifth, censorship does not come only from people outside the school. Administrators, other teachers or librarians, or the school board may initiate an incident. That often surprises some English teachers or librarians. It should not.

Sixth, censorship is, for too many educators, like cancer or a highway accident. It happens only to other people. Most incidents happen to people who know "it couldn't happen to me." It did and it will.

Seventh, schools without clear and established and school board–approved policies and procedures for handling censorship are accidents waiting to happen. Every school should develop a policy and a procedure that helps both educators and objectors when an incident arises. The aim of both policy and procedures should be to ensure that everyone has a fair hearing, not to stall or frustrate anyone.

SUE ELLEN BRIDGERS
on the Elimination of Choices

I admit to being slow about getting involved in censorship issues. When, early in my career, I heard tales of *Home Before Dark* being relegated

to the "protected" shelf in some elementary school libraries, I shrugged it off. I was amused by the few critical letters I received, especially one that castigated me for the use of a single word which had kept the book out of a church library without letting me in on what the offensive word was. I could laugh off such nitpicking because I felt secure in my own belief system. I saw myself as a moral person writing about peole struggling to find meaning in life. What could be suspect in that? Well, a lot.

Only a few months ago, *All Together Now* was withdrawn from an approved reading list although all the seventh graders in that school district had read and enjoyed the book. I spoke with these children, examined the thoughtful, creative art projects they had done about the book, read some of the essays they had written in response to their reading. Their excitement and interest in my visits in their district was the kind of boost writers long for and yet, because of the protest of one parent who felt a minor character acted in a suggestive manner (flirty, she called it), next year's seventh graders won't be reading that book. A committee

Eighth, if one book is removed from a classroom or library, no book is safe any longer. If a censor succeeds in getting one book out, every other person in the community who objects to another book should, in courtesy, be granted the same privilege. When everyone has walked out of the library carrying all those objectionable books, nothing of any consequence will be left no matter how many books remain. Some books are certain to offend some people and be ardently defended by others. Indeed, every library will have books offensive to someone, maybe everyone. After all, ideas do offend many people.

Ninth, educators and parents should, ideally, coexist to help each other for the good of the young, but the clash of parents with some educators appears to be sadly inevitable. Some people would prefer to see young adults *educated,* which means allowing them to think and wonder about ideas and to consider the consequences of those ideas. Others would prefer to see young people *indoctrinated* into certain community or family values or beliefs or traditions and to eschew anything controversial. With so little in common between these two philosophies of schooling, disagreement is not only natural but certain.

of administrators and teachers took the path of least resistance and as a result, several hundred children gave up an experience that is their right—the right to read, to think, to know.

What then do censors want? To eliminate our choices—my choices of what to write, teachers' choices of what to recommend or require, and the students' right to be exposed to new ideas and difficult questions and to practice making intelligent decisions based on what they've learned.

What do writers want? I want to write stories that compel me to grow, that force me to think beyond my own life in an exploration of another person's psyche, that stretch and strengthen my technical skills. I want to write without the threat of censorship at my shoulder. I want the confidence and the responsibility that freedom brings.

What do teachers want? Oh, I hope you want to open doors. I hope you want to know your students in personal ways that can be enhanced by reading and talking together. I hope you want to say good-bye every summer to kids whose reading and writing skills have improved.

And yet, I know that many of you are fearful and with reason. Stories of ruined careers, of administrators and school boards abandoning dedicated teachers to twist in the wind are not uncommon anymore. Books that are meaningful to young people and that reflect their personal struggles are bound to be questioned by people who want to eliminate for others the right to question.

The fact is that young adult literature of quality depends on you; it must be introduced and made accessible in the classroom. Many of us on this side of the books intend to keep on writing stories that explore both the emotional and the social issues that touch young people. We can do that as long as you are there on the other side reading, thinking, dreaming with your students. Both of us must meet the challenge by supporting each other, always aware that the kid with the book is what really matters.

Sue Ellen Bridger's books include *Home Before Dark*, Knopf, 1976; *All Together Now*, Knopf, 1979; *Notes for Another Life*, Knopf, 1981; and *Permanent Connections*, HarperCollins, 1987.

Censors seem unwilling to accept the fact that the more they attack a book, the greater the publicity and likelihood that more young adults will read the offensive book. In their messianic drive to eliminate a book, censors create a wider and wider circle of readers. In some cases with older or more obscure works, they revive something that has been virtually dead for years.

Censors will not believe that in trying desperately to keep young people pure and innocent they often expose those young people to the very thing the censors abhor. Several years ago, a group violently objected to a scholarly dictionary that contained some "offensive" words. Worried that others might not believe all those degrading, evil, pernicious words were so easily found in one work, censors compiled a sort of digest of "The Best Dirty Words in _____," duplicated the list, and disseminated it to anyone curious, including the very students censors claimed to be protecting. More than one censor has read the "offensive" parts of a book aloud at a school board meeting to prove the point while young students raptly listened.

Censors often have a simplistic belief that there is an easily established and absolute relationship between books and deeds. A bad book, however defined, produces bad actions. What one reads, one immediately imitates. To read profane language automatically leads to young people swearing. Presumably, nonreading youngsters who swear must eagerly await more literate fellows to instruct them in the art of the profane. To read about seduction is to wish to seduce or to be seduced (although it is possible the wish may precede the book). To read about crime is to wish to commit that crime, or at the very least something vaguely antisocial. Anthony Comstock loved to visit boys in jail because when he asked what led them into the world of crime, they told him exactly what he wanted to hear (as they knew full well), that dime novels and drinking and shooting pool were *the* sources of all their present misery.

Censors seem to have limited, if any, faith in the ability of young adults to read and think. Censors wonder if young people can handle controversial, suspect books like Huxley's *Brave New World* or Salinger's *The Catcher in the Rye,* since the young are so innocent and pure and untainted by contact with reality. That may have been what caused one censor who objected to Ann Head's *Mr. and Mrs. Bo Jo Jones* and Paul Zindel's *The Pigman* to announce to an audience, "Teenagers are too young to learn about pregnancy."

Censors alternately love and hate English teachers and librarians. Censors would appear to hate what educators use, but censors would also appear to approve of great literature, particularly the classics. Being essentially nonreaders, they know little about literature but that it must be uplifting and noble and fine. They may claim to have read the uplifting when they were young, "back when schools knew what they were doing," but they often cannot remember titles; when they do their comments suggest the book was read in an emasculated child's edition. Censors assume that classics have no objectionable words or actions or ideas. So much for *Crime and Punishment, Oedipus Rex, Hamlet, Madame Bovary, Anna Karenina,* and most other classics. For censors, the real virtue of great literature is that it is old, dusty, and hard to read, in other words, good for young people.

Censors care little what others believe. Censors are ordained by God to root out evil, and they are divinely inspired to know the truth. Where teachers and librarians may flounder searching for the truth, censors need not fumble, for they *know.* They are sincerely unable to understand that others may regard the censors' arrogance as sacrilegious, and they rarely worry, since they represent the side of morality. One censor counts for any number of other parents. When Judy Blume's *Deenie* was removed from an elementary library in the Cotati-Rohnert Park School District, California, in October 1982, a trustee said that a number of parents from a nearby college wanted the book retained, but "the down-to-earth parents who have lived in the district for quite awhile didn't want it,"[26] and that was clearly that. No one counted the votes, but no one needed to. Orwell knew what he was talking about when he wrote, "All animals are equal but some are more equal than others." Censors would agree with Orwell's comment if not his ironic intention.

Finally, censors use language carelessly or sloppily. Sometimes they cannot possibly mean what they say. The administrator who said, "We don't wish to have any controversial books in the bookstore or the library," either did not understand what the word *controversial* meant or was speaking gibberish (the native tongue of embarrassed administrators talking to reporters who think they may have a juicy story here). Three adjectives are likely to pop up in the censor's description of objectionable works: *filthy, obscene,* or *vulgar* along with favored intensifiers like *unbelievably, unquestionably,* and *hopelessly* though a few censors favor oxymoronic expressions like *pure garbage* or *pure evil.* Not one of the adjectives is likely to be defined operationally by censors who assume that *filth* is *unquestionably filth,* and everyone shares their definition. Talking with censors is, thus, often difficult, which may disturb others, although it is often a matter of sublime indifference to the censors. If talking is difficult, communicating with them is usually nigh unto impossible.

ATTACKS ON MATERIALS

Who Are the Censors?

There are three reasonably distinct kinds of censors and pressure groups: (1) those from the right, the conservatives; (2) those from the left, the liberals, and (3) an amorphous band of educators and publishers and editors and distributors who most other educators might assume would be opposed to censorship. The first two groups operate from different guiding principles, or so one would assume. But it is sometimes easy for educators to be confused, whether the attack stems from the right or the left, the coercive methods, the censorial rhetoric, and the messianic fervor seem so similar. The third group is unorganized and functions on a personal, ad hoc, case-by-case approach, although people in the group are more likely than not to feel sympathetic to the conservative case for censorship.

An incredible number of small censorship or pressure groups on the right continue to *worry* educators (worry in the sense of alarm *and* harass). Many are better known for their acronyms, which often sound folksy or clever—for example, Save Our Schools (SOS); People of America Responding to Educational Needs of Today's Society (PARENTS); Citizens United for Responsible Education (CURE); Let's Improve Today's Education (LITE); American Christians in Education (ACE); and everyone's favorite, Let Our Values Emerge (LOVE). Probably the most powerful, far beyond the state boundary implied by the title, was Parents of New York—United (PONY-U). Chapter 9 in Ed Jenkinson's *Censors in the Classroom: The Mind Benders* summarizes quite well the major groups, big or small.

With few exceptions, these groups seem united in announcing that they want to protect young people from insidious forces that threaten the schools, to remove

& People for the American Way - against censorship

any vestiges of sex education and secular humanism from classes or libraries, to put God back into public schools, and to restore traditional values to education. Very few announce openly that they favor censorship of books or teaching materials, although individual members of the groups may so proclaim. Indeed, what is particularly heartening about the groups is that many of them maintain that they are anticensorship, although occasionally a public slip occurs. The president of the Utah chapter of Citizens for Decency was quoted as saying:

> I am opposed to censorship. We are not a censorship organization. But there are limits to the First Amendment. People have the right to see what they want on television, but that has nothing to do with the right to exhibit pornography on television. We're not stopping anyone from buying books and magazines or going to the movies they want. They just can't do it in Utah. Let them go to Nevada. Nobody there cares.[27]

Whether anyone from Nevada with a similar anticensorial attitude responded with a suggestion that people from Nevada seeking cheap thrills should go to Utah is unknown. Something similar to the preceding comment came from the Rev. Ricky Pfeil. Wheeler, Texas, apparently has its moral problems with objectionable movies like *Porky's* and *Flashdance* and *E.T.* (Pfeil's argument against the latter film was, "The film's an attempt to show something supernatural and it's not God. There's only one other power that's supernatural and that's Satan.") The good minister also is against censorship, as he said:

> You know, I am not for censorship. People have a right to see what they want or read what they want, but I'd just as soon they go to Los Angeles to get a copy of *Playboy* magazine. I'm responsible for here. Evil left unchecked will go rampant. God tells me what to do.[28]

Given the doublespeak of Ms. Brimhall and the Rev. Pfeil, readers will admire the honest and the original constitutional interpretation of the Rev. Vincent Strigas, co-leader of the Mesa (Arizona) Decency Coalition. Slashing merrily away at magazines that threatened the "moral fiber" of residents, the Rev. Strigas answered complaints about his approach:

> Some people are saying that we are in violation of First Amendment rights. I do not think that the First Amendment protects people [who sell] pornographic materials. The Constitution protects only the freedom to do what's right.[29]

Surely there is no ambiguity in that message.

Best known of all censors in America today are Mel and Norma Gabler, who operate a small but powerful company out of their Longview, Texas, home. Educational Research Analysts came about when the Gablers found a vast difference between their son's American history text and ones they remembered.

Norma Gabler appeared before the State Board of Education in 1962 and went largely ignored. Upset, she came home and did her spadework on offensive textbooks. (Most texts seem to be offensive to the Gablers until they help writers and publishers to correct the material and remove secular humanism and anything that might prove offensive to Christians or any proponents of traditional values). Now Educational Research Analysts crank out thousands of pages of textbook analyses and reviews to aid any school or school board in selecting the best, the most proper, and the most accurate texts by the Gablers' standards. Readers who wish to know more about the Gablers or their organization should read William Martin's "The Guardians Who Slumbereth Not," a model of fair play reporting by a writer who does not agree with the Gablers on fundamental points but who clearly likes and admires their openness and caring.

Whatever else conservative groups may agree or disagree on, they seem united in opposing secular humanism and the teaching of evolution. Secular humanism is both too large and too fuzzy to handle adequately in a few paragraphs (or even a short chapter). Briefly, if inexactly, conservatives appear to define secular humanism as any teaching material that denies the existence of (or ridicules the worth of) absolute values of right and wrong. Secular humanism is said to be negative, anti-God, anti-American, antiphonics, and antiafterlife and pro-permissive, pro–sexual freedom, pro–situation ethics, pro-socialism, and pro–one worldism. Conservatives hopelessly intolerant about secular humanism often have problems explaining what the term means to outsiders, or even insiders, usually defining the presumably philosophical term operationally and offering little more than additional examples of the horror that secular humanism implies. Such was the case when secular humanism reared its ugly head at a meeting of the Utah Association of Women.

One woman says with disgust that two recent school board members didn't know what secular humanism was; thus they weren't qualified to run for office. Lots of "tsks" run through the group until a young woman visitor apologizes for her ignorance and asks, Just what is secular humanism? There is an awkward silence. No one gives a definition, but finally they urge her to attend a UAW workshop on the subject. Later in the meeting, during a discussion of unemployment a vice-president says, "Our young people are only taught to do things that give them pleasure. That's secular humanism."[30]

Fortunately for educators already concerned about the many pressure groups from the right, only one pressure group from the left need concern them, but that one group is worrisome. The Council on Interracial Books for Children was formed in 1965 to change the all-white world of children's books and to promote literature that more accurately portrayed minorities or reflected the goals of a multiracial, multiethnic society. They offer meetings and publications to expedite their goals, but for most teachers, the CIBC is best known for its often excellent *Bulletin*.

No humane person would disagree with the CIBC's goals. And, as it has maintained over the years, the CIBC does not censor teaching or library materials. It has, however, perhaps inadvertently, perhaps arrogantly, been guilty of coercing educators into not purchasing or stocking or using books offensive to the CIBC or its reviewers. Its printed articles have attacked Paula Fox's *The Slave Dancer,* Ouida Sebestyen's *Words by Heart,* and Harper Lee's *To Kill a Mockingbird* and, by implication, have criticized those who stocked or taught these books.

The CIBC has argued that *evaluation* is hardly identical with *censorship,* and no one would dispute an organization or journal's right to criticize or lambast any book with which it disagreed for whatever reason. But the CIBC and the *Bulletin* are unable to see any distinction between *Bulletin* reviews and reviews appearing in the *New York Times Book Review,* the *Horn Book Magazine, School Library Journal,* or *Voice of Youth Advocates,* not a difference in quality but in kind. *Bulletin* reviews are, whether the CIBC accepts it or not, a call for censorship based on social awareness. If book reviewer X reviews a YA book in any national publication except for the CIBC *Bulletin,* readers may disagree with the reviewer's opinion, but in any case readers will decide on their own whether they wish to buy or reject the book. Differences in taste are so commonplace that almost no one would attack someone else for choosing or not choosing to purchase on literary merit or personal taste. And, as anyone knows who reads many reviews of the same book, literary merit is an inexact term used to justify personal judgments.

But literary merit does not loom large in the reviews in CIBC's *Bulletin.* Replacing it are terms like *racist, sexist, handicappist,* and *ageist,* all of them personal judgments, none of them objective, although doubtless all are used sincerely and, in the case of a favorite author gone awry, sometimes sadly. If librarians purchase or teachers use a book attacked in the *Bulletin,* those educators had better be prepared to defend it against the true believer who will often assume the worst about them, that they are racist or sexist or worse. In most cases, it is less troublesome simply to avoid buying or using any book that has aroused the ire of the CIBC or a CIBC reviewer. The CIBC carries greater weight with librarians and teachers and school officials than it apparently is willing to recognize, and it is hardly a secret—save perhaps to the CIBC— that it is regarded by many as a censor. And supporters of the CIBC are almost certain to assume the worst about anyone who dares to criticize the organization, witness the letters to the editor that followed Lillian Gerhardt's editorial "The Would-be Censors of the Left" in the November 1976 *School Library Journal* or Nat Hentoff's article "Any Writer Who Follows Anyone Else's Guidelines Ought to Be in Advertising" a year later in the same magazine.

The case for the racist-free library is carried to its absurd conclusion by Bettye I. Latimer in "Telegraphing Messages to Children about Minorities." After defining censorship as the "actual destruction of a book through banning, exiling, or burning it, so that no one has access to it," Latimer proclaims that she is "strongly opposed to censorship for adult readers, since adults are responsible for their own values," but that apparently does not hold true for young people:

> I am *not* suggesting censorship for books that are racist-oriented. I *am* suggesting that we remove these books to archives. This will permit scholars and researchers to have access to them. Since old racist books have no use in constructing healthy images for today's children, they need to be put in cold storage. As for contemporary racist books, educational institutions ought to stop purchasing and thereby stop subsidizing publishers for being racist.
>
> Finally, I would like to see librarians, teachers, and reading coordinators reeducate themselves to the social values which books pass on to children. I invite them to learn to use antiracist criteria in evaluating and assessing books.[31]

Amidst all the noble sentiments in these words, some people will sense a hint of liberal censorship or pressure at work. All censors, whatever their religious or sociological biases, *know* what is good and bad in books and are only too willing to *help* the rest of us fumbling mortals learn what to keep and what to exile (or put in the archives).

The third kind of censorship or pressure group comes from within the schools, teachers or librarians or school officials who either censor materials themselves or support others who do. Sometimes these educators do so fearing reprisals if they do not. Sometimes they do so because they fear being noticed, preferring anonymity at all costs. Sometimes they are fearful of dealing with reality in literature. Sometimes they regard themselves as highly moral and opposed to whatever they label immoral in literature. Sometimes they prize (or so claim) literary merit and the classics above all other literature, and refuse to consider teaching or recommending anything recent or second-rate, however they define those terms.

Fear permeates many of these people. A survey of late 1960s Arizona censorship conditions among teachers uncovered three such specimens:

> I would not recommend any book any parent might object to.

> The Board of Education knows what parents in our area want their children to read. If teachers don't feel they can teach what the parents approve, they should move on.

> The English teacher is hired by the school board, which represents the public. The public, therefore, has the right to ask any English teacher to avoid using any material repugnant to any parent or student.[32]

Lest readers assume that Arizona is unique in certifying these nonprofessionals, note these two Connecticut English Department Chairs quoted in

JUDY BLUME
on Censorship

When I began to write, more than twenty years ago, I didn't know if anyone would publish my books, but I wasn't afraid to write them. I was lucky. I found an editor and publisher who were willing to take a chance. They encouraged me. I was never told that I couldn't write. I felt only that I had to write the most honest books I could. Books that came from deep down inside—books about real people, real families, real feelings— books that left the reader hopeful (because I am basically an optimist), without tying up all the loose ends. It never occurred to me, at the time, that what I was writing was controversial. Much of it grew out of my own feelings and concerns when I was young.

There were few challenges to my books then, although I remember the night a woman phoned, asking if I had written *Are You There God? It's Me, Margaret*. When I replied that I had, she called me a Communist and slammed down the phone. I never did figure out if she equated Communism with menstruation or religion.

But in 1980, following the presidential election, everything changed. The censors crawled out of the woodwork, seemingly overnight, organized and determined. Not only would they decide what their children could read, but what all children could read. Challenges to books quadrupled within months. And we'll never know how many teach-

Diane Shugert's "Censorship in Connecticut" in the Spring 1978 *Connecticut English Journal:*

At this level, I don't feel it's [censorship] a problem. We don't deal with controversial material, at least not in English class.

We have no problems at all in my department. The teachers order books directly and don't clear them with me or with a committee. But *I* receive the shipments. Copies of books that I think to be inappropriate simply disappear from the book room.[33]

In a letter to the book review editor of the *School Library Journal,* a librarian told how she had been approached by a parent objecting to words in Alice Childress' *A Hero Ain't Nothin' But A Sandwich.* The librarian particularly

ers, school librarians, and principals quietly removed books to avoid trouble.

I believe that censorship grows out of fear, and because fear is contagious, some parents are easily swayed. Book banning satisfies their need to feel in control of their children's lives. This fear is often disguised as moral outrage. They want to believe that if their children don't read about it, their children won't know about it. And if they don't know about it, it won't happen.

Today, it's not only language and sexuality (the usual reasons for banning my books) that will land a book on the censors' hit list. It's Satanism, New Age-ism, and a hundred other *isms*, some of which would make you laugh if the implications weren't so serious. Books that make *kids* laugh often come under suspicion; so do books that encourage kids to think, or question authority; books that don't hit the reader over the head with moral lessons are considered dangerous. (My book, *Blubber*, was banned in Montgomery County, Maryland, for *lack of moral tone*, but in New Zealand it is used in teacher-training classes to help explain classroom dynamics.) Censors don't want children exposed to ideas different from their own. If every individual with an agenda had his/her way, the shelves in the school library would be close to empty. I wish the censors could read the letters kids write.

Dear Judy,
I don't know where I stand in the world.
I don't know who I am. That's why I read,
to find myself.

Elizabeth, age 13

But it's not just the books under fire now that worry me. It is the books that will never be written. The books that will never be read. And all due to the fear of censorship. As always, young readers will be the real losers.

But I am encouraged by a new awareness. This year I've received a number of letters from young people who are studying censorship in their classes. And in many communities across the country, students from elementary through high school are becoming active (along with caring adults) in the fight to maintain their right to read and their right to choose books. *They* are speaking before school boards, and more often than not, when they do, the books in question are returned to the shelves.

Only when *readers* of all ages become active, only when *readers* are willing to stand up to the censors, will the censors get the message that they can't frighten us!

Copyright © 1992, Judy Blume

Judy Blume's books include *Tiger Eyes*, Bradbury, 1981; *Just As Long As We're Together*, Orchard/Watts, 1987; *Then Again, Maybe I Won't*, Bradbury, 1971; and *Letters to Judy: What Kids Wish They Could Tell You*, Putnam, 1986.

objected to the book's listing among the "Best Books of the Year for 1973." She wrote:

> ■ Our school strongly recommends you remove this book from your list as profanity at the junior high level is not appropriate in a library book.[34]

More recently, the book was the subject of a school hearing when two Arizona mothers argued, "Most kids don't have the maturity to handle this." A junior high school principal agreed when he said, "I would like to see it banned altogether. That kind of language is not acceptable. I don't want any book on the shelf that would result in a student being disciplined if he used that language. Otherwise, our disciplinary policy will go out the window."

The December 1973 *School Library Journal* carried an article by Mary F. Poole objecting to Johanna Reiss's *The Upstairs Room:*

> The book proved to be a well-told account of a truly horrible situation. It is peopled with well delineated characters, who are in truth, "people with weaknesses and strengths," an aim of the author which was accomplished quite well: so the more than 50 irreverent expletives and the use of one four-letter word in the book are mere baggage or are used for their shock appeal, their monetary value, out of unconcern for the name of God, or to prove that the author is not a prude. Take your choice.[35]

The question of whether an author can make a valid moral or psychological point with "strong language," a typical euphemism in such cases, raged in letters in the following issues.

Similarly, Patty Campbell's "The YA Perplex" column in the December 1978 *Wilson Library Bulletin* led to increased letters as Campbell noted, "Judging from the letters to the editors in various library publications, obscene language rings alarm bells for most librarians."[36] She proceeded to review three possibly controversial novels—Fran Arrick's *Steffie Can't Come Out to Play,* Kin Platt's *The Doomsday Gang,* and Sandra Scoppettone's *Happy Endings Are All Alike.* Sure enough, controversy produced letters, the best or most typical from an admitted self-censoring high school librarian. After announcing that he had played football and coached for eleven years—proving, one can assume, that he was a real man, not a wimp—he added:

> I have a philosophy of what it should be like within the walls and pages (especially pages) of a library. Two different worlds? You bet.
>
> Do I want our teens to see a sugarcoated world through rose-colored glasses? Why not? Is there anything wrong with reading about the good things that happen? . . . Is it wrong for a character of fiction to say "gosh darn" instead of "damn it"?
>
> In my library censorship lives, and I'm not ashamed or afraid to say it, either. I have books like *The Boy Who Could Make Himself Disappear* on my shelves, but these are few and far between. To all you so-called liberal librarians out there in city or country schools now condemning this letter, I say to you: "The kids of today are great! Do you want to help give them a boost or a bust?"[37]

And at least one book distributor was only too willing to help librarians precensor books. The Follett Library Book Company of Crystal Lake, Illinois (not to be confused with Follett Publishing Company in Chicago), has for several years marked titles with a pink card *if* three or more customers had objected to the vocabulary or illustrations or subject matter of a book. The cards read:

■ Some of our customers have informed us of their opinion that the content or vocabulary of this book is inappropriate for young readers. Before distributing this book, you may wish to examine it to assure yourself that the subject matter and vocabulary meet your standards.[38]

Publishers, too, have been guilty of rewriting texts or asking authors to delete certain words to make books or texts more palatable to highly moral librarians or communities. "Expurgation Practices of School Book Clubs" in the December 1983 *Voice of Youth Advocates* and Gayle Keresey's "School Book Club Expurgation Practices," in the Winter 1984 *Top of the News* uncovered censorship practices in Scholastic Book Club selections, as titles were changed and deletions of offensive words or ideas occurred between the hard-back edition and its publication in a paperback club edition.

What Do the Censors Censor?

The answer to the question of what censors censor is easy—almost anything. Books, films, magazines, anything that might be enjoyed by someone is likely to feel some censor's scorn and moral wrath.

Some works, however, are more likely to be attacked. Judging from state and national surveys of censorship conditions, these works are almost certain to be objected to last year, this year, next year, and for years to come.

J. D. Salinger's *The Catcher in the Rye* (seemingly on every censor's hit list and leading every survey but one as the most widely censored book in America)

John Steinbeck's *Of Mice and Men* and *The Grapes of Wrath*

Go Ask Alice

Joseph Heller's *Catch-22*

Aldous Huxley's *Brave New World*

William Golding's *Lord of the Flies*

Harper Lee's *To Kill a Mockingbird*

Kurt Vonnegut's *Slaughterhouse-Five*

Judy Blume's *Forever*

Slightly behind these ten golden favorites come these adult works widely read by young adults:

Ken Kesey's *One Flew Over the Cuckoo's Nest;* Ernest Hemingway's *The Sun Also Rises, For Whom the Bell Tolls,* and *A Farewell to Arms;* F. Scott Fitzgerald's *The Great Gatsby;* Eve Merriam's *The Inner City Mother Goose;* Claude Brown's *Manchild in the Promised Land;*

Gordon Parks' *The Learning Tree;* George Orwell's *1984* and *Animal Farm;* Jerzy Kosinski's *The Painted Bird;* Mark Twain's *Adventures of Huckleberry Finn;* and Alexander Solzhenitsyn's *One Day in the Life of Ivan Denisovich.*

Along with these come young adult novels:

Judy Blume's *Deenie* and *Are You There, God? It's Me, Margaret;* Robert Cormier's *The Chocolate War* and *After the First Death;* Paula Fox's *The Slave Dancer;* Alice Childress' *A Hero Ain't Nothin' But a Sandwich;* Johanna Reiss's *The Upstairs Room;* Rosa Guy's *Ruby;* M. E. Kerr's *Dinky Hocker Shoots Smack;* S. E. Hinton's *The Outsiders;* Paul Zindel's *The Pigman* and *My Darling, My Hamburger;* and Norma Klein's *Mom, the Wolfman and Me.*

And who could forget favorites like *The American Heritage Dictionary* and *Romeo and Juliet* and *Othello* and *The Merchant of Venice*? Or short stories (and films) like Shirley Jackson's "The Lottery" or Ambrose Bierce's "An Occurrence at Owl Creek Bridge"? Or modern plays like Thornton Wilder's *Our Town* or Tennessee Williams' *The Glass Menagerie* or *Summer and Smoke* or Arthur Miller's *Death of a Salesman* or *All My Sons?*

Readers surprised to discover an obvious censorial title not on the preceding list should feel free to add whatever they wish. Anyone who wishes to expand the list (easy and probably necessary for some) should casually read any issue of the *Newsletter on Intellectual Freedom* or skim through James E. Davis' *Dealing with Censorship* or any other book on censorship. The list of objectionable works could go on and on and on and on.

Why Do the Censors Censor What They Do?

Why censors censor what they do is far more important and far more complex than what they censor. Unfortunately for readers who want simple answers and an easy-to-remember list of reasons, the next paragraphs will certainly be disappointing.

In "Censorship in the 1970s; Some Ways to Handle It When It Comes (and It Will)" in early 1974, Donelson listed eight different kinds of materials that get censored. Those that censors

1. deem offensive because of sex (usually calling it "filth" or "risqué" or "indecent")
2. see as an attack on the American dream or the country ("un-American" or "pro-commie")
3. label peacenik or pacifistic (remember the Vietnam War had not yet become unpopular with the masses)
4. consider irreligious or against religion or, specifically, un-Christian

5. believe promote racial harmony or stress civil rights or the civil rights movement ("biased on social issues" or "do young people have to see all that ugliness?")
6. regard as offensive in language ("profane" or "unfit for human ears")
7. identify as drug books, pro or con ("kids wouldn't hear about or use drugs if it weren't for these books")
8. regard as presenting inappropriate adolescent behavior and therefore likely to cause other young people to act inappropriately.[39]

In an article entitled "Dirty Dictionaries, Obscene Nursery Rhymes and Burned Books," published in James E. Davis' 1979 *Dealing with Censorship,* Ed Jenkinson added fourteen more likely targets, including young adult novels, works of "questionable" writers, literature about or by homosexuals, role playing, texts using improper grammar, sexist stereotypes, and sex education. In a *Publishers Weekly* article the same year,[40] Jenkinson listed forty targets, with new ones being sociology, anthropology, the humanities generally (if secular humanism is bad, so then must be humanism or anything that sounds like humanism, and that easily extends to humanities), ecology, world government, world history that mentions the United Nations, basal readers lacking phonics, basal readers with many pictures or drawings, situation ethics, violence, and books that do not promote the Protestant ethic or do not promote patriotism. A year later, Jenkinson had expanded his list to sixty-seven, with additions including "Soviet propaganda," citizenship classes, black dialects, uncaptioned pictures in history texts, concrete poetry, magazines that have ads for alcohol or contraceptives, songs and cartoons in textbooks, and "depressing thoughts."[41] The last of the objections is truly depressing, apparently for censors and educators alike.

SOME COURT DECISIONS WORTH KNOWING ABOUT

Legal battles and court decisions often seem abstract and dull and irrelevant to practical matters for too many educators, but several court decisions have been significant and have affected thousands of educators who hardly knew the battles had taken place, much less their disposition. A brief run-through of two kinds of decisions, those involving attempts to define obscenity and its supposed influence on readers and viewers and those directly involving schools and school libraries, may be helpful to readers.

Court Decisions about Obscenity and Attempting to Define Obscenity

Since censors frequently bandy the word *obscene* in attacking books, teachers and librarians should know something about the history of courts vainly attempting to define the term.

Although it was hardly the first decision involving obscenity, the first decision announcing a definition of and a test for obscenity came about in an English case in 1868. *The Queen v. Hicklin* (L.R. 3Q.B. 360) concerned an ironmonger who was also an ardent antipapist. He sold copies of *The Confessional Unmasked: Showing the Depravity of the Romish Priesthood, the Iniquity of the Confessional and the Questions Put to Females in Confession,* and although the Court agreed that his heart was pure, his publication was not. Judge Cockburn announced a test of obscenity that was to persist in British law for nearly a century and in American law until the 1930s:

> I think the test of obscenity is this, whether the tendency of the matter charged as obscenity is to deprave and corrupt those whose minds are open to such immoral influences, and into whose hands a publication of this sort may fall.

Clearly, but not exclusively, Cockburn was attempting to protect young people.

In 1913 in *United States v. Kennerly* (209 F. 119), Judge Learned Hand ruled against the defendant since his publication clearly fell under the limits of the Hicklin test, but he added:

> I hope it is not improper for me to say that the rule as laid down, however consonant it may be with mid-Victorian morals, does not seem to me to answer to the understanding and morality of the present time, as conveyed by the words, "obscene, lewd, or lascivious." I question whether in the end men will regard that as obscene which is honestly relevant to the adequate expression of innocent ideas, and whether they will not believe that truth and beauty are too precious to society at large to be mutilated in the interest of those most likely to pervert them to base uses.

Then in 1933 and 1934, two decisions (5 F. supp. 182 and 72 F. 2d 705) overturned much of the Hicklin test. James Joyce's *Ulysses* had been regarded as obscene by most legal authorities since its publication, largely for Molly Bloom's soliloquy. The novel was stopped by Customs officials and tried before Judge John M. Woolsey of the Federal District Court for Southern New York. Woolsey found the book "sincere and honest" and "not dirt for dirt's sake" and ruled that in matters determining what is obscene, the work *must* be judged as a whole, not on the basis of its parts. An appeal to the Federal Circuit Court of Appeals in 1934 led to Judge Learned Hand's upholding Woolsey's decision.

In 1957 in *Butler v. Michigan* (352 U.S. 380), Butler challenged a Michigan statute that tested obscenity in terms of its effect on young people, arguing that this restricted adult reading to that fit only for children. Mr. Justice Frankfurter agreed, and wrote:

> The State insists that, by thus quarantining the general reading public against books not too rugged for grown men and women in order to shield

juvenile innocence, it is exercising its power to promote the general welfare. Surely, this is to burn the house to roast the pig. . . . The incidence of this enactment [the Michigan statute] is to reduce the adult population of Michigan to reading only what is fit for children.

Frankfurter agreed with Butler and declared the Michigan statute unconstitutional.

Later in 1957 in *Roth v. United States* (354 U.S. 476), the U.S. Supreme Court announced that obscenity was not protected by the Constitution, for "implicit in the history of the First Amendment is the rejection of obscenity as utterly without redeeming social importance." (That phrase, "without redeeming social importance" was to cause problems for several years thereafter.) Reading for the majority, Justice Brennan added a new definition of obscenity:

Obscene material is material which deals with sex in a manner appealing to prurient interest.

And a new test:

whether to the average person, applying contemporary community standards, the dominant theme of the material taken as a whole appeals to prurient interest.

Roth rejected the Hicklin test (already in patches) as "unconstitutionally restrictive of the freedoms of speech and press."

Jacobellis v. Ohio (84 S. Ct. 1676) in 1964 further refined the *Roth* test when Justice Brennan announced that the "contemporary community" standard referred to national standards, not local standards though Chief Justice Warren angrily dissented, arguing that community standards meant local and nothing more.

In 1966 in *Memoirs v. Attorney General of Massachusetts* (86 S. Ct. 975) Justice Brennan further elaborated on the *Roth* test:

Under this definition, as elaborated in subsequent cases, three elements must coalesce: it must be established that (a) the dominant theme of the material taken as a whole appeals to prurient interest in sex; (b) the material is patently offensive because it affronts contemporary community standards relating to the description or representation of sexual matters; and (c) the material is utterly without redeeming social value.

The *Ginsberg v. New York* (390 U.S. 692) decision in 1968 did not develop or alter the definition of obscenity, but it did introduce the concepts of variable obscenity and caused some concern for librarians and English teachers. Ginsberg, who operated a stationery store and luncheonette, had sold "girlie" magazines to a sixteen-year-old boy in violation of a New York statute that declared illegal the sale of anything "which depicts nudity" and "was harmful" to anyone under seventeen years of age. Ginsberg maintained that New York State was without power to draw the line at the age of seventeen. The Court dismissed his argument, sustained the New York statute, and wrote:

> The well-being of its children is of course a subject within the State's constitutional power to regulate.

The Court further noted, in lines that proved worrisome to anyone dealing in literature, classic or modern or what-have-you:

> To be sure, there is no lack of "studies" which purport to demonstrate that obscenity is or is not "a basic factor in impairing the ethical and moral development of . . . youth and a clear and present danger to the people of the state." But the growing consensus of commentators is that "while these studies all agree that a causal link has not been demonstrated, they are equally agreed that a causal link has not been disproved either."

Those words were lovingly quoted by censors across the nation, although few of them bothered to read the citations in the decision that suggested the dangers of assuming too much either way about the matter.

Then in 1973, five decisions were announced by the Court. The most important, *Miller v. California* (413 U.S. 15) and *Paris Adult Theatre II v. Slaton* (413 U.S. 49), enunciated a new (or more refined) test, one designed to remove all ambiguities from the past tests and to endure. That the test proved as ambiguous and as difficult to enforce and understand as previous tests should come as no surprise to readers. After attacking the 1957 *Roth* test, the majority decision read by Chief Justice Burger in *Miller* provided this three-pronged test of obscenity:

> The basic guidelines for the trier of fact must be: (a) whether "the average person, applying contemporary community standards" would find that the work, taken as a whole, appeals to the prurient interest; (b) whether the work depicts or describes in a patently offensive way, sexual conduct specifically defined by the applicable state law; and (c) whether the work taken as a whole lacks serious literary, artistic, political or scientific value.

To guide state legislatures with "a few plain examples of what a state statute could define for regulation under the second part (b) of the standard announced in this opinion," the Court provided these:

> (a) Patently offensive representations or descriptions of ultimate sexual acts, normal or perverted, actual or simulated.
> (b) Patently offensive representations or descriptions of masturbation, excretory functions, and lewd exhibition of the genitals.

After this so-called Miller catalogue, Burger announced that "contemporary community standards" meant state standards, not national standards.

Paris Adult Theatre II repeated and underscored *Miller* and added more worrisome words about the dangers of obscenity and what it can lead to. Chief Justice Burger, again, for the majority:

> But, it is argued, there is no scientific data which conclusively demonstrated that exposure to obscene material adversely affects men and women or their society. It is urged on behalf of the petitioner that, absent such a demonstration, any kind of state regulation is "impermissible." We reject this argument. It is not for us to resolve empirical uncertainties underlying state legislation, save in the exceptional case where that legislation plainly impinges upon rights protected by the Constitution itself. . . . Although there is no conclusive proof of any connection between antisocial behavior and obscene material, the legislature of Georgia could quite reasonably determine that such a connection does or might exist.

In other words, no proof exists that obscenity does (or does not) lead to any certain antisocial actions (or nonactions), yet state legislatures can assume or guess that such a relationship may exist and pass legislation to that effect.

Justice Brennan dissented, noting that the dangers to "protected speech are very grave" and added that the decision would not halt further cases before the Court:

> The problem is that one cannot say with certainty that material is obscene until at least five members of this Court, applying inevitably obscure standards, have pronounced it so.

To few observers' surprise, Brennan's prophecy proved correct.

On January 13, 1972, police in Albany, Georgia, seized the film *Carnal Knowledge* (starring Jack Nicholson) and charged the manager with violating a state statute against distributing obscene material. He was convicted in the Superior Court and the decision was affirmed by a divided vote in the Georgia State Supreme Court. In 1974, the U.S. Supreme Court announced its decision in *Jenkins v. the State of Georgia* (94 S. Ct. 2750), Justice Rehnquist reading the unanimous decision to reverse the Georgia Supreme Court opinion. Although *Carnal Knowledge* had been declared obscene by state standards and although it had a scene showing simulated masturbation, Rehnquist stated that "juries do not have unbridled discretion" in determining obscenity and that *Carnal Knowledge* had nothing that fell "within either of the two examples given in *Miller*."

The history of litigation and court decisions about obscenity and its definition are hardly models of clarity or consistency. Anyone interested in more details of this frustrating but fascinating story should read that marvelous book by Felice Flanery Lewis, *Literature, Obscenity and Law*.

Court Decisions About Teaching and School Libraries

If the implications of court decisions about obscenity are a bit vague, decisions about teaching and school libraries are not notably better. Courts are notoriously leery of decisions involving schools and libraries, but a few decisions, not unsurprisingly ambiguous, are worth noting about school libraries.

The U.S. Supreme Court had ruled in *Tinker v. the Des Moines (Iowa) School District* (393 U.S. 503) in 1969:

> First Amendment rights, applied in light of the special characteristics of the school environment, are available to teachers and students. It can hardly be argued that either students or teachers shed their constitutional rights to freedom of speech or expression at the schoolhouse gate.

But the Courts, federal or state, seemed unwilling to extend those rights to the school library in *Presidents Council, District 25 v. Community School Board No. 25* (457 F. 2d 289) in 1972. A New York City school board voted 5–3 in 1971 to remove all copies of Piri Thomas' *Down These Mean Streets* from junior high libraries because of its offensive nature and language. The U.S. Court of Appeals, Second Circuit, held for the school board. The book, so the Court decided, had dubious literary or educational merit, and since the state had delegated the selection of school materials to local school boards and there was no evidence of basic constitutional impingement by the board, the Court saw no merit in the opposing view.

Presidents Council was cited for several years thereafter as the definitive decision, but since it was not a Supreme Court decision, it served as precedent only for judges so inclined. A different decision prevailed in *Minarcini v. Strongsville (Ohio) City School District* (541 F. 2d 577) in 1977. The school board refused to allow a teacher to use Heller's *Catch-22* or Vonnegut's *God Bless You, Mr. Rosewater,* ordered Vonnegut's *Cat's Cradle* and Heller's novel removed from the library, and proclaimed that students and teachers were not to discuss these books in class. The U.S. District Court found for the school board, but on appeal to the U.S. Circuit Court of Appeals, the three-member panel reversed the lower court. Judge Edwards focused on the main issues of the case in eloquent words widely quoted and much admired by school librarians:

> A library is a storehouse of knowledge. When created for a public school it is an important privilege created by the state for the benefit of the students in the school. That privilege is not subject to being withdrawn by succeeding school boards whose members might desire to "winnow" the library for books the content of which occasioned their displeasure or dis-approval. Of course, a copy of a book may wear out. Some books may become obsolete. Shelf space alone may at some point require some selection of books to be retained and books to be disposed of. No such rationale is involved in this case.

The opinion of the Court that library books gained a tenure of sorts and could not easily be culled by a school board was at odds with the parallel U.S. Circuit Court in *Presidents Council,* but again, the Ohio decision served as precedent only if judges in other Federal District Courts (or Federal Appeals Courts) wished to so use it.

A year later in *Right to Read Defense Committee of Chelsea (Massachusetts) v. School Committee of the City of Chelsea* (454 F. Supp. 703) in the U.S. District Court for Massachusetts, another decision supported the rights of students and libraries. The librarian of Chelsea High School ordered and made available a paperback anthology, *Male and Female under Eighteen,* containing a poem by a student, "The City to the Young Girl," which had, as the judge wrote, "street language." A parent felt the language was "offensive" and called the board chairman, who was also the editor of the local paper. The chairman-editor concluded that the poem was "filthy" and contained "offensive" language and should be removed from the library. He scheduled an emergency meeting of the school committee to consider the subject of "objectionable, salacious and obscene material being made available in books in the High School Library" and wrote an article for his newspaper about the matter, concluding with these words:

> Quite frankly, I want a complete review of how it was possible for such garbage to even get on bookshelves where 14-year-old high school ninth graders could obtain them.

The superintendent urged caution and noted that the book could not be removed from the library without a formal review, but the chair was adamant. When the librarian argued that the poem was not obscene, the chair-editor wrote in his newspaper:

> [I am] shocked and extremely disappointed to have our high school librarian claim there is nothing lewd, lascivious, filthy, suggestive, licentious, pornographic or obscene about this particular poem in this book of many poems.

The school committee claimed "an unconstrained authority to remove books from the shelves of the school library." Although the judge agreed that "local authorities are, and must continue to be, the principal policymakers in the public schools," he was more swayed by the reasoning in *Minarcini* than in *Presidents Council.* He wrote:

> The Committee was under no obligation to purchase *Male and Female* for the High School Library, but it did. . . . The Committee claims an absolute right to remove *City* from the shelves of the school library. It has no such right, and compelling policy considerations argue against any public authority having such an unreviewable power of censorship. There is more

at issue here than the poem *City*. If this work may be removed by a committee hostile to its language and theme, then the precedent is set for removal of any other work. The prospect of successive school committees "sanitizing" the school library of views divergent from its own is alarming, whether they do it book by book or one page at a time.

What is at stake here is the right to read and be exposed to controversial thoughts and language—a valuable right subject to First Amendment protection.

What may prove to be the most significant decision about school libraries began in September 1975 when three members of the Island Trees (New York) School Board attended a conference sponsored by the conservative Parents of New York—United (PONY-U). After examining lists of books deemed "objectionable" by PONY-U, the three returned home, checked their district's school libraries, and found several suspect works—Bernard Malamud's *The Fixer*, Vonnegut's *Slaughterhouse-Five*, Desmond Morris' *The Naked Ape*, Piri Thomas' *Down These Mean Streets*, Langston Hughes' edition of *Best Short Stories of Negro Writers*, Oliver LaFarge's *Laughing Boy*, Richard Wright's *Black Boy*, Alice Childress' *A Hero Ain't Nothin' But a Sandwich*, Eldridge Cleaver's *Soul on Ice,* and *Go Ask Alice.* In February 1976, the board gave "unofficial direction" that the books be removed from the library and delivered to the board for their reading.

Once the word got out, the board issued a press release attempting to justify its actions, calling the books "anti-American, anti-Christian, anti-Semitic, and just plain filthy" and argued:

> It is our duty, our moral obligation, to protect the children in our schools from this moral danger as surely as from physical or medical dangers.

When the board appointed a review committee—four members of the school staff and four parents—they politely listened to the report suggesting that five books should be returned to the shelves, and that two should be removed (*The Naked Ape* and *Down These Mean Streets*); then they ignored their own chosen committee. (The board did return one book to the shelves, *Laughing Boy*, and placed *Black Boy* on a restricted shelf available only with parental permission.) Stephen Pico, a student, and others brought suit against the board, claiming that their rights under the First Amendment had been denied by the board.

The U.S. District Court heard the case in 1979 and granted a summary judgment to the board. The court held that the state had vested school boards with broad discretion to formulate educational policy, and the selection or rejection of books was clearly within their power. The court found no merit in the First Amendment claims of Pico et al. A three-judge panel of the U.S. Court of Appeals for the Second Circuit (638 F. 2d 404) reversed the District Court's decision 2–1 and remanded the case for trial. The case then, although not directly, wended its way to the U.S. Supreme Court, the first such case ever to be heard at that level.

In a strange and badly fragmented decision—and for that reason it is unclear just how certainly it will serve as precedent—Justice Brennan delivered the plurality (*not* majority) opinion in *Board of Education, Island Trees Union Free School District v. Pico* (102 S. Ct. 2799). He immediately emphasized the "limited nature" of the question before the court, for "precedents have long recognized certain constitutional limits upon the power of the State to control even the curriculum and classroom," and he further noted that *Island Trees* did not involve textbooks "or indeed any books that Island Trees students would be required to read." The case concerned only the removal, not the acquisition, of library books. He concluded the first section of his opinion by pointing out that the case concerned two questions:

First, Does the First Amendment impose *any* limitations upon the discretion of petitioners to remove library books from the Island Trees High School and Junior High School? Second, if so, do the affidavits and other evidential materials before the District Court, construed most favorably to respondents, raise a genuine issue of fact whether petitioners might have exceeded those limitations?

Brennan proceeded to find for Pico (and ultimately for the library and the books):

. . . we think that the First Amendment rights of students may be directly and sharply implicated by the removal of books from the shelves of a school library.

Petitioners emphasized the inculcative function of secondary education, and argue that they must be allowed *unfettered* discretion "to transmit community values" through the Island Trees schools. But that sweeping claim overlooks the unique role of the school library. . . . Petitioners might well defend their claim of absolute discretion in matters of *curriculum* by reliance upon their duty to inculcate community values. But we think that petitioners' reliance upon that duty is misplaced where, as here, they attempt to extend their claim of absolute discretion beyond the compulsory environment of the classroom, into the school library and the regime of voluntary inquiry that there holds sway.

Petitioners rightly possess significant discretion to determine the content of their school libraries. But that discretion may not be exercised in a narrowly partisan or political manner. . . . Our Constitution does not permit the official suppression of ideas. Thus whether petitioners' removal of books from their school libraries denied respondents their First Amendment rights depends upon the motivation behind petitioners' actions. If petitioners *intended* by their removal decision to deny respondents access to ideas with which petitioners disagreed, and if this intent was the decisive factor in petitioners' decision, then petitioners have exercised their discretion in violation of the Constitution.

Four pages follow before Justice Blackmun's generally concurring opinion and Justices Burger, Rehnquist, Powell, and O'Connor offered their stinging dissents, but it is clear that school librarians won something, although precisely what and how much will need to be resolved by future court decisions.

It is equally clear that secondary teachers lost something in *Island Trees*. In an understandable ploy, the American Library Association, the New York Library Association, and the Freedom to Read Foundation submitted an *Amicus Curiae* brief which sought to distinguish between the functions of the school classroom and the school library, a distinction that worked to the advantage of the school librarian but certainly not to that of the classroom teacher. Apparently, Brennan bought the argument as readers will see, comparing Brennan's words with those from the following brief:

> ▉ This case, however, is about a library, not a school's curriculum. This is an extremely important distinction for the evaluation of the First Amendment interests at stake here.
>
> The school board below banned books from a library. Thus, this case does not present an issue concerning the board's control of curriculum, i.e., what is taught in the classroom. We freely concede that the school board has the right and duty to supervise the general content of the school's course of study.

Whether these words will cause serious disagreements between teachers and librarians remains to be seen. Certainly, that phrase, "we freely concede," has rankled a number of English teachers who recognized that *Island Trees* was a serious setback for intellectual freedom in the classroom.

Anyone who assumed that *Pico* settled school censorship problems must have been surprised by five court decisions from 1986 through 1989. These decisions might have been expected to clear up the censorial waters; instead they made the waters murkier and murkier.

On July 7, 1986, the U.S. Supreme Court announced its decision in *Bethel School District v. Fraser* upholding school officials in Spanaway, Washington, who had suspended a student for using sexual metaphors in describing the political potency of a candidate for student government. Writing the majority opinion in the 7–2 decision, Chief Justice Burger said, "Surely it is a highly appropriate function of public school education to prohibit the use of vulgar and offensive terms in public discourse. . . . schools must teach by example the shared values of a civilized social order." To some people's surprise, Justice Brennan agreed with Justice Burger that the student's speech had been disruptive, although Brennan refused to label the speech indecent or obscene.

That decision worried many educators, but a lower court decision on October 24, 1986, frightened more teachers. *Mozert v. Hawkins County (Tennessee)*

Public Schools began in September 1983 when the school board of Hawkins County refused a request by parents to remove three books in the Holt, Rinehart and Winston reading series from the sixth-, seventh-, and eighth-grade program. The parents formed Citizens Organized for Better Schools and ultimately brought suit against the school board. U.S. District Judge Thomas Hull dismissed the lawsuit, but on appeal before the Sixth Circuit of the Court of Appeals, a panel of three judges remanded the case back to Judge Hull.

Not all the testimony in the trial during the summer of 1986 concerned humanism, particularly secular humanism, but so it seemed at times. Vicki Frost, one of the parents who initiated the suit, said that the Holt series taught "satanism, feminism, evolution, telepathy, internationalism, and other beliefs that come under the heading of secular humanism."[42] Later she explained why parents objected to any mention of the Renaissance by saying that "a central idea of the Renaissance was a belief in the dignity and worth of human beings," presumably establishing that teaching the Renaissance was little more than teaching secular humanism.

Judge Hull ruled in favor of the parents on October 24, 1986, but the U.S. Sixth Circuit Court of Appeals later overturned Hull's decision. Worse yet for the fundamentalist parents, the U.S. Supreme Court refused to hear an appeal of the Court of Appeals' ruling in February 1988. Beverly LaHaye, leader of the Concerned Women for America, who had filed the original suit in 1983 and whose group had helped finance the legal fees for the parents, said, "School boards now have the authority to trample the religious freedom of all children." Other people, notably educators, were grateful to the court for giving them the right to teach.

While Mozert worked its way through the courts, an even more troublesome and considerably louder suit was heard in Alabama. Judge Brevard W. Hand had earlier helped devise a suit defending the right of Alabama to permit a moment of silence for prayer in the public schools. The U.S. Supreme Court overturned Judge Hand's decision so he devised another suit, *Smith v. School Commissioners of Mobile County, Alabama,* alleging that social studies, history, and home economics textbooks in the Mobile public schools unconstitutionally promoted the "religious belief system" of secular humanism, as Judge Hand wrote in his March 4, 1987, decision maintaining that forty-four texts violated the rights of parents.

The decision was both silly and certain, but those who feared the boogeyman of secular humanism celebrated for a few weeks. Then, late in August 1987, the Eleventh U.S. Circuit Court of Appeals reversed Judge Hand's decision. The Court of Appeals did not address the question of whether secular humanism was a religion, but it did agree that the forty-four texts did not promote secular humanism. Phyllis Schlafly said she was not surprised by the ruling, but it mattered little, since the decision would be appealed to the U.S. Supreme Court. Oddly enough for a case that began so loudly, the plaintiffs were mute, the date for the appeal quietly passed, and all was silence.

The fourth case, *Hazelwood School District v. Kuhlmeier,* will trouble many educators, although nominally the case was concerned with school journalism and the publication of a school newspaper. The case began in 1983 when the principal of a high school in Hazelwood, Missouri, objected to two stories in the school newspaper dealing with teenage pregnancy and divorce's effects on young people.

Associate Justice Byron White wrote the majority opinion in the 5–3 decision announcing that educators (i.e., administrators) are entitled to exercise great control over student expression. And although the case presumably dealt only with a school newspaper, White's words—inadvertently or not—went further. White wrote:

> The policy of school officials toward [the school newspaper] was reflected in Hazelwood School Board Policy 348.51 and the Hazelwood East Curriculum Guide. Board Policy 348.51 provided that "school-sponsored publications are developed within the adopted curriculum and its educational activities."

And later after commenting about needed school standards and the right of administrators to set standards, White added:

> This standard is consistent with our oft-expressed view that the education of the nation's youth is primarily the responsibility of parents, teachers, and state and local school officials, and not of federal judges.

Kirsten Goldberg warned only a month later that the consequences of *Hazelwood* would likely extend beyond school newspapers and be far more serious than most teachers had thought.

> Less than a month after the U.S. Supreme Court's decision expanding the power of school officials to regulate student speech, lower courts in three widely differing cases have cited the ruling in upholding the actions of school administrators.
>
> The court decisions, which came less than a week apart, support a Florida school board's banning of a humanities textbook, a California principal's seizure of an "April Fool's" edition of a school newspaper, and a Nebraska school district's decision not to provide meeting space to a student Bible club.[43]

The Florida decision was particularly troubling and hinted that parallel decisions citing *Hazelwood* as precedent might be on the way. *Virgil v. School Board of Columbia County, Florida* concerned a challenge to a school board's decision to stop using a humanities text in a high school class since it contained Chaucer's "The Miller's Tale" and Aristophanes' *Lysistrata,* two works that parents had objected to. After a formal complaint had been filed in April 1986, the school board appointed an advisory committee and then ignored that committee when it recommended keeping the text. Parents filed an action against the school board. In the district court decision in January 1988, Judge Black agreed with the parents that the school board had overestimated the potential harm to students of Chaucer or Aristophanes, but she concluded that the board had the power as announced in *Hazelwood* to decide as it had.

The parents appealed to the Eleventh Circuit of Appeals, which, as in the district court, fell back on *Hazelwood* for precedent for curricular decisions, not merely those concerned with school newspapers. As Judge Anderson wrote in his decision of January 1989:

> In applying the *Hazelwood* standard to the instant case, two considerations are particularly significant. First, we conclude that the Board decisions at issue were curricular decisions. The materials removed were part of the textbook used in a regularly scheduled course of study in the school. . . .
>
> The second consideration that is significant in applying the *Hazelwood* standard to this case is the fact that the motivation for the Board's removal of the readings has been stipulated to be related to the explicit sexuality and excessively vulgar language in the selections. It is clear from *Hazelwood* and other cases that this is a legitimate concern.

Judge Anderson found that the school board had acted appropriately, although in the last paragraph he and the court distanced themselves from the folly of the board's decision to ban two classics.

> We decide today only that the Board's removal of these works from the curriculum did not violate the Constitution. Of course, we do not endorse the Board's decision. Like the district court, we seriously question how young persons just below the age of majority can be harmed by these masterpieces of Western literature. However, having concluded that there is no constitutional violation, our role is not to second-guess the wisdom of the Board's action.

Florida teachers must have been touched by those words.

Joan DelFattore's *What Johnny Shouldn't Read: Textbook Censorship in America* is a recent scholarly and readable work which admirably covers major court decisions involving teachers and librarians.

Extralegal Decisions

Most censorship episodes do not result in legal hearings and court decisions. Teachers or librarians come under attack and unofficial rumor-mongering charges are lodged because someone objects and labels the offending work "obscene" or "filthy" or "pornographic." The case is heard in the court of public opinion, sometimes before the school board, with few legal niceties prevailing. The censors (and too often the school board) almost never operate under any definitions of obscenity that a court would recognize, but their interpretations of the issues are operationally effective for their purposes. The book may not always be judged as a whole book (although individual parts may be juicily analyzed), and the entire procedure may be arbitrary and capricious. The decision, once announced, rapidly disposes of the offending book and frequently the teacher or librarian to boot, a variation of old-fashioned Western justice at work. Extralegal trials need not be cluttered with trivia like accuracy or reasoning or fairness or justice. Many of the eighteen censorship incidents described earlier in this chapter were handled extralegally.

Why would librarians or teachers allow their books and teaching materials to be so treated? Court cases cost money, lots of money, and unless a particular case is likely to create precedent, many lawyers would discourage educators from going to the courts. Court cases, even more important, cause friction within the community and—surprising to many neophyte teachers and librarians—cause almost equal friction among a school's faculty. A teacher or librarian who assumes that all fellow teachers will support a case for academic freedom or intellectual freedom is a fool. Many educators, to misuse the word, will have little sympathy for troublemakers or their causes. Others will be frightened at the prospect of possibly antagonizing their superiors. Others will "know their place" in the universe. Others are morally offended by anything stronger than *darn* and may regard most of modern literature (and old literature) as inherently immoral and therefore objectionable to high school students' use. Others will find additional or different reasons aplenty for staying out of the fray. And that, more likely than not, is the reason most censorship episodes do not turn into court cases.

WHAT TO DO BEFORE AND AFTER THE CENSORS ARRIVE

Certain steps should be taken by librarians and teachers, preferably acting in concert, to prepare for censorship.

Before the Censors Arrive

Teachers and librarians should have some knowledge about the history of censorship and why citizens would wish to censor (see the books and articles listed at the end of the chapter). They should keep up-to-date with censorship problems and court decisions and what books are coming under attack for what reason. That means they should read the *Newsletter on Intellectual Freedom, School Library Journal, English Journal, Wilson Library Bulletin, Journal of Youth Services in Libraries,* and *Voice of Youth Advocates,* along with other articles cited in the bibliography that concludes each issue of the *Newsletter.* A lot of work? Of course, but better than facing a censor totally ignorant of the world of censorship.

They should develop clear and succinct statements, devoid of any educational or library or literary jargon, on why they teach literature or stock books. These statements ought to be made easily available to the public, partly to demonstrate educators' literacy—always an impressive beginning for an argument—and to make parents feel that someone intelligent works in the school, partly because teachers and librarians have a duty to communicate to the public what is going on and why it goes on.

They need to develop and publicize procedures for book selection in the library or the classroom. Most parents have not the foggiest notion how educators go about selecting books, more or less assuming it comes about through sticking pins through a book catalogue. It might be wise to consider asking some parents to assist teachers and librarians in selection, partly to let parents learn how difficult the matter is, partly to use their ideas (which might prove surprisingly helpful).

They need to develop procedures for handling censorship, should it occur. The National Council of Teachers of English monographs *The Students' Right to Read* and *The Students' Right to Know* should prove helpful, as should the American Library Association's *Intellectual Freedom Manual,* both for general principles and for specific suggestions. Whether adopted from any of these sources or created afresh, the procedure should include a form to be completed by anyone who objects to any teaching material or library book, and a clearly defined way in which the matter will be handled after completion of the form. (Will it go to a committee? How many are on the committee? Are people outside the school on the committee? How many teachers? Administrators?) The procedural rules must be openly available for anyone to consult, the procedures must apply to everyone (no exceptions should be allowed, no matter whether the complainant is the local drunk or the school board president), every complainant must be treated courteously and promptly, and the procedures must be approved by the school board. If the board does not approve the procedures, they have no legal standing. If the school board is not periodically reminded of the procedures—say, every couple of years—it may forget its obligation. Given the fact that many school boards will change membership slightly in three or four years and may change their entire composition within five or six, teachers and librarians should take it upon themselves to remind the board. Otherwise, an entirely new board may wonder why it should support something it neither created nor particularly approves of.

Teachers who assign long works (other than texts) for common reading should write rationales, statements aimed at parents but open to anyone, explaining why the teacher chose *1984* or *Silas Marner* or *Manchild in the Promised Land* or *Hamlet* for class reading and discussion. Rationales should answer the following, although they should be written as informal essays, not answers to essay tests: (1) Why would the teacher use this book with this class at this time? (2) What specific objectives—not couched in behavioral terms unless the

Some materials are essential for librarians and teachers who want to keep up-to-date on censorship.

teachers are anxious to alienate parents—literary or pedagogical, is the teacher aiming at? (3) How will this book meet those objectives? (4) What problems of style, tone, theme, or subject matter exist, and how will the teacher face them? Answering those questions should force teachers to take a fresh look at the book and think more carefully about the possibilities and problems inherent in the book. Rationales are *not* designed to protect the teacher by showing careful advance preparation before teaching, although clearly such rationales would be valuable should censorship strike. Rather, rationales should be written for public information easily available to anyone interested as part of the professional responsibility of teachers. Diane Shugert offers a number of sample rationales in the fall 1983 *Connecticut English Journal* and in "How to Write a Rationale in Defense of a Book" in James Davis' *Dealing with Censorship*.

Educators should woo the public to gain support for intellectual and academic freedom. Any community will have its readers and former teachers interested in students' freedom to read. Finding them ahead of time is part of teachers' and librarians' jobs. Waiting until censorship strikes is too late. Pat Scales's ideas about working with parents in the November 1983 *Calendar* (distributed by the Children's Book Council) are most helpful. Scales was talking to a parent who helped in Scales's school library and who had picked up copies of Maureen

Daly's *Seventeenth Summer* and Ann Head's *Mr. and Mrs. Bo Jo Jones* and wondered about students reading books with such provocative covers. Scales asked the mother to read the books before forming an opinion. From that experience came a program called "Communicate Through Literature" with monthly meetings to discuss with parents the reading that young adults do. And we shouldn't forget about discussing the topic of censorship with our current students (see Focus Box 12.1). They may well be the parents who in a few years will be on the school board or on the library's board of trustees.

Educators should be prepared to take on the usual arguments of censors—for example, that educators are playing word games when we insist that we select and some parents try to censor. There is a distinction between *selection* and *censorship*, no matter how many people deliberately or inadvertently misuse or confuse the two. The classic distinction was drawn by Lester Asheim in 1952:

> ▌ Selection begins with a presumption in favor of liberty of thought; censorship with a presumption in favor of thought control. Selection's approach to the book is positive, seeking its values in the book as a book, and in the book as a whole. Censorship's approach is negative, seeking for vulnerable characteristics wherever they can be found anywhere in the book, or even outside it. Selection seeks to promote the right of the reader to read; censorship seeks to protect not the right—but the reader himself from the fancied effects of his reading. The selector has faith in the intelligence of the reader; the censor has faith only in his own.
>
> In other words, selection is democratic while censorship is authoritarian, and in our democracy we have traditionally tended to put our trust in the selector rather than in the censor.[44]

Finally, teachers and librarians should know the organizations that will be most helpful if censorship does strike. Diane Shugert's "A Body of Well-instructed Men and Women: Organizations Active for Intellectual Freedom," in James Davis' *Dealing with Censorship,* has a long list of such groups. But here are six national groups every educator ought to know:

The American Civil Liberties Union; 132 W. 43rd St.; New York, NY 10036

The Freedom to Read Foundation; 50 E. Huron St.; Chicago, IL 60611

The National Coalition Against Censorship; 2 W. 64th St.; New York, NY 10023

People for the American Way; 2000 M St., N.W.; Washington, DC 20036

SLATE (Support for the Learning and Teaching of English); National Council of Teachers of English; 1111 Kenyon Road; Urbana, IL 61801

The Standing Committee on Censorship; % National Council of Teachers of English; 1111 Kenyon Road; Urbana, IL 61801

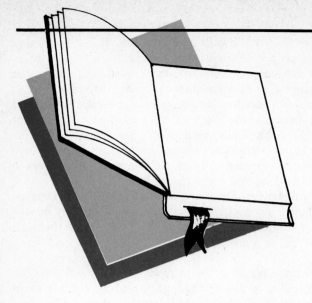

Two Children's Novels and Six YA Novels About Kids and Censorship

The Day They Came to Arrest the Book by Nat Hentoff. Delacorte, 1982. Almost a text of what happens when people of good will and different viewpoints debate whether *Huckleberry Finn* ought to be taught today, given the racial climate.

Freddy's Book by John Neufeld. Random House, 1973. Young Freddy sees the word *fuck* written on the wall and wonders what it means and why it causes such intense and embarrassed reactions from adults he asks for help.

A Matter of Principle by Susan Beth Pfeffer. Delacorte, 1982. Seven students publish an underground high school newspaper, in part to get back at a teacher and an administrator. The principal threatens to suspend them.

Maudie and the Dirty Book by Betty Miles. Knopf, 1980. Two sixth-grade girls read *The Birthday Dog* to first-graders, the children ask some questions about sex education, the girls are in trouble, and they learn something about community pressures and adults.

The Ninth Issue by Dallin Malmgren. Delacorte, 1989. Students at Nathan Hale High try to breathe life into a dead school paper by taking up real and significant issues and learn that reality easily leads to controversy.

A Small Civil War by John Neufeld. Fawcett, 1982. A small-town councilman attacks Steinbeck's *The Grapes of Wrath* and demands that it be removed from the tenth-grade English curriculum.

Strike! by Barbara Corcoran. Atheneum, 1983. Barry and his father take opposite sides, again, when the Committee for a Balanced Curriculum interferes with the curriculum and recommends that books be removed from the school library.

The Trouble with Mothers by Margery Facklam. Clarion, 1989. It's bad enough that people know Luke because his mother teaches history. When she writes *The Passionate Pirate* under a pen name, things seems safe until the "Crusade for a Clean America" discovers his mother's book.

After the Censors Arrive

Teachers and librarians should begin by refusing to panic, easier said than done but essential. Censors always have one advantage. They can determine the time and the place for the attack. No matter how well prepared the teacher or the librarian, only the censor can say *when*.

Educators should not be too surprised or appalled to discover that not all their fellow teachers or librarians will rush in with immediate support. If teachers and librarians assume they represent the entire cause by themselves, they are far better off and considerably less likely to be instantly disillusioned.

Educators ought to urge the potential censors to talk first to the teacher or librarian in question before completing the complaint form, not to stall the objectors but to assure everyone of fair play all around. Teachers or librarians may discover what others have before, that objectors sometimes simply want to be heard and their complaints treated with dignity and dispatch. Sometimes, teachers and librarians may even be able to talk calmly—once the need to battle has died down—with the objectors and to reason with them, which is not exactly the same as convincing them that the teachers or librarians are necessarily right. The objectors may even see why the offending work was assigned or recommended, sometimes even seeing the difficulty in choosing a book for a class or an individual. Many teachers and librarians, although by no means all, agree that if parents ask that their child not be required to read a certain book, educators must agree to find a substitute book. If a substitute book is to be found and if it is to meet a different fate than the first book, parents must help in selecting the new book. Most objectors are deadly serious about their children's education, and they will understand why the substitute book should not be easier or shorter (thus rewarding the student) or harder and longer (thus unduly punishing the student). Finding another book approximately as long and as difficult as the original choice is no easy matter, but parents who demand substitutes must help, lest the teacher offend once more.

Librarians and teachers must treat objectors with every possible courtesy, although courtesy may not always be what educators first consider. Objectors should be expected to complete the school's forms detailing the objection, but the forms should be easily accessible and politely distributed. The complaint form should *never* be used to stall objectors. If it is so long that objectors get discouraged, the school may win one battle, but it will have produced one disgruntled citizen, and at school bond time, one irritated citizen and friends are quite enough to harm the cause of education.

Last, a committee (spelled out in detail prior to the censorship) meets to look at and discuss the complaint. After considering the problem but before arriving at a decision, the committee must meet with the teacher or librarian in question *and* the objectors to hear their cases. The committee will then make its decision and forward it to the highest administrator in the school, who will forward it to the superintendent, who will forward it to the school board. That body, already aware of the policy and procedures much earlier adopted to handle such matters, will consider this objection and make its decision, probably after at least one open meeting.

In no case and at no level should the actions of the educators or administrators or the school be viewed as pro forma. They should be considered as thoughtful actions to resolve a problem, not as an attempt to create newer and bigger ones. Objectors should feel that they have been listened to and courtesy has been extended them at all levels and all stages.

We believe that the school—classroom or library—must be a center of intellectual ferment in the community. This implies not that schools should be radical, but that they should be one place where freedom to think and inquire is protected, where ideas of all sorts can be considered, analyzed, investigated, discussed, and their consequences thought through. We believe librarians and English teachers must protect these freedoms, not merely in the abstract but in the practical, day-by-day world of the school and library. To protect those freedoms we must fight censorship, for without them no education worthy of the name is possible.

NOTES

[1] Colin Campbell, "Book Banning in America," *New York Times Book Review,* December 20, 1981, p. 1.

[2] Comstock's life and work have been the subject of many books and articles. Heywood Broun and Margaret Leech's *Anthony Comstock: Roundsman of the Lord* (Albert and Charles Boni, 1927) is amusing and nasty and still worth reading. A brief overview of Comstock's life can be found in Robert Bremner's introduction to the reprinting of *Traps for the Young* (Harvard University Press, 1967), pp. vii–xxxi. See also Paul S. Boyer's *Purity in Print: The Vice-Society Movement and Book Censorship in America* (Scribner, 1968) and Robert W. Haney's *Comstockery in America: Patterns of Censorship and Control* (Beacon Press, 1960).

[3] Arthur E. Bostwick, *The American Public Library* (Appleton, 1910), pp. 130–31.

[4] *Library Journal* 21 (December 1896): 144.

[5] "Unexpurgated Shakespeare," *Journal of Education* 37 (April 13, 1883): 232.

[6] "What Books Do They Read?" *Common School Education* 4 (April 1890): 146–47.

[7] Evaline Harrington, "Why Treasure Island?" *English Journal* 9 (May 1920): 267–68.

[8] *Tempe* (Arizona) *Daily News,* February 22, 1990, pp. A-1, A-7.

[9] *Idaho Language Arts News,* April 1990, p. 1.

[10] *Newsletter on Intellectual Freedom* 39 (July 1990): 128.

[11] *Los Angeles Times,* May 3, 1990, pp. E-1, E-6; *Chicago Tribune,* June 3, 1990, pp. I-1, I-16; *Newsletter on Intellectual Freedom* 39 (September 1990): 161; *American Teacher* 75 (September 1990): 6.

[12] *Newsletter on Intellectual Freedom* 40 (January 1991): 12.

[13] *Newsletter on Intellectual Freedom* 40 (January 1991): 12.

[14] *Newsletter on Intellectual Freedom* 40 (March 1991): 43–44.

[15] *Newsletter on Intellectual Freedom* 40 (March 1991): 45–46.

[16] *Newsletter on Intellectual Freedom* 40 (March 1991): 43.

[17] *Newsletter on Intellectual Freedom* 40 (July 1991): 130.

[18] *Newsletter on Intellectual Freedom* 40 (July 1991): 107–108.

[19] *Newsletter on Intellectual Freedom* 40 (July 1991): 108.

[20] *Newsletter on Intellectual Freedom* 40 (July 1991): 110.

[21] *Newsletter on Intellectual Freedom* 40 (November 1991): 198.

[22] *Newsletter on Intellectual Freedom* 41 (January 1992): 9.

[23] *Newsletter on Intellectual Freedom* 41 (January 1992): 5–6.

[24] *Tempe* (Arizona) *Daily News,* August 9, 1991, p. B-1.

[25] *Arizona Republic,* February 16, 1992, p. A-4.

[26] *San Francisco Examiner,* October 8, 1982, p. B-4.

[27] Louise Kingsbury and Lance Gurewell, "The Sin Fighters: Grappling with Gomorrah at the Grass Roots," *Utah Holiday* 12 (April 1983): 46.

[28] Lee Grant, "Shoot-Out in Texas," Calendar section, *Los Angeles Times,* December 25, 1983, p. 21.

[29] *Phoenix Gazette,* June 10, 1981, p. SE-6.

[30] Kingsbury and Gurwell, p. 52.

[31] Bettye I. Latimer, "Telegraphing Messages to Children About Minorities," *Reading Teacher* 30 (November 1976): 155.

[32] *Arizona English Bulletin* 11 (February 1969): 37.

[33] Diane Shugert, "Censorship in Connecticut,"

Connecticut English Journal 9 (Spring 1978): 59–61.

[34]*School Library Journal* 21 (December 1974): 34.

[35]*"The Upstairs Room:* Room for Controversy," *School Library Journal* 20 (December 1973): 67.

[36]*Wilson Library Bulletin* 53 (December 1978): 340.

[37]*Wilson Library Bulletin* 53 (February 1979): 421.

[38]*Publishers Weekly* 215 (April 30, 1979): 24.

[39]Ken Donelson, "Censorship in the 1970s: Some Ways to Handle It When It Comes (and It Will)," *English Journal* 63 (February 1974): 47–51.

[40]"Protest Groups Exert Strong Impact," *Publishers Weekly* 216 (October 29, 1979): 42–44.

[41]"Sixty-seven Targets of the Textbook Protesters," *Missouri English Bulletin* 38 (May 1980): 27–32.

[42]*Arizona Republic,* July 12, 1986, p. D-3.

[43]Kirsten Goldberg, "Censorship Decision Is Rapidly Coloring Other School Cases," *Education Week* 7 (February 17, 1988): 1.

[44]Lester Asheim, "Not Censorship but Selection," *Wilson Library Bulletin* 28 (September 1953): 67. See also Asheim's later article, "Selection and Censorship: A Reappraisal," *Wilson Library Bulletin* 58 (November 1983): 180–84. Julia Turnquist Bradley's "Censoring the School Library: Do Students Have the Right to Read?" *Connecticut Law Review* 10 (Spring 1978): 747–75, also draws a distinction between *selection* and *censorship*.

A STARTER BIBLIOGRAPHY ON CENSORSHIP

Bibliographical Sources

McCoy, Ralph E. *Freedom of the Press: An Annotated Bibliography*. Southern Illinois University Press, 1968.

————. *Freedom of the Press: A Bibliocyclopedia Ten-Year Supplement*. Southern Illinois University Press, 1979.

Newsletter on Intellectual Freedom. A bimonthly edited by Judith Krug with a sizable bibliography concluding each issue. Available from the American Library Association, 50 East Huron Street, Chicago, IL 60611.

Two Basic Policies

Burress, Lee and Edward B. Jenkinson. *The Students' Right to Read*, 3rd ed. National Council of Teachers of English (NCTE), 1982. NCTE's official policy statement.

Intellectual Freedom Manual, 3rd ed. American Library Association (ALA), 1989. ALA's official policy statement along with a mass of material.

Books

Ahrens, Nyla H. *Censorship and the Teaching of English: A Questionnaire Survey of a Selected Sample of Secondary Teachers of English*. Dissertation, Teachers College, Columbia University, 1965.

Bosmajian, Haig A., ed. *Censorship: Libraries and the Law*, Neal-Schuman, 1983. Censorship cases.

————. *The First Amendment in the Classroom*, 5 volumes. Neal-Schuman. No. 1, *The Freedom to Read*, 1987; No. 2, *Freedom of Religion*, 1987; No. 3, *Freedom of Expression*, 1988; No. 4, *Academic Freedom*, 1989; and No. 5, *The*

Freedom to Publish, 1989. Censorship cases.

Boyer, Paul S. *Purity in Print: The Vice-Society and Book Censorship in America.* Scribner's, 1968.

Burress, Lee and Edward B. Jenkinson. *The Students' Right to Know.* National Council of Teachers of English, 1982.

Censorship Litigation and the Schools. American Library Association, 1983.

Cline, Victor B., ed. *Where Do You Draw the Line?* Brigham Young University Press, 1974.

Davis, James E., ed. *Dealing with Censorship.* National Council of Teachers of English, 1979.

DelFattore, Joan. *What Johnny Shouldn't Read: Textbook Censorship in America.* Yale University Press, 1992. Court cases involving textbooks.

DeGrazia, Edward, ed. *Censorship Landmarks.* R. R. Bowker, 1969. Censorship cases.

Fiske, Marjorie. *Book Selection and Censorship: A Study of School and Public Libraries in California.* University of California Press, 1968.

Geller, Evelyn. *Forbidden Books in American Public Libraries, 1876–1939: A Study in Cultural Change.* Greenwood Press, 1984.

Haight, Anne Lyons. *Banned Books*, 4th ed. R. R. Bowker, 1978.

Hefley, James C. *Textbooks on Trial.* Victor Books, 1976. A defense of Mel and Norma Gabler's work.

Hentoff, Nat. *The First Freedom: The Tumultuous History of Free Speech in America.* Delacorte, 1980.

Jenkinson, Edward B. *Censors in the Classroom: The Mind Benders.* Southern Illinois University Press, 1979.

———. *The Schoolbook Protest Movement: 40 Questions and Answers.* Phi Delta Kappa Educational Foundation, 1986.

Lewis, Felice Flanery. *Literature, Obscenity and Law.* Southern Illinois University Press, 1976. The best book in the field.

Moffett, James. *Storm in the Mountains: A Case Study of Censorship, Conflict, and Consciousness.* Southern Illinois University Press, 1988.

Noble, William. *Bookbanning in America. Who Bans Books?—And Why?* Paul S. Eriksson, 1990.

Oboler, Eli, ed. *Censorship and Education.* H. W. Wilson, 1981.

O'Neil, Robert M. *Classrooms in the Crossfire: The Rights and Interests of Students, Parents, Teachers, Administrators, Librarians, and the Community.* Indiana University Press, 1981.

Reichman, Henry. *Censorship and Selection: Issues and Answers for Schools.* American Library Association, 1988.

Robbins, Jan C. *Student Press and the Hazelwood Decision.* Phi Delta Kappa Educational Foundation, 1988.

West, Mark, ed. *Trust Your Children: Voices against Censorship in Children's Literature.* Neal-Schuman, 1988. YA authors speak out about censorship.

Articles

"Are Libraries Fair: Pre-Selection Censorship in a Time of Resurgent Conservatism," *Newsletter on Intellectual Freedom* 31 (September 1982): 151, 181–88. Comments by Cal Thomas, conservative syndicated columnist, and Nat Hentoff, *Village Voice* columnist.

Asheim, Lester. "Not Censorship, but Selection," *Wilson Library Bulletin* 28 (September 1953): 63–67. The most widely quoted statement on the distinction between selection and censorship.

———. "Selection and Censorship: A Reappraisal," *Wilson Library Bulletin* 58 (November 1983): 180–84.

Avery, Kay Beth and Robert J. Simpson. "The Constitution and Student Publications: A

Comprehensive Approach." *Journal of Law and Education* 16 (Winter 1987): 1–61.

Baker, Mary Gordon. "A Teacher's Need to Know Versus the Student's Right to Privacy," *Journal of Law and Education* 16 (Winter 1987): 71–91.

Bernays, Anne. "I Don't Want to Read a Novel Passed by a Board of Good Taste," *Chronicle of Higher Education* 37 (March 6, 1991): B-1, B-3.

Booth, Wayne C. "Censorship and the Values of Fiction," *English Journal* 53 (March 1964): 155–64.

Bradley, Julia Turnquist. "Censoring the School Library: Do Students Have a Right to Read?" *Connecticut Law Review* 10 (Spring 1978): 747–75.

Briley, Dorothy. "Are the Editors Guilty of Precensorship?" *School Library Journal* 29 (October 1982): 114–15.

Broderick, Dorothy. "Censorship— Reevaluated." *School Library Journal* 18 (November 1971): 30–32.

———. "Serendipity at Work," *Show-Me Libraries* 35 (February 1984): 13–14.

Bryant, Gene. "The New Right and Intellectual Freedom." *Tennessee Librarian* 33 (Summer 1981): 19–24.

Burger, Robert H. "The Kanawha County Textbook Controversies: A Study of Communication and Power," *Library Quarterly* 48 (April 1982): 584–89.

Burress, Lee A. "How Censorship Affects the School," Wisconsin Council of Teachers of English, *Special Bulletin No. 8* (October 1963): 1–23.

Campbell, Colin. "Book Banning in America." *New York Times Book Review* December 20, 1981, pp. 1, 16–18.

"Censorship: An American Dilemma," *Publishers Weekly* 230 (July 11, 1986): 30–46.

Clark, Todd, ed. "The Question of Academic Freedom," *Social Education* 39 (April 1975): 202–52.

Click, J. William, and Lillian Lodge Kopenhaver. "Few Changes Since *Hazelwood,*" *School Press Review* 65 (Winter 1990): 12–27.

Donelson, Kenneth L. "Almost 13 Years of Book Protests . . . Now What?" *School Library Journal* 3 (March 1985): 93–98.

———. "Shoddy and Pernicious Books and Youthful Piety: Literary and Moral Censorship, Then and Now," *Library Quarterly* 51 (January 1981): 4–19.

———. "You Can't Have That Book in My Kid's School Library: Books Under Attack in the *Newsletter on Intellectual Freedom* 1952–1989," *High School Journal* 74 (October–November 1990): 1–7.

"Expurgation Practices of School Book Clubs," *Voice of Youth Advocates* 6 (Fall 1981): 97–101.

Faaborg, Karen Kramer. "High School Play Censorship: Are Students' First Amendment Rights Violated When Officials Cancel Theatrical Productions?" *Journal of Law and Education* 14 (October 1985): 575–94.

FitzGerald, Frances. "A Disagreement in Baileyville." *New Yorker* 59 (January 16, 1984): 47–90.

Glatthorn, Allan A. "Censorship and the Classroom Teacher," *English Journal* 66 (February 1977): 12–15.

Groves, Cy. "Book Censorship: Six Misunderstandings," *Alberta English '71* 11 (Fall 1971): 5–7.

Hentoff, Nat. "Any Writer Who Follows Anyone Else's Guidelines Ought to Be in Advertising," *School Library Journal* 24 (November 1977): 27–29.

———. "School Newspapers and the Supreme Court." *School Library Journal* 34 (March 1988): 114–16.

———. "When Nice People Burn Books." *Progressive* 47 (February 1983): 42–44.

Hillocks, George, Jr. "Books and Bombs: Ideological Conflicts and the School—A

Case Study of the Kanawha County Book Protest," *School Review* 86 (August 1978): 632–54.

Hirschoff, Mary-Michelle Upson. "Parents and the Public School Curriculum: Is There a Right to Have One's Child Excused from Objectionable Instruction?" *Southern California Law Review* 50 (1977): 871–959.

Janeczko, Paul. "How Students Can Help Educate the Censors," *Arizona English Bulletin* 17 (February 1975): 78–80.

Jenkinson, David. "Censorship Iceberg: Results of a Survey of Challenges in Public and School Libraries," *Canadian Library Journal* 43 (February 1986): 7–21.

Kamhi Michelle Marder. "Censorship vs. Selection—Choosing the Books Our Children Shall Read," *Educational Leadership* 39 (December 1981): 211–15.

Keresey, Gayle. "School Book Club Expurgation Practices," *Top of the News* 40 (Winter 1984): 131–38.

Kingsbury, Louise, and Lance Gurwell. "The Sin Fighters: Grappling with Gomorrah at the Grass Roots," *Utah Holiday* 12 (April 1983): 42–61.

Kopenhaver, Lillian Lodge, David L. Martinson, and Peter Habermann. "First Amendment Rights in South Florida: View of Advisors and Administrators in Light of *Hazelwood*," *School Press Review* 65 (Fall 1989): 11–17.

Macrorie, Ken. "A Letter to the Supreme Court about American Students' Writing." *Middlebury College Breadloaf News* 4 (Summer 1990): 2–13.

Martin, William. "The Guardians Who Slumbereth Not," *Texas Monthly* 10 (November 1982): 145–50.

Merrill, Martha. "Authors Fight Back: One Community's Experience," *Library Journal* 112 (September 1985): 55–56.

Moffett, James. "Hidden Impediments to Improving English Teaching," *Phi Delta Kappan* 67 (September 1985): 50–56.

Nelson, Jack L., and Anna S. Ochoa. "Academic Freedom, Censorship, and the Social Studies," *Social Education* 51 (October 1987): 424–27.

Niccolai, F.R. "Right to Read and School Library Censorship." *Journal of Law and Education* 10 (January 1981): 23–26.

O'Malley, William J. (S.J.). "How to Teach 'Dirty' Books in High School," *Media and Methods* 4 (November 1967): 6–11.

Orleans, Jeffrey H. "What Johnny Can't Read: 'First Amendment Rights' in the Classroom," *Journal of Law and Education* 10 (January 1981): 1–15.

Peck, Richard. "The Genteel Unshelving of a Book," *School Library Journal* 32 (May 1986): 37–39.

———. "The Great Library-Shelf Witch Hunt," *Booklist* 88 (January 1, 1992): 816–17.

Pico, Steven. "An Introduction to Censorship." *School Library Media Quarterly* 18 (Winter 1990): 84–87. Pico was the plaintiff in *Pico v. Island Trees*.

"Rationales for Commonly Challenged Taught Books," *Connecticut English Journal* 15 (Fall 1983): entire issue.

Reed, Michael. "What Johnny Can't Read: School Boards and the First Amendment," *University of Pittsburgh Law Review* 42 (Spring 1981): 653–57.

Rossi, John et al., eds. "The Growing Controversy Over Book Censorship," *Social Education* 46 (April 1982): 254–79.

Russo, Elaine M. "Prior Restraint and the High School 'Free Press': The Implications of *Hazelwood School District vs. Kuhlmeier*," *Journal of Law and Education* 18 (Winter 1989): 1–21.

Schrader, Alvin M. "A Study of Community Censorship Pressures on Canadian Public Libraries." *Canadian Library Journal* 49 (February 1992): 29–38.

Simmons, John. "Censorship and the YA

Book," *ALAN Review* 16 (Spring 1989): 14–19.

Small, Robert C., Jr. "Censorship and English: Some Things We Don't Think About Very Often (but Should)," *Focus* 3 (Fall 1976): 18–24.

Stielow, Frederick J. "Censorship in the Early Professionalization of American Libraries, 1876 to 1929," *Journal of Library History* 18 (Winter 1983): 37–54.

Strike, Kenneth A. "A Field Guide of Censors: Toward a Concept of Censorship in Public Schools," *Teachers College Record* 87 (Winter 1985): 239–58.

Sutton, Roger. "What Mean We, White Man?" *Voice of Youth Advocates* 15 (August 1992): 155–58.

Tollefson, Alan M. "Censored and Censured: Racine Unified School District vs. Wisconsin Library Association," *School Library Journal* 33 (March 1987): 108–12.

Valgardson, W.D. "Being a Target," *Canadian Library Journal* 48 (February 1991): 17–18, 20.

Watson, Jerry J., and Bill C. Snider. "Educating the Potential Self-censor," *School Media Quarterly* 9 (Summer 1981): 272–76.

West, Celeste. "The Secret Garden of Censorship: Ourselves." *Library Journal* 108 (September 1983): 1651–53.

Whaley, Elizabeth Gates. "What Happens When You Put the Manchild in the Promised Land? An Experiment with Censorship," *English Journal* 63 (May 1974): 61–65.

A BRIEF HISTORY OF ADOLESCENT LITERATURE

While we wouldn't argue with teachers and librarians that the best way to know adolescent literature is to read widely in contemporary books, a case can be made that professionals ought to know the history of their own fields for at least three reasons.

First, they ought to know not merely where they are but also how they got there, and too many teachers and librarians are unaware of their history. We were, for too many of us, miraculously born from nothing as a profession the day before yesterday. More than just being aware of a mixture of fascinating historical tidbits, knowing our common backgrounds gives us a sense of the past and a way of knowing why and how certain kinds of books have consistently proved popular and where books today came from.

Second, for anyone who cares about the mores and morals of our time reflected in adolescent books, there's a fascination in knowing how they came to be. And there is no better way to see what adults wanted young people to accept as good and noble at any point in history than to examine adolescent books of the time. The analysis may breed some cynicism as we detect the discrepancies between the lessons taught by a Felsen or an Alger or a Stratemeyer Syndicate author and the truth about the world of the time, but the lessons are none the less important, and not necessarily less sincere.

Third, and this may be difficult to believe for those who haven't dipped into books out of the past, many of the older books are surprisingly fun to read. We're not suggesting that many deserve to be reprinted and circulated among today's young adults, only that librarians and teachers may discover that books as different as Mabel Robinson's *Bright Island* (1937) or John Tunis' *Go, Team, Go!* (1954) or John Bennett's *Master Skylark* (1897) are fun, or that other books like Ralph Henry Barbour's *The Crimson Sweater* (1906) or Susan Coolidge's

What Katy Did (1872) or Mary Stolz's *Pray Love, Remember* (1954) are not without their charm.

For the convenience of readers, we've divided this chapter into roughly equal parts, 1800–1900, 1900-1940, and 1940–1966.

1800–1900: A CENTURY OF PURITY WITH A FEW PASSIONS

Prior to 1800, literature read by children and young adults alike was largely religious. Such books as John Bunyan's *The Pilgrim's Progress* (1678) reminded young people that they were merely small adults who soon must face the wrath of God. In the 1800s, the attitude of adults towards the young gradually changed. The country expanded, we moved inevitably toward an urban society, medical knowledge rapidly developed, and young people no longer began working so early in their lives. The literature that emerged for young adults remained pious and sober, but it hinted at the possibility of humanity's experiencing a satisfying life here on earth. Books reflected adult values and fashions, but of this world, not merely the next.

Alcott and Alger

Louisa May Alcott and Horatio Alger, Jr., were the first writers for young adults to gain national attention, but the similarity between the two ends almost as it begins. Alcott wrote of happy family life. Alger wrote about broken homes. Alcott's novels were sometimes harsh but always honest. Alger's novels were romantic fantasies. Alcott's novels are still read for good reason. Alger's novels are rarely read save by the historian or the specialist.

The second daughter of visionary Amos Bronson Alcott, Louisa May Alcott lived her youth near Concord and Boston with a practical mother and a father who was brilliant, generous, improvident, and impractical. The reigning young adult writer of the time was Oliver Optic (the pen name of William T. Adams), and Boston publishers Roberts Brothers were eager to find a story for young adults that would compete with Optic. Thomas Niles, Roberts' representative, suggested in September 1866 that Louisa May Alcott write a girls' book, and in May 1868 he gently reminded her that she had agreed to try.

She sent a manuscript to Niles, who thought parts of it dull, but other readers at the publishers office disagreed, and the first part of *Little Women: Meg, Jo, Beth, and Amy. The Story of Their Lives. A Girl's Book* was published September 30, 1868. With three illustrations and a frontispiece for $1.50 a copy, *Little Women* was favorably reviewed, and sales were good, here and in England. By early November 1868, Alcott had begun work on the second part, which was published on April 14, 1869.

Little Women has vitality and joy and real life devoid of the sentimentality common at the time, a wistful portrait of the life and world Alcott must have wished she could have lived. The Civil War background is subtle, expressing the loneliness and never-ending war far better than many adult war novels, for all their suffering, pain, and horror. Aimed at young adults, *Little Women* has maintained steady popularity with them and children. Adults reread it (sometimes repeatedly) to gain a sense of where they were when they were children.

Son of an unctuous Unitarian clergyman, Horatio Alger, Jr., graduated from Harvard at eighteen. Ordained a Unitarian minister in 1864, he served a Brewster, Massachusetts, church only to leave it two years later under a cloud of scandal and claims of sodomy, all hushed at the time. He moved to New York City and began writing full-time.

The same year, he sent *Ragged Dick; or, Street Life in New York* to Oliver Optic's magazine, *Student and Schoolmate,* a popular goody-goody magazine. Optic recognized salable pap when he spotted it, and he bought Alger's book for the January 1867 issue. Published in hardcover in 1867 or 1868, *Ragged Dick* was the first of many successes for Alger and his publishers, and it is still

The names of Horatio Alger, Jr., and Harry Castlemon were well known as authors of boys' books during the last half of the 19th century.

his most readable work, probably because it was the first from a mold that soon became predictably moldy.

The plot, as in most Alger books, consisted of semiconnected episodes illustrating a boy's first steps toward maturity, respectability, and affluence. Ragged Dick, a young bootblack, is grubby but not dirty, he smokes and gambles occasionally, but even the most casual reader recognizes his essential goodness. Through a series of increasingly difficult-to-believe chapters, Ragged Dick is transformed by the model of a young man and the trust of an older one into respectability. But where the sequence of events was hard to believe, Alger now makes events impossible to believe as he introduces the note that typified his later books. What pluck and hard work had brought to Dick is now cast aside as luck enters in—a little boy falls overboard a ferry, Dick saves the child, and a grateful father rewards Dick with new clothes and a better job.

Some readers inaccurately label Alger's books "rags to riches" stories, but the hero rarely achieves riches, though at the close of the book he is a rung or two higher on the ladder of success than he has any reason to deserve. "Rags to respectability" would be a more accurate statement about Alger's work.

Other Series Writers

The Boston publishing firm of Lee and Shepard established *the* format for young adult series, and to the distress of teachers, librarians, and parents, series books became the method of publishing for many young adult novels, though the format would be far more sophisticated when Edward Stratemeyer became the king of series books a few years later. If sales were any index, readers delighted in Lee and Shepard's 440 authors and 900 books published in 1887 alone.

Four series writers were especially popular. Under the pen name of Harry Castlemon, Charles Austin Fosdick wrote his first novel, *Frank the Young Naturalist* (1864), while in the navy. Castlemon's novels are close to unreadable today, but his books were popular well into the twentieth century. Oliver Optic, the pen name of William Taylor Adams, was a prolific writer of more than 100 books. *The Boat Club* (1885), his first book and the first of the six-book Boat Club series, ran through sixty editions.

Martha Finley (pen name of Martha Farquharson) wrote the amazingly popular Elsie Dinsmore series, twenty-eight volumes carrying Elsie from girlhood to grandmother. A favorite with young women who seemingly loved crying over every other page, Elsie is persistently and nauseatingly docile, pious, virtuous, sweet, humble, timid, ignorant, good, and lachrymose. Published in 1867 and running to an incredible number of editions after that, *Elsie Dinsmore* opened with the ever-virtuous and Christian Elsie awaiting the return of her cold father. His return proves again how unloving he is and how patient Elsie is. Elsie exhibits virtues no matter what happens to her, and much does, for she is no actor, but only a reactor. Susan Coolidge (pen name of Sarah Chauncey

Woolsey) wrote only a few books, but one series rivalled Alcott's books with many girls. *What Katy Did* (1872) featured tomboy Katy Carr, her widowed doctor father, her sisters and brothers, and an invalid aunt. While too much of the book is concerned with retribution for Katy's obstinacy, Katy is prankish and fun and essentially good.

The Two Most Popular Types of Novels: Domestic and Dime Novels

In 1855, Nathaniel Hawthorne wrote his publisher bitterly lamenting the state of American literature

> America is now wholly given over to a d—d mob of scribbling women, and I should have no chance of success while the public taste is occupied with their trash—and should be ashamed of myself if I did succeed. What is the mystery of these innumerable editions of *The Lamplighter,* and other books neither better nor worse?—worse they could not be, and better they need not be, when they sell by the 10,000?[1]

The trash was the domestic novel. Born out of belief that humanity was redeemable, the domestic novel preached morality; woman's submission to man; the value of cultural, social, and political conservatism; a religion of the heart and the Bible; and the glories of suffering.

Most domestic novels concerned a young girl, orphaned and placed in the home of a relative or some benefactor, who meets a darkly handsome young man with shadows from his past, a man not to be trusted but worth redeeming and converting. Domestic novels promised some adventure amidst many moral lessons. The heroines differed more in names than characteristics. Uniformly submissive to—yet distrustful of—their betters and men generally, they were self-sacrificing and self-denying beyond belief or common sense, and interested in the primacy of the family and marriage as the goal of all decent women. Domestic novels were products of the religious sentiment of the time, the espousal of traditional virtues, and the anxieties and frustrations of women trying to find a role in a changing society.

Writing under the pen name of Elizabeth Wetherell, Susan Warner wrote more then twenty novels and the first domestic novel, *The Wide, Wide World* (1850). As much as forty years later, the novel was said to be one of the four most widely read books in America, along with the Bible, *The Pilgrim's Progress,* and *Uncle Tom's Cabin.* An abridged edition was published in England in 1950 by the University of London Press, and the Feminist Press republished Warner's book in 1987.

The novel was rejected by several New York publishers. George Putnam was ready to return it but decided to ask his mother to read it. She did, she loved it, she urged her son to publish it, and the book was out in time for the

Christmas trade. Sales slowly picked up, and the first edition sold out in four months. Translations into French, German, Swedish, and Italian followed, and by 1852, *The Wide, Wide World* was in its fourteenth printing.

The author's life paralleled that of her heroine, Ellen Montgomery. Warner's father was pathetically and persistently broke, and while the fictional world is not quite so ugly, Ellen's mother dies early and her father is so consumed with family business that he asks Aunt Fortune Emerson to take over Ellen's life. Ellen, to her aunt's irritation, forms a firm friendship with the aunt's intended. Ellen's closest friend—the daughter of the local minister—is doomed to die soon, and succeeds in doing just that. In the midst of life, tears flow. And when Ellen and her friends are not crying they are cooking. Warner's novel taught submission, the dangers of self-righteousness, the virtues of a steadfast religion. Despite all the weeping, or maybe because of it, the book seemed to have been read by everyone of its time. E. Douglas Branch called it, "The greatest achievement of any of the lady novelists."[2]

Warner's popularity was exceeded only by Augusta Jane Evans Wilson for her *St. Elmo* (1867). Probably no other novel so literally touched the American landscape—13 towns were named, or renamed, St. Elmo, as were hotels, railroad coaches, steamboats, one kind of punch, and a brand of cigars. The popularity of Wilson's book may be gauged by a notice in a special edition of *St. Elmo* "limited to 100,000 copies." Only *Uncle Tom's Cabin* had greater sales, and Wilson was more than once called by her admirers, the American Brontë.

Ridiculously melodramatic as the plot of *St. Elmo* is, it was so beloved that men and women publicly testified that their lives had been permanently changed for the better by reading it. The plot concerns an orphaned girl befriended by a wealthy woman whose dissolute son is immediately enamored of the young woman, is rejected by her, and leaves home for several years, returns to plead for her love, is again rejected, and eventually becomes a minister to win the young woman's hand. They marry, another wicked man reformed by the power of a good woman.

If domestic novels took women by storm, dime novels performed almost the same miracle for men. They began when two brothers, Erastus and Irwin Beadle, republished Ann S. Stephens' *Malaeksa: The Indian Wife of the White Hunter* in June 1860. The story of a hunter and his Indian wife in the Revolutionary War days in upper New York state may be as melodramatic as any domestic novel, but its emphasis is more on thrills and chills than tears, and it apparently satisfied and intrigued male readers. Indeed, 65,000 copies of the 6- by 4-inch book of 128 pages sold in almost record time. The most popular of the early dime novels, also set in the Revolutionary period, appeared in October 1860. *Seth Jones: or, The Captives of the Frontier* sold 60,000 copies the first day; at least 500,000 copies were sold in the United States alone, and it was translated into ten languages.

For several years, dime novels cost ten cents, ran about 100 pages in a

These two half dime novels illustrate the promised action, the purple prose, and the erudite vocabulary of their day.

7- by 5-inch format, and were aimed at adults. Some early genius of publishing discovered that many readers were boys who could hardly afford the dime cost. Thereafter, the novels dropped to a nickel, though the genre continued to be called the *dime novel*. The most popular dime novels were set in the west— and the west of dime novels increasingly meant Colorado and points west— with wondrous he-men like Deadwood Dick and Diamond Dick. Dime novels developed other forms, like mysteries and even early forms of science fiction, but none were so popular or so typical as the westerns.

Writers of dime novels never pretended to be writing great literature, but they did write satisfying thrills and chills for the masses. The books were filled with stock characters. Early issues of the *Library Journal,* from 1876 onward for another thirty years, illustrate how many librarians hated dime novels for their immorality; but in truth dime novels were moral. The Beadles sincerely believed that their books should represent sound moral values, and what the librarians objected to in dime novels was nothing more than the unrealistic melodramatic plots and the stereotyped characters, more typical of the time than just the dime novel.

Bad Boy and Adventure Novels

Beginning with Thomas Bailey Aldrich's *The Story of a Bad Boy* in 1870, a new kind of literature developed around bad boys, imperfect but tough and realistic and anything but the good-little-boy figures in too many unrealistic books of the time. *The Story of a Bad Boy,* part-novel, part-autobiography, was an immediate success with readers and critics.

Mark Twain's *The Adventures of Tom Sawyer* (1876) and *Adventures of Huckleberry Finn* (1884) culminated and ended the genre. Aldrich and Twain told of real boys, sometimes moral or cruel or silly but always real. Other books once popular in the same strain, for example, George Wilbur Peck's *Peck's Bad Boy and His Pa* (1883), stressed silliness or prankishness to extremes.

A few adventure novels of the time deserve mention if for no other reason than that they remain readable even today. Noah Brooks's *The Boy Emigrants* (1876) is a romanticized but fascinating tale of boys traveling across the plains. Kirk Munroe is undeservedly ignored today, but his story of a young boy working in the mines, *Derrick Sterling* (1888), is great fun to read. John Bennett's *Master Skylark: A Story of Shakespeare's Time* (1898) is a witty and adventure-filled story, and John Meade Falkner's *Moonfleet* (1898) is almost as good a tale of piracy and derring-do as Robert Louis Stevenson's *Treasure Island* (1883).

The Development of the American Public Library

The development of the public library was as rocky and slow as it was inevitable. In 1731, Benjamin Franklin suggested that members of the Junto, a middle class social and literary club in Philadelphia, share their books with other members. That led to the founding of the Philadelphia Library Company, America's first subscription library. Other such libraries followed, most of them dedicated to moral purposes, as the constitution of the Salisbury, Connecticut, Social Library announced: "The promotion of Virtue, Education, and Learning, and . . . the discouragement of Vice and Immorality."[3]

In 1826, the governor of New York urged that school district libraries be established, in effect using school buildings for public libraries. Similar libraries were established in New England by the 1840s and in the midwest shortly thereafter. Eventually, mayors and governors saw the wisdom of levying state taxes to support public libraries in their own buildings, not the schools, and by 1863, there were 1,000 public libraries spread across the country.

The first major report on the developing movement came in an 1876 document from the U.S. Bureau of Education. Part I, "Public Libraries in the United States of America, Their History, Condition, and Management," contained 1,187 pages of reports and analyses on 3,649 public libraries with holdings of three hundred volumes or more.

That same year marks the beginning of the modern library movement. Melvil

Dewey, then assistant librarian in the Amherst College Library, was largely responsible for the October 4, 1876, conference of librarians which formed the American Library Association the third day of the meeting. The first issue of the *American Library Journal* appeared the same year (it was to become the *Library Journal* the following year), the world's first professional journal for librarians. While there had been an abortive meeting in 1853, the 1876 meeting promised continuity the earlier meeting had lacked.[4]

In 1884 Columbia College furthered the public library movement by establishing the first school of Library Economy (later to be called Library Science) under Melvil Dewey's leadership.

Excellent as these early public libraries were, they grew immeasurably under the impetus of Andrew Carnegie's philanthropy. A Scottish immigrant, Carnegie left millions of dollars for the creation of public libraries across America.

Fiction and Libraries

The growth of public libraries presented opportunities for pleasure and education of the masses, but arguments about the purposes of the public library arose almost as fast as the buildings. William Poole listed three common objections to the public library in the October 1876 *American Library Journal:* the normal dread of taxes; the more philosophical belief that government had no rights except to protect people and property—that is no right to tax anyone to build and stock a public library; and concern over the kinds of books libraries might buy and circulate.[5] In this last point, Poole touched upon a controversy that raged for years, that is, whether a public library is established for scholars or the pleasure of the masses. Poole believed that a library existed for the entire community or else there was no justification for a general tax.

Poole's words did not quiet critics who argued that the library's sole *raison d'etre* was educational. Waving the banner of American purity in his hands, W.M. Stevenson maintained:

> ▪   If the public library is not first and foremost an educational institution, it has no right to exist. If it exists for mere pleasure, and for a low order of entertainment at that, it is simply a socialistic institution.[6]

Many librarians of the time agreed. Probably, a few agree even today.

The problem lay almost entirely with fiction. Indeed, the second session of the 1876 American Library Association meeting was devoted to "Novel Reading," mostly but not exclusively about young people's reading. A librarian announced that his rules permitted no fiction in his library. His factory-patrons might ask for novels, but he recommended other books and was able to keep patrons without supplying novels. To laughter, he said that he had never read novels so he "could not say what their effect really was."[7]

Teachers worried almost as much as librarians. A principal of a large endowed academy was approvingly quoted by a librarian for having said:

> ▪ The voracious devouring of fiction commonly indulged in by patrons of the public library, especially the young, is extremely pernicious and mentally unwholesome.[8]

That attitude persisted for years and is occasionally heard even today among teachers and librarians.

▪ *1900–1940: FROM THE SAFETY OF ROMANCE TO THE BEGINNING OF REALISM*

During the first forty years of the twentieth century the western frontier disappeared, and the country changed from an agrarian society to an urban one. World War I brought the certainty that it would end all wars. The labor movement grew along with Ford's production lines of cars, cars, cars. President Hoover came along, then the Wall Street crash of 1929 and the Great Depression. By 1938, three million young people from sixteen through twenty-five were out of school and unemployed, and a quarter of a million boys were on the road. Nazi Germany rose in Eastern Europe, and in the United States Roosevelt introduced the "New Deal." When the end of the Depression seemed almost in sight, the New York World's Fair of 1939 became an optimistic metaphor for the coming of a newer, better, happier, and more secure life. But World War II lay just over the horizon, apparent to some, ignored by most.

Reading Interests vs. Reading Needs

In the high schools, which enrolled only a tiny fraction of the country's eligible students, teachers faced pressure from colleges to prepare the young for advanced study, which influenced many adults to be more intent on telling young people what to read than in finding out what they wanted to read. Recreational reading seemed vaguely time-wasting, if not downright wicked. Young people nevertheless found and read books, mainly fiction, for recreation. Popular choices were series books from Stratemeyer's Literary Syndicate, including Tom Swift, Nancy Drew, the Hardy Boys, Baseball Joe, and Ruth Fielding. Non-Stratemeyer series books were also popular, as were individual books written specifically for young adults, along with some classics and best-sellers selected by the Book-of-the-Month Club when it began in 1926 and the Literary Guild when it began a year later.

Arguments over what students choose to read have raged for years, and the end is unlikely to precede the millennium. In 1926 when Carleton Washburne and Mabel Vogel put together the lengthy *Winnetka Graded Book List,* they explained, "Books that were definitely trashy or unsuitable for children, even though widely read, have not been included in this list."[9] Apparently enough people were curious about the trashy or unsuitable to lead the authors to add two supplements.[10] *Elsie Dinsmore* was among the damned, and so were Edgar Rice Burroughs' *Tarzan of the Apes,* Eleanor Porter's *Pollyanna,* Zane Grey's westerns, books from the Ruth Fielding and Tom Swift series, Mark Twain's *Tom Sawyer Abroad,* and Arthur Conan Doyle's *The Hound of the Baskervilles.* However, *The Adventures of Sherlock Holmes* was considered worthy of inclusion.

Representative of the other side of the argument is this statement by English professor William Lyon Phelps:

> I do not believe the majority of these very school teachers and other cultivated mature readers began in early youth by reading great books exclusively; I think they read *Jack Harkaway, an Old Sleuth,* and the works of Oliver Optic and Horatio Alger. From these enchanters they learned a thing of tremendous importance—the delight of reading. Once a taste for reading is formed, it can be improved. But it is improbable that boys and girls who have never cared to read a good story will later enjoy stories by good artists.[11]

Girls' Books and Boys' Books

Up to the mid 1930s, teachers and librarians frequently commented that girls' books were inferior to boys' books. Franklin T. Baker wrote that with the obvious exception of Alcott, girls' books of 1908 were "painfully weak" and lacking "invention, action, humor."[12] Two years later Clara Whitehill Hunt agreed that many girls' books were empty, insipid, and mediocre.[13] In 1935, Julia Carter broke into a review of boys' nonfiction with what appeared to be an exasperated obiter dictum:

> Will someone please tell me why we expect the *boys* to know these things and still plan for the girls to be mid-Victorian, and consider them hoydens beyond reclaiming, when instead of shrieking and running like true daughters of Eve, they are interested in snakes and can light a fire with two matches?[14]

Such writers as Caroline Dale Snedeker, Cornelia Meigs, Jeanette Eaton, Mabel Robinson, and Elizabeth Forman Lewis responded to these kinds of criticism by writing enough good girls' books that in 1937 Alice M. Jordan wrote as if the difference in quality was a thing of the past:

There was a time not long ago when the boys had the lion's share in the yearly production of books intended for young people. So writers were urged to give us more stories in which girls could see themselves in recognizable relationship to the world of their own time, forgetting perhaps that human nature does not change and the vital things are universal. Yet, nonetheless, the girls had a real cause to plead and right valiantly the writers have responded.[15]

Critics believed then, as they continued to insist for years, that girls would read boys' books but boys would never read girls' books. At least part of the problem lay with stereotypes of boys' and girls' roles as expressed by two writers. Clara Vostrovsky, author of the first significant reading interest study, went back to ancient times for her stereotypes, suggesting that it was "probable" that the differences in reading interests between boys and girls lay "in the history of the race."[16] Psychologist G. Stanley Hall predicted reading interests of girls and boys on psychological differences:

Boys love adventure, girls sentiment. . . . Girls love to read stories about girls which boys eschew, girls, however, caring much more to read about boys than boys to read about girls. Books dealing with domestic life and with young children in them, girls have almost entirely to themselves. Boys, on the other hand, excel in love of humor, rollicking fun, abandon, rough horse-play, and tales of wild escapades. Girls are less averse to reading what boys like than boys are to reading what girls like. A book popular with boys would attract some girls, while one read by most girls would repel a boy in the middle teens. The reading interests of high-school girls are far more humanistic, cultural and general, and that of boys is more practical, vocational, and even special.[17]

The simple truth, perhaps too obvious and discomforting to be palatable to some parents, English teachers, and librarians, was that boys' books were generally far superior to girls' books. That had nothing to do with the sexual or psychological nature of boys or girls but rather with the way authors treated their audience. Many authors insisted on making their girls good and domestic and dull (if a heroine were allowed some freedom to roam outside the house, she soon regretted it or grew up, whichever came first), perhaps because they thought parents and librarians wanted books that way. Boys were allowed outside the house to find work and responsibilities, of course, but also to find adventure and excitement in their books.

The Changing English Classroom

By 1900 the library played a significant role in helping young adults find reading materials. Although many librarians reflected the traditional belief that classics should be the major reading of youth, other librarians helped young adults find a variety of materials they liked, not trash, but certainly popular books.

This would rarely have been true of English teachers, saddled as they were with responsibility for preparing young adults for college entrance exams. At first, these exams simply required some proof of writing proficiency, but in 1860 and 1870, Harvard began using Milton's *Comus* and Shakespeare's *Julius Caesar* as alternative books for the examination. Four years later, Harvard required a short composition based on a question about one of the following: Shakespeare's *The Tempest, Julius Caesar,* and *The Merchant of Venice,* Goldsmith's *The Vicar of Wakefield,* or Scott's *Ivanhoe* and *The Lay of the Last Minstrel.*

In 1894, the prestigious Committee of Ten on Secondary School Studies presented its report, and English became an accepted discipline in the schools, though not yet as respectable as Latin. Chaired by controversial Harvard president Charles W. Eliot, the committee was appointed by the National Education Association in July 1892 and met later that year to determine the nature, limits, and methods appropriate to many subject matters in secondary school. Samuel Thurber of the Boston Girls' High School was unable to promote his belief that a high school curriculum should consist almost entirely of elective courses, but as chairman of the English Conference, his report liberalized and dignified the study of English. Two important recommendations were that English be studied five hours a week for four years and that uniform college entrance examinations be established throughout the country.

The result was the publication of book lists, mainly classics, as the basis of entrance examinations. Plays and books such as Shakespeare's *Twelfth Night* and *As You Like It,* Milton's Books I and II from *Paradise Lost,* Scott's *The Abbot* and *Marmion* or Irving's *Bracebridge Hall* virtually became the English curriculum as teachers, inevitably concerned with their students' entry into college, increasingly adapted the English curriculum to fit the list.

The National Council of Teachers of English (NCTE) Begins

Out of the growing protest about college entrance exams, a group of English teachers attending a national Education Association Table formed a Committee on College Entrance Requirements in English to assess the problem through a national survey of English teachers. The committee uncovered hostility to colleges presumptuous enough to try to control the secondary English curriculum through the guise of entrance examinations. John M. Coulter, a professor at the University of Chicago, tried to sound that alarm to college professors, but without much success:

The high school exists primarily for its own sake; and secondarily as a preparatory school for college. This means that when the high school interest and the college interest comes into conflict, the college interest must yield.

It also means that the function of a preparatory school must be performed only in so far as it does not interfere with the more fundamental purpose of the high school itself.[18]

Some irate teachers recognized that the problem of college control would hardly be the last issue to face English teachers and formed the nucleus of the National Council of Teachers of English. The First Annual Meeting in Chicago on December 1 and 2, 1911, was largely devoted to resentment about actions of the National Conference on Uniform Entrance Requirements, particularly because that body had representatives from twelve colleges, two academies, and only two public high schools (principals, not English teachers). Wilbur W. Hatfield, then at Farragut High School in Chicago and soon to edit the *English Journal,* relayed instructions from the Illinois Association of Teachers of English that the new organization should compile a list of comparatively recent books suitable for home reading by students and that they should also recommend some books of the last ten years for study because the "present custom of using only old books in the classroom leaves the pupil with no acquaintance with the literature of the present day," from which students would choose their reading after graduation.[19]

James Fleming Hosic's 1917 report on the *Reorganization of English in Secondary Schools,* part of a larger report published under the aegis of the U.S. Bureau of Education, looked at books and teaching in ways that must have seemed muddle-headed or perverse to traditionalists. Looking at literature for the tenth, eleventh, and twelfth grades, Hosic chose works that pleased many, puzzled others, and alienated some. He explained that English teachers should lead students to read works in which they would, "find their own lives imaged in this larger life," and would gradually attain from the author's "clearer appreciation of human nature, a deeper and truer understanding. . . . It should be the aim of the English teacher to make [reading] an unfailing resource and joy in the lives of all."[20] Hosic's list included classics as well as modern works such as Helen Hunt Jackson's *Ramona* and Owen Wister's *The Virginian* for the tenth grade; Rudyard Kipling's *The Light That Failed* and Mary Johnston's *To Have and To Hold* for the eleventh grade; and John Synge's *Riders to the Sea* and Margaret Deland's *The Awakening of Helena Richie* for the twelfth grade. Teachers terrified by the contemporary reality reflected in these books— and perhaps equally terrified by the possibility of throwing out age-old lesson plans and tests on classics—had little to fear. In many schools, nothing changed. *Silas Marner, Julius Caesar, Idylls of the King, A Tale of Two Cities,* and *Lady of the Lake* remained the most widely studied books. Most books were taught at interminable length in what was known as the "intensive" method with four to six weeks—sometimes even more—of detailed examination, while horrified or bored students vowed never to read anything once they escaped high school. A 1927 study by Nancy Coryell offered proof that the "intensive" method produced no better test results and considerably more apathy toward literature than the "extensive" method in which students read assigned works faster.[21] But again, in many schools nothing changed.

Fortunately, the work of two college professors influenced more English teachers. A 1936 study by Lou LaBrant on the value of free reading at the Ohio State University Laboratory School revealed that students with easy access to different kinds of books and some guidance read more, enjoyed what they read, and moved upward in literary sophistication and taste.[22] Earlier, University of Minnesota professor Dora V. Smith discovered that English teachers knew next to nothing about books written for adolescents. She began the long process of correcting that situation by establishing the first course in adolescent literature. She argued that it was unfair to both young people and their teachers "to send out from our colleges and universities men and women trained alone in Chaucer and Milton and Browning to compete with Zane Grey, Robert W. Chambers, and Ethel M. Dell."[23]

The School Library

The development of the school library was almost as slow and convoluted as the development of the public library. In 1823, Brooklyn's Apprentice Library Association established a Youth Library where "Boys over twelve were allowed . . . as were girls whose access to the library were limited to one hour an afternoon, once a week." And in 1853, Milwaukee School Commissioner Increase A. Lapham provided for a library open Saturday afternoons and recommended that schools spend $10 a year for books. Rules for the Milwaukee library were clear and more than a bit reminiscent of rules in some school and public libraries until the 1940s:

> (1) Only children over ten years old, their parents, teachers, and school commissioner could withdraw books; (2) books might be withdrawn between 2:00 p.m. and sunset on Saturdays and kept for one week; (3) withdrawals were limited to one book per person; and (4) fines were to be assessed for overdue or damaged books.[24]

Writers in the early years of the *Library Journal* encouraged the cultivation of friendly relations between "co-educators."[25] The National Education Association formed a Committee on Relations of Public Libraries to Public Schools, and its 1899 report announced that "The teachers of a town should know the public library, what it contains, and what use the pupils can make of it. The librarian must know the school, its work, its needs, and what he can do to meet them."[26]

A persistent question was whether schools should depend on the public library or establish their own libraries. In 1896, Melvil Dewey recommended to the NEA that it form a library department (as it had for other subject disciplines) since the library was as much a part of the educational system as the classroom.

The previous year, a branch of the Cleveland, Ohio, Public Library was established within Central High School, and in 1899, a branch of the Newark, New Jersey, Public Library was placed in a local high school. In 1900, Mary Kingston became the first library school graduate appointed to a high school library (Erasmus High School in Brooklyn). In 1912, Mary E. Hall, librarian at Girls' High School in Brooklyn, argued the need for many more professionally trained librarians in high school libraries.

■ (1) The aims and ideals of the new high school mean we must stop pretending that high school is entirely college preparatory. "It realizes that for the great majority of pupils it must be a preparation for life." (2) Modern methods of teaching demand that a textbook is not enough. "The efficient teacher today uses books, magazines, daily papers, pictures, and lantern slides to supplement the textbook." (3) Reading guidance is easier for the school librarian than the public librarian. "The school librarian has the teacher always close at hand and can know the problems of these teachers in their work with pupils."[27]

In 1916, C. C. Certain, as head of an NEA committee, began standardizing high school libraries across the country. He discovered conditions so mixed, from deplorable (mostly) to good (rarely) that his committee set to work to establish minimum essentials for high schools of various sizes. Two reports from the U.S. Office of Education indicate the growth of high school libraries. A 1923 report found only 947 school libraries with more than 3,000 volumes, and these were mostly in the northeastern part of the country. Six years later, the 1929 report found 1,982 school libraries with holdings of more than 3,000 volumes, and the libraries were more equally spread over the country with New York having 211 such libraries and California having 191. However, the steady growth of high school libraries slowed drastically during the Depression.

Edward Stratemeyer's Literary Syndicate

Whatever disagreements librarians and English teachers may have had about books suitable for young adults, they bonded together, although ineffectively, to oppose the books produced by Edward Stratemeyer and his numerous writers. Stratemeyer founded the most successful industry ever built around adolescent reading. In 1866, he took time off from working for his stepbrother and wrote on brown wrapping paper an 18,000-word serial, *Victor Horton's Idea,* and mailed it to a Philadelphia weekly boys' magazine. A check for seventy-five dollars arrived shortly, and Stratemeyer's success story was underway. By 1893 Stratemeyer was editing *Good News,* Street and Smith's boys' weekly, building circulation to more than 200,000. This brought his name in front of the public, particularly young adults. Even more important, he came to know staff writers such as William T. Adams, Edward S. Ellis, and Horatio Alger, Jr. When

Optic and Alger died leaving some uncompleted manuscripts, Stratemeyer was asked to finish the last three Optic novels, and he completed (or possibly wrote from scratch) at least eleven and perhaps as many as eighteen Alger novels.

His first hardback book published under his own name was *Richard Dare's Venture; or, Striking Out for Himself* (1894), first in a series he titled Bound to Succeed. By the close of 1897, Stratemeyer had six series and sixteen hardcover books in print. A major breakthrough came in 1898. After Stratemeyer sent a manuscript about two boys on a battleship to Lothrop and Shepard, one of the most successful publishers of young adult fiction, Admiral Dewey won his great victory in Manila Bay. A Lothrop editor asked Stratemeyer to place the boys at the scene of Dewey's victory. He rewrote and returned the book, and *Under Dewey at Manila; or, The War Fortunes of a Castaway* hit the streets in time to capitalize on all the publicity. Not one to miss an opportunity, Stratemeyer used the same characters in his next books, all published from 1898 to 1901 under the series title Old Glory. Using the same characters in contemporary battles in the Orient, Stratemeyer created another series called Soldiers of Fortune, published from 1900 through 1906.

By this time Stratemeyer had turned to full-time writing and was being wooed by the major publishers, notably Grossett & Dunlap and Cupples & Leon. For a time he turned to stories of school life and sports, the Lakeport series (1904–1912), the Dave Porter series (1905–1919), and the most successful of his early series, the Rover Boys (thirty books published between 1899 and 1926). These books were so popular that somewhere between five or six million copies were sold worldwide, including translations into German and Czechoslovakian.

But Stratemeyer aspired to greater things. Between 1906 and 1910, he approached both his publishers, suggesting they reduce the price of his books to fifty cents. The publishers may have been shocked to find an author willing to sell his books for less money, but, as they soon realized, mass production of fifty-centers increased their revenue and Stratemeyer's royalties almost geometrically.

But an even greater breakthrough came at roughly the same time, when he evolved the idea of his Literary Syndicate. Stratemeyer was aware that he could create plots and series faster than he could possibly write them. He advertised for writers who needed money and sent them sketches of settings and characters along with a chapter-by-chapter outline of the plot. Writers had a few weeks to fill in the outlines, and when the copy arrived, Stratemeyer tightened the prose and checked for discrepancies with earlier volumes of the series. Then the manuscript was off to the publisher and checks went out to the authors, from fifty to 100 dollars, depending upon the writer and the importance of the series.

Attacks on Stratemeyer were soon in coming. Librarian Caroline M. Hewins criticized both Stratemeyer's book and the journals that praised his output:

Stratemeyer is an author who misuses "would" and "should," has the phraseology of a country newspaper, as when he calls a supper "an elegant affair" and a girl "a fashionable miss," and follows Oliver Optic closely in his plots and conversations.[28]

Most librarians supported Hewins, but their attacks hardly affected Stratemeyer's sales. A far more stinging and effective attack came in 1913 from the Boy Scouts of America. Chief executive James E. West was disturbed by the deluge of inferior books and urged the organization's Library Commission to establish a carefully selected and recommended library to protect young men. Not long afterward, Chief Scout Librarian Franklin K. Mathiews urged Grosset & Dunlap to make better books available in fifty-cent editions—to compete with Stratemeyer—and on November 1, 1913, the first list appeared in a Boy Scout publication, "Safety First Week."

But that was not enough to satisfy Mathiews, who in 1914 wrote his most famous article under the sensational title "Blowing Out the Boy's Brains,"[29] a loud and vituperative attack, sometimes accurate but often unfair. Mathiews' attack was mildly successful for the moment though how much harm it did to Stratemeyer's sales is open to question. Stratemeyer went on to sell more millions of books. When he died in 1930, his two daughters ran the syndicate, which still persists, presumably forever.

Series books were inevitably moral. Whatever parents, teachers, or librarians might have objected to about the unrealistic elements of the books or the poor literary quality, they would have agreed that the books were clearly on the side of good and right, if simplistically so. Series books—and many adult books as well—repeatedly underlined the same themes. Sports produced truly manly men. Foreigners were not to be trusted. School, education, and life should be taken seriously. The outdoor life was healthy, physically and psychologically. Good manners and courtesy were essential for moving ahead. Work in and of itself was a positive good and would advance one in life. Anyone could defeat adversity, any adversity, *if* that person had a good heart and soul. The good side (ours and God's) always won in war. Evil and good were clearly and easily distinguishable. And good always triumphed over evil (at least by the final chapter).

The Coming of the "Junior" or "Juvenile" Novel

Although for years countless books had been published and widely read by young adults, the term *junior* or *juvenile* was first applied to young adult literature during the early 1930s. Rose Wilder Lane's novel *Let the Hurricane Roar* had been marketed by Longmans, Green, and Company as an adult novel. A full-page blurb on the front cover of the February 11, 1933, *Publishers Weekly* bannered THE BOOK THAT MAKES YOU PROUD TO BE AN AMERICAN! and quoted an unnamed reader, presumably an adult, saying, "Honestly, it makes me ashamed of cussing about hard times and taxes." The tenor of the ad and ones to follow suggest an adult novel likely to be popular with young adults as well. It had been the same with the earlier serialization of the novel in the *Saturday Evening Post,* and also with the many favorable reviews. But, sometime later in 1933, Longmans, Green began to push the novel as the first of their series of "Junior Books," as they termed them.

That the company wanted to attract young adults to Lane's novel is not difficult to understand. Lane wrote of a threatening frontier world she had known in a compelling manner certain to win readers and admirers among young adults. *Let the Hurricane Roar* tells of newly married David and Molly and their life on the hard Dakota plains. David works as a railroad hand for a time, Molly waits for her baby to arrive, and both strive for independence and the security of owning their own fifty-acre homestead. When they realize that dream and the baby is born, all looks well, but David overextends his credit, grasshoppers destroy the wheat crop, and no nearby employment can be found. David heads east to find work and later breaks his leg, leaving Molly isolated on the Dakota plains for a winter. Neighbors flee the area, and Molly battles loneliness, blizzards, and wolves before David returns. In summary, *Let the Hurricane Roar* sounds melodramatic, but it is not. In a short, quiet, and loving work, Lane made readers care about two likable young adults living a tough life in a hostile environment. The book's popularity is attested to by its twenty-six printings between 1933 and 1958 and a recent TV production and reissue in paperback under the title *Young Pioneers.*

The development of publishing house divisions to handle books lying in limbo between children's and adults' books grew after *Let the Hurricane Roar,* although authors of the time were sometimes unaware of the "junior" or "juvenile" branches as was John T. Tunis when he tried to market *Iron Duke* in 1934 and 1935. After sending the manuscript to Harcourt, Tunis was invited into the president's office. Mr. Harcourt clearly did not want to talk about the book, but instead took the startled author directly to the head of the Juvenile Department. He explained that Harcourt wanted to publish the book as a juvenile, much to Tunis' bewilderment and dismay, since he had no idea what a "juvenile" book was. Thirty years later he still had no respect for the term which he called the "odious product of a merchandising age."[30]

Books That Young Adults Liked

Among the most popular books prior to World War I were those featuring a small child, usually a girl, who significantly changed people around her. At their best, they showed an intriguing youngster humanizing sterile or cold people. At their worst (and they often were), they featured a rapturously happy and miraculously even-dispositioned child who infected an entire household— perhaps a community—with her messianic drive to improve the world through cheer and gladness.

The type began promisingly with Kate Douglas Wiggin's *Rebecca of Sunnybrook Farm* (1904). Nothing Wiggin wrote surpassed *Rebecca,* which sold more than a million and a quarter copies between 1904 and 1975. Living in a small town during the 1870s, the optimistic heroine is handed over to two maiden aunts while her parents cope with a large family. She is educated despite her imperfections, high spirits, and rebelliousness, and at the close of the books seems cheerfully on her way upward to a better life.

Anne of Green Gables (1908) by Lucy Maud Montgomery was a worthy successor. As in Wiggin's book, Anne travels to an alien society. Here a childless couple who wants to adopt a boy gets Anne by mistake. Anne changes the couple for the better, but they also change her, and Anne's delightfully developed character goes far to remedy any defects in the book.

Wiggin and Montgomery generally managed to skirt the sea of sentimentalism, that fatal syrupy deep beloved by bad writers. Occasionally, Rebecca and Anne waded out dangerously far, but their common sense, their impulsiveness, and their ability to laugh at themselves brought them back to shore. After them came the disaster: authors and character so enamored of humanity, so convinced that all people were redeemable and so stickily and uncomplainingly sweet and dear that they drowned in goodness while many readers gagged. Eleanor Porter wrote the genre's magnum opus and destroyed it with *Pollyanna* (1913). *Pollyanna* is usually remembered as a children's book, but it began as a popular adult novel, eighth among best-sellers in 1913 and second in 1914.

Westerns provided a different type of popularity. The closing of the West heightened interest in an exciting, almost magical, era. A few writers, aiming specifically at young adults, knew the West so well that they became touchstones for authenticity in other writers. In *Pawnee Hero Stories and Folk Tales* (1898) and *By Cheyenne Campfires* (1926), George Bird Grinnell established an honest and generally unsentimentalized portrait of Indian life. Both he and Charles A. Eastman often appeared on reading interest studies as boys' favorites. Joseph Altsheler wrote more conventional adventure tales, including *The Last of the Chiefs* (1909) and *The Horsemen of the Plains* (1910). Far more sentimental but much more popular was Will James's *Smoky, The Cowhorse* (1926), originally published as an adult novel but soon read by thousands of young adults and twice filmed to appreciative audiences. The best-written and most sensitive western for young people was Laura Adams Armer's *Waterless Mountain* (1931). Unfortunately, enthusiastic librarians and teachers had little success in getting teenagers to read this slow-moving and mystical story about a young Navajo boy training to become a Medicine Priest.

The first great writer to focus on the West and its mystique of violence and danger mixed with open spaces and freedom was Owen Wister, whose *The Virginian: A Horseman of the Plains* (1902) provided a model of colloquial speech and romantic and melodramatic adventure for novelists to follow. The best of Zane Grey's books—certainly the most remembered and probably the epitome of the overly romanticized western—was *Riders of the Purple Sage* (1912), which was filled with such classic elements as the mysterious hero, the innocent heroine, evil villains, and the open land. Although Grey has been criticized by librarians and teachers—who seem in general to have read little or nothing of his work—anyone who wishes to know the western dream must read Grey.

With more young adults attending school and with the steadily rising popularity of sports—especially college football and professional baseball—more school-sports stories appeared. William Gilbert Patten, under the pen name of Burt L. Standish, was the first to introduce a regular, almost mythic, sports character recognized throughout America—Frank Merriwell. The Frank Merriwell books began as short stories later fashioned into hardback books. Three other writers who stand out for their realistic sports books include Owen Johnson with his *The Varmint* (1910), *The Tennessee Shad* (1911), and *Stover at Yale* (1911), which attacks snobbery, social clubs, fraternities, and anti-intellectualism. Ralph Henry Barbour wrote an incredible number of fine books, beginning with *The Half-Back* (1899). He invented the formula of a boy attending school and learning who and what he might become through sports. William Heyliger followed in a similar pattern with *Bartley: Freshman Pitcher* (1911) and his Lansing and St. Mary's series.

School stories for girls never had a similar number of readers, but a few deserve reading even today, including Laura Elizabeth Richard's *Peggy* (1899) and Marjorie Hill Allee's *Jane's Island* (1931) and *The Great Tradition* (1937). Best of them all is Mabel Louise Robinson's *Bright Island* (1937) about spunky Thankful Curtis who was raised on a small island off the coast of Maine and later attends school on the mainland.

1940–1966: FROM CERTAINTY TO UNCERTAINTY

During the 1940s, the United States moved from the Depression into a wartime and then a postwar economy. World War II caused us to move from hatred of Communism to a temporary brotherhood, followed by Yalta, the Iron Curtain, blacklisting, and Senator McCarthy. We went from "Li'l Abner" to "Pogo," and from Bob Hope to Mort Sahl. Problems of the time included school integration, racial unrest, civil rights, and riots in the streets. We were united about World War II, unsure about the Korean War, and divided about Vietnam. We went from violence to more violence and the assassinations of John Kennedy and Malcolm X. The twenty-five years between 1940 and 1965 revealed a country separated by gaps of all kinds: generational, racial, technological, cultural, and economic.

Educators were as divided as anyone else. Reading interest studies had become fixtures in educational journals, but there was little agreement about the results. In 1946, George W. Norvell wrote, "Our data shows clearly that much literary material being used in our schools is too mature, too subtle, too erudite to permit its enjoyment by the majority of secondary-school pupils.[31] Norvell offered the advice that teachers should give priority to the reading interests of young adults in assigning materials that students would enjoy and in letting students select a portion of their own materials based on their individual interests. He thought that three-fourths of the selections currently in use were uninteresting, especially to boys, and that "to increase reading skill, promote the reading habit, and produce a generation of book-lovers, there is no factor so powerful as interest."[32]

Other researchers supported Norvell's contention that young adults' choices of voluntary reading rarely overlapped books widely respected by more traditional English teachers. In 1947, Marie Rankin surveyed eight public libraries in Illinois, Ohio, and New York and discovered that Helen Boylston's *Sue Barton, Student Nurse* was the most consistently popular book.[33] Twelve years later, Stephen Dunning surveyed fourteen school and public libraries and concluded that the ten most popular books were Maureen Daly's *Seventeenth Summer*, Henry Gregor Felsen's *Hot Rod*, Betty Cavanna's *Going On Sixteen*, Rosaumnd Du Jardin's *Double Date*, Walter Farley's *Black Stallion*, Sally Benson's *Junior Miss*, Mary Stolz's *The Sea Gulls Woke Me*, Rosamund Du Jardin's *Wait for Marcy*, James Summers' *Prom Trouble*, and John Tunis' *All American*.[34]

Near the height of the outpouring of published studies, Jacob W. Getzels assessed the value of reading interest surveys and found most of them wanting in "precision of *definition*, rigor of *theory*, and depth of *analysis*."[35] He was, of course, right. Most reports were limited to a small sample from a few schools and little was done except to ask students what they liked to read. But the studies at least gave librarians and teachers insight into books young adults liked and brought hope that somewhere out there somebody was reading—a hope that for librarians and teachers needs constant rekindling.

In the mid-1950s, G. Robert Carlsen summarized the findings of published reading interest surveys as showing that young people select their reading first to reassure themselves about their normality and their status as human beings and then for role-playing.

> With the developing of their personality through adolescence, they come to a partially integrated picture of themselves as human beings. They want to test this picture of themselves in the many kinds of roles that it is possible for a human being to play and through testing to see what roles they may fit into and what roles are uncongenial.[36]

Carlsen's observations tied in with those of University of Chicago psychologist Robert J. Havighurst, who outlined the developmental tasks necessary for the healthy growth of individuals. (See Chapter One, p. 41, for the tasks that Havighurst thought crucial to adolescence.)

An outgrowth of the tying together of reading interests and psychology was an interest in bibliotherapy. In 1929, Dr. G. O. Ireland coined the term while writing about the use of books as part of his treatment for psychiatric patients.[37] By the late 1930s and early 1940s, articles about bibliotherapy became almost commonplace in education journals, and by the 1950s, the idea of using books to help readers come to terms with their psychological problems was firmly entrenched. Philosophically, it was justified by Aristotle's *Poetics* and the theory of emotional release through catharsis, a theory with little support except for unverifiable personal testimonials.

One clear and easy application of bibliotherapy was the free reading program (sometimes too clear and too easy for the inept psychologist/English teacher who, finding a new book in which the protagonist had acne, sought the acne-ridden kid in class saying, "You must read this—it's about you"). Lou LaBrant, popularizer of free reading, sounded both a recommendation and a warning when she wrote:

> Certainly I can make a much wiser selection of offerings if I understand the potential reader. . . . [but] This does not mean, as some have interpreted, that a young reader will enjoy only literature which answers his questions, tells him what is to be done. It is true, however, that young and old tend to choose literature, whether they seek solutions or escape, which offers characters or situations with which they can find a degree of identification.[38]

The Rise of Paperbacks

Young adult readers might assume paperbound books have always been with us. But despite the success of dime novels and libraries of paperbacks in the late 1800s, paperbacks as we know them entered the mass market in 1938 when Pocket Books offered Pearl Buck's *The Good Earth* as a sample volume in mail-order tests. In the spring of 1939, a staff artist created the first sketch of Gertrude the Kangaroo with a book in her paws and another in her pouch. It became Pocket Books' trademark. A few months later, the company issued ten titles in 10,000-copy editions, most of them remaining best-sellers for years. Avon began publishing in 1941, Penguin entered the United States market in 1942, and Bantam, New American Library, Ballantine, Dell, and Popular Library began publishing in 1943. By 1951, sales had reached 230 million paperbacks annually.

Phenomenal as the growth was, paperbacks were slow to appear in schools despite an incredible number of titles on appropriate subjects. Librarians complained that paperbacks did not belong in libraries because they were difficult to catalog and easy to steal. School officials maintained that the covers were lurid and the contents little more than pornography. As late as 1969, a New York City high school junior explained, "I'd rather be caught with Lady Chatterley in hardcover than *Hot Rod* in paperback. Hard covers get you one detention, but paperbacks get you two or three."[39]

Regardless of "official" attitudes, by the mid-1960s paperbacks had become a part of young adults' lives. They are easily available, comfortably sized, and inexpensive. And fortunately not all school personnel were resistant. The creation of Scholastic Book Clubs and widespread distribution of Reader's Choice

Catalogs helped paperbacks get accepted in schools and libraries. Eventually, Dell's Yearling and Mayflower books became the major suppliers of books written specifically for young adults.

Changes and Growth in Young Adult Literature

From 1941 to 1965, the quality of young adult literature rose steadily, if at times hesitatingly and uncertainly. Series books, so popular from 1900 to the 1940s, died out—except for Stratemeyer Syndicate stalwarts Nancy Drew, the Hardy Boys, and the new Tom Swift, Jr., series. They were killed by increasing reader sophistication combined with the wartime scarcity of paper. Many of the books that replaced the series celebrated those wonderful high school years by focusing on dating, parties, class rings, senior year, the popular crowd, and teen romances devoid of realities like sex. The books often sounded alike, and read alike, but they were unquestionably popular.

Plots were usually simple with only one or two characters being developed while others were stock figures or stereotypes. Books dealt almost exclusively with white, middle-class values and morality. The endings were almost uniformly happy and bright, and readers could be certain that neither their morality nor their intelligence would be challenged.

Taboos may never have been written down, but they were clear to readers and writers. Certain things were not to be mentioned—obscenity, profanity, suicide, sexuality, sensuality, homosexuality, protests against anything significant, social or racial injustice, or the ambivalent feelings of cruelty and compassion inherent in young adults and all people. Pregnancy, early marriage, drugs, smoking, alcohol, school drop-outs, divorce, and alienation could be introduced only by implication, and only as bad examples for thoughtful, decent young adults. Consequently, YA books were often innocuous and pervaded by a saccharine didacticism.

Despite these unwritten rules, some writers transcended the taboos and limitations and made it possible for Stanley B. Kegler and Stephen Dunning to write in 1960, "Books of acceptable quality have largely replaced poorly written and mediocre books."[40] Among the authors bringing about this welcome change were four who appealed largely to girls (Florence Crannell Means, Maureen Daly, Mary Stolz, and James Summers) and four who appealed largely to boys (Paul Annixter, Henry Gregor Felsen, Jack Bennett, and John Tunis).

Means was unusual in developing minority protagonists. *Tangled Waters* (1936) about a Navajo girl on an Arizona reservation, *Shuttered Windows* (1938) about a black girl in Minneapolis who goes to live with her grandmother in South Carolina, and *The Moved Outers* (1945) about Japanese Americans forced into a relocation camp during World War II are rich portraits of young people with problems not easily solved.

During this period, Daly published only *Seventeenth Summer* (1942), which was incredibly popular and is still occasionally read, although by younger girls than its original audience. Daly was a college student when she wrote her story about shy and innocent Angie Morrow and her love for Jack Duluth during the summer between high school and college.

Stolz, the most prolific of the four, is still publishing. She writes magic, quiet, introspective books that appeal mostly to readers more curious about character than incident. Things happen in her books, but the focus is always on people—always lovingly developed. Her two best works are *Pray Love, Remember* (1945) and *A Love, or a Season* (1964). The former is a remarkable story of Dody Jenks, a popular and lovely and cold young woman who likes neither her family nor herself. The latter is a story of quiet and uneventful love suddenly turning torrid before either girl or boy is old enough to handle sex.

Summers' two best books are *Ring Around His Finger* (1957), a tale of young marriage told from the boy's point of view, and *The Limit of Love* (1959), a fine delineation of a sexual affair between two children. The girl begins to grow up, while the boy remains a boy dedicated to proving that the girl is ruining his life. Although both books were more about boys than girls, the readers were usually girls, curious about a boy's point of view. Critics worried about Summers' honesty, presumably fearing that YA readers were too young to handle the emotional intricacies of sex.

Howard A. Sturzel, under the pen name of Paul Annixter, wrote widely, but best known is *Swiftwater* (1950), a story mixing animals, ecology, symbolism, and some stereotyped characters into a rousing tale that remains a better than respectable book.

Felsen wrote run-of-the-mill prose, but not one of his fans cared since Felsen wrote about the joys and dangers of cars. *Hot Rod* (1950), *Street Rod* (1953), and *Crash Club* (1958) were widely read, often by boys who had never before read a book all the way through. Felsen was didactic, but his fans read for the material on cars and ignored his lessons. His best book was unquestionably *Two and the Town* (1952) about a young couple forced to marry. Tired as the book seems now, it was a groundbreaker widely opposed by teachers and librarians.

Bennett, a South African journalist, wrote several remarkable books for young boys including *Jamie* (1963), *Mister Fisherman* (1965), and *The Hawk Alone* (1965), a brilliant book that never received its due. It's about an old white hunter who has hunted everything, done everything, and outlived his time.

Tunis, an amateur athlete and sports reporter, was the best of these writers. *Iron Duke* (1938), his first YA novel, is about a high school runner who wants to enter the big time at Harvard. What that book promised, *All American* (1942) delivered in its attack on prejudice aimed at both Jews and blacks and the win-at-all-costs attitude. *Yea! Wildcats* (1944) eloquently mixes basketball with incipient totalitarianism in a small Indiana town, while *Go, Team, Go* (1954) is a fine story about the pressures brought to bear on high school coaches. Tunis preached too often, and sometimes the preaching was simply too much for readers to bear, but he knew sports and he cared deeply about boys and about games. At his best, he is still worth reading, and several of his books have recently been reissued.

Other Books Popular with Young Adults

Young adult reading during these twenty-five years fell loosely into the six areas of careers; sports and cars; adventure and suspense; love, romance, passion, and sex; society's problems; and personal problems and initiation.

Emma Bugbee, a reporter for the *New York Tribune,* began a deluge of career books with her *Peggy Covers the News* (1936). She wrote five Peggy Foster books that conveyed the ambivalent excitement and boredom of getting and writing the news. In presenting the picture of a young woman breaking into a male-dominated profession, the books served a purpose for their time. By far the most popular career books were about nursing, led by Helen Boylston's seven Sue Barton books followed by Helen Wells's twenty Cherry Ames books. Wells also wrote thirteen books about flight stewardess Vicki Barr. Lucile Fargo's *Marion Martha* (1936) treated librarianship, while Christie Harris' *You Have to Draw the Line Somewhere* (1964) was about fashion designing.

Whatever freshness the vocational novel may once have had, by the late 1940s it was a formula and little more. Early in the book the insecure hero/heroine (more often the latter) suffers a mixture of major and minor setbacks, but, undaunted, wins the final battle and a place in the profession. The novel passes rapidly and lightly over the job's daily grind, focusing instead on the high

These books reflect the enthusiasm for women's liberation that followed (or contributed to?) women getting the right to vote. After World War II, this enthusiasm suffered a relapse, only to be revived during the 1970s when books advocating similar career aspirations again appeared.

points, the excitement and events that make any job potentially, if rarely, dramatic.

We have already mentioned John Tunis and Henry Gregor Felsen in the sports and car category. Another notable is basketball writer John F. Carson with his *Floorburns* (1957), *The Coach Nobody Liked* (1960), and *Hotshot* (1961). C. H. Frick (pen name of Constance Frick Irwin) used clever plot twists to make her sports novels different. *Five Against the Odds* (1955) features a basketball player stricken with polio while *The Comeback Guy* (1961) focuses on a too-popular, too-successful young man who gets his comeuppance and works his way back to self-respect through sports. Nonfiction was not yet as popular as it would become but Jim Piersall's *Fear Strikes Out* (1955) and Roy Campanella's *It's Good to Be Alive* (1959) attracted young readers.

Until the late 1940s interest in adventure or suspense was largely fulfilled by various kinds of war books including vocational nonfiction such as Carl Mann's *He's in the Signal Corps Now* (1943) and vocational novels such as Elizabeth Lansing's *Nancy Naylor, Flight Nurse* (1944). More popular were true stories about battles and survivors including Richard Tregaskis' *Guadalcanal Diary* (1943), Ernie Pyle's *Here Is Your War* (1943) and *Brave Men* (1944), Robert Trumbull's *The Raft* (1942), and Quentin Reynolds' *70,000 to One* (1946).

Perhaps as a reaction to the realities of war, the most popular series of books for both adults and young adults during the 1950s and 1960s centered about the fascinating James Bond, Agent 007. Ian Fleming caught the mood of the time with escapist excitement tinted with what appeared to be realities.

Also far removed from the grim realities of World War II were three historical novels which appealed to some young adults. Elizabeth Janet Gray's *Adam of the Road* (1942) revealed the color and music of the Middle Ages as young Adam Quartermain became a minstrel. Marchette Chute's *The Innocent Wayfaring* (1943) covers four days in June 1370 when Anne runs away from her convent school to join a band of strolling players, while in Chute's *The Wonderful Winter* (1954), young Sir Robert Wakefield, treated like a child at home, runs off to London to become an actor in Shakespeare's company.

Writers for young adults contributed several fine romances, including Margaret E. Bell's Alaskan story *Love Is Forever* (1954), Vivian Breck's superior study of young marriage in *Maggie* (1954), and Benedict and Nancy Freedman's *Mrs. Mike,* set in the northern Canadian wilderness. Elizabeth Goudge's *Green Dolphin Street* had everything working for it—a young handsome man in love with one of a pair of sisters. When he leaves and writes home his wishes, the wrong sister accepts. The true love, apparently overwhelmed by his unfaithfulness, becomes a nun. Passion, love, and adventure are all handled well by a first-rate writer. Kathleen Winsor was also one of a kind, though what one and what kind was widely debated. When her *Forever Amber* (1944) appeared, parents worried, censors paled, and young adults smiled as they ignored the fuss and read the book.

Young people, especially in the last year or two of high school, have often been receptive to books about human dilemmas. Between 1940 and 1966, society changed rapidly and drastically with deeply disturbing consequences. There was a growing awareness that the democracy described in our Constitution was more preached than practiced. As the censorship applied to John Steinbeck's *The Grapes of Wrath* (1939) and *Of Mice and Men* (1937) lessened—although it never entirely disappeared—young readers read of the plight of migrant workers and learned that all was not well. Many were deeply disturbed by Alan Paton's stories of racial struggles in South Africa, *Cry the Beloved Country* (1948) and *Too Late the Phalarope* (1953). Still more were touched by the sentiment and passion of Harper Lee's *To Kill a Mockingbird* (1960) set in the American South.

Richard Wright and his books *Native Son* (1940) and *Black Boy* (1945) served as bitter prototypes for much black literature. The greatest black novel, and one of the greatest novels of any kind in the last fifty years, is Ralph Ellison's *Invisible Man* (1952). Existential in tone, *Invisible Man* is at different times bawdy (the incest scenes remind readers of Faulkner without being derivative), moving, and frightening, but always stunning and breathtaking.

Three black nonfiction writers are still read. Claude Brown painted a stark picture of black ghetto life in *Manchild in the Promised Land* (1965), while Malcolm X and Alex Haley, the latter better known for *Roots,* painted a no more attractive picture in *The Autobiography of Malcolm X* (1965). The most enduring work may prove to be Eldridge Cleaver's *Soul on Ice* (1968), an impassioned plea by a black man in prison who wrote to save himself.

Writings about blacks aimed at young adults were not long in coming. Lorenz Graham presented realistic black characters in *South Town* (1958), which today seems dated, *North Town* (1965), and *Whose Town?* (1969). Nat Hentoff's first novel for young adults, *Jazz Country* (1965), is a superb story of a white boy trying to break into the black world of jazz. It's an unusual topic, and perhaps neither blacks nor whites are comfortable with the themes or the characters, which is sad because Hentoff is a remarkable, compassionate, and honest writer. Nonfiction writing for young adults about African Americans was mostly biographical. In the late 1940s and early 1950s, Shirley Graham wrote good biographies of Frederick Douglass, Benjamin Banneker, Phillis Wheatley, and Booker T. Washington. Elizabeth Yates won applause and the Newbery Award for *Amos Fortune, Free Man* (1950). However her account of a slave who gained freedom in 1801 and fought the rest of his life for freedom for other blacks has been attacked by some groups as paternalistic, a word overused by black critics who assume that any white writer is inherently incapable of writing about blacks.

Intrigued and concerned as many young adults were about social issues and dilemmas, something far more immediate constantly pressed in upon them—their own personal need to survive in an often unfriendly world. Anne Emery's books preached the status quo, especially acceptance of parental rules, but they also touched on personal concerns with her best book being *Married on Wednesday* (1957). Mina Lewiton's *The Divided Heart* (1947) is an early study of the effects of divorce on a young woman, while Lewiton's *A Cup of Courage* (1948) is an honest and groundbreaking account of alcoholism and its destruction of a family. Later, Zoa Sherburne proved more enduring with her portrait of alcohol's effects in *Jennifer* (1959), although her best and most lasting book is *Too Bad About the Haines Girl* (1967), a superb novel about pregnancy, honest and straightforward without being preachy.

But something far more significant happened during this period, which was that the *bildungsroman,* a novel about the initiation, maturation, and education of a young adult, grew in appeal. Most bildungsroman were originally published for adults but soon read by young adults. Dan Wickenden's *Walk Like a Mortal* (1940) and Betty Smith's *A Tree Grows in Brooklyn* (1943) were among the first. None of these books won the young adult favor or the adult opposition as did J. D. Salinger's *The Catcher in the Rye* (1951). It is still the most widely censored book in American schools and still hated by people who assume that a disliked word (*that* word) corrupts an entire book. Holden Caulfield may indeed be vulgar and cynical and capable of seeing only the phonies around him, but he is also loyal and loving to those he sees as good or innocent. For many young adults, it is the most honest and human story they know about someone they recognize (even in themselves)—a young man caught between childhood and maturity and unsure which way to go. Whether *Catcher* is a masterpiece like James Joyce's *Portrait of the Artist as a Young Man* depends on subjective judgment, but there is no question that Salinger's book captured— and continues to capture—the hearts and minds of countless young adults as no other book has.

Many teachers and librarians would have predicted just as long a life for John Knowles's *A Separate Peace* (1961) and William Golding's *Lord of the Flies* (1955), but fame and longevity are sometime things, and despite many articles in *English Journal* about the literary and pedagogical worth of both books, they seem to be in a state of decline.

The Rise of Criticism of Young Adult Literature

Today we take criticism of young adult literature as discussed in Chapter Ten for granted, but it developed slowly. In the 1940s, journals provided little information on, and less criticism of, young adult literature except for book lists, book reviews, and occasional references in articles on reading interests or improving young people's literary taste. The comments that did appear were often more appreciative than critical, but given the times and the attitude of many teachers and librarians, appreciation or even recognition may have been more important than criticism.

In 1951, Dwight L. Burton wrote the first criticism of young adult novels, injecting judgments along with appreciation as he commented on works by Dan Wickenden, Maureen Daly, Paul Annixter, Betty Cavanna, and Madeleine L'Engle. Concluding his article, Burton identified the qualities of the good young adult novel and prophesied its potential and future:

■   The good novel for the adolescent reader has attributes no different from any good novel. It must be technically masterful, and it must present a significant synthesis of human experience. Because of the nature of adolescence itself, the good novel for the adolescent should be full in true invention and imagination. It must free itself of Pollyannaism or the Tarkington-Henry Aldrich-Corliss Archer tradition and maintain a clear vision of the adolescent as a person of complexity, individuality, and dignity. The novel for the adolescent presents a ready field for the mature artist.[41]

In 1955, Richard S. Alm provided greater critical coverage of the young adult novel.[42] He agreed with critics that many writers presented a "sugar-puff story of what adolescents should do and should believe rather than what adolescents may or will do and believe." He cited specific authors and titles he found good and painted their strengths and weaknesses in clear strokes. He concluded by offering teachers some questions that might be useful in analyzing the merits of young adult novels.

A year later, Emma L. Patterson began her fine study of the origin of young adult novels showing that "The junior novel has become an established institution,"[43] Her command of history, her knowledge of trends in young adult novels, her awareness of shortcomings and virtues of the novels, and her understanding of the place of young adult novels in schools and libraries made her article essential reading for librarians and teachers.

Despite the leadership of Burton, Alm, and Patterson, helpful criticism of young adult literature was slow in arriving, but biting criticism was soon forthcoming. Only a few months after Patterson's article, Frank G. Jennings' "Literature for Adolescents—Pap or Protein?"[44] appeared. The title was ambiguous, but if any reader had doubts about where Jennings stood, the doubt was removed with the first sentence, "The stuff of adolescent literature, for the most part, is mealy-mouthed, gutless, and pointless." The remainder of the article added little to that point, and although Jennings overstated his case, Burton, Alm, Patterson, and other sensible supporters would have agreed that much young adult literature, like much adult literature, was second-rate or worse. Jennings' article was not the first broadside attack, and it certainly would not be the last.[45]

Much of the literature written for young adults from 1940 through 1966 goes largely and legitimately ignored today. But some writers are still read, and more important than mere longevity is the effect that these authors had on books appearing after 1966. Readers before then could not have anticipated S. E. Hinton's *The Outsiders* or Paul Zindel's *The Pigman,* which were to appear in only a year or two, much less Isabelle Holland's *The Man Without a Face,* Norma Klein's *Mom, The Wolfman and Me,* Rosa Guy's *Ruby,* or Robert Cormier's *The Chocolate War.* These iconoclastic, taboo-breaking novels and others of today would not have been possible had it not been for earlier novels that broke ground and prepared readers, teachers, librarians, and even some parents, for contemporary novels.

◼ NOTES

[1] Caroline Ticknor, *Hawthorne and His Publisher* (Houghton Mifflin, 1913), p. 141.

[2] E. Douglas Branch, *The Sentimental Years, 1836–1860* (Appleton, 1934), p. 131.

[3] Jesse H. Shera, *Foundations of the Public Library: The Origins of the Public Library Movement in New England, 1629–1885* (The University of Chicago Press, 1949), p. 238.

[4] A brief summary of the 1853 and 1876 library conventions can be found in Sister Gabriella Margeath, "Library Conventions of 1853, 1876, and 1877," *Journal of Library History* 8 (April 1973): 52–69.

[5] William F. Poole, "Some Popular Objections to Public Libraries," *American Library Journal* 1 (October 1876): 48–49.

[6] W. M. Stevenson, "Weeding Out Fiction in the Carnegie Free Library of Allegheny, Pa.," *Library Journal* 22 (March 1897): 135.

[7] "Novel Reading," *American Library Journal* 1 (October 1876): 98.

[8] "Monthly Reports from Public Librarians upon the Reading of Minors: A Suggestion," *Library Journal* 24 (August 1899): 479.

[9] Carleton Washburne and Mabel Vogel, *Winnetka Graded Book List* (American Library Association, 1926), p. 5.

[10] Carleton Washburne and Mabel Vogel, "Supplement to the Winnetka Graded Book List," *Elementary English Review* 4 (February 1927): 47–52; and 4 (March 1927): 66–73.

[11] William Lyon Phelps, "The Virtues of the Second-Rate," *English Journal* 16 (January 1927): 13–14.

[12] Franklin T. Baker, *A Bibliography of Children's Reading* (Teachers College, Columbia University, 1908), pp. 6–7.

[13] Clara Whitehill Hunt, "Good and Bad Taste in Girls' Reading," *Ladies Home Journal* 27 (April 1910): 52.

[14] Julia Carter, "Let's Talk About Boys and Books," *Wilson Bulletin for Librarians* 9 (April 1935): 418.

[15] Alice M. Jordan, "A Gallery of Girls," *Horn Book Magazine* 13 (September 1937): 276.

[16] Vostrovsky, p. 535.

[17] G. Stanley Hall, "Children's Reading: As a Factor in Their Education," *Library Journal* 33 (April 1908): 124–25.

[18] J. M. Coulter, "What the University Expects of the Secondary School," *School Review* 17 (February 1909): 73.

[19] Wilbur W. Hatfield, "Modern Literature for High School Use," *English Journal* 1 (January 1912): 52.

[20] *Reorganization of English in Secondary Schools,* Department of the Interior, Bureau of Education, Bulletin 1917, No. 2. (Government Printing Office, 1917), p. 63.

[21] Nancy Gillmore Coryell, *An Evaluation of Extensive and Intensive Teaching of Literature: A Year's Experiment in the Eleventh Grade,* Teachers College, Columbia University, Contributions to Education, No. 275 (Teachers College, Columbia University, 1927).

[22] Lou LaBrant, *An Evaluation of the Free Reading Program in Grades Ten, Eleven, and Twelve for the Class of 1935.* The Ohio State University School, Contributions to Education No. 2 (Ohio State University, 1936). See also Lou LaBrant, "The Content of a Free Reading Program," *Educational Research Bulletin* 16 (February 17, 1937): 29–34.

[23] Dora V. Smith, "American Youth and English," *English Journal* 26 (February 1937): 111.

[24] Graham P. Hawks, "A Nineteenth-Century School Library: Early Years in Milwaukee,"

Journal of Library History 12 (Fall 1977): 361.

[25]S. Swett Green, "Libraries and School," *Library Journal* 16 (December 1891): 22. Other representative articles concerned with the relationship include Mellen Chamberlain, "Public Libraries and Public School," *Library Journal* 5 (November–December 1880): 299–302; W. E. Foster, "The School and the Library: Their Mutual Relations," *Library Journal* 4 (September–October 1879): 319–41; and Mrs. J. H. Resor, "The Boy and the Book, or The Public Library a Necessity," *Public Libraries* 2 (June 1897): 282–85.

[26]"The Report of the Committee on Relations of Public Libraries to Public Schools," *NEA Journal of Proceedings and Addresses of the 38th Annual Meeting* (The University of Chicago, Press, 1899), p. 455.

[27]Mary E. Hall, "The Possibilities of the High School Library," *ALA Bulletin* 6 (July 1912): 261–63.

[28]Caroline M. Hewins, "Book Reviews, Book Lists, and Articles on Children's Reading: Are They of Practical Value to the Children's Librarians?" *Library Journal* 26 (August 1901): 58. Attacks on series books, especially Stratemeyer's books, persisted thereafter in library literature. Mary E. S. Root prepared a list of series books not to be circulated by public librarians, "Not to Be Circulated," *Wilson Bulletin for Librarians* 3 (January 1929): 446, including books by Alger, Finley, Castlemon, Ellis, Optic, and others, the others being heavily Stratemeyer. Two months later, Ernest F. Ayers responded, "Not to Be Circulated?" *Wilson Bulletin for Librarians* 3 (March 1929): 528–29, objecting to the cavalier treatment accorded old favorites and sarcastically adding, "Why Worry about censorship so long as we have librarians?" Attacks continue today. Some librarians and English teachers to the contrary, the Syndicate clearly is winning, and students seem to be pleased.

[29]Franklin K. Mathiews, "Blowing Out the Boy's Brains," *Outlook* 108 (November 18, 1914): 653.

[30]John Tunis, "What Is a Juvenile Book?" *Horn Book Magazine* 44 (June 1968): 307.

[31]George W. Norvell, "Some Results of a Twelve-Year Study of Children's Reading Interests," *English Journal* 35 (December 1946): 532.

[32]Norvell, "Some Results . . . ," p. 536.

[33]Marie Rankin, *Children's Interests in Library Books of Fiction,* Teachers College, Columbia University, Contributions to Education, No. 906 (Teachers College, Columbia University, 1947).

[34]Stephen Dunning, "The Most Popular Junior Novels," *Junior Libraries* 5 (December 15, 1959): 7–9.

[35]Jacob W. Getzels, "The Nature of Reading Interests: Psychological Aspects" in *Developing Permanent Interests in Reading,* ed. Helen M. Robinson, Supplementary Education Monographs, No. 84, December 1956 (University of Chicago Press, 1956), p. 5.

[36]Robert Carlsen, "Behind Reading Interests," *English Journal* 43 (January 1954): 7–10.

[37]G. O. Ireland, "Bibliotherapy: The Use of Books as a Form of Treatment in a Neuropsychiatric Hospital," *Library Journal* 54 (December 1, 1929): 972–74.

[38]Lou LaBrant, "Diversifying the Matter," *English Journal* 40 (March 1951): 135.

[39]S. Alan Cohen, "Paperbacks in the Classroom," *Journal of Reading* 12 (January 1969): 295.

[40]Stanley B. Kegler and Stephen Dunning, "Junior Book Roundup—Literature for the Adolescent, 1960," *English Journal* 50 (May 1961): 369.

[41]Dwight L. Burton, "The Novel for the Adolescent," *English Journal* 40 (September 1951): 363–69.

[42]Richard S. Alm, "The Glitter and the Gold," *English Journal* 44 (September 1955): 315.

[43]Emma L. Patterson, "The Junior Novels and How They Grew," *English Journal* 45 (October 1956): 381.

[44]*English Journal* 45 (December 1956): 226–31.

[45]See, for example, Alice Krahn, "Case Against the Junior Novel," *Top of the News* 17 (May 1961): 19–22; Esther Millett, "We Don't Even Call Those Books!" *Top of the News* 20 (October 1963): 45–47; and Harvey R. Granite, "The Uses and Abuses of Junior Literature," *Clearing House* 42 (February 1968): 337–40.

■ OTHER TITLES MENTIONED IN THE TEXT OF CHAPTER THIRTEEN

Alcott, Louisa May. *Little Women: Meg, Jo, Beth, and Amy. The Story of Their Lives. A Girl's Book.* 1968.

———. *Little Women: Meg, Jo, Beth, and Amy. Part Second.* 1869.

Aldrich, Thomas Bailey. *The Story of a Bad Boy.* 1870.

Alger, Horatio. *Ragged Dick: or Street Life in New York.* 1867.

Allee, Marjorie Hill. *The Great Tradition.* 1937.

———. *Jane's Island.* 1931.

Altsheler, Joseph. *The Horsemen of the Plains.* 1910.

———. *The Last of the Chiefs.* 1909.

Annixter, Paul (real name Howard A. Sturzel). *Swiftwater.* A. A. Wyn, 1950.

Appleton, Victor (Stratemeyer Syndicate pseudonym). Tom Swift series, 1910–1935.

Armer, Laura. *Waterless Mountain,* 1931.

Barbour, Ralph Henry. *The Crimson Sweater.* 1906.

———. *The Half-Back.* 1899.

Bell, Margaret Elizabeth. *Love Is Forever.* Morrow, 1954.

Bennett, Jack. *The Hawk Alone.* Little, Brown, 1965.

———. *Jamie.* Little, Brown, 1963.

———. *Mister Fisherman.* Little, Brown, 1963.

Bennett, John. *Master Skylark: A Story of Shakespeare's Time.* 1897.

Benson, Sally. *Junior Miss.* Doubleday, 1947.

Boylston, Helen Dore. *Sue Barton, Student Nurse.* Little, Brown, 1936.

Breck, Vivian. *Maggie.* Doubleday, 1954.

Brooks, Noah. *The Boy Emigrants.* 1876.

Brown, Claude. *Manchild in the Promised Land.* Macmillan, 1965.

Buck, Pearl. *The Good Earth.* John Day, 1931.

Bugbee, Emma. *Peggy Covers the News.* Dodd, Mead, 1936.

Burroughs, Edgar Rice. *Tarzan of the Apes.* 1914.

Campanella, Roy. *It's Good to Be Alive.* Little, Brown, 1959.

Carson, John F. *The Coach Nobody Liked.* Farrar, Straus & Giroux, 1960.

———. *Floorburns.* Farrar, Straus & Giroux, 1957.

———. *Hotshot.* Farrar, Straus & Giroux, 1961.

Castlemon, Harry (real name, Charles Austin Fosdick). *Frank the Young Naturalist.* 1864.

Cavanna, Betty. *Going on Sixteen.* Ryerson, 1946.

Chute, Marchette. *The Innocent Wayfaring.* Scribner, 1943.

———. *The Wonderful Winter.* Dutton, 1954.

Cleaver, Eldridge. *Soul on Ice.* McGraw-Hill, 1968.

Coolidge, Susan (real name, Sarah Chauncey Woolsey). *What Katy Did.* 1872.

Cormier, Robert. *The Chocolate War.* Pantheon, 1974.

Daly, Maureen. *Seventeenth Summer.* Dodd, Mead, 1942.

Deland, Margaret. *The Awakening of Helena Richie*. 1906.

Doyle, Arthur Conan. *The Adventures of Sherlock Holmes*. 1891.

———. *The Hound of the Baskervilles*. 1902.

DuJardin, Rosamund. *Double Date*. Longman, 1953.

———. *Wait for Marcy*. Longman, 1950.

Ellison, Ralph. *Invisible Man*. Random House, 1952.

Emery, Anne. *Married on Wednesday*. Ryerson, 1957.

Falkner, John Meade. *Moonfleet*. 1898.

Fargo, Lucile Foster. *Marian Martha*. Dodd, Mead, 1936.

Farley, Walter. *Black Stallion*. Random House, 1944.

Felsen, Henry Gregor. *Crash Club*. Random House, 1958.

———. *Hot Rod*. Dutton, 1950.

———. *Street Rod*. Random House, 1953.

———. *Two and the Town*. Scribner, 1952.

Finley, Martha (real name, Martha Farquharson). *Elsie Dinsmore*. 1867. The series ran from 1867–1905.

Freedman, Benedict and Nancy. *Mrs. Mike*. Coward, McCann, & Geoghegan, 1947.

Frick, Constance H. *The Comeback Guy*. Harcourt Brace Jovanovich, 1961.

———. *Five Against the Odds*. Harcourt Brace Jovanovich, 1955.

Golding, William. *Lord of the Flies*. Coward, McCann, 1955.

Goudge, Elizabeth. *Green Dolphin Street*. Coward, McCann, 1944.

Graham, Lorenz. *North Town*. Crowell, 1965.

———. *South Town*. Follett, 1958.

———. *Whose Town?* Crowell, 1969.

Gray, Elizabeth. *Adam of the Road*. Viking, 1942.

Grey, Zane. *Riders of the Purple Sage*. 1912.

Grinnell, George Bird. *By Cheyenne Campfires*. 1926.

———. *Pawnee Hero Stories and Folk Tales*. 1899.

Guy, Rosa. *Ruby*. Viking, 1976.

Haley, Alex. *Roots*. Doubleday, 1976.

Harris, Christie. *You Have to Draw the Line Somewhere*. Atheneum, 1964.

Hentoff, Nat. *Jazz Country*. HarperCollins, 1965.

Heyliger, William. *Bartley: Freshman Pitcher*. 1911.

Hinton, S. E. *The Outsiders*. Viking, 1967.

Holland, Isabelle. *The Man Without a Face*. Lippincott, 1972.

Jackson, Helen Hunt. *Ramona*. 1884.

James, Will. *Smoky, the Cowhorse*. 1926.

Johnson, Owen. *Stover at Yale*. 1911.

———. *The Tennessee Shad*. 1911.

———. *The Varmint*. 1910.

Johnston, Mary. *To Have and to Hold*. 1900.

Joyce, James. *Portrait of the Artist as a Young Man*. 1914.

Klein, Norma. *Mom, the Wolfman and Me*. Random House, 1973.

Knowles, John. *A Separate Peace*. Macmillan, 1960.

Lane, Rose Wilder. *Let the Hurricane Roar*. 1933.

———. *The Young Pioneers* (reissue of *Let the Hurricane Roar*). 1976.

Lansing, Elizabeth. *Nancy Naylor, Flight Nurse*. Crowell, 1944.

Lee, Harper. *To Kill a Mockingbird*. Lippincott, 1960.

Lewiton, Mina. *A Cup of Courage*. McKay, 1948.

———. *The Divided Heart*. McKay, 1947.

Malcolm X and Alex Haley. *The Autobiography of Malcolm X*. Grove, 1965.

Mann, Carl. *He's in the Signal Corps Now*. McBride, 1943.

Means, Florence Crannell. *The Moved-Outers*. Houghton Mifflin, 1945.

———. *Shuttered Windows*. Houghton Mifflin, 1938.

———. *Tangled Waters: A Navajo Story*. Houghton Mifflin, 1936.

Montgomery, Lucy Maud. *Anne of Green Gables*. 1908.

Munroe, Kirk. *Derrick Sterling*. 1888.

Optic, Oliver (real name, William Taylor Adams). *The Boat Club*. 1855.

Paton, Alan. *Cry, the Beloved Country*. Scribner, 1948.

_____. *Too Late the Phalarope*. Scribner, 1953.

Peck, George Wilbur. *Peck's Bad Boy and His Pa*. 1883.

Piersall, James Anthony and Albert Hirschberg. *Fear Strikes Out*, Little, Brown, 1955.

Porter, Eleanor. *Pollyanna*. 1913.

Pyle, Ernie. *Brave Men*. Holt, 1944.

_____. *Here Is Your War*. Holt, 1943.

Reynolds, Quentin. *70,000 to One*. Random House, 1946.

Richards, Laura Elizabeth. *Peggy*. 1899.

Robinson, Mabel Louise. *Bright Island*. 1937.

Salinger, J. D. *The Catcher in the Rye*. Little, Brown, 1951.

Sherburne, Zoa. *Jennifer*. Morrow, 1959.

_____. *Too Bad about the Haines Girl*. Morrow, 1967.

Smith, Betty. *A Tree Grows in Brooklyn*. HarperCollins, 1943.

Standish, Burt L. (real name, William Gilbert Patten). Frank Merriwell series, 1901–1911.

Steinbeck, John. *The Grapes of Wrath*. Viking, 1939.

_____. *Of Mice and Men*. Viking, 1937.

Stevenson, Robert Louis. *Treasure Island*. 1883.

Stolz, Mary. *A Love, or a Season*. HarperCollins, 1953.

_____. *Pray Love, Remember*. HarperCollins, 1954.

_____. *The Seagulls Woke Me*. HarperCollins, 1951.

For information on the availability of paperback editions of these titles, please consult the most recent edition of *Paperbound Books in Print*, published annually by R. R. Bowker Company.

Stratemeyer, Edward. Dave Porter series. 1905–1919.

_____. Lakeport series. 1904–1912.

_____. Old Glory series. 1898–1901.

_____. *Richard Dare's Venture; or, Striking Out for Himself*. 1894.

_____. Rover Boys series. 1899–1926.

_____. Soldiers of Fortune series, 1900–1906.

_____. *Under Dewey at Manila; or, The War Fortunes of a Castaway*. 1898.

_____. *Victor Horton's Idea*. 1886.

Summers, James. *The Limit of Love*. Ryerson, 1959.

_____. *Prom Trouble*. Ryerson, 1954.

_____. *Ring Around Her Finger*. Westminster, 1957.

Tregaskis, Richard. *Guadalcanal Diary*. Random House, 1943.

Trumbull, Robert. *The Raft*. Holt, 1942.

Tunis, John. *All-American*. Harcourt, 1938.

_____. *Go, Team, Go!* Morrow, 1954.

_____. *Iron Duke*. 1938.

_____. *Yea! Wildcats*. Harcourt, 1944.

Twain, Mark (real name, Samuel Clemens). *Adventures of Huckleberry Finn. 1884.*

_____. *The Adventures of Tom Sawyer*. 1876.

Wetherell, Elizabeth (real name, Susan Warner). *The Wide, Wide World*. 1850.

Wickenden, Dan. *Walk Like a Mortal*. Morrow, 1940.

Wiggin, Kate Douglas. *Rebecca of Sunnybrook Farm*. 1904.

Wilson, Augusta Jane Evans. *St. Elmo*. 1867.

Winsor, Kathleen. *Forever Amber*. Macmillan, 1944.

Wister, Owen. *The Virginian: A Horseman of the Plains*. 1902.

Wright, Richard. *Black Boy*. HarperCollins, 1940.

_____. *Native Son*. HarperCollins, 1940.

Yates, Elizabeth. *Amos Fortune, Free Man*. Aladdin, 1950.

Zindel, Paul. *The Pigman*. HarperCollins, 1968.

The following sources are designed to aid professionals in the selection and evaluation of books and other materials for young adults. An attempt was made to include sources with widely varying emphases. However, in addition to these sources—most of which appear at regular intervals—many specialized lists are prepared by committees and individuals in response to current and/or local needs. Readers are advised to check on the availability of such lists with librarians and teachers. For purposes of comparison, the 1992 prices are included, but readers should expect that many of them will have risen because of inflation.

The ALAN Review. (Assembly on Literature for Adolescents, National Council of Teachers of English. Order from William Subick, NCTE, 1111 Kenyon Rd.; Urbana, IL 61801. $15 for three issues.)

Since 1973, this publication has appeared three times a year. It is currently edited by Robert Small and Leila Christenbury and is unique in being devoted entirely to adolescent literature. Each issue contains "Clip and File" reviews of approximately forty new hardbacks or paperbacks and several feature articles, news announcements, and occasional reviews of professional books.

Best Books for Junior High Readers by John T. Gillespie (R. R. Bowker, 1991, 567 pp. $39.95.)

Each of the 6,848 books listed in this collection for students ages twelve to fifteen received two positive recommendations in standard reviewing sources. Fiction is arranged according to genre; nonfiction is arranged according to common subjects studied in junior high schools. Also recommended is Gillespie's *Best Books for Senior High Readers* (R. R. Bowker, 1991).

Best Videos for Children and Young Adults: A Core Collection for Libraries. (ABC–CLIO, 1990, 185 pp.)

Annotations, evaluations, and suggestions for use are given for over 300 videos, excluding feature films and music videos.

Book Bait: Detailed Notes on Adult Books Popular with Young People, edited by Eleanor Walker. (4th ed., 1988. American Library Association; 50 E. Huron St.; Chicago, IL 60611. $17.50.)

A useful bibliography for bridging the gap between young adult and adult novels, this listing contains 100 books with extensive annotations that include plot summaries, discussions of appeal to teenagers, hints for booktalks, and suggested titles for use as follow-ups. Arrangement is alphabetical by author; subject and title indexes are appended.

Booklist. (American Library Association; 50 E. Huron St.; Chicago, IL 60611. $56 for twenty-two issues.)

The size of the reviews of either books or media varies from twenty-word annotations to 300-word essays. "Books for Young Adults" (ages fourteen through eighteen) is a regular feature. Occasionally, books in both the children's and adult sections are also marked YA. A review constitutes a recommendation for library purchase, with stars being given to books having exceptionally high literary quality. *Booklist* publishes special-interest lists fairly regularly and also the best-book lists produced by various groups affiliated with the American Library Association.

Books for the Teen Age. (Annual ed. Office of Young Adult Services; New York Public Library. Order from Office of Branch Libraries; NYPL; 455 Fifth Avenue; New York, NY 10016. $6 per copy plus $1 handling charge for up to five copies.)

The 1,250 recommendations in this booklet come from the young adult librarians in the eighty branches of the New York Public Library. Annotations are minimal; grouping is by subject, with titles and authors indexed.

Books for You: A Booklist for Senior High Students, edited by Shirley Wurth and the Committee to Revise the Senior High Reading List. (11th ed., 1993. National Council of Teachers of English; 1111 Kenyon Rd.; Urbana, IL 61801. $16.95 nonmembers, $12.95 members.)

Part of NCTE's Bibliography Series, this booklist is published approximately every five years and includes only books published during the assigned years. The over 1,000 annotations of both fiction and nonfiction are written to students and organized under some fifty categories.

Bulletin of the Center for Children's Books. (Editor, Betsy Hearne; Executive Editor, Roger Sutton. Published by the University of Illinois Press for the Graduate School of Library and Information Science; 54 E. Gregory Dr.; Champaign, IL 61820. Editorial offices at 1512 N. Fremont St., Suite 105; Chicago, IL 60622.)

This is the journal founded by Zena Sutherland and published by the University of Chicago Press until the recent closing of Chicago's Graduate Library School. In each issue, the *Bulletin* reviews approximately sixty new books for children and young adults. It has been known for the consistency of its reviews and for including discussions of developmental values and curricular uses.

Celebrate the Dream by the New York Public Library. (Order from Office of Branch Libraries; NYPL; 455 Fifth Ave.; New York, NY 10016. $5 per copy plus $1 handling charge for up to five copies.)

Books annotated in this guide explore the black experience in the United States and abroad.

Characters from Young Adult Literature by Mary Ellen Snodgrass. (Libraries Unlimited, 1991.)

A collection of comments on YA material, ranging in time from Shakespeare's *Julius Caesar* (1598) to Norma Fox Mazer's *After the Rain* (1987), with stopovers in *The Chocolate War, A Day No Pigs Would Die, Gentlehands, The Outsiders, The Pigman, Summer of My German Soldier,* and *The Year without Michael.*

Children's Literature in Education: An International Quarterly. (Human Sciences Press; 233 Spring St., New York, NY 10013. Individuals $50 per year; K–12 Schools, $20.)

This British/American cooperative effort is edited by Anita Moss from the United States and Geoff Fox from Great Britain. The editors show a preference for substantive analysis rather than pedagogical advice or quick once-overs. A good proportion of the articles are about YA authors and their works.

English Journal. (National Council of Teachers of English; 1111 Kenyon Rd.; Urbana, IL 61801. $35 for eight issues, which includes membership in NCTE. $40 for institutions.)

Aimed at high school English teachers, nearly every issue contains at least a few reviews and/or articles about young adult literature.

High Interest—Easy Reading: A Booklist for Junior and Senior High School Students, edited by William G. McBride. (6th ed., 1990. National Council of Teachers of English; 1111 Kenyon Rd.; Urbana, IL 61801. $8.95 nonmembers, $6.95 members.)

Nearly 400 annotations are written so as to appeal directly to students. The books, mostly fiction, are grouped into twenty-three categories, including adventure, death, ethnicity, friendship, how-to, humor, love and romance, and social problems.

The Horn Book Guide to Children's and Young Adult Books and *Horn Book Magazine.* (The Horn Book, Inc.; 14 Beacon St.; Boston, MA 02108-3718. Magazine [six issues], $34 for new subscribers, $38 for renewals. Guide [two issues], $50. Combination magazine and guide $65.)

Since 1924, the *Horn Book Magazine* has been devoted to the critical analysis of children's literature through both articles and reviews. Popular appeal takes a back seat to literary quality in the selection of titles for review. In a typical issue, seven or eight adolescent novels will be reviewed under the heading of "Stories for Older Readers." A new service begun by the editors in 1990 is the *Horn Book Guide,* which gives brief annotations and a numerical ranking from 1 (outstanding) to 6 (unacceptable) for some 4,000 books published in the United States (including books published in Spanish), Canada, and Australia.

Interracial Books for Children Bulletin. (Council on Interracial Books for Children; 1841 Broadway; New York, NY 10023. Send stamped envelope [52¢] for subscription and catalogue information.)

Nearly all reviews and articles in this twenty-five-page bulletin are written for the purpose of examining the relationship between social issues and how they are treated or reflected in current fiction, nonfiction, and curriculum materials.

Journal of Reading. (International Reading Association; 800 Barksdale Rd.; Box 8139; Newark, DE 19711–8139. $41 for libraries; $38 for individuals, which includes membership in the International Reading Association.)

The audience for this journal is high school reading teachers. Although most of the articles are reports on research in the teaching of reading, some articles focus on reading interests and literature. Reviews of new young adult books are also included.

Journal of Youth Services in Libraries. American Library Association, 50 E. Huron St., Chicago, IL 60611. $40.00 for yearly subscription of four issues.

Articles cover both children's and YA literature as well as research and professional interests of librarians. Until 1987, the name was *Top of the News*.

Junior High School Library Catalog, edited by Richard H. Isaacson and Gary L. Bogart. (5th ed. H. W. Wilson Company; 950 University Ave.; Bronx, NY 10452. $80.)

Designed as a suggested basic book collection for junior high school libraries, this volume is divided into two major parts. The first includes an annotated listing by Dewey Decimal Number for nonfiction, author's last name for fiction, and author's/editor's last name for story collections. The second part relists all books alphabetically by author, title, and subject. This outstanding reference tool for junior high school librarians is revised approximately every five years with frequent supplements.

Kirkus Reviews. (Kirkus Service, Inc.; 200 Park Ave. South; New York, NY 10003. $75 for the children's and young adult section.)

Kirkus reviews are approximately 200 words long. The big advantage of this source is its timeliness and completeness, made possible by its being published on the first and the fifteenth days of each month.

Kliatt Young Adult Paperback Book Guide. (425 Watertown St.; Newton, MA 02158. $33 for three issues, with five interim supplements.)

Because teenagers prefer to read paperbacks, this source serves a real need by reviewing all paperbacks (originals, reprints, and reissues) recommended for readers ages twelve through nineteen. A code identifies books as appropriate for advanced students, general young adult readers, junior high students, students with low reading abilities, and emotionally mature readers who can handle "explicit sex, excessive violence and/or obscenity." Reviews are arranged by subject. An index of titles and a directory of cooperating publishers are included.

New York Times Book Review. (New York Times Company; 229 W. 43rd St.; New York, NY 10036. 52 issues, $39.)

The currency of the reviews makes this an especially valuable source. Also, because well-known authors are often invited to serve as critics, the reviews are fun to read.

Nonfiction for Young Adults: From Delight to Wisdom by Betty Carter and Richard F. Abrahamson. (Oryx Press, 1990.)

"You need this book," was the headline leading off the *School Library Journal* review of Carter and Abrahamson's book. We agree, as reflected by the number of times we refer to it.

Notable Children's Trade Books in the Field of Social Studies. (National Council for the Social Studies and the Children's Book Council. Single copies available free if an envelope stamped for three ounces is provided to the Children's Book Council; 568 Broadway; New York, NY 10012.)

This list is published each spring in *Social Education*. Many of the recommended books are appropriate for junior and early senior high students.

School Library Journal and *Star Track* supplement. (Cahners Publishing Co.; Bowker Magazine Group; 245 W. 17th St.; New York, NY 10011. $59 for subscriptions; send to P.O. Box 1978, Marion, OH 43305–1978.)

The most comprehensive of the review media, *SLJ* reviews both recommended and not recommended books. Reviews are written by a panel of 400 librarians who are sent books, media, and/or computer materials appropriate to their interests and backgrounds. Starred reviews signify exceptionally good books. A *Star Track* supplement is published every six months that brings all the starred reviews together in an attractive and convenient booklet.

Senior High School Library Catalog, edited by Ferne Hillegas and Juliette Yakkov. (13th ed. H. W. Wilson Company, 1987; 950 University Ave.; Bronx, NY 10452. $96.)

Using the same format as the *Junior High School Library Catalog* (see earlier), this invaluable resource lists some books appropriate for both junior and senior high school collections as well as those aimed specifically at readers in grades 10 through 12. Like its companion volume, it is produced approximately every five years with frequent supplements.

Voice of Youth Advocates (VOYA). (Scarecrow Press; P.O. Box 4167; Metuchen, NJ 08840. Editorial correspondence to Dorothy M. Broderick; 1226 Cresthaven Dr.; Silver Spring, MD 20903. $27 for six issues.)

One of the aims of this publication, founded in 1978, is "to change the traditional linking of young adult services with children's librarianship and shift the focus to connection with adult services." Feature articles are especially good because they present viewpoints not commonly considered. About one-fourth of the journal is devoted to reviews in the categories of pamphlets, mysteries, science fiction, audiovisual, adult and teenage fiction and nonfiction, and professional books.

Wilson Library Bulletin. (H. W. Wilson Co.; 950 University Ave.; Bronx, NY 19452. $46 for eleven issues.)

Although the focus of the *Wilson Library Bulletin* is much broader than young adult librarianship, "The Young Adult Perplex" is a regular feature that reviews current books. Other columns of interest to YA teachers and librarians include "Front Row Center," "SF Universe," and "Video Shopper."

Young People's Books in Series: Fiction and Non-Fiction, 1975–1991, edited by Judith K. Rosenberg with C. Allen Nichols. (Libraries Unlimited, 1992.)

Your Reading: A Booklist for Junior High and Middle School Students, edited by Alleen Pace Nilsen and the Committee to Revise the Junior High/Middle School Reading List. (1991. National Council of Teachers of English, 1111 Kenyon Rd.; Urbana, IL 61801. $16.95 nonmembers, $12.95 members.)

Part of the NCTE Bibliography Series, this one includes annotations of more than 1,000 recommended books published during 1988, 1989, and 1990.

APPENDIX B   *SOME OUTSTANDING BOOKS AND ARTICLES ABOUT YOUNG ADULT LITERATURE*

The following represents our personal choices. We followed our ground rules of the first edition. That may explain, if not justify, why some works were included or excluded. Brief explanations are given where titles are not self-explanatory.

1. Books or articles were primarily about young adult literature, not on the psychology of the young, cultural milieu, literary history, or literary criticism.
2. Books or articles had to cover more than one author. No matter how good articles were on Cynthia Voigt or Leon Garfield or Robert Cormier, we ignored them in favor of articles with broader implications.
3. Books and articles had to excite us.
4. No books and articles were chosen to balance out the list. We chose what we did because we believe in them.
5. Readers will, again, find no books or articles by Nilsen or Donelson. Those desperate to see our work included will search in vain. Readers may continue to assume that we believe none of our work belongs in a list of "outstanding" works, that we long for professional oblivion, or that we are modest to a fault.

■ BOOKS

Histories of Young Adult Literature

Avery, Gillian. *Childhood's Pattern: A Study of the Heroes and Heroines of Children's Fiction, 1770–1950.* London: Hodder and Stoughton, 1975.

Bingham, Jane, and Grayce Scholt. *Fifteen Centuries of Children's Literature: An Annotated Chronology of British and American Works in Historical Context.* Greenwood Press, 1980.

Cadogan, Mary, and Patricia Craig. *You're a Brick, Angela! A New Look at Girls' Fiction from 1839 to 1975.* London: Victor Gollancz, 1976. Still one of the most delightful and wittiest commentaries on girls' books.

Campbell, Patricia J. *Sex Education Books for Young Adults, 1892–1979.* R. R. Bowker, 1979. Always accurate, often funny.

Children's Fiction, 1876–1984. 2 vols. R. R. Bowker, 1984.

Crouch, Marcus. *The Nesbit Tradition: The Children's Novel in England 1945–1970.* London: Ernest Benn, 1972.

_____. *Treasure Seekers and Borrowers: Children's Books in Britain 1900–1960.* London: Library Association, 1962.

Darling, Richard. *The Rise of Children's Book Reviewing in America: 1865–1881.* R. R. Bowker, 1968. A fascinating study of early children's and YA books, book reviewing, and book reviewers.

Darton, F. J. Harvey. *Children's Books in England: Five Centuries of Social Use*. 2nd ed. Cambridge, England: Cambridge University Press, 1958. First published in 1932. Informative, if a bit stuffy.

Egoff, Sheila. *The Republic of Childhood: A Critical Guide to Canadian Children's Literature in English*. 2nd ed. Toronto: Oxford University Press, 1975.

_____. *Worlds Within: Children's Fantasy from the Middle Ages*. American Library Association, 1988.

Girls' Series Books: A Checklist of Hardback Books Published 1900–1975. Children's Literature Research Collections, University of Minnesota Library, 1978. Basic for any work with girls' series books.

Howarth, Patrick. *Play Up and Play the Game: The Heroes of Popular Fiction*. London: Eyre Methuen, 1973.

Hudson, Harry K. *A Bibliography of Hard-Cover Boys' Books*. rev. ed. Tampa, FL: Data Print, 1977. Basic for any work with boys' series books (and fun to skim through).

Jackson, Mary V. *Engines of Instruction, Mischief, and Magic: Children's Literature in England from Its Beginnings to 1839*. University of Nebraska Press, 1989. Beautifully illustrated background material.

Kiefer, Monica. *American Children Through Their Books, 1700–1835*. University of Pennsylvania Press, 1948.

Kloet, Christine A. *After Alice: A Hundred Years of Children's Reading in Britain*. London: Library Association, 1977. Published for an exhibition at the Victoria and Albert Museum of Childhood, 1977–1978.

MacLeod, Anne Scott. *A Moral Tale: Children's Fiction and American Culture, 1820–1860*. Archon Books, 1975.

Mason, Bobbie Ann. *The Girl Sleuth: A Feminist Guide*. Feminist Press, 1975. Perceptive, chatty, and witty words about girls' series books, especially Nancy Drew.

Meigs, Cornelia, et al. *A Critical History of Children's Literature*. rev. ed. Macmillan, 1969. Encyclopedic history of YA literature (and children's literature, of course) from the beginning.

Musgrave, P. W. *From Brown to Bunter: The Life and Death of the School Story*. London: Routledge and Kegan Paul, 1985.

Nye, Russel. *The Unembarrassed Muse: The Popular Arts in America*. Dial, 1970.

Quigly, Isabel. *The Heirs of Tom Brown: The English School Story*. London: Chatto and Windus, 1982.

Rowbotham, Judith. *Good Girls Make Good Wives: Guidance for Girls in Victorian England*. Oxford, England: Basil Blackwell, 1989.

Sloane, William. *Children's Books in England and America in the Seventeenth Century*. Columbia University Press, 1955.

Townsend, John Rowe. *25 Years of British Children's Books*. London: National Book League, 1979. Not easily found but this sixty-page pamphlet is worth the search.

_____. *Written for Children: An Outline of English-Language Children's Literature*. 3rd ed. Lippincott, 1988. The most readable history.

Criticism of Young Adult Literature

Broderick, Dorothy M. *Images of the Black in Children's Fiction*. R. R. Bowker, 1973. Racism in YA literature.

Carter, Betty, and Richard F. Abrahamson. *Nonfiction for Young Adults: From Delight to Wisdom*. Oryx Press, 1990.

Chambers, Aidan. *Reluctant Reader*. London: Pergamon Press, 1969. This reads better the older it gets. Sympathetic and practical ideas about getting hard-to-reach readers to read.

Children's Literature Review. Gale Research Co., 1976–. A continuing series and an excellent source of material on YA books.

Christian-Smith, Linda K. *Becoming a Woman*

through Romance. Routledge and Kegan Paul, 1990.

Contemporary Literary Criticism. Gale Research Co., 1973–. A continuing series.

Dixon, Bob. *Catching Them Young: Political Ideas in Children's Fiction*. London: Pluto Press, 1977.

_____. *Catching Them Young: Sex, Race and Class in Children's Fiction*. London: Pluto Press, 1977.

Egoff, Sheila A. *Thursday's Child: Trends and Patterns in Contemporary Children's Literature*. American Library Association, 1981. One of the great books in the field, basic reading.

Ettinger, John R., and Diana L. Spirt, eds. *Choosing Books for Young People*. Vol. 2: *A Guide to Criticism and Bibliography, 1976–1984*. American Library Association, 1982.

Harrison, Barbara, and Gregory Maguire, eds. *Innocence and Experience: Essays and Conversations on Children's Literature*. Lothrop, 1987.

Hazard, Paul. *Books, Children and Men*. trans. Marguerite Mitchell, Horn Book, 1944. About all sorts of readers. A seminal book impossible to overrate.

Hearne, Betsy, and Marilyn Kaye, eds. *Celebrating Children's Books: Essays on Children's Literature in Honor of Zena Sutherland*. Lothrop, 1981.

Hendrickson, Linnea. *Children's Literature: A Guide to the Criticism*. G. K. Hall, 1987.

Howard, Elizabeth F. *America as Story: Historical Fiction for the Secondary Schools*. American Library Association, 1988.

Inglis, Fred. *The Promise of Happiness: Value and Meaning in Children's Fiction*. Cambridge, England: Cambridge University Press, 1981.

Kohn, Rita, compiler. *Once Upon . . . A Time for Young People and Their Books: An Annotated Resource Guide*. Scarecrow Press, 1986.

Lynn, Ruth Nadelman. *Fantasy Literature for Children and Young Adults*. R. R. Bowker, 1989.

MacCann, Donnarae, and Gloria Woodward, eds. *The Black American in Books for Children: Readings on Racism*. Scarecrow Press, 1972.

Salmon, Edward. *Juvenile Literature as It Is*. London: Henry J. Drane, 1888. Forward-looking views on children's and YA books. A remarkable book.

Shields, Nancy E. *Index to Literary Criticism for Young Adults*. Scarecrow Press, 1988.

Sloan, Glenna. *The Child as Critic*. Teachers College Press, 1975. Northrop Frye's theories applied to children's and YA literature.

Street, Douglas, ed. *Children's Novels and the Movies*. Ungar, 1984.

Sutherland, Zena. *The Arbuthnot Lectures: 1970–1979*. American Library Association, 1980.

Libraries and Young Adult Literature

Bodart, Joni. *Booktalking and School Visiting for Young Adult Audiences*. H. W. Wilson, 1980.

_____. *Booktalk 2: Booktalking for All Ages and Audiences*. H.W. Wilson, 1985.

Books for the Teen Age. New York Public Library, published annually.

Edwards, Margaret A. *The Fair Garden and the Swarm of Beasts: The Library and the Young Adult*. rev. ed. Hawthorn, 1974. Some of the problems but mostly the joys of working with YA's.

Field, Carolyn W., ed. *Special Collections in Children's Literature*. American Library Association, 1982.

Gillespie, John T. *More Juniorplots: A Guide for Teachers and Librarians*. R. R. Bowker, 1977.

Gillespie, John T., and Diana L. Lembo. *Juniorplots: A Book Talk Manual for Teachers and Librarians*. R. R. Bowker, 1967.

Gillespie, John T., and Corinne Naden. *Juniorplots 3: A Book Talk Guide for Use with Readers, Ages 12–16*. R. R. Bowker, 1987.

———. *Seniorplots: A Book Talk Guide for Use with Readers, Ages 15–18*. R. R. Bowker, 1989.

Hinckley, Karen, and Barbara Hinckley. *America's Best Sellers: A Reader's Guide to Popular Fiction*. Indiana University Press, 1989.

Marshall, Margaret R. *Libraries and Literature for Teenagers*. London: Andre Deutsch, 1975.

Rochman, Hazel. *Tales of Love and Terror: Booktalking the Classics, Old and New*. American Library Association, 1987.

Roe, Ernest. *Teachers, Librarians, and Children: A Study of Libraries in Education*. Archon Books, 1965. Superb, maybe the best of the lot. First published in Australia.

Rosenberg, Betty. *Genreflecting: A Guide to Reading Interests in Genre Fiction*. 2nd ed. Libraries Unlimited, 1987.

English Classrooms and Young Adult Literature

Beach, Richard, and James Marshall. *Teaching Literature in the Secondary School*. Harcourt Brace Jovanovich, 1991.

Burton, Dwight L. *Literature Study in the High Schools*. 3rd ed. Holt, 1970. For many teachers and librarians, *the* book that introduced them to YA books.

Carlsen, G. Robert. *Books and the Teen-Age Reader*. 2nd ed. HarperCollins, 1980.

Corcoran, Bill, and Emrys Evans, eds. *Readers, Texts, Teachers*. Boynton/Cook, 1987. A great collection of criticism and pedagogy.

Crowley, Sharon. *A Teacher's Introduction to Deconstruction*. National Council of Teachers of English, 1989.

Evans, Tricia. *Teaching English*. London: Croom Helm, 1982.

Fader, Daniel. *The New Hooked on Books*. Berkley, 1976. First published in 1966 and revised in 1968, Fader's book made English teachers take YA books seriously. The book lists are dated, but Fader's enthusiasm and caring aren't.

Farrell, Edmund J., and James R. Squire, ed. *Transactions with Literature: A Fifty-Year Perspective*. National Council of Teachers of English, 1990. Essays honoring Louise M. Rosenblatt.

Moran, Charles, and Elizabeth F. Penfield, eds. *Conversations: Contemporary Critical Theory and the Teaching of Literature*. National Council of Teachers of English, 1990.

Peck, David. *Novels of Initiation: A Guidebook for Teaching Literature to Adolescents*. Teachers College, 1989.

Probst, Robert E. *Response and Analysis: Teaching Literature in Junior and Senior High School*. Boynton/Cook, Heinemann, 1988. A rarity: brilliant pedagogy with understandable and usable material on literary criticism.

Protherough, Robert, Judith Atkinson, and John Fawcett. *The Effective Teaching of English*. London: Longman, 1989. The best text today on teaching English.

Purves, Alan C., Theresa Rogers, and Anna O. Soter. *How Porcupines Make Love II: Teaching a Response-Centered Literature Curriculum*. Longman, 1990.

Richter, David H., ed. *The Critical Tradition: Classic Texts and Contemporary Trends*. Bedford Books, St. Martin's Press, 1989. Plato to Wordsworth to Eliot to Langer on standard texts along with selections from contemporary critical schools—Marxist, psychological, formalism, structuralism and semiotics, poststructuralism, feminist, and reader-response. An unwieldy set of texts but generally helpful.

Rosenblatt, Louise M. *Literature as Exploration*. 4th ed. Modern Language Association, 1983.

Sample, Hazel. *Pitfalls for Readers of Fiction*. National Council of Teachers of English, 1940. Too little known and appreciated, many insights into reading popular fiction.

Scholes, Robert. *Textual Power: Literary Theory and the Teaching of English*. Yale University Press, 1985.

Thomson, Jack. *Understanding Teenager's Reading: Reading Processes and the Teaching of Literature*. Norwood, Australia: Australian Association for the Teaching of English, 1987.

Authors of Young Adult Literature

Cech, John, ed. *American Writers for Children, 1900–1960. Dictionary of Literary Biography*. Vol. 22: Gale Research Co., 1983.

Chevalier, Tracy. *Twentieth Century Children's Writers*. 3rd ed. St. Martin's Press, 1989.

Commire, Anne, ed. *Something About the Author*. Gale Research Co., 1971. A continuing series about authors and books. Indispensable.

———. *Yesterday's Authors of Books for Children*. Gale Research Co., 1977. Lives of authors who died before 1961.

de Montreville, Doris, and Elizabeth D. Crawford, eds. *Fourth Book of Junior Authors and Illustrators*. H. W. Wilson, 1978.

de Montreville, Doris, and Donna Hill, eds. *Third Book of Junior Authors*. H. W. Wilson, 1972.

Estes, Glenn E., ed. *American Writers for Children Before 1900. Dictionary of Literary Biography*. Vol. 42: Gale Research Co., 1985.

———. *American Writers for Children Since 1960: Fiction. Dictionary of Literary Biography*. Vol. 52: Gale Research Co., 1986.

———. *American Writers for Children Since 1960: Poets, Illustrators, and Nonfiction Authors. Dictionary of Literary Biography*. Vol. 61: Gale Research Co., 1987.

Gallo, Donald R., ed. *Authors' Insights: Turning Teenagers into Readers and Writers*. Boynton/Cook; Heinemann, 1992.

———. *Speaking for Ourselves: Autobiographical Sketches by Notable Authors of Books for Young Adults*. National Council of Teachers of English, 1990. From Joan Aiken to Paul Zindel, 92 sketches from important YA writers.

Fuller, Muriel, ed. *More Junior Authors*. H. W. Wilson, 1963.

Haviland, Virginia, ed. *The Openhearted Audience: Ten Authors Talk About Writing for Children*. Library of Congress, 1980.

Helbig, Alethea K., and Agnes Regan Perkins. *Dictionary of American Children's Fiction, 1859–1959*. Greenwood Press, 1985.

———. *Dictionary of American Children's Fiction, 1960–1984*. Greenwood Press, 1986.

———. *Dictionary of British Children's Fiction*. Greenwood Press, 1989.

Holtze, Sally Holmes, ed. *Fifth Book of Junior Authors and Illustrators*. H. W. Wilson, 1987.

———. *Sixth Book of Junior Authors and Illustrators*. H. W. Wilson, 1989.

Huffman, Miriam, and Eva Samuels, eds. *Authors and Artists for Young Adults*. Gale Research Co., 1989.

Jones, Cornelia, and Olivia R. Way. *British Children's Authors: Interviews at Home*. American Library Association, 1976.

Kirkpatrick, D. L., ed. *Twentieth-Century Children's Writers*. 3rd ed. Macmillan, 1990.

Kunitz, Stanley J. and Howard Hatycraft, eds. *The Junior Book of Authors*. 2nd ed. rev.: H. W. Wilson, 1951.

Rees, David. *The Marble in the Water: Essays on Contemporary Writers of Fiction for Children and Young Adults*. Horn Book, 1980.

_____. *Painted Desert. Green Shade: Essays on Contemporary Writers of Fiction for Children and Young Adults*. Horn Book, 1984.

_____. *What Do Draculas Do? Essays on Contemporary Writers of Fiction for Children and Young Adults*. Scarecrow Press, 1990.

Roginski, Jim. *Behind the Covers: Interviews with Authors and Illustrators of Books for Children and Young Adults*. Libraries Unlimited, 1985.

_____. *Behind the Covers: Interviews with Authors and Illustrators of Books for Children and Young Adults*. Vol. 2. Libraries Unlimited, 1989.

Sarkissian, Adele, ed. *Writers for Young Adults: Biographies Master Index*. Gale Research Co., 1984.

Townsend, John Rowe. *A Sense of Story: Essays on Contemporary Writers for Children*. Lippincott, 1971.

Ward, Martha E., and Dorothy A. Marquardt, eds. *Authors of Books for Young People*. 3rd ed. Scarecrow Press, 1990.

Weiss, M. Jerry, ed. *From Writers to Students: The Pleasures and Pains of Writing*. International Reading Association, 1979.

Wintle, Justin, and Emma Fisher, eds. *The Pied Pipers: Interviews with the Influential Creators of Children's Literature*. Paddington Press, 1974.

Books of Readings about Young Adult Literature

Broderick, Dorothy M., ed. *The VOYA Reader*. Scarecrow Press, 1990. Articles from the *Voice of Youth Advocates*.

Egoff, Sheila, G. T. Stubbs, and L. F. Ashley, eds. *Only Connect: Readings in Children's Literature*. 2nd ed. Oxford University Press, 1980.

Fox, Geoff, et al., eds. *Writers, Critics, and Children: Articles from Children's Literature in Education*. Agathon Press, 1976.

Haviland, Virginia, ed. *Children and Literature: Views and Reviews*. Scott, Foresman, 1973.

Salway, Lance, ed. *A Peculiar Gift: Nineteenth Century Writings on Books for Children*. London: Kestrel, 1976.

Varlejs, Jana, ed. *Young Adult Literature in the Seventies: A Selection of Readings*. Scarecrow Press, 1978.

ARTICLES IN PERIODICALS

History and Young Adult Literature

Ashford, Richard K. "Tomboys and Saints: Girls' Stories of the Late Nineteenth Century." *School Library Journal* 26 (January 1980): 23–28.

Cantwell, Robert. "A Sneering Laugh with the Bases Loaded." *Sports Illustrated* 16 (April 23, 1962): 67–70, 73–76. Baseball novels for boys, particularly by Barbour and Heyliger.

Carlsen, G. Robert. "Forty Years with Books and Teen-Age Readers." *Arizona English Bulletin* 18 (April 1976): 1–5. From 1939 to 1976 in YA literature.

Crandall, John C. "Patriotism and Humanitarian Reform in Children's Literature, 1825–1860." *American Quarterly* 21 (Spring 1969): 3–22.

Edwards, Margaret A. "The Rise of Teen-Age Reading." *Saturday Review of Literature* 37 (November 13, 1954): 88–89, 95. The state of YA literature in the 1930s and 1940s and what led to it.

Evans, Walter. "The All-American Boys: A

Study of Boys' Sports Fiction." *Journal of Popular Culture* 6 (Summer 1972): 104–121. Formulas underlying boys' school sports books, especially Barbour and the series books.

"For It Was Indeed He." *Fortune* 9 (April 1934): 86–89, 193–194, 204, 206, 208–209. An important, influential, and biased article on Stratemeyer's Literary Syndicate.

Geller, Evelyn. "The Librarian as Censor." *Library Journal* 101 (June 1, 1976): 1255–58. Social control as censorship in late-nineteenth-century library selection.

———. "Tom Sawyer, Tom Bailey, and the Bad-Boy Genre." *Wilson Library Bulletin* 52 (November 1976): 245–50.

Hutchinson, Margaret. "Fifty Years of Young Adult Reading, 1921–1971." *Top of the News* 29 (November 1973): 24–53. "A survey of the field (of) young adult reading for the past fifty years by examining articles indexed in *Library Literature* from its inception in 1921."

Kelly, R. Gordon. "American Children's Literature: An Historiographical Review." *American Literary Realism, 1870–1910* 6 (Spring 1973): 89–107.

Lapides, Linda F. "A Decade of Teen-Age Reading in Baltimore, 1960–1970." *Top of the News* 27 (Spring 1971): 278–291.

Morrison, Lillian. "Fifty Years of 'Books for the Teen Age.'" *School Library Journal* 26 (December 1979): 44–50.

Radnor, Rebecca. "You're Being Paged Loudly in the Kitchen: Teen-Age Literature of the Forties and Fifties." *Journal of Popular Culture* 11 (Spring 1978): 789–99. Ways in which YA writers for girls influenced young women.

Repplier, Agnes. "Little Pharisees in Fiction." *Scribner's Magazine* 20 (December 1896): 718–24. The didactic and joyless goody-goody school of YA fiction in the last half of the nineteenth century.

Trensky, Anne. "The Bad Boy in Nineteenth-Century American Fiction." *Georgia Review* 27 (Winter 1973): 503–17.

Vostrovsky, Clara. "A Study of Children's Reading Tastes." *Pedagogical Seminary* 6 (December 1899): 523–35. A pioneer account of the kinds of books young people read.

Criticism and Young Adult Literature

Abrahamson, Jane. "Still Playing It Safe: Restricted Realism in Teen Novels." *School Library Journal* 22 (May 1976): 38–39.

Brewbaker, James M. "Are You There, Margaret? It's Me, God—Religious Contexts in Recent Adolescent Fiction." *English Journal* 72 (September 1983): 82–86.

Campbell, Patty. "Perplexing Young Adult Books: A Retrospective." *Wilson Library Bulletin* 62 (April 1988): 20, 22, 24, 26. Campbell looks back on ten years of her YA column.

Carlsen, G. Robert. "For Everything There Is a Season." *Top of the News* 21 (January 1965): 103–110. Stages in reading growth.

———. "The Interest Rate Is Rising." *English Journal* 59 (May 1970): 655–59.

Carver, Nancy Lynn. "Stereotypes of American Indians in Adolescent Literature." *English Journal* 77 (September 1988): 25–32.

Early, Margaret J. "Stages of Growth in Literary Appreciation." *English Journal* 49 (March 1960): 161–67. A seminal article.

Edwards, Margaret A. "A Time When It's Best to Read and Let Read." *Wilson Library Bulletin* 35 (September 1960): 43–47. Myths of buying books for young adults demolished.

Engdahl, Sylvia. "Do Teenage Novels Fill a Need?" *English Journal* 64 (February 1975): 48–52.

Evans, Dilys. "The YA Cover Story." *Publishers Weekly* 232 (July 24, 1987):

112–15. Differences between hardcover and paperback covers on YA books.

Gauch, Patricia. "'Good Stuff' in Adolescent Fiction." *Top of the News* 40 (Winter 1984): 125–29.

Green, Samuel S. "Sensational Fiction in Public Libraries." *Library Journal* 4 (September–October 1879): 345–55. Extraordinarily forward-looking intelligent comments about young adults and their books. The entire issue is worth reading, particularly papers by T. W. Higginson (pp. 357–59), William Atkinson (pp. 359–62), and Mellen Chamberlain (pp. 362–66).

Hanckel, Frances, and John Cunningham. "Can Young Gays Find Happiness in YA Books?" *Wilson Library Bulletin* 50 (March 1976): 528–34.

Hentoff, Nat. "Fiction for Teen-Agers." *Wilson Library Bulletin* 43 (November 1968): 261–64. The shortcomings of YA fiction.

———. "Tell It as It Is." *New York Times Book Review* May 7, 1967, pp. 3, 51.

Hinton, Susan. "Teen-Agers Are for Real." *New York Times Book Review.* August 27, 1967, pp. 26–29. Brief and excellent.

Hipps, G. Melvin. "Adolescent Literature: Once More to the Defense." *Virginia English Bulletin* 23 (Spring 1973): 44–50. Nearly thirty years old and still one of the best rationales for adolescent literature.

"Is Adolescent Literature Worth Studying?" *Connecticut English Journal* 10 (Fall 1978). Robert P. Scaramella, "Con: At the Risk of Seeming Stuffy," pp. 57–58; Robert C. Small, Jr. "Pro: Means and Ends," pp. 59–63.

Janeczko, Paul B. "Seven Myths About Adolescent Literature." *Arizona English Bulletin* 18 (April 1976): 11–12.

Kraus, W. Keith. "Cinderella In Trouble: Still Dreaming and Losing." *School Library Journal* 21 (January 1975): 18–22. Pregnancy in YA novels from Felsen's *Two*

and the Town (1952) to Neufeld's *For All the Wrong Reasons* (1973).

———. "From Steppin' Stebbins to Soul Brothers: Racial Strife in Adolescent Literature." *Arizona English Bulletin* 18 (April 1976): 154–60.

Martinec, Barbara. "Popular—But Not Just a Part of the Crowd: Implications of Formula Fiction for Teenagers." *English Journal* 60 (March 1971): 339–44. Formulaic elements in six YA novelists.

Matthews, Dorothy. "An Adolescent's Glimpse of the Faces of Eve: A Study of the Images of Women in Selected Popular Junior Novels." *Illinois English Bulletin* 60 (May 1973): 1–14.

———. "Writing About Adolescent Literature: Current Approaches and Future Directions." *Arizona English Bulletin* 18 (April 1976): 216–19.

McDowell, Myles. "Fiction for Children and Adults: Some Essential Differences." *Children's Literature in Education* 4 (March 1973): 48–63.

Meltzer, Milton. "Where Do All the Prizes Go? The Case for Nonfiction." *Horn Book Magazine* 52 (February 1976): 17–23.

Merla, Patrick. "'What is Real?' Asked the Rabbit One Day." *Saturday Review* 55 (November 4, 1972): 43–49. The rise of YA realism and adult fantasy, twenty years old and still valid.

Mertz, Maia Pank, and David A. England. "The Legitimacy of American Adolescent Fiction." *School Library Journal* 30 (October 1983): 119–23.

Peck, Richard. "In the Country of Teenage Fiction." *American Libraries* 4 (April 1973): 204–207.

———. "Some Thoughts on Adolescent Literature." *News from ALAN* 3 (September–October 1975): 4–7.

Peck, Richard, and Patsy H. Perritt. "British Publishers Enter the Young Adult Age." *Journal of Youth Services in Libraries*

1 (Spring 1988): 292–304. Useful survey of British YA publishers.

Pollack, Pamela D. "The Business of Popularity: The Surge of Teenage Paperbacks." *School Library Journal* 28 (November 1981): 25–28.

Popkin, Zelda F. "The Finer Things in Life." *Harpers* 164 (April 1932): 602–11. Contrasts between what young adults like to read and what parents and other adults want kids to read.

Root, Sheldon L. "The New Realism—Some Personal Reflections." *Language Arts* 54 (January 1977): 19–24.

Ross, Catherine Sheldrick. "Young Adult Realism: Conventions, Narrators, and Readers." *Library Quarterly* 55 (April 1985): 174–91.

Silver, Linda R. "Criticism, Reviewing, and the Library Review Media." *Top of the News* 35 (Winter 1979): 123–30. The entire issue on reviewing YA books is fine, particularly "What Makes a Good Review? Ten Experts Speak" (pp. 146–52) and Patty Campbell's "Only Puddings Like the Kiss of Death: Reviewing the YA Book" (pp. 161–62).

Small, Robert C., Jr. "The Literary Value of the Young Adult Novel." *Journal of Youth Services in Libraries* 5 (Spring 1992): 277–85.

Stanek, Lou Willett. "The Junior Novel: A Stylistic Study." *Elementary English* 51 (October 1974): 947–53.

Sutton, Roger. "The Critical Myth: Realistic YA Novels." *School Library Journal* 29 (November 1982): 33–35.

————. "What Mean We, White Man?" *Voice of Youth Advocates* 15 (August 1992): 155–58.

Townsend, John Rowe. "Didacticism in Modern Dress." *Horn Book Magazine* 43 (April 1967): 159–64. Argues that nineteenth-century didacticism is remarkably like didacticism in modern YA novels.

————. "Standards of Criticism for Children's Literature." *Top of the News* 27 (June 1971): 373–87.

Unsworth, Robert. "Holden Caulfield, Where Are You?" *School Library Journal* 23 (January 1977): 40–41. A plea for more books about males by males.

Wigutoff, Sharon. "Junior Fiction: A Feminist Critique." *The Lion and the Unicorn* 5 (1981): 4–18.

Wilson, David E. "The Open Library: YA Books for Gay Teens." *English Journal* 73 (November 1984): 60–63.

Using Young Adult Literature in Classrooms and Libraries

Abrahamson, Dick, and Eleanor Tyson. "What Every English Teacher Should Know About Free Reading." *ALAN Review* 14 (Fall 1986): 54–58, 69.

Applebee, Arthur N. "Stability and Change in the High-School Canon." *English Journal* 81 (September 1992): 27–32.

Broderick, Dorothy M. "Serving Young Adults: Why We Do What We Do." *Voice of Youth Advocates* 12 (October 1989): 203–206.

Chelton, Mary K. "Booktalking: You Can Do It." *School Library Journal* 22 (April 1976): 39–43. Practical and fun to read and do.

Hopkins, Dianne McAfee. " Challenges to Materials in Secondary School Library Media Centers: Results of a National Survey." *Journal of Youth Services in Libraries* 4 (Winter 1991): 131–40.

Janeczko, Paul B. "Seven Myths About Teaching Poetry, or, How I Stopped Chasing Foul Balls." *ALAN Review* 14 (Spring 1987): 13–16.

Lesesne, Teri S. "Developing Lifetime Readers: Suggestions from Fifty Years of

Research." *English Journal* 80 (October 1991): 61–64.

Mearns, Hughes. "Bo Peep, Old Woman, and Slow Mandy: Being Three Theories of Reading." *New Republic* 48 (November 10, 1926): 344–46.

Nelms, Ben F. "Reading for Pleasure in Junior High School." *English Journal* 55 (September 1966): 676–81.

Peck, Richard. "Ten Questions to Ask About a Novel." *ALAN Newsletter* 5 (Spring 1978): 1, 7.

Probst, Robert E. "Adolescent Literature and the English Curriculum." *English Journal* 76 (March 1987): 26–30.

———. "Mom, Wolfgang, and Me: Adolescent Literature, Critical Theory, and the English Classroom." *English Journal* 75 (October 1986): 33–39.

———. "Three Relationships in the Teaching of Literature." *English Journal* 75 (January 1986): 60–68.

Robertson, Sandra L. "Text Rendering: Beginning Literary Response." *English Journal* 79 (January 1990): 80–84.

Scharf, Peter. "Moral Development and Literature for Adolescents." *Top of the News* 33 (Winter 1977): 131–36. Lawrence Kohlberg's six stages of moral judgment applied to YA books.

Scoggin, Margaret C. "Do Young People Want Books?" *Wilson Bulletin for Librarians* 11 (September 1936): 17–20, 24.

Schontz, Marilyn Louise. "Selected Research Related to Children's and Young Adult Services in Public Libraries." *Top of the News* 38 (Winter 1982): 125–42. Includes an excellent list of sources.

Small, Robert C., Jr. "The Junior Novel and the Art of Literature." *English Journal* 66 (October 1977): 56–59.

———. "Teaching the Junior Novel." *English Journal* 61 (February 1972): 222–29.

Spencer, Patricia. "YA Novels in the AP Classroom: Crutcher Meets Camus." *English Journal* 78 (November 1989): 44–46. See also Tim McGee, "The Adolescent Novel in AP English: A Response to Patricia Spencer." *English Journal* 81 (April 1991): 57–58.

Thurber, Samuel. "An Address to Teachers of English." *Education* 18 (May 1898): 515–26. The best writer of his time, and one of the best English teachers of any time, on getting young people excited about literature.

Vogel, Mark, and Don Zancanella. "The Story World of Adolescents in *and* out of the Classroom." *English Journal* 80 (October 1991): 54–60.

ACKNOWLEDGMENTS

(p. 555) From "The Virtues of the Second-Rate" by William Lyon Phelps, from *English Journal,* January 1927, Vol. 16, No. 1. Copyright 1927 by the National Council of Teachers of English. Reprinted by permission of the publisher and the author.

(p. 555) From "A Gallery of Girls" by Alice M. Jordan. Reprinted from *Horn Book Magazine,* September–October 1937. Copyright 1937 by The Horn Book, Inc.

(p. 566) From "Behind Reading Interests" by G. R. Carlsen from *English Journal,* January 1954, Vol. 43, No. 1. Copyright © 1954 by the National Council of Teachers of English. Reprinted by permission of the publisher and the author.

(p. 566) From "Bibliotherapy and the School Librarian" by Willard A. Heaps. Reprinted with permission from *The Library Journal,* October 1, 1940. R. R. Bowker Co./A Xerox Corporation.

PHOTO AND ILLUSTRATION CREDITS

(p. 1) Jacket cover from *In Lane Three, Alex Archer* by Tessa Duder. Text copyright © 1987 by Tessa Duder. Cover art copyright © 1991 by Ben Stahl. Used by permission of Bantam Books, a division of Bantam Doubleday Dell Publishing Group, Inc. Cover of *Phoenix Rising or How to Survive Your Life* by Cynthia D. Grant. Copyright © 1989 by Cynthia D. Grant. Reprinted by permission of HarperCollins Publishers. Cover of *The Contender* by Robert M. Lipsyte. Copyright © 1967 by Robert W. Lipsyte. Reprinted by permission of HarperCollins Junior Books. Cover of *Heartbeats and Other Stories* by Peter D. Sieruta. Copyright © 1989 by Peter D. Sieruta. Reprinted by permission of HarperCollins Publishers. Cover of *Cat, Herself* by Mollie Hunter. Copyright © 1985 by Maureen Mollie Hunter McIlwraith. Reprinted by permission of HarperCollins Publishers. Cover of *A Solitary Blue* by Cynthia Voigt. Copyright © 1983 by Cynthia Voigt. Published by Atheneum. Reprinted by permission of Macmillan Publishing Company.

(p. 24) Cover of *Black Ice* by Lorene Cary. Copyright © 1991 by Lorene Cary. Reprinted by permission of Alfred A. Knopf, Inc.

(p. 33) Jacket cover from *Ruby* by Rosa Guy. Copyright © 1976 by Rosa Guy. Used by permission of Bantam Books, a division of Bantam Doubleday Dell Publishing Group, Inc.

(p. 33) Jacket cover from *Ruby* by Rosa Guy. Copyright © 1976 by Rosa Guy. Used by permission of Dell, a division of Bantam Doubleday Dell Publishing Group, Inc.

(p. 38) Christopher Knight

(p. 42) Anon Rupo

(p. 50) Taryn Nilsen

(p. 84) Cover of *Losing Joe's Place* by Gordon Korman. Copyright © 1990 by Gordon Korman Enterprises, Inc. Reprinted by permission of Scholastic, Inc. Cover of *Chain of Fire* by Beverley Naidoo. Illustrations by Eric Velasquez. Text copyright © 1989 by Beverley Naidoo. Illustrations copyright © 1990 by Eric Velasquez. Reprinted by permission of HarperCollins Publishers.

(p. 90) Cover of *Witch Baby* by Francesca Lia Block. Copyright © 1991 by Francesca Lia Block. Reprinted by permission of HarperCollins Children's Books, a division of HarperCollins Publishers. Cover of *Maus II: A Survivor's Tale and Here My Troubles Began* by Art Spiegelman. Copyright © 1986, 1989, 1990, 1991 by Art Spiegelman. Reprinted by permission of Pantheon Books, a division of Random House, Inc.

(p. 99) Cover of *Melusine: A Mystery* by Lynne Reid Banks. Copyright © 1988 by Lynne Reid Banks. Reprinted by permission of HarperCollins Junior Books. Cover of *Now is Your Time! The African-American Struggle for Freedom* by Walter Dean Myers. Copyright © 1991 by Walter Dean Myers. Reprinted by permission of HarperCollins Children's Books, a division of HarperCollins Publishers. Cover of *Up Country* by Alden R. Carter. Copyright © 1989 by Alden R. Carter. Reprinted by permission of Scholastic, Inc. Cover of *Tunnel in the Sky* by Robert A Heinlein. Copyright © 1955 by Robert A. Heinlein. A Charles Scribner's Sons Books for Young Readers. Reprinted by permission of Macmillan Publishing Company. Cover of *Tehanu: The Last Book of Earthsea* by Ursula K. LeGuin. Copyright © 1990 Ursula K. LeGuin. A Jean Karl Book, Atheneum. Reprinted by permission of Macmillan Publishing Company.

(p. 123) Jacket cover from *Children of the River* by Linda Crew. Copyright © 1989 by Linda Crew. Used by permission of Dell, a division of Bantam Doubleday Dell Publishing Group, Inc. Jacket cover from *A Summer Life* by Gary Soto. Copyright © 1990 by University Press of New England. Used by permission of Dell, a division of Bantam Doubleday Dell Publishing Group, Inc.

(p. 124) Phil Cantor

(p. 135) HarperCollins

(p. 159) Cover of *Fell* by M. E. Kerr. Copyright © 1987 by M. E. Kerr. A Harper Keypoint Book. Reprinted by permission of HarperCollins Publishers.

(p. 159) Cover of *Fell* by M. E. Kerr. Copyright © 1987 by M. E. Kerr. Reprinted by permission of HarperCollins Publishers.

(p. 178) Cover of *The Moves Make the Man* by Bruce Brooks. Copyright © 1984 by Bruce Brooks. Cover art © 1987 by Richard Williams. Cover © 1987 by Harper & Row Publishers. Reprinted by permission of HarperCollins Publishers. Cover of *The Brave* by Robert Lipsyte. Copyright © 1991 by Robert Lipsyte. Reprinted by permission of HarperCollins Children's Books. Jacket cover from *The Shadow Brothers* by A. E. Cannon. Copyright © 1990 by A. E. Cannon. Used by permission of Delacorte Press, a division of Bantam Doubleday Dell Publishing Group, Inc.

(p. 198) Jacket cover from *Whispers from the Dead* by Joan Lowery Nixon. Copyright © 1989 by Joan Lowery Nixon. Used by permission of Dell, a division of Bantam Doubleday Dell Publishing Group, Inc. Cover of *The Tricksters* by Margaret Mahy. Copyright © 1986 by Margaret Mahy. A Margaret K. McElderry Book. Reprinted by permission of Macmillan Publishing Company. Cover of *Ghostly Tales of Love & Revenge* by Daniel Cohen. Cover illustration by Stephen Marchesi. Reprinted by permission of G. P. Putnam's Sons.

(p. 219) One map from *The Stone and the Flute* by Hans Bemmann, translated by Anthea Bell (Penguin Books, 1987), copyright © Hans Bemmann, 1987, originally published 1983, Edition Weitbrecht in K Thienemanns Verlag Stuttgart. Reproduced by permission of Penguin Books Ltd.

(p. 246) From *Motel of the Mysteries* by David Macaulay. Copyright © 1979 by David Macaulay. Reprinted by permission of Houghton Mifflin Company.

(p. 254) Cover of *Voices from the Civil War* by Milton Meltzer. Copyright © 1989 by Milton Meltzer. Reprinted by permission of HarperCollins Children's Books, a division of HarperCollins Publishers.

(p. 303) Catherine Noren

(p. 314) D. Wingar

(p. 315) Cover of *The New York Times Book of Science Literacy*. Jacket design by Murray Greenfield © Random House, Inc. Reprinted by permission of Random House, Inc. Cover of *The Riddle of the Rosetta Stone: Key to Ancient Egypt* by James Cross Giblin. Copyright © 1990 by James Cross Giblin. Artwork © 1990 by HarperCollins Publishers. Reprinted by permission of HarperCollins Publishers. Cover of *An Ancient Heritage: The Arab-American Minority* by Brent Ashabranner. Text copyright © 1991 by Brent Ashabranner. Photographs copyright © 1991 by Paul Conklin. Reprinted by permission of HarperCollins Publishers.

(p. 329) Cover of *Changing Bodies, Changing Lives*, Revised and updated by Ruth Bell and other co-authors. Jacket design © Random House, Inc. Reprinted by permission of Random House, Inc.

(p. 331) Warren Budd

(p. 344) Nadine Edris

(p. 346) Cover of *My Friend's Got This Problem, Mr. Candler* by Mel Glenn. Text copyright © 1991 by Mel Glenn. Photographs copyright © 1991 by Michael J. Bernstein. Reprinted by permission of Houghton Mifflin Company. All rights reserved.

(p. 361) Beth Bergman, *Sentinel/Enterprise*

(p. 364) Cover of *Center Stage: One-Act Plays for Teenage Readers and Actors* edited by Donald R. Gallo. Copyright © 1990 by Donald R. Gallo. Reprinted by permission of HarperCollins Publishers. Cover of *Lost in Yonkers* by Neil Simon. Original art by Craig Nelson © 1991 by Serino Coyne, Inc. Jacket design © Random House, Inc. Reprinted by permission of Random House, Inc.

(p. 393) Jill Paton Walsh

(p. 402) Cover of *The VOYA Reader* edited by Dorothy M. Broderick, 1990. Reprinted by permission of Scarecrow Press, Inc. Cover of *Novels of Initiation: A Guidebook for Teaching Literature to Adolescents* by David Peck. Reprinted by permission of Teachers College Press. Cover

of *Nonfiction for Young Adults: From Delight to Wisdom* by Betty Carter and Richard F. Abrahamson. Copyright © 1990 by The Oryx Press, 4041 N. Central at Indian School Rd., Phoenix, AZ 85012. Used by permission of the Oryx Press. Cover of *Writers, Critics, and Children*, ed. by Geoff Fox, Graham Hammond, Terry Jones, Frederic Smith, Kenneth Sterck, 1976. Reprinted by permission of Agathon Press, Inc.

(p. 454) Wendy Gavin Gregg

(p. 458) Cover art by Alan Adler for *The Effective Teaching of English* by Robert Protherough, Judith Atkinson, and John Fawcett used by permission of Alan Adler. Copyright © 1992 Alan Adler. Cover of *Response and Analysis* by Robert E. Probst (Boynton/Cook Publishers, Portsmouth, NH, 1988). Reprinted with permission. Cover of *Book-banning in America* by William Noble. Reprinted by permission of Paul S. Eriksson Publishers. Cover of *Teaching Literature in the Secondary School* by Richard Beach and James Marshall. Cover © 1990, Craig McClain Photography. Cover of *Teaching Literature in Middle and Secondary Grades* by John S. Simmons and H. Edward Deluzian. Copyright © 1992 by Allyn and Bacon. Reprinted by permission of the publisher.

(p. 470) Jan Hall

(p. 482) Davis S. Strickler/The Picture Cube

(p. 495) Cover of *Scary Stories 3: More Tales to Chill Your Bones* by Alvin Schwartz. Text copyright © 1991 by Alvin Schwartz. Illustrations © 1991 by Stephen Gammell. Reprinted by permission of HarperCollins Children's Books, a division of HarperCollins Publishers. Cover of *Vampires, A Collection of Original Stories* edited by Jane Yolen and Martin H. Greenberg. Copyright © 1991 by Jane Yolen and Martin H. Greenberg. Reprinted by permission of HarperCollins Children's Books, a division of HarperCollins Publishers.

(p. 514) George Cooper

(p. 534) Cover from *The First Freedom* by Nat Hentoff. Copyright © 1980 by Namar Productions, Ltd. Jacket design copyright © 1980 by Mike Stromberg. Reprinted by permission of Delacorte Press, a division of Bantam, Doubleday, Dell Publishing Group, Inc. Cover from *Dealing with Censorship* edited by James E. David. Reprinted by permission of the National Council of Teachers of English. Cover from *The Students' Right to Read*. Reprinted by permission of the National Council of Teachers of English. Cover from *The Students' Right to Know* by Lee Burress and Edward B. Jenkinson. Reprinted by permission of the National Council of Teachers of English. Cover from *Censors in the Classroom* by Edward B. Jenkinson. Copyright © 1979 by Southern Illinois University Press. Reprinted by permission of Southern Illinois University Press.

(p. 570) Ruthe S. Wheeler, *Janet Hardy in Radio City*. Chicago: The Goldsmith Publishing Company, 1935, cover. Cover of *Polly Learns to Fly* by Lillian Elizabeth Roy, 1932. Reprinted by permission of Grosset and Dunlap. Ruthe S. Wheeler, *Helen in the Editor's Chair*. Chicago: The Goldsmith Publishing Company, 1932, cover.

SUBJECT INDEX

CRITICS AND COMMENTATORS

AUTHOR AND TITLE INDEX

604